McFarland Classics

Adir. *The Great Clowns of American Television*

Anderson. *Science Fiction Films of the Seventies*

Archer. *Willis O'Brien*

Benson. *Vintage Science Fiction Films, 1896–1949*

Bernardoni. *The New Hollywood*

Broughton. *Producers on Producing*

Byrge & Miller. *The Screwball Comedy Films*

Chesher. *"The End": Closing Lines...*

Cline. *In the Nick of Time*

Cline. *Serials-ly Speaking*

Darby & Du Bois. *American Film Music*

Derry. *The Suspense Thriller*

Douglas. *The Early Days of Radio Broadcasting*

Drew. *D.W. Griffith's* Intolerance

Ellrod. *Hollywood Greats of the Golden Years*

Erickson. *Religious Radio and Television in the U.S., 1921–1991*

Erickson. *Syndicated Television*

Fernett. *American Film Studios*

Frasier. *Russ Meyer—The Life and Films*

Fury. *Kings of the Jungle*

Galbraith. *Motor City Marquees*

Harris. *Children's Live-Action Musical Films*

Harris. *Film and Television Composers*

Hayes. *The Republic Chapterplays*

Hayes. *3-D Movies*

Hayes. *Trick Cinematography*

Hill. *Raymond Burr*

Hogan. *Dark Romance*

Holland. *B Western Actors Encyclopedia*

Holston. *Starlett*

Horner. *Bad at the Bijou*

Jarlett. *Robert Ryan*

Kinnard. *Horror in Silent Films*

Langman & Gold. *Comedy Quotes from the Movies*

Levine. *The 247 Best Movie Scenes in Film History*

McGee. *Beyond Ballyhoo*

McGee. *The Rock & Roll Movie Encyclopedia of the 1950s*

McGee. *Roger Corman*

McGhee. *John Wayne*

Mank. *Hollywood Cauldron: Thirteen Horror Films*

Martin. *The Allied Artists Checklist*

Nollen. *The Boys: ...Laurel and Hardy*

Nowlan. *Cinema Sequels and Remakes, 1903–1987*

Okuda. *The Monogram Checklist*

Okuda & Watz. *The Columbia Comedy Shorts*

Parish. *Prison Pictures from Hollywood*

Pitts. *Western Movies*

Quarles. *Down and Dirty: Hollywood's Exploitation Filmmakers*

Selby. *Dark City: The Film Noir*

Sigoloff. *The Films of the Seventies*

Slide. *Nitrate Won't Wait*

Smith, L. *Famous Hollywood Locations*

Smith, R.D. *Ronald Colman, Gentleman of the Cinema*

Sturcken. *Live Television*

Tropp. *Images of Fear*

Tuska. *The Vanishing Legion: ...Mascot Pictures*

Von Gunden. *Alec Guinness*

Von Gunden. *Flights of Fancy*

Warren. *Keep Watching the Skies!*

Watson. *Television Horror Movie Hosts*

Watz. *Wheeler & Woolsey*

Weaver. *Poverty Row HORRORS!*

Weaver. *Return of the B Science Fiction and Horror Heroes*

West. *Television Westerns*

Syndicated Television

The First Forty Years, 1947–1987

by
Hal Erickson

McFarland & Company, Inc., Publishers
Jefferson, North Carolina, and London

The present work is a reprint of the library bound edition of
Syndicated Television: The First Forty Years, 1947–1987, *first
published in 1989*. **McFarland Classics** *is an imprint of
McFarland & Company, Inc., Publishers, Jefferson, North
Carolina, who also published the original edition.*

Library of Congress Cataloguing-in-Publication Data

Erickson, Hal, 1950–
    Syndicated television : the first forty years, 1947–1987 / by Hal
Erickson.
       p.   cm.
    Bibliography: p. 375.
    Includes index.
    ISBN 0-7864-1198-8 (softcover : 50# alkaline paper) ∞
    1. Television programs—United States—Plots, themes, etc.
2. Television programs—United States—Dictionaries.   3. Television
programs—United States—History.   I. Title.
PN1992.55.E67   2001   016.79145'75—dc19   89-42583

British Library cataloguing data are available

On the cover: Vanna White, letter-turner for *Wheel of Fortune* (Photofest)

Manufactured in the United States of America

McFarland & Company, Inc., Publishers
Box 611, Jefferson, North Carolina 2864
www.mcfarlandpub.com

For Joanne
and Brian and Peter

Table of Contents

Introduction
and Acknowledgments

There are three basic types of television syndication. The first is the off-network distribution of network-series reruns. That's not what this book is about. The second is the local-station distribution of theatrical feature films, short subjects and cartoons. That's not what this book is about. The third is the distribution of programs either made exclusively for non-network play, or of programs perhaps intended for network telecasts but ultimately making their debuts in syndication. This is called "first-run" syndication, and *that's* what this book is about.

Syndicated Television is the story of the first forty years of first-run TV syndication, from 1947's *Public Prosecutor* to the latest syndicated output of 1987, including *Star Trek: The Next Generation, Friday the 13th* and *Win, Lose or Draw.* I'd like to have included every syndicated release ever filmed or taped, but that would have resulted in a gargantuan work. Certain genres, or program categories, such as Religious, Sports and Informational shows, have yielded so much product that I've had to streamline and concentrate on highlights. Of the major genres (Adventure [including mystery], Comedy, Drama, and Westerns), every time I'm satisfied that these have been completed, there are last-minute additions, corrections, and discoveries — indicating that somewhere out there may still be lurking yet-undiscovered gems awaiting the next television historian foolhardy enough to take on a project like this.

Many of the television-industry terms used in this book, such as "stripping," "day and date" and "access time," are explained in the text. One term that you'll see a lot of is "syndie." This abbreviation of "syndicated" is an invention of the show-biz trade paper *Variety* — one of the main research sources used for this book.

And while we're on that subject, we'll mention other publications helpful in getting this volume together. Of utmost service were two weekly magazines, *TV Guide* and *Broadcasting,* which should be made required reading for any curriculum on television history. Also of service were

American Film Magazine, Films in Review and the now-defunct *Panorama,* as well as the media sections of such weeklies as *Time* and *Newsweek.* Useful tidbits of information were gleaned from several daily papers, among them the *New York Times,* the *Los Angeles Times,* the *Chicago Sun-Times* and *Chicago Tribune,* and the *Milwaukee Journal* and *Milwaukee Sentinel.*

Outside of specialized books on individual types of television programs, the best overall source for television history is Vincent Terrace's intimidatingly thorough *Encyclopedia of Television: Series, Pilots and Specials (1937–1984)* (Zoetrope, New York, 1986). Space restrictions have prohibited me from going into detail on the cast and production credits of the many series listed in my book, so those interested in such minutiae as who played whom or who wrote or directed what are referred to the *Encyclopedia of Television.* A few comments: Terrace tends to list some syndicated programs as network shows, simply because they were carried by network stations in the biggest cities; there are also several programs listed as series which never got past the pilot-episode stage. I am also proud to say that I was able to uncover some bits of information (and obscure series) overlooked by the eagle-eyed Terrace and staff. But since this sort of churlish nit-picking leaves my book wide open for similar criticism, I'll stop right here.

Other helpful volumes included Alex McNeil's *Total Television* (Penguin, 1980; second edition, 1984) and the yearly *Television and Motion Picture Almanac.* Useful to a lesser degree (because it confines itself only to a hundred or so top-rated "syndies") was Tim Brooks and Earle Marsh's *The Complete Directory to Prime Time Network TV Shows,* which has since first published in 1979 by Ballantine Books undergone three revised editions. Another 1979 Ballantine product, *The TV Guide Almanac* (edited by Craig T. Norback and Peter G. Norback and the editors of *TV Guide*) helped in matching many syndie series with their distributing companies.

Since much more has been written about network programs than about their non-network counterparts, a great deal of my research was primary, including the rewarding (but exhausting) task of screening videotapes of many older programs listed in my book. This project also led me to the University of Wisconsin–Madison's Film Research Center, which houses an enormous collection of material from syndie–TV pioneer Fred W. Ziv. Included in this collection is an indispensible dissertation on Ziv's career, written for the University of Michigan by Morleen Getz Rouse in 1976. For this and so much more, many thanks to the always-helpful University of Wisconsin library staff.

Also many thanks to friends who helped me with their own recollections of days wasted before the tube as children (even as you and I), and with their own collections of classic–TV videotapes (all scrupulously legal):

John Bierman, Carl Bobke, Dennis Couch, Wayne and Rita Hawk, Ron Killian, Steve Lutomski and David Seebach. Special thanks to Lee Mathias, who knows the publishing business like the back of his hand.

Gratitude is extended lovingly to my parents, who put up the money to have my text photo-copied (though I suspect this was so they could show their friends what a smart kid they had), and who were among the first on their block to buy a TV back in 1950.

Finally, there aren't enough thanks available to honor the people to whom this book is dedicated: my wonderful wife Joanne, who when I was laid off from work asked me, "Why don't you use this time to get that book done?"; and my two sons, Brian and Peter, who unlike their father show no inclinations of turning into couch potatoes.

Hal Erickson
Milwaukee
August, 1988

A Note on the
Program Listings

The television programs listed herein are those that were in syndication but not seen on the major American networks (ABC, CBS, NBC, and — in the 1950's — DuMont). Certain series or specials that were previously telecast on networks outside the United States (such as Britain's BBC) are included if they made their American debuts in first-run syndication. Also included are several programs that were first seen on the various cable services which popped up in the '70's and '80's, since these efforts are still outside the realm of the major United States networks.

These series are listed first by program category or "genre," then alphabetically within those genres. Series using numbers as titles, such as *$100,000 Pyramid,* are listed as if the number was spelled out. The genres are

Adventure/Mystery
Children's
Comedy
Drama
Game/Quiz
Informational
Music/Variety
Religious

Specials/Miniseries/
   Mini-Networks
Sports
Talk/Interview
Travel/Documentary
Westerns
Women's

Finally: Programs are listed in those decades where they made their first documented appearances. Thus, you won't find *The Phil Donahue Show* in the section on the 1970's, since Donahue's debut took place in the '60's. Nor will you find *Truth or Consequences* in the 1980's, despite its recent incarnation in 1986, though you'll find that incarnation referred to in the notes on *Truth or Consequences* in the 1960's section.

Syndication in a
150-Year Nutshell

Let's go back to 1841; but stay tuned. We'll be back in a moment.

Normally, the actual inauguration of a new president wasn't priority news in the first half of the 19th century. But when President John Tyler was sworn in a mere month after newly elected William Henry Harrison had taken the vows (and a mere few days after Harrison died), it was "dog-bites-man" time. Just as today, inquiring minds wanted the news, but most newspapers, even those within a 100-mile radius of Washington, wouldn't have the inauguration story for weeks, maybe months. But after the *New York Sun* was given the story by mounted messenger, the *Sun* decided to expedite things by dispatching several more couriers to deliver the story swiftly to all the other papers in New York State, spreading the news to outlying rural regions faster than ever before. And so, in addition to the war with Mexico, John Tyler was also memorable as the spiritual father of newspaper syndication.

With the advent of telegraphy, syndicated news was further advanced; the telegraph was especially handy during the Civil War of the 1860's since, as everyone in the country was involved, everyone wanted to stay abreast of late-breaking events. The *State Journal* of Madison, Wisconsin, enjoyed a brisk wartime business distributing news bulletins, with the added fillip of syndicated advertisements: already syndication was a handy conduit for merchandising, and we're getting closer to the television era all the time.

Wisconsinite Ansel Nash Kellogg, whose Baraboo newspaper was a client of the *State Journal,* was struck with the postwar thought that syndication might be a sweet business to indulge in himself. Kellogg set up his own distribution company, farming out his news bits with the added attraction of human-interest pieces and humorous anecdotes. So now syndication was turning into an *entertainment* medium.

Chicago was the news-syndication capital of the 1870's, the city being located strategically between New York and the land west of the Mississippi. Several Chicago-based companies thrived by nationally scattering

1

comic pieces, serials, illustrations and, by 1875, the stereotype plates needed for front-page composition. Within the next decade, O.J. Smith's Chicago offices and Joseph Pulitzer's *New York World* were specializing in syndicating fiction, humor and drawings. Amidst all the "big boys," there were mavericks. S.S. McClure tried to convince the popular magazine bearing his name to resell its articles to local papers, but *McClure's* wanted no part of this plan; so McClure set up his own personal syndicate, making things attractive by giving his material free of charge to one major newspaper per state, in exchange for that newspaper's distributing the galley proofs to other papers and depositing the profits with McClure. This was one of the first examples of an "independent" entrepreneur bucking the majors in the marketplace; it would not be the last.

In the 1890's, most papers retained their own staffs of "star" writers and illustrators. One of the bigger publishers, San Francisco's William Randolph Hearst, was so enchanted by the illustrated comic stories he'd seen in various European periodicals that he decided to create his own "funnies" section, eventually introducing full color to the printing process. Hearst then shipped out the best of his comic strips to Hearst publications throughout the country; his rivals, most notably Joe Pulitzer, followed suit with their own funny papers. Color comics ended up being the biggest selling point for these competing syndicates. Small papers without full-time cartoonists on their staffs could now provide Sunday-supplement chuckles simply by purchasing whole blocks of funnies from the majors. To step up distribution, regional syndicates sprouted up all over; in 1915, Hearst consolidated all his regionals to form King Features, then created United Press International simply by merging his own International News service with the rival United Press. Merge and splurge; everybody was doing it. Syndication, need it be said, was Big Business.

As syndication flourished, so did specialization. The Bell Syndicate, like its owner, John Wheeler, was devoted to creating new sales and mechanical techniques in shipping out its comics product. Newspaper Enterprise Association, catering to small rural papers, sold whole blocks of its material in package deals, specializing in family-oriented features and children's comics. Publishers' Syndicate, tackling a more metropolitan market, trafficked in the more serious continuing-story comic strips. Plenty of diversification in the years prior to 1920, but the various syndicates were united in that they represented the most powerful mass communication and entertainment form of its time. And then came Radio.

Radio's evolution was astonishingly similar to the life story of the news services. Its first technological leap forward, KDKA–Pittsburgh's coverage of the 1920 Harding-Cox elections, was yet another "new president" story. The Radio Corporation of America (RCA) reasoned that the future of radio lay in a nationwide hook-up—a "network" of stations, similar to the big newspaper chains. To usher in its new National Broadcasting Company in 1926, RCA relied not on the spreading of news that put radio on the map, but on singers, actors, comedians: Entertainment. The newest news medium became big business by becoming the newest amusement medium. Shades of Ansel Nash Kellogg's syndicated bits-o'-fun back in the 1860's! And it followed, as it did in Kellogg's time, that radio entertainment was accompanied by nationally broadcast advertisements; radio quickly outstripped the newspapers as the primary merchandise mart of the nation.

Foremost among the pioneer radio entertainers were Freeman Gosden and Charles Correll, a couple of white-faced actors who starred in a blackface comedy serial titled *Amos 'n' Andy*. In 1928, Gosden and Correll, with visions of fat bank accounts dancing in their heads, asked their home radio station, WMAQ–Chicago, for permission to record their nightly *Amos 'n' Andy* broadcast and then distribute the records to stations outside the Chicago area. WMAQ agreed, providing the boys continued doing their nightly program live; so after each evening's live broadcast, the stars went to a recording studio and re-enacted the evening's script on a ten-inch wax disc. Copies of these discs were then shipped out to thirty independent radio stations. This "chainless chain," the very first example of syndicated radio, boosted the popularity of *Amos 'n' Andy,* increased sales of radio sets throughout the country, and led to Gosden and Correll's long-term NBC contract beginning in 1929.

Once electrical transcriptions were proven to be a practical means of wide-range fun-spreading (and once the records stopped sounding as though the actors were speaking into a muslin curtain), the two major networks, NBC and the new Columbia Broadcasting System, thought about using recordings full-time—and just as quickly abandoned that thought. The official reason, the networks claimed, was that the fans *wanted* the immediacy and spontaneity of live radio. There was, of course, a real reason lurking in there. Networks and sponsors had complete control over *live* broadcasts, especially in terms of financial remuneration. But recordings would cut those profits up; who knew who'd use those records in years to come? Another network? Another sponsor? Or, heaven forbid, the radio stars themselves? How could networks and sponsors maintain creative and financial control over those stars, once the stars began recording on their own, merchandising on their own, calling the shots on their own? Anarchy! Pestilence!

But not every local radio station was affiliated with a major network. This didn't hurt the big-time, metropolitan stations, most of which had their own in-house talent pool. But small-time outfits with weaker signals needed to fill their air time with something more than the birth reports and the hog futures. So, just as small-town newspapers relied on syndication to fill in the blanks, so did small-town radio outlets.

Once record discs running as long as fifteen minutes a side became a reality in the mid-'30's, any number of quarter-hour syndie radio series went into distribution. Some began as local shows with strong regional followings: Chicago's *The Air Adventures of Jimmy Allen,* Nashville's *Asher and Little Jimmy,* even Duluth's *Detectives Black and Blue.* Other syndies were based on well-established literary properties, like *Chandu the Magician.* Major properties original to radio began emerging. When George Trendle's WXYZ–Detroit split away from CBS in 1933, Trendle set up his own ad hoc network to broadcast his popular *Lone Ranger* series. From there, WXYZ's penny-whistle hookup formed the nucleus of the Mutual Network in 1934. Mutual delivered a lot of its programming live, but unlike NBC and CBS, Mutual had no qualms about sending programs out on disc; with silent gaps in the recordings left open for local commercials, Mutual was able to build support for its programs with regional sponsorship. Local advertisers considered too insignificant for the bigger networks could add their own ads to Mutual's slick transcriptions, while other sponsors liked the fact that the Mutual recorded output could be broadcast any time of the day, a much more flexible setup than the rigidly regulated time slots of NBC and CBS. California's Don Lee was able to put together his own big-time West Coast network by relying almost exclusively on Mutual's discwork.

While radio syndicators grew rich, radio actors got their next few meals and not much else. The going rate for an actor in syndication was in the neighborhood of $3.50 per show, a pretty rundown neighborhood even in the '30's. And on top of that, there were no "residuals"—no remuneration to the performers when the recordings were run a second, fourth or fifteenth time. Radio actress Mary Jane Higby, in her wonderful book *Tune in Tomorrow,* recalled that the "syndie" actor had very few fringe benefits to compensate for the low wages. The wax used in the early days for recordings was expensive; programs were recorded straight through, as there was no way to edit them, and if a mistake was made, the wax matrix had to be scraped clean for re-use, a process which could and did take hours. Most actors working on these records did so in the evenings, after a busy day with the networks, which meant that some recording sessions wound up being all-night marathons, all-night turning in to all-morning whenever a boo-boo required more matrix-scraping and more retakes. Poor Gale Gordon once condemned himself and his fellow performers to a purgatory of retakes on a transcribed series titled *Don Hancock* when he inadvertently referred to the hero as Dan Hoe-Cake.

By and by, cheaper acetate was used for the discs, allowing technicians to discard a bad recording inexpensively and then quickly set up a new disc on the occasion of a fluffed line. But there was still no method of editing, and retakes continued to eat up time, until Bing Crosby's people brought magnetic recording tape back from Germany following World War II.

Tape *could* be edited, on the spot, and now recording sessions took on the tranquility of a visit to the masseur. Bing Crosby's decision to use audio tape on his weekly show, allowing him to work whenever he felt like it without being bound to live-radio time restrictions (leaving him plenty of time for the golf course), eventually led to industry-wide adoption of magnetic tape — to the approbation of veteran actors who no longer had to put in third-shift hours.

But we digress; back to syndication in the 1930's. This could really be a seat-of-the-pants business, as witness a recorded program in which an actor named Dugan played all the parts, did all the sound effects, then personally peddled the wax discs, station by station, in his rickety old sedan. It was Frederick W. Ziv who brought sophistication to syndication, turning it into a science, combining modern recording techniques with a masterful sense of merchandising.

A Cincinnati-based ad man and scriptwriter, Fred Ziv formed his own ad agency in 1930, promptly developing a locally sponsored series on Cincy's WLW starring one Oklahoma Bob Albright. Ziv would explain in later years that he'd gone into radio because, whereas print advertising was an overstocked and highly regimented field, radio advertising was still making up its own rules and allowing the inexperienced a bit of growing room. So Ziv created his *own* market, carefully manning his staff with loyal, hardworking folks who ate and slept the concept of packaging radio entertainment. His second-in-command, John L. Sinn, remained with Ziv for three decades, attaining the presidency of Ziv's television division and ending up as a top exec at United Artists when that company absorbed Ziv in 1961.

By the late '30's, Ziv had determined that syndication was the road to travel; this way, his company would be paid outright for its programs, avoiding the usual percentages handed over to the networks. Ziv made his product desirable by offering an outlet for local sponsors; his first "big" property was a Cincinnati variety show designed to hawk the wares of a local bakery, but its title, *The Freshest Thing in Town,* was open-ended enough to appeal to bakeries outside Cincinnati. The producer was still aiming at the nation's breadbasket when, in 1949, he offered his *Cisco Kid* television series to Inter-State Bakeries, a company which franchised its facilities to local bread firms like Ward's, Mrs. Karl's and Butternut.

Moving to Chicago at the end of the '30's to be closer to the major midwestern broadcasting hub, Ziv added to his empire; like William Randolph Hearst before him he bought a lot of smaller concerns, banking against the day that he'd turn them all into one big moneymaking ball of wax. One of Ziv's major acquisitions was the "World Library," the largest collection of royalty-free recorded music in existence, allowing the producer to score his series without dealing with the powerful and costly music agency ASCAP. And, in addition to picking up rerun rights to such popular former network programs as *Easy Aces* and *Lightning Jim,* Ziv acquired *first*-run radio rights to established literary properties like *Philo Vance, Boston Blackie* and *The Cisco Kid.* Then, to attract "star" talent, Ziv cooked up percentage-of-profits deals for movie actors such as Ronald Colman, Humphrey Bogart and Lauren Bacall, and for top-rank radio songsmiths like Wayne King, Guy Lombardo and Kenny Baker. These luminaries were given their own syndicated series, enjoying wider distribution and a heftier chunk of the profits than they ever would have enjoyed as "live" performers on the networks; it was a far cry from the $3.50-per-episode days of Dan Hoe-Cake.

When television was established as a here-to-stay medium in 1948, Fred Ziv tackled the new medium like a man devouring sirloin, setting up a television-film factory of the first calibre. His enthusiasm for television was not shared by the major motion picture studios, which regarded it as dangerous competition, dangerous because its entertainment was free. Columbia Pictures president Harry Cohn, for example, would greet potential television-film producers with free-association insults concerning those producers' ancestry and sexual preferences. M-G-M head Louis Mayer was less volatile, but no less adamant; he decreed that no one on the M-G-M payroll was even allowed to *own* a television set. Further building up big-studio hostility against television was the fact that the government was forcing the "majors" to cease the practice of block-booking—the forcing of theatres to accept a bunch of "B" pictures in exchange for the rights to run the studios' "A" product. This move would lead eventually to a monopoly-busting ruling forcing the studios into divestiture of their movie-theatre chains. The top movie factories, therefore, were not about to involve themselves in television, a medium ruled by the dictates of the Federal Communications Commission and thus even further under the government's thumb than the studios. Only Paramount Pictures entertained plans to expand into television, but the studio's involvement with the old DuMont Television Network led to conflict-of-interest suits that dashed the Paramount plans early on.

With the big studios snubbing it, television had to turn to the radio networks for support—hardly a major move, since both NBC and CBS had been running limited TV service since 1941. With no major-league film product at its disposal, television stuck with live broadcasting, and once more, the top networks decided that live television equalled total control over talent and content. Take a hike, film people.

But just as in radio's heyday, local TV channels had schedule gaps to fill, and could not make do with test patterns and recorded music forever. Alas, most of the film available to television in the late '40's were industrial films, educational reels, and the dregs of Hollywood's "B" and "C" pictures. What was needed was new, quality product.

The independent filmmakers were the first to respond. Hal Roach, whose studio hadn't picked up the momentum it had enjoyed before the war, went into television-film production to survive, leasing his studio facilities to other independents as well. Jerry Fairbanks, a producer of novelty theatrical shorts, developed much of the earliest made-for-TV celluloid; it was Fairbanks who produced television's very first syndicated item, a weird combination detective series and game show starring John Howard and titled *Public Prosecutor* (1947). With his specially patented five-camera filmmaking technique (five cameras covering each scene from different angles to cut down on production time), Fairbanks also churned out television's first syndicated sitcom, *Jackson and Jill;* a semitravelogue, *Goin' Places with Uncle George;* and a union-free musical/variety item filmed in Mexico, *Club Paradise* (also titled *Variety Musicale*). And Fairbanks was distributor for the pioneer made-for-TV cartoon series *Crusader Rabbit,* filmed on the very cheap in the garage studio of a real-estate salesman named Jay Ward. All of this happened *before* 1950.

Fairbanks and Hal Roach were making television film, but not real *series,* not in the 39-week-per-year, 30- and 60-minute formats established in radio. In point of fact, Fairbanks' films were designed as filler, to plug up odd-length schedule gaps: *Goin' Places* ran 10 minutes a show, the *Crusader Rabbits* were 19½ minutes each, and the *Public Prosecutors* a clumsy 17 minutes. Fairbanks was still in the short subject business.

The first group of films sent out as a weekly, 60-minute series weren't made for television at all, but were William Boyd's *Hopalong Cassidy* B westerns, produced for theatres in the '30's and '40's. By 1948, Boyd had sunk all his money into buying up the television rights to the *Cassidy* shows, courting both bankruptcy and a breakdown, because he devoutly believed that TV was ripe for plucking. How right he was. Boyd's westerns weren't masterpieces, but they had an identifiable central character, something missing from most of the second-string movies filling the airwaves at the time. By 1949, the syndication of *Hopalong Cassidy* had put Boyd in the millionaire bracket, and the merchandising of Hopalong Cassidy tie-in toys, games and costumes became a bonanza. The Cassidy flicks would be picked up by NBC before the end of 1949, but the precedent had been set; the way to go, TV-filmwise, was in syndication.

In 1948, Frederick Ziv was, like his colleagues, testing the television-syndie waters with 15-minute fillers. Enter another "accumulation"; Ziv purchased the vast General Film Library (so vast that it had storehouses on both coasts) and began assembling priceless newsreel footage from the General Film vaults. The results were two long-running series, *Yesterday's Newsreel* and *Sports Album*. After the financial windfall from these efforts engendered good will from the local channels, Ziv set about going into all-new, television-film work with one of his surefire radio properties. *Boston*

Blackie was Ziv's first choice, but the *Hopalong Cassidy* mania forced the producer's thoughts to turn westward; as a result, 1950's *The Cisco Kid* turned up as Ziv's first non-newsreel TV effort. For the same monetary considerations he'd had in his radio days, Ziv bypassed the networks and went straight into syndication; and, just as in the radio era, Ziv sent his sales teams out full-force to capture the local markets. It is said that Ziv sales reps were required to appear at out-of-town sales meetings wearing Cisco Kid hats.

Cisco, and most all the rest of Ziv's earliest television work, was filmed in color. Modern television historians have cited this decision as proof that Ziv had a gift of prophecy, and was as early as 1950 foreseeing the all-color 1960's. In truth, it was the opinion of the entire industry in 1950 that color television, full-time, would be adopted in a matter of months. The FCC was all prepared to adopt the CBS network's "color-wheel" process, which was crystal clear and life-like, but was incompatible with existing television receivers. This meant that if CBS got the go-ahead, viewers would *have* to buy color sets or else watch screenfuls of fuzzy blobs on their black-and-whites. Film producers like Ziv and Jerry Fairbanks converted to color because they were betting on the CBS process, a safe enough bet at the time. No one could have foreseen that NBC would come up with a *compatible* color system, which would allow the viewers to keep their old sets and watch the color shows in black-and-white with no trouble at all, and which, after a drawn-out battle with CBS' system, would end up as the color method adopted by the FCC. It would be many years before the saleability of color TV would enable Ziv to make his investment in Eastman color film stock pay off.

During the *Cisco Kid* era, Ziv was one of several producers leasing space at the old Eagle-Lion movie studio; by 1955, he'd owned Eagle-Lion outright, but until that time, the venerable "B" factory would be one of several studios renting out to television filmmakers. Since most of these plants, including General Service, RKO-Pathé, Hal Roach and Nassour Studios, had in the past loaned studio space to shoestring-budgeted B-movie producers, it seemed to logically follow that many of the first television filmmakers were graduates of Poverty Row. William F. Broidy, a top banana at Monogram pictures, was responsible for *Wild Bill Hickok* (1951); Producers Releasing Corporation president Leon Fromkess put up the money for *Ramar of the Jungle* (1952); and the largest of the B-pic studios, Republic, was the first Hollywood studio to enter regular television work, Republic chieftain Herbert Yates eventually earning an Emmy for his troubles with the syndicated *Stories of the Century* (1954).

Even after the networks started scheduling more and more filmed programs, several television producers stuck with syndication, where the money wouldn't have to be divvied up with ABC, CBS or NBC. Some film firms, like Gross-Krasne (created by Universal exec Jack Gross and Monogram producer Philip Krasne), started out by supplying the networks, then opted for exclusive syndicated sales. Guild Films, created by adman Reuven Kaufman and producer-writer W. Lee Wilder in 1952 for the purpose of nationally syndicating local Los Angeles programs, stayed with syndication and never left it. Screen Gems, the television subsidiary of Columbia Pictures, originally produced programs for both network and non-network; by the end of the '50's, Screen Gems was so swamped with work that it set up two different production units, one for network series, one for syndies.

The FCC gave syndication a major boost in 1952, the year that the FCC lifted its "freeze" on granting new television station licenses — a freeze imposed in 1949 in order to study the qualifications of the applicants, the potential of television's Ultra High Frequency band (channels 14–83), and the future of colorcasting. Once the freeze was unfrozen, brand-new television channels bred like rabbits; before the lift, Ziv would have been satisfied with 33 or so sales on *Cisco Kid* or *Boston Blackie,* but by 1954, if Ziv wasn't selling its series to 100 or more markets, somebody wasn't doing his job.

As the call went out for more and better product, several new syndie producers entered the fray. Foremost was Management Corporation of America, or MCA. Technically, talent agencies weren't allowed to produce their own shows, but MCA's Revue Studios (headquartered for many years at Republic) had gotten special dispensation from Screen Actors Guild president Ronald Reagan, who by a curious coincidence was managed by MCA. Obliged by law in 1959 to get out of the talent-agency business, MCA remained in the production end, acquiring Gross-Krasne's valuable United Televisions Programs distribution arm in the process, as well as the whole Universal Pictures lot, gradually emerging as the largest television-film manufacturer in the Free World.

Largely by dealing with new stations not immediately hooked up to the networks in the early '50's and therefore more dependent on filmed material, MCA, Ziv, and the other syndicators steadily built up their industry influence. In 1955, the demise of the DuMont Network (always the also-ran in the ratings race) left large holes in many a local station's airtime, so the syndie mills rushed to the rescue. That same year, statistics were compiled revealing that 25 to 75 percent of a filmed series' revenue was accrued in local reruns. The three major networks, having long before set up film divisions of their own, fattened their bank balances not only by controlling syndication of their network castoffs, but by developing their own *first*-run syndicated shows. As of 1955, syndication was a $150 million a year business, which broke down to about a million bucks' profit per series. A million *1955* bucks.

Detractors grumbled that syndication was television's "poor relation," lacking the production polish of series financed by the networks and the big sponsors. Syndication's stars, many of whom had gone into that field because they'd been ignored by the networks, went on the defensive. Richard Carlson, star of Ziv's *I Led Three Lives,* spoke for many in 1955 when he said, "Who gives a damn about production values on TV? Nobody. The major film studios who went into TV have learned that production values will not sustain any show. What the people want is a story and people they don't resent in their living rooms." Carlson added that "TV film syndication will be bigger than anyone today dreams."

How true. By the late '50's, syndication was gangbusters. Many first-run syndies were scheduled in "access slots" like 7:00–8:00 p.m. and 11:00–11:30 p.m. (EST), periods during which there was little or no network activity. As late as 1959, both NBC and ABC had lots of "down time," usually between 10 and 11 p.m.; syndicators moved in, attracted regional sponsors, and cleaned up. Non-net fare built up a large and loyal following: Desilu's *Whirlybirds,* for instance, could always be counted upon to out–Nielsen CBS' *What's My Line?* in Milwaukee. And it was standard operating procedure in the '50's for network affiliates to bump the weaker network shows in favor of syndies; there was little point in losing viewers with a basement-ratings network public affairs program when a station could kidnap those viewers and thousands more besides with Ziv's *Sea Hunt.* Incidentally, *Sea Hunt* was a prime example of a series that did far better in syndication that it could ever have on a network. In its prime, it ran in over 200 markets, a boast that even the best ABC Network offering couldn't make in those days.

It looked as though the syndication boom would last forever, but the dark clouds began a-gathering in 1960. In that year, all three networks increased their broadcast time, biting into those valuable access slots. The late night popularity of NBC's Jack Paar and those glittering packages of new-to-television Hollywood "A" pictures eroded the hold that the syndies had enjoyed after 11 p.m. In 1961, new FCC chairman Newton Minow started pushing local stations to run network public-service shows, so the locals complied, squeezing out even more syndication time. Escalating production costs hardly helped the situation, either.

Adding to the crisis facing first-run syndication was the damned popularity of all those network reruns. Why, reasoned MCA, should lots of good dough be shelled out to develop new syndie properties when MCA could reap the same revenue at far less cost with repeats of the studio's old NBC-network cop show *M Squad?* Worse news for the syndie field came when hour-long network programs came into vogue; when one of these 60-minuters went into local distribution, that was *two* half-hours gone.

First-run syndicated dramatic, comic and adventure shows all but vanished during the 1960's. The few exceptions were mostly foreign imports. This was an outgrowth of a trend started in the late '50s, when so many American series had found berths on television schedules in Great Britain, Canada and Australia that, to protect their *own* product, these countries set up "quota" systems. For example, Londoners were permitted to see only 15 percent's worth of American series on their tellies; the remaining 85 percent had to be produced by studios in the British Empire. American producers came up with a devilishly clever solution: the international co-production. If, say, an English or Canadian series featured casts and production facilities from Hollywood, that series could pass as an American show—yet, having been filmed in England or Canada, it qualified as a domestic product and thereby satisfied the quota restrictions. The financial advantage of this set-up to American studios included the lower production costs abroad, as well as the utilization of "frozen funds"—profits which those studios had built up in foreign countries and which by law could be spent only *in* those countries. Foreign producers also prospered, battening on profits made on co-productions which often exceeded those made on series produced exclusively within their own boundaries. In the early '60's, Britain's BBC network financed a number of television series so expensive that they could not hope to show a profit if run exclusively in England. Their salvation came about with the fact that fewer first-run American syndies were being produced by that time, causing U.S. syndicated-series distributors to literally beg for new product from other sources. Thus began the practice of shipping British programs to America, not only meeting the new demand but retaining the lucrative foreign-market sales which England had first tapped during the '50's. To be sure, several of these imports gathered dust, but others—*The Saint* from England, *The Littlest Hobo* from Canada, *Skippy* from Australia—did very well indeed in the States.

Another, cheaper method for distributors to stay alive in the 1960's syndie field was that chattering beastie, the talk show. This sort of program could be made on cost-efficient videotape (introduced in syndication as early as 1958), with a whole week's worth of programs taped during one or two marathon sessions, keeping studio costs low, profits high. David Susskind blazed the trail in this field, followed by entertainers Steve Allen, Merv Griffin and Mike Douglas, and provocateurs William F. Buckley, Joe Pyne and Alan Burke. The talkshow craze inspired a lot of able people to go the gabfest route, including Pat Boone, Donald O'Connor, and Joe Namath. Able people who soon learned that there was more to sustained success than a desk, a couch, and the Gabors.

One other low-cost method of thriving in syndication came about after the networks started cancelling such long-running game shows as Ralph Edwards' *Truth or Consequences* and Goodson-Todman's *What's My*

Line? They were too tired-blooded, too 1950's. The Edwardses and the Goodson-Todmans responded by pitching camp in the syndication wilds, going market-by-market with their time-tested wares. The result was the mid–'60's second coming of game shows in syndication—leading to a *third* coming back on the networks.

Elements contributing to the new burst of syndie activity in the 1960's included the 1964 law requiring that new television sets include the UHF band on their channel selectors, resulting in the births of hundreds of new television stations eager and willing to be provided for; and the "color boom" of 1965–66, brought about by the unanimous decision of all three networks to commence full-time colorcasting. With very few color network reruns in distribution at that time, television stations with gleaming new color equipment swiftly gobbled up syndication's steady diet of first-run color gameshows, cartoons, travelogues, huntin'-fishin' expeditions, and (the wheel turns) repeats of old color syndies from the '50's like *Cisco Kid, Superman* and *Science Fiction Theatre.*

By 1969, however, there was plenty of ex-network color material in syndication, discouraging syndie producers from going beyond such proven commodities as games, talk and travelogue. Would there ever be another "Golden Age" of syndication as in the 1950's, wherein new, diverse syndicated material—comedies, dramas, adventure, variety—would proliferate? There would, but it would take an act of government to provide it.

In 1971, the FCC determined that the networks had had too much control over television content for too long. The first step to lessen this hold was to force the networks to relinquish their film-syndication divisions; the next step was to wrest a half-hour's worth of airtime nightly from the networks, usually the 7:30–8:00 p.m. slot, and return it to the local outlets. This was done in the hopes that the locals, and the first-run syndicators, would be encouraged to develop new, unusual and creative programming to fill the space. This was the P.T.A.R.—the Prime Time Access Rule.

Hooray, cried the local outlets. Now we can make hay with those valuable network reruns. Not so, replied the FCC in 1972, particularly in the top fifty markets. Access Time had to be filled with first-run, non-network programming, period. However, the first new syndies to profit from P.T.A.R. were such recent network castoffs as *Wild Kingdom, Lassie, Hee Haw* and *Lawrence Welk*—all four permitted to flourish in Access so long as the bulk of their episodes were new, non-network-rerun, made-for-syndication installments. The same happened to the first-run syndie versions of old game shows like *Let's Make a Deal* and *To Tell the Truth.* Ditto such recently exhumed corpses as *This Is Your Life* and *You Asked for It.*

In the interest of "diversification," for which P.T.A.R. had purportedly been created, producers here and abroad began to supply such access-minded first-run syndies as *Primus, Monty Nash* and *The Protectors.* Some of these series, like *Ozzie's Girls* and *Young Dr. Kildare,* were but half-hearted imitations of old network favorites. Others, like *Dusty's Trail,* gave new meaning to the word "inept."

Several new syndies of the '70's were offered on a "barter" basis, with their sponsors handing the series out free or at minimal cost to local stations in exchange for free advertising time. The barter system had made its mark in 1955 thanks to film distributor Matty Fox, who set up a deal with the California softdrink manufacturer Cantrell & Cochrane to distribute some 725 pictures made between 1929 and 1953 by the RKO–Radio company— the first television package from a major movie studio. To spark local sales of his C&C package, Fox talked the International Latex Corporation into acting as national sponsor for the films, International Latex receiving free ad space in return. After the incredible C&C sales boom that followed, one would think that "barter" would become the principal method of moving syndicated product; unfortunately, barter wound up with a very checkered history, thanks to syndies which gave viewers a maximum of advertising with a bare minimum of entertainment. Typical was the alleged *Hoot Gibson Show* (circa 1952), wherein a miserable parade of musical acts shared time with an endless commercial for a ratty-looking line of chinchillas.

The most infamous barter release of 1971, Colgate-Palmolive's *Dr. Simon Locke,* wasn't much of an improvement over Hoot Gibson and his chinchillas; made on what looked like a budget of $18, *Locke's* primary appeal was that it didn't cost anything to run. Fortunately, bartered series did improve, with programs like Chevrolet's *Stand Up and Cheer* and Bristol-Myers' *In Search of...* brightening their access slots with good entertainment value. And as the 1980's came closer, soaring production costs made it virtually impossible for local stations to run syndies if they *weren't* offered on a barter basis.

As P.T.A.R. became a way of life, some syndicators' ambitions grew, with producers striving to please with out-of-ordinary product. When they scored, as did Independent Television Corporation with *The Muppet Show,* there was little that the networks could offer that was finer.

But by the late '70's, with notable exceptions like Norman Lear's *Mary Hartman—Mary Hartman,* syndicated television had settled into a syndrome of gameshows, talk, music-variety and kidstuff. There were, however, still those distributors who saw possibilities in syndication beyond "more of the same." There were even those syndicators who dreamed of challenging the ABC-CBS-NBC triumvirate with an independent "Fourth Network."

Nothing new here. Ever since the death of the DuMont hookup in 1955, ambitious programmers have tried to create network-like syndie systems.

In 1957, National Telefilm Associates, riding the crest of a wave after its enormously successful television distribution of 20th Century–Fox's old Shirley Temple pictures, began forming plans for a fourth network that would have the time-slot flexibility of syndication but would match the production gloss and benefits to affiliates of the three major "webs." Producing its series through the facilities of Desilu, Television Programs of America and 20th Century–Fox (which somewhere down the line had acquired a half-interest in the new network), NTA added to its schedule such videotaped series as *Divorce Court* and began lining up affiliate stations, even buying important channels in such big markets as New York and Minneapolis. With WNTA–Manhattan as its flagship, the "NTA Film Network" officially debuted in October of 1958. But there was a flaw. NTA may have had network ambitions, but it was still at heart a syndication service. The new NTA affiliates didn't take it very well when their "parent" network continued selling syndies to their rival channels. If NTA had had a full-time, seven-day-per-week network manifest, this might not have been a problem; but the company just didn't have enough product for its affiliates to justify NTA's continued outside sales. National Telefilm got off to a very bad start, condemning its network aspirations to a short and not too sweet life.

Flash-forward to 1967: Self-made millionaire Dan Overmyer announces that he's going to set up a nationwide alternative to standard network fare. Overmyer's United Network premieres in May with a live talk show from Las Vegas. One month later, the United Network's first, last and only offering is a live talk show from Las Vegas.

Another flash-forward, to 1977: Lining up 94 television stations (including several influential "independent," or non-network-affiliated channels), MCA creates Operation Prime Time. OPT's first presentation, a star-studded miniseries titled *Testimony of Two Men,* causes enough of a crease in the ratings to warrant future operations, resulting over the next ten years in such multipart projects as *The Kent Family Chronicles, A Woman Called Golda* and *Hoover vs. the Kennedys.* To sustain its cash flow between specials, OPT has had to create bread-and-butter weekly series; hence such programs (distributed through Operation Prime Time's distributor, Television Program Entertainment) as *Solid Gold* and *Entertainment Tonight.*

Also in 1977, syndication was graced with *The Mobil Showcase Network,* created by Mobil Oil for the avowed purpose of upgrading commercial television with high-brow BBC imports like *Edward the King* and *Nicholas Nickleby.* Was there a reason, beyond Art? Well, remember that Mobil Oil, like all the big oil firms, was under fire in the late '70's for reasons clear to those of us who suffered through escalating utility prices and long service-station lines. Mobil had designed a group of commercials to put forth its side of the energy-crisis story, but the big networks rejected this witch's brew of advertising and editorializing; so Mobil offered its *Showcase* specials to an alignment of local stations, promising that the programs would be run without commercial interruption — save for one three-minute allegorical ad at the beginning of each program, wherein a group of cute bunnies and squirrels would explain in pantomime why the viewers should stop bellyaching and love Mobil.

Talk shows thrived in '70's syndication, but by the end of the decade the Mervs, Mikes and Dinahs, with their couchbound showbiz prattle, had begun to give way to spicy controversy-baiting tyros like Phil Donahue. Syndie chat shows began concerning themselves less with plugging new series, new movies and personal appearances, and started delving into the tricky business of coping with a difficult, complex modern world. As the '70's became the '80's, people like Jim Nabors and Alan Thicke, who persisted in the here's-the-hottest-young-new-comic approach, fell by the wayside as programs like *Hour Magazine* tempered their "fluff" content with vital issues of the day, a progression leading to the ultimate syndicated majority of Oprah Winfrey and her compatriots.

It hardly needs to be said that the 1980's brought in several new developments. Of major significance to syndication was the satellite dish. In the past, the syndie practice of "bicycling" tapes from station to station — using one taped copy of a program to service several television outlets, telecasting that copy on one channel and then immediately shipping it to the next market — resulted in some first-run programs not running in many cities until several months after the taping date (a '50's plan to pipe programs over relay cables, for each station's videotaping convenience, was never adopted). Satellite technology allowed local channels to telecast syndicated shows the very same day, sometimes the very same moment, at their inception. For better or worse, this technology has made possible *Entertainment Tonight,* newsman Geraldo Rivera's highly rated ego trips, and the home shopping shows.

Weekend syndication in the 1980's became the province of *Solid Gold* and *Star Search*-style variety series, the increasingly flamboyant wrestling matches, and Robin Leach's show-and-tell spectacles. A new development, which like most new developments wasn't new at all but a revival of a practice that had been going on since the 1950's, was the habit of taking old network series that had run their course and then making new episodes for first-run syndication — series like *Fame, It's a Living* and *Star Trek.* The nice part about this trend is that it created a new, hungry market for first-run, original syndies, resulting in such syndication-only endeavors as *Tales from the Darkside, Small Wonder* and *What a Country!*

Most of these new efforts were far removed from brilliance — some, in fact, were barely tolerable. At the very least, they were an alternative to the syndie variety-talk-game treadmill of the '80's. Still, old ways were the best ways to most non-network producers, so it's not surprising that the most popular syndicated series of all time was the 1980's version of a time-tested NBC network game show, *Wheel of Fortune.*

Of special significance to syndication in this last decade was the decision to relax several old FCC regulations. One such regulation used to govern the amount of advertising allowed on children's shows. After the FCC backed away from limiting this amount, syndication responded with a multitude of new cartoon shows created primarily to peddle "action figures" (that's ad-man talk for plastic dolls with moveable arms). The kids watch *GI Joe* or *He-Man* and buy the GI Joe and He-Man toys. Kids buy the toys, watch the series. It isn't likely to end in our lifetime.

Deregulation also resulted in a wider television market. Owners of TV station groups were no longer limited to the number of channels they were allowed to own, nor did they have to promise to operate primarily "in the public interest." Between 1980 and '85, nearly 300 new independent TV channels were born, operating in no interest other than their own well-being. All those new outlets needed things to show; hence, we have in the 1980's seen the biggest syndication boom in television history.

And, since 1987, we've also seen the latest "fourth network"— publishing mogul Rupert Murdoch's 100-plus-affiliate Fox Television Network. And this one isn't about to fold its tent overnight.

Who knows where it will all end? We *can* tell you where most of it began.

The 1950's

A 1954 edition of *Broadcasting* Magazine listed the genre-types of syndicated programs in order of popularity. Leading the pack with 38 percent of the audience were Adventure/Mystery series; they were followed by Dramas, Westerns, Comedies, Children's shows, Music/Variety, Informational (or Instructional), Travel/Documentary, Game or "Quiz" shows, Talk/Interview series, Religious programs, and (the magazine's designation, not ours) Women's shows. Syndicated sports programs were curiously left off the list, perhaps on the theory that wrestling, auto-racing and bowling weren't considered to *be* sports; we'll include them in our 1950's overview all the same.

Adventure/Mystery

On and off the networks, these were the most popular. They also weren't hard to produce for the most part, since they usually used contemporary clothing, inexpensive location shooting, and about six basic plotlines. Taking few chances, most producers based their series on established literary and radio characters, guaranteed audience favorites. The U.S.–U.S.S.R. Cold War which hung over the decade like a black fog resulted in a plethora of espionage shows, more so than during the spy craze of the 1960's. Comic-strip characters were plentiful, spurred on by the early syndie successes of *Flash Gordon, Terry and the Pirates,* and especially *The Adventures of Superman.* The popularity of *Ramar of the Jungle* led to a steady safari of jungle programs, endearingly nicknamed "The Straw Hut Circuit" by the trade papers of the time. And there were always producers who strove to save a buck or two in labor costs by filming in foreign countries.

Then as now, the public was inscrutable in choosing favorites. The two biggest hits of the decade were a "quickie" designed to fill a release commitment and an underwater epic that had been turned down by all three networks. We'll get to *Highway Patrol* and *Sea Hunt* when the alphabet permits.

17

Adventures of a Jungle Boy (1957). One of two series filmed in Kenya by former child actor George Breakston Jr. and Gross-Krasne Productions (see also *African Patrol*), designed to capitalize on 1957 headlines concerning the efforts of several African nations to declare independence — and also designed to take advantage of the ongoing rerun popularity of *Ramar of the Jungle*. Teenager Michael Carr Hartley was "Boy," a plane-crash orphan growing up in the Kenyan wilds; Ronald Adam co-starred as Laurence, a medical researcher. 39 episodes.

The Adventures of Falcon (1954). Michael Arlen's devil-may-care sleuth with a shady past had been the hero of a sprightly B-picture series from RKO Radio in the 1940's. In these movies, the Falcon's antagonists were mainly murderers and jewel thieves; on the 39-week NBC Films TV series, the character was altered to accommodate the Cold War. He was now international secret agent Michael Waring, whose code name was "Falcon." One concession to Michael Arlen's original character was that, as played by Charles McGraw, the Falcon was rougher and tougher than RKO's suave brother act of George Sanders and Tom Conway.

The Adventures of Fu Manchu (1955). In 1951, the NBC network financed a pilot film for a series based on Sax Rohmer's diabolical Dr. Fu Manchu; it was filmed in New York by producers Lester Schwinn and Herbert Bayard Swope Jr. and starred John Carradine as Fu and Cedric Hardwycke as his Scotland Yard nemesis Sir Nayland Smith. The pilot didn't sell, but was a welcome addition to anthology series for years afterward. In 1955, Republic Pictures paid a reported $4,000,000 to the Sax Rohmer estate for the rights to the Fu Manchu characters. Judging by Republic's subsequent 26-week TV series, that's where *all* the money went. *Fu Manchu* was pasted together with chunks of stock footage from Republic's serial vaults. Demonic Dr. Fu was played by Glenn Gordon in a manner reminiscent of the old vaudeville sketch "Fun in a Chinese Laundry," while Lester Stevens walked through the Nayland Smith part. The series would have been utterly worthless had it not been for the breathtakingly underdressed presence of pin-up girl Laurette Luez as a Manchu minion. Connoisseurs of bad movies will remember Ms. Luez as the star of the 1950 triumph *Prehistoric Women*.

The Adventures of Superman (1952–57). Here is a syndie series that truly needs no introduction. The 104-episode saga of Jerry Siegel and Joe Schuster's "Man of Steel" hasn't stopped playing since it debuted courtesy of Kellogg's Cereals and Motion Pictures for Television (distribution was later handled by Flamingo Films). George Reeves played both Superman and his alter-ego, *Daily Planet* reporter Clark Kent. Fellow reporter Lois Lane was portrayed by Phyllis Coates, then by Noel Neill. Rounding out the cast were Jack Larson as cub reporter Jimmy Olsen, John Hamilton as editor Perry White, and Robert Shayne as Inspector Henderson. With *Superman* still in active syndication, and with Gary Grossman's book *Superman: Serial to Cereal* the definitive work on the subject, there's little to say that hasn't already been said—except for one recently unearthed fact.

It's been reported that the first 26 black and white *Supermans,* filmed on the RKO-Pathé lot in 1951, were held back for release by Kellogg's until March of 1953, and then shown only in late-afternoon kiddie slots. But a foray into some yellowed TV schedules has revealed that *Superman* was being test-marketed as early as the fall of 1952, with several cities, notably Chicago, running the series in adult prime time. This lends credence to the claim that Robert Maxwell, *Superman's* first producer, regarded the series as a fantasy for grownups, and explains why those first episodes were so overloaded with tense melodrama and brutal murders. Of course, by the time *Superman* began filming in color in 1954, the series, under the guiding hand of new producer Whitney Ellsworth, was strictly a kid's show. As such, *Superman* fit in comfortably with the ABC network's 1957–58 late afternoon lineup, where 39 episodes of the series were rerun, still boasting the sponsorship of Kellogg's Cereals.

The Adventures of William Tell (1958). *William Tell,* an NTA release, was filmed on location in Switzerland by a lot of the production people who'd worked on the CBS networker *Robin Hood* (1955–58). Conrad Philips starred as the Swiss folk hero, and was outacted each week by the splendidly named Willoughby Goddard as the evil Gessler. Oddly, though *Tell* was shot in Europe by a British crew, the series was carefully monitored by the Hollywood actors' unions, who saw to it that pay-scales were strictly enforced down to the lowliest bit player. The unions might have done better to find these actors some other work, for the 39-week *William Tell* was a cheapjack affair that ran out of excitement early on. Apparently the only person who really liked this show was the program manager at WGN–Chicago, where *William Tell* remained a fixture of the all-night schedule as late as 1982.

The Affairs of China Smith (1952). Also: **The New Adventures of China Smith** (1955). Originally titled *Captain China,* this entry starred movie badguy Dan Duryea as an Irish-American soldier of fortune, tooling around Singapore armed with little more than a brogue and an excess of nerve. Duryea's character was a tonic to viewers fed up with ultra-clean Lone Ranger types; China Smith was a liar, a thief, and a rat with women. But because his adversaries were either Communists or bigger crooks than he, China Smith remained a favorite with the viewers.

Mr. Smith was not, however, a favorite of the American Federation of TV and Radio Artists. It seemed that *China Smith* producer Bernard Tabakin, deciding that nothing in Hollywood looked anything like Singapore and that nothing in Hollywood was as cheap as Mexican labor, filmed the series' first six episodes in Mexico. AFTRA called Tabakin on the carpet for allegedly taking bread from the mouths of Hollywood union members, forcing the producer to film the rest of *Smith's* 26 episodes in Los Angeles and San Francisco. This labor vs. management debacle discouraged other TV producers from making plans for extensive filming in Mexico; TV series that would venture South of the Border in the future would do so only with production crews well stocked with Hollywoodites.

The first 26 *China Smiths* made a wad of dough for Dan Duryea (as did an additional 26 filmed by NTA in 1955 and bearing the innovative title *The New Adventures of China Smith*); the series didn't hurt the careers of its production people, either. *Smith's* associate producer Buck Houghton went on to a producer's berth on CBS' *Schlitz Playhouse,* thence to a three-year stint with the classic *Twilight Zone.* Dan Duryea's chief director and drinking buddy Robert Aldrich graduated to top motion pictures like *The Dirty Dozen, Flight of the Phoenix* and *The Longest Yard.* And Aldrich's director of photography on those last two films—as well as on the 1953 Dan Duryea picture *World for Ransom,* filmed while *China Smith* was on production hiatus—was Joseph Biroc, yet another *Smith* alumnus, who'd win a 1974 Oscar for his work on *The Towering Inferno.*

African Patrol (1957). The second of George Breakston Jr./Gross-Krasne's "jungle" syndies of 1957 (see also *Adventures of a Jungle Boy*), *African Patrol* starred John Bentley as Kenya-based Inspector John Derek. Derek put in his time trailing criminals who'd been foolish enough to attempt escape into the Kenyan wilds, and sometimes performed such tricky efforts as directing a delicate medical procedure via walkie-talkie. *African Patrol's* 39 installments were filmed in remarkable haste; the news headlines about the political turmoil in Africa forced Gross-Krasne to rush the series into an October '57 release before there were even 13 episodes in the can. Despite the speed, *African Patrol* was one of the handsomer "Straw Hut" endeavors of the era.

The Big Story (1957). Created for radio by Bernard F. Procktor in 1947, *Big Story* was an anthology of major scoops turned in by real-life newspaper reporters, often at risk of life and limb. The TV version of *Big Story* first ran live and on film over NBC from 1949 until 1957, at which time Official Films released 39 new *Big Story* half-hours for syndication. These were significant in that they represented the first regular-series work for their host-narrator, Burgess Meredith.

Bold Venture (1959). One of Ziv Productions' biggest radio moneyspinners was 1950's *Bold Venture.* It starred Humphrey Bogart as Slate Shannon, owner of a Cuban hotel and skipper of the charter-boat "Bold Venture." Lauren Bacall (Mrs. Bogart) played Slate's "ward," Sailor Duval. If the whole thing sounded a lot like the Bogart-Bacall movie *To Have and Have Not,* what a coincidence *that* was. One neat touch on the series was having its scenes bridged with expository songs sung by Calypso artist "King Moses." By late 1958, Calypso music was all the rage, and so was Ziv's TV syndie *Sea Hunt.* Cashing in on both trends, Ziv produced a 39-week TV version of *Bold Venture,* with emphasis on the music and the seafaring business. Dane Clark, who'd made his movie debut in a Humphrey Bogart picture, stepped into Bogey's Slate Shannon role; Sailor Duval was portrayed by TV-anthology regular Joan Marshall, while King Moses was played by actor-singer Bernie Gozier. The series' locale was shifted from Cuba to the Bahamas, a nod to the political climate of early 1959. Ziv's relationship with regional sponsors was a happy one at the time, and the company could usually count on at least 180 sales for each new syndie release; *Bold Venture* got 184. The series' producers, Morton Fine and David Friedkin, had been scriptwriters for the radio *Bold Venture;* Fine and Friedkin would later enjoy a three-year hitch on the Cosby-Culp series *I Spy.*

Border Patrol see *United States Border Patrol*

Boston Blackie (1951–52). Boston Blackie, the reformed-crook-turned-sleuth created by Jack Boyle in the early 20th century, was a proven media commodity long before television. Blackie had appeared in movies since 1918 (most notably in a breezy Columbia "B" series starring Chester Morris) and on radio since 1944, first on the NBC network, then in a syndicated effort recorded at the studios of WOR–New York by Ziv Productions. Ziv secured TV rights to the property from Jack Boyle's widow, and once the company's *Cisco Kid* got off the ground in 1951, Ziv rented studio space at Eagle-Lion, churning out 58 full-color *Boston Blackie* half-hours.

Although the TV series wasn't cheap — it cost $21,000 per episode, some five thousand more than the average filmed series of 1951 — *Boston Blackie* never lost its B-picture "look," since most of the production money went to crew-member overhead, color film stock, and the salaries of stars Kent Taylor (Blackie) and Lois Collier (Blackie's girl Mary). To accelerate production, Ziv adopted an assembly-line shooting method, filming up to three episodes simultaneously. To keep a keen eye on the budget, Fred Ziv hired Maurice "Babe" Ungar as production manager. Ungar not only kept track of every penny spent, but also made sure that Ziv's story-content rules were strictly enforced. Ziv preferred plots which thrust Blackie into exotic settings (even if those settings were close-to-studios spots like the Santa Monica amusement pier and San Francisco's Japanese Gardens), and hated stories that had anything to do with knives. Most of the *Blackie* scripts vetoed by Ungar involved blades in the back.

As was customary in filmed TV of the time, *Boston Blackie's* supporting casts were comprised of the finest 100-dollar-a-day players available, including John Eldredge, Herb Vigran, John Doucette and Ben Welden. Sportscaster Tom Hanlon, narrator of Ziv's *Sports Album* (1948), appeared as a news vendor who'd show up halfway through the story to say "We'll be right back." The local commercial that followed was generally for a bank or a brewery, the two foremost syndie sponsors of the early '50s. Unlike Ziv's *Cisco Kid, Boston Blackie* was considered an "adult" series, and as such was usually scheduled in a late-evening slot, often just before the 11 o'clock news. The "adult" stories might seem a tad juvenile today, but in 1951, *Boston Blackie* was a pleasant way for viewers in 33 cities to while away half an hour.

Cannonball (1958). Robert Maxwell, producer of Television Programs of America's CBS-networker *Lassie,* stayed on payroll when T.P.A. was absorbed by Independent Television Corporation in 1958. Maxwell's first ITC syndie was *Cannonball,* a weekly saga of two long-haul truck drivers filmed in both the U.S. and Canada to satisfy the quota restrictions of both countries. Paul Birch starred as Mike "Cannonball" Malone, with William Campbell as his partner Jerry Austin. The 39 *Cannonballs* thrived in syndication, offering a little something for everyone. Action fans were served a diet of smugglers, hijackers and wildcat truckers. Drama fans enjoyed tales of the drivers' domestic difficulties and their coping with such professional hazards as "tunnel vision" and fatigue. And kids were entranced by *Cannonball's* whale of a theme song, wherein a squad of he-man choristers would rhapsodize over "the rumble of the Diesel, the shiftin' of the gear."

Captain David Grief (1956). Guild Films picked up distribution rights for this filmed-in-Mexico cheapie starring serial hero Maxwell Reed as Captain Grief. Stuck with a lemon, Guild resolved to make lemonade. The company piled up several sales by promoting the fact that the series' 26 episodes were shot in color, and emphasizing that *Captain David Grief* was the first television series based on the works of Jack London. But few markets bothered to renew their contracts after the first year, even when Guild reissued the program as *Jack London Stories.* What little professional veneer *Captain David Grief* might have had was due to its director, *Superman* regular Harry Gerstad.

Captured (1953). At closer glance, NBC Films' *Captured* was the network series *Gangbusters,* with nine new episodes filmed for syndication. Hosting was onetime Boston Blackie of the silver screen Chester Morris.

Charlie Chan see *The New Adventures of Charlie Chan*

Charter Boat see *Crunch and Des*

China Smith see *The Affairs of China Smith*

City Detective (1953–54). MCA/Revue's 65-episode *City Detective* might well have been dismissed as more of the same had it not been for two strong, driving forces. One force was MCA, which did its talent-agency best to promote the series, racking up a then-record 117 syndie sales. The other, even more formidable force was the series' star. Rod Cameron, a minor action-movie star of the 1940's, entered television when good picture roles became scarce; *City Detective* was the first of three percentage-of-profits deals between Cameron and MCA. Aware that his series' critics dismissed him as merely "acting with his fists," Cameron seasoned his portrayal of Lt. Bart Grant with humor, a way with the ladies, and a penchant for undercover-work disguises (three ingredients which later would be ingrained in the movie work of Blake Edwards, who for a while was a writer and associate producer of *City Detective*). Lt. Grant may not have been the most original thing to come down the pike, but Rod Cameron added a third dimension to the character's existing two — and in so doing became an instant TV favorite. A canny businessman, Cameron knew that his *City Detective* residuals wouldn't have been as fat had a major television network been claiming a percentage of the action, and as a result the actor vowed to remain in syndication for the rest of his TV career. By 1960, Cameron was drawing over $200,000 per annum in residuals on no fewer than three MCA syndies: *City Detective, State Trooper* and *Coronado 9.* That's a total of 218 non-network half-hours.

With so much good fortune coming his way, Rod Cameron could be excused for chalking up some of his success to superstition. Actress Beverly Garland had guest-starred on the *City Detective* pilot; it sold. In 1956, Cameron hired Garland for the *State Trooper* pilot; it sold. So when it came time in 1959 to film the pilot for *Coronado 9,* Cameron again called upon the talented Miss Garland — and got yet another sale. Never underestimate the Philosophy of the Rabbit's Foot.

Code Three (1956). Hal Roach Studios' response to the success of *Highway Patrol* (which see), *Code Three* was initially planned for an ABC network run, but ended up in syndication via MCA. The series' title was drawn from the Los Angeles County Sheriff's Department's designation for any crime involving immediate action: murder, manslaughter, grand theft, kidnapping. Richard Travis and a beardless, pre–*Dukes of Hazzard* Denver Pyle were prominent among the regulars; *Code Three's* authenticity was assured by its occasional host, L.A. County Sheriff Eugene W. Biscialuz.

Colonel March of Scotland Yard (1953). Imported from Britain by Official Films, *Colonel March* was the only weekly series based on the stories of prolific mystery writer John Dickson Carr (a.k.a. Carter Dickson). Boris Karloff excelled as the erudite, eye-patched Colonel March, head of Scotland Yard's Department of Queer Complaints ("queer" meant "unusual" back then). Directing several solid *March* episodes was Cy Enfield, whose crowning cinematic achievement was 1964's *Zulu;* another future director of note, John Schlesinger, popped up on a *March* adventure as a villain. Official sold this above-average series on the basis of Col. March's intellect; the ad copy asked "Remember when a detective could count to ten?"

Congressional Investigator (1959). Despite a title given timeliness in 1959 by real-life congressional crimefighting, this 39-weeker was strictly routine, usually consigned to late-late-night time slots. The main investigator was played by Edson Stroll, later a juvenile lead in Three Stooges comedies and a supporting clown on *McHale's Navy.*

Copter Patrol see *The Whirlybirds*

Counterspy (1959). An obscure television incarnation of an old radio spy series, *Counterspy* might have fared better had it starred Reed Hadley, who played lead character David Harding in the pilot film. After all, Hadley had a good syndie track record thanks to his *Racket Squad* reruns. Instead, the unremarkable Don Megowan wound up as David Harding.

Counterthrust (1958). In direct contrast to *Counterspy,* ABC Films' *Counterthrust* did feature a syndie favorite: Tod Andrews, star of the smash-hit *Gray Ghost.* Still, this international intrigue affair didn't make it past 13 episodes. Perhaps audiences were as sick of the 1950's spy-show cycle as they'd be of the second such cycle ten years later.

The Count of Monte Cristo (1955–56). George Dolenz (father of The Monkees' Mickey) played fight-for-right Edmond Dantes in this economical but entertaining 78-week version of Alexandre Dumas' adventure novel. Television Programs of America claimed that some scenes were shot on standing sets left over from the 1934 film version of *Monte Cristo,* and this might well have been true, since Edward Small, the producer of the '34 movie, was chairman of the board at T.P.A. Most of the series was lensed at Hal Roach Studios, until producer Rudy Flotow moved production to England, there to take advantage of all that eyefilling 19th-century architecture (not to mention the lower labor costs). *Count of Monte Cristo,* one of the better "literary" syndies (programs inspired by the Classics), was for one whole week the top-rated non-network program in New York City.

Craig Kennedy, Criminologist (1951). Inspired by *Boston Blackie,* the Weiss Brothers warmed up another early 20th-century pulp-novel sleuth for television: Columbia University crime expert Craig Kennedy. Donald Woods was rather stolid in the admittedly stiff-necked leading role, but the Weisses managed quite a few sales on the basis of a neat promotional gimmick. The producers promised that should the first 13 weeks of *Craig Kennedy* fail to outrate their competition, the remaining 13 episodes would be given out free of charge. Whether or not the Weiss boys ever had to ante up is unknown, but we do know that *Craig Kennedy* was the first filmed TV series ever shown in U.S. Army hospitals abroad.

Cross Current see *Foreign Intrigue*

Crunch and Des (1955). An NBC Films release, based on characters created by Philip Wylie for *The Saturday Evening Post.* Forrest Tucker received solo star billing as Crunch Adams, who with pal "Desperate" Smith (Sandy Kenyon) ran a charter-boat service in the Bahamas. Their boat was called the *Poseidon,* but stayed rightside-up anyway. Filmed at RKO-Pathé and on location in Bermuda, *Crunch and Des* was typical mid–50's action fare with the usual day-player supporting casts, featuring occasional newcomers such as strapping young George Kennedy. Like many syndies, *Crunch and Des* was sold by NBC Films directly to major sponsors who'd cover several markets at once. These advertisers frequently signed long-term exclusivity contracts, so when NBC wanted to send out *Crunch and Des* reruns in 1957, they were re-titled *Charter Boat* in some markets. One year later, the *Sea Hunt* craze compelled NBC to *re-*retitle *Crunch and Des* as *Deep Sea Adventures.* It was always smart in the syndication game to squeeze the last possible drop of profits out of a property.

Dangerous Assignment (1952). Television version of a pedestrian radio spy series starring Brian Donlevy as suave, dinner-jacketed undercover agent Steve Mitchell. Donlevy claimed that Mitchell was based on the actor's favorite movie role, that of a slick con man in *Nightmare* (1942). The star was permitted a lot of personal input with *Dangerous Assignment;* in fact, this 52-week NBC Films release was a product of Donlevy Development Enterprises. With Brian Donlevy allegedly giving his all to the series, it is a puzzlement that his performance on *Dangerous Assignment* was so relentlessly sluggish, right down to his ho-hum reaction to the dagger which whizzed past his head in the opening credits.

Dateline Europe see Foreign Intrigue

Deadline (1959). Despite an unappetizing title and the none-too-original premise of dramatizing actual events in the lives of news reporters (see *The Big Story*), Flamingo Films' *Deadline* scored high profits by making its plotlines secondary to its violent-action content. Paul Stewart hosted the series' 39 episodes, starring in 13.

Decoy see Policewoman Decoy

Deep Sea Adventures see Crunch and Des

Dial 999 (1958). *Dial 999* (the title referred to the telephone exchange for Scotland Yard's emergency calls) was produced by Ziv in conjunction with Harry Alan Towers' Towers of London Productions, using "frozen funds" accrued by Ziv in England. Robert Beatty starred as a Canadian detective working at "The Yard."

Dick Tracy (1952). Chester Gould's jut-jawed comic strip detective first appeared on the ABC television network in 1950. Ralph Byrd, who'd been playing Tracy in the movies on and off since 1937, was the star. United Television Productions filmed 39 more episodes for syndication following the ABC run, just before Ralph Byrd's sudden death in 1952. *Dick Tracy's* producer-director team of Robert M. Snader and Duke Goldstone would later attain the pinnacle of syndicated success with *The Liberace Show.*

Dr. Fu Manchu see The Adventures of Fu Manchu

Ellery Queen (1954). "Ellery Queen" was the joint pen name of the writing-team cousins Frederick Dannay and Manfred Lee, and also the name of Manfred and Lee's fictional intellectual sleuth. Several actors took turns playing Ellery Queen on network television since 1950, but when T.P.A. filmed a syndicated *Ellery Queen* on the Roach and Goldwyn lots in 1954, the role went to Hugh Marlowe, the first actor to play Queen on radio in 1939. When the CBS network announced plans for a new version of the durable detective property in 1957, the 39 syndie *Ellery Queens* were renamed *Mystery Is My Business.*

Fabian of Scotland Yard (1955). Bruce Seton portrayed Inspector Fabian in this British cops-and-robbers opus syndicated in America by CBS Films. The enormous success of *Highway Patrol* led CBS to believe that they'd realize even more revenue off of *Fabian* by re-christening the one-season series as *Patrol Car.*

The Falcon see **The Adventures of Falcon**

The Files of Jeffrey Jones (1953). The CBS network enjoyed an unexpected success in 1952 with a so-so private eye show, *Cases of Eddie Drake*—but only indirectly. *Drake* had been filmed for CBS in 1949, but the network saw no potential in the project, and sold it to the DuMont Network, where *Eddie Drake* scored a hit. CBS Films responded by assembling a lookalike syndie project with the *Eddie Drake's* star (Don Haggerty) and producer (Lindsley Parsons), and the result was 26 weeks' worth of *The Files of Jeffrey Jones.* All that set Jeffrey Jones apart from his detective-show brethren was his rabid enthusiasm over professional sports events.

Flash Gordon (1952). Alex Raymond's comic strip *Flash Gordon,* already a popular cinema attraction via the serials starring Buster Crabbe as the dauntless space-traveller, was turned into a television series by Intercontinental Films under the aegis of Hollywood producer Edward Grushkin and West Berlin's Wenzel Luedtke. A bizarre crazy-quilt of papier-mâché sets and wooden acting, *Flash* was filmed in Berlin, which explained why the principal mode of transportation in the 21st century seemed to be the Volkswagen. Buster Crabbe clone Steve Holland played Gordon, Irene Champlin was Dale Arden, and the villains were usually gangster and spy types in spacesuits. The series' curious emphasis on beatings and bondage represented its only concession to any audience other than the kiddie trade. *Flash Gordon's* American distributor was Motion Pictures for Television (MPTV), a firm created by Matty Fox to release independently produced Hollywood movies to television. Matty Fox's theory was that syndication was the way to travel in the world of filmed television; true to his beliefs, Fox stayed out of the networks until the end of the '50s, by which time he'd become one of the leaders of the pay–TV movement.

The Flying Doctor (1959). Filmed in England, Gross-Krasne's *Flying Doctor* was based on a real-life airborne medical service which tended to patients in the farther reaches of Australia. Richard Denning starred, but the most appealing character was Denning's superior, played by Peter Madden as a man who was totally blind, but a brilliant, active physician all the same.

Foreign Intrigue (1951–55). *Foreign Intrigue* managed during its four-year first-run syndie career to garner three Emmy nominations, invite the participation of three major distributors (NBC Films, Official Films and the J. Walter Thompson agency), and make history as the first filmed American series to play on Canadian television. So popular was the series that, when it was being handled by NBC Films, clips from *Foreign Intrigue* showed up in a promotional film for NBC's *network* shows. *Intrigue's* producer was a peripatetic 27-year-old American millionaire named Sheldon Reynolds, who preferred travelling the privileged circles of international society and European royalty. Through friends and friends of friends, Reynolds secured production facilities and financial backing for his series, attracting American viewers in the early '50s by offering them something they weren't getting from their average domestic television product: breathtaking glimpses of the glamour spots of Europe. In the bargain, Reynolds took advantage of low-cost European labor to get millions of dollars' worth of entertainment value at bargain-basement prices.

Foreign Intrigue's first 78 episodes were shot in Paris and Stockholm, and starred Jerome Thor and Synda Scott as two correspondents for the "Consolidated News Service." When the workload on Thor and Scott got too heavy, Reynolds set up a "second-string" cast featuring Robert Arden and Dorein Denning as two more reporters on the Consolidated payroll. In its third 39-week season, *Foreign Intrigue* traversed the Continent with a new star-team: James Daly and Ann Preville as yet still two more news service correspondents. Common to all episodes in the series' first three seasons were the newspersons' tendencies to stick their noses into espionage and Communist-bashing. Also "constant" in those first three years, appearing in supporting and bit roles, was Nicole Millenaire, better known in Europe as the Duchess of Bedford. A close friend of Sheldon Reynolds, the duchess was invaluable in rounding up her society chums to play minor roles and dress extras; she also functioned as *Intrigue's* production assistant, even doubling for actors in long shots and car chases.

The series' format was totally overhauled for its final 39 episodes in 1954; gone were all those news correspondents, replaced by something out of *Casablanca*. Gerald Mohr starred as Chris Storm, a Vienna-based hotel owner who permitted his inn to be used as a way-station for Iron Curtain refugees and victims of international crooks. Even in these final episodes, Sheldon Reynolds strove for quality beyond picture-postcard views of Europe; the scripts had strong story values, so that even when the plots weren't logical, they were expertly put together and *seemed* to make sense. Reynolds carried this quality over into his next project, 1954's *Sherlock Holmes.*

Even as *Foreign Intrigue* played for top sponsors in first-run, Official Films was recycling the series' reruns under new titles. The Thor-Scott episodes were reissued as *Dateline Europe* in 1953; one year later, the Daly-Preville installments were issued anew as *Overseas Adventure;* and in 1955, the Gerald Mohr episodes showed up as *Cross Current*. Further adding to his own bank balance, Sheldon Reynolds pasted three of the early Thor-Scotts together as a "feature film" for Scandinavian release. And in 1956, Reynolds produced and directed a Technicolor *Foreign Intrigue* theatrical picture starring no less than Robert Mitchum.

The Four Just Men (1959). A collaboration of American producer Jack Wrather and British mogul J. Arthur Rank, ITC's *Four Just Men,* filmed at Pinewood Studios in England, was a beautiful job by any standards. The series had its roots in a 1920's novel by that legendary story machine Edgar Wallace (filmed by Ealing Studios in 1939). The four heroes of the television version had been World War II guerrilla fighters, reteamed in the late '50s by the man who'd commandeered their last great wartime mission in order to combat modern-day tyranny, injustice and crime. The quartet consisted of two Americans, one an expatriate living in Paris, the other a news correspondent; a British private detective; and an Italian hotel owner. In a burst of "spare no expense," *Four Just Men* was lavishly mounted (its principal director was the high-priced Basil Dearden) and sumptuously location-filmed all over England and Europe. And its four rotating stars were not the usual syndicated–TV aggregate of former greats in professional decline, but four performers at the top of the heap: Dan Dailey, Richard Conte, Jack Hawkins and Vittorio de Sica. The result was 1959's best-looking syndie, a series that sold far and wide throughout the world. But its $50,000-per-episode budget was way too high to accrue big profits in the syndicated market of the day, so *Four Just Men* classed itself out of filming any more than 39 episodes. It was just too good to last.

Fu Manchu see **The Adventures of Fu Manchu**

The George Raft Casebook see **I'm the Law**

Grand Jury (1959). A swiftly assembled series made to capitalize on real-life legal actions against major crime figures occurring in the late '50s, Desilu/NTA's *Grand Jury* was *so* rapidly put together that only three episodes had made it to film by the time of its premiere in October, 1959. While NTA made every effort to sell the series on its "public service" angle, *Grand Jury's* million dollars' worth of prerelease sales was due more to the series' violence quotient. Like many syndies of the era, the 39 *Grand Jurys* were excessively brutal to remain competitive with network action shows, which were then under pressure to tone things down. Lyle Bettger and Harold J. Stone, usually seen in their television work on the other side of the law, starred as the principal Grand Jury investigators.

The Gray Ghost (1957). But for an accident of timing, Lindsley Parsons/CBS Films' *The Gray Ghost* might have produced more than 39 episodes. The first of several syndies to cash in on America's upcoming Civil War Centennial, *Gray Ghost* was based on the true exploits of Major John Mosby of the 43rd Battalion, 1st Virginia Cavalry, Army of the Confederacy. Mosby was played by New York–born Tod Andrews, who was drawn to the role because of Mosby's distaste for violence, making him a far more complex and compelling character than the usual television hero. Mosby's nickname sprang from his quiet elusiveness while he acted as an undercover spy against the North. *Gray Ghost's* greatest fan following quite naturally came from below the Mason-Dixon line — and therein lay the reason for the series' premature shutdown. The Civil Rights movement was at long last picking up steam in 1957, especially after the desegregation of Little Rock High School. Popular though *Gray Ghost* may have been, it did have a Confederate hero, and was thus perceived by some civil rights activists as espousing the Confederate cause — which was tantamount in those troubled times to embracing racial intolerance. It didn't matter that *Gray Ghost* avoided the black-white issue like a case of measles; CBS Films decided it was best to drop this hot potato before it was allowed to burn. This didn't prevent CBS from collecting profits from the 39 episodes already in syndication, however, nor did it prevent the company from keeping interest in *Gray Ghost* alive by issuing statements that the series might resume production, or perhaps even matriculate into a feature film.

Harbor Command (1957). An economic recession in 1957 resulted in increased production costs for filmed syndies; as a result, non-network programs that didn't perform spectacularly seldom got past 39 episodes. Ziv's *Harbor Command,* starring Wendell Corey, fell victim to this new stringency. Ziv secured more than 150 first-run sales on the basis of its "A *commanding* role — a *commanding* performance" publicity hype, but when all was said and done, *Harbor Command* was merely *Highway Patrol* at sea, and as such wasn't considered worthy of a second season.

Hawkeye and the Last of the Mohicans (1957). A Canadian-American coproduction for TPA, *Hawkeye* was taken as far as possible from the works of James Fenimore Cooper. John Hart, who'd demonstrated his utter lack of star quality when he briefly replaced Clayton Moore on *The Lone Ranger,* kept his record intact in the role of 18th-century frontiersman Hawkeye. His Indian chum Chingachcook was played by Lon Chaney Jr., and you know you're in trouble with a series in which Lon Chaney Jr. is the best actor. A major attraction in the Canadian kiddie–TV trade, *Hawkeye* was strictly Amateur Night in the Great White North, so you'd think that the series wouldn't pass muster with adults. And you'd be wrong. *Hawkeye* was one of TPA's strongest '57 properties, its 26 episodes drawing fans from all viewer age groups. All this proved, perhaps, that if you had a frontier hero, an Indian companion, and a series that looked enough like a western to satisfy western-happy viewers of the time, you had it made.

Highway Patrol (1955–59). Eventually weighing in at 155 episodes, Ziv's *Highway Patrol* began as a virtual throwaway, slapped together in a dark corner of Eagle-Lion studios to meet Ziv's October 1955 release commitment. *Patrol* star Broderick Crawford had some name value thanks to his 1949 Oscar for *All the King's Men,* but his career had rollercoastered from the heights to the depths with such frequency that he was hardly everyone's first choice for enduring television-series success (Crawford's off-screen reputation as a premiere elbow-bender helped not at all). A Screen Gems pilot for a potential Crawford vehicle, *Manhunt,* proved unsuccessful, but it convinced Ziv Productions that the actor could carry a goodly amount of authority and conviction to the role of Capt. Dan Matthews in *Highway Patrol*—for at least 39 weeks.

Every expense was spared in keeping *Highway Patrol* fast and cheap. Although its stories occasionally brought in elaborate hardware like helicopters or tanks, the series' pinchpenny budget was typified by an early episode in which a three-minute robbery/murder/escape sequence was filmed in one single, static take. The thriftiness extended to *Highway Patrol's* well-remembered theme music, which was drawn from Ziv's vast library of royalty-free tunes and had previously been used on the radio version of *Mr. District Attorney.*

Yet somehow, *Highway Patrol* took off. By 1956, the series was attracting big sponsors and huge ratings everywhere it played; other Hollywood producers rushed about creating imitation Highway Patrols like *Code Three* and *State Trooper;* and Ziv Productions found itself building its entire 1956–57 ad campaign around *Highway Patrol's* track record. Fred Ziv's "minor" time-filler was a major smash. Ziv eventually formulated an explanation of the series' popularity. The producer insisted that it was due in part to the public's ongoing *Dragnet*-inspired fascination with police procedure, jargon, and state-of-the-art law enforcement hardware. But the most vital ingredient to *Patrol's* success, claimed Ziv, was Broderick Crawford's curt, clipped acting technique, exemplified by his frequent barked-out radio commands of "Ten-Four!" and "Twenty-One Fifty Bye!" Ziv noted that Crawford's style had carried over into the series' "look," resulting in tight closeups and rapid-fire editing. In short, Brod Crawford did not act on *Highway Patrol; Highway Patrol* acted *like* Brod Crawford.

Given in later years to lampooning his Capt. Matthews role on such comedy shows as *Saturday Night Live,* Crawford never joked about the positive effect *Highway Patrol* had on his life: it made him a millionaire, prolonged his career, and even allowed him to direct on occasion. Nor did Crawford feel that syndicated TV was a step below network quality: "I see no difference," he once said, "except that in syndication you get your money quicker." *Highway Patrol* not only benefited Crawford, but turned out to be the biggest money-maker Ziv ever had; it was still turning a profit in mid–60's reruns. The series even obliged Ziv to set up a subsidiary company, Economee Films, in 1957. Ziv's policy was to sell its first-run series directly to regional sponsors; Economee handled Ziv's reruns, offering them directly to local TV stations. To avoid competition with the first-run *Patrol* episodes, Economee's repeats were given the logical title *Ten-Four.* And there was definitely a demand for those repeats: at one juncture in 1959, *Highway Patrol* was running on *three* New York City channels each week. It also owned the distinction of being the first American series shown on West Germany's commercial television channel—conjuring up irresistible images of Broderick Crawford grabbing his radio microphone and shouting, "Sehn-FIER!"

Hollywood Off-Beat (1952). Jerry Fairbanks production, starring Melvyn Douglas as disbarred lawyer Steve Randall, who became a private eye in order to clear himself. *Hollywood Off-Beat* is included here as an example of those hybrid series which ran both as syndicated programs and as network offerings, using the same episodes (on DuMont and CBS, this show was titled *Steve Randall*). In noting this series, we acknowledge all the other "hybrids" like *Racket Squad, The Roy Rogers Show* and *Sky King,* which fluctuated between network play and syndication.

Hudson's Bay (1958). Forgotten 39-week Canadian costumer starring Barry Nelson as an 18th-century explorer. *Hudson's Bay* floundered when United Artists television failed to line up any sales, and didn't do much better when reissued in 1959 and 1960. The adventure-syndie market was too glutted with product to make room for something as unremarkable as *Hudson's Bay.*

I Led Three Lives (1953–55). Fred Ziv had wanted to film a television version of his radio syndie *I Was a Communist for the FBI,* the saga of real-life double agent Matt Cvetic, but the TV rights eluded him. Ziv latched onto a similar property, *I Led Three Lives;* this was the true story of Herbert A. Philbrick who, like Cvetic, posed as a Communist on behalf of the Federal Government (Philbrick's "third life" was as a Boston ad man). Richard Carlson, another second-string movie star seeking to extenuate his career by entering television, played Herb Philbrick in 117 extremely popular half-hours. The real Philbrick, a shy man not given to self-promotion, was suddenly turned into an Instant Celebrity thanks to the series, then sucked into a maelstrom of lecture tours and personal appearances—and loving every minute of it!

I Led Three Lives has long been the whipping-boy of television historians and sociologists. Because the principal villains were American "Reds," the series has been perceived as supporting and encouraging the Hollywood "blacklist"—that scurrilous tally of actors and writers denied TV and movie work during the '50s because of their political beliefs—and the antics of Senator Joe McCarthy. Some latter-day critics have gone so far as to claim that *I Led Three Lives* was responsible for the anti–Red paranoia all by itself. But as we've seen with such previously mentioned syndies as *China Smith* and *Foreign Intrigue, I Led Three Lives* was hardly unique in its use of Commies as convenient bad-guys. Moreover, Ziv's series did not subscribe to the McCarthy/Blacklist notion that a person's eccentricities automatically made that person a subtle Communist. If anything, *Three Lives* strove to *avoid* subtlety: the villains exchanged furtive glances, perspired like pigs, and were given to declaring that they wouldn't rest until "the last American flag is cut up for so much cotton waste." Most viewers in 1953, as well as several television critics working on the more "liberal" newspapers and magazines, understood that *Three Lives* used Communist villains because they were timely. And crude though the series may have been, *I Led Three Lives* never stooped to the level of the 1951 movie version of *I Was a Communist for the FBI,* which tacitly suggested that *every* effort at social reform, even the Civil Rights movement, was Communist-inspired.

Richard Carlson—whose participation in the series made him quite wealthy, his only "complaint" (which smacked of PR-man flack) being that his own family preferred watching an Ann Sothern sitcom that ran opposite *I Led Three Lives* in Los Angeles—insisted that his series was entertainment, not didactic: "In our series, we don't preach the anti–Communist doctrine ... we assume people know Communism is evil." Fred Ziv himself showed where *he* stood by regularly hiring victims of the Blacklist for his many TV and radio series. Existing prints of *I Led Three Lives* bear out the "entertainment only" stance of Ziv and Carlson. The melodrama in the series grew not as much from the exposure of enemies in our midst as from whether or not Herb Philbrick would be found out and killed by his "comrades" before the episode was over. It's best to say that *I Led Three Lives* was popular because it was a tense, tautly directed, thoroughly professional job. And to leave it at that.

I'm the Law (1953). Also known as *The George Raft Casebook* in deference to its star, MCA's *I'm the Law* was a product of comedian Lou Costello's production company, filmed concurrently with *The Abbott and Costello Show* at Hal Roach Studios. George Raft signed on to play Lt. George Kirby because he was a pal of the series' executive producer, Lou Costello's brother Pat, with whom Raft had appeared in vaudeville. The very ordinary *I'm the Law* had one intriguing production highlight: the day that Raft and the Costello brothers were approached by a team of Hollywood money men, who offered a six-figure sum for permission to re-cut several of the series' episodes into a theatrical feature film. George Raft refused, a decision that he'd never understand and would have cause to regret until his dying day. Promised $90,000 for his work in the 26-week *I'm the Law,* Raft saw every penny evaporate when Lou Costello was pounced upon by the I.R.S. for back taxes.

International Detective (1959). Official Film's *International Detective* was a year-long fictionalization of the files of the William J. Burns detective agency. It is of interest primarily because its producer-director was Eddie Sutherland, a Hollywood giant of the '30s reduced to working in Europe on the cheap in the '50s, and because its star was Art Fleming, some five years away from his tenure on the game show *Jeopardy.*

Interpol Calling (1959). Producers Jack Wrather and J. Arthur Rank were obliged to produce two British-made series for ITC release. The brilliant *Four Just Men* was one; *Interpol Calling,* starring the unexciting Charles Korvin in 39 uninvolving stories, was the other.

I Spy (1955). By no stretch of imagination could this Guild Films syndie be confused with the later Robert Culp-Bill Cosby series. The original 39-week *I Spy,* filmed in England, was an anthology of true espionage tales, many of them set in Centuries Past. The series had one of the most arresting openings in all television; the camera zoomed in on a super-tight closeup of a wide-open human eye. Most of the episodes didn't sustain the visual dynamics of that opener, but were competent jobs under the supervision of B-quickie veteran William Berke. "Anton the Spymaster," the host, was played by Raymond Massey, who felt no need to mention this fact in either of his autobiographies.

Ivanhoe (1958, 1972). Produced with American funds in England by ITC, *Ivanhoe* was released stateside by Screen Gems. Roger Moore, later star of TV's *The Saint,* got his first series exposure as Sir Walter Scott's noble knight. Anticipating CBS' *Afternoon Specials* by nearly two decades, Screen Gems sent out a schoolroom "study guide" to be used by *Ivanhoe's* younger viewers. The guide never explained why the Jewish characters so important to Walter Scott's original story were conspicuous by their absence. *Ivanhoe* re-emerged, this time with more fidelity to the source material, as a British 10-parter released in America as part of 1972's *Family Classics Theatre;* Eric Flynn emulated his father Errol in the leading role.

The Jack London Stories see *Captain David Grief*

The Joe Palooka Story (1953). Ham Fisher's soft-hearted comic-strip pugilist had been knocking around the funnies since 1928 and in movies since 1934. The last cinematic Joe Palooka was Joe Kirkwood Jr., who starred in a late–40's series of Monogram B's. Kirkwood bought the television rights, set himself up as producer-star on the Republic Pictures lot, and ground out 39 episodes of *The Joe Palooka Story* for Guild Films syndication. Cathy Downs was Joe's girl Ann Howe, Sid Tomack and Luis Van Rooten both played Joe's manager Knobby Walsh, and the character of "Clyde the Trainer" was added, based on and played by "Slapsie" Maxie Rosenbloom. Sold on promises of non-stop, slam-bang action, the leisurely *Joe Palooka* merely danced around the ring; and frankly, Joe Kirkwood Jr. the producer should have fired Joe Kirkwood Jr. the actor.

Jungle Boy see *The Adventures of a Jungle Boy*

Jungle Jim (1955). Screen Gems entered the "Straw Hut Circuit" with 26 half-hours of *Jungle Jim.* Created by cartoonist Alex Raymond the same day he'd created *Flash Gordon* in 1934, dauntless African guide Jungle Jim was the subject of a high-grossing series of Columbia B-flicks starring former Tarzan Johnny Weissmuller and produced by King of the Quickies Sam Katzman. Critics never warmed to these cheapies, but TV station managers, remembering the sounds of turnstyles clicking whenever the latest *Jungle Jim* epic played the neighborhood theatres, helped Columbia's subsidiary Screen Gems make $250,000 worth of prerelease sales for the TV *Jim.* Series producer Harold Greene out–Katzmaned Sam Katzman in keeping his low-budget effort even lower by pumping the episodes full of thrifty stock footage. Johnny Weissmuller was back as Jungle Jim, this time saddled with a son named Skipper (Martin Huston) who said "Holy Toledo" all the time. Jim's Hindu assistant Kasseem was played by Frederick Norman, who later bleached his hair, changed his name to Dean Fredericks, and starred in his own comic-strip-cum-TV-series, NBC's *Steve Canyon* (1958).

Lock-Up (1959–60). Like *Highway Patrol*, Ziv's *Lock-Up* was a rush job, hooked together to fill an impending release commitment — and like *Highway Patrol*, the 78-episode *Lock-Up* did far better than many more costly syndicated ventures of 1959. The series' working title, *Philadelphia Lawyer*, referred to its inspiration, real-life attorney Herbert L. Maris, who during his long career had kept some three hundred innocents from unjust prison terms and death sentences. After reading a magazine story about Maris, Ziv executive Herbert Gordon went to work on a series about the attorney. The lead role went to MacDonald Carey, who welcomed the opportunity to play a character less passive than in his earlier Ziv vehicle, *Dr. Christian*. In answer to fans who wanted the all-business Herb Maris to pursue a more active love life, Olive Carey (no relation to MacDonald but the widow of Western star Harry Carey) was added to the cast as Maris' mother-hen secretary, ever eager to match up her boss with an eligible young damsel. The real Herbert Maris made no comment on this embroidery of his romantic pursuits, nor did he go the Herb *(I Led 3 Lives)* Philbrick route of capitalizing on his new "celebrity" (since he was nearly eighty, there wouldn't have been much point). Maris did like MacDonald Carey, however, and was more than cooperative in sharing his private files with Ziv's writing staff.

The Lone Wolf (1954). The Lone Wolf, Louis Joseph Vance's thief-turned-private-eye, was another of a long line of similar B-movie-series heroes converted into syndie–TV protagonists. Gross-Krasne Productions made a $2.8 million deal with actor Louis Hayward, who was part-owner of the rights to 13 of Vance's Lone Wolf novels, to star in and co-produce the new series. MGM scenarist William Kozlenko confidently adapted those novels into 78 half-hour scripts, but *The Lone Wolf* lasted only the standard 39 weeks. It was a smooth job, but withal just another show with a smart-lipped detective. Evidently because its distributor was worried that viewers might mistake *The Lone Wolf* for an animal show, the series was retitled *Streets of Danger*.

Long John Silver (1955). Bearing only the vaguest resemblance to Robert Louis Stevenson's *Treasure Island*, *Long John Silver* was filmed in color in Australia by Jay-Kay Productions and distributed in America by CBS Films. It was far and away the sloppiest of the "literary" syndies of the era, but was also a lot more fun, thanks to its chops-licking star. Robert Newton, who'd already played bold buccaneer Silver in two feature films, distributed more ham than the Armour Star company in his 26 weeks of "arr-mateys" and eyeball-rolling. There was a supporting cast, but who cared?

The Man Behind the Badge (1954). *The Big Story* producer-creator Bernard F. Procktor developed a similar true-story anthology about the workaday policeman and other uniformed officials. As with *Big Story*, *Man Behind the Badge* ran first as a live networker (CBS, 1953–54) before MCA committed 39 half-hours to film for syndication. Charles Bickford hosted both versions; the filmed *Man Behind the Badge* was produced at the increasingly crowded Eagle-Lion studios.

The Man Called X (1956). Cultured secret agent Ken Thurston, also known as "The Man Called X," had hop-scotched around all the major networks in his own radio series since 1944, with Ziv handling the property's sporadic syndication. Thurston battled the Nazis during the war, the Communists afterward (the bad guys were played by the same actors with the same accents). After *I Led Three Lives* ran its course in 1955, Ziv felt that the Spy Genre was still exploitable, so an updated filmed version of *The Man Called X* was warmed up for television. Herbert Marshall, who'd played Ken Thurston on radio, was sixtyish, weary of the role, and hampered with a wooden leg; thus, Barry Sullivan was television's action-prone and disguise-happy Thurston. This proved a boon for Sullivan in the form of profits-percentages and frequent directorial assignments on Ziv's other series. Like most Ziv productions, *Man Called X* enjoyed the services of a technical adviser, in this case former intelligence officer (and best-selling author) Ladislas Farago. *Man Called X* was given Ziv's usual big-bang promotion, its ads "excusing" the series' violence by explaining that a loyal secret agent must be willing to commit murder in the battle against Communism. The series was quite profitable, but escalating production costs made further filming beyond the first 39 installments impractical.

Mandrake the Magician (1954). ABC Films' *Mandrake* starred real-life magician Coe Norton as the comic-strip illusionist created by Lee Falk and Phil Davis. Ex-wrestler and future John Ford stock-company actor Woody Strode played Mandrake's hulking assistant Lothar. Perhaps because filmed magic tricks were seldom terribly convincing, no one cared for *Mandrake* much—least of all ABC, which pulled the series' 39 episodes out of circulation early on. This series is now so obscure that a 1979 *Mandrake* TV movie is generally regarded as the character's video debut.

Manhunt (1959–60). *Manhunt* hadn't made the grade as a pilot for a Broderick Crawford vehicle in 1954, but Screen Gems' second crack at the property in 1959 resulted in a 78-week run. *Manhunt's* budget was so miserly that its stars, Victor Jory and Patrick McVey, were compelled to buy coffee for themselves and their crew out of their own pockets when filming on location. The series bore more than a passing resemblance to CBS' long-running *Lineup*, the main difference being that *Lineup* was based on the "actual files" of the San Francisco Police Department, while *Manhunt's* stories were drawn from the records of the San Diego cop shop. Victor Jory insisted, understandably so, that *Manhunt* was superior to *Lineup*, citing as his series' chief appeal the warm rapport between himself and co-star Pat McVey (Jory played Lt. Howard Finucane, while McVey was police reporter Ben Andrews). Screen Gems viewed *Manhunt* as the least expensive means of screen-testing its new male contractees, which is why Victor Jory had a new "young assistant" every few episodes. Jory, who could be quite irascible at times, welcomed the musical-chairs casting because he liked to see himself as a nurturer of fresh new talent. However, the only fledgling actors on *Manhunt* who got anywhere were Todd Armstrong, star of Columbia's 1963 feature film *Jason and the Argonauts,* and Charles Bateman, the lead of Screen Gems' 1960 syndie *Two Faces West.* And while Victor Jory didn't mind giving new performers a break, he didn't suffer "method actors" too well. After one would-be Brando wasted production time by running around in circles to get "in the mood," Jory got in his own mood by walking off the set and going home.

Martin Kane see *The New Adventures of Martin Kane*

Mickey Spillane's Mike Hammer (1958–59). Ever since Mickey Spillane's *I the Jury* became required reading for adolescent males of all ages in 1951 (there were those who could quote its last page from memory), Spillane's unscrupulous, unethical and ungrammatical private eye Mike Hammer had been bulldozing his way through several movies and a radio series, most of these incarnations almost as violent but never as sexy as the original. After a false-start pilot film starring Brian Keith, Darren McGavin became television's Hammer in an MCA series filmed in New York and syndicated starting in January of 1958. The notoriously hard-to-please McGavin liked Mike Hammer, saying "He's a nonconformist, and aggressively so." That wasn't the half of it. It didn't take long for media critics to single out *Mike Hammer* as the bloodiest, most violent new series of 1958. (What did these critics *expect* from a Spillane character, *Ozzie and Harriet?*) While a model of restraint by today's standards, *Mike Hammer* was pretty raw meat in an era when the networks were being cautioned to tone down the violence on their programs. But MCA thoroughly understood *Hammer's* audience, which responded with "More of the same, please"; *Mike Hammer* enjoyed 78 money-making episodes, and remained a local-ratings attraction as late as 1964.

Mister District Attorney (1954). Like so many Ziv projects, *Mr. District Attorney* sprang from a popular radio series. David Brian had starred as D.A. Paul Garrett on Ziv's radio-syndie version of the property, and revived the role on Ziv's full-color, 52-episode television version. (A live *District Attorney* had previously run in the early '50s on the CBS TV network starring Jay Jostyn, who'd been the lead in the long-running *network* radio version of *Mr. District Attorney.*) Assisting David Brian was the usual "girl Friday," played by former Miss U.S.A. (and former Mrs. Jack Webb) Jackie Loughery. A police officer from the real-life Los Angeles District Attorney's office acted as the series' technical advisor. That officer later forsook the badge for the typewriter and entered television on a full-time basis. His name is Gene Roddenberry. Of *Star Trek* fame.

Mystery Is My Business see *Ellery Queen*

The New Adventures of Charlie Chan (1957). These were called "New Adventures" so as not to be confused with the "old" ubiquitous Charlie

Chan B-pictures of the '30s and '40s. T.P.A. distributed the British-produced *New Adventures of Charlie Chan*. In time-honored Hollywood tradition, a non–Oriental was cast as Chan: J. Carroll Naish, who'd ironically played a villain in *Charlie Chan at the Circus* (1936). Charlie's "Number One Son," the traditional comic relief in the Chan movies, was played by nightclub funnyman James Hong. There were 39 "New Adventures."

The New Adventures of China Smith see *The Affairs of China Smith*

The New Adventures of Martin Kane (1957).

Like Ellery Queen, fictional sleuth Martin Kane had been played by four different actors since his live-television debut in 1949. William Gargan, the first TV Kane (he'd originated the role on radio), returned to the fold in 39 "New Adventures" filmed in England and Europe by Towers of London and Ziv Productions. In later years, Gargan evinced a preference for the filmed *Martin Kanes* over his live television version. The actor was particularly proud of an episode shot in Denmark's Elsinore castle; the Danish Government had banned filmmakers from Elsinore, so the *Kane* film crew had to smuggle in their camera equipment under their coats.

New Orleans Police Department (1956).

Forgettable cop show starring Stacy Harris as Beaujac, a New Orleans-based detective. This and a dramatic anthology, *The Tracer,* were the only products of Minot Films, a company created in a vain attempt to turn Louisiana into a major filmmaking center.

New York Confidential (1958).

The successful distribution of TPA's 39 location-filmed *New York Confidential* episodes was helped along by a mammoth publicity blitz, including a series of personal appearances by series star Lee Tracy (who played reporter Lee Cochran). During a stop in Tulsa, Oklahoma, the series was heralded by a Hollywood-style premiere, and capped with taped promotional spots for *New York Confidential* featuring Lee Tracy, which Tulsa's KDTA ran during a telecast of the 1945 film *Betrayal from the East* — also featuring Lee Tracy. The television series was based on a best-selling book by Jack Lait and Lee Mortimer, whose virulent anti–Communist stance frequently lapsed into tastelessness (they once referred to New York's Mayor Fiorello LaGuardia as a "pink stinkweed"). Television's *New York Confidential* did without the book's red-baiting, substituting sentimental human interest stories and fist-happy melodrama, and including such eye-popping camerawork as recording a suicidal descent out of a high-rise window from the jumper's point of view.

N.O.P.D. see *New Orleans Police Department*

Not for Hire (1959).

California National Productions (formerly NBC Films) shot *Not for Hire* in Hawaii, concurrently with their ABC network series *Philip Marlowe. Not for Hire* starred Ralph Meeker as Sgt. Steve Dekker, an operative for the Army Criminal Investigations Division and therefore "not for hire" as a private eye. The series was a garden-variety mellerdrammer save for some surprisingly frank (by 1959 standards) plot devices. In the first episode, it was learned that a policewoman's trigger-happy tendencies stemmed from a pathological hatred of men—she'd been gang-raped as a teenager. But while the censors tolerated this turn of events, *Not for Hire* wasn't entirely censor-free. Nearly all of the series' regional sponsors were tobacco companies, which meant that the producers had to be *very* careful who was seen smoking on-screen and who wasn't. *Not for Hire* could touch upon the topic of rape— but couldn't show cigarettes dangling from the lips of the villains.

Official Detective (1957). This Desilu/NTA 39-weeker, like its radio-series predecessor, was based on the true-story files of *Official Detective* Magazine. Although the series' sales started slowly, they quickly picked up steam, and by 1960, *Official Detective* was sturdy enough for the NBC-owned television station in Chicago to drop one of its own network's Friday offerings and telecast *Official Detective* reruns in prime time. NTA's promotional campaign for the series included the requisite personal appearances from *Detective's* otherwise tactiturn host-narrator Everett Sloane and a Hollywood press junket honoring members of the local police departments from the series' biggest markets. Each of *Official Detective's* scripts was carefully checked for accuracy by the Philadelphia-based researchers of *O.D.* Magazine (a favorite no-no was the misuse and misrepresentation of firearms), and the episodes themselves were filmed in the presence of on-set law enforcement technical advisers. One of these was a policewoman whose job it was to instruct actresses in the art of judo. Since *Official Detective's* stories covered a wide range of locales, the series was able to accommodate guest actors as varied as Broadway character man Ned Glass and onetime cowboy star Johnny Mack Brown.

Orient Express (1953). Espionage anthology from PSI Films, mostly made up of failed series pilots. The best of these, "Man of Many Skins," starred Erich Von Stroheim as a detective who solved crimes by assuming the mental and physical traits of the criminal.

Overseas Adventure see Foreign Intrigue

Paris Precinct (1955). M.P.T.V. release, filmed in France and starring Louis Jourdan and Claude Dauphin as a pair of Paris plainclothesmen. The series hoped to emulate the success of *Foreign Intrigue* by using locations and actors previously seen on *Intrigue,* but *Paris Precinct* suffered from anemic scriptwriting. Reissued as *World Crime Hunt.*

Passport to Danger (1954). Hal Roach/ABC Films' *Passport to Danger* was a *Foreign Intrigue*-ish spy caper starring dapper Cesar Romero as Steve McQuinn, a diplomatic courier duped into a life of espionage. Romero cheerfully admitted at the time that he was doing these 39 half-hours merely for the money, and it was the star's less-than-serious approach to his work that gave *Passport to Danger* its charm.

Patrol Car see *Fabian of Scotland Yard*

Police Call (1955). Journeyman MCA anthology, given variety by drawing its stories out of police files from all over the world.

Policewoman Decoy (1957). Beverly Garland was considered a "good luck charm" by virtue of the number of pilot films featuring her as guest-star which made it to the series stage. With Official Films' *Decoy,* Garland was finally rewarded with a 39-week series all her own. As undercover cop "Casey" Jones, the actress posed as hookers, gun molls, singers and nurses in the line of duty; in so doing, Beverly Garland was in the enviable position of having steady series work while still playing a multitude of widely different characters. What a shame, then, that the Manhattan-filmed *Decoy,* despite the artistry of its star and a corps of top New York supporting talent (including such young hopefuls as Ed Asner and Phyllis Newman), was weighed down with excessive bloodshed and gratuitous violence. Its scripts were chock-full of sex maniacs, serial killers, robbers who ordered their victims to beg for their lives, and at least one sicko with an unnatural affection for his revolver. But sadistic though it was, *Policewoman Decoy* definitely had its fingers on the public's pulse; the series remained in the syndicated Top-Ten ratings long after production closed down. The television executives who purchased *Decoy* understood their audience equally as well; on the basis of a pilot and a premise, the series was partially financed by a consortium of major independent TV channels. Publicity stunts on behalf of *Decoy* contained a lot more lightheartedness than ever was seen on the series itself. Most notable was a cute ploy in Boston wherein genuine policewomen stormed a local TV station and "arrested" several film editors — for the crime of being film editors.

Ramar of the Jungle (1952–53). The prime mover of television's Straw Hut Circuit, *Ramar of the Jungle* starred beefcake movie hero Jon Hall as Kenya-based Dr. Tom Reynolds, known to the local tribesmen as "Ramar" (allegedly native-ese for "White Witch Doctor"). Aware that the Arabian Nights/South Seas "A" pictures he'd headlined in the 1940's were on their way out, Jon Hall moved into television as soon as the opportunity presented itself. Hall wisely reasoned that a Western or detective series would make him just one more cowboy or cop in an overstocked TV barrel. He planned instead to translate the exotic ambience of his movie vehicles to the small screen with an "African jungle" setting; and, since Hall was no youngster and since the old beefcake was beefing up in the wrong places, the actor decided to cast himself in a more "mature" role than mere adventurer. It was future *Ramar* director Rudy Flotow who suggested that Hall play a doctor. While he'd never give Olivier any sleepless nights, Jon Hall was utterly acceptable to viewers as "Ramar"; more importantly, he was hero-worship material for the kiddie set. Hall had to carry *Ramar* by sheer strength of personality, for the series was a

"B" effort through and through; its budget was microscopic, its acting and directing just this side of mediocre, its "authenticity" provided by stock footage, and its depiction of "primitive" blacks embarrassing even by 1952 standards. Despite the almost unanimous critical panning of Jon Hall's acting abilities, the fact is that *without* Hall, *Ramar of the Jungle* would have been just so much rubber foliage on the Eagle-Lion studios' backlot.

Eagle-Lion, incidentally, was once known as Producers Releasing Corporation, and it was former PRC president Leon Fromkess who controlled Arrow Productions, *Ramar's* production company. Arrow was absorbed by T.P.A. in 1953, with Fromkess going along as T.P.A.'s chief "line" producer (the producer who remained on-set during a series' filming). In 1959, T.P.A. merged with Independent Television Corporation; it was ITC which, in the early '60s, made even more money off the already lucrative 52-episode *Ramar of the Jungle* by stringing together several of those episodes into ersatz "feature films."

Rescue Eight (1958–59). Screen Gems' *Rescue Eight* (initially titled *Dial 1116*) eschewed the heavy violence typical of television in 1958, and was thus suitable for all ages. Created by George Draine and voice-over specialist Paul Frees, *Rescue Eight's* format was pretty well defined in its opener, "The Ferris Wheel," scripted by future *Star Trek* stalwart Gene L. Coons. The syndie series' formula included an exotic location riddled with potential danger-traps, and a victim, preferably a pretty girl or a small child, trapped dangerously. It was then up to *Rescue Eight's* team of paramedics (Lang Jeffries and Jim Davis) to come clanging to the rescue. The series' excitement level was matched by its topnotch location photography, a specialty of executive producer Herbert B. Leonard, as witness his *Naked City* and *Route 66*. *Rescue Eight* was good for two full first-run seasons.

Sailor of Fortune (1957). This Canadian series, syndicated in the States by RKO Films, starred CBC newsman-turned-actor Lorne Greene as sea captain "Mitch" Mitchell. *Sailor of Fortune* sank from sight in 1957, only to resurface three years later to cash in on Lorne Greene's *Bonanza*-induced celebrity status. But bad is not good, and *Sailor* fell from grace for the last time.

The Scarlet Pimpernel (1956). Baroness Orczy's "damn'd elusive Pimpernel" (or "curs'd elusive Pimpernel" as he was designated for American consumption) was brought to television with 39 British-filmed episodes from Towers of London productions, syndicated in America by Official Films. Marius Goring, who'd previously starred in a radio *Pimpernel* from the same production company, revived his role as Sir Percy Blakeney, fop by day, rescuer of guillotine-bound French aristocrats by night. Goring gave a good account of himself, even though his swashbuckling was hampered by his middle-aged avoirdupois, and the TV *Pimpernel* was a serviceable if somewhat austere "literary" syndie. Goring's assistant rescuer on the series was played by star-in-the-making Robert Shaw.

Sea Hunt (1958–61; 1987). Producer Ivan Tors dreamed up *Sea Hunt* during pre-production of Tors' feature film *Underwater Warrior,* a yarn about World War II–vintage Navy frogmen (this was Tors' official story, though he'd be sued in 1963 by another producer-writer who claimed that *Sea Hunt* had been swiped from an unsold pilot titled *Underwater Legion*). Tors hired Lloyd Bridges, whose only previous connection with deep-sea work had been the 1948 Monogram quickie *Sixteen Fathoms Deep,* to play ex–Navy man Mike Nelson, *Sea Hunt's* diver-for-hire. The producer then tried peddling the series concept to the three major networks, and was turned down flat by all three. "No potential in an underwater show!" they declared as though those words were carved upon Mt. Sinai. Besides, hadn't Lloyd Bridges belonged to that "Pinko" Actor's Lab theatre group in the '30s? Hadn't he committed such "subversive" acts as inviting black people to his house for dinner? Yes, Lloyd Bridges was one more guilt-by-flimsy-association victim of a blacklist. But one of the few producers who hired the actor during his dark days was Fred Ziv, and it was Ziv who at long last saw potential in *Sea Hunt.* The producer bought the series for syndication, and on the basis of his impressive track record was able to line up 100 markets before *Sea Hunt's* January 1958 debut. Within two months, the series was Number Two in the nationwide non-network ratings; by 1960, *Sea Hunt* was playing in 203 out of 243 potential markets, and would later peak at 210. It was second only to *The Liberace Show* as the biggest syndicated hit of the 1950's.

Television viewers, especially those in land-locked midwestern communities, were fascinated to the point of hypnosis by the world beneath the waves, especially when that world was magnificently photographed by *Sea Hunt's* Lamar Boren (who could spend a whole day submerged in his plastic protection bubble with naught but a bag of sandwiches and bananas to keep him going). *Sea Hunt* offered adventure on a scale as limitless as the sea itself; the series cost Tors and Ziv $40,000 an episode (pretty steep for a show without big casts or elaborate sets), but paid back every penny and then some, running and rerunning to new young fans for two decades. Lloyd Bridges may have commented on occasion that he felt *Sea Hunt* was beneath his talents, but he never complained about his annual $250,000 profits-percentage take, nor of the millions he made in residuals thereafter.

While Bridges did most of his own stunts in and out of the water — he even wrestled an alligator once, though the beast had considerably shown up for work with its jaws wired shut — Ricou Browning was *Sea Hunt's* all-around stunt man and technical advisor. Browning, who'd once played the Creature from the Black Lagoon, did the underwater work that took place in waters too deep for the average actor. Miss Zale Perry doubled for the female guest-stars, and like Browning, offered technical advice on location. That location was generally the crystal-clear waters of Silver Springs, Florida, though *Sea Hunt* made occasional jaunts to Mexico and the Caribbean; when pressed for time, Ivan Tors would film in any body of water that was handy, notably in the near-to-Hollywood port of Santa Barbara.

In addition to Browning and Perry, *Sea Hunt's* advisory council included former frogman John Lindbergh (son of Charles) and a crack research team from California's Scripps Institute of Oceanography. It's no surprise that the series' authenticity level was flawless, though in the early episodes Lloyd Bridges dove alone or without a spotter, something that real-life divers considered the height of unprofessionalism. Later scripts were rewritten to indicate that one of Mike Nelson's pals, usually named "Jose," was on Nelson's boat to monitor the undersea activity.

Like many a syndie, *Sea Hunt* featured a number of future stars in the supporting casts, most notably Leonard Nimoy and, in a bad-guy role two decades before *Dallas,* Larry Hagman. But while it's been reported that Lloyd Bridges' sons Beau and Jeff made their acting debuts on *Sea Hunt,* the fact is that both boys had been appearing in movies since their diaper days.

After 156 episodes, Ziv's *Sea Hunt* folded its fins in 1961. Twenty-six years later, a new *Sea Hunt* bobbed into view from MGM/United Artists. In fine old Ziv tradition, 1987's *Sea Hunt* was hastily created merely to meet a release commitment as soon as possible. Former TV Tarzan Ron Ely took over as Mike Nelson (Lloyd Bridges wasn't interested in eating yesterday's stew), and this time was paired with a pretty 15-year-old daughter (who was studying to be an oceanographer), played with refreshing spunk and self-assuredness by Kimberly Sissons. While the new *Sea Hunt* seemed more cut-and-dried and less spontaneous than the original, it had the benefit of state-of-the-art, full-color underwater camerawork. It was also entertaining to watch the stars pretend to be swimming comfortably while shivering in the ice-cold waters of British Columbia.

Secret File USA (1954). Lumbering 26-week spy series filmed in Amsterdam, Holland by Cinetone Studios and distributed by Official Films. Robert Alda played Maj. William Morgan, an Army intelligence officer who hunted down Commie agents all over the world. Alda's son Alan would later don khaki himself for a rather lengthier hitch on *M*A*S*H.*

Sergeant Preston of the Yukon (1958). A radio creation of George W. Trendle (of *Lone Ranger* fame), Canadian mountie Sgt. Preston had been on the CBS TV network since 1955 in the person of actor Richard Simmons (definitely *not* the exercise guru of the '80s). After *Sergeant Preston* ended its network run, Skinner Productions filmed 26 additional color episodes for syndication, again starring Simmons as Preston and the World's Stupidest Dog (forever wagging its tail when attacking the villains) as Yukon King.

Sergeant Steve Dekker see *Not for Hire*

Sheena, Queen of the Jungle (1955). The most famous of the comic-book female Tarzans, Sheena was created in 1937 by Will Eisner and S.M. Iger. The *Sheena* comics displayed a disturbing tendency towards featuring beautiful, barely dressed women in situations of bondage and torture. None of this kinkiness was translated to the 26-week television version of *Sheena* from Nassour Productions and ABC Films, though true to her comic book counterpart, TV's Sheena was still able to punch out any man her size and any animal *any* size. Statuesque Anita Ekberg had been slated to play Sheena, but when she failed to show up for location shooting in the jungles of Mexico, she was replaced by the equally impressive Irish McCalla. Standing 6 foot 1, McCalla was *so* impressive that the Nassour Brothers couldn't find her a female stand-in, so Sheena's stunts were performed by a gentleman named Raoul Gaona. Although obviously cast because she successfully filled out Sheena's brief leopardskin attire, Irish McCalla was an intelligent, creative woman who brought the two-dimensional heroine to life. Like most syndicated stars, McCalla was disdainful of guest actors who regarded syndie work as "slumming." One such insufferable character actor, who'd managed to alienate everyone on the *Sheena* crew, learned that Irish McCalla was something of an expert on African languages, so he insisted that she translate one of his speeches into Swahili. The actress sweetly taught this would-be Barrymore a speech, let everyone else on the set know what the speech *really* meant, then sat back during filming to watch cast and crew dissolve into laughter as the pompous actor proclaimed in flawless Swahili, "One, two, three, four, five! Birds have two legs! I do not read! Get lost!"

Sheriff of Cochise (1956–57); **U.S. Marshal** (1958–59). One of the best of the imitation *Highway Patrols,* Desilu/NTA's *Sheriff of Cochise* starred onetime Republic star John Bromfield as Sheriff Frank Morgan of Cochise County, Arizona. Within a year of its debut, the slickly entertaining *Sheriff* attained enough of a following to turn Arizona's real Cochise County (a conservative community of about 32,000 people) into a big-time tourist attraction. During the County's July 4th festivities in 1957, John Bromfield was guest of honor, the parade's Grand Marshal, and was even sworn in as a *genuine* deputy sheriff. After 78 episodes, *Sheriff of Cochise* was getting old, at least according to its producer Mort Briskin, and needed a new coat of paint. So Briskin filmed an episode wherein Sheriff Morgan escorted a crazed-killer convict (played with bug-eyed venom by a young Jack Lord) to the nearby United States marshal. The prisoner murdered the marshal and escaped, obliging Morgan to assume the marshal's job so he'd have jurisdiction to track down the killer himself. The plan was to offer this episode as a pilot for a "new" syndie, *U.S. Marshal;* if the pilot failed to sell, it would be *Sheriff of Cochise's* final installment. It sold. John Bromfield became U.S. Marshal in the series of the same name, putting in 78 more weeks in uniform. In 1960, NTA lumped these episodes together with the *Sheriff of Cochise* adventures into a new rerun package entitled — and they must have stayed up all night thinking of this one — *Man from Cochise.*

Sherlock Holmes (1954). Sir Arthur Conan Doyle's master detective had been a sporadic visitor to TV anthologies since the medium's infancy in the 1930's. Plans for a filmed *Sherlock Holmes* weekly series were formulated in 1951 by producers Irving Allen and Albert "Cubby" Broccoli, but were vetoed at the last minute by Sir Arthur's mercurial son Adrian Conan Doyle. It took the Machiavellian machinations of Sheldon *(Foreign Intrigue)* Reynolds to talk the younger Conan Doyle into giving the green light for a *Holmes* television series. Reynolds filmed the subsequent 39-week project in Paris, which explains why one of Sherlock's adventures took him to the top of the Eiffel Tower. Nicole Millenaire, a.k.a. the Duchess of Bedford, was promoted from Reynolds' production assistant to line producer for the new *Sherlock Holmes.* The Duchess was compelled to use all her inbred diplomacy to handle her actors' personality quirks: Archie Duncan, who played Inspector Lestrade, insisted that each day's filming be halted at 4 p.m. for a proper British teatime, while guest star Paulette Goddard caused no end of delays on location because of her superstitious fear of cemeteries and the color green. Sherlock Holmes himself was played by Ronald Howard (son of Leslie), who was a bit on the callow side for "The Master" but did his best to please. Far better cast was Howard Marion-Crawford, who brought to his role of Dr. Watson the dignity and intellect that had been undermined by years of Nigel Bruce in the *Holmes* movies. Matty Fox's MPTV handled American distribution for *Sherlock Holmes;* Fox eventually gave the property to Guild Films in exchange for a piece of Guild. Over two decades later, Sheldon Reynolds dug into his file of European connections to finance a new *Sherlock Holmes* series, taped in Poland and starring Geoffrey Whitehead; this version went directly to PBS stations in America, where Holmes has made his television home ever since.

Soldiers of Fortune (1955). John Russell and Chick Chandler played a pair of globetrotting adventurers-for-hire in this juvenile adventure show produced by MCA/Revue and sponsored in most markets by Seven-Up. If the 52-week series resembled an old-time serial on occasion, that was because *Soldiers of Fortune* was filmed at Republic Studios, utilizing that operation's topnotch team of stuntmen.

Special Agent 7 (1958). It sounded like a spy show, but TPA's *Special Agent 7* actually told 26 stories involving an operative from the Treasury Department (Lloyd Nolan) who went after tax frauds. Nolan was a hero only if you hadn't been audited lately.

State Trooper (1956–58). MCA/Revue's attempt to emulate *Highway Patrol's* success with State Trooper paid off to the tune of 104 episodes. This was the second of three syndie-series packages involving MCA, producer Richard Irving, and star Rod Cameron (*City Detective* was the first, 1960's *Coronado Nine* the third). Cameron had originated the role of Nevada state trooper Rod Blake on an episode of the NBC network anthology *Star Stage,* but insisted that the *State Trooper* series itself be syndicated rather than network-cast, a decision that fattened Mr. Cameron's bank-account considerably. *State Trooper* was filmed with high professional gloss, taking full advantage of the scenic splendors of Las Vegas, Reno and Lake Tahoe.

Streets of Danger see *The Lone Wolf*

Stryker of Scotland Yard (1955). British cop series (titled merely "Stryker of the Yard" in England, where they knew what "the Yard" meant), starring Clifford Evans. Republic Pictures' TV subsidiary Hollywood Television Service handled the series in the States.

Superman see The Adventures of Superman

Sword of Freedom (1957).

Lavishly produced but sluggishly paced 39-weeker filmed in Europe, *Sword of Freedom* took place during the Italian Renaissance, so it's not surprising that its swashbuckling hero (Edmond Purdom) was a Cellini-like painter. *Sword* sold so poorly in America that Official Films ended up offering the series as a part of a budget-priced package deal together with the more popular *Decoy* and *The Big Story*.

Tales of the Vikings (1959).

United Artists Television's *Tales of the Vikings* was filmed 'midst the snowcapped mountainous splendor of West Germany. Its 39 episodes looked more expensive than was actually the case thanks to the utilization of the completely furnished Norse villages, authentic costumes and scale-model ships originally built for Kirk Douglas' 1958 feature film *The Vikings;* it may be unnecessary to add at this point that the television series was produced by Kirk Douglas' Bryna Productions. Jerome Courtland starred as the Adonis-like Viking captain Eric; Courtland's stand-in was the equally handsome Ryan O'Neal.

Ten-Four see Highway Patrol

Terry and the Pirates (1952).

Milton Caniff's comic-strip flyboy buzzed into television with 26 episodes shot on the RKO-Pathé lot by Don Sharpe Enterprises and DougFair productions. (Guess what son of a famed movie swashbuckler owned DougFair?) The series was sponsored nationally by Canada Dry during its first run, then syndicated by Official Films thereafter. Terry was portrayed by John Baer, who later made media history by being the first actor to play John F. Kennedy (on the "PT 109" episode of CBS' *Navy Log*). Rolypoly William Tracy was Terry's charter-plane-service partner Hotshot Charlie, while Mari Blanchard and Sandra Spence took turns playing the toothsome Burma (nowhere near as sexy as her comic-strip original). Also on hand were Terry's Chinese assistant Chopstick Joe (Jack Reitzen) and slinky Oriental villainess the Dragon Lady (Gloria Saunders). Both of these "Chinese" characters were about as Oriental as matzo-ball soup, and it is their demeaning characterizations which make the otherwise competent *Terry and the Pirates* an unlikely candidate for latter-day revival.

This Man Dawson (1959).

"Drawn from today's headlines," Ziv's 39-week *This Man Dawson* was all about a police department official named Dawson (Keith Andes) and his fight against political and corporate corruption in an unnamed big city. Ziv's prerelease preparation for *Dawson* was to have Keith Andes become a virtual walking encyclopedia on Police Procedure; the actor even sat in on a three-man panel which screened applicants for the Los Angeles Police Department, and on more than one occasion it was Andes who cast the deciding vote. After *This Man Dawson* folded, Andes became a welcome fixture on the lecture circuit, campaigning on behalf of better working conditions and higher pay for our Boys in Blue. *This Man Dawson* was produced by two old radio hands, William *(Cannon)* Conrad and Elliot Lewis.

The Three Musketeers (1955). Filmed in Italy by IFE/Thetis Productions, the 26-week *Three Musketeers* had lain unopened on the shelf for nearly three years before being picked up for American distribution by ABC Films. The series was related to the Alexandre Dumas novels in name only (in one episode, the 16th-century heroes took on a band of counterfeiters); it was so budget-conscious that one of the original Musketeers, Athos, was completely written out, making D'Artagnan (Jeffrey Stone) the third Musketeer. The other two were played by Paul Campbell and Peter Trent.

Tomahawk (1957). Canada's answer to Disney's amazingly popular *Davy Crockett* television films was supposed to have been a series about famed Canadian frontiersman Pierre Radisson. Jacques Godet was star of this series, and its producers, anticipating a merchandising windfall, cluttered department stores with "Radisson hats," which looked a lot like Davy Crockett's coonskin caps without the tails. Alas, *Radisson* laid a large and noxious egg; it did even worse when distributed in the United States under the deceptive "Western" title *Tomahawk*. As for all those Radisson hats, there are Canadian store owners who insist to this day that they were forced to hastily sew on coon's tails to the useless merchandise in hopes of fooling the Davy Crockett fans.

Top Secret U.S.A. (1954). MCA/Revue espionage quickie inspired by *I Led Three Lives*. Starring as operatives of the Bureau of Science Information were Paul Stewart and young Gena Rowlands.

United States Border Patrol (1959). The powerful and influential American Oil Company announced in early 1959 that it would ever after devote all its television advertising to syndicated programming. In the words of an Amoco spokesman, syndication was "local, identifiable, flexible, programmable." The company's first big step in the syndie world was to line up 59 markets for CBS Films' new *United States Border Patrol*—even though the series had barely started filming. The last of the *Highway Patrol* clones of the '50s (there would be a miserable cheapie from Crosby-Brown Productions, *Squad Car,* in 1960), *U.S. Border Patrol* starred Richard *(Captain Midnight)* Webb as Patrol deputy Don Jagger. The 39-week series wasn't all that much, but Amoco's support enabled *Border Patrol* to get top-dollar bookings for several seasons to come.

U.S. Border Patrol see immediately previous entry

U.S. Marshal see *Sheriff of Cochise*

The Vikings see *Tales of the Vikings*

Walter Winchell File (1958). A single-season network effort which continued filming episodes for the syndie market after its cancellation, Desilu's *Walter Winchell File* was the best of the legendary columnist's many television projects (topped only by Winchell's offscreen narration of Desilu's later *The Untouchables*). The stories on this anthology were allegedly drawn from Winchell's news-reporter experiences, with old Walter himself showing up on each installment just when the story was getting hot.

Waterfront (1954–55). A tugboat called the "Cheryl Ann" (played by a *real* tug called the "Milton S. Patrick") was setting for Roland Reed/Hal Roach's *Waterfront,* starring Preston Foster as "Cap'n John" Herrick. Television critics had a grand time wondering if any genuine San Pedro harbor tug captain ever had as many adventures as did Cap'n John, but none of these scoffers could deny that the 76-episode *Waterfront* boasted a fine production polish and immense audience appeal. What set this series apart from most actionfests was that Cap'n John was head of a close-knit family, including a wife (Lois Moran) and two grown sons. When not cruising perilous waters, *Waterfront* resembled a TV sitcom minus the laughtrack. This was no accident; though the series was created by Ben Fox, the prime mover on *Waterfront* was producer Roland Reed, who'd long been the proponent of the television "family unit" as witness his comedy series *Beulah, The Stu Erwin Show* and *My Little Margie*. Reed wasn't about to forsake a winning formula for an adventure-only series. Adding to *Waterfront's* familial warmth were Preston Foster's occasional vocal duets with supporting actor Pinky Tomlin, a 1930's-era crooner who'd parlayed a ditty titled "The Object of My Affections" into a lengthy career. *Waterfront's* deft blend of action, family values and song kept the property afloat in reruns for over a decade, a fact that delighted and enriched its longtime distributor MCA.

The Whirlybirds (1957–59). A CBS Films release, produced by Desilu. Kenneth Tobey and Craig Hill were Chuck and P.T., owner-operators of Whirlybirds Inc., a charter helicopter service. That copter (actually manned by stunt pilots Earl Gilbreath and Rod Parker) was the *real* star of *The Whirlybirds,* spending a lot of screen time rescuing lost children or trapped explorers, transporting precious cargo, hunting down desperadoes and just plain joyriding. *Whirlybirds* premiered just around the time that the television Western craze was shifting into gear, so its appeal was greatly enhanced by the viewers' perception of *Whirlybirds* as an airborne Western. Since many episodes were produced by Republic shoot-'em-up specialist John H. Auer, and since most of the location scenes were filmed at the Iverson Ranch, scene of many a video horse opera, *Whirlybirds'* connection to the Western form was more than tenuous. As with most of the Desilu product, the series gave good exposure to new talent, including a gangly young fellow named James Coburn. Because of its strict avoidance of gratuitous violence, *Whirlybirds* weathered the clean-up-TV brigades of the late '50s and lasted 110 episodes.

Legend has it that *Whirlybirds* had been commissioned by CBS as a network prime time series, but that no sponsor could be located for the show, forcing CBS to turn the property over to its syndication division. The more pragmatic truth is that CBS decided from the start that *Whirlybirds* would make more money as a syndie because its wide-ranging audience appeal would perform just as well in a late-afternoon kid's time slot in one city as it would in a 10:30 p.m. adult slot in another. CBS Films had no trouble whatever lining up sponsors for *Whirlybirds,* most prominently a 95-market commitment from Continental Oil. And in 1958, CBS pulled the familiar syndie hat-trick of redistributing 39 *Whirlybirds* reruns as *Copter Patrol.*

White Hunter (1957). Its title seemingly calculated to enrage proponents of African self-rule, Telestar's *White Hunter* was a yawner starring Rhodes Reason.

William Tell see **The Adventures of William Tell**

World Crime Hunt see **Paris Precinct**

Children's

While some adventure and western syndies had a great deal of kiddie appeal, syndicated series designed with children specifically in mind weren't all that plentiful in the 1950's. The networks held the moppet monopoly with their well-stocked Saturday mornings full of puppet shows and outer-space sagas; local stations leaned toward their moneymaking "Uncle" and "Captain" hosts who presided over screaming studio audiences and introduced ancient theatrical two-reel comedies while dispensing long-winded commercial pitches. These "locals" ran plenty of cartoons, but most of them had been made for the movie houses; the current blizzard of made-for-TV animation was a mere gentle breeze in the '50s until a company called Hanna-Barbera pitched camp.

Most kiddie syndies doggedly imitated the already-established network hits. One children's-show form that syndication could honestly call its own was the "franchise," which involved series concepts created by national distributors (commercial tie-ins and all), and then sold or bartered in exchange for ad time to local stations that didn't have the resources (or imagination) to come up with concepts of their own. The two biggest franchises of the '50s featured a fright-wigged freak named Bozo and an electronic pre-school calling itself *The Romper Room.*

The Adventures of Blinky (and others) (1950–59). Early network children's television concentrated on puppet and marionette shows because they were cheap to put together and because the close-up camerawork vital to such programs hid the fact that early TV studios were cramped and none too attractive. Once NBC's *Howdy Doody* and *Kukla Fran and Ollie* were established, local stations followed suit with their own puppet shows, many of them making it into syndication.

A rundown of the various and sundry puppet plays dotting the syndie landscape would include *The Adventures of Blinky* (1952), featuring "real person" Michael Mann metamorphosing into a puppet for 15 minutes daily; *Barnyardville Varieties* (1951), a color-filmed prehistoric *Muppet Show* complete with a pushy female pig; the Christmastime favorite *Betsy and the Magic Key* (1952); *Don Q, Dick and Alladin* (1953), expurgated Arabian-Nights stories; *Gigi and Jock* (1955), which sounded like and was a doggie duo; *Jump Jump of Holiday House* (1951), featuring a puckish elf; and *Willie Wonderful* (1952), an echo of the old *Barnaby* comic strip headlining a small boy and his con-man fairy godfather.

Most of these properties were regionally distributed, made their money, then disappeared and were forgotten. Some were still making the rounds by the end of the decade, albeit in revised form. *Gigi and Jock,* for example, reappeared as a series of public-service ads, while *Willie Wonderful* popped up as a half-hour promotional film for Lionel Trains.

The Amazing Tales of Hans Christian Andersen (1954). A sparkling package of familiar fairy tales filmed in Andersen's beloved Copenhagen in color by Scandinavian-American Productions, then syndicated in America by Interstate Television. Hosting these 26 tales were George and Gene Bernard, whose specialty was a "record act" — the brothers lip-synched to popular recordings. Well, that's how Jerry Lewis got started.

Barnyardville Varieties see *The Adventures of Blinky*

Betsy and the Magic Key see *The Adventures of Blinky*

Big Mac and His Magic Train (1959). A "franchise" put together by United Artists Television and the Nabisco Company. Local stations had the choice of using a pre-filmed "Big Mac" (a railroad engineer with a predilection for puns and pies-in-the-face, a la Soupy Sales) or hiring a "Big Mac" host of their own. Either way, Mac's antics were designed as "wrap-arounds" for a package of old two-reel Warner Bros./Vitaphone comedies starring people like Bob Hope, Shemp Howard and Fatty Arbuckle. Unfortunately, these slapped-together '30s shorts had none of the staying power of such TV two-reel favorites as The Three Stooges, Laurel and Hardy and The Little Rascals, so Big Mac's train chugged into the sunset in 1960.

The Blue Fairy (1958). Peabody-award-winning children's series produced on videotape by WGN–Chicago. *The Blue Fairy* didn't perform any ratings magic when put into national syndication, but the series did wonders for its star, Brigid Bazlen. MGM studios awarded Miss Bazlen with a movie contract, leading to choice supporting parts in such films as *The Honeymoon Machine* (1961) and *How the West Was Won* (1962).

Bobo the Hobo (1955). Filmed in color, *Bobo the Hobo* was a puppet/live-action hybrid; the marionettes' mouths were electronically manipulated by the jaw movements of the voice actors. Bobo's voice was supplied by Bret Morrison, who once induced goosebumps as radio's Shadow.

Bozo the Clown (1956–   ). Created for a series of Capitol records in the early '40s, Bozo the Clown was to have made his television debut in a filmed live-action series produced by Elmo Williams and directed by Les Goodwyns in 1951. This didn't come about, but five years later, actor/producer/entrepreneur Larry Harmon bought the TV and merchandising rights to "The World's Most Famous Clown" and vowed to "Bozo-ize the World." (Later on, Harmon secured the rights to another valuable property and promised to "Laurel and Hardy-ize the World." What a world.) Harmon's plans involved franchising his Bozo audience-participation series concept to local stations, then to personally supervise the training of the local Bozos (though there are many of these who insist that they've never met Mr. Harmon). The producer even set up his own animation studios — later named Filmation — and ground out 156 five-minute Bozo cartoons for Jayark Films release. Anyone who's ever endured these things will take with several tons of salt Jayark's ad-campaign assurance of "magnificent animation." The *Bozo* machine hit its peak in the mid-1960's with 240 Bozo shows running throughout the world. Some of the local Bozos, like Boston's Frank Avruch, made the corny clown their life's work. (Avruch was in fact featured in two separate syndicated *Bozo* five-a-day "strips," one in 1965 and another ten years later, distributed to stations too budget-conscious to produce their own kid's shows.) There were other Bozos who didn't quite have Larry Harmon's concept nailed down, such as the Milwaukee-based Bozo of the early '80s who tried converting the clown into an innuendo-laden FM deejay type. Or the poor soul in Green Bay, Wisconsin, whose Bozo wig didn't arrive in time, forcing him to go before the cameras with his head wrapped in a towel. As of this writing, the best-known Bozo in the Free World is Joey D'Auria, who presides over an elaborate daily on Chicago "superstation" WGN.

Over the past 25 years, a notorious "urban legend" had sprung up around Bozo. The story goes that a local Bozo was trying to calm an unruly kid, who then stopped the show cold by yelling "Cram it, Clown!" Though people of all ages insist that they "saw" this incident, it's never been confirmed. But it makes a swell story.

Captain Hartz and His Pets (1954). A weekly half-hour, sponsored by a major pet-food concern known as Hartz-Mountain. Phil Lord played the captain.

Captain Z-Ro (1955). A well-written Los Angeles local series tapped for national distribution by Atlas Films. Captain Z-Ro was a space traveller who deployed an elaborate time machine. The Captain was played by Roy Steffins, the series' producer, who curiously sported a villainous-looking black mustache and goatee.

The Chimps (1951). Bing Crosby productions cooked up a deal with Courneya Films for 52 half-hours of a detective spoof featuring a cast of chimpanzees, recruited from the World Jungle Compound at Thousand Oaks, California. The chimps were outfitted with business suits, invernesses and deerstalkers, then given full dominion over scale-model sets and midget motorcars (the series was titled *Chimplock Hums* until the Conan Doyle estate got wise). The results were just about what one would expect; still, United Television Productions did excellent business with *The Chimps* for quite a few seasons. The simians' voices were provided by Daws Butler (later a mainstay at Hanna-Barbera) and Marion Richman. One of the "star" chimps ended up acting opposite Ronald Reagan in *Bedtime for Bonzo* (1952).

Colonel Bleep (1957). From Soundac Color Productions: primitively animated cartoon adventures of a cosmic cop from the "Planet Pheutoria."

Crusader Rabbit (1957). This pioneer made-for-TV cartoon series first appeared as a group of two-reelers animated by Jay Ward and Alexander Anderson, and distributed by Jerry Fairbanks starting in 1949. Because of a drawn-out lawsuit involving the animators, Fairbanks and NBC Films, this earlier *Crusader Rabbit* was off the screen as much as on during the '50s. In 1957, Jay Ward sold the rights to the characters of Crusader Rabbit and Rags the Tiger (precursors to Ward's Rocky Squirrel and Bullwinkle Moose) to Shul Bonsall, who filmed 260 color five-minute *Crusader* cartoons. Ward's earlier shorts had compensated for their barely extant animation with first-rate satiric scripts; Shul Bonsall's cartoons were better produced, but lacked Jay Ward's comic bite.

Cyclone Malone (1950). A puppet-show western from KNBH–Los Angeles, *Cyclone Malone* went the national syndication route through UTP.

Don Q, Dick and Alladin see *The Adventures of Blinky*

Gigi and Jock see *The Adventures of Blinky*

Hans Christian Andersen see *The Amazing Tales of Hans Christian Andersen*

Huckleberry Hound (1958–61). Fired from their longtime cartoon-director posts at MGM in 1957, Willian Hanna and Joseph Barbera immediately set up their own shop and went into television work. Their first group of cartoons, *Ruff and Reddy,* was merely "filler" for an NBC-network kiddie host and two bird puppets. What Hanna and Barbera longed for was a cartoon series over which they could exercise creative control—consisting totally of their animation, minus a "live" host. The dream came true when Hanna-Barbera, in concert with Kellogg's Cereals and Screen Gems, assembled their first weekly, half-hour syndicated series: *Huckleberry Hound.* Huckleberry, a tophatted blue dog, starred in his own six-minute cartoon and acted as "host" for the vehicles of animated characters Yogi Bear, Booboo Bear, Pixie and Dixie the mice and Mr. Jinks the cat. All of these "new" characters were rooted in Hanna-Barbera's MGM work. Huckleberry was patterned after MGM's Droopy the Dog, Yogi Bear's ancestor was Barney Bear, and of course, Pixie and Dixie and Jinks were the television equivalent of Tom and Jerry. The TV-cartoon characters also put in "box-office duty" in the Kellogg's Cereal ads; *Huckleberry Hound* was a "package" in every sense of the word.

Originally, Huck Hound was to have had a different voice for each cartoon; Bogart's voice in cop stories, Gary Cooper's in westerns, etc. This was scrapped in favor of Huck's familiar Tennessee Ernie southern drawl, created by voice-actor Daws Butler. The superb work of Butler and fellow voice-artist Don Messick, and the clever (at first!) scripts of former Warner Bros. cartoon scenarists Warren Foster and Michael Maltese, made *Huckleberry Hound* a favorite of all ages. The series may have won a 1959 Emmy as "Best New Children's Series," but research revealed that a goodly portion of its audience was of voting age. Bars were known to close whenever *Huckleberry Hound* was on, Jack Webb tossed off a wisecrack about the character in his 1959 movie *-30-,* and the series was running in prime time in several markets as late as 1961.

It may be hard to believe that a series format and animation style (or lack of style) which today seems trite and tiresome was greeted so enthusiastically in 1958. Remember, though, that while the classic cartoons of the '30s and '40s far outclass anything made by Hanna-Barbera for television, those old cartoons were also full of dated wartime references and ethnic jokes that either alienated or confused young viewers in the '50s, Also, the rich color and carefully detailed animation in those earlier cartoons meant little on the black-and-white television screens of the time. *Huckleberry Hound* was both up-to-date and easy on the eyes. It was also full of appealing, loveable characters whom audiences took to their hearts immediately. Though the series may seem unfunny and primitive today, it pleased viewers in 1958 enough to form the foundation of the Hanna-Barbera Empire—and to invite other producers into the heretofore sparsely populated world of TV animation. For better or worse.

Jim and Judy in Teleland (1952). One of the few pre–Hanna/Barbera cartoon syndies which amounted to anything, Television Screen Productions' *Jim and Judy in Teleland* had the clever premise of Jim and Judy climbing right into their TV set en route to adventure. Yes, yes, there were those adults who lambasted the series, claiming it would inspire the kids at home to try climbing into their own sets. These adults never *were* kids.

Johnny Jupiter (1954). *Johnny Jupiter* first ran on both the ABC and DuMont networks, then as a filmed five-a-week syndie. The network versions were brimming with wickedly witty in-jokes about the politics of the Television Industry (the story concerned an Earthman who communicated with the citizens of Jupiter by means of a two-way TV); the syndicated version settled for standard one-line gags about nothing in particular.

Jump Jump of Holliday House see *The Adventures of Blinky*

The Magic Lady and Boko (1951). Syndicated by Telemount, a company specializing in distributing the product of Paramount Pictures' KTLA–Los Angeles, *The Magic Lady and Boko* was a fun-'n'-magic outing starring Geraldine Larsen as the lady and popular Hollywood midget Jerry Maren as Boko the Elf.

Quick Draw McGraw (1959–61). The second Hanna-Barbera/Screen Gems/Kellogg's Cereals cartoon syndie, *Quick Draw McGraw* was one of the better H-B products, which to some cartoon fans may not be saying much, but will have to do for now. Hanna-Barbera intended *Quick Draw* to be a satire of 1959 Network Television: Quick Draw McGraw, a gun-toting horse, lampooned westerns, the cat-and-mouse detective duo Snooper and Blabber kidded private eye shows, and Augie Doggy and Doggy Daddy poked fun at sitcoms. Perhaps because there was definite satiric focus (most Hanna-Barbera efforts threw in jokes whether they fit the situation or not), the humor of *Quick Draw McGraw* was fairly sharp and snappy — not in the league of Jay Ward's brilliant *Rocky and His Friends,* but amusing all the same.

Romper Room (1953–   ). The oldest and most durable of the kiddie "franchise" shows, *Romper Room* was the brainchild of Baltimore television producer Bert Claster. Claster came to the conclusion in 1953 that there wasn't anything on the tube *specifically* for preschool children. At the time, Claster's wife Nancy was a nursery-school teacher. Claster simply moved Nancy's classroom before the WBAL-TV cameras every morning and titled the new series *Romper Room.* Once the project took off (it was especially popular with young mothers looking for a convenient "baby-sitter" for their restless offspring), the Clasters were approached with an offer of a CBS-network time slot. Bert and Nancy felt that *Romper Room's* basic appeal was its usage of local children and teachers, an appeal that might dissipate with a coast-to-coast hookup. To retain its "local" flavor, the Clasters offered *Romper Room* as a franchise package, providing the format, the Romper Room games and toys, and a training program for local hostesses on a station-by-station basis. By 1957, there were 22 *Romper Rooms* in the country, and after the Clasters made their first foreign sale in 1959, the number of versions increased to 130 worldwide. Several million dollars ended up coming the Clasters' way, mostly from profits on the Romper Room toys, many of these tied in with the "Do Bee" and "Don't Bee" characters used on the programs to help children learn right from wrong. With merchandising so much a part of its educational pursuits, it's no surprise that the Claster company is now a division of Hasbro Toys.

The *Sesame Street* beachhead of 1969 lessened *Romper Room's* hold on the preschool market; the series was down to 46 markets by 1977, most of these running tapes of the WFLD–Chicago version hosted by the Clasters' daughter Sally. (Around this time, the series endured the reprimands of various pressure groups because the *Romper Room* hostesses encouraged the kiddies to say

Grace before eating!) As of 1987, many cable services carried WWOR–New York's *Romper Room,* shown at the ungodly hour of 6 a.m. and hosted by the nice, no-nonsense Molly McCloskey Barber.

Sleepy Joe (1950). Jimmy Scribner, famed in broadcast circles as the man who played all the roles on the old radio series *The Johnson Family,* created the kid's series *Sleepy Joe* for KTSL–Los Angeles in 1949; it ran briefly that same year over the fledgling ABC TV network. Scribner donned blackface to play Sleepy Joe, a lazy storyteller who spoke in an outrageous minstrel-show dialect. When *Sleepy Joe* was filmed for syndication, the lead character became a puppet, no less offensive than before.

Time for Beany (1950–53). An oasis of brilliance in a sea of puppet-show mediocrity, *Time for Beany* was the saga of a little boy named Beany (after his propellor-equipped headgear), his sea-captain Uncle Horatio Huffen-puff, and the boy's pet, Cecil the Seasick Sea Serpent. The series was created by former Warner Bros. animation director Bob Clampett, who provided the voice of Cecil; other voices were superbly supplied by Stan Freberg and Daws Butler, who never failed to embroider their roles with a surplus of ad-libs. *Time for Beany's* specialty was gentle satire of the showbiz world in particular and the state of the world in general, and as such the series attracted as many old fans as young when it first ran locally on KTLA–Los Angeles. (Actor Lionel Barrymore loved the show, but had to watch it at his local tavern because his MGM bosses forbade Barrymore from owning his own TV!) Bill Scott, later co-producer of *Rocky and His Friends,* honed his comic gifts on several *Beany* scripts, helping the series to win three Emmies before 1952. While some fans may remember *Time for Beany* as a network show, the fact is that the series was shown nationally on a strictly syndicated basis, distributed by both Tele-mount and UTP. These kinescopes were still surefire ratings-winners as late as 1958. Clampett's property finally did make it to the ABC network in 1962, not in its original puppet-show form but as a cartoon series titled *Beany and Cecil.* While the animation was several notches above the TV norm and the scripts just as laugh-filled as in the old "live" days, the new *Beany and Cecil* lacked the freshness, the audience involvement, and most of all the irrepressible ad-libbing that graced the late, great *Time for Beany.*

Willie Wonderful see *Adventures of Blinky*

Comedy

Of all filmed television, comedy series are the hardest to do well. They require expert timing, which means more rehearsal time. They require the right talent, which means hiring comedy actors very much in demand and not inexpensive. They require a certain level of consistency, which means hiring larger writing staffs. Comedies have traditionally been the costliest series to make (*Amos 'n' Andy* was the most expensive filmed show of 1951), so it's not surprising that, until very recently, syndication producers without the financial backing of networks and national sponsors have shied away from comedies. But the 1950's yielded several notable syndie attempts — and not a few ignoble failures.

The Abbott and Costello Show (1951–52). This series came about because Lou Costello wanted to own outright, on film, the sketches and routines made famous by himself and his longtime partner Bud Abbott. MCA, which represented the team, approached both NBC and CBS with a proposed Abbott and Costello filmed series. Conflicts over time slots and telecasting days led MCA/Revue to peddle the show in syndication (armed in several regions by the strong sponsorship of Chevrolet), and most markets first saw *The Abbott and Costello Show* in the last days of 1952. A year earlier, filming had commenced at Hal Roach Studios, with costs kept in check by adopting an assembly-line shooting method, filming odd bits from several different episodes on any given day. Since Abbott and Costello could recite their routines in their sleep, they didn't see the need for much rehearsal time. This was good whenever Lou Costello would perk up a sagging script with his manic ad-libbing, but bad whenever that manic ad-libbing threw off the supporting actors' timing. Most of the regular supporting cast — Hillary Brooke, Sidney Fields, Gordon Jones, Joe Besser — had worked with the team before and were conditioned to Costello's improvising. But some guest actors, unsure of when to jump in with their lines, looked — and acted — completely baffled. Bud and Lou themselves floundered on occasion; when doing their classic "Who's on First" routine, Costello got so lost that Abbott virtually had to start the bit over twice! Still, the lunatic quality of the first 26 *Abbott and Costello Shows* could be gut-funny. But for the second group of 26, director Jean Yarborough decided to forego gags-for-gags' sake and concentrate on coherent story lines. The second-season *Abbott and Costellos* were relatively unified sitcoms, most of them written by comedy-film veteran Clyde Bruckman, who indulged his usual habit of lifting gags, routines and sometimes entire storylines from films he'd worked on in the past — notably the shorts and features of Buster Keaton. While the last season of *Abbott and Costello* made more sense, the team's enthusiasm was flagging to the point of ennui. Frequently the funniest thing on these programs was the shrill, tacked-on laughtrack.

After a season of *Abbott and Costello* reruns in the CBS network's Saturday morning kiddie block, distribution shifted from MCA to Sterling Television. Sterling discovered that it had its best results reselling the reruns to markets that had already run the series, which is why some cities saw *Abbott and Costello* over and over and why others never saw it at all. Today, the series' pure-gag format has made it a welcome alternative to the usual syndie-sitcom syndrome, so *Abbott and Costello* has ended up the only non-network comedy show of the '50s to remain in active distribution in the '80s. Its current syndicator has sped up the action in those sluggish second-season installments with a tape-transfer process called Lexicon. Every little bit helps.

Art Linkletter and the Kids (1952; 1960). A series of 15-minute interviews featuring the chortling Mr. Linkletter and those kids who said the darndest things, unleashed by CBS Films in 1952 and reactivated with new material by Programs for Television Inc. eight years later. A matter of taste, but Linkletter's effort was heaps better than a similar-vintage filler, *Oh Baby!*, which featured eternal gameshow host Jack Barry and a panel of comics providing "funny" voice-overs for baby pictures.

Colonel Humphrey Flack (1958). Colonel Flack, the soft-hearted con man who fleeced only criminals and other tricksters who'd victimized the needy, first appeared in a series of *Saturday Evening Post* stories by Everett Rhodes Castle. Flack's television debut, in the person of actor Alan Mobray, came about on a 1953 episode of *Plymouth Playhouse;* later that year, Mobray continued as Flack in a series of 39 live half-hours over the DuMont Network. These were so well received that DuMont shipped out kinescopes to its many non-affiliates. In 1958, *Colonel Flack's* original producers Wilbur Stark and Jerry Layton dug up those 39 DuMont scripts and filmed them as Desilu; directing most of them was John Rich, best known for his later work on such sitcoms as *The Dick Van Dyke Show* and *All in the Family*. Returning to the fold was Alan Mobray, who fit the role of Flack like a glove, and Frank Jenks, who played the Colonel's nervous aide "Patsy" Garvey. Reviewers carped about the requisite laughtrack on CBS Films' syndicated version of *Flack* and expressed the wish that Mobray would find a more "dignified" vehicle (man does not live by *King Lear* alone), but most everyone else was happy with the new series — everyone except the fellow who wrote the first *Flack* script for *Plymouth Playhouse,* who subsequently sued producers Stark and Layton for a piece of the residuals.

Duffy's Tavern (1954). The long-established radio version of *Duffy's Tavern,* created by and starring Ed Gardner, had resisted a "visualization" when made into a dismal motion picture in 1945, but nobody learned their lesson and tried nine years later to bring the property to television. The 39-week TV *Tavern* was a trial balloon for the newly created production coalition of Hal Roach Studios and Motion Pictures for Television, part of a master plan to produce high-quality series exclusively for syndication. *Duffy's Tavern* was the first and last step in this plan; the operative word, you see, was "quality." The series was woefully cookiecutter in design, the roughneck appeal of the radio version nullified by TV-sitcom cliches. While Ed Gardner was pretty good reviving his radio role as Archie, malaprop-laden manager of the unseen Duffy's greasy-spoon eatery, he was saddled with lines and situations that went beyond tiresome. Worst of all, the TV Duffy's Tavern didn't even *look* like the fly-ridden, rotting establishment so well conveyed to the imagination via radio; on television, the Tavern was four flat walls, two tables, two checkered tablecloths, and that's all she wrote. Roach/MPTV took a bath with *Duffy's Tavern,* eventually selling the mess to Guild Films in 1956. Guild tried to get some mileage out of this lemon by playing up the fact that the series had been shot in color. Better it should have been strangled in its sleep.

The Fabulous Fraud see *Colonel Humphrey Flack*

The Eddie Cantor Comedy Theatre (1955). Ziv Productions lucked into an extremely valuable commodity in late 1954 in the form of song/dance/laughs man Eddie Cantor. Cantor had been plying his trade in all phases of show business for nearly half a century, but a recent heart attack had forced the venerable entertainer to halt the grind. Still yearning to remain in the Public Eye, Cantor decided upon a filmed television series — which could be shot *once,* then rerun indefinitely so Cantor could show up once a week while still relaxing at home. The result was *The Eddie Cantor Comedy Theatre,* a full-color humorous anthology in which host Eddie wove his way through each episode on the pretext that he was "backstage" supervising things. This was Ziv's costliest series thus far ($53,000 per episode), one which warranted a larger-than-usual promotional campaign. One of the cuter publicity stunts was the holding of local "Five Daughters" contests, with big prizes given to fathers who'd matched Mr. Cantor in the number of female offspring. The push worked: *Comedy Theatre's* prerelease sales surpassed anything Ziv had offered up to January of 1955.

So that Ziv could offer the series to *two* sponsors per market, 38 episodes were filmed instead of the usual 39, allowing an equal number of episodes for both advertisers. Most of the playlets supported Ziv's boast that each story had been written with a particular guest star in mind: Basil Rathbone, Charles Coburn and Joe E. Brown were among the celebrities whose stories matched their distinctive talents. But last-minute changes did occur. A role written for Rudy Vallee, that of a kidnapped millionaire who stingily refused to pay his ransom, worked just as well for Vincent Price, while in one Aladdin's-lamp farce, Eddie Cantor *himself* was replaced by Buster Keaton. Some of the best *Comedy Theatres* were musical mini-revues; one of these gave audiences the frightening spectacle of seeing The Three Stooges in living color. Throughout it all, Eddie Cantor was the trouper's trouper, performing as though he'd never heard the words "heart attack." Cantor may not have been everyone's favorite (his tastes in music and comedy seemed to have undergone an attack of arrested development in the 1920's), but *The Eddie Cantor Comedy Theatre* was a solid vehicle, one in which the Ziv organization could take justifiable pride.

Glencannon (1959). Gross-Krasne-Silleman/NTA's *Glencannon* was a comedy-adventure series based on the stories by Guy Gilpatric. Thomas Mitchell, in the last of three lucrative profits-percentage deals with Gross-Krasne (see also *Mayor of the Town* and *O. Henry Playhouse* in the "Drama" section), played Colin Glencannon, captain of the freighter "Inchcliffe Castle." To look at the series' location work, purportedly set in the Caribbean and at California's San Pedro Harbor, one would never guess that *Glencannon* was filmed entirely in England. Thomas Mitchell's star value enabled NTA to make over a million dollars in prerelease sales to 91 stations. And while the series itself wasn't remarkable, *Glencannon* represented a rare attack of integrity on the part of its producers, who spent several thousand dollars just before its release to *remove* the series' canned laughtrack.

The Goldbergs (1954). Created by its star Gertrude Berg for radio in 1929, *The Goldbergs* wasn't essentially a comedy, but had for most of its media life been a daily serial with humorous undertones. Mrs. Berg's story of a Jewish family in the Bronx had been seen on all four major television networks since 1949, sometimes as a live serial, sometimes a filmed half-hour weekly. After its final network cancellation in 1954, Mrs. Berg was determined to keep *The Goldbergs* alive, and Gertrude Berg was not one to be easily dissuaded; 39 new *Goldbergs* were shot in New York, then syndicated by Guild Films. By 1954, ethnic humor was on the outs; the Goldbergs retained their essential Jewishness in the syndie version, but were "assimilated" a bit by moving from their Bronx tenement to a cozy suburban home (complete with overstocked closet) in the town of Haverville. While Mrs. Berg may have changed the locale, she saw to it that her characters remained consistent and believable, even when wrestling with the most motheaten of standard sitcom situations. At Berg's insistence, the series had no laughtrack, but there were indeed laughs, not of the belly variety but more in the way of gentle chuckles. Retained from *The Goldbergs'* earliest TV days were its theme music, "Toselli's Serenade," and Molly Goldberg's opening greeting from her kitchen window—although Molly no longer exchanged gossip (and Maxwell House Coffee commercials) with her unseen tenement neighbor Mrs. Bloom.

The Great Gildersleeve (1955). Hal Roach/NBC Films' *The Great Gildersleeve* fell into the "typical TV sitcom" pattern, but since the radio version that had been playing since 1941 had always been locked in that same pattern, few *Gildersleeve* fans were disappointed. Willard Waterman, who'd played radio's Throckmorton P. Gildersleeve since 1950, was the ideal visualization of the town of Summerfield's corpulent, conceited water commissioner (much more so than the original radio "Gildy," Harold Peary, who'd been obliged to gain a great deal of weight for his *Gildersleeve* movies). The 39 television *Gildersleeves* did excellent business on the basis of the radio series' following, but the visual version was a bit too complacently reminiscent of every other TV comedy—right down to that damned laughtrack.

The Hank McCune Show (1953). The spectacularly unfunny *Hank McCune Show,* which ran on the NBC network in 1950, is usually given a footnote in television histories as the first filmed sitcom to use a prerecorded laughtrack—or at least, to admit to doing so. The dumbo-eared Hank McCune was an Air Force buddy of Samuel Z. Arkoff, who'd developed the *McCune Show* as a live New York local series in 1949 and who'd later be co-founder of American International Pictures. United Television Productions released a batch of newly filmed *Hank McCunes* for syndication in 1953, featuring the "star" as a young man incapable of performing the smallest task without creating catastrophe. The syndie was just as atrocious as the network version; its rare moments of fun were provided by reliable supporting players Hanley Stafford and Florence Bates.

How to Marry a Millionaire (1958–59). When 20th Century–Fox acquired half-control of the proposed "NTA Film Network" in 1957, the studio rifled through its old movie properties in search of suitable TV-series material (a practice Fox continued for the next twenty years, as witness such series as *Voyage to the Bottom of the Sea* and *M*A*S*H*). After considering titles like *Cheaper by the Dozen, Chicken Every Sunday* and *Mr. Belvedere,* Fox found that the only reheated movie idea that "flew" as a potential series was *How to Marry a Millionaire,* a variation of Fox's favorite film plot: three pretty girls on the prowl for rich husbands. *Millionaire* had been Fox's first Cinemascope comedy in 1953, starring Betty Grable, Lauren Bacall and Marilyn Monroe. The TV version was likewise used as an excuse by the studio to show off three of its contract actresses: Merry Anders, Lori Nelson, and (in the Monroe part) Barbara Eden. These ladies promoted the series with a whirlwind prerelease national tour, culminating in a studio-arranged night on the town with three genuine millionaires in Chicago. In October 1958, *How to Marry a Millionaire* debuted. To engender ratings, NTA "triple-billed" the series on three different New York City channels during the month of November. Critics were cool to *Millionaire,* citing its slick production values and its stars' beauty as the series' only tangible assets, but the show did well enough in the big-city markets to warrant a second season. Production on the last 26 episodes was held up briefly when co-star Lori Nelson left for what she hoped were bigger things (they weren't); she was replaced by Lisa Gaye. As it happened, only Barbara Eden was able to finesse her *Millionaire* work into a lasting career. While Eden was starring in *I Dream of Jeannie* in 1966, her *Millionaire* co-star Merry Anders could be seen in the role of a girl drowned in a phone booth (you had to be there) on an episode of *Get Smart.*

Life with Buster Keaton (1951). Part of silent-film comedian Buster Keaton's phoenix-like comeback in the early '50s was a live weekly series from KTTV–Los Angeles. Keaton played a clerk in a sporting-goods store who dreamed of life in the fast lane: Buster the Great Detective, the Great Sportsman, the Great Lover. The popularity of *Life with Buster Keaton* led KTTV to try syndication. Kinescopes—films taken directly off the TV screen of live broadcasts—were used, and these had all the aesthetic value of a bowl of oatmeal. So KTTV withdrew its kinescopes, and set about filming a Keaton series at the Nassour Studios facilities which KTTV would eventually purchase for its own. Two of Buster's pals from the silent days were recruited for the project: gagman Clyde Bruckman and director Mal St. Clair. Sad to say, the resulting half-hours nearly scuttled the reputation that Keaton had been so painfully rebuilding. *Life with Buster Keaton* was pasted together so quickly that Buster might just as well have been performing underwater. Mal St. Clair took ill and was replaced by increasingly incompetent directors, while Clyde Bruckman, who unlike Keaton had never learned the art of abstention from spirits, indulged in his characteristic lazy pilfering of comic routines that had worked in films of the past but which had lost their sparkle over the years. For reasons that defied logic, KTTV retained the one truly weak aspect of the live Keaton series, a motley group of puppets who'd been around to fill up airtime not involving Buster. There was no point to having these cloth creations appear in the filmed series to exchange limp one-liners with Keaton, who'd never been a fast-patter specialist. *Life with Buster Keaton* was Death with Agony.

Life with Elizabeth (1953–54). Years before *The Mary Tyler Moore Show* and *Golden Girls,* Betty White had been a full-fledged, very popular sitcom star. Her first vehicle, originally titled *Hello Darling,* was *Life with Elizabeth,* which ran live on KLAC–Los Angeles starting in 1952. Betty played a perky newlywed, while L.A. TV personality Del Moore portrayed her befuddled hubby. KLAC executive Don Fedderson, later the guiding force behind *My Three Sons* and *Family Affair,* was producer-director; the series' property man was future blood-and-guts film director Sam Peckinpah! The syndicated *Life with Elizabeth* was shot at Nassour Studios and distributed by Guild. The series had a time slot flexibility unmatched by most other syndies; each episode was divided into three short sketches, allowing local stations to run *Elizabeth* as either 65 half-hour weeklies or 195 ten-minute daily fillers.

Meet Corliss Archer (1954). Miss Corliss Archer first drew breath as a character in F. Hugh Herbert's mildly risque teen-romance play *Kiss and Tell* (the film version of which starred a blossoming Shirley Temple). *Meet Corliss Archer* debuted on the CBS radio network in 1943, and as a live weekly on the CBS television hookup in 1951. When Ziv Productions acquired the property for syndication in 1954, Ann Baker, a competent actress if a bit long in tooth for a teenager, became the fourth young lady to play the TV-radio version of Corliss. Syndie-TV stalwart John Eldredge and silent-film star Mary Brian were cast as Corliss' long-suffering parents. (Parents of television teens were always long-suffering. It was part of the job description.) Hy Averback, later most closely associated with Walter Brennan's sitcom *The Real McCoys,* produced the 39 filmed *Corliss Archers* and also provided the sardonic narration for the series. Viewers and reviewers found this narration, and the drawn caricatures that popped up on-screen during each installment to comment upon the tangled plotlines, to be the freshest and most entertaining aspects of *Meet Corliss Archer.* The series was a surprisingly pedestrian choice for Ziv Productions' entree into television situation comedy (plus laughtrack), but the Ziv sales department did the trick again, planting *Corliss Archer* into 105 first-run markets. When the property was later handed over to Ziv's rerun subsidiary Economee Films, *Meet Corliss Archer* became a register-ringer all over again. Ziv didn't become an industry leader without knowing its audience.

Oh, Baby see *Art Linkletter and the Kids*

This Is Alice (1958). Building a lineup of first-run syndies for its incipient "fourth network" in 1957, NTA reasoned that situation comedies were sure tickets to success. That was true only if the shows were good. *This Is Alice,* filmed mostly in Atlanta by Desilu, starred child actress Patty Ann Gerrity as little-miss-fixit Alice Holliday. When the pilot for *Alice* was filmed, Patty Ann was eight years old and cute as a button; by the time the series debuted in October of 1958, Miss Gerrity was only too aware of how cute she was. Her portrayal of Alice was tiresome enough without her tendency to look directly at the camera, grin toothily, and snap her fingers (with accompanying musical "sting") whenever hitting upon a great idea. Even the polished work of Phyllis Coates and Tommy Farrell as Alice's parents was unable to stem the drivel. The nicest thing one can say about *This Is Alice* is that it lasted only 39 weeks.

Tugboat Annie (1958). "Tugboat Annie" Brennan, formidable skipper of the good tug "Narcissus," came to the public by way of Norman Reilly Raine's short stories in that cornucopia of syndie-series concepts, *The Saturday Evening Post*. Since 1933, Annie had been played in films by such earthy actresses as Marie Dressler, Marjorie Rambeau and Jane Darwell, so television's Annie, the weatherbeaten Minerva Urecal, was maintaining a fine tradition. TPA commissioned *Tugboat Annie* in 1954, and a pilot film, costing a then-record $130,000, was completed two years later. The subsequent 39 episodes were filmed in Canada; TPA was contractually obligated to run the series first over Canadian network TV, where it was sponsored by Lever Bros. and became a major hit of the 1957–58 season. The excellence of the Canadian ratings led to big American sales for the series. One can imagine the dismay of American TV station managers who'd shelled out good money for *Tugboat Annie,* only to discover after its fall 1958 premiere that the two-year-old property was a mishmash of banal plotlines, syrupy pathos and cut-rate slapstick (sample gag: Annie, believing she's dead, tests out her "ghostly" skills by trying to walk through a wall. She fails). *Tugboat Annie* didn't exactly lose money, and was still making sales to fresh new markets like Alaska and Hawaii into the '60s. But the series was a rather drippy end to an appealing character.

Drama

"Drama," a loose term at best, could generally be broken down on '50s television into two categories. There were the Anthologies — featuring different casts and stories each week, but presided over by a celebrity host — and there were what best can be labelled Semi-Anthologies. These series featured continuing, regular cast members and/or a permanent location (a small town, a hospital or whatever), but offered different supporting casts each week. The regulars would become intertwined in the trials and tribulations of the guest actors, and usually would determine the outcome of the plotlines.

The Big Attack see Citizen Soldier

Broadway Television Theatre (1952). This super-ambitious undertaking of WOR–New York offered weekly hour-long versions of famous plays (usually cleaned up for TV consumption), featuring well-known character actors and second-echelon Hollywood stars. The plays were presented live — with a brand-new performance every night of the week! The "best" performance was kinescoped and syndication nationally. Unfortunately, local stations — then as now — were hesitant to hand over an hour's worth of air time to a "prestige" item.

Citizen Soldier (1958). Flamingo Films' *Citizen Soldier* was part of a then-current trend of "military" anthologies, both on network *(Navy Log)* and off *(Silent Service)*. This series of World War II stories had the odd distinction of being the only dramatic program in which none of the cast members were given screen credit; that's because the casts of *Citizen Soldier* were made up entirely of genuine military personnel. This deployment of the military got the series' producers into a lot of hot water, not from the military brass who didn't want their troops thus occupied, but from the Screen Actors' Guild, which *did* want its troops thus occupied. *Citizen Soldier* was foredoomed anyway. The series lacked the budget for the expected big-battle scenes, so director Harry Gerstad had to concoct new ways to make clips from old training films and newsreels look exciting. With little action and no stars, *Citizen Soldier* stayed on permanent sick-leave, even when re-issued as *The Big Attack*.

Conrad Nagel Theatre (1954). Early talkie matinee idol Conrad Nagel hosted this anthology from Guild Films, noteworthy for its emphasis on "new talent discoveries."

The Crown Theatre Starring Gloria Swanson (1953). Silent-screen superstar Gloria Swanson was swamped with television offers following her spectacular comeback in the 1950 picture *Sunset Boulevard.* While conducting an interview show on New York's Channel 13, Swanson was offered a filmed series by Mexico's Tele-Voz studios, but that was squelched when Hollywood's unions clamped down on below-the-border production. Eventually, Bing Crosby Productions came up with an attractive anthology: *Crown Theatre Starring Gloria Swanson,* a lucrative 26 weeks from CBS Films.

Divorce Court (1958–61; 1965; 1969; 1984–   ). Inspired by the surprise success of CBS' 1957 series *Perry Mason,* television's first "courtroom cycle" began as a group of locally produced programs. It was fairly simple for local stations searching for low-cost, in-house programming to build a courtroom set, hire a retired judge (or an actor who looked like a judge), round up several practicing attorneys who, denied permission to advertise on television, welcomed the free publicity of on-camera exposure, cast several inexpensive actors to make like litigants and spectators, then base the scripts on existing court records. Presto — instant TV show!
    Leader of the pack was *Divorce Court,* which KTTV–Los Angeles ran in prime time, out-rating the network competition. NTA decided to add *Divorce Court* to its new ad-hoc network in 1958; the hour-long weekly series made history as the first syndicated program to be offered on videotape. (Kinescopes were offered to local stations without tape facilities.) Actor/lawyer Voltaire Perkins played the judge, and Bill Walsh was the whispering "commentator." The true-life cases dramatized on *Divorce Court* were usually in the lurid/sensational category. The series' raw, spontaneous energy stemmed from the fact

that no one—not even the producer—knew how Judge Perkins would rule in any given case. There was no rehearsal, no formal script. Each actor/litigant was given three fact-sheets about his or her character: the first sheet contained the truth about the litigant, the second listed a set of lies that the actor would try to palm off as the truth, and the third outlined hidden facts that would come to light under cross-examination. One male "litigant" got so wound up in his performance that he accused his "wife" of adultery—a tidbit not covered by *any* of his fact-sheets.

Storer Television redistributed the first 130 *Divorce Courts* as a daily strip after production ceased in 1961. A mid-decade boost in daytime-TV profits led Storer to tape 130 new, half-hour *Divorce Courts* in 1966, and another 130 in 1969. Voltaire Perkins was back as the judge, with Colin Male on hand as the unctuous commentator. Keeping in step with the times, both daily packages were raunchier and more suggestive than the original series. In 1984, the popularity of the syndicated *People's Court* inspired a *fourth* daily go-round for the warhorse *Divorce Court,* produced by Storer in association with Blair Television. This version starred retired jurist William B. Keene (famous for his participation in the Charles Manson murder trial) as the judge, with gameshow veteran Jim Peck as the commentator. The cases heard on this most recent *Divorce Court* dealt with such standard 1980's buzz-topics as homosexuality, child molestation and S & M. Still, the newest *Court* wasn't all that different from the 1958 original. Once again, no one knew ahead of time how the judge would render his decision. Once again, the litigants were actors, but the lawyers genuine (though not necessarily *divorce* lawyers). And once again, the judge called the attorneys together for consultation every ten minutes or so—*just* in time for the commercial break.

Divorce Hearing (1958). Another Los Angeles local courtroom show given a national break, Interstate TV's *Divorce Hearing,* unlike *Divorce Court,* was an "actuality" show. Los Angeles marriage counselor Dr. Paul Popenoe listened, in closed quarters, to pretrial complaints offered by real-life divorce-bound couples. The contestants were actually repeating complaints that they'd already offered Dr. Popenoe at earlier meetings, with expletives deleted for the television cameras (one gentleman insisted that his married life was "H-E-double-L!"). Making audiences feel less like voyeurs, most *Divorce Hearings* ended positively, with the lugubrious Dr. Popenoe urging the couples to give things another chance.

Dr. Christian (1956). Ziv's *Dr. Christian* rode in on a wave of popular '50s medical series like *Medic* and *Janet Dean, R.N.* Dr. Paul Christian had initially put up his shingle at CBS radio in 1937, with Jean Hersholt in the title role; Hersholt also starred in several RKO *Dr. Christian* movies, which like the radio series emulated their star's real-life humanitarian work. But Jean Hersholt was mortally ill with cancer when filming began on the 39 TV *Christians.* Shortly before his death, the gallant actor, shrunken to 95 pounds, guested in the *Christian* pilot to turn over his small-town practice to his "nephew" Mark Christian, played by MacDonald Carey. While he was handsomer and more romantic than Mr. Hersholt, Carey couldn't hope to match the older actor's charisma, but he was authoritative enough in the Dr. Christian role to appear in filmed promotional spots on behalf of local medical charities and health programs. While he professed in later years to finding his Dr. Christian character somewhat wishy-washy, MacDonald Carey has persisted in a television medical career to this day via his long-running role as a doctor in the NBC soapera *Days of Our Lives.*

Dr. Hudson's Secret Journal (1955–56). In his 1929 novel *Magnificent Obsession,* Lloyd C. Douglas created the kindly, selfless, somewhat mystical Dr. Wayne Hudson. Hudson was killed off halfway through the book, but made such an impression on the readers that Douglas wrote a "prequel" to *Magnificent Obsession* in 1939, composed in the form of a private journal, written in code, that Dr. Hudson was supposed to have kept during his early years in medicine. This diary of the care and treating of troubled souls was titled—surprise!—*Dr. Hudson's Secret Journal.* Gross-Krasne bought the television rights to the property in 1955, proving that Dr. Hudson had retained his popularity to the tune of 78 episodes. Starring as Wayne Hudson was John Howard, who'd appeared in 1947's *Public Prosecutor* and thus was the "oldest" star in syndication; Howard's interpretation of Hudson was as altruistic as ever, though he was a bit better off financially than his literary counterpart, able to support a daughter (Cheryl Callaway) and that requisite of syndie-drama heroes, the all-knowing housekeeper (Olive Blakeney). Also appearing as Hudson's protegee was Joe Walker, who'd won the role in a nationwide talent hunt. Because of the religious undertones prevalent in all of Lloyd C. Douglas' work, *Dr. Hudson's Secret Journal* usually ran on Sunday.

Douglas Fairbanks Jr. Presents (1952–55). American-born Doug Fairbanks Jr. was (and is) a devout Anglophile, so it's not surprising that his syndie-anthology series was mostly filmed at Elstree Studios, just outside London. NBC distributed Fairbanks' series in America, the NBC-owned stations getting first dibs. Like many another syndicated program, *Douglas Fairbanks Jr. Presents* was retitled in deference to its sponsor in several markets: it was known as *Rheingold Theatre* in New York City, while stations in Wisconsin ran it as *Triangle Theatre* in honor of Blatz Beer's three-cornered logo. By any name, the series was a class act. While budgets and production schedules were corset-tight, the series *looked* lavish and expensive, using many of Elstree's magnificent standing sets and the best English and European locations available. (Fairbanks frequently had to use as many as three different locales for a single exterior scene; local officials, jealously guarding their scenic attractions, were forever shooing his crew away.) If *Fairbanks Presents* had any kind of through-line, it was "irony": the dictator thwarted by his own brother, the village buffoon becoming a millionaire, the army deserter redeemed by love at the expense of freedom. Fairbanks himself appeared in a variety of colorful roles, most enjoyably as renegade poet Francois Villon. The 117 half-hour playlets shifted distribution in mid-decade from NBC to ABC Films, ever racking up new sales to stations that hadn't existed when *Douglas Fairbanks Jr.*

Presents debuted in 1952. Additionally, NBC Films bundled up the first few seasons of *Fairbanks* in 1954 as a "new" package hosted by Walter Abel and titled *Paragon Playhouse*.

The Ella Raines Series see *Janet Dean, Registered Nurse*

The Errol Flynn Theatre (1956). We'd like to say that Official Films' British-American *Errol Flynn Theatre* was the freshest, most innovative anthology of 1956 — but we can't. Mr. Flynn's life of drinks, drugs and damsels had made the fortyish actor look like a candidate for Social Security. He hosted with a minimal expense of energy, and occasionally starred in the pedestrian playlets, often in the company of then-wife Patrice Wymore. But the old swash had long become unbuckled. Flynn's anthology was a carbon copy of everyone else's anthology, right down to having the host sit before a studio fireplace in the opening. Would that the set had caught fire....

The Ethel Barrymore Theatre (1953). The septuagenarian "First Lady of the American Theatre" was lured before the cameras to host her own filmed anthology, distributed by Interstate TV. Noted Hollywood directors Lewis Allen and Gerald Mayer handled most of the 26 dramas, with Ethel Barrymore herself starring in four episodes.

Favorite Story see *My Favorite Story*

Flight (1958). *Flight,* a 39-week Air Force omnibus hosted by General George C. Kenney, was released by California National Productions in hopes of matching the success of the same company's seabound syndie, *Silent Service*. In truth, *Flight* was the better of the two anthologies, since its aerial photography had a momentum and thrill value lacking in *Silent Service's* submarine scenes. But *Flight's* maudlin, cliched scripts couldn't maintain the euphoria of the flying sequences. Still, sales were good, even to educational stations who were attracted by *Flight's* documentary-style air footage.

The Gloria Swanson Show see *Crown Theatre Starring Gloria Swanson*

Henry Fonda Presents the Star and the Story (1954). Four Star Productions, set up by actors Dick Powell, Charles Boyer, Ida Lupino and David Niven to create TV showcases for that formidable foursome, added to its successful CBS network anthology *Four Star Playhouse* the equally star-studded Official Films syndie *Henry Fonda Presents the Star and the Story*. The series of 39 stories was entertaining, but the anthology form was getting terribly standardized by 1954.

His Honor, Homer Bell (1955). An NBC Films release starring respected character actor Gene Lockhart as a small-town justice of the peace. Homer Bell came equipped with the usual sassy housekeeper (Jane Moultrie) and an endless barrage of sage advice for his friends and neighbors. The "youth angle" so vital to TV executives was handled by the Judge's pretty daughter Casey (Mary Lee Dearing). Since *Homer Bell* was set in a Frontier town and since it had plenty of chuckles to offset the more serious stories, NBC Films was able to promote the 39-week series as a western, a comedy, or a drama. Or a western-comedy-drama.

Homer Bell see above

Inner Sanctum (1954). Created in 1941 by Himan Brown, *Inner Sanctum* had been one of radio's premiere anthologies of horror and grim irony, spawning a series of pulp novels and a Universal Pictures "B" series starring Lon Chaney Jr. On radio, host Raymond Edward Johnson opened the "squeaking door" (the world's only copyrighted sound effect) to each week's *Inner Sanctum;* in the films, David Hoffman appeared as a disembodied head floating in a crystal ball to intone the pre-credits introductions. *Inner Sanctum's* television host Paul McGrath (who'd been hosting the radio version since 1945) was unseen, but still ushered in each week's drama to the sound of that faithful squeaking door. Himan Brown and Galahad Productions' 39 New York-filmed *Inner Sanctums* were issued by NBC Films; they were serviceable, but lacked the extra dimension of stirring the audience's imagination that had distinguished the radio version.

Janet Dean, Registered Nurse (1954). Ella Raines, a movie star of the '40s who came out of both a retirement and a marriage in England in the '50s, and Joan Harrison, best remembered as Alfred Hitchcock's TV producer, teamed in 1953 to form Cornwall Productions. With Peter Godfrey in the director's chair, Cornwall turned out a 39-week vehicle for Miss Raines, *Janet Dean, Registered Nurse,* released with great fanfare by MPTV in 1954. This group of stories about an R.N. who moved from job to job had its share of wounded hoodlums and gun-wielding dope fiends, but the best *Janet Deans* were emotional dramas concerning such subjects as child abuse, parental neglect, mistreatment of the mentally disabled and the shutting out of the elderly — dramas usually dismissed by critics of the '50s as "Women's Stories." Ignoring the ignorant, fans of *Janet Dean* — including members of several medical organizations who honored the series with a number of awards — kept the series in rerun circulation until the early '60s.

The Lilli Palmer Theatre (1952). NBC Films, hoping that the lightning which accompanied its Doug Fairbanks Jr. anthology would strike twice, released *The Lilli Palmer Theatre.* All the Fairbanks ingredients were there: glamorous host, international production, eager sponsors at the ready. But Lilli Palmer had other professional fish to fry, so NBC was obliged to trot out the same 26 *Palmer Theatres* year after year.

Mayor of the Town (1954). From 1942 through '49, *Mayor of the Town* was a radio vehicle for the bluster and fluster of Lionel Barrymore, who appeared as Springdale's Mayor Russell. As early as 1951, Barrymore was slated for a television version of the series, but by the time Rawlins-Grant Productions and Gross-Krasne Films were ready to shoot the series in 1954, Barrymore was too ill to appear (he died that same year). Another Oscar-winner, Thomas Mitchell, was engaged to play TV's Mayor Russell, enabling Gross-Krasne's distributor UTP to sell the series on the basis of Mitchell's cinema track record. *Mayor of the Town* was the first of three liaisons between Thomas Mitchell and Gross-Krasne, none of them lasting past 39 episodes but all of them making piles of cash for the people involved. While no one could really replace Lionel Barrymore, Mitchell emerged as an agreeable TV personality thanks to this series. His Mayor Russell was abetted by the inevitable housekeeper (Kathleen Freeman, in a role played on radio by Agnes Moorehead) and the usual young ward, a tow-headed kid named Butch (David Saber). UTP (and later MCA) managed to have *Mayor of the Town* running in virtually every important market by early 1955; strangely, this rather prestigious property didn't appear in the valuable Los Angeles market until Richfield Oil assumed sponsorship of *Mayor of the Town* in the fall of 1956.

Men of Annapolis (1956). Aiming for its first network sale, Ziv Productions offered two "officer's-academy" anthologies to CBS in 1956. While to the naked eye the only difference between *West Point* and *Men of Annapolis* was the usual distinction between the Army and the Navy, CBS decided upon *West Point,* leaving *Men of Annapolis* to make do with syndication, where it did well indeed thanks to the nationwide sponsorship of Cities Service Gasoline. *Annapolis,* a series of dramatized true-life stories about the famed Naval Academy, was filmed in part on the Maryland campus of Annapolis itself. The entertainment level on both *West Point* and *Men of Annapolis* was fairly even; if you liked stories of hazing, protocol, and tradition, you'd probably like both series. The two properties were also equally expensive, averaging some $40,000 an episode — which may explain why *West Point,* with its network backing, lasted 78 episodes, while *Annapolis* managed only 39. The series' lofty budget, by the way, was publicly defended by *Men of Annapolis'* producer-director, who declared that the only way syndicated television could stay on a par with the networks was to pump up production costs. Those sentiments were expressed by William Castle, who later produced and directed several delightful, gimmick-laden horror films *(The Tingler, House on Haunted Hill),* which were among the *cheapest* Hollywood product of their time.

My Favorite Story (1952–53). *My Favorite Story* had been a Ziv radio syndie anthology hosted by Ronald Colman starting in 1946. The series featured celebrities introducing their "favorite" tales from classic literature, usually (and economically) public-domain pieces by Tolstoy, Poe, de Maupassant and the like. Ronald Colman bypassed the television version of *Favorite Story,* so Ziv engaged another star who was working on one of the company's radio properties: Adolphe Menjou, who was then hosting an interview syndie with his wife Veree Teasdale. Ziv reasoned that Menjou could transfer his patented charm to the TV *Favorite Story;* as it happened, the company caught the actor at the right psychological moment. Menjou's cheery cooperation with the House Un-American Activities Commission, where he'd helped finger Hollywood's "Commies" by claiming he could smell them out, had made the actor *persona non grata* with filmmakers who resented informers of any political persuasion (it's been noted that the anti–Red purges in Hollywood produced no heroes or villains, only victims). When Ziv came up with *My Favorite Story,* Adolphe Menjou frankly needed the work. The 52-week anthology made him a star all over again; while the actor would never qualify for any Mr. Nice Guy award, Menjou suddenly found himself graciously accepting both praise and criticism for his new series from strangers in the street. As Menjou himself observed, *Favorite Story* transformed him from Unapproachable Star to a weekly friend of everyone's family.

As it had on radio, *My Favorite Story* employed as head writers Jerome Lawrence and Robert E. Lee. The team had been with Ziv since the '40s, and would remain with the company until graduating to Broadway fame with such hit plays as *Auntie Mame* and *Inherit the Wind.*

Night Court USA (1958). Banner Films' 78-installment *Night Court* starred radio's onetime Mr. District Attorney, Jay Jostyn, as the Judge. This entry into the late–50's courtroom cycle was the only one not using any "real people": all of the participants, including attorneys, were actors recreating actual cases. Producer-director Sandy Howard apparently searched high and low for the most sensational, titillating cases to dramatize for the series, stopping just this side of *really* bad taste. Drug abuse and sexual misconduct were given special consideration, though *Night Court* always had time for such tickle-and-tease cases as a pretty girl brought up on charges for nude sunbathing.

The O. Henry Playhouse (1956). 39-week Gross-Krasne/MCA anthology based on the surprise-ending tales of William Sidney Porter, who wrote under the nom de plume "O. Henry." Thomas Mitchell hosted as an unnamed "storyteller" who collected odd anecdotes from odder people. *O. Henry Playhouse* was the second Thomas Mitchell/Gross-Krasne syndie of the '50s, and eventually netted the actor $150,000 (over and above his weekly $2000 salary) — a rather better situation than the one which faced the real William Sidney Porter, who died with 37 cents in his pocket.

In a 1958 article, *TV Guide* used *O. Henry Playhouse* to illustrate the ins and outs of the syndication business. Amidst tallies of money earned and spent, the article revealed that Gross-Krasne would make 40 prints of each *O. Henry* episode and ship them C.O.D. to the top 40 markets running the series (including Philadelphia, where the anthology debuted in October 1956). These 40 prints were telecast and then sent back to Gross-Krasne to be cleaned and spliced, then shipped out to their *next* 40 markets. This is why *O. Henry Playhouse* was still being first-run in some cities as late as 1958 — *and* why Gross-Krasne didn't really make a profit on the series until that time, not with their initial investment of nearly $1,350,000. Syndication could be lucrative, but one had to persist in it to survive — it wasn't a game for producers with but one or two concepts to their names.

When Standard Oil said "hands off," they meant it. *Play of the Week* was occasionally edited for time, but seldom for content. Only once did censorship prevail when the phrase "son of a bitch" was changed — to "bastard" (this was a time when network censors had coronaries over such words as "damn" and "guts"). There was a brief period when ratings were low and Standard Oil was going to ax the series, but were dissuaded after 22,000 viewers sent in written support for *Play of the Week* (cash contributions were promptly sent back). This viewer loyalty repeated itself when *Play of the Week* began making syndication sales in early 1960. Stations in such markets as Los Angeles, Chicago, Philadelphia and Cincinnati had assumed that they'd merely acquired a low-revenue *succès d'estime,* and then were bowled over by the viewer and sponsor support they received. *Play of the Week* continued making new sales, mostly to educational outlets, long after production ended in 1961. (David Susskind had bowed out of the proceedings after the first season, to be replaced by *Studio One's* mentor Worthington Miner.) *Play of the Week* closed out the 1950's as one of the boldest syndicated achievements in the days just before PBS cornered the market on American Culture.

Rendezvous (1958). Hosted by Charles Drake, *Rendezvous* was a minor anthology originally slated for the CBS network. When its intended time slot was overtaken by Westinghouse's *Desilu Playhouse, Rendezvous* was syndicated by CBS Films, and did better financially as a syndie than ever would have been possible on the network.

Science Fiction Theatre (1955–56). This two-season anthology was Ziv's first association with producer Ivan *(Sea Hunt)* Tors. After a moderately successful movie career, Tors was frustrated because studio executives preferred science-fiction films with bug-eyed monsters and beautiful girls over the more cerebral and speculative brand of sf. One of Tors' pet scripts, concerning the invention of an artificial space satellite, was rejected by every film producer in Hollywood (this was, need one say, several years before Sputnik). Ivan Tors took his satellite story, combined it with several other "unmarketable" science fiction scripts, and sold the whole package as a weekly series to Ziv. *Science Fiction Theatre* was often wildly fanciful, but virtually every episode had its basis on a reasonably plausible scientific theory. Example: the theory of "freezing" the dead in hopes of bringing them back to life in the future resulted in a story about a scientist (Virginia Bruce) who revived an ancient mastodon found frozen in an iceberg, then suffered the anguish of a "biological mother" when the beast withered and died. Other episodes theorized on retarding the aging process, accelerating the growth of intelligence, time-displacement, telekinesis, and the possibility of extraterrestrial visitation; one story starred MacDonald Carey as the subject of an LSD experiment. Each script represented the diligent research of *Science Fiction Theatre's* three-person staff, all dedicated to thinking "five moves ahead," as Ivan Tors put it.

Radio announcer and erstwhile actor Truman Bradley became famous a *Science Fiction Theatre's* host, lending credibility to his introductions handling an array of robots, computers (a favorite Ivan Tors prop) and of

Paragon Playhouse see *Douglas Fairbanks Jr. Presents*

Parole (1959). Produced by Fred Becker and released by Telestar, *Parole* was an "actuality" courtroom syndie featuring films of real parole hearings various prisons; the series was available in 15- or 30-minute installments.

The Passerby (1953). An oddity of early television, the 15-minute playlet popped up now and then on film. *The Passerby*, a group of quarter hour terror tales, was one of the earliest projects of Ely Landau, who later guided the destinies of the "NTA Film Network."

The People's Court of Small Claims (1958). Another "actuality" show, this ABC Films release was about the same in content as the similar titled hit syndie of the 1980's. But Orrin B. Evans, who presided over the small claims arguments in the 1958 *People's Court,* wasn't quite the compleat entertainer that Judge Joseph Wapner later turned out to be.

Play of the Week (1959–60). *Play of the Week* was a felicitous collaboration between the NTA Film Network's head man Ely Landau and television "spectacular" producer David Susskind. Landau had dreams of making his Manhattan TV station WNTA a fountain of cultural events; Susskind longed to produce the sort of plays rejected by the networks as "uncommercial." Caught up in the project was Standard Oil of New Jersey, who underwrote the series with the promise not to dictate story content. (This hands-off proviso was, believe it or not, the *sponsor's* idea.) Fifty-two two-hour *Play of the Weeks* were videotaped at WNTA at a cost of $40,000 each, roughly a third the weekly cost of a 60-minute filmed show. The actors, even the Big Names, worked for a flat $650 per program. (Helen Hayes insisted that she be paid no more than $500.) Directors, adapters and staff likewise cut their salaries to the bone; Susskind worked for literally nothing.
   The series premiered over WNTA on October 12, 1959, with *Medea,* starring Judith Anderson. The next production, Graham Greene's *Power and the Glory,* featured Telly Savalas and Peter Falk in minor roles. Falk would work on the series again, as would another newcomer, Robert Redford. Major talents seen on *Play of the Week* included Lillian Gish, Burgess Meredith, Walter Matthau, Larry Blyden, Nancy Walker, Uta Hagen, Luther Adler, Tammy Grimes, Arthur Drake and Margalo Gillmore; also given work by Susskind were several performers who'd been blacklisted by the major networks, among them Zero Mostel and Lee Grant. *Play of the Week's* repertoire included esoterica like Beckett's *Waiting for Godot* and heavy fare like Turgenev's *A Month in the Country* ("too downbeat," one can hear the networks saying); counterbalancing these plays were such harmless pieces of froth as *The Girls in 509* and *Thieves' Carnival.* The jewel in *Play's* crown was a two-part, four-hour presentation of O'Neill's *The Iceman Cometh,* directed by Sidney Lumet and starring Jason Robards Jr. One of the few great plays *not* seen was *Death of a Salesman;* playwright Arthur Miller rejected Susskind's $50,000 offer for the rights because Miller was holding out for a network deal.

then-futuristic paraphernalia. Casts were drawn from the ranks of Basil Rathbone, Pat O'Brien, Gene Lockhart, Marshall Thompson and Hugh Beaumont; the series' best-known director was Jack Arnold, the helmsman of such '50s sf film classics as *The Incredible Shrinking Man.* Presold in 58 markets for its spring 1955 debut, *Science Fiction Theatre* tripled that number within a year. Its 78 episodes — 39 in color — remained a breadwinner for Ziv's successor United Artists television well into the late 1960's.

The Silent Service (1957–58). NBC Films' 1957 contribution to the military-anthology sweepstakes was *Silent Service,* a 78-episode bouquet to the submarine brigade of World War II created and hosted by Rear Admiral (Ret.) Thomas M. Dykers. Obtaining full U.S. Navy cooperation by showing submarine life in the best possible light (there was none of that *Das Boot* fatalism here), Dykers was able to film his series "on location," as it were, in the cramped confines of a genuine sub, the USS *Sawfish.* For conning tower scenes, *Silent Service's* camera crew had only a 6-foot-diameter working space, so a wide-angle-lensed camera had to be lowered by rope, tripod and all, into the hatch. The authenticity extended to using real sailors to fill the bit and extra roles (leads were handled by Hollywood professionals), and to basing the scripts on true stories of wartime heroics. After each week's half-hour, Adm. Dykers would interview the actual person whose experiences had just been dramatized. Without taking anything away from these gallant men, the fact was that most of them hadn't spoken in public since their First Grade Thanksgiving pageant. These well-intentioned interviews never failed to slow the episode's pace to a walk — a dangerous thing, especially since the direction on *Silent Service,* to quote *Variety,* had "all the animation of a still life." Even so, the painstaking authenticity of the series (an attractive angle to viewers who were war veterans themselves) helped keep *Silent Service* in syndication's "Top Ten" until filming ceased in 1958. One year later, news headlines about Adm. Hyman Rickover's nuclear submarine program turned *Silent Service* into a hot property all over again. NBC Films' publicity people added a soupçon of sex appeal to the all-male anthology by sending out a "Miss Silent Service" to promote the series, usually by posing in a bathing suit and illustrating the "Silent" part of the title by holding her fingers in her ears. Miss Silent Service of 1958 was Barbara Eden.

The Star and the Story see *Henry Fonda Presents the Star and the Story*

Studio 57 (1955). Sponsored by Heinz' 57 Varieties, *Studio 57* had been one of the last filmed anthologies on the disintegrating DuMont Network when, in 1955, MCA/Revue filmed a batch of new episodes for syndication. *Studio 57* did better locally than it had on its threadbare network, even though it wasn't much more than a mild compendium of reasonably well-cast melodramas.

Target (1958). Ziv's second Adolphe Menjou-hosted anthology (see *My Favorite Story*), *Target* kept its prerelease promise to offer nail-biting tales in which ordinary people found themselves "targeted" by Danger, human or otherwise. The series' sales were brisk before and after its March 1958 release, but *Target* fell victim to Rumor. An unconfirmed report came out that Ziv would film only 38 episodes of the series, whether it was successful or not. By the time Ziv was able to issue a statement, *Target* had been dropped by one of its largest East Coast sponsors in favor of new syndies like *Glencannon* and *New York Confidential*. Thanks to hearsay, Ziv couldn't have gotten sponsor support for a second season of *Target* even if it had tried.

This Is Charles Laughton (1953). There'd been plans afoot since the dawn of filmed television to produce dramatic readings from the classics by top-flight performers. Mr. and Mrs. James Mason and Richard Burton had some success along these lines, but the best of these efforts was in the form of producer Paul Gregory's *This Is Charles Laughton*. Laughton's props for this 15-minute weekly were a book and a lectern; his "supporting cast" was himself. The ever-insecure star, known for his lapses into excess, welcomed the 15-minute confinement as a way of keeping himself under control and maintaining subtlety — subtlety by Charles Laughton standards, of course, but effective nonetheless. Most critics welcomed *This Is Charles Laughton,* the one carp coming from the *Los Angeles Daily News:* "Aside to Charles: It would be nice if you would have your suit pressed before appearing in front of the TV cameras."

The Tracer (1956). This was the one-and-only success from the short-lived firm of Minot Films. Onetime Eagle-Lion Studios executive Charles M. Amory had originally formed Minot as a New Orleans-based producer of industrial films; Minot became part of U.M. & M. Television in 1954, a company that was at first the sales-rep arm of Motion Pictures for Television but which eventually became the TV distributor of Paramount Pictures' short subjects (including the ever-popular *Betty Boop* cartoons). After UM&M was absorbed by NTA, Charles Amory was so tantalized by the El Dorado-like possibilities of TV syndication that he re-formed Minot Films, hoping to turn New Orleans into the Hollywood of the South. But by 1958, with only *The Tracer* and the humdrum cop series *N.O.P.D.* in his manifest, Amory became discouraged by the headaches of production overhead and folded his Minot Films tent for good. Ironically, *The Tracer* was starting to flourish even as Amory called it quits. The series was the brainchild of Dan Eisenburg, who'd founded the Tracers Company in 1924 as a means of locating heirs to unclaimed legacies. At the end of each *Tracer* episode, a list of these missing heirs was rattled off, and viewers hearing their own names or the names of friends were encouraged (as if encouragement was needed) to contact Dan Eisenburg immediately. The 39 *Tracer* dramas themselves, starring Jim Chandler as the head tracer, were well below the standards set by Hollywood-made syndies, but the series got by with its weekly promise of lost riches found. *The Tracer* ended up helping nearly two thousand people claim close to $1,700,000 in inheritances; the luckiest single claimant ($20,000 worth) was a patient at a St. Louis mental hospital!

The Unexpected (1952). Hosted by Herbert Marshall and written by the workhorse team of Jerome Lawrence and Robert E. Lee, Ziv's *The Unexpected* offered tales in which Fate Itself determined the outcome. An overworked Fate was still doing its trick some 15 years later when *The Unexpected* became the number one television hit in Thailand.

The Veil (1958). Adequate psychic-phenomena anthology from Official Films; Boris Karloff hosted.

The Whistler (1954). Like *Inner Sanctum, The Whistler* was a suspense anthology with an unseen host that had been on radio (since 1943) and in "B" movies (1944–46) before becoming a filmed syndie series. Lindsley Parsons/CBS Films' television *Whistler* offered 39 neat little hoist-on-one's-own-petard morality plays. As in the *Whistler* movies, the offscreen narrator was depicted as a shadow on the wall, and as in the radio version, the Whistler was played by two people: Bill Forman did the talking, while Dorothy Roberts whistled Wilbur Hatch's eerie 13-note theme song. The TV series sold quite well, lining up not only its old radio sponsor (Signal Oil) but the sponsor of the radio version of *Inner Sanctum* (Lipton Tea)—before a single *Whistler* episode had been filmed. But like *Inner Sanctum,* the attractively produced TV *Whistler* lacked the appeal to the Mind's Eye that had been so essential an ingredient of the radio series—and of all Radio, for that matter.

Game/Quiz

This sort of programming was as a rule in the hands of the big networks and major sponsors in the '50s. In fact, it was *very* much in these hands until network and sponsor excesses led to the infamous "cheating scandals" of 1958. Audience participation, giveaways, even good old Bingo could be found on local stations back when they could afford local live programming. Filmed syndie fun-and-games, crowded out by its "live" competition, was but a minor marketplace commodity.

Capsule Mysteries (etc.) (1950–59). Many syndie guessing-games were five-minute fillers, designed to plug up odd scheduling holes or to encourage call-ins and postcards from the viewers (just to let station managers know that there *were* viewers). Typical were Charles Michelson's *Capsule Mysteries,* Walter Schwimmer's *Movie Quick Quiz* and PSI TV's *Viz-Quiz,* all "open-ended" brain-teasers which allowed home contestants to come up with the solutions. One item that was all over the place was the 5-minute "horserace" contest, usually run as filler during local sports programs. These were either animated-cartoon events, with clues to the races' outcomes given via cartoon sight gags, or were filmclips from actual (but unidentified) races. Once again, prizes awaited the lucky viewers who picked the winners. The most durable program of this kind, Walter Schwimmer's *Let's Go to the Races,* survived into the late '70s, when for a brief time it was offered as a half-hour weekly.

Home Run Derby (1959–61). Hosted during three consecutive baseball seasons by Mark Scott, Ziv's *Home Run Derby* featured guest big-league ballplayers who'd square off weekly to see who could hit furthest and mostest. The series never failed to rack up big sales, but the transitory nature of sports fame (the big leaguer of today is the swimming-pool salesman of tomorrow) made *Home Run Derby* virtually unsaleable in reruns.

Juke Box Jury (1958). Los Angeles deejay Peter Potter's *Juke Box Jury,* wherein a celebrity panel determined the hit potential of new songs ("Will it be a hit? [Clang!] Or a miss? [Thud!]") had run locally in Los Angeles for years, enjoying a short network life in 1953. Through the miracle of videotape, NTA was able to peddle a 60-minute, weekly *Juke Box Jury* nationally in 1958. Host Potter's appeal lay in his just-folks approach to decisions made by himself and his panel; he cheerfully admitted that he'd been wrong when he predicted that such tunes as Ross Bagdasarian's "Witch Doctor" and Fats Domino's "My Blue Heaven" would go nowhere. The syndicated *Jury* ran until 1959, when Potter moved from one L.A. TV station to another and his series was put on "temporary syndication hiatus." Temporary for over thirty years now.

Let's Go to the Races see *Capsule Mysteries*

Movie Quick Quiz see *Capsule Mysteries*

Pantomime Quiz (1950). First seen over KTTV–Los Angeles in 1948, Mike Stokey's celebrity version of the old parlor game "Charades" (later network TV's favorite summer replacement) made it to the CBS network in 1949, its East Coast viewers seeing the show via kinescope. A better-quality filmed version of *Pantomime Quiz* was briefly syndicated to non–CBS markets by Consolidated Films.

Viz Quiz see *Capsule Mysteries*

Informational

Syndicated news and current-events shows had to be filmed in the '50s and thus weren't all that current after all (communications satellites were still the stuff of sci-fi pulp novels). Most of the "informational" efforts were Hobby and How-To shows. In those days before the nationwide Educational TV movement, a few commercial stations offered what were known as "classroom" series — though what often passed for "educational" were merely re-cycled filmclips from newsreels and theatrical documentaries.

Dave Elman's Curiosity Shop (1952). There wasn't a local '50s TV station that existed without at least one "hobby" show. Among the few that got into syndication was one starring "the dean of American Hobbyists" — Dave Elman, whose *Hobby Lobby* radio series had started in 1938. Amidst trotting on fellow amateur artisans and their odd basement-built creations, Elman amazed his fans with his *Britannica*-like knowledge on the subject of what Mankind did with its spare time.

Ding Dong School (1959). Named in honor of the ringing school bell that opened each broadcast, *Ding Dong School* was an NBC daily from 1952 until 1956, when the network squeezed it out in favor of an expanding "adult" morning schedule. ITC revived the property for 1959 syndication, its 130 videotaped half-hours still making sales into 1961. *School's* hostess was the kindly, matronly, slightly patronizing "Miss Frances" Horwich. Although she was considered by many grown-ups to be the "ideal" kid's-show host, the now middle-aged fans of *Ding Dong School* will generally opine that Miss Frances got harder to take the older one became.

Handyman (1955). Home-improvement series hosted by radio commentator Norman Brokenshire. The host had the advantage of being plump, middle-aged and slightly dishevelled — not unlike most of his fans.

Junior Crossroads see *Junior Science*

Junior Science (1954). Kid-oriented filmed series like *Junior Crossroads* and *Movietone Children's Newsreel* were never quite able to shake the condescending nature of their titles. MPTV's full-color *Junior Science* was despite its tune-out of a title a real winner, demonstrating the delights of creation and discovery in and out of the classroom lab. Dr. George Wendt was host.

Kieran's Kaleidoscope (1952). This one began live on NBC in 1948, but is best remembered in its ABC Films syndicated version. The 104 15-minute *Kaleidoscopes* were narrated by John F. Kieran, the resident genius of radio's *Information Please*. Kieran's carefully selected filmclips were enhanced by his astounding expertise on virtually *any* given subject. But while he might have been "Mr. Know-All," Kieran had the rare ability to talk to children without talking down to them.

Learn to Draw (approximately 1952–59). What aspiring young artist of the '50s can forget *Learn to Draw,* with its organ-rendered theme music ("The Artist's Waltz"), host Jon Gnagy's goatee and checkered shirt, and his limitless supply of charcoal and paper? So entranced were viewers by Gnagy's theory that one could learn to draw by utilizing "the circle, the square and the cone," that no one really cared that *Learn to Draw* was little more than a 15-minute commercial for Gnagy's huge art supplies store in Paramus, New Jersey.

The Magic Eye (1959). Science series shown principally on the five CBS-owned outlets.

Movietone Children's Newsreel see Junior Science

Shakespeare on TV (1954). Like Alistair Cooke, Deems Taylor and the aforementioned John Kieran, University of Southern California English professor Frank Baxter was a "pop intellectual," the sort who could make complex theories and facts simple to the average Joe by using words of one syllable. Dr. Baxter was a genial ham who appeared in a variety of educationally oriented series both on and off the networks; one of the best was *Shakespeare on TV,* an enjoyable group of 15-minute lectures that helped make Shakespeare seem as up-to-date to '50s audiences as Paddy Chayefsky or Rod Serling. In 1964, Dr. Baxter commemorated the Bard of Avon's 400th birthday with another Shakespearean syndie, NTA's *The Fair Adventure.*

Music/Variety

Filmed musical/variety series had a tough time competing with their live-television counterparts. Adding to the cost of committing star-studded, full-orchestra shows to film was a new bogeyman called "residuals." James C. Petrillo, bantam president of the American Federation of Musicians, so hamstringed TV filmmakers with rules concerning pay-scales for musicians' reruns and recordings that many producers went outside the United States to get their music union-free. (Petrillo also managed to get residuals for musicians who'd scored some of the theatrical movies then being shown on television. Even the movie stars themselves couldn't get a deal like that!) Thus it was that most TV musical shows were presented live; Petrillo couldn't demand residual payments on a program that was aired once and *only* once. Filmmakers weren't so lucky, and were forced to offer their musicales with smaller casts and smaller budgets to compensate for residuals. As a result, their efforts looked pretty threadbare in comparison to the poshness of the network product. Musical syndies had to rely on personalities rather than production values; one of those personalities, a chap who called himself Liberace, became the first musical superstar of the 1950's.

The Ames Brothers (and other 15-minute favorites) (1955–58). MCA's *The Ames Brothers* did quite well, and might have run indefinitely had not the group jealously broken up once its baritone, Ed Ames, started getting more fan mail than his siblings. *Ames Brothers* was one of several economically produced 15-minute series spotlighting a popular musical star or singing group. These fillers were quite handy when local stations wanted to bridge schedule gaps between their own efforts and the evening network lineups. Some of these quarter-hour epics featured such now-forgotten luminaries as Jill Corey and Charlie Applewhite. Others had no set star but offered a variety of talent, like MCA's *Playhouse 15*. The best of the batch might well have been Screen Gems' *The Patti Page Show* (1955–56). This "pocket musical" maintained a topicality rare on filmed TV; ten minutes of each *Patti Page Show* would be filmed weeks ahead of distribution, but the final five minutes would be held open to allow Patti to sing the broadcast week's latest hit tune.

Country-Western Shows (1950–59). The proliferation of Country-Western syndies in the '50s can be traced to a spot of trouble brewing since the 1940's. The all-powerful ASCAP music agency, which represented the biggest musical performers and songwriters, was in position not only to charge exorbitant rates for broadcasts but to dictate *how* the music would be performed. Exasperated, radio and television producers created their own agency, Broadcast Music International. BMI represented low-cost performers of ethnic music, South American tunes and other specialized audience entertainment — including Country/Western. The "down home" boom had its best showing on *Grand Ole Opry,* which began its Saturday-night radio run on WSM–Nashville in 1925 and is still to this day booming out its weekly 50,000 watts' worth. Television's *Grand Ole Opry* has been seen sporadically on network, in syndication, and latterly over its own cable service. The most notable batch of *Opry* half-hours were shot in color by Flamingo Films in 1954; these have survived in excerpt form ever since, most recently in the 1983 Time-Life syndie retrospective *Classic Country.* Some of the *Opry* stars of the '50s branched out to do their own syndicated series, notably such talent as Foy Willing and Webb Pierce, but their efforts were usually "regionals," produced for limited audiences and seldom making the coast-to-coast route. Other C-and-W offerings broadened their appeal with slick production values and a few songs outside the Country-Western range. *The Eddy Arnold Show* (Schwimmer, 1954), Tex Ritter's *Ranch Party* (Screen Gems, 1958) and *Country Style USA* (a 1958 vehicle for Milton Berle discovery Charlie Applewhite) were among the handful of syndie hoedowns that made it to the larger TV markets.

Country Style USA see *Country-Western Shows*

The Eddy Arnold Show see *Country-Western Shows*

The Florian ZaBach Show (1954). After striking gold with its *Liberace Show,* Guild Films cast about for another pop-music phenomenon that would match the success of the elegant Mr. L. One of Guild's stars was mile-a-minute violin virtuoso Florian ZaBach, whose fan following was within shouting distance of Liberace's. Giving the 39-week *Florian ZaBach Show* a little bit of visual dynamics was a $7000-per-show special effect: a miniaturized "dancing pixie" (Mary Ellen Terry), who flitted across the screen while the nimble-fingered ZaBach sawed away.

Foy Willing see *Country-Western Shows*

Frankie Fontaine (1955). Years before obtaining TV immortality as loveable cretin Crazy Guggenheim on *The Jackie Gleason Show,* comic Frank Fontaine hosted a New York-filmed variety series syndicated by Associated Artists Productions.

The Frankie Laine Show (1955). More from Guild Films. Frankie Laine and co-star Connie Haines strutted their stuff for 39 weeks.

Get Set, Go (1958). New York-based series with Chuck Richardson and Sue Ann Langdon, which got set and went in less than a year.

The Grand Ole Opry see *Country-Western Shows*

The Guy Lombardo Show (1954). An MCA syndie which scotched the popular belief that bandleader Lombardo and his "Royal Canadians" showed up only on New Year's Eve.

Jill Corey see *The Ames Brothers*

Les Paul and Mary Ford (1951–54). The five-minute musical filler had been part of television since the beginning, including Screen Gems' early series of recording artists lip-synching to their hits. No one succeeded within the 300-second limit as well as "electronic music" pioneer Les Paul and his wife Mary Ford, whose five-a-week minimusicales could be seen virtually everywhere at any time.

The Liberace Show (1953–55). Strictly a Los Angeles local celebrity in the '40s (but a wealthy one), pianist Wladziu Valentino Liberace built up a large, loquacious if not gushing following. Responding to this, NBC-TV gave Liberace his own 15-minute live series in 1952; it didn't last, but was enough to convince the star that his future lay in TV—and that his financial future would be better served with the profits attending a *filmed* series. In early 1953, Liberace entered into $1,500,000 worth of contractual agreements with Guild Films. Participants in this venture included Guild producer Don *(Life with Elizabeth)* Federson and the producer-director team of Robert Snader and Duke Goldstone, late of UTP's *Dick Tracy* series. The ensuing half-hours were filmed on a miserly weekly budget of $13,000, with Liberace's "cast" consisting of his violinist brother George and a small band of sidemen. Following Guild's promotional device of giving away free Liberace records in the nation's department stores, *The Liberace Show* made its official syndie bow on February 18, 1954, over Denver's KBTV. The series began with only 23 markets; it would peak two years later at 217. *The Liberace Show* was literally the biggest syndicated hit of the decade. The star enhanced his new-found national celebrity with a series of S.R.O. personal appearances (as well as a best-forgotten feature film, *Sincerely Yours*); before a heart problem forced him to curtail his activities, Liberace had filmed 117 half-hours. By 1958, New Yorkers could watch the series six times per week in its tenth rerun!

What can account for this? *Liberace's* program content was nothing you couldn't hear over the radio. The extent of its "production values" was typified when Liberace wore a Lone Ranger mask while playing "The William Tell Overture." And most male viewers were left unmoved by Liberace's flamboyance. (During this time, the "Liberace joke" became a generic term referring to a cheap laugh gotten by poking fun at any male star's eccentricities.) But Liberace's millions of fans couldn't *all* be wrong. Asked to explain the phenomenon, Guild executive Will Lane, ever the company man, suggested it was due to the promotional expertise of Guild president Reuven Kaufman. Director Duke Goldstone chalked it down to Liberace's essential humility. The star's personal manager noted Liberace's intimate style, holding to the theory of "basic magnetism." And Liberace himself believed in the old Right Place–Right Time saw: "I discovered at the time that TV viewers were composed essentially of family units. I appealed to them and became part of their simple way of life." Whatever the case, Liberace's series was not only the cornerstone of a spectacular career, but was also the one series that made the syndie-musical format commercially realistic.

Mantovani (1959). One of the few syndie-variety outings which maintained an illusion of network quality was *Mantovani,* 39 easy-listening half-hours hosted by John Conte, taped by Towers of London in England and syndicated in the U.S. by NTA. Aimed at the Lawrence Welk crowd, Mantovani's dentist-office tunes could be heard wafting through the ether until the first syndicated "disco craze" of the early '60s.

The Patti Page Show see **The Ames Brothers Show**

Playhouse 15 see **The Ames Brothers Show**

Ranch Party see **Country-Western Shows**

The Ray Anthony Show (1956; 1969). Dipping once more into its talent-agency pool, MCA came up with a one-season syndie for orchestra leader Ray Anthony. Anthony was back with a taped package for Official Films in 1969.

The Rosemary Clooney Show (1955). All 39 *Rosemary Clooney Shows* opened with the star belting out her early–50's hit "Come On'a My House." Clooney's was the best of MCA's musical syndies of the era, featuring strong vocal backup from a group called the Hi-Lo's (later the singers on the Hertz man-in-the-driver's-seat ads of the 1960's) and offbeat guest stars like Buster Keaton, Boris Karloff and Vincent Price.

Showtime see **Frankie Fontaine**

The Webb Pierce Show see **Country-Western Shows**

Religious

This designation did not in the 1950's refer so much to "televangelists" (a word that didn't exist then) as it did to the many filmed dramatic anthologies underwritten by various religious denominations. Television religion also manifested itself in a handful of children's shows—which unlike many later kid-oriented religious syndies were more fun than dogma.

The Bible Puppets (late 1950's). Just what the title implied: Biblical tales enacted by puppets. A similar children's series, *Through the Porthole,* used a continuing cast of puppet characters to illustrate how religion could be applied to the hassles of modern life. Both these series were 15-minute weeklies.

Bishop Fulton J. Sheen (1958–61). Bishop Sheen was one of the few "personality preachers" who managed to bridge the gap between religion and entertainment. It's now part of television folklore that the Bishop's DuMont network series *Life Is Worth Living* (1952–55), a lively group of sermons delivered before a studio audience, was the only program to successfully hold its own opposite Milton Berle's Tuesday night extravaganza on NBC. After an ABC network run in 1957, NTA Films put together a package of kinescopes of the Bishop's programs and syndicated same as *The Best of Bishop Sheen.* In 1958, NTA taped 13 brand-new half-hour sermons, a policy the company would follow for the next four seasons. Once more, the showbiz-savvy Bishop Sheen got prime time bookings and respectable ratings. The Bishop had a happy knack of making points without clubbing the viewers with piety, and when compared to some of today's humorless shouters and thumpers, Bishop Sheen's happy knack was a knack and a half.

The Christopher Program (1952–69); **Christopher Closeup** (1969–　). Originally titled *What Can One Person Do?,* the 15-minute *Christopher Program* was the brainchild of Fr. James Keller, founder of the Christophers. In his prime, Fr. Keller was one dynamite public relations man; in some markets, his Sunday morning program ran on as many as three different channels. He also was adept at persuading such talent as Rosalind Russell, Pat O'Brien, Ann Blyth and Ed Herlihy into participating in *The Christopher Program's* playlets, dramatic readings and interviews, all of which put forth the philosophy that "It is better to light one candle than to curse the darkness." The series went full-color and expanded to half an hour in the late '60s, and by decade's end was titled *Christopher Closeup.*

Faith for Today (1950–　). Produced by the Seventh Day Adventist Church and originally an ABC network show, *Faith for Today* was for many years a quasi-interview series, with host the Rev. William A. Sagal discussing life's problems with actors posing as victims of those problems.

Family Theatre (1951–58). *Family Theatre* had been a weekly radio anthology for the Mutual network; it was created by Father Patrick Peyton, who advocated nothing more radical than daily family prayer. ("The family that prays together, stays together; and a world of prayer will be a world of peace.") The radio version presented a rich variety of dramas ranging from cozy domestic plays to spy melodramas and even science-fiction yarns. The television *Family Theatre,* produced in color by Jerry Fairbanks, was more traditional, its half-hours devoted to periodic holiday specials, but was entertaining enough to break into prime time once in a while. The one *Family Theatre* that got the most air-time was an Easter program from the early '50s featuring an earnest performance from a young James Dean.

The Hour of St. Francis (1951–63). Filmed its first few seasons by William F. Broidy Productions, *The Hour of St. Francis* (actually a *half*-hour) was an intriguing anthology put together by four stagestruck Franciscans: Father Terence Cronin, Edward Henriques, Carl Holtschneider and Hugh Noonan. The four priests not only wrote and directed the plays but even occasionally ran the sound and camera equipment, much to the dismay of grizzled union technicians who didn't know the proper way to tell a Franciscan Father to mind his own business. Leaning towards domestic dramas, *St. Francis* branched out once in a while with an allegory: one well-distributed 1962 playlet starred Henry Daniell as a bureaucratic Satan.

Off to Adventure (1958–60). More travelogue than tract, *Off to Adventure* was a color 15-minute children's show which transported its audience to various religious capitals of the world.

Oral Roberts (1955–67; 1969–   ). Because of certain FCC restrictions which we'll discuss in later chapters, most of the '50s "electronic evangelists" were strictly local acts. Oral Roberts was one of the few whose weekly sermons achieved national distribution. Not that Roberts, whose programs during this decade were heavily into spectacular (and to the critical eye, not altogether convincing) acts of faith-healing, was universally accepted. In fact, when Roberts was starting out, the only broadcasters who'd run his series were those super-powered radio stations located south of the Mexican border who'd run anything for a price. At that, Roberts was luckier than his contemporary "healer," A.A. Allen, a man whose arm-waving style was to influence the "supersaver" television-religious movement for years. Allen's program was even more outrageous than Roberts', and the very few television channels that picked it up usually dropped it in a hurry amidst an avalanche of viewer complaints. At any rate, Allen's personal life (which included several violent alcoholic episodes) and his mysterious hotel-room death in 1970 have rather obscured his TV work, giving many historians the mistaken impression that Oral Roberts alone fostered the faith-healing "genre" that persists to this day.

Oral Roberts' first syndie was shot in a revival tent before an enthusiastic congregation, and survived in this manner for twelve seasons. By 1967, the laying-on-of-hands school was losing its TV audience, so Roberts left the air, took stock of himself, and in 1969 reappeared with a more conventional sermon-and-song color weekly, *Oral Roberts and You*. Roberts' audience peaked in 1977, after which there was a levelling-off in his ratings and his station lineup. It's worth noting that Roberts' viewership shot up substantially in 1980 and again in 1987 — and that 1980 was the year that Roberts claimed he'd had a vision of a 900-foot high Jesus and 1987 was the year Roberts threatened that he'd "be called back to Heaven" unless he could raise several million dollars in a hurry. In network television, this is called "stunting."

The Pastor (1955). One of two anthologies underwritten by the Methodists; the other was *The Way*. Both bore the influence of *This Is the Life* (which see).

Talk Back (circa 1959). What made *Talk Back* stand out among the rest of the religious anthologies was that its dramas were "open-ended." The stories would build to a climax, then leave things hanging; it was then up to a local host and/or studio audience to determine the outcome. The series was quite flexible; it could be presented as a religious or "mainstream" half-hour depending upon whether or not the local host was a clergyman. When Norman Lear syndicated a similar open-ended series, *The Baxters*, in 1979, enough time had passed for Lear's product to be hailed as innovative.

This Is the Answer (1958–61). The Southern Baptist Convention's entry into the religious-anthology market.

This Is the Life (1953–   ). The Lutheran Church, Missouri Synod, began *This Is the Life* in network prime time, running variously on ABC and DuMont during 1952. On this version there appeared a continuing cast of characters — a family named Fisher — who faced life's triumphs and tragedies with a firm belief in God and Providence. When the series went into syndication, the cast of regulars was dropped (their episodes were rerun as *The Fisher Family*), and *This Is the Life*, filmed by the Roland Reed unit at Hal Roach Studios, became a weekly anthology. Even back in the censor-bound 1950's, *This Is the Life* dealt with stories of moral hypocrisy, race prejudice, urban blight, juvenile delinquency and other aberrations. By the '60s, there were playlets involving sex crimes and drug abuse. Most of the stories were resolved, directly or indirectly, by the deus-ex-machina arrival of a Lutheran minister, who was usually the best looking, most articulate character on the show. The casts, generally comprised of Hollywood's best character people and stars-to-be, were always scrupulously sincere, though it was offsetting to see such clashes in style as having a kidnap victim recite scripture to the villains while being bound and gagged. In the early 1970's, This Is the Life Inc. created two similar anthologies: *Patterns for Living* (one episode of which starred Suzanne Somers as a girl tired of being a sex object) and the Spanish-language *Esta Es la Vida*. The color-videotaped *This Is the Life* of the 1980's remained a thriving property in hundreds of international markets, and added to its industry prestige with two Emmy Awards given in one single year—though admittedly, the "best religious series" category isn't as crowded as it once was.

Through the Porthole see *Bible Puppets*

The Way see *The Pastor*

What's Your Trouble (1952–53). Dr. Norman Vincent Peale, advocate of The Power of Positive Thinking, could always be counted on for a few annual filmed words of advice. His 1952 syndie co-starred Mrs. Peale.

Sports

Like news, sports was almost exclusively a "live" attraction in the '50s. But filmed sports syndies did get made and definitely got seen, especially on small-market stations that otherwise would have had to fill time with shaky remote broadcasts of the local Slow Pitch Softball games.

Baseball (1950–59). Thanks to a confining FCC rule, baseball wasn't the big ratings pull in the '50s that it is today. It seemed that if you lived in a city with a major league team, the network baseball games were blacked out in your area—even if your team wasn't playing! Banking on a marketful of hungry viewers, an enterprising Chicagoan named Peter DeMet assembled 26 hour-long cutdowns of 1959's best ball games, signed "voice of the Cubs" Jack Brickhouse to provide play-by-play, then distributed *Major League Baseball* through Official Films just after World Series week in '59. That same year, producer Max Cooper and director Ed Scherer colloborated on a taped 90-minute weekly titled *Winter Baseball.* These games featured top big-league talent and were recorded in Havana, Cuba, through the facilities of television station CMQ. There might have been a 1960 season of *Winter Baseball* had it not been for the political capriciousness of an ex-ball player by the name of Fidel Castro.

Bowling (1950–59). Since many local channels didn't have the equipment to set up remote telecasts at the local lanes, filmed bowling syndies were strong sales items. Some of the earlier series in this category were none too carefully made, so there was justifiable pride in the ad-claims of Walter Schwimmer's *Championship Bowling,* which promised that the package contained no kinescopes and that each match had been covered by five—count 'em, five—film cameras. Female bowling fans were as well served as the males with ABC Films' *Bowling Queens* (1957), hosted by a Chicago radio personality who called himself (and in 1987 *still* called himself) "Tenpin Tattler."

Bowling Queens see **above**

Championship Bowling see above

Football (1950–59). Pro football was several years removed from its "TV's Number One Sport" status back in the '50s. This could be attributed to several reasons, among them the fact that baseball had been around longer, had more teams and one more major league than football, or the fact that football would have to wait for colorcasts, the minicamera and the "instant replay" of the '60s to match the thrill of watching a live game. Most syndicated gridiron activity was confined to the filmclip-interview format, as presented by such seasonal series as Notre Dame coach Frank Leahy's *Football Forecasts* (1956) and onetime West Point star Glenn Davis' *See the Pros* (1958). In 1960, Peter De Met and Official Films followed up their popular *Major League Baseball* with another package of 26 hour-long abridgments titled *Pro Football Highlights* — and, as with the earlier series, made a mint in markets where pro-ball telecasts were few and far between.

Football Forecasts and Pro Football Highlights see above

Major League Baseball see Baseball

Racing Shows (1950–59). Always welcome on '50s television were auto-racing events (with some viewers, sad to say, tuning in on the off-chance of witnessing some blood and guts). Since live races were inclined to have dull stretches, filmed events, which could be thrillingly photographed from a variety of angles and then edited to the bone, were surefire ratings-grabbers. Stock Car Races Inc. had an ingenious setup wherein the company would offer its filmed races in chunks ranging from 10 minutes to a full hour, depending on the local outlet's needs. It wasn't uncommon for some locals to buy footage from several different sources, then devote an entire weekend afternoon to filmed motor events; viewers could tune in any time of the day and know that whatever they'd be watching, it wouldn't be standing still. In 1959, WFBM–Indianapolis came up with an action-packed, full-color half-hour titled *Speedway International,* which mopped up on the weekend-syndie market until ABC knocked the locals out of the box with 1961's *Wide World of Sports.*

See the Pros see Football

Speedway International see Racing Shows

Telesports Digest (1953–mid '60s). MCA's answer to Ziv's pioneer 15-minute filmclip series *Sports Album* was *Telesports Digest,* which was not a newsreel retrospective like *Sports Album* but an up-to-date rundown of the week's sports events. Harry Wismer produced and narrated.

Winter Baseball see Baseball

Wrestling (1950–59). We aren't about to risk life and limb by suggesting that television wrestling isn't altogether spontaneous. Let's just note that, because televised matches always managed to resolve themselves within the tight time limits of '50s television, and because the "highlights" always seemed to take place conveniently within camera range, wrestling was the ideal "sports event" of TV's first decade. Then as now, it was bold, bigger-than-life entertainment (though not as Hollywoodized as it would become in the '80s), with just as rowdy a fan following as it enjoys today. For those early 50's TV outlets whose schedules couldn't accommodate the network wrestling events, KTLA–Los Angeles began distributing its filmed *Wrestling from Hollywood* in 1950. The financial returns inspired a deluge of filmed grappling matches from such cities as New York, Chicago, Indianapolis, Cincinnati and Dallas (remember *Texas Rasslin'?*). And there was women's wrestling, a favorite of kids who'd come to school with tales of torn brassieres — stories just as authentic as *Bozo's* "Cram it, Clown!" legend.

For the next thirty years, wrestling would fall in and out of favor, though of course it never completely disappeared. By the '60s and '70s, few wrestling programs were nationally syndicated; most were regionally distributed to promote upcoming live events. Note: during the '60s, one brave soul in North Dakota attempted to syndicate matches featuring the sort of "legitimate" wrestling seen in colleges and at the Olympics. The poor guy lost his shirt. Some audiences *want* style without substance.

Talk/Interview

This type of syndie carried over two time-honored radio traditions: "commentary," assessing the facts behind the news, or "fluff," featuring movie stars and such folks whose opinions were neither given nor taken seriously. The Talk/Interview form took a more sober-sided approach after Mike Wallace's ABC network interviews began turning into interrogations (sweaty closeups and all), a precedent followed by most of Wallace's colleagues at the NTA Film Network.

Alex in Wonderland (1959). Sardonic humorist Alexander King made no secret of the demons which plagued his psyche during his frequent visits to Jack Paar's NBC program, nor did King hesitate to somewhat sadistically feed on Paar's own insecurities. While Alex King was very funny in his own perverse way, he was definitely an acquired taste. His NTA syndicated talkfest, *Alex in Wonderland,* was sent out in the fall of 1959; by the end of the year it was being shown on one whole station.

Clete Roberts (1951–53). During the Korean War, Los Angeles newsman Clete Roberts achieved national prominence through a series of on-the-spot interviews with the U.N. forces involved in that "police action," which were distributed in the States by U.S. Television News. This is the same Clete Roberts who, over twenty years later, "interviewed" the cast members of *M*A*S*H* on that series' famous black-and-white "documentary" episode.

Confidential File (1955). KTTV–Los Angeles commentator Paul Coates had been doing his interview/documentary series *Confidential File* locally for several seasons before Guild Films produced a 39-week syndie version of the show. This version, produced by Coates and Jim Peck and sometimes directed by Irvin *(The Empire Strikes Back)* Kershner, dealt with sensational subjects like drug addiction, shoddy medical practices, mental retardation and political corruption. Anticipating such later "actuality" shows as *60 Minutes,* it was common for several of Coates' interviewees to wear masks to hide their identities. Unlike *60 Minutes, Confidential File* had no qualms about re-staging crucial incidents to bring their stories into sharper focus; and like every interview show before or since, there were lurid stories thrown in just to keep the viewers alert, such as tales about the perils facing aspiring starlets or the alleged connection between comic books/teen movies/rock-'n'-roll and juvenile delinquency. Paul Coates' sincerity was never in doubt, though he could be a bit priggish, especially when not in full possession of the facts. Coates returned to syndication in 1960 with a five-a-week taped interview from KTTV.

Double Play with Durocher and Day (1952). A frothy brew of show-talk, sports-gab and audience-participation contests, UTP's *Double Play* was hosted by baseball manager Leo Durocher and his then-wife, glamorous actress Laraine Day.

George Jessel's Show Business (1959). Venerable vaudevillian Jessel's Los Angeles-based hour was syndicated on videotape by NTA. Famous guests appeared for nothing or next to nothing, allegedly for the privilege of saying anything they felt like saying without fear of censorship, but more likely because they owed favors to dear old Georgie. The lukewarm response to this syndie would seem to bear out the adage of the network executive who said that "thirteen weeks of Jessel would be misery unto Eternity."

Henry Morgan and Company (1959). Sharp-witted satirist Henry Morgan, who'd managed to lose nearly every network job he'd ever had because of his wicked habit of ridiculing his sponsors, proved a surprisingly friendly host on his NTA interview show. But the comedy sketches on *Henry Morgan and Company* indicated that the star found the whole talkshow format to be fundamentally ridiculous. Sadly, that sort of David Letterman stuff did not go over too well in 1959, and Henry Morgan lasted only 16 weeks.

The Mike Wallace Interview (1959–61). Mike Wallace's reputation had been built up through his local New York and ABC network interview series with the famous and notorious; Wallace's go-for-the-jugular style, amplified with tight, uncomfortable closeups of his guests as they were bombarded with prickly devil's-advocate questions, was pretty radical when his NTA syndie went national in 1959. But the law of diminishing returns eventually worked against Wallace. When you've seen one fat politician squirm as his lies are thrown back at him, you've seen them all, and after a season or so, *The Mike Wallace Interview* became dangerously predictable.

Operation Success (1954). This weekly featured journalist Quentin Reynolds interviewing the rich and/or famous, who'd impart their theories on attaining the Golden Ring. Most of the guests advocated hard work and persistence. This much we could have gotten from Mom and Dad.

Washington Merry-Go-Round (1954–57). Since most regular newsmen weren't allowed to voice personal opinions, viewers who wanted something more than mere headlines turned to the commentators, many of whom sidestepped network restrictions by appearing locally or in syndication. MPTV's *Washington Merry-Go-Round* was an interview/commentary hosted by the highly opinionated Drew Pearson.

Washington Spotlight (1953). UTP's contribution to the interview/opinion genre was hosted by Marquis Childs.

Zero 1960 (1958–60). A faintly mystical, fairly bizarre series of talks, predicated on the theory expounded by some religious leaders and psychics that the world would end in the year 1960. For some strange reason, *Zero 1960* was cancelled in 1961.

Travel/Documentary

Travelogues and documentaries weren't precisely twin genres, but shared enough characteristics to be bracketed together in the minds of many television industryites. Both forms featured carefully chosen filmclips on single themes or subjects, bound together with narration and appealing to the 1950's stay-at-homes who desired a broader view of the world around them. Documentaries were first on the scene with Ziv's *Yesterday's Newsreel* (1948); travelogues followed suit when famed globetrotter Burton Holmes assembled a package of snippets from his best theatrical shorts for TV consumption in 1949.

The Air Force Story (early 1950's). Thanks to such popular efforts as *Victory at Sea* and *Crusade in Europe,* war documentaries were plentiful in the '50s. *The Air Force Story,* a batch of 15-minute fillers of obvious origin, was a staple of early-morning and weekend-afternoon schedules. The Air Force added to its manifest late in the decade with a syndie study of jet propulsion titled *Contrails.*

Americans at Work and ***Industry on Parade*** (circa 1951–58). While many of the quarter-hour fillers underwritten by this or that business concern were mostly self-promotional flackery, some were superbly put together and managed to entertain as well as advertise. *Americans at Work,* distributed (as if there was any doubt) by the AFL-CIO, was a fine paean to organized labor. NBC Films and the National Association of Manufacturers came up with the equally splendid *Industry on Parade,* which was honored with occasional network play and a 1954 Peabody Award. Certainly *Industry* had one of the most stirring openings of any series: a close shot of a screeching noon whistle, with the words "INDUSTRY ON PARADE" emblazoned on the screen in big block letters. No wonder many stations ran this series first thing in the morning!

The Big Picture (1951–70). The U.S. Army's self-congratulatory *Big Picture* was first seen on WTOP–Washington D.C., then syndicated by the Department of Defense. Mixed in with the usual Signal Corps war footage were a number of well-produced modern and "home-front" military stories, and at least one program on Communist excesses in Korea which incurred the wrath of several local censors. Narrating the series for many years was Capt. Carl Zimmerman, who went on to a three-decade career as a highly respected Milwaukee newscaster. *The Big Picture,* the sort of series that not only received awards but presented them to stations who'd had the "good citizenship" to run the show, was shooting some 13 to 20 yearly half-hours well into the color television era; during the '50s, it was an off-and-on visitor to the ABC network as well.

Alas, this often worthwhile documentary has in recent years achieved a negative fame thanks to several *Big Pictures* containing tragically ludicrous misinformation concerning the effects of nuclear radiation on human beings. Whether these episodes were misleading by accident or design is secondary to the fact that the episodes are currently used by anti-nuclear organizations as prime examples of the "Big Lie Theory." Thus it is that *Big Picture* has become the anti-nuke version of *Reefer Madness.*

Bold Journey (1959). This documentary of world adventure ran on ABC from 1956 to 1959, then was expanded with a group of new half-hours for syndication. In its syndie installments, *Bold Journey* was narrated by its creator, Jack Douglas, whose documentary career began in association with Col. John D. Craig (see *Danger Is My Business*). Douglas would soon become one of the most prolific syndie-documentary producers, explaining the volume of his work by observing that the more series he had in distribution, the less chance of suffering if one or two of them were cancelled. The producer also explained that he preferred syndication to network because, while network producers lived or died if their series were cancelled on a 200-plus station hookup, "with my products in syndication, I can lose a dozen stations and it really doesn't matter much; the show goes on each week in all the other markets and I can go on sleeping well at night." While *Bold Journey* was a relatively unrehearsed "reality" show, Jack Douglas would later advance the theory that some documentaries were better served with a little bit of re-staging for dramatic effect. The producer would call such series "Docu-Matics" (see *Seven League Boots*).

Contrails see *The Air Force Story*

Crusade in the Pacific (1951). Dwight D. Eisenhower's best-selling book *Crusade in Europe* had been the basis for a compelling 26-part series put together by The March of Time Inc. and network-run on ABC in 1949. So well did this series perform in reruns that March of Time's Richard De Rochemont spliced together another 26 half-hours exclusively for syndication, titled *Crusade in the Pacific*. Narrated by March of Time's "voice of doom" Westbrook Van Voorhees, *Pacific* was a superlative work that pre-dated NBC's more celebrated *Victory at Sea* by a year. The opening episode of *Crusade in the Pacific* generated extra-special attention when the film was telecast over WJZ–New York on October 30, 1951, the same night as the film's *theatrical* release at New York's Guild Newsreel Theatre.

Danger Is My Business (1958). This full-color NTA release depicted danger-prone folks in hazardous professions, and was narrated by Jack Douglas. *Danger Is My Business'* creator was Col. John D. Craig, who'd written the book upon which the series was based. After a full life of neck-rising adventure, Col. Craig had been appointed head of all American combat photographers' units during World War II, and later supervised the 54-man crew that filmed the Pacific A-Bomb tests. Applying his cinematic skills to TV, Craig explained "I had an idea . . . that each film should be a quest, not just a series of pretty pictures." Col. Craig stuck to that idea from his first syndie (1954's *I Search for Adventure*) to his last (1965's *Of Lands and Seas*). Never was there a "pretty picture" in a Craig production that did not advance the adventure.

Global Zobel (and other one-shots) (1954–59). With virtually every local channel offering at least one weekly show to adventurers ·and their glorified home movies, the travelogue business was a flourishing one in the 1950's. Los Angeles became the travel-show capital of the country, with many of the syndicated efforts getting their start on one of L.A.'s four independent outlets. Former Hollywood publicity man Myron Zobel did just fine with his *Global Zobel* years before going national in 1959. Gunther Less made a career out of a single property, *Journey to Adventure,* which began in 1954 and was still running into the '80s. Likewise, the Linker Family parlayed their one syndie hit, *Wonders of the World,* into a lifetime of lecture tours. But for every success, there were plenty of one-series wonders who were brilliant at taking "pretty pictures" but hopeless when called upon to narrate them.

High Road to Danger (1959). Actor Steve Brodie was host/participant in *High Road to Danger* (not to be confused with an ABC series of 1959, *John Gunther's High Road*), 39 filmed expeditions — 13 in color — released by United Artists TV.

I Search for Adventure (1954). Col. John D. Craig's first syndie, based on his own 1938 book and distributed by Bagnall Productions. Each episode was one of Craig's beloved "quests," culled from either the Colonel's own film backlog or from location footage shot by the expeditionists who appeared as guest narrators.

Industry on Parade see Americans at Work

It Seems Like Yesterday (1953). Blatant imitation of Ziv's *Yesterday's Newsreel,* given prestige by the stentorian narration of news commentator H.V. Kaltenborn.

Journey to Adventure see Global Zobel

Jungle Macabre (1953). Despite its lurid title, Guild's *Jungle Macabre* wasn't all that macabre, but its 15-minute glimpses of Nature's most unusual jungle wildlife weren't dull, either.

Kingdom of the Sea (1956). First-rate color underwater footage adorned this 41-episode John D. Craig project. It was produced by Jack Douglas, narrated by Bob Stevenson and syndicated by Guild.

The Michaels in Africa (1959). Togetherness on the veldt, filmed and narrated by George and Marjorie Michael. The series' attitude towards the "humble" African natives was better summed up by the title of the Michaels' 1966 syndie, *B'wana Michael.*

Movie Museum (1953). Manhattan television pianist Paul Killiam first rose to prominence by providing mocking, sarcastic narration to silent films of the pre–1920 era. Somewhere along the line, Killiam fell in love with his object of ridicule, and became a leading film historian and preservationist, amassing one of the world's largest silent-celluloid collection—a collection which included virtually the entire output of director D.W. Griffith during his years at Biograph Studios. Together with producer Saul J. Turrell of Sterling Films and researcher William K. Everson, Killiam put together 130 15-minute silent-film vignettes under the title *Movie Museum.* Killiam's garrulous narration made these vintage shadow-plays seem as contemporary as the latest wide-screen talkie blockbuster, especially when he pointed out cinema techniques invented for the old films which were still in use half a century later. In the mid–70's, *Movie Museum* was revived for public and cable TV, minus some of Paul Killiam's more superfluous (but well-intentioned) narration but with the addition of newly unearthed film and film facts.

Noah Beery Jr. (1952). Even character actor Noah Beery Jr. hopped on the syndie travel-doc bandwagon with a delightful travelogue featuring himself and his children; released by Courneya Films.

Seven League Boots (1959). An ITC release, *Seven League Boots* was Jack Douglas' first "Docu-Matic," showing thrillseekers the world over re-enacting their most perilous exploits.

Treasure (1959). This color, 39-week study of treasure hunters and treasures hunted was the first major syndie release of Teledynamics, a company created by one Bill Burrud. Burrud's initial foray into the travel-doc field was a Los Angeles local of 1952, *Open Road.* This was followed by Burrud's longest-running local property, *Wanderlust,* which did only middling business as a 1957 black-and-white syndie but scored when revived in color eight years later. After *Treasure,* Bill Burrud spent the next several years churning out syndie after syndie, nearly all of them devoted to his two pet topics — exploration and animals. The producer could honestly boast that he could put together a top-quality half-hour for as little as $12,500 a week, simply by retaining a skeleton film crew and by purchasing most of his footage from independent filmmakers. When asked why he specialized in animal shows, Burrud was only half-kidding when he replied "Monkeys don't get residuals." Despite the seeming cynicism, Bill Burrud became an ardent pro-animal advocate, using his later syndies as entertaining soapboxes for his views on conservation and animal rights. It's ironic that the gruesome 1984 videotape release *Faces of Death,* which features such scenes as a primitive tribe bashing in the skulls of monkeys and then eating their brains, was distributed by a company run by Burrud's children!

Uncommon Valor (1955). An NBC Films 26-week hitch with Marine Corps documentary footage, hosted by General Holland A. "Howlin' Mad" Smith.

Wanderlust see *Treasure*

War in the Air (1956). As if to say "Hey, fellows, *we* were in that war, too!" the British Broadcasting Corporation issued 26 weeks' worth of *War in the Air,* which got some big-city airtime in America.

What Are the Odds? (1958). Inspired by the successful ABC network series *You Asked for It,* Official's *What Are the Odds* was a filmed parade of curious facts, freaks of nature and strangely shaped human beings hosted by Bob Warren. Comprised mostly of cheap stock footage, *Odds* was pepped up by having Warren rattle off an endless stream of statistics, quoting the odds on certain things happening and others not. Interviews on this series were of the triumph-over-the-odds school, featuring guests as diverse as novelist Romaine Gary and entertainer Sammy Davis Jr.

Wonders of the World see *Global Zobel*

Westerns

It once was axiomatic that no western ever lost money. This was seldom truer than in the world of '50s television, with its B-movie-style shoot-'em-ups (filmed in great part by B-movie veterans) at the beginning of the decade, and the talky, occasionally Freudian "adult westerns" at the end. Syndie sagebrushers tended to reflect prevalent network styles; as with adventure/mystery programs, non-network producers liked to play safe with established trends.

The Adventures of Kit Carson (1951–55). Like many western syndies, MCA/Revue's *Kit Carson* had a national sponsor in its first seasons, Coca-Cola. This is why each *Carson* episode opened with old-timer Hank Patterson recalling Kit's exploits to a group of beaming youngsters, all of whom were drinking a brownish beverage from hourglass-shaped bottles. Filmed at Republic Studios, the 104-episode *Kit Carson* was for a time syndicated television's top-rated western. Today it is largely forgotten. Perhaps this is because *Carson* was so derivative of most of the other westerns of its era that one wonders why the producers were never sued. The series even gave Kit Carson a funny Mexican sidekick à la the Cisco Kid's pal Pancho; in fact, the only difference between Cisco's Pancho and Carson's El Toro (Don Diamond) was that the latter was younger and had his tongue hanging out for every pretty girl in sight. Former RKO leading man Bill Williams played Kit Carson; he approached the role as a job of work, with minimal exertion of personality or enthusiasm, and when the series ended, Williams declared publicly that he never wanted anything to do with *Kit Carson* ever again. Such words were the "kiss of death" to a syndicated western, where continuous personal appearances were ever so important. Eventually MCA retired *Kit Carson* to its vaults, so totally forgetting the property that its copyright was allowed to lapse. Scattered episodes therefore exist in many of those public-domain video-cassettes so beloved of ardent collectors.

Annie Oakley (1952–56). Gene Autry's Flying A Productions maintained a level of production quality and fast-action content that was the envy of the industry. One of Flying A's best, most representative series began life as *Annie Oakley and Tagg,* an exciting if historically suspect account of the famous 19th-century sharpshooter and her younger brother. Tagg's name was dropped from the title when well-known child actor Billy Gray (later a regular on *Father Knows Best*) was replaced by Jimmy Hawkins. Annie Oakley herself was portrayed by Gail Davis; although the twentyish actress had been a western leading lady for several years, she got the Oakley role largely on the strength of a guest appearance as a tomboy on Flying A's *Range Rider.* Davis not only conveyed the necessary pluck and perkiness of Annie Oakley, but was an expert rider, roper and markswoman in her own right. The actress played Annie until 1956, but Gene Autry's characteristically tight contract required her to keep her hair up in "Oakley"-style pigtails for personal appearances until 1960 (rather limiting her "outside" work). *Annie Oakley* premiered via CBS Films in January 1954, sponsored by Canada Dry and TV Time Popcorn. Little-boy viewers normally shunned TV series starring icky old girls, but *Annie Oakley* contained enough of Flying A's traditional action-adventure to keep pre-puberty males tuning in — not to mention those *post*-puberty boys who were interested whenever Gail Davis strolled into view.

Boots and Saddles (1957). The title of this California National Productions release was derived from the bugle call used to summon U.S. Cavalrymen to their horses. Filmed on location in Kanab, Utah, *Boots and Saddles* told stories of the American 5th Cavalry, vintage 1870. The regular cast-list read like a syndie-TV Who's Who: Patrick McVey, David Willock, John Alderson and Michael Hinn. One actor who'd been hired for a continuing role was fired for "incompetence." That actor was Gardner McKay, who later learned his trade well enough to star in three seasons' worth of ABC's *Adventures in Paradise*.

Buffalo Bill Junior (1954). 26-week Flying A production created as a vehicle for Dick Jones, who'd costarred as "Dick West" in the company's *Range Rider*. Jones, who played a youthful Texas marshal, had been acting since childhood, including a stint in Hal Roach's Our Gang, the "lead" in Disney's cartoon feature *Pinocchio* (he supplied the voice and posed for the animators), and several seasons as radio's Henry Aldrich. Evidently he picked up some business acumen from Flying A boss Gene Autry; after *Buffalo Bill Jr.* ended, Dick Jones went into the real-estate business, where he made more money than he'd ever accumulated during his showbiz career.

Casey Jones (1957). Although the real-life railroad engineer Casey Jones was a native of Tennessee and had worked for the Midwest and Central line, most of Screen Gems' 26 *Casey Jones* episodes chugged far enough into the Frontier to qualify the series as a western. Alan Hale Jr. starred as Casey, and since the real Casey's widow was still alive when the series was filmed, it would have been churlish not to write Mrs. Jones into the scripts (she was played by Mary Lawrence). *Casey Jones* was popular with everyone but the Brotherhood of Railroad Engineers, who refused to endorse the series because Alan Hale Jr. was forced by cramped studio space to mount his engine's cabin from the wrong side.

Cavalcade of the West (1954). Although he'd been a western star since the silents, Col. Tim McCoy was better known to some people as an expert on Indian customs and sign language. His *Cavalcade of the West,* a Los Angeles local which Mercury International syndicated as a group of 15-minute color films, was a likeable oddity—no action or gunplay, simply a fascinating glimpse at western and Indian lore.

The Cisco Kid (1950–55). *The Cisco Kid* was in development long before it became Ziv's first half-hour weekly television series. O. Henry's "Robin Hood of the Old West" (who in the O. Henry original acted more like the Sheriff of Nottingham) had been showing up in movies since 1913. During the 1940's, producer Philip Krasne made a brace of *Cisco Kid* B-series starring Duncan Renaldo as Cisco, and while western purists aren't overly fond of Renaldo's interpretation of the role, the actor was johnny-on-the-spot when Krasne and Ziv began working on radio and television deals involving the character. In 1949, Ziv formed two separate Cisco Kid corporations, one for filming the pilot of a *Cisco* TV series, the other to merchandise Cisco Kid toys (hey there, Hopalong Cassidy!). Duncan Renaldo's co-star in the pilot was comic-dialectician Leo Carillo as funny-sidekick Pancho. Ziv lined up a powerful national sponsor in the form of Interstate Bread, then pre-tested the pilot in cities with heavy Hispanic populations. After all existing TV markets purchased the property, *Cisco Kid* premiered in March of 1951. By 1960, Ziv had grossed $11,000,000 on the 155-episode series; distribution has changed hands quite often since then. *Cisco Kid* is still in circulation, still turning a profit after nearly forty years. It may look crude and raw when compared to the MTV-style action efforts of the '80s, but *Cisco Kid* retains its honest vitality and willingness to please the crowd.

As Ziv's first big series, *Cisco Kid* was the proverbial oldest child, subject to rules and restrictions that would be relaxed for later productions. No knives were allowed on *Cisco,* nor were any stories involving elements like witchcraft or the supernatural that might scare the kiddies. Writers were instructed to avoid such "slow-down" devices as mules, cumbersome props or elderly people. (One rejected *Cisco* script featured an old man who travelled in a mule-drawn bathtub.) Writers were encouraged to incorporate new-fangled inventions like the steam engine or telephone, or exotic animals like elephants or camels, into their traditional cowboy plotlines. Above all, each episode had to contain at least three major action sequences—and at no time could Cisco or Pancho be bested in combat unless they were heavily outnumbered. This last point was typical of the ego-massaging that went on. A great deal of rivalry existed between Duncan Renaldo and Leo Carillo, so the writers saw to it that Pancho got as much screen-time as Cisco, and that Cisco never gave Pancho direct orders; Pancho would "pitch camp" or "go to town" only on his own volition. Nor was Duncan Renaldo vanity-free. Directors were told never to ask the star to remove his hat. It was not only a Cisco Kid trademark, but it neatly covered Renaldo's receding hairline.

Everyone knows that *Cisco Kid* was one of the earliest series filmed in color, a fact that kept the property alive in the first years of the '60s color boom. Why, then, do several episodes exist that were clearly filmed in black and white? The answer was both simple and costly. During the 1953 season, Fred Ziv wasn't sure that color film was showing up properly on black-and-white TV screens. Rather than risk a dark, muddy TV image, Ziv shot each 1953 *Cisco* episode *twice,* once in color, once in black-and-white.

Cowboy G-Men (1952). Though its title seems to be the ultimate in contrivance, Telemount-Mutual's *Cowboy G-Men* was actually an above-average account of Federal Operatives in the West of the 1870's, boasting likeable performances from stars Russell Hayden and Jackie Coogan and taut direction from film-cultist favorite Lesley Selander. It's hardly unusual that the 26 *Cowboy G-Men* episodes were in color. What *is* unique is the fact that the series' producers, anticipating a possible future technological advance, filmed the series' final 13 episodes in 3-D.

Death Valley Days (1952–70; 1974). This indefatigable western anthology started in 1930 as a simple commission job for Mrs. Ruth Woodman, a young advertising copywriter for the McCann-Erickson agency. Pacific Coast Borax, a small company specializing in cleaning products, was the latest McCann-Erickson client, and wished to break into radio. Assigned to create a series for Borax, Mrs. Woodman lifted the legend of the discovery of Borax in Death Valley verbatim from the company's publicity handouts and wrote a script titled "She Burns Green." The Pacific Coast people so loved the script that they wanted Mrs. Woodman to write *all* future stories for their new *Death Valley Days*. Knowing little and caring less about Death Valley, Mrs. Woodman rapidly boned up on the history of the desert region and took long trips to the valley, where with the help of a leather-skinned "desert rat" named Wash Cahill she interviewed every survivor of Death Valley's frontier days. Before long, Ruth Cornwall Woodman was America's foremost authority on Death Valley lore, and stayed with *Death Valley Days* throughout its network radio run from 1931 to 1945. In 1951, Pacific Coast Borax decided to have a whack at television, so Mrs. Woodman was rehired to assemble a filmed version of *Death Valley Days*. (The pilot episode was, inevitably, "She Burns Green.") This time, the Borax people decided to peddle the series, commercials and all, directly to local stations who needed to plug up unsponsored holes in their non-network schedules.

Most early *D.V.D.* dramas were filmed at Gene Autry's Flying A facilities, but as the series' popularity grew, so did its budgets, and soon the producers were filming all over California, Utah, Arizona, Nevada and Oregon. The first producer for *DVD's* Filmmasters Productions was Darryl McGowran, the first director McGowran's brother Stuart. Martin Skiles arranged the music, including the lone bugle call that had been the series' trademark since the radio days. Guest stars included such luminaries as Yvonne DeCarlo, Pat O'Brien, John Carradine, Red Buttons, Neville Brand, James Franciscus, Fess Parker, Tony Martin, Howard Keel, and, as they say at awards banquets, a host of others. All of the stories on the series had their foundation in true events from Death Valley's history, and Mrs. Woodman was positively wizard in finding factual tales connecting the valley with the likes of Calamity Jane, Abe Lincoln and William Randolph Hearst. So long as she cast no aspersions on their products, Pacific Coast Borax gave Mrs. Woodman leeway on story content, enabling her to do tales that no other western of the time would touch — including a 1953 drama depicting a family of black frontiersmen. Actually it was the series' fans, not its sponsors, who had the final word. (*Death Valley Days* was a syndie "Top Ten" attraction well into the '60s.) Mrs. Woodman *listened* to those fans, even going as far as publicly apologizing for such goofs as showing the head of a Mormon wagon train drinking a cup of coffee.

Thirty new *Death Valley Days* were filmed per year; when the series switched to color in 1964, the added costs trimmed the yearly episode quote down to 20. The program's first brush with color had been its 30th episode, 1953's "The Big Team Rolls," which made history by being the first TV half-hour filmed in the expensive Technicolor process previously reserved for big-budget motion pictures.

Radio's *Death Valley Days* had been hosted and narrated by "The Old Ranger," a tobacco-spitting, mud-caked saddle bum. Such an image was hardly beneficial to a sponsor with a line of soap products, so television's Old Ranger was brushed off and cleaned up—even unto wearing a necktie—in the person of down-to-earth character actor Stanley Andrews. For most viewers, Andrews was The Old Ranger to the letter, and the actor obligingly played no other role from 1952 to his death in 1963. Unless you've been on Mars all your life, you'll know that Andrews' replacement as *DVD* host was Ronald Reagan. Since Reagan's older brother Kyle was an executive at McCann-Erickson, who distributed the series, Ronnie's casting may at first glance strike of nepotism. Not so. Kyle Reagan did *not* hire his brother until the younger Reagan's audience appeal had been tested, and proven, by an appearance in a well-distributed Borax commercial.

Reagan's tenure on *Death Valley Days* was brief. When the actor began his 1965 campaign for governor of California, his *DVD* appearances were edited from telecasts in that state lest his opponents demand equal time; the actor was replaced by several old friends, including Robert Taylor and Rosemary DeCamp. Once Reagan was elected and left showbiz for good (so they say), Taylor took over as *Death Valley's* host, while DeCamp handled the Borax commercials. Robert Taylor died in 1969, and was succeeded by Dale Robertson, who stayed with *Death Valley Days* until production shut down in 1970. Four years later, Les Walwork and Associates thought the world was ready for 24 brand-new *DVD* episodes, hosted by and occasionally starring singer Merle Haggard. These sub-par efforts had nothing to do with Pacific Coast Borax, Mrs. Ruth Woodman's original concept, nor the glory that once was *Death Valley Days*. For all intents and purposes, the series retired in 1970 while it was still a force to reckon with in the world of syndication.

Now follow closely. Starting in 1960, Peter Robeck Productions set up a deal with McCann-Erickson to re-distribute *Death Valley Days* reruns under new titles. Borax would not sponsor these repeats, but would offer them to local stations in exchange for ad time on other programs. The first bundle of reruns was 1960's *The Pioneers,* 104 episodes with "non-star" casts hosted by Will Rogers Jr. Fifty-two more repeats were issued as *Trails West* in 1962, emceed by that eminent cowpoke Ray Milland. Nineteen sixty-three brought forth *Western Star Theatre,* with Rory Calhoun hosting; these 67 reruns featuring big name casts and occasional big name directors like Richard Boone. And in 1969, 52 full-color *Death Valley Days* reruns *not* starring either Ronald Reagan or Robert Taylor appeared under the heading *Call of the West,* hosted this time around by John Payne. By 1970, it was quite possible during any given week in Los Angeles to watch a first-run *Death Valley Days* episode and all *four* of the series' rerun "offspring."

The Fast Guns see Stories of the Century

Frontier Doctor (1956). Republic Pictures appointed one of its contract singing cowboys, Rex Allen, to star in 39 half-hours as Bill Baxter, *Frontier Doctor.* Amidst the miles of stock footage that typified Republic's TV product,

Frontier Doctor was pretty good, with decent story values and a reasonably three-dimensional hero who spent as much time battling health-standard ignorance and resistance to new medical methods as he did punching out bad guys. For non-doctor fans, Republic reissued the series under the catch-all title *Man of the West*.

Hopalong Cassidy (1952). After several profitable seasons of distributing his old movies to television, William Boyd responded to public demand with 39 new *Hopalong Cassidy* half-hours filmed at the Corriganville Ranch and distributed by NBC Films. At age 60, Boyd looked as sharp as ever in his all-black "Hoppy" costumes; he was ably assisted by Edgar Buchanan as Red Connors. Competently if economically produced, the new *Hopalong Cassidys* ended each week with William Boyd exercising his "role-model-for-youth" prerogative to deliver important messages to his "podners": Don't Litter, Trust the Police, Beware the Friendly Stranger, and so on.

Judge Roy Bean (1955). Edgar Buchanan's reward for faithful service as everybody's comic sidekick was his own 39-week vehicle, Screencraft's *Judge Roy Bean*. (There'd been plans a few years earlier by Tele-Voz to shoot a *Judge Bean* series in Mexico, starring another stalwart western supporting actor, Chill Wills.) The Judge, Langtry, Texas' "only law west of the Pecos," was in real life an unregenerate scoundrel, notorious for his left-handed, self-serving style of jurisprudence. Television's Judge Bean was dry-cleaned into a big-hearted rascal who twisted legalities solely in the interest of justice and fair play. Once accustomed to fabrication, the series' producers had no qualms about giving the judge a pretty niece (Jackie Loughery), who in a pinch could be counted on to draw a derringer from the folds of her petticoat. Also supporting Edgar Buchanan were Jack Beutel as Bean's deputy (Beutel's last role of note was as Jane Russell's main squeeze in the notorious 1943 film *The Outlaw*) and Russell Hayden, who doubled as *Judge Roy Bean's* producer. Hayden shot the series in future-saleable color at the least possible cost in a California tourist-trap called "Pioneertown."

Kit Carson see *The Adventures of Kit Carson*

Lash of the West (1952). This miserable excuse for a western was the first syndie release of Guild Films. Shot during what must have been a lunch break at Nassour Studios, *Lash* ripped off the format established by NBC's *The Gabby Hayes Show*. The resistible B-flick star Al "Lash" LaRue would be seen swapping tales with some pals, then he'd segue with an "I remember the time..." into a clip from a vintage Lash LaRue theatrical western of dubious merit. At fifteen minutes, these doses of LaRue were about a quarter-hour too long (and hard to understand, thanks to the star's well-oiled slurring of lines); but Lash LaRue's marginal name value helped *Lash of the West* make money for Guild, even — incredibly — attaining some network exposure.

MacKenzie's Raiders (1958). With television gearing up for the upcoming Civil War Centennial, and with CBS Films' *Gray Ghost* knocking 'em dead in the syndie ratings, Ziv's *MacKenzie's Raiders* was a shoo-in for success. Based on a real-life military unit, the Raiders were Northern Civil War vets working for the U.S. 4th Cavalry some four years after the hostilities. This was a period when Mexican bandits and terrorists were making attacks in the United States, secure that they wouldn't be pursued into Mexico because the two countries weren't at war. But with full government sanction (and the understanding that, should they be caught or killed, the secretary or somebody would disavow all knowledge of their actions), MacKenzie's Raiders made more than one unofficial foray south of the border to bring the miscreants to justice. As Col. Ranald MacKenzie, Richard *(I Led Three Lives)* Carlson essayed his second American hero for Ziv (what simpler times, when perpetrators of covert activities were called "heroes"). For authenticity's sake, MacKenzie's Raiders weren't the usual passel of Hollywood pretty-boys but pock-marked, weathered character actors like Louis-Jean Heydt and Morris Ankrum. Handsomely assembled by producers Elliot Lewis and Lou Breslow, *MacKenzie's Raiders'* 100 prerelease sales made it an instant smash, but like many other syndies of that period, its production costs made a second season virtually impossible.

Man of the West see Frontier Doctor

Man Without a Gun (1958–59). Setting their sights on the "adult western" market, the NTA Film Network began work on *Man Without a Gun* a year before its deubt. The project first appeared as a one-shot on the NTA-produced network series *The 20th Century–Fox Hour* entitled "Man of the Law." Former *Our Miss Brooks* regular Robert Rockwell starred as Adam McLean, a Dakota-territory newspaper editor who advocated the superiority of the pen over the six-gun but wasn't above bashing a few of the bad guys' heads together just to get their attention. "Man of the Law's" producer Peter Packer replaced Robert Rockwell with Rex Reason when *Man Without a Gun* proper began filming. Since the hero didn't pack a gun and since a western wouldn't be a western without at least *one* good guy toting firearms, Mort Mills was co-starred as the conventional Sheriff Frank Talman. The series' opener, directed by later *Maverick* mainstay Douglas Heyes, featured a bravura performance by Richard Jaeckel as a sneering villain. Compared to colorful guest stars like Jaeckel, Rex Reason looked a little over-starched, but critics welcomed him as at least one western hero who favored intellect over instinct. Filmed at 20th Century–Fox and Corriganville, *Man Without a Gun* lasted 52 episodes, and proved the most profitable series the NTA Film Network would have outside the talk-show field.

The Range Rider (1951–52). Flying A Productions' first fling at syndication (through CBS Films), *Range Rider* was a vehicle for that amazing stunt artist Jock — then billed as Jack — Mahoney. The series' strong suit was action, action, and more action. Other early westerns (notably *The Lone Ranger*) kept budgets in control by cutting corners in the action department, concentrating instead on plot and dialogue. *Range Rider's* plotlines were elemental at best; its fans wanted and got non-stop riding, fighting, stunting. Another plus was Jock Mahoney's unpretentious approach to his work. One of the few stunters who could act as well as he moved, Mahoney was thoroughly convincing as the shy stranger who thwarted the machinations of the baddies with a minimum of wasted action. And there was none of the Lone Ranger's pompous speechmaking, either; when Range Rider showed his young saddle pal Dick West (Dick Jones) the proper way to build a fire, he built the fire — he didn't recite the history of the forest. Range Rider's utter avoidance of acting superior to those younger than himself helped the kids at home to accept the character as a friend whom they'd want to visit once a week. Sometimes those visits were once a day, since *Range Rider* was the first major syndie to be "stripped" five times a week in many markets. This was a carryover from the series' first telecast week, when WCBS–New York ran daily *Range Rider* episodes as a ploy to attract sponsors. It was common for some markets to run the program as often as *eight* times weekly, so CBS Films periodically withdrew its 76 *Range Riders* from distribution just to avoid oversaturation. (*Range Rider,* along with two other Flying A syndies, *Annie Oakley* and *Buffalo Bill Jr.,* ran as part of the ABC network's weekend-morning schedule in 1964–65 after ABC Films bought Flying A outright from Gene Autry.)

While no one made as much money off *Range Rider* as did Gene Autry, the series did a world of good for Jock Mahoney's subsequent acting career, and even enhanced his private life. Mahoney's leading lady on two consecutive *Range Riders* in 1951 was Margaret Field; the two co-stars eventually fell in love and were married. It was the second time around for both. Jock Mahoney adopted Margaret's two daughters, one of whom now acts under the name of Sally Field.

Shotgun Slade (1959–60). With westerns, westerns everywhere in 1959, there was no room for the minimalism of *Cisco Kid.* The "gimmick" western abounded both on and off the networks, said "gimmick" usually being the type of gun used by the hero. Frank Gruber, an excellent but otherwise traditional western writer, decided to be competitive by creating a series that out-gimmicked everybody. That series was *Shotgun Slade* (an MCA package originally intended for the NBC network), which had enough "novelty value" for three different series. Shotgun Slade (Scott Brady) had a two-in-one shotgun, with each barrel a different caliber. Slade's adventures were musically scored with an anachronistic *Peter Gunn*-style jazz beat supplied by Gerald Fried. And the supporting casts were, well, unorthodox. The first *Slade* starred comedian Ernie Kovacs as a bearded, villainous miner; he was so good that *Variety* suggested a full-time western career for Kovacs "if he ever gives up his cigar and the Nairobi Trio." Future guest stars were professional — but not professional actors. War hero "Pappy" Boyington played a rancher, ex-football star Elroy "Crazylegs" Hirsch a saloonkeeper, and country-western troubadors Johnny Cash and Jimmy Wakely posed as lawmen. Other bit parts were filled by celebrated sports figures, though Scott Brady never fulfilled his dream of acting opposite Yogi Berra. The novelty value inherent in *Shotgun Slade* kept viewers tuning in for two seasons, even after most of them deduced that at base, the series was just another western. Because the gimmickry made it difficult to accept the show as a western pure-and-simple, local stations advertised *Slade* as everything from a cowboy private-eye show to a comic satire of the cowboy genre. Seen today, *Shotgun Slade* is as much a victim as a product of its gimmick-laden era, and doesn't stand up even as well as *Cisco Kid*.

Steve Donovan (1952). NBC Films peddled this one under several titles: *Steve Donovan, Steve Donovan—Western Ranger, Western Marshal*. By any name, it smelled. Fresh from his production duties on *The Lone Ranger,* Jack Chertok pitched camp at Hal Roach Studios to dole out 26 half-hours starring movie second lead Douglas Kennedy as Steve Donovan and grizzled old Eddy Waller as Donovan's grizzled old sidekick Rusty. *Donovan* had little to recommend it; Douglas Kennedy looked uncomfortable trying to carry the show, action scenes were stilted, stories were dishwater dull. That the series got sold at all is a tribute to the diligence of NBC Films. *Steve Donovan* made its first big sales in 1952, just after the FCC lifted its freeze on granting new television station licenses. Another round of sales occurred after the death of the DuMont network left schedule holes on local stations who'd been carrying DuMont's *Captain Video* in 1955. And *Donovan's* last big go-round was a result of the network western boom of 1957–58. *Steve Donovan* made the Top Ten ratings list in several markets—nevertheless.

Stories of the Century (1954). Western fans eagerly awaiting the first television series from the fabled Republic Pictures were less than thrilled when that series turned out to be merely an imitation *Death Valley Days*. *Stories of the Century* (originally and more accurately titled *Outlaws of the Century*) was a 39-week history of the West's most colorful scofflaws. While it followed the anthology form, it wasn't really an anthology, since it had several continuing characters: railroad detective Matt Clark (Jim Davis) and Matt's female aides Frankie (Mary Castle) and Jonesy (Kristine Miller). Republic fast-action maestro William Witney directed the few scenes on *Stories of the Century* that hadn't been lifted from the studio's vast stock-footage library. Those generous helpings of Republic's past cinema triumphs made the series look more expensive than it was; *Stories* was impressive-looking enough to win a 1954 Emmy, beating out even *Death Valley Days*. Ever able to wring out the last dollar, Republic later reissued *Stories of the Century* as *The Fast Guns*.

Tombstone Territory (1959). After a 65-week network run on ABC, Ziv's *Tombstone Territory* didn't really start bringing home the bacon until it entered syndication with 26 new episodes. The series starred Richard Eastham as the editor of the Tombstone (Arizona Territory) *Epitaph,* with Pat Conway handling the rough stuff as Sheriff Clay Hollister. The stories, all allegedly drawn from "the yellowed pages" of the *Epitaph,* were on occasion written by Sam Peckinpah.

"26" Men (1957–58). ABC Films' *"26" Men* was produced by Russell Hayden, who'd previously produced and acted in *Judge Roy Bean* and starred in *Cowboy G-Men*. Tris Coffin and Kelo Henderson starred as Ryning and Travis, two Arizona Rangers. The real Rangers had been created in 1901 by the territorial legislature to keep the peace, but to avoid vigilantism, the lawmen could never exceed 26 in number: 2 officers, 4 sergeants, 20 privates. It was a voluntary unit, and the Rangers had to provide their own weapons, supplies and horses. In the spirit of authenticity (and economy), producer Hayden required that the location sites used in filming the series had to "volunteer" their own supporting and bit players. Many of the Phoenix and Tucson residents drafted as cast members were more or less playing themselves, such as an Episcopal canon cast as a clergyman, but there were always little surprises like the Arizona juvenile officer who specialized in mustachioed bad guys. This was *"26" Men's* basic gimmick, and it's a good thing that it was an appealing one, for the series didn't offer much in the way of production values or action scenes. The show's shabby look wasn't helped by its principal director, Reg Browne, who'd made his reputation filming the lowest of low-budget western films of the early '50s. The series' second season was an improvement over its first, with better stories and reliable character actors, but that still wasn't saying much. Still, *"26" Men* was one of those curious syndies that caught on with the public (78 episodes' worth) despite its faults. Certainly its reputation was enhanced by schoolkids who'd warble its jaunty theme song by Hal Hopper ("This is the story of Twenty-Six Men/Who rode the Arizona Territory...") *ad nauseum,* much to the chagrin of their elders.

Union Pacific (1958). California National Productions added to its roster of syndie moneymakers with *Union Pacific,* loosely based on Cecil B. DeMille's 1939 railroad epic and filmed in part at DeMille's old stamping grounds, Paramount. Jeff Morrow starred as railroad supervisor Bart McClelland, with Judd Pratt as his chief surveyor. The "Miss Kitty"-type role was played by Susan Cummings as the proprietor of a camp-following dance hall. Viewers with long memories will recall Miss Cummings as the woman who screamed "It's a cookbook!" at the end of the 1962 *Twilight Zone* shocker "To Serve Man."

Western Marshal see *Steve Donovan*

Wild Bill Hickok (1951–58). William F. Broidy Productions entered TV in 1951 with grandiose plans for several elaborate series, but the only project that went anywhere was the decidedly unelaborate *Wild Bill Hickok.* The star was Guy Madison, whose movie career had skyrocketed a few years earlier (he was billed *above* Robert Mitchum in 1946's *Til the End of Time,* which co-starred *Kit Carson's* Bill Williams) but had sputtered out by 1951. *Hickok* made Madison a big name all over again, with enough star value to resume his movie career and enough "youth appeal" to make him a number one kid's idol. While his performance was convincing, Madison's interpretation of James Butler Hickok had about as much to do with truth as the Tooth Fairy.

The series understandably ignored the real Hickok's poor eyesight and bouts with the bottle, and once even contrived to have Wild Bill witness the arrival of Halley's Comet, a phenomenon that occured two years before Hickok was born and three decades after he died. The kids, of course, didn't give a rap about authenticity — *Wild Bill Hickok* was real enough to satisfy them through 112 episodes. Besides, to most kids the *real* star of the show was ratchet-voiced Andy Devine as Bill's sidekick Jingles Jones (a character created from whole cloth by series director Tommy Carr). Devine never gave less than his best to the show; he even supplied his own horse for the riding scenes, and used a special gun which emitted a faint "pop" so as not to frighten the poor animal. Devine and Madison got along famously, so *Wild Bill Hickok's* production schedule ran smoothly until 1958. After distribution deals with both ABC and Flamingo Films, Broidy Productions got a budget boost by tying up with Screen Gems for the final 13 *Hickoks,* which were filmed in color. Still, no penny was ever frivolously spent on the *Hickok* set, its economizing extending to the theme music, which was drawn from "stock" themes previously heard in the B-western product of Monogram and PRC Studios. *Hickok's* frugality was, however, glaring only when Allied Artists (Monogram's successor) would splice together two or more *Wild Bill* episodes as a theatrical feature film.

Wild Bill Hickok was a high grosser for its longtime sponsor, Kellogg's Cereals. Kellogg's stuck with the property from its first days in syndication through its brief rerun life on the ABC network, and even in its spinoff as a radio series that like the television version starred Guy Madison and Andy Devine. When you see a *Hickok* rerun today, you'll see Wild Bill firing his gun at the camera in the opening scene. You won't see the smoke clear to reveal a box of Kellogg's Sugar Pops. That was yesterday, and yesterday's gone.

Women's

Presumptuous though this designation may be, "women's shows" was a label accepted with minimal resistance in the 1950's. Only on rare occasions was this opprobrious label applied to programs that required the viewer to exercise her intellect. Most syndies for women were cotton-candy interview shows, cooking opuses wherein viewers were talked down to, foolish game shows, and exercise sessions.

The Ed Allen Show see below

Exercise Shows (1952–59). The theory behind most of these series was that housewives put on weight because they didn't do any physical labor (a theory in frequent dispute). Syndicators started sending out grunt-and-puffers with Guild's daily *It's Fun to Reduce* in 1953. Most of the series' hosts were men; local talent like Chicago's Paul Fogarty and Dayton, Ohio's Andy Marten were satisfied with their viewership and didn't try to crack the national scene. On the other hand, California's Jack LaLanne acted like he was big time even when nobody'd ever heard of him, performing such eye-catching stunts as dragging tugboats by his teeth under the Golden Gate Bridge. LaLanne's "inhale— exhale" syndie began in 1958, and, allowing for a couple of production hiatuses, remained in circulation for the next twenty years. Jack never seemed to stop moving on his show, ever conscious that he was on national television, and by God had better *perform!* For him, it worked; LaLanne looked better in his seventies than did most men a third his age. Jack's most serious rival was Detroit's Ed Allen, whose syndication career began in 1959 and didn't let up until 1980; Allen's best group of shows were color-taped in the mid–60's amidst the outdoor grandeur of the Bahamas. Less flamboyant than LaLanne, Ed Allen was just as unshirking in giving his viewers a real workout. Like most exercise stars, both LaLanne and Allen offered their series to local markets on a "barter" basis, in exchange for the free opportunity of hawking their lines of physical-fitness equipment and pamphlets.

First Date (1952). This ancestor of *The Dating Game* began locally in New York and was hosted by the pomade-haired Renzo Cesana, who reportedly set female hearts a-flutter as an oily character called "The Continental."

Gourmet Club (1958). One of the few cooking shows to go national; hosting was Dione Lucas.

It's Fun to Reduce see *Exercise Shows*

Jack LaLanne see *Exercise Shows*

Ladies Be Seated (1955). A title that wouldn't get to first base today, *Ladies Be Seated* had been an audience-participation networker on radio and television until 1949, then was brought back from the dead for syndication. One of its producers was Greg Garrison, later responsible for such dignified celebrations of womanhood as *The Golddiggers*.

Women in the News (1950). This laudable 10-minute filler from United Artists attempted to show the contributions made by women in the fields of science, education, government, and even the military. But TV station managers of the time saw less potential in series like *Women in the News* than they did in the inane-chatter syndies hosted by such personalities as Wendy Barrie and Ilka Chase. So far as the television industry was concerned, the only time a woman should appear in the news was wearing a bathing suit and trying to fry an egg on the sidewalk on the first day of summer. And that's the way it was.

The 1960's

The revolutionary 1960's were years of radical changes on the syndicated television scene. For starters, the faces of those running the syndie field began to change. Ziv Productions was sold in 1961 to United Artists and became merely a distributor, not a producer; Ziv's Eagle-Lion Studios facility was torn down to make way for a shopping center in 1963. That same year, Hal Roach Studios, beleaguered by several improvident business deals, was sold at auction and likewise bulldozed into oblivion. Gross-Krasne became Gross-Krasne-Silleman, then disappeared when Mickey Silleman moved to NTA. Guild Films merged with Official, while Television Programs of America was absorbed by ITC, which in turn became a cog in the Associated Television wheel run by England's Sir Lew Grade. Screen Gems would merge with its parent company Columbia before the decade was over. MCA acquired Universal Pictures, leaving its old Republic Studios headquarters to Four-Star and CBS Films. And Desilu, camped on the old RKO lot, was sold to Gulf and Western Oil, then merged with another Gulf and Western acquisition, RKO's next-door neighbor Paramount.

CBS, NBC and ABC continued putting up money for their network shows, but all three firms were out of the first-run filmed syndie business by 1962. Thereafter, the three networks' film divisions would devote themselves to handling the work of independent producers, mostly musical and game-show syndies.

The young turks running 1960's syndication included the "Station Groups"—companies owning major television stations in several important cities. Westinghouse, which brought us radio station KDKA back in 1920, kept up a steady flow of '60s taped series and specials, and by 1969 was officially known as "Group W." The Metropolitan Broadcasting Company, risen from the ruins of the old DuMont network, absorbed producer David Wolper's company in 1964, and later, armed with an arsenal of taped syndie material, closed out the decade under the name of "Metromedia." Also joining the "distributors club" were Philadelphia's Kaiser and Triangle companies, Chicago's Field Communications and WGN–Continental, and

Cincinnati's Avco and Taft. After years in the hands of Hollywood, syndicated television became the property of television itself.

The onetime front-running syndie genres — Adventure/Mystery, Comedy, Drama, Western — virtually vanished from the first-run field, succumbing to an increase in network reruns. A few of the old genres — Talk/Interview, Music/Variety, Children's and Game Shows — suddenly had greatness thrust upon them. Informational programs (including several "Women's" shows, the new liberation movement making that irksome label virtually obsolete) functioned fitfully on commercial TV, conserving their energies for the blossoming public television market. Travel/Documentary continued to thrive, enhanced by a mid-decade demand for more full-color product. And with the added bonuses of color and videotape coupled with the disadvantages of higher production costs, a lot of syndie producers forsook weekly series in favor of one-shot specials — and it didn't take long for the airwaves to become thick with oneshots.

Adventure/Mystery

The '60s Adventure/Mystery menu contained several warmed-over concepts from previous decades, as well as some "new" series that actually had been completed in the 1950's. Production on American-made syndie series dwindled to a halt by 1963, when the adventure field was turned over to government-imposed "quota" imports from England, Canada and Australia.

Adventures of the Sea Hawk (1961). Veteran syndication star John Howard starred as seaborne research professor John Hawk in this 39-week series. It had originally been location-filmed as *Caribbean Adventure* in 1958, but was too low-key and leisurely to foster sales in that violence-prone TV year. When TV Marketeers picked up the retitled *Sea Hawk* for 1961 release, company president Wynn Nathan plotted to use the series' lack of violence to its advantage. Nathan declared that with the public hue and cry over television mayhem, *Sea Hawk's* minimal action content made the property the perfect panacea to the complainers. Nice try, Wynn, but no cigar. And very few sales.

Adventures of the Sea Spray (1968). Screen Gems issued 32 color episodes of this Australian effort from Crawford Productions, starring Walter Brown as a famed author encountering danger and delight aboard his yacht.

Assignment: Underwater (1960). An NTA vehicle for former *Kit Carson* lead Bill Williams (a champion swimmer in his college days), who played professional diver Bill Greer. Is there a remote possibility that *Assignment: Underwater* was a derivation of *Sea Hunt?* Not according to NTA's advertising copy, which carefully ticked off the differences between the two series. *Sea Hunt's* location work was confined to the waters surrounding the continental United States, while *Assignment: Underwater* was filmed in such '60s "hot spots" as Hawaii, Alaska, Korea, even Cuba. *Sea Hunt* seldom had more than one or two on-set technical advisors at any given time, while *Assignment* had a full-time staff of five. And while *Sea Hunt's* Mike Nelson (Lloyd Bridges) was a loner, *Assignment's* Bill Greer had an eight-year-old daughter (Diane Mountford). In one respect, the two series were indeed different. *Sea Hunt* was still rerunning its 156 episodes in 101 markets as late as 1966, while *Assignment: Underwater* stayed afloat for only 39 weeks and was but a tic on television's memory bank by 1962.

The Beachcomber (1961). Filmmasters/ITC's *The Beachcomber* anticipated the 1969 NBC series *Then Came Bronson* by detailing the adventures of an ulcerated executive who scooted the rat race in search of the Good Life. But whereas *Bronson's* hero took to the road on a motorcycle, *Beachcomber's* John Lackland (Cameron Mitchell) became a beach bum on the South Pacific isle of Amura. To avoid having Lackland arrested each week for vagrancy, the 39 scripts contrived to have him employed to pursue and pummel the Bad Guys from time to time; so much for "fresh concepts." Supporting Mitchell in the role of "Captain Huckabee" was Don Megowan, a replacement for the pilot episode's Huckabee, Adam *(Batman)* West.

The Blue Angels (1960). California National Productions' 32-week *Blue Angels* didn't try to imitate anything else on television in 1960, yet still carried with it echoes of the "military series" trend of 1957–58; and no wonder, since NBC had initially planned to schedule the as-yet-unfilmed *Blue Angels* in its fall 1958 network lineup. Produced by Sam Gallu with the assistance of Hollywood-Navy liaison man Donald Baruch, *Blue Angels* was a stirring tribute to the Navy's elite corps of precision jet pilots. Though the series had a cast of regulars, the debut episode was essentially a documentary narrated by Ernest Borgnine, and it was the fantastic aerial photography in this first *Blue Angels* that cinched the show's 132 first-run sales. *Angels* ran into the same logjam that vexed CNP's earlier *Flight;* in the air, the pilots were stars, but on solid ground they were just another bunch of good-looking guys (played by Dennis Cross, Don Gordon, Mike Galloway and other beefcake types) on the prowl for good-looking girls. The bathos-and-brawls scripts brought the audience interest engendered by the flying scenes down in flames. Some critics even found the aerial scenes tiresome, *Variety* noting that the camerawork was "tricky to the point of being intrusive." Nonetheless, *Blue Angels* was a success, helped by publicity tie-ins including live appearances by the real Blue Angels in those cities showing the series, and a release date coinciding with the 50th anniversary of naval aviation.

The Brothers Brannagan (1960). With ever-escalating production costs combined with frequent Hollywood labor strikes, several producers moved out of Hollywood in search of trouble-free locations. Phoenix, Arizona, became the production site for CBS Films' *Brothers Brannagan,* produced by Wilbur *(Colonel Flack)* Stark. Aside from its locale, *Brothers* was strictly formula private-eye stuff. Steve Dunne and Mark Roberts played P.I.s Mike and Bob Brannagan, and though Bob had a way with witty epigrams, the two brothers were so hard to tell apart that one reviewer had to identify the boys by their suit colors.

The Case of the Dangerous Robin (1960). This Ziv production was presold to 189 markets, a feat more attributable to Ziv's previous record than to the merits of the series itself. The 38 *Dangerous Robins* starred Rick *(Combat!)* Jason as the latest in a long line of insurance investigators. Robin was "individualized" solely by his preference for judo and karate over gunplay.

The Cheaters (1961). British series with American John Ireland as still another insurance detective. This ITC release was typical of such imports as Australia's *Homicide* and the European *The Adventurers,* shipped to America to meet quota requirements and then consigned to take up shelf space in the U.S.

Coronado Nine (1960). Third and final MCA/Rod Cameron syndie deal (produced by Richard Irving, who'd previously helmed Cameron's MCAers *City Detective* and *State Trooper*). Rod Cameron joined the private-eye fraternity as gun-for-hire Dan Adams, whose telephone exchange was revealed in the series title. *Coronado Nine* was set in San Diego, giving Cameron ample opportunity to engage in *Sea Hunt*-style histrionics in and around the blue Pacific. While it met with a deluge of prerelease sales, the new Cameron vehicle was too much the mixture as before to last past 39 weeks; but the star wasn't crying himself to sleep, not with his *City Detective* making new sales all the time and his *State Trooper* reruns still playing in 162 markets by 1963.

Dangerous Robin see **The Case of the Dangerous Robin**

The Everglades (1961). Non–Hollywood "runaway" production, lensed by Ziv–United Artists in the swamplands of Florida. *The Everglades* starred Ron Hayes as Florida State Ranger Link Vail, and the series was basically *Highway Patrol* with alligators. Even so, *Everglades* survived as a "Top Ten" syndie by virtue of its acting (including a guest shot by Florida native Burt Reynolds), its superb hand-held photography, and the decision to shoot 18 of its 36 episodes in color.

Exclusive (1960). *Exclusive,* an anthology based after a fashion on the real-life adventures of America's Overseas Press Club, had been targeted for ABC's 1959 network schedule, but newspaper shows seemed played out by that time, so sponsors weren't buying. ABC decided to recoup its investment in the existing 13 European-filmed *Exclusives* by syndicating the property through its film division. Those 13 half-hours built up such viewer and (come-lately) sponsor enthusiasm that it was too bad *Exclusive's* production unit had disbanded and its producer-director Eddie Sutherland had retired by 1960.

The Forest Rangers (1965). Coproduced by the Canadian Broadcasting Corporation and Astral Productions, *Forest Rangers* was an outdoors adventure aimed at a family audience. Stories were pure Smokey-the-Bear, but the series became the Number One kid's attraction on Canadian television, and its emphasis on ecology earned *Forest Rangers* several major awards. More important to its United States syndie career was the fact that the 78 *Forest Rangers* were filmed in color, this at a time when American TV stations, having shelled out for expensive new color equipment, were panting for tinted product to run in weekday-afternoon strips. NBC Films did quite well peddling the series, though, curiously, few sales were made in markets with large forest preserves of their own (in Wisconsin, for example, *Forest Rangers* was never shown). For the record, the adult cast of *Rangers* included Graydon Gould, Michael Zenon, and Canadian television stalwart Gordon Pinset, with six youngsters of various sexes and sizes as the Junior Rangers.

The Ghost Squad (1962). Though its title smacked of the supernatural, ITC's *Ghost Squad* was comprised of 26 hour-long tales of Scotland Yard's undercover unit. Starring was Sir Donald Wolfit, the legendary British actor-manager parodied by Albert Finney in the 1983 film *The Dresser*. Wolfit saw no need to leash his play-to-the-balcony technique for the more intimate television camera; when *Ghost Squad* went into a second season on British television, Wolfit had been replaced by younger, subtler, and frankly less colorful actors. A well-crafted London-filmed cop show, *Ghost Squad* suffered in America because of its 60-minute length. Local station managers were having enough trouble drumming up sponsors for hour-long reruns of such American network series as *Riverboat* and *Wire Service;* why should they bother with an untested import with "unknown" stars like *Ghost Squad?*

Gideon CID (1966). ITC did reasonably well peddling *Gideon* in the United States despite its hour length. The main character, a middle-aged family man who happened to be Chief Inspector of Scotland Yard's criminal investigation division (and who was played by John Gregson), already had several thousand American fans thanks to the "Gideon" novels by John Creasey.

The Inspector see *The Pursuers*

Johnny Midnight (1960). Released by MCA, Jack Chertok Productions' New York-filmed *Johnny Midnight* began its one-season run in January 1960. It was yet one more "confidential investigator" yarn, the twist being that Midnight (Edmond O'Brien) had once been an actor; his sleuthing took him to the same Broadway–Park Avenue circles he'd traversed while thesping. (Midnight was the only hard-boiled private eye of the 1960's who had that crime-story staple of the '30s, a Japanese houseboy.) Besides a few months' steady work, Edmond O'Brien's take on *Johnny Midnight* included a few extra years of good health; Jack Chertok would not allow O'Brien to step before the cameras until the actor had shed several pounds through an all-vegetable diet.

King of Diamonds (1961). No new syndie of 1961 was as eagerly anticipated as Ziv–UA's *King of Diamonds*. Ziv built its entire 1961–62 ad promotion around the series, stressing the star power of Broderick *(Highway Patrol)* Crawford, the impressive credits of producer-director John Rich, and the female-viewer value of Crawford's "exciting" young costar Ray Hamilton. To make sure that no one would miss the ballyhoo, Ziv had its *Diamonds* trade-magazine ads decorated with jewel-like Halloween glitter. Broderick Crawford was so anxious to break from his *Highway Patrol* character to play John King, globetrotting troubleshooter for the International Diamond Industry, that he signed a long-term contract with Ziv — thus ending his chances of replacing the late Ward Bond on the NBC network smash *Wagon Train*. Promised a substantial share of *Diamond's* profits, Crawford gleefully dreamed of a windfall exceeding his riches accrued by *Highway Patrol*.

Ziv gave *King of Diamonds* a lavishness far in excess of its usual product, presenting a wide range of lightning-paced adventures dealing with John King's battle against a cartel of villains who helpfully listed themselves in the yellow pages as the Illicit Diamond Buyers Inc. There was even time for Brod Crawford to dally with beautiful ladies, a far cry from the *Highway Patrol* era when the actor didn't even have to shave every day. Its potential audience aroused, Ziv was able to premiere *King of Diamonds* in 118 markets, and for a while the series did "Top Ten" business.

But this was 1961. The series was way too expensive to survive without the financial backing of a big network or major sponsor. Several of the stations who'd bought *Diamonds* were network-owned, and thus forced to shunt the series to weaker time slots when their networks began expanding their evening schedules. A powerful "anti-violence" campaign was then in full swing, affecting every action show on television. And on top of everything, in their zeal to create a thrilling series in the "I-want-it-done-yesterday" world of 1961, Ziv forgot that Broderick Crawford's basic appeal on *Highway Patrol* had been the clipped austerity of his acting style. Put bluntly, Crawford was in over his head as the smooth, well-travelled John King, a role someone like Michael Rennie or James Mason could have played blindfolded. So despite its initial success, *King of Diamonds* lasted but a year. Its disappointing financial returns, together with Broderick Crawford's recent and costly marital breakup, depleted the star's bank account, *Highway Patrol* residuals and all. And the series' inability to cope in the marketplace utterly squashed assurances made by Ziv–UA president John L. Sinn early in 1961 that Ziv was committed to syndication and would forever provide a strong supply of non-network series.

The Littlest Hobo (1963–64; 1982). The Storer Stations Group latched upon a winner when it handled American distribution of the Canadian-made *Littlest Hobo*. Based upon a 1958 B-picture "sleeper," the 58-episode *Hobo* was produced by the McGowran Brothers of *Death Valley Days* fame, and offered the adventures of London, a magnificent German shepherd who, apparently immune to all leash, quarantine and inoculation laws, travelled without a master from city to city. Storer's publicity department claimed that London could understand over 4000 different words in three different languages, accounting for the dog's occasional sidetrips to Europe and the Orient. Promising a range of stories "from Hitchcock suspense to Lucy-type humor," *Littlest Hobo's* producers did their best to provide a variety of plots, though most episodes ended with a *Lassie*-type nick-of-time rescue. Guest stars included old reliables like Keenan Wynn and Bill Williams, up-and-comers like Pat Harrington Jr. and Henry Gibson, and even Edgar Bergen and Charlie McCarthy, whose appearance was an effort to create a "spinoff" weekly series for the ventriloquist-dummy team. Tapping the same all-ages demographic group that had enjoyed *Lassie* for many years, *Littlest Hobo* was a syndie bell-ringer, and might have lasted past two seasons had not production ceased abruptly due to a lawsuit between the McGowran Brothers and Storer over rights to the "London" character. Even so, *Hobo* stayed alive in reruns until Storer temporarily left the syndication business in 1969. A new, full-color *Littlest Hobo* (with of course a new "London") surfaced on Canadian television in 1982, and while it was an immediate success, the series hasn't made the journey across the U.S.–Canada border as of this writing.

Man of the World (1964). ITC had every confidence that its *Man of the World* (released in Britain in 1962) would do as well in America as the company's *The Saint* (which see). Not only did *Man of the World* follow *Saint's* tried-and-true international espionage path—one *World* episode took place in South Vietnam, this at a time when other action shows were pretending that *that* patch of land didn't exist—but its star, as photo-journalist Michael Strait, was Craig Stevens, a cash-value American television attraction thanks to the rerun success of his *Peter Gunn* series. *Man of the World's* British TV ratings had been strong enough to produce a spinoff, a tongue-in-cheek endeavor starring Carlos Thompson titled *The Sentimental Agent*. ITC's hopes to match that success in America began to soar when 20 American markets picked up *Man of the World* solely on the strength of the earlier *Saint*. Those hopes turned to dust when ITC realized late in 1964 that few stations outside those first 20 markets wanted anything to do with the new series. One problem was that ITC had not stuck to its original plan of filming *World* in color, a major goof in the first year of the '60s color-TV boom. The other stumbling block was, as with so many other imports, the series' cumbersome 60-minute length. To make back its $3 million investment, ITC spliced the 20 *Man of the Worlds* into 10 two-hour "movies," shipping them to stations that were begging for brand-new first-run features. The American failure of *Man of the World* foredoomed the chances of its spinoff *Sentimental Agent* (by many accounts the better of the two series) getting any U.S. play.

Miami Undercover (1961). Filmed in the fall of 1959 by United Artists' Aubrey Schenck–Howard W. Koch Productions, *Miami Undercover* starred

Lee Bowman, who was old enough to know better, as a private eye kept in the employ of the Miami Hotel Owners' Association. Bowman's assistant was portrayed by ex-boxer Rocky Graziano, and perhaps to offset Rocky's well-pummelled homeliness, *Miami Undercover's* gimmick was to "guest-star" a different beauty contest winner each week, the size of her role contingent on her ability to walk and chew gum at the same time. The 38 Florida-filmed episodes weren't bad in their own low-budget way, but the syndication market in 1959 was very tight, with most available time slots going to earlier bidders and series renewals; besides, there were already far too many private-eye shows on the scene anyway. It wasn't until January 1961 that United Artists, with the aid of the company's recently purchased Ziv Productions sales team, was able to line up 141 markets for *Miami Undercover,* and then only because Ziv–UA didn't have any new product to meet its January release commitment.

The Pursuers (1964). In the shadow of ITC's *Saint,* M&A Alexander distributed the British-made *The Pursuers,* a Scotland-Yarder starring Louis Hayward, whom the Alexanders hoped would be remembered by viewers as the first actor to play the movie "Saint" back in 1938. Coming at the tail-end of the recent cop-show cycle, *The Pursuers* made no headway, not even when NTA reissued the series in 1966 as *The Inspector.*

R.C.M.P. (1960). Contractually obligated to run on the Canadian Broadcasting Corporation a year before its American release, *R.C.M.P.* (that stands for Royal Canadian Mounted Police, but you already knew that) was the result of a collaboration including the CBC, Canada's Crawley Films and Britain's BBC. $1,400,000 were sunk into the series' 39 episodes, produced by Canadian George Gorman and Americans Harry Horner and Bernard Girard (the two-nation dichotomy extended to the cast, with Canada's Don Francks and Giles Pelletier sharing billing with Boston's John Perkins). The most important contributor to *R.C.M.P.* was Ed Fowlie, the British special-effects wizard who'd spent most of 1957 blowing up the Bridge on the River Kwai in the movie of the same name. Fowlie faced and conquered such challenges as making a hound look like a fox for an animal-fight sequence, and convincing viewers that a dog team was pulling a sled when in fact the sled was being pushed by the camera crew (the dogs wouldn't travel on an unmarked path). Bolstered by an endorsement from the Mounties themselves, *R.C.M.P.* swept the Canadian ratings; but when Hollywood's California National Productions picked up the series for U.S. syndication, *R.C.M.P.* ended up the poorest performer in what was otherwise CNP's best year. It could be that with all those astronauts suiting up for spaceflight in 1961, most American viewers didn't give two maple leaves for any mountie other than Nelson Eddy or Dudley Do-Right.

Ripcord (1961–62). Ziv–UA's *Ripcord* was in the skilled hands of producers Maurice Ungar and Leon Benson and director Joe Wonder, graduates all of Ziv's production-manager pool. The stars were Larry Pennell and Ken Curtis as Ted McKeever and Jim Buckley, owners of a parachute service and school called Skydivers, Inc. Storylines were locked snugly into the *Sea Hunt-Whirlybirds* mold, but *Ripcord's* main attraction was not its plotlines but the heartstopping aerial camerawork of Monroe Atkins and the gasp-inducing feats of stunt pilot Cliff Winters and stunt skydiver Lyle Cameron. Adding to the thrill quotient was a real-life incident in 1962 that came close to killing everyone involved. While filming a typical action sequence some 5000 feet in the sky, two planes collided in mid-air, forcing pilot Winters to crash land. Luckily, no one was seriously hurt, and even more luckily, Monroe Atkins had captured the entire near-catastrophe on film. One whole *Ripcord* episode was built around the accident footage, while another adventure used the incident as its climax. To their everlasting credit, the Ziv–UA people kept details of the accident hushed up until *after* both episodes went into release, thus avoiding the temptation of stirring up ghoulish sensationalism. *Ripcord's* first-season revenue from its 110 markets enabled the series to up the budget to include color film for its final 36 episodes, a move that would keep the series alive and kicking in reruns after color television became the rule rather than the exception. A great family favorite, *Ripcord* was a happy and profitable farewell to the Ziv Productions unit of old, just before its disappearance into United Artists' sea of subsidiaries.

Royal Canadian Mounted Police see *R.C.M.P.*

The Saint (1963–66). Despite its disappointing *Ghost Squad* (1962), ITC hoped that the 60-minute first-run format would find a home in American syndication. In 1963, ITC began its U.S. promotion of *The Saint,* which had been running on England's BBC since '62. Simon Templar, a.k.a. "The Saint," had been created in the 1930's by novelist Leslie Charteris, originally as a criminal who fought in a cold-blooded fashion against bigger, better organized crooks. In typical Hollywood fashion, the longer The Saint remained a movie-series character at RKO (played by such roguish charmers as Louis Hayward and George Sanders), the more "purified" he became. Unhappy at how the character was handled by the movies, Leslie Charteris formed his own production company in the early '50s for the purpose of filming a *Saint* TV-er starring David Niven. These plans went awry, and it wouldn't be until the next decade that Sir Lew Grade's Associated Television would commit *The Saint* to the small screen. Producers Robert S. Baker and Monty Berman, remembering that an unfamiliar cast had hurt the American chances of many an earlier British series, hired as their Simon Templar Roger Moore, recognizable the world over through his rerun appearances in *Ivanhoe* and *Maverick*. Templar had by now evolved into a tuxedoed James Bondish troubleshooter (to make sure Roger Moore fit that tux, the producers ordered him to lose some of his middle-aged spread), but his American debut came a year or so before the Great Spy Boom of the 1960's, so no network space was available for *The Saint*. ITC was compelled to line up a few dozen U.S. TV stations in syndication, eventually attaining the all-important New York market when that city's WNBC ran out of *Desilu Playhouse* reruns for its Sunday 11:15 p.m. slot.

At $100,000 per episode the most expensive English series filmed to date without American co-financing, *The Saint* looked (and was) slicker and more lavish than any previous British import. The first three black-and-white *Saint* seasons—those seen in syndication—had the advantageous participation of good supporting casts (though actress Dawn Addams was rather over-used) and the best of Britain's budget-film directors: Freddie Francis, John Llewellyn Moxey, Anthony Bushell, the incredibly prolific Roy Baker, and eventually Roger Moore himself. *The Saint* looked as though it would be a syndie smash forever, but the spy craze kicked off by NBC's *Man from U.N.C.L.E.* suddenly made NBC reconsider *The Saint* for network exposure. A switch to color was a foregone conclusion (this being 1966), but the attendant upping of production costs to accommodate color filming led to corner-cutting in other aspects of the series, and eventually *The Saint,* previously an entity unto itself with no two episodes being quite the same, turned into a formula affair, with the plotlines becoming as derivative as derivative could be. What once was a beacon of freshness on the syndie horizon was now just another network espionage effort. In its prime, though, *The Saint* was a superior work, the one series that encouraged television to continue setting its sights toward England for top-drawer filmed fare.

The Sea Hawk see *Adventures of the Sea Hawk*

Sea Spray see *Adventures of the Sea Spray*

Seaway (1966). Produced by Canada's ASP Productions in association with the CBC network, *Seaway* was the costliest Canadian filmed series made up until 1965, so much so that additional funding was provided by Britain's Associated Television in exchange for British TV and ITC syndication rights. Stephen Young and Austin Willis starred as security agents working the various ports serviced by the St. Lawrence Seaway, but the weekly hour-long series was less a cop show than it was Canada's answer to Hollywood's *Route 66.* The stars travelled to a different scenic locale each week, then took a back seat as the guest star bore the brunt of the plot. The storylines had holes that one could drive trucks through, but the guest roster was impressive by any nation's television standards: included were Herschel Bernardi, Ralph Bellamy, Nehemiah Persoff, Albert Dekker, Susan Oliver, Marisa Pavan, Lloyd Bochner, Gary Lockwood, J.D. Cannon, and, at the very outset of their careers, Susan Clark and Faye Dunaway. Despite healthy early ratings on CBC, *Seaway* faltered and died after 30 episodes. According to executive producer Maxine Samuels, the series' black-and-white photography couldn't compete with the full-color programs available to and dearly coveted by Canadian viewers in 1965–66. In hopes of reviving *Seaway,* Samuels shot its last two episodes in color, then campaigned to sell the series to an American network, perhaps as a summer replacement. It was too late; *Seaway* would have to make do in U.S. syndication. ITC sent the show out in 1966, and then in 1969, this latter release taking advantage of *Seaway* star Stephen Young's popularity as Carl Betz' assistant on the ABC network series *Judd for the Defense.* But though it was well above average, *Seaway* suffered in syndication, with *Perry Mason* reruns grabbing all the best 60-minute local slots.

Shannon (1961). The adventure-syndie swansong of Screen Gems Productions. There was nothing off the beaten path about Shannon (George Nader), who was yet another insurance sleuth. The series' appeal lay in Shannon's snazzy Buick convertible, which functioned as his "office," replete with weaponry, telephone and tape recorder. This was ambrosia to television detective fans, and also kept production costs low by keeping the series "on location" and eliminating the building of expensive sets. At a time when the average network half-hour filmed on a three-day schedule, *Shannon* was getting three programs in the can per six-day week; so short was production time that co-star Regis Toomey obligingly kept his hat on during his scenes to save the few minutes it would have taken to powder his bald head. Making up for the series' thriftiness was director Fred Jackman, who during his years as cinematographer for Columbia's B westerns and two-reelers had learned how to make something from nothing. Jackman's fast-moving direction helped keep *Shannon* in the top-ratings ranks, even making it to Number One Syndie of 1963 in the powerful Detroit market.

Skippy, the Bush Kangaroo (1968–69). Brought over from Australia by United Artists, *Skippy* scored with the two ingredients proven surefire by Ivan Tors' series *Flipper* and *Gentle Ben:* exotic animals and freckle-faced kids. The animal was the titular Skippy, and the kids were the children of a ranger (Ed Devereaux) for Australia's Watarah National Park. Beautifully photographed in color and nationally sponsored by old syndie reliable Kellogg's Cereals, *Skippy* hippity-hopped through 91 innocuous episodes. Reruns were still being seen in 1987 over the CBN cable service and in a French-language version shown on Canadian TV.

Tallahassee 7000 (1961). More from Florida; Screen Gems' January '61 release *Tallahassee 7000* was noteworthy only in that its detective hero was played by Walter Matthau, taking a 26-week respite from his "scowling villain" period.

The Third Man (1960–61). Co-produced in Britain by Pinewood Studios and in Hollywood by 20th Century–Fox, *The Third Man* was distantly related to the 1949 film of the same name. The villain of this Graham Greene creation was the charming but utterly reprehensible Harry Lime (Orson Welles), who came to a well-deserved end after selling diluted penicillin to Viennese children's hospitals. As was customary, Orson Welles stole the picture, and was awarded with a *Third Man* radio series, taped in Britain. Here, the black-market-medicine angle was allowed to lapse, and Harry Lime became a mildly larcenous soldier-of-fortune whose essential decency always got in the way. By the time Harry Lime was being prepared for his TV debut in 1958, all criminal tendencies had vanished, and what remained was an international businessman dedicated to battling injustice. All that was left of the original

Third Man was Anton Karas' Oscar-winning (and oftimes irritating) zither-music score. James Mason was supposed to have been television's Harry Lime, but walked out in a huff when details of certain clauses in his contract were made public by a London tabloid. He was replaced by Michael Rennie, who like James Mason had a catnip effect on the vital 18- to 49-year-old female viewership. Distribution rights for *Third Man* were divided between ITC, which handled the series' debut on British television in 1959, and NTA, which oversaw American syndication starting in 1960.

The original *Third Man* movie was released in subtly different versions to American and British audiences; likewise, the TV series was very much a dual-market job, with European actress Mai Zetterling guesting on the first British episode, while Suzanne Pleshette was guest-star on the American premiere. Most performers on the series utilized the "mid–Atlantic accent" preferred on British-American coproductions so that the dialogue would be decipherable to both markets; no one was more adept at this accent than Michael Rennie's co-star, Brooklyn native Jonathan Harris, who'd use the same vocal affectation even more effectively as resident badguy on CBS' *Lost in Space*. The producers' decision to convert Harry Lime from sociopathic snake to semi-saint turned out to be a sound one. *Third Man* was a hit all over the world, its 76 installments capturing top ratings in all 146 of its first-run American markets. Enriched by the series was Budweiser Beer, who sponsored *Third Man* in all U.S. cities except New York, which was Rheingold country.

Whiplash (1961). Best described by everyone who's ever tried to describe it as an "Australian Western," ITC's *Whiplash* starred American actor Peter Graves as Chris Cobb, owner-operator of a stagecoach service during Australia's 19th-century Gold Rush days. The plotlines seldom strayed far from accepted American cowboy formula, but the out-of-ordinary location-filmed backdrops of *Whiplash* kept its 38 episodes in lucrative U.S. syndication throughout the 1961–62 season.

World of Giants (1960). Lensed in England, William Alland Productions' *World of Giants* was a well-made if prosaic saga of a secret agent (Marshall Thompson) who'd been "miniaturized" to help him solve unsolvable mysteries. Actually, the title was something of a misnomer, since it was the star and not the rest of the "world" that was of unusual size, but *World of Giants* was at least a better title than its original *The Little Man*. Thirteen episodes were filmed and firmly set for CBS' network schedule in 1958, then less firmly set for 1959. On both occasions, CBS decided that there wasn't room for another science-fiction affair on the network (CBS had *Invisible Man* in '58, *Twilight Zone* in '59), so the existing *Giants* episodes were syndicated courtesy of United Artists Television.

Zero One (1964). Hollywood's MGM Studios bankrolled half the production costs of a half-hour BBC adventure series, 1962's *Zero One,* in hopes of a future American network sale. No network evinced interest, so MGM sent the property into the syndie pool, which didn't seem like much of a gamble in

1964 since *Zero One* had done very well on Canadian network television. The series depicted the exploits of an investigator (Dennis Patrick) hired by various airlines to prevent skullduggery aboard their jet flights. Each week's adventure was bolstered by a guest star drawn from the British-luminary ranks of Margaret Rutherford and George Coulouris. But *Zero One* was stymied in America by the fact that an airline-based action series by its very nature dealt with hijackings, crashes and bombs-on-board. In weekly doses, such plot devices tended to scare off potential sponsors, not simply the airlines themselves, but American food and utility companies with fat airline contracts. (This problem was averted in Canada by having the series sponsored by General Motors; what better advertising for an auto concern than a series which implied that air travel might not be terribly safe?) Add to the sponsor dilemma the fact that most American stations liked to play safe with proven syndie properties like the onetime network series *The Rifleman* and *Leave It to Beaver* — the two biggest local-market moneymakers of 1964 — and you have in a nutshell, or a cockpit, the story of *Zero One's* American demise.

Children's

The 1960's were the decade of the animated cartoon, which was usually more cartoon than animated. With Hanna-Barbera leading the parade, the television-cartoon racket grew to gargantuan dimensions — and these dimensions became "Godzillan" when the Japanese got into the act. Puppet shows, considered a dead form after the cancellations of *Kukla, Fran and Ollie* and *Howdy Doody,* were given a shot in the arm by British producers Gerry and Sylvia Anderson. And the "Uncle" and "Captain" hosts, holdovers from the previous decade, hung around until PBS' *Sesame Street* changed the face of children's television in 1969.

Abbott and Costello (1966). It was true then, it's true today; whenever cartoon producers run out of ideas for new characters, they turn to pre-tested "live" performers. Hanna-Barbera's 156 five-minute *Abbott and Costello* cartoons were painful to behold, but they did give work to the heavily-in-debt Bud Abbott, who provided the voice for his animated likeness. Stan Irwin impersonated the long-dead Lou Costello.

The Amazing 3 (1967). Released in Japan by Mushi Productions as *Wonder Three,* this was one of several Japanese-made series re-edited and re-dubbed for American consumption in the '60s (see notes on *Astro Boy*). The "three" were outer-space aliens who'd been sent to Earth to determine whether or not this "warlike" planet should be destroyed to preserve universal peace. To avoid detection, the alien trio disguised themselves as animals — a horse, a dog, and a duck — and made their true purpose known only to young Earthling Kenny Carter.

Animatoons (1967) and ***Mel-o-toons*** (1960). Both of these cartoon series would better have been titled "Illustrated Radio-Toons." *Animatoons,* narrated by Nancy Berg, were five-minute groups of static poses designed to tell such classic fairytales, fables, and stories as "Cinderella," "Pinocchio," and "Treasure Island." *Mel-o-toons,* released by United Artists, predated the rock-video craze of the '80s with cartooned illustrations of those old children's records (the yellow ones, with red labels) which told famous stories or played favorite tunes.

Astro Boy (1963). Mushi Productions, a Japanese animation firm founded in 1961 by comic-strip artist Osamu Tezuka, began its television career with a cartoon version of Tezuka's most popular character. *Tetsuwan-Atom* ("The Mighty Atom") was a pint-sized android who, under the tutelage of the kindly Dr. Ochanomizu, was launched into a crime-fighting career. The excellence of *Tetsuwan-Atom's* Japanese TV ratings inspired NBC Films to bring the property to the United States, where it was "Americanized" by redubbing the soundtracks and renaming the protagonists. Dr. Ochanomizu was now called "Dr. Elefun," in honor of his prominent proboscis, while Tetsuwan-Atom's American name was "Astro Boy." What the 153 *Astro Boys* lacked in animation (movement was frequently suggested by quick cutting from pose to pose, even "dissolving" between still pictures), they made up for in speed and clever plotlines. *Astro Boy's* goldmine take in the United States prompted other distributors to seek out saleable commodities in the land of the Rising Sun.

Batfink (1967). Witless and practically animationless cartoon spoof of the *Batman* television series, which was itself a spoof. Actor and old-time-radio historian Frank Buxton gave voice to the lead character of this Hal Seegar/Screen Gems effort.

Beetle Bailey see ***King Features Trilogy***

Big World of Little Adam (1964). This Banner Films release (often misnamed "Little Atom" in television history books) consisted of animated propaganda on behalf of the U.S. Air Force.

Billy Bang Bang (1962). Somebody's idea of humor, MGM's *Billy Bang Bang* offered five-minute mutilations of old silent Bob Custer westerns, "improved" with squeaky small-boy narration.

Birthday House (1966). This award-winning morningtime daily, emceed by Paul *(Mr. I. Magination)* Tripp, began its run locally on WNBC–New York in 1963. By the time the series was released for national syndication, *Birthday House* had been cancelled by WNBC to make way for less costly *Bachelor Father* reruns.

Captain Fathom see ***Clutch Cargo***

Captain Scarlet and the Mysterons (1968). ITC released this series in America after its fabulously successful prime time career in England. *Captain Scarlet* was the latest product of Century 21, a firm run by Gerry and Sylvia

Anderson. Their specialty was "Supermarionation," a moving-puppet process combining electrical impulses with the traditional strings. *Captain Scarlet* embraced the Andersons' two favorite plot devices: setting the action in the 21st century and pitting the heroes against a well-organized contingent of extraterrestrial bad guys. In this case, the villains were "The Mysterons," Martians intent on invading Earth in their UFO's. In fact, the Andersons' first live-action series *UFO* (1970) was a loose remake of *Captain Scarlet.*

Chatter's World (1960). Saul Turrell's Sterling Films had the nerve to perpetrate another cute chimpanzee with a dubbed-in human voice on the world — and to convince stations to buy the show.

The Chuckleheads (1962). One of many silent-comedy excerpt packages aimed at the kiddie trade, *Chuckleheads* was drawn from the Weiss Brothers' backlog of mediocre silent two-reelers starring Ben Turpin, Snub Pollard, Jimmy Aubrey and the ever-popular Poodles Hanneford.

Clutch Cargo (and other Cambria productions) (1960–65). Cambria's *Clutch Cargo* was the ultimate "limited animation" series of the 1960's — in fact, it offered virtually no animation at all! *Clutch* creator Clark Haas called Cambria's process "motorized movement." If a character had to walk across the screen, a cardboard cutout of the character would be jogged by hand past the background. If a windmill or propellor was called for, we'd see a genuine miniature moving windmill or propellor. And if a character blew bubble gum or smoked — you guessed it. The upshot of this was that *Clutch Cargo* had to rely heavily on dialogue to keep things moving, and the Cambria people even had a gimmick for that. Synchro-Vox, a process first developed in the '50s for "talking animal" commercials, was used whenever a *Clutch Cargo* character had to speak. The voice actor would be filmed in close-up, a mask obscuring all but the actor's lips; this film would then be grafted onto a drawing of the cartoon character, creating the illusion that the drawing possessed human lip movements! (The makeup required to match the skin color of the voice-actors with the cartoon characters made it seem as though everyone on the series was wearing lipstick.) A slick trick, Synchro-Vox was the only truly memorable aspect of the otherwise leaden *Clutch Cargo.* Cambria's 1961 *Space Angel* took the company's corner-cutting to the limit; the hero's face was covered by a space helmet, and thus required *no* lip movements. A later Cambria cartoon series, *Captain Fathom* (1965), was shot in something called "Superanivision." Super it wasn't, but at least the characters *moved* now and then.

Comedy Capers see The Mischief Makers

Courageous Cat (1960). Sam Singer-Telefeatures' *Courageous Cat* coasted on a single gimmick: the hero, a cowled-and-caped superfeline, had a pistol for every occasion, such as an "umbrella gun," a "parachute gun" and a "bullet-proof-vest gun." Hilarious, right? This animated syndie's career was revivified after 1966 thanks to the popularity of television's *Batman.* And as fate would have it, the creator of *Courageous Cat* was writer/artist Bob Kane . . . who'd created *Batman* back in 1939.

Cyborg Big "X" (1965). A human's brain in a robot's body. That's pretty much the whole story on this Japanese import, released in the United States by Transglobal. Created by Osamu *(Astro Boy)* Tezuka for the comics pages under the title *Big X*.

A Day with Doodles (1965). The 1960's offered a brisk traffic in short comedy fillers, featuring everything from comedians *(The World of Dayton Allen)* to gagged-up newsreels *(This Funny World);* and though most of these were allegedly adult-oriented, they often found homes on children's programs. One of the most widely distributed fillers, NTA's *A Day with Doodles,* was also the saddest. Doodles Weaver, once the star of his own NBC variety series, plodded through these ill-timed slapstick vignettes in what seemed to be an alcoholic daze.

Deputy Dawg (1960). *Deputy Dawg* was Terrytoons/CBS Films' foray into the cartoon syndie territory staked out by Hanna-Barbera. (Terrytoons had been one of the first major animation firms to sell its theatrical backlog, including *Mighty Mouse* and *Heckle and Jeckle,* to network television.) The Deputy, a bucolic southerner whose Crazy Guggenheim-type voice was provided by Dayton Allen, wasn't a whole lot better animated than the general TV-cartoon standard, but the cartoons moved quickly and scripts were just a bit funnier than usual. The half-hour *Deputy Dawg* was a lucrative addition to many a local station's 6–7 p.m. lineup, frequently seen in direct competition with the Hanna-Barbera stuff. The last of the *Deputy Dawgs,* completed in 1963, were directed by a young Ralph Bakshi, light-years removed from his X-rated animated features *Fritz the Cat* and *Heavy Traffic.*

Dick Tracy (1961). United Productions of America's 130 five-minute *Dick Tracy* cartoons were as formula-bound as a kabuki dance. Every one of the cartoons began with Tracy getting his orders from his chief, then relaying those orders to one of his comic assistants (typical TV-animation characters all, with names like "Heap O'Calorie" and "Joe Jitsu"). Halfway through the five minutes, all action would screech to a halt as the assistants would report their progress to Tracy, whose absence during most of the proceedings was a better "joke" than the scriptwriters ever came up with. This ritualization wore out its welcome quickly with older viewers, but was a big hit with the kids, who evidently liked nothing better than *Tracy's* repetition and predictability. The one vestige remaining from Chester Gould's original *Dick Tracy* comic strip was the grotesque lineup of villains, including such classic Gould creations as Flat-Top, Pruneface, B-B Eyes and Mumbles. Sadly, these colorful reprobates were robbed of their uniqueness by UPA's decision to make their voices "accessible" to 1960's viewers: B-B Eyes sounded like Edward G. Robinson, for example, while Flat-Top sounded like Peter Lorre. Even so, it was the voice-work of talent like Mel Blanc, Paul Frees, Benny Rubin, Howard Morris and Everett Sloane (who played Tracy) that gave these cartoons what little verve they had.

Diver Dan (1961). Almost surrealistically bad, *Diver Dan* was a series of five-minute color shorts featuring live actors playing Diver Dan and Minerva the Mermaid, and a group of marionettes (with such gut-busting names as "Baron Barracuda" and "Finley Haddock") as their fishy friends and enemies. One would have to search far and wide for any other series that would have its leading lady kidnapped by a fish puppet one-eighth her size. *Diver Dan* was produced in, of all places, Philadelphia.

Dodo, the Kid from Outer Space (1965). At a time when Japanese cartoons imitated the plots and characters of other countries' animated series, Halas & Batchelor/Embassy's *Dodo* boldly bucked the trend. It was a British imitation of the Japanese product.

The Eighth Man (1965). A bionic-crimefighter series from Japan's TCJ Productions, *The Eighth Man* (released in the United States by ABC Films) was based on a popular comic strip by Jiro Kuwata and Kazumaza Hirsi, titled simply *8 Man*.

Felix the Cat (1960). Trans-Lux, a company who'd once been in the theatre-chain business, contracted with Pat Sullivan's representatives for television rights to Sullivan's *Felix the Cat,* a highly regarded animated character of the silent era. The resulting 260 cartoons were produced on a skin-tight budget by New York's Joe Oriolo studios. While many viewers disputed the series' theme-song promise that "You'll laugh so hard, your sides will ache/ Your heart will go pitter-pat," *Felix* had the advantage of newness and color, and remained in demand for years; some markets renewed the property as far ahead as 1970!

Foo Foo and *Snip Snap* (1961). The initials H and B may have stood for Hanna-Barbera so far as American cartoon fans were concerned, but in England they stood for the husband-wife animation firm of Halas and Batchelor (best known in this country for their cartoon-feature version of George Orwell's *Animal Farm*). Two Halas-Batchelor products made their way to the U.S. via Interstate Television in 1961. *Foo Foo* was an animated cartoon, done in the modernistic style of the U.P.A. Studios, about a transparent man in a pencil-sketch world, while *Snip Snap* was stop-motion model animation, featuring a dog made out of paper and a pair of scissors. Neither series was Disney calibre, but *Foo Foo* was the better of the two, only because the stories told on *Snip Snap* were absolutely impossible to follow.

The Funny Company (1963). Mattel Toys' *Funny Company* compensated for its poor animation and cliched cartoon characters ("Super Chief," "Terry Dactyl" and so forth) with some truly worthwhile live-action educational filmclips, dispensed by "The Weisenheimer," a giant computer.

The Funny Manns (1960). After several seasons' association with NBC's *Howdy Doody,* producers Nick Nicholson and Roger Muir signed with California National Producions to produce 130 10-minute installments of *Funny Manns*. Consummate comic actor Cliff Norton lent his wealth of characterizations to his appearances as various branches of the "Mann" family:

Police Mann, Milk Mann, Sailor Mann, etc. (he stopped before he got to Thomas Mann). Norton's vignettes were filmed in clusters at a Greenwich Connecticut studio, with Nick Nicholson playing Norton's stooge. Each episode began with a few sight gags, after which Cliff Norton would explain that he'd learned all about his station in life from one of his various "uncles"; Norton would then narrate some silent footage of one of those "uncles" in action, who turned out to be the two-reel clowns featured in the vast library of silent-comedy material owned by CNP's parent company NBC. Laden with appalling one-liners and atrocious puns, Norton's narration was very basic stuff; still, *Funny Manns* caught on, and wound up as CNP's biggest moneymaker of 1961. And we all know what effect *that* had on the copycat world of TV syndication.

Gigantor (1965). *Gigantor,* a cartoon robot designed for war but reprogrammed into an agent for peace, was originally called *Tetsujin 28g0* ("Iron Man No. 28") after the Mitsuteru Yokoyama comic strip upon which it was based. This TCJ Production was brought to America by Trans-Lux.

Gumby (1966). Stop-motion-model animator Art Clokey's lovable little eraser-boy first appeared as an NBC Saturday morning show in 1957, spun off from a regular feature on *The Howdy Doody Show.* Gumby's movements were made possible through a process called Pixillation (see notes on *Davey and Goliath* in the upcoming section on religious shows in the 1960's); "pixillated" could also describe Clokey's sense of humor, which was laden with visual puns, instant miniaturization of the characters, whimsical ignorance of the laws of gravity, and speed — speed — speed! Joining Gumby and his horse Pokey in their new adventures, shot in color for syndication in 1966, were such characters as a dinosaur named Prickle and a dog named "Nopey" (so called because the only word he could say was "No!"); if anything, the gags on the new cartoons were wilder, and the sense of humor more esoteric, than in 1957. *Gumby* returned with a set of parents and a group of antagonists called "The Blockheads" in a series of half-hour adventures in 1988, beyond the scope of this text but worth noting as one of the best-produced (and one of the farthest off the wall) daily cartoon strips of its time.

The Hanna-Barbera Cartoons (Lippy the Lion, Touche Turtle, Wally Gator) (1962). Hoping to take home a larger profits slice, Hanna-Barbera released its first syndie package without the national sponsorship of Kellogg's cereals in 1962. *The Hanna-Barbera Cartoons* were sold directly to local stations, who'd then come up with sponsors of their own. The package was made up of 156 color cartoon shorts, with three new animated stars in 52 cartoons apiece. Creativity was hardly a consideration: the "new" stars were cut from Hanna-Barbera's old cloth. *Wally Gator* was Yogi Bear in a city zoo instead of a national park; *Touche Turtle* was an amphibian version of El Kabong, a Zorro parody introduced on H-B's *Quick Draw McGraw;* and while *Lippy the Lion* had no predecessor, Lippy's sidekick, Hardy-Har-Har the nonlaughing hyena, was already familiar to fans of Hanna-Barbera's *Snooper and Blabber* cartoons.

Joe 90 (1969). The last "Supermarionation" project of Gerry and Sylvia Anderson's Century 21, this young-boy-in-space adventure ran to excellent response in England in 1968 before being distributed Stateside by ITC.

Johnny Cypher in the Dimension Zero (1967). Still another outer-space cartoon, 7 Arts' *Johnny Cypher* was put together with the Xeroxed-animation process popularized by *The Marvel Super Heroes* (which see).

Johnny Sokko and His Flying Robot (1968). A rare live-action half-hour from Japan's Mushi Studios, *Johnny Sokko* was a futuristic adventure with Mitsundbu Kaneko in the title role. The series' bad-robot-turned-good premise was borrowed from Mushi's 1965 cartoon *Gigantor*.

Judo Boy (1969). Mushi martial-arts cartoon series.

Kimba the White Lion (1966). Created for the funny papers by Osumu *(Astro Boy)* Tezuka, *Jungle Tatei* ("Jungle Emperor"), the story of a little white lion, was rendered into animation by Mushi in 1965, and had the distinction of being Japanese television's first color series. NBC Films snatched up the property for the states, changed the names of the characters to such All-American monickers as "Dan'l Baboon" and "Pauley Cracker the Parrot," and thus *Kimba the White Lion* was born.

The King Features Trilogy (Beetle Bailey, Krazy Kat, Snuffy Smith) (1963). Following the success of their made-for-TV *Popeye* cartoons (which see), King Features Television dug into their newspaper-syndicate files for more old comicstrip properties that might "fly" as animated stars. King Features producer Al Brodax then commissioned the same companies that had worked on *Popeye,* including Paramount/Famous Studios, to grind out 150 color cartoons divided equally among KF's newest stars: Beetle Bailey, Krazy Kat and Snuffy Smith. Not as bad as they might have been under the assembly-line circumstances (*Beetle Bailey* even had a theme song by Paramount's Oscar-winning tunesmiths Jay Livingston and Ray Evans), the new cartoons still suffered from predictable gags and repetitive plots. Paramount Pictures was given first crack at distribution, releasing the cartoons to theatres in 1962, a year before their television issue. (Compared to the great cartoons of old, these new shorts looked like kindergarten finger-paintings when projected on the Big Screen.) When King Features syndicated the shorts to television, they were anxious that they not be thrown in minus fanfare as filler for the nation's various "Cartoon Carnivals." To that end, the cartoons were sent out as part of a franchised package, utilizing a "corner drugstore" setting wherein local kiddie hosts would be garbed as soda jerks and would give the new cartoons the "showcase" treatment they supposedly deserved. Nowadays, *The King Features Trilogy* is given the treatment it *really* warrants; it's tossed in to take up space on early-morning cartoonfests.

Krazy Kat see above

Laurel and Hardy (1966). Three operations were involved in bringing the 156 *Laurel and Hardy* cartoons into being: Larry Harmon Productions, David Wolper Productions, and Hanna-Barbera. A plague on all their houses. Once again, a great live-action property was shrunken to cookie-cutter standards. Even the fairly good Laurel and Hardy voice impersonations by Larry Harmon and Jim MacGeorge were small help. The only bright point of this dim property was that a good portion of the cartoons' profits went to Stan Laurel's widow.

Lippy the Lion see The Hanna-Barbera Cartoons

Little Joe (1967). Did anyone *ever* see this Spangler release about the cartoon adventures of a bee?

Mack and Myer for Hire (1963). Few remember *Mack and Myer for Hire,* Trans-Lux's entry into the live-action-comedy market engendered by *Funny Manns,* but in 1963 this series of 15-minute skits was hailed by the trade press (and its own publicity) as the long-overdue return of "classic" slapstick comedy. Veteran burlesquers Mickey Deems and Joey Faye were Mack (cleaned up from "Muck" before the series' release) and Myer, two monumentally inept workmen who laid waste to job after job. Mickey Deems doubled as director for the 200 New York-filmed shorts; producer Sandy Howard aspired to recreate the Mack Sennett days with an arsenal of comedy props ("2000 sight gags! 1078 falls! 296 pies!" boasted the ads) and an army of supporting clowns. Appearing as minor characters were double-talk master Al Kelly, Sid "Tell Ya What I'm Gonna Do" Stone, and Kenny "Senator Claghorn" Delmar. Playing to neat financial returns, *Mack and Myer* deserved at least an E for Effort, and might be worth rewatching today.

Magilla Gorilla (1964). Released in January of 1964, Hanna-Barbera's *Magilla Gorilla* half-hour went out with the national sponsorship of Ideal Toys. Ideal was then cleaning up with toys and games based on Hanna-Barbera characters like Yogi Bear and Pebbles Flintstone. (Pebbles had in fact been "born" to promote a new line of dolls and building blocks.) *Magilla* was chockfull of such round-edged characters as Mushmouse, Punkin Puss, Ricochet Rabbit and Droopalong Coyote, all suitable for transformation into dolls and bubble-soap bottles. This series was one of the first syndicated cartoon properties created expressly to sell toys, a practice that would grow into a science by the 1980's (see also *Peter Potamus*).

Marine Boy (1966). The future of television animation was determined — or foredoomed — when the inevitable happened and American producers began shipping their Hollywood-born scripts to Japanese studios for low-cost animation work. All this started in 1966 when 7 Arts contracted with H. Fujita Studios for a campy super-guy saga, *Marine Boy,* which turned out to be 7 Arts' biggest worldwide grosser of the year.

The Marvel Super Heroes (1966). The *Batman* craze of 1966 was a boon to producer Steve Krantz, who a year earlier had negotiated with Marvel Comics for the right to produce a series of television cartoons based on Marvel "stars" Captain America, The Hulk, Iron Man, Sub-Mariner and The Mighty Thor. Krantz engaged the Grantray-Lawrence company to write the scripts and commission the animation. Grantray-Lawrence tried to justify their use of a limited-animation technique that even outlimited Hanna-Barbera by explaining that, since the fans of Marvel Comics had always used their imaginations to "fill in" the movements of the comics' characters, why not encourage the TV viewers to use their imaginations as well? No one mentioned the economic reasons behind this artistic corner-cutting, but the public needn't be burdened with the facts. Saving *The Marvel Super Heroes* from total mediocrity was the fact that the character artwork was done not by Grantray-Lawrence's hirelings, but by Marvel's own staff of comic artists. This was accomplished through a copying process called Xerography, which transferred Marvel's drawings to the animation cels. While said animation was tacky at best, *The Marvel Super Heroes* contained some of the best-rendered and detailed character design ever seen on any TV cartoon series. Best of the batch were the *Mighty Thor* cartoons, filmed by Paramount/Famous Studios under the guidance of animation veteran Shamus Culhane. Despite the severe artistic limits of Xerography, Culhane's efforts far outclassed anything else in the TV-animation field of the time. *Super Heroes* was an instant hit, running in prime time in several markets. But the down-side of this popularity was that it led other producers to employ the Xerography process, glutting the market with cheap copy-machine cartoonery.

Mel-o-toons see *Animatoons*

The Mighty Hercules (1962). Trans-Lux's *Mighty Hercules* wasn't as big a seller as the company's *Felix the Cat,* and in a way this was understandable: Felix was after all an old family friend to most viewers, but who outside Steve Reeves' fans knew Hercules? The *Batman* mania of 1966 somewhat improved *Hercules'* syndie career.

Mighty Mr. Titan (1965). This Trans-Lux cartoon release about a super-robot was seen briefly, then utterly forgotten.

The Mischief Makers (and other National Telepix triumphs) (1961–62). If ever an award is given for wholesale butchery, it should go to National Telepix. The company's first release, *The Mischief Makers,* consisted of 13-minute cutdowns of Hal Roach's *Our Gang* silent films, with a few of Roach's *Dippy Doo-Dads* (two-reelers starring monkeys) and the Stern Bros.' *Buster Brown* shorts thrown in. National Telepix's next project was *Comedy Capers,* a package of abridged silent comedies featuring such people as Laurel and Hardy, Ben Turpin, Charlie Chase and Billy Bevan. By rights, these films should have induced as much loud laughter as they had thirty years earlier, but National Telepix's policy was to slice and dice the shorts until continuity and coherence were all but obliterated. The company even removed the dialogue subtitles, so that most of the shorts made no sense whatsoever. Little kids didn't seem to care about the hashed-up plots as long as the sight gags were left in, so both *Mischief Makers* and *Comedy Capers* made enough money to permit National Telepix to perpetrate another crime against humanity. *Wally Western* (1962) recut old Ken Maynard, Tex Ritter and Hoot Gibson westerns into ersatz cliffhangers. This stuff was then overladen with funny commentary—"funny" only if one's taste was in one's mouth.

Mister Magoo (1960). United Productions of America, whose *Gerald McBoing Boing* and *Mister Magoo* cartoons of the 1950's were Oscar-winning material, responded to the shrinking theatrical-cartoon market by going whole-hog into television. After a run of *Gerald McBoing Boing* on CBS, UPA entered syndication with *Mr. Magoo*. The company signed a distribution deal with Kellogg's Cereals, with Kellogg's assuming that it would have the final word on program content. But in an eleventh-hour decision, UPA decided that it would brook no sponsorial interference, and abruptly withdrew from its arrangement with Kellogg's; the cartoon company managed to sell *Magoo* on its own to 150 markets. Stuck for a 1960–61 first-run cartoon release, Kellogg's commissioned Hanna-Barbera to come up with a quickie *Magoo* replacement—and that's how *Yogi Bear* was born.

Filmed using the assembly-line methods that UPA had disdained in its theatrical work, the 130 five-minute *Magoos* were occasionally amusing, with good voice work from Jim Backus as Magoo and Richard Crenna as a hamster named Hamlet. But UPA quickly drove *Magoo* into the ground with repetition and cliche, stretching the single joke of Mr. Magoo's nearsightedness well past its comic value. As cartoon historian Leonard Maltin once observed, it was virtually impossible for anyone unfamiliar with UPA's theatrical product to believe that Mr. Magoo was once a genuinely hilarious character. Remember, however, that *Mr. Magoo* was *new!* and *in color!!* The cartoons sold like the proverbial hotcakes in 1960, with some stations scheduling the shorts in prime time. It was popular enough to enable UPA to sell its next project, *Dick Tracy,* without even making a pilot film.

Mister Piper (1962). A curious attempt by ITC to make headway in the American market with a British kiddie series. Alan Crofoot played Mr. Piper.

The New Adventures of Pinocchio (1961). Canada's Video Crafts, an animation firm run by Arthur Rankin Jr. and Jules Bass, entered the kiddie-syndie scene in concert with the Canadian Crawley Films and the American Storer Stations group. This contingent figured it had the "built-in-appeal" angle of the business licked by bringing to television two beloved children's favorites, Carlo Collodi's *Pinocchio* and L. Frank Baum's *Wizard of Oz. New Adventures of Pinocchio,* available as either 130 five-minute shorts or 26 half-hours, was filmed in "Animagic," an animated-puppet process. The only problem was that the series was filmed in such a hurry that the animation was invariably off in its timing, with characters jerking and floating instead of moving smoothly. None of the 19th century Italian milieu of Collodi's original was retained; instead, Pinocchio's adventures were "modernized" by having the puppet hero run up against beatniks, avaricious movie producers, and even the Loch Ness monster. *Pinocchio* did good business throughout Canada and the States, though an attempted spinoff series, *Willy Nilly,* came to naught (see also *Tales of the Wizard of Oz).*

The New Adventures of Popeye see *Popeye the Sailor*

The New Three Stooges (1965). This Cambria/Heritage cartoon outing consisted of 156 five-minute shorts, with voices provided by the then-current members of the venerable comedy team: Moe Howard, Larry Fine and "Curly" Joe DeRita. In addition to their voiceovers, the Three Stooges appeared in the liver-spotted flesh in 40 live-action color vignettes used as "wraparounds" for the cartoons. These were directed by old Stooge crony Edward Bernds, with featured appearances by two supporting actors from the team's two-reeler days, Emil Sitka and Harold Brauer; also appearing was Margaret Brown, actress wife of Cambria production head Dick Brown. While the live-action scenes were passable, the cartoons were putrid enough to make one thankful that plans to animate the adventures of other "real people" like Jack E. Leonard and The Marx Brothers never came to fruition.

The Nutty Squirrels (1960). "The Nutty Squirrels" was the name of a recording group which lifted the sped-up style of "Alvin and the Chipmunks" for use in a novelty record, the lyrics of which consisted primarily of the phrase "Uh-oh!" The Squirrels may have ripped off the Chipmunks, but they beat Alvin and company to television by a full year with a series of five-minute *Nutty Squirrels* cartoons, which boasted an attractive modernistic design and little else. Transfilm/Wilde produced; Flamingo Films released.

Out of the Inkwell (1962). Videohouse's *Out of the Inkwell* was a stab at reviving Max Fleischer's 1920's cartoon character Koko the Clown. Producer Hal Seegar enlisted animation directors Shamus Culhane and Myron Waldman, the vocal skills of Larry Storch as Koko, and for the pilot episode, Max Fleischer himself. Despite the input, the results were in the "less said the better" category.

Peter Potamus (1964). Hanna-Barbera/Ideal Toys' September 1964 cartoon release, *Peter Potamus,* premiered over the same 151 markets carrying the same combination's earlier *Magilla Gorilla.* As with *Magilla, Peter Potamus's* "stars" (the title character, Breezly Bear and Sneezly Seal, and "The Three Goofy Guards") were developed for the chief purpose of providing Ideal with a new line of Hanna-Barbera toys. Both *Magilla Gorilla* and *Peter Potamus* resurfaced on the ABC network's weekend-morning schedule in 1966.

Pinocchio see *The New Adventures of Pinocchio*

Planet Patrol (1964). Wonderama's British-filmed *Planet Patrol,* a second-string imitation of Gerry and Sylvia Anderson's Supermarionation releases, was picked up by M&A Alexander for an undistinguished American run.

Popeye the Sailor (1960). The principal motivating factor behind King Features' made-for-TV *Popeye* cartoons was supposed to have been the "fact" that children were beginning to tire of watching the old Paramount *Popeyes* produced between 1933 and 1957. (Did anyone ever *ask* these kids?) That was part of the story. Also contributing to the creation of the new *Popeyes* was the fact that, while King Features controlled the character rights to the spinach-munching sailor, the company had had to share the TV profits with Associated Artists Productions, who'd licensed the old cartoons to television. The fate (and most of the profits) of the 210 new *Popeye* shorts would be in the hands of King Features and King Features alone. With no studio of its own, K.F. developed its cartoon storyboards in its offices, then farmed out the animation work to several different shops: Paramount/Famous Studios, Larry Harmon Productions, Total TV Productions (then busy with NBC's *King Leonardo*), the Czechoslovakia-based studios of Gene Deitch, and Britain's Halas and Batchelor. The lion's share of the new cartoons were made at the independent facilities of Jack Kinney, who'd once directed the exploits of Goofy for Walt Disney. To say that the results were inconsistent would be giving them a break. The best-animated *Popeyes,* those filmed by Gene Deitch, had the weakest gags, while many of the funnier scripts were rendered by Jack Kinney, whose studio ground out *Popeyes* of unrivalled sloppiness and ineptitude. The only constant factors of all these cartoons were the basic character design and the always-delightful voice-work of Jack Mercer (Popeye), Mae Questel (Olive Oyl) and Jackson Beck (Brutus and Everyone Else). But there's little point in tearing these cartoons down; they fulfilled a demand in 1960–62, and were lucrative enough to be coveted for a time by both the NBC and CBS networks. And thanks to the fact that the new *Popeyes* were all in color (many of the theatrical shorts were made in black and white), 90 percent of the stations that had bought the television cartoons in 1960 were renewing their contracts in 1965. The *Popeyes* made money, reasoned King Features, so why should they be made better?

Prince Planet (1966). At a time when color was the principal selling angle for cartoon syndies, the Japanese producers of *Prince Planet* improvidently filmed their property in black and white. American International was the unlucky U.S. distributor.

Q.T. Hush (1960). Q.T. Hush was a private eye whose shadow had a mind of its own in this animated quickie released by M&A Alexander.

Rocket Robin Hood (1967). The title told all in this second collaboration between producer Steve Krantz and animator Shamus Culhane (see

Marvel Super Heroes). After this series, Paramount Pictures withdrew its financial backing from Culhane, leaving Krantz to thereafter seek out cartoon directors with less skill and ambition.

Rod Rocket (1963). Serialized outer-space cartoons; worth noting because one of the producers was Lou Scheimer, who with Norman Prescott would later create Filmation Studios, one of the foremost instigators of science-fiction/fantasy TV cartoons of the '70s and '80s.

Roger Ramjet (1965). CBS Films' limited-animation *Roger Ramjet* won points as a blue-ribbon satire of the whole kiddie-adventure genre. Ramjet was a musclebound hero whose "proton pills" gave him the strength of 20 atom bombs for 20 seconds. His principal antagonists were a rival good-guy who sounded like Burt Lancaster and a bunch of villains who acted like Lennie in *Of Mice and Men*. Garry Owens' voice work did full justice to the hilarious scripts.

Sinbad Junior (1965). American International cartoon release about a young seafarer who travelled in the company of a wisecracking parrot.

Skyers Five (1967). United Artists' *Skyers Five* was still more Xerography, that triumph of technology over talent.

Snip Snap see *Foo Foo*

Snuffy Smith see *The King Features Trilogy*

The Soupy Sales Show (1965; 1979). Soupy Sales, the eternal "local host" with regional programs in Cincinnati and Detroit to his credit, flirted off and on with the ABC network from 1955 through '61, but didn't make his national reputation until he moved to Los Angeles. There, his berserk mixture of pie-throwing, abysmal puns and "inside jokes" made Soupy the court jester of showbiz hipsters, even allowing him to deliver on-camera pies to the celebrated countenances of Frank Sinatra and Burt Lancaster. Soupy went East in 1964 to launch a daily show on WNEW–New York, and as usual drew swift attention to himself. First, he introduced a silly dance called "the Mouse," then endured a celebrated suspension from WNEW after inviting the kiddie viewers to pick their daddies' pockets and mail in those little green pieces of paper, on the promise that Soupy would send them a postcard from Venezuela. This oft-told story is true, more than can be said for an urban legend concerning a dirty joke supposedly told on the air by Sales, the punch-line of which was "Every time *I* see 'F,' *you* see 'K'!"

Cashing in on Soupy's notoriety, Screen Gems syndicated 260 taped half-hour *Soupy Sales Shows* from WNEW in 1965. After a lengthy distribution, all 260 shows suddenly disappeared from the face of the earth! The story goes that WNEW bulk-erased the tapes for future use. Whatever the reason, Soupy was back in 1979 with a daily color series taped at KCOP–Los Angeles for

Golden West Television, wherein he deliberately repeated his "best" routines (and revived his old puppet supporting cast of White Fang, Black Tooth, Pookie and Hippy) so that he'd have a little something to leave for Posterity.

Space Angel see Clutch Cargo

Space Giants (1969). Mushi Films' second live-action adventure series (see *Johnny Sokko*) was a save-the-world caper, with the usual heroic robots battling evil prefabricated prehistoric monsters from the planet Rodak. We're not making any of this up.

Speed Racer (1967). H. Fujita Studios' follow-up to *Marine Boy* (1966), *Speed Racer* was a 52-episode cartoon series with scripts written in Hollywood and animation turned out in Japan. Speed Racer not only drove his "Special Formula Mark Five" racing car, but he drove other American producers into the arms of Japanese animators. A Trans-Lux release, *Speed Racer* was arguably the best cartoon of its kind, if there was such a thing.

Spunky and Tadpole (1960). This boy-and-his-bear cartoon yarn, from Beverly Hills Productions and Telemet, had the advantageous contribution of voice-actor Don Messick, but in animation style and story substance *Spunky and Tadpole* looked like an ice cream commercial.

Stingray (1965). Gerry and Sylvia Anderson's first color Supermarionation project, *Stingray* took place not in the Andersons' beloved Outer Space but in the Inner Space beneath the ocean's surface. The time-frame was still the 21st century, however, and the puppet-heroes were still a bunch of crime-fighters, this time known as the World Aquanaut Security Council. ITC's American distribution of *Stingray* was benefitted by a new consortium of television stations, the Development Program Associates. D.P.A. was created to increase the market for first-run color syndies by lining up choice timeslots. The 22 D.P.A. members secured evening-hour bookings for *Stingray* (some in prime time), broadening the audience of what otherwise might have been just another gapfiller for the daytime moppet-TV ghetto.

Supercar (1962). The first Supermarionation effort from the Andersons' Century 21, *Supercar* ran through the auspices of Associated Television during British-TV prime time in 1961. The title referred to the name of a 21st-century crimefighting concern headed by bushy-eyebrowed marionette Mike Mercury, and also to Mercury's main mode of transportation: a souped-up vehicle that could travel by land, sea or air. When ITC first brought *Supercar* to America in early 1962, many stations followed Britain's lead by running the 39 episodes in the evening hours, since not much else existed in the first-run syndicated-adventure line at the time. Most of *Supercar's* later markets aired the program during standard weekend and afternoon children's slots, with such regional sponsors as Colorforms Inc. and Marx Toys. The ratings and earnings of *Supercar* cemented Gerry and Sylvia Anderson's reputation in the States, though on a technical level this earliest example of Supermarionation wasn't that far advanced from the Howdy Doody era; the black strings used to manipulate the puppets were all too obvious, and the fixed grins on the characters' faces rather undermined the "danger" they were supposed to be experiencing at every turn.

Tales of the Wizard of Oz (1961). Video Crafts' companion piece to its *New Adventures of Pinocchio* (1961) was limited animation at its most primitive, with the character designs far more interesting than the characters themselves. Although producers Arthur Rankin Jr. and Jules Bass purportedly had all the characters in L. Frank Baum's *Oz* stories at their disposal, they used only those that had lapsed into "public domain" — which happened to be the characters immortalized in MGM's 1939 *Wizard of Oz* feature film. Apparently to avoid any possible legal tangles, Rankin and Bass took great pains not to pattern the cartoon characters' personalities after Judy Garland, Ray Bolger, Jack Haley, Bert Lahr et al; the animated Tin Man's heartlessness, for example, was manifested in his volatile temper. Ironically, the cartoon Wizard of Oz was given a W.C. Fields-type voice; one wonders if Rankin and Bass knew that Fields had been MGM's first choice to play the movie "Wizard." Updated with devices like quiz programs and guided missiles, the 1961 *Oz* cartoons were soon more out-dated than Baum's books ever would be, but were popular enough to spawn an animated one-hour special produced by Rankin and Bass for the NBC network in 1965. This program established the two Canadian producers in the "seasonal special" racket; since that time, Rankin and Bass have come up with such perennial holiday favorites as *The Little Drummer Boy, Frosty the Snowman* and *Rudolph the Red-Nosed Reindeer.*

This Funny World see *A Day with Doodles*

Thunderbirds (1967); **Thunderbirds 2086** (1985). A worldwide favorite long before its American television debut, Century 21/ITC's *Thunderbirds* was the costliest Supermarionation production to date. It was the saga of yet another futuristic crimefighting team, this time devoted to stopping major crimes *before* they happened, and was made available as either 32 hour episodes or 64 half-hour cliffhangers. Benefitting *Thunderbirds'* American career was the series' resemblance to CBS's live-action espionager *Mission: Impossible,* even though *Thunderbirds* premiered on British televison a full year before *Mission* made its television bow. The characters and situations on *Thunderbirds* were revived by Gerry Anderson in 1984 for an animated series, *Thunderbirds 2086,* which ran first on cable TV in America before entering commercial syndication in 1985.

Tintin (1963). This small-boy comic-strip hero created by Dutch artist "Herge" was popular and beloved the world over — except, apparently, in the United States, where attempts made by NTA to syndicate the animated version of *Tintin* (with the requisite "Americanized" character names) led to a riot of silence.

Touche Turtle see ***The Hanna-Barbera Cartoons***

Ultraman **(1966).** United Artists Japanese import; this live-action outer space melange was created and coproduced by Eiji Tsuburaya, the special-effects master who unleashed Godzilla on a tinker-toy Tokyo in the 1956 film classic.

Wally Gator see ***The Hanna-Barbera Cartoons***

Wally Western see ***The Mischief Makers***

Wizard of Oz see ***Tales of the Wizard of Oz***

World of Dayton Allen see ***A Day with Doodles***

Yogi Bear **(1961–62).** When the pullout of UPA's *Mr. Magoo* left Kellogg's Cereals without a January 1961 syndie release, Kellogg's persuaded Hanna-Barbera (then producing two cartoon series for the breakfast-food concern) to come up with a hasty substitute. Just *how* hasty was evidenced by the fact that not one of the "stars" of H-B's *Yogi Bear* was a new creation—all of them had been test-marketed on the company's earlier series. Yogi Bear had of course been a headliner on *Huckleberry Hound* (his replacement on that series was Hokey Wolf, one of Hanna-Barbera's many Phil Silvers derivations) while Yakky Doodle the baby duck and Snagglepuss the Shakespearean lion had been supporting players on both *Huckleberry* and *Quick Draw McGraw.* As early as 1961, Hanna and Barbera were living up to the motto "Nothing succeeds like Past Success."

Comedy

Outside of the above-mentioned children's shows of a humorous nature (not to mention other programs which were unintentionally funny), the 1960's syndication field produced only three bona fide comedy half-hours.

Fractured Flickers **(1963).** Produced by Jay *(Bullwinkle)* Ward and released by Desilu, *Fractured Flickers* took the bewhiskered device of hoking up old movies with new, comically sarcastic dialogue, but managed to freshen up that old gimmick to pay off in a load of genuine laughs and a bundle of sales—including an important sale to the five ABC-owned outlets. It was the prevailing industry theory in 1963 that Jay Ward's promotional stunts were funnier than his series themselves; Ward's prerelease hoopla for *Flickers* included an expensive "First Coney Island Film Festival," staged at the amusement park in August of '63 with a full cadre of tuxedoed "presenters" and pneumatic bathing beauties. All of the awards were won by *Fractured Flickers* (collusion, perhaps?), in categories like "Best Film Made Without a Camera," "Most Serious Comedy," and "Best Foreign Film Made with an All-Male Cast, Except for Six Leading Ladies and Other Women." Ward himself copped the prize for "Nicest, Most Talented Producer."

Hosted by Hans Conried (then the voice of Snidely Whiplash in Ward's *Dudley Do-Right* cartoons), *Fractured Flickers* was 26 weeks of potted silent and early-talkie pictures, offering such highlights as Marlene Dietrich cracking elephant jokes, cowboy star William S. Hart as a used-horse dealer, and Lon Chaney Sr.'s Hunchback of Notre Dame reborn as a college cheerleader majoring in rope-climbing. (This last "revision" sparked a lawsuit from Lon Chaney Jr.) It can't be denied that the series' humor was, to quote *Variety,* "a big favorite with audiences whose taste [ran] to hotfoots, itching powders, dribble glasses and baby pictures with captions." Well, watch *Fractured Flickers* in rerun sometime on one of the cable services and you'll realize that there's a little of the dribble-glass freak in all of us.

Hot Off the Wire see *The Jim Backus Show*

The Jim Backus Show (1960). This CNP release, originally titled *Press Time,* was shown in many markets under the title *Hot Off the Wire.* Jim Backus starred as Mike O'Toole, the fast-lipped head of a fifth-rate, ever-in-debt newspaper wire service. The 39-week series went the route of such past newspaper pictures as *The Front Page* by building its comedy (laughtrack and all) on ultra-melodramatic storylines: two of the best episodes concerned a mad bomber and a gang of vicious juvenile delinquents. But when the writers' attempts at heavy drama lapsed, as they often did, into banality (there was even the old bromide about the reclusive millionaire who willed her fortune to her cat), *The Jim Backus Show* could count on the ebullience of its star to deflect attention from the dusty plotlines. Backus' rapid-fire delivery of salty dialogue and boundless energy kept things going at a hectic, hilarious clip, with the star showing not a trace of fatigue when he added to his burden by embarking on a back-breaking national tour to promote his series. Indeed, so much time was taken up by this tour that one *Jim Backus* episode contrived to have Mike O'Toole locked in a rolltop desk so that Backus could pre-record his dialogue and be free for extra personal appearances. As if this workload wasn't enough, Jim Backus was busy at the same time with his voiceovers for the syndicated *Mr. Magoo.* Local station managers had to be very careful not to schedule *The Jim Backus Show* opposite *Magoo* lest Backus end up competing with himself — which is precisely what happened in 1965 when NBC's *Famous Adventures of Mr. Magoo* went head-to-head with CBS's *Gilligan's Island.*

Mister Ed (1961). Although best remembered for its astonishing five-season run on CBS (1961–66), *Mister Ed* spent the first 39 weeks of its life in syndication. Director Arthur Lubin, who'd spent several years directing the adventures of Francis the Talking Mule for the movies, had since 1954 been trying to peddle a series starring a gabby horse; along the way, he managed to get financial support from comedian George Burns and *Burns and Allen Show* producer Al Simon. But he couldn't get funnyman Alan Young, then a major television variety star, interested in playing the horse's human straight man — nor could he get any of the three networks to give his series concept the tiniest bit of consideration. The first *Ed* pilot, filmed in 1957 with Scott McKay playing opposite the horse, was met with further disdain and difference. Things began to jell in 1960; Alan Young, after several years' inactivity as a TV "draw," signed on to play Mister Ed's owner Wilbur Post. Al Simon filmed a second pilot for Filmways Productions. But still the networks weren't buying. That might have been the end of *Mister Ed* had it not been for the arrival of a force even stronger than a 1960 network — a national sponsor. The automaking firm of Studebaker-Lark liked *Mister Ed* (even though its equestrian star represented a rival form of transportation) and agreed to sponsor the series in nationwide syndication, providing that the top 25 markets run *Ed* in the best-rated syndie time slots. Slowly but surely, *Mister Ed* built its audience after its January '61 debut. Helping the series was a "mystique" angle; Filmways coyly refused to reveal the name of the actor who dubbed in Mister Ed's voice, even though clues managed to "leak out" to the trade papers daily. After a while, it was common knowledge that Ed's voice emanated from the larynx of western star Allan "Rocky" Lane (though he never received billing), but the guessing-game kept viewers who'd otherwise have galloped away from a talking-animal comedy tuning in out of curiosity. Once it was established as a crowd-pleaser, *Mister Ed* suddenly became most attractive to CBS, a network that previously had been one of the loudest and most vehement in turning down the series; CBS picked up the show, and the rest was television sitcom history. Incidentally, it's easy when watching *Mister Ed* reruns to spot the episodes that had initially run in syndication; they're the ones that play Jay Livingston and Ray Evans' horse-is-a-horse-of-course theme music *without* the lyrics.

Drama

Straightforward dramatic series were scarce in '60s syndication. The format was engulfed in the decade's early years by the networks (who'd played out the anthology form by mid-decade and thereafter concentrated on specials), and by 1969, drama was almost solely the province of public television.

The Age of Kings (1961); **Spread of the Eagle** (1963). Spurred on by the unexpected success they'd experienced by underwriting 1959–60's *Play of the Week,* Standard Oil provided financial support to a 15-part BBC product, *The Age of Kings.* Released in America in January 1961 by Metropolitan Broadcasting, *Kings* covered, in chronological form, Shakespeare's "histories": *Richard II, Henry IV, Henry V, Henry VI* and *Richard III,* presented in weekly installments of 60 or 90 minutes. The British actors who appeared were uniformly excellent but light on "star names," though astute viewers might have spotted potential in a young Sean Connery, who played

Hotspur in the first *Henry* plays. To clarify points of British history obscure to American viewers, Standard Oil hired Shakespeare specialist Dr. Frank Baxter to introduce the segments. *Age of Kings* picked up a Peabody award in 1962, the same year its spiritual predecessor, *Play of the Week,* was feted at the Monte Carlo Television Festival. By this time, both series were seen almost exclusively on public TV, as was BBC's *Spread of the Eagle,* which serialized Shakespeare's "Roman" works: *Coriolanus, Antony and Cleopatra,* and *Julius Caesar.*

Best of the Post (1960). This anthology of stories that first appeared in *The Saturday Evening Post* had been in the works on the MGM lot since 1957, undergoing a number of production-personnel changes, settling finally on Jack Wrather Productions and ITC distribution. Filming was held up for a while when the Powers-That-Were decided that *Best of the Post* was a lousy series title, a problem solved when the *Saturday Evening Post* said that if the title went, so would the magazine's cooperation. The *Post's* large-scale promotional blitz enabled ITC to tote up several strong sales before the anthology's premiere in the fall of 1960. After filming four of the first 13 dramas in color, Wrather Productions decided to "go color" for the remaining 13, a smart move that guaranteed *Best of the Post* a sturdy rerun career. The 30-minute dramas were forced by a limited budget to avoid massive action scenes, even in stories set in the Old West, but this reliance in human drama over violence endeared the series to television stations wishing to counter-program against such blood-letters as *The Untouchables,* the better to curry favor with the increasingly militant FCC. The attractively produced *Best of the Post* gave full head to such scene-stealers as Alan Mobray, Charles Coburn, Peter Lorre, Everett Sloane and Buddy Ebsen, and spelled an entertaining *finis* to the Hollywood-filmed syndie-anthology form.

The Human Jungle (1964). This British series, filmed in 1963, starred Herbert Lom, a year away from his descent into movie "insanity" as Dreyfus in the Inspector Clouseau films, as cool-calm-collected psychiatrist Roger Corder. (Lom was then lean and handsome enough to make *Human Jungle* a hit with Britain's female viewers.) Corder's specialty was high-profile patients who couldn't cope with their high-pressure lifestyles. Most English critics applauded *Human Jungle's* production expertise, though many felt that it was too simplistic in its solutions for delicate mental and emotional crises. United Artists Television, sensing an upcoming American trend in psych-series thanks to NBC's *The Eleventh Hour* and ABC's *The Breaking Point,* picked up 26 *Human Jungle* 60-minute episodes and managed to make 18 U.S. sales. But by the time *Jungle* made its American premiere in 1964, both *Eleventh Hour* and *Breaking Point* had been cancelled. End of the trend that never was, and virtually the end of any American life for *The Human Jungle.*

On Stage (1962). Canada's bid for television-anthology prestige was first seen in the states on the RKO-General stations, then syndicated by RKO's own Worldcorporation. *On Stage* was a bit more adventuresome than such predecessors as *Play of the Week* in that it offered new, untested plays with mostly unknown acting talent.

The Robert Herridge Theatre (1960). Widely hailed as the best new series of 1960, CBS Films' *Robert Herridge Theatre* might have done better had it undergone a title change; few viewers outside the urban wine-and-cheese crowd knew that Robert Herridge was the innovative producer behind such CBS series as *Camera Three* and *The Seven Lively Arts*. The best of the Manhattan-filmed *Herridge Theatres* was its Christmas release, "Girl on the Road," starring Salome Jens in Louis Adamic's tale of a lonely hitchhiker.

Scarlet Hill (1965). A mid–1960's boost in daytime-TV profits led syndicators on the hunt for daylight-hour material. Even syndie serials were given a brief whirl, the first of these being Canada's *Scarlet Hill,* a genteel variation of *Peyton Place* set in a New York boarding house and starring Beth Lockerbie and Lucy Warner. *Scarlet Hill* enjoyed a short period of outrating its New York City competition, but the novelty soon tarnished and viewers returned to their American soaps and game shows.

Spread of the Eagle see The Age of Kings

Strange Paradise (1969). Another Canada-taped serial was tried out for U.S. syndication in 1969, this one distributed by Metromedia to capitalize on the success of ABC's supernatural soaper *Dark Shadows*. But where *Dark Shadows* dealt with spooks and vampires, Metromedia's *Strange Paradise* concerned itself with voodoo. Colin Fox was double-cast as the modern-day resident of a mysterious Caribbean island and the spirit of the hero's ancestor, whose demonic influence pervaded the goings-on in the serial's 195 episodes. Quite a few of the new UHF stations that had sprouted up in the 1960's were obsessed with the belief that *Strange Paradise* would be the profit-grabber that *Highway Patrol* had been ten years earlier; many of these channels followed the lead of a VHF independent in Minneapolis which scheduled *Paradise* in nightly prime time. But the euphoria was short-lived. *Strange Paradise* was played out in such a funky manner that viewers weren't sure if the series was on the level or whether it was designed as a derisive "camp" of *Dark Shadows*. A Philadelphia station was first to drop the series from its nighttime schedule, after only two weeks; outlets in New York and Los Angeles rapidly followed suit. Some of these defectors rescheduled *Paradise* during daytime, but many others dropped the series entirely. In desperation, *Strange Paradise's* producers brought in former *Dark Shadows* producer Robert Costello to revamp (or maybe revampire) the series. The effort was wasted. By the summer of 1970, the only station still running *Strange Paradise* in prime time was a San Francisco UHF-er that didn't sign on until late in the afternoon anyway. Thanks to *Paradise's* dismal showing, the syndie serial market would have to wait for 1976's *Mary Hartman, Mary Hartman* before being taken seriously again. A voodoo curse, perhaps?

Game/Quiz

Although they'd been around since the first flicker of TV's cathode light in the 1940's, game shows were pretty much network affairs and largely ignored by syndication. But by 1965, prime time quiz shows were on their way out, and daytime quizzers were giving way to less costly, more profitable sitcom reruns. Those game shows still on the air had ceased their live telecasts long before, and were economically videotaping a week's worth of programs in single sessions, thus cutting down studio rentals. This taping policy would in time be adopted by syndication, providing local channels with 2½ weekly hours of "strip" entertainment at a fraction of the normal cost, a savings passed on to the buying stations. This financial consideration, together with the growing need for color material, turned the game show form into syndication's "late bloomer."

The Anniversary Game (1969). In 1968, the ABC network encouraged (a better word than "pressured") its five owned-and-operated stations to develop series for potential syndication. WXYZ–Detroit's contribution was *The Anniversary Game,* which ran daily on the ABC o-and-o's and weekly as a national syndie starting in January 1969. The host was Al Hamel, one of those ever-grinning wisecrackers who've always populated the game show industry. The game in this case involved married couples' competing with other married couples for the ususal "fabulous prizes."

Beat the Clock (1969–74). Mark Goodson and Bill Todman, whose syndie career began with the 1968 revival of their recently cancelled networker *What's My Line?,* spent most of their later career exhuming their old network properties for local distribution. *Beat the Clock,* a daily that required its contestants to finish silly stunts within set time-limits, had been seen on both CBS and ABC from 1950 through 1962. Replacing the late Bud Collyer as host for the syndicated *Clock* was Jack Narz for the first season, Gene Wood for the rest of the run. The one cosmetic format change from *Beat the Clock's* network days was the addition of celebrity contestants for the syndie edition. To lower an already lowered budget, *Beat the Clock* was taped in Montreal, Quebec, where studio and labor costs were minimal compared to Hollywood and New York; 20th Century–Fox Television handled distribution.

Beat the Odds (1969). *Beat the Odds* did nothing of the kind; like many another first-run game show syndie, it couldn't "beat the odds" against a series without a strong network history (like *Beat the Clock*) surviving past 13 weeks. For the record, *Beat the Odds* was emceed by Johnny Gilbert, and was something of a predecessor to *Wheel of Fortune* with its spinning-wheel and fill-in-the-blank wordbuilding.

Everything's Relative (1965). Hosted by actor Jim Hutton (father of current star Timothy Hutton), NBC Films' *Everything's Relative* was founded on the premise of having family members determine just how one member would answer a given question. That member would then participate in "zany" on-camera stunts.

Fast Draw (1969). Johnny Gilbert bounced back from the failure of *Beat the Odds* to host the equally unsuccessful *Fast Draw*. This 7 Arts release, a precursor to 1987's *Win Lose or Draw,* required that celebrities and "civilians" figure out clues given in hastily drawn sketches. Fast, but no draw.

The Game Game (1969). Producer Chuck Barris, whose 1960's reputation rested on his two ABC-network projects *The Dating Game* and *The Newlywed Game,* launched his syndie career with CBS Films' *Game Game.* Not as "gamy" as Barris' later extravaganzas, this daily was hosted for its single season by Jim McKrell, and its contest questions were of a psychological bent. A team of professional head-doctors would determine the answers that a typical group might give to a question. It was then up to the contestants and a team of celebrities to match those answers. Simple?

He Said—She Said (1969). Goodson-Todman's only failure in the '60s syndie field (in terms of longevity, that is) was its one release without a network background. G-T had intended this husband-wife quizzer to bow on NBC as *It Had to Be You,* but the network balked and the series ended up in syndication as *He Said—She Said.* Hosted by Joe Garagiola, *He Said* was a "barter" program, sent out virtually free to stations by Holiday Inns Inc. and American Home Products in exchange for *gratis* ad time. In 1969, Barter was one of several syndication routes; by the next decade, Barter became the cheapest, most expedient means of syndie survival.

The Liars' Club (1969; 1975–76). Ralph Andrews Productions/Metromedia's *Liars' Club* first appeared with Rod Serling as host in 1969; this briefie exists today only as a packet of written transcripts in the University of Wisconsin's Serling collection. Metromedia brought *Liars' Club* back with Bill Armstrong hosting in 1975; the show did better this time, perhaps because it had a better class of liars. Actress Betty White was "permanent panelist" on the '70s version, the object of which was for the contestants to decide which celebrity panelist was telling the truth in describing the purpose of an odd-looking item. Producer Andrews described Betty White as a "Godsend" for her ability to weave the most outrageous fabrications with a sweet, straight face. *Liars' Club* ended up a family affair in 1976 when Bill Armstrong was replaced by Betty White's husband, Allen Ludden.

Matches 'n' Mates (1967). Nicholson-Muir, the production team who'd assembled *The Newlywed Game* for Chuck Barris, was responsible for *Matches 'n' Mates,* syndicated by Taft Communications and 20th Century–Fox TV. On this daily excursion, host Art James required competing married couples to match questions with answers. The gimmick was that both question and answer were unknown quantities, identified only by labels like "Question A" and "Answer B." Typical match-ups included "It's considered bad manners to eat.... Your neighbors." A real knee-slapper.

The Movie Game (1969–71). One of the few syndie game shows that enjoyed long-range success without a previous life as a network series, *Movie Game* was produced by Henry Jaffe and Bob Silver, and hosted by Sonny Fox and then by Larry Blyden. The daily series capitalized on the then-burgeoning movie-trivia craze; celebrity panelists would play on behalf of non-celebs from the studio audiences (and write-in contestants from the home viewership). The luminaries on *Movie Game* were not the standard selection of game show regulars, but honest-to-goodness STARS like Bob Hope, Bing Crosby, James Stewart, Robert Culp, Joan Collins, Burgess Meredith and Rowan and Martin, most of them appearing for the pittance of $150 per episode simply because they themselves were fans of *The Movie Game* and had *asked* to appear. Viewers were surprised at how little veterans like Hope or Crosby knew about the history of the industry that had sustained them, while comparative youngsters like Don Adams and Mel Torme proved to be veritable IBM machines of trivia. The most fun was in watching the Friday installment of *Movie Game,* which was taped just after dinner break, during which time many of the star panelists had quaffed a few. It was then that incorrigible adlibbers like Dick Martin and George Carlin got away with quips and double-entendres that never would have passed the network censors, and that stars like Joan Collins would admit to walking around their homes buff-naked, "and not just for the titillation." Colgate-Palmolive offered *Movie Game* on a barter basis.

Oh, My Word (1966). On this obscure weekly from 7 Arts, Jim Lange hosted as celebrities tried to provide definitions for odd words.

Pay Cards (1968). Nicholson-Muir/Taft (with added funding by the Kaiser Stations Group) replaced their *Matches 'n' Mates* with the daily *Pay Cards,* a show best described as a dressed-up television poker game. Hopes for the series were high but *Pay Cards* folded within a year.

P.D.Q. (1965–70). Four-Star's *P.D.Q.* was hosted by Dennis James, who'd been in television since 1938(!). Despite the standard "law" that syndies without prior network track records were doomed to short lives, *P.D.Q.* lasted four seasons, thanks partially to support from the NBC-owned stations and the contingent of local channels known as Development Program Associates (see the notes on the '60s children's series *Stingray*). *P.D.Q.* was predicated on the contestant's swift identification of words revealed letter-by-letter on a gameboard, a format later adopted by NBC's *Baffle.* Three contestants were pulled from that gypsy tribe known as "celebrities," and this was what got *P.D.Q.* into trouble with the FCC. As expected, these celebrities liked to give out with funny adlibs, and since not every star was a Nipsey Russell who supplied his own material, most of the "adlibs" were prepared before showtime by professional gag writers. The jokes had little if anything to do with playing *P.D.Q.'s* game itself, but they did constitute "pre-show coaching" — a practice forbidden by the FCC ever since the game show cheating scandals of 1958. Thus it is that game shows featuring quip-happy celebrities are required to carry a disclaimer, flashed onscreen at the end of the program, that some of the contestant's responses were prepared in advance. There's no law governing just how *long* that disclaimer must be displayed, however, and if one sneezes, one usually misses it.

Perfect Match (1967). No relation to *Matches 'n' Mates,* Screen Gems' *Perfect Match* was a seminal version of the '80s syndie *Love Connection.* Hosted by Dick Enberg, *Perfect Match* brought couples together with the then-new process of Computer Dating. While *Match* wound up being seen in only nine markets, it was low-budget enough to pay its way.

Queen for a Day (1969). Not every resurrected network show was a syndie hit. *Queen for a Day* had been a long-running network wallow in human misery, with a woman becoming "Queen" on the basis of how many hard knocks she'd taken in life. Metromedia's daily *Queen* revival, hosted by Dick Curtis, was less smarmy than in its Jack Bailey-hosted network days. It was also far less successful, indicating that perhaps there was still a market for smarm in 1969.

Stump the Stars (1969). *Stump the Stars* was merely the new title given Mike Stokey's old summer-replacement favorite (and syndication pioneer) *Pantomime Quiz.* Official Television's attempt at a daily version of this ancient wheeze came a-cropper, despite guest-lists including such "now people" as Deanne Lund and Roger C. Carmel (who must, one supposes, nowadays be called "then people").

To Tell the Truth (1969–77; 1980). Goodson-Todman's much-parodied quiz show, in which a celebrity panel had to figure out which of three contestants was actually the person all three claimed to be, ended its 12-year network run in 1968. One year later, a daily *To Tell the Truth* appeared, taped in marathon sessions at New York's Ed Sullivan Theatre (Goodson-Todman's headquarters for their syndie *What's My Line?*). The new *Truth* carried over its basic network format and most of its star panelists, including Bill Cullen, Kitty Carlisle, Peggy Cass and Orson Bean; Garry Moore filled the host's chair left vacant by the death of the series' longtime emcee Bud Collyer. *To Tell the Truth* was distributed by Firestone Sales, a company created by former Four-Star executive Len Firestone which evolved into one of the foremost traffickers in game shows for the next two decades. Viacom's 1980 version of *To Tell the Truth,* hosted by Robin Ward, came at a time when audiences were more satisfied with non-think gamefests like *Family Feud.* Peggy Cass was back as *Truth's* permanent panelist, Soupy Sales was "semi-permanent," and the audience was definitely temporary.

Truth or Consequences (1966–74; 1977; 1987). Invented in 1940 by Ralph Edwards as a parody of radio giveaway shows, *Truth or Consequences* built up such a following that it ended up more popular than the programs it was lampooning. *T or C* was based on the average person's willingness to behave like an ass before a national audience (if the contestant couldn't answer a simple question, that contestant was then required to indulge in a crazy stunt), and enjoyed such an enthusiastic response that a small New Mexico town was renamed "Truth or Consequences" in the show's honor. Television's *T or C* began in 1950, hosted first by Edwards, then by Jack Bailey, and finally by Bob Barker, who stayed with the series until its cancellation by NBC in 1965. (NBC replaced it with something called *Fractured Phrases*. Please note that there is no such town as Fractured Phrases, New Mexico.) Convinced that there was a dance or two left in the old property, Edwards talked David Wolper/Metromedia into reheating *T or C* for daily strip syndication, with the same host (Bob Barker) and same format as in its last network days. Premiering first on the Metromedia-owned stations in 1966, the attendant high ratings led to the series' national distribution. *Truth or Consequences* remained a top-rater in its time slots for the next six seasons. That's time *slots,* plural. The beauty of *T or C* was an audience appeal so broad that it could be telecast anytime of the day — from early morning to just after the late news — and still count on a loyal viewership. The series' low production costs and its command of all demographic groups helped spark the Great Game Show Rebirth of the 1960's.

By 1977, Chuck Barris had cornered the market on audience-participation shows wherein contestants behaved like jerks (i.e. *The Gong Show*); thus when Ralph Edwards and Viacom came up with a *New Truth or Consequences* hosted by Bob Hilton, the onetime industry leader was perceived as a mere camp-follower of the Barris brigade. Ten years later, Edwards-Billett Productions and Lorimar Telepictures hoped that the old magic would rub off on its latest *Truth or Consequences,* produced by onetime Barris associate Chris Bearde. The 1987 *T or C* was hosted by Larry Anderson, assisted by Murray Langston, who'd been *Gong Show's* "unknown comic." This new nightly version bore the heavy influence of the David Letterman style of smirky put-down humor. On the original *T or C,* Bob Barker always made us believe that he was pulling for the contestants no matter how ridiculously they were behaving. The new series' Larry Anderson did little to hide his contempt for the participants, suggesting that he'd rather be anywhere else than hosting a game show. After 13 weeks, Anderson got his "wish." *Truth or Consequences* was honored as the first syndie of the 1987–88 season to halt production and vanish from the airwaves.

What's My Line? (1968–74). *What's My Line* was the show wherein a celebrity panel tried to guess the occupations of the contestants, whose cash intake increased the longer the panel was stumped. At the end of each half-hour program, the panelists were blindfolded and attempted to determine the identity of the "mystery guest." This was the format for the longest-running prime time network game show in history; *What's My Line?* lasted on CBS from 1950 through 1967, and was the cornerstone of the Goodson-Todman game show empire. CBS dropped the series on the theory that *Line* was played out; Goodson-Todman felt otherwise, and after toying with the notion of reviving their onetime CBS property *I've Got a Secret,* used *What's My Line?* as their entree into the world of weekday syndication. This decision must have required some soul-searching, as the producers had gone on record in early '67 condemning videotape for robbing game programs of their spontaneity and allowing them to be tampered with by network censors. But with all their prime time networkers having been axed by 1968, Goodson-Todman had no choice but to switch on the tape machine for the syndie *What's My Line.* The series' producer Gil Fates worked up an agreement with CBS Films (later Viacom) in which CBS would distribute *Line* and assume half the production costs—said costs kept in check by adopting the five-shows-in-one-day taping procedure.

Because the new *What's My Line?* would have to appeal to as wide a demographic viewership as *Truth or Consequences* (flexibility is still the biggest selling angle for game-syndies), the evening-dress formality and intellectual appeal that had been the *Line's* network trademarks were dispensed with. Illustrative of this change was the replacing of *Line's* wit-in-residence Bennett Cerf with Soupy Sales, whose wit was frequently qualified with the prefix "nit." Of all the original series' panelists, only Arlene Francis remained a regular in syndication. Hoping to appeal to the 1968 crowd, *Line's* question-and-answer sessions were sped up, with a lightning-round session added in which several contestants appeared onstage at once. There was even a bit of "sex appeal" in the form of a "Girl Friday" named Jennifer Wood. CBS Films' promotional copy for *What's My Line?* stressed the participation of such "now people" panelists as Alan Alda, Meredith MacRae and Godfrey Cambridge. Apparently less dignified than such old-time *Line* regulars as John Daly and Dorothy Kilgallen, these new now people were required to participate when the contestants demonstrated their skill in their chosen professions. On the first syndie episode, the panel had to help a lady pretzel-bender. Imagine Dorothy Kilgallen bending pretzels.

Two inaccurate assumptions have haunted the syndicated *What's My Line* for years. One involves President Jimmy Carter, who while he was governor of Georgia appeared as a "mystery guest." It's been reported that Carter was so obscure at the time that the panel failed to identify him; but Gil Fates has noted in his behind-the-scenes book about the series that Gene Shalit correctly identified Mr. Carter—though it took two rounds of questions to do so. The other misapprehension is that *What's My Line?* was cancelled upon the death of its host, actor Larry Blyden (who'd taken over from *Line's* original syndie emcee, former weatherman Wally Bruner, in 1972). Actually, the final episode was taped in December of 1974, several months before Blyden's fatal auto accident. What killed *What's My Line?* was that, even though it remained popular, it hadn't lined up any new local-station sales by the spring of '75. So after 25 years, that was that.

Win with the Stars (1968). A Bing Crosby/Walter Schwimmer weekly hosted by Allen Ludden, and produced by Ludden's own Albet company. This guess-the-song affair was essentially *Name That Tune* with celebrities. Ludden was seen to better advantage in the color network reruns of *Password* then making the syndie rounds.

Informational

Most syndicated offerings in this category went straight to the expanding public TV market, but not all. With the elimination of the "Women's Show" tag, this informational field began to embrace many of the cooking and exercise shows. And if one wasn't careful, one might have gotten a little book-learning from a few of the commercial-TV educational endeavors.

Bonnie Prudden see *Exercise Shows*

The Carlton Fredericks Show (1967). The outspoken Mr. Fredericks, whose opinions on nutrition and health had prompted a few lawsuits in his time, had a high-toned weekly in 1967 from Triangle/ABC.

Consult Dr. Brothers see *Dr. Joyce Brothers*

Debbie Drake see *Exercise Shows*

Dr. Joyce Brothers: Consult Dr. Brothers (1961); **Tell Me Dr. Brothers** (1964). Psychologist Joyce Brothers, who came to fame after appearing as a boxing expert on the *$64,000 Question* (she later admitted she had no interest in boxing, but had boned up on the subject as a mental exercise), dispensed advice on marriage, children and coping on two '60 syndies. The first, *Consult Dr. Brothers,* was a 15-minute daily; the second, *Tell Me Dr. Brothers,* was also a daily, but ran 30 minutes and was taped in color. It was Dr. Brothers' practice to update and amend advice she'd given on earlier appearances; she certainly wouldn't want to go on record today saying (as she did in 1960) that one shouldn't worry about children who starve themselves to gain attention.

Doctor's House Call (1965). 200 five-minute fillers hosted by Dr. James Fox; taped at KSTP-Minneapolis/St. Paul.

Exercise Shows (1960–69). No longer were exercise shows mere daily rituals of bend-and-stretch; now they also gave tips on nutrition, recreation, and mental relaxation. Nor were they strictly the province of male hosts. Joining Ed Allen and Jack LaLanne in the jumping-jack sweepstakes were Bonnie Prudden, Gloria Roeder and Debbie Drake. Prudden, who was first seen on NBC's *Today Show* in the '50s, had a color daily subtitled "Better Health Through Better Living." Roeder's *Exercise with Gloria* (Triangle) began its daily color run in 1965, the same year Bonnie Prudden made her syndie bow.

And most popular was leotard-clad Debbie Drake, whose 15-minute daily debuted in Indianapolis in 1960, then was distributed by Banner Films. Drake returned in 1969 with a new color project, *Debbie Drake's Dancercize,* which anticipated the success of aerobic-dancing television series and videocassettes in the 1980's. Alas, by that decade Debbie Drake had dropped totally from public view, victim of a crushing series of personal setbacks and radical physical changes.

Exercise with Gloria see above

The Fair Adventure see *Shakespeare on TV* (1950's Informational series)

The Galloping Gourmet (1968–71).

Chasing all cooking-show competition out of the kitchen was Scotsman Graham Kerr, who after a television career in New Zealand moved to CJOH–Ottawa where, as "The Galloping Gourmet," he became the most popular pot-and-pan attraction of the '60s. Produced by Kerr's wife Treena, *The Galloping Gourmet* was so named because of the Kerrs' habit of traversing the globe in search of rare gourmet recipes, and also from Graham's tendency to race around his TV kitchen, flirting with the studio audience ladies while imbibing considerable quantities of cooking sherry and other potables. Kerr brought the otherwise highfalutin world of gourmet cookery down to earth by cracking jokes about his craft and making no effort to cover up kitchen booboos, but it was obvious from the resultant delectable dishes that Kerr knew his trade. The daily *Galloping Gourmet* bartered in the United States by the Young and Rubicam agency (representing American Can, American Cyanimid and Hunt and Wesson), proved so successful that Canadian television took to running the series in prime time. Production came to a sudden halt when Graham and Treena Kerr were involved in a serious auto accident in 1971. *Gourmet* reruns filled the air until 1974, at which time, and amidst tearful public confessions of impropriety and infidelity, the Kerrs found Jesus. Graham Kerr returned in 1975 with the daily five-minute *Take Kerr,* where he'd soberly (in every sense of the word) give cooking tips, then close with an inspirational Biblical passage. There was no doubt that Kerr was sincere. There was also no doubt—and no offense intended in the observation—that Kerr was far less fun to watch.

The Inquiring Mind see *University of Michigan Series*

It's Academic (1966).

Once CBS' scholarly quizzer *G.E. College Bowl* was established, several local markets trotted out the brainiest of their high schoolers for weekly television question-and-answer shows of their own. After a few seasons as a New York local, *It's Academic* (NBC Films) went national as a franchise, offering title and format to regional stations and local hosts.

James Beard (1963).

Another cook-show host, whose Screen Gems weekly made the rounds until Mr. Beard became a fixture of public TV.

Joyce Brothers see *Dr. Joyce Brothers*

Let's Talk About (1961). Hearst/Official's *Let's Talk About* was a series of 10-minute extraordinary explorations of ordinary things, not unlike NBC's later kid's series *Hot Dog.*

Science in Action (1963). After thriving locally in Los Angeles since 1949, *Science in Action,* hosted by Earl S. Herald, was distributed by NBC films in early 1963.

Step This Way (1966). Dance-lesson weekly, hosted by Gretchen Wyler and featuring guest terpsichoreans. Distributed by Triangle, with barter assistance from Colgate-Palmolive.

Tell Me Dr. Brothers see *Dr. Joyce Brothers*

University of Michigan Series (1964–66). Although Michigan had very little in the way of public, noncommercial television in the '60s, the University of Michigan did fairly well distributing several half-hour syndies to commercial outlets. The best of these were *The Inquiring Mind,* a science series hosted by John Arthur Hanson, and a brief series showing the activities of the Interlochen Camp for artistically gifted youngsters.

Yoga for Health (1962; 1968). Richard and Diane Hittelman, California-based advocates of the Lotus Position, hosted this daily from Ross-Danzig Productions; the Hittelmans taped a new batch in color towards the end of the decade.

Zoorama (1962). Emceed by Bob Dale, *Zoorama* (Trans-Lux) was a fascinating daily visit to the denizens of the San Diego Zoo. *Zoorama* would surface briefly on the CBS network in 1965, then return to syndication three years later.

Music/Variety

Videotape did wonders for the syndicated music-variety field. Where once the spontaneity and immediacy of musical performances had been mitigated by the flatness of black-and-white film, color videotape had a live urgency, making viewers feel that they were watching their favorites at the very moment of performance. Nowhere did videotape do more for proliferation of product than in the two musical styles with the biggest turn-over of hit tunes: Country-Western and Rock-and-Roll.

An Evening With... (1966). 26-week WGN/Continental series staged in a "lounge" setting. Spotlighted in this half-hour weekly were such names as

Dennis Day, Louis Prima, Phil Ford and Mimi Hines, Gretchen Wyler and Hildegarde.

The Barbara McNair Show (1969–70). While black entertainers made great strides in television of the '60s, it would be presumptuous to suggest that they'd truly conquered past obstacles. This was, after all, the decade in which Mississippi's public TV stations refused to air *Sesame Street* because it showed black and white children playing together, and in which Petula Clark received threatening letters for holding hands with Harry Belafonte on an ABC special. Those black performers who fared best were "established" personalities who'd made their television reputations on "mainstream" variety shows. One of the most successful on the syndie scene was Barbara McNair, who hosted two seasons' worth of a weekly variety hour. *The Barbara McNair Show* was the first hit for the Canada-based musical-show packaging firm of Winters-Rosen Productions.

Barn Dance see *Country-Western Shows*

The Big Bands (1965). 20th Century–Fox Television's *Big Bands* featured weekly half-hour helpings of the swinging sounds of Count Basie, Duke Ellington, Lionel Hampton, Woody Herman, Sammy Kaye, Guy Lombardo and others, including — by proxy — Glenn Miller and the Dorseys. *Big Bands'* biggest moment was December 31, 1966, when a New York independent channel ran four hours' worth of the series back-to-back to ring in the New Year.

The Bill Anderson Show see *Country-Western Shows*

The Bobby Lord Show see *Country-Western Shows*

Broadway Goes Latin (1962). Hit Broadway scores were reorchestrated and performed by top "ethnic" performers in this ITC weekly hosted by Edmondo Ros.

The Buck Owens Show see *Country-Western Shows*

Colorful World of Music (1964). Five-minute vignettes from the classics, depicted pantomimically by the Podrecca Puppet Theatre, which like many European acts got its big American break on *The Ed Sullivan Show*.

Country Carnival; Country Music Carousel; A Country Place see below

Country-Western Shows (1960–69). By 1966, Country-Western was in control of 25 percent of the broadcast-music market. Most weekly musical hoedowns were syndicated regionally by Nashville-based Show Biz Inc., with occasional releases from Screen Gems, Desilu and Official Films; Buck Owens was entrepreneur enough to distribute his *Buck Owens Show* through his own company. The chronicler of C-and-W is reduced to mere list maker, since to the *non*devotee of country music, it's hard to tell the many '60s television series apart. Occasionally, a maverick like Leroy Van Dyke would bridge the gap between country and mainstream (Van Dyke and his entourage even wore tuxedoes). Otherwise, the shows all tended to look and sound alike: *The Bill Anderson Show, The Bobby Lord Show* (followed by *The New Bobby Lord Show*), *Country Carnival, Country Music Carousel, A Country Place, The Ernest Tubb Show, Flatt and Scruggs, The Judy Lynn Show, The Kitty Wells/ Johnny Wright Family Show, Music City USA, The Stoneman Family, The Wilburn Brothers.* All toe-tappin' fun, but with little to distinguish one from another, except perhaps for regular appearances of stars-to-be like Loretta Lynn on *The Wilburn Bros.* and Loretta's sister Crystal Gayle on *A Country Place.* Longest-lasting of the personality-oriented C-W series was *The Porter Wagoner Show,* which started syndication in 1960 and was still at it over twenty years later; by that time, Wagoner's most famous protegee, Dolly Parton, had starred in a syndie of her own.

Not *all* of these series emanated from Nashville. Avco's Cincinnati-based *Midwestern Hayride,* a sometimes network drop-in, had built up so many color half-hours that by 1966 it was running in some cities as a daily strip. WGN–Chicago's *Barn Dance,* another old property, was likewise revved up for syndication in '66, hosted by WGN's agriculture expert Orion Samuelson. And Canada, with an enormous C-W following all its own, brought to U.S. syndication two of the CBC's longest-running favorites, *Don Messer's Jubilee* (1960) and *The Tommy Hunter Show* (1966).

Della (1969). To make certain that Worldcorporation's daily half-hour starring singer Della Reese wouldn't be lumped together with such talkfests as *The Virginia Graham Show,* its ad copy promised "no desk, no couch, no chairs — all performance!"

The Discophonic Scene (1966). The discotheque craze of the mid–1960's resulted in this weekly from the Tigris and Euphrates of Rock-n-Roll, Philadelphia. *Discophonic Scene,* distributed variously by Triangle and 7 Arts, was hosted by Jerry Blavat. A disc jockey known as "The Geator with the Heater," Blavat had attracted national attention by being the only white d.j. on an all-black Philly radio station, and by publicizing the fact that he supplemented his minimum-wage radio job with over $130,000-per-year's worth of personal appearances. A onetime assistant to Dick Clark, Blavat at first patterned his series after Clark's *American Bandstand,* then retooled the program in its second season to include segments on "vital teen issues."

Don Messer's Jubilee see *Country-Western Shows*

The Ernest Tubb Show see *Country-Western Shows*

Evening at the Palladium (and other ITC monthlies) (1961–65). The syndicated-special trend started in 1961, when ITC decided to release its

British-taped *Evening at the Palladium* on a monthly basis. ITC felt that, with the upsurge in theatrical movie sales to television, the company's more prestigious variety shows would better compete with the old movies if treated as infrequent "Special Events" rather than run-of-the-mill weeklies. Jo Stafford's monthly ITC specials, "theme" shows based upon the time of year, lasted until 1965. And ITC handled another packet of 12 British-made specials starring syndication's favorite son, Liberace.

An Evening with Liberace see above

Feliciano (1969). Jose Feliciano's variety weekly, distributed by the Spanish International Network, was performed entirely in Spanish, anticipating the bilingual UHF-TV market of the '70s and '80s.

Festival of the Performing Arts (1962). A grab-bag of musical and dramatic performances for the summer-viewing crowd, courtesy of producer David Susskind.

Flatt and Scruggs see Country-Western Shows

Great Music from Chicago (1962–66). Hour color weekly from WGN/Mid-America with the Chicago Symphony Orchestra.

Hawaii Calls (1966). A 25-year-old Mutual radio series produced at Waikiki and subsidized by Hawaii's tourism bureau, *Hawaii Calls* TV-debuted from the same location and with the same producer (Webley Edwards) as in its radio days. Distributed by Cardinal Films, the weekly was filmed in color, and would have been foolish not to be.

Here Come the Stars (1968–69). So many venerable performers showed up on Four-Star's *Here Come the Stars* that even middle-aged critics begged host-creator Georgie Jessel to offer fewer old favorites like Jack Benny and George Burns and more new young performers. Staged in the manner of a weekly testimonial (Jessel's specialty), *Here Come the Stars* was Georgie's most successful bid for TV exposure.

Hollywood A Go Go (1965). Practically every big city of the '60s had its own television disco show, with paisley-shirted kids frugin' and groovin' to the rhythm of rock records, illuminated by psychedelic colored lights. Hosted by future *Star Search* producer Sam Riddle, KHJ–Los Angeles' *Hollywood A Go Go* was given two seasons' national syndication by Four-Star. The series' live-talent roster outdistanced anything most other local dance shows could come up with; included were Little Richard, The Platters, Gary Lewis and the Playboys, The Serendipity Singers, Neil Sedaka and Tina Turner.

Hurdy Gurdy (1967). Even the barbershop and beer-hall tunes of the Gay '90s were given space in the '60s. *Hurdy Gurdy* started as a KABC–Los

Angeles special before its weekly career via ABC's Circle 7 productions. Regulars included Jack Benny's singing-commercial quartet, The Sportsmen.

Jazz Scene USA (1962). Oscar Brown Jr. hosted this weekly from Desilu. Meadowlane Enterprises, headed by comedian/jazz expert Steve Allen, handled the production end.

The Jerry Lester Show (1962). If former *Tonight Show* hosts Steve Allen and Jack Paar could have their own TV series in 1962, reasoned Canada's Arrowhead Productions, the time was ripe for a vehicle built around the talents of NBC's *first* late-night emcee, Jerry Lester. Like Lester's *Broadway Open House* (NBC 1950–51), the weekly *Jerry Lester Show* was a potpourri of Catskill-mountain comedy, brassy music and wacky audience-participation stunts. But Jerry Lester was definitely a child of his time—and that time was not A.D. 1962.

The Jo Stafford Show see Evening at the Palladium

The John Gary Show (1968). After a good summer's exposure as Danny Kaye's replacement on CBS, pop singer John Gary was awarded his own syndie in 1968, taped in Miami Beach. *The John Gary Show* was designed as a launching pad for a new non-network distribution concept: WGN–Continental and Scripps-Howard Broadcasting coproduced the series, leading industryites to speculate that other major station groups would go the "collaboration" route as a challenge to the networks. All speculation ended when Scripps-Howard pulled out, leaving WGN to finance the final 13 *John Garys* all by itself.

The Judy Lynn Show see Country-Western Shows

The Kitty Wells-Johnny Wright Family Show see Country-Western Shows

The Las Vegas Show (1967). Ohio-based self-made millionaire Daniel H. Overmyer plunged into show business by buying a UHF station in Toledo, which he named with becoming Ted Turner-like modesty WDHO-TV. The UHF market of the mid–60's, opened up after the 1964 FCC law requiring that all American-made television sets carry the UHF band as well as channels 2 through 13, was ripe for plucking by a shrewd operator like Overmyer; he erected four more UHF outlets in early 1965 to create the "Overmyer Network" (O.N.). "I'm against smut," Overmyer boldly declared for the benefit of those in favor of smut, and began carefully monitoring the programs on his five stations for offensive material. Soon he started developing his own programs, and this taste of production supervision led to the decision to expand the O.N. into a nationwide hook-up. Overmyer enticed potential UHF affiliates with promises of a 50–50 profits split—something the FCC had been trying to get the major networks to do with *their* affiliates for years. Now that he had the FCC on his side, Overmyer set about making his O.N. lineup more attractive than the already-available syndicated product. With lofty statements that syndication merely recycled "past mistakes," Overmyer vowed to knock the syndies off the map by encouraging his O.N. affiliates to create new "network" series of their own. The ABC network had to a lesser scale been buying the best its affiliates had to offer for years, so who better to guide the destinies of O.N. than former ABC president Oliver Treyz? The fact that Treyz had previously been involved in an abortive "fourth network" plan with ex–NBC president Pat Weaver was ignored by the Overmyer publicity machine.

The Overmyer Network's predebut affiliate lineup in the fall of 1966 was anywhere from 75 to 125 local channels, depending on which publicity release one believed. O.N.'s management assured the affiliates of 56 hours per week of original programming, with emphasis on in-depth news reports produced by United Press International, sports events, and such "wholesome" fare as a cartoon series based on the Bible and an Edgar Allan Poe anthology.

If you're wondering what all of this information is doing in the "Music/Variety" section, the answer is that the only series definitely locked into Overmyer's early 1967 schedule involved neither Poe nor the Prophets, but was instead a nightly two-hour variety show from Las Vegas—a curious locale for a network which was "against smut." On May 1, 1967, *The Las Vegas Show* debuted on Overmyer's hookup, which now was known as the United Network. Hosted by comic Bill Dana from the stage of the Hotel Hacienda, *Las Vegas'* opener featured such top talent as Don Adams, Xavier Cugat, Abbe Lane and Pete Barbutti, either appearing on the Hacienda stage or telecast remote from other clubs. Subsequent programs were equally star-studded, and it looked as though the United Network was on its way.

But ... the United Network's avowed target was Middle America, and *Las Vegas'* lounge acts and cliqueish showbiz chatter were aimed at an entirely different crowd. There was the additional problem of Daniel Overmyer's $250,000,000 personal wealth, which may not seem like much of a problem until one realizes that it takes a lot more than a piddling $250,000,000 to keep a network running past its first year. Overmyer soon came to grips with the fact that a full schedule of expensive programs like *Las Vegas* would soon bankrupt him; it was also painfully obvious that *Las Vegas* just didn't have the sufficient number of viewers to survive. Daniel Overmyer's later legal tangles with the FCC aren't worth relating here. Let's just close by noting that on June 5, 1967, the United Network came to an end—making *The Las Vegas Show* the first series in history to leave the air because its network was cancelled.

Let's Sing Out! (1965). Canadian folk-singing series, hosted by Oscar Brand. It's a safe bet that Mr. Brand didn't trot out any of the bawdy sea ballads he'd performed on several "party" records.

The Lloyd Thaxton Show (1964–66). Straddling the fence between folk music and rock was MCA's *Lloyd Thaxton Show,* which started locally on KCOP–Los Angeles in 1962. Like Dick Clark, Thaxton was a teenshow host, producer, and nurturer of new talent. Unlike Clark, Thaxton was also an accomplished musician in his own right, with a guitar or piano never far from reach on his daily series. Guests on *The Lloyd Thaxton Show* ranged from country warblers to Beatle clones, with the more extroverted of his audience members given permission to cut loose during the program's "dance band" sequence. Ample time was given to the offbeat as well, including an incredible appearance by Burgess Meredith, decked out in his Penguin costume from *Batman,* lip-synching to a novelty record he'd cut based on his piscatorial TV alter ego.

Midwestern Hayride see *Country-Western Shows*

Murray the K (1967). As musical styles changed seemingly by the hour in the late '60s, syndie producers had trouble keeping apace, especially with a gap of several weeks—or months—from the time a program was taped to the time of its release. Four-Star tried to maintain a semblance of currency with a "retrospective" approach. The company's monthly specials, hosted by New York deejay Murray the K, featured recaps of the past month's hit tunes.

Music City USA see *Country-Western Shows*

Night Train (1966). Though seldom seen in markets where racial tensions ran high, 7 Arts' *Night Train* was one of the best TV pipelines for black entertainers and rhythm-n-blues hits.

One Man Show (1969). A variation on *An Evening With...*, ABC Films' *One Man Show* interspersed its stars' monologues with glimpses of those stars at home and at play. Unfortunately, such potent talents as Groucho Marx and Redd Foxx were compromised by *One Man Show's* efforts to create, with garish lighting and cramped staging, the "feel" of a real nightclub performance—efforts that succeeded only in making the show look cheesy and amateurish.

Playboy's Penthouse (1960–61); *Playboy After Dark* (1968–69). Whenever a variety show tries to convince its audience that it's being taped under "real-life" conditions, it doesn't take long for the viewers to wise up to the artifice. Such a fate befell a brace of syndies hosted by *Playboy* magazine editor Hugh Hefner. The first, taped at WBKB–Chicago and syndicated by Official, was *Playboy's Penthouse.* The milling guests and the strategically placed Playboy "bunnies" were meant to suggest that the "Penthouse" of the title was Hefner's genuine stamping grounds. To maintain the illusion of an unending party, the "guest's" drinking glasses contained real booze; much was made of this, evidently on the assumption that viewers would find irresistible the spectacle of well-dressed drunks listing to and fro in their comfy chairs. The first *Penthouse* guest was Crown Prince of Scatology Lenny Bruce, who, unshackled by network censors, was given a fairly free hand. That Bruce was rather dull this time out was not evident to the on-screen "audience," who laughed knowingly at every one of Lenny's bon mots, sometimes even before he'd said them. Hefner's second-season-opener guest star, Sammy Davis Jr., remembered what Bruce and the on-camera yokkers had apparently forgotten — when one is on a television show, one might pay a little attention to the home viewers, who'd also like to be entertained.

Hefner's next syndie bid was a two-season Screen Gems issue, *Playboy After Dark*. Once more, every effort was made to convince the audience that the show was being taped during a genuine *Playboy* party, this time through the use of naughtier repartee and hand-held camerawork. And once more, the results looked more sloppy than off-the-cuff. After each guest star did his or her turn on *Playboy After Dark*, Hugh Hefner would puff on his pipe and pontificate on the guest star's merits with the philosophical solemnity of Immanuel Kant. Small wonder that viewers were delighted when guest comic Don Rickles lumbered toward the camera and barked, "All right. Where's the dummy with the pipe?"

The Porter Wagoner Show see *Country-Western Shows*

Scene 70 (1969). Typical of syndication's lag-behind attempts to keep abreast of changing '60s musical styles, *Scene 70* was outdated even before 1970 came into being.

The Screen Gems Specials (1966–67). Monthly hour-long concerts produced by Jackie Barnett, with stars drawn from the ranks of Julie London, Duke Ellington and Ella Fitzgerald.

Shivaree (1965). Disco time again, this time taped weekly at KABC–Los Angeles and dispensed in 30-minute doses to the other four ABC-owned outlets. Gene Weed hosted.

Show Street (1964). Comedienne Phyllis Diller emceed this amateur-talent parade, distributed by ABC Films to the five ABC-owned channels but barely seen elsewhere.

Something Special (1966). Ten music/comedy specials with the usual big names, from Four-Star TV.

Spotlight on Stars (1965). ITC monthly package, this one from Canada.

The Stoneman Family see *Country-Western Shows*

The Tommy Hunter Show see *Country-Western Shows*

Upbeat (1966–71). The most durable of the 1960's syndies to spotlight new black talent, *Upbeat* was hosted by Don Webster, color-taped at WUAB–Cleveland, and syndicated by Century Communications.

The Wilburn Brothers see *Country-Western Shows*

Your All-American College Show (1968–70). Harking back to the days of *The Original Amateur Hour* and *Talent Scouts, Your All-American College Show* was a slick color concoction bartered by Colgate-Palmolive. Talented teens (all scrupulously well-scrubbed and short-haired) from the nation's colleges were judged by celebrities; hosts included Rich Little, Dennis James, and the original *Talent Scout* mentor himself, Arthur Godfrey.

Religious

Long-established "personality" preachers like Bishop Sheen, Oral Roberts and Billy Graham continued to thrive in syndication, though the "televangelist takeover" had yet to arrive. Some television ministers tended to exhibit politics slightly to the right of Genghis Khan, but their targets in the '60s tended to be integration, rock-and-roll and anyone named Kennedy — not that current bugaboo, "Secular Humanism." Religious dramatic anthologies diminished in number, victims of escalating costs. And children's religious indoctrination was helped along by a pair of 15-minute color weeklies, one of which, *Davey and Goliath,* can still be seen.

Davey and Goliath (1960–65). Distributed by the National Council of Churches, *Davey and Goliath* was the saga of little Davey Hanson and his talking dog Goliath, who spoke only to his master. This animated 15-minute series came from the studios of *Gumby* creator Art Clokey; like *Gumby, D and G* was filmed in a stop-motion puppet process called "Pixillation." The program dealt in a low-key, entertaining manner with such weighty topics as race prejudice, responsibility to society, illness and death. A typical crisis of faith occurred when Davey was locked in a moving freight train. The boy's fears of being all alone were mollified by the rhythmic sound of the train wheels, which seemed to say "God is everywhere ... God is everywhere...." Though the animation wasn't always perfect, few could fault *Davey and Goliath* for its good intentions. The series was expanded in 1965 to include a group of half-hour holiday specials.

Day of Discovery (1968–   ). Created and for many years hosted by Richard De Haan and Paul Van Gorder, *Day of Discovery* was a straightforward half-hour of religious songs and Scriptural interpretations — minus the hyperbole and distortions that often accompany such readings on Sunday morning television.

I Believe in Miracles (1965–75). Kathryn Kuhlman was one of the few female evangelists to attain a national audience in the '60s. Her overenthusiastic *I Believe in Miracles,* though widely parodied and lampooned, lasted for ten years before Kuhlman's death in 1975.

Insight (1960–   ). The one successful religious-anthology newcomer of the decade was *Insight,* created by Paulist Priest Fr. Ellwood Keiser. At first a standard weekly sermon, *Insight* blossomed once Father Keiser decided that the best way to convey his messages was through hard-hitting dramatic presentations. Free of commercial-television taboos, *Insight* was allowed to offer themes and storylines normally diluted or ignored by the networks: the series dealt with drug abuse, rape, abortion, Vietnam, even the Afterlife in several allegorical tales set in Heaven, Hell or Limbo. This was the sort of material usually rejected out of hand by the networks as too "artsy" or provocative, but it was the order of the day for two decades on *Insight.*

By offering total artistic freedom in lieu of big salaries (participants on the series received union scale, and all of them gave the money back to the Paulists voluntarily), Father Keiser was able to build a talent pool that put many a "mainstream" television series to shame. Executive producer of *Insight* for many years was John Meredyth Lucas, onetime guiding force behind CBS's *Mannix;* directors included Marc Daniels of *I Love Lucy* fame and film actor Richard *(West Side Story)* Beymer; and among the contributing writers was Rod Serling, who penned a neat antifascist playlet, "The Hate Syndrome," in 1967. The stars, all eager to tackle the sort of meaty roles denied them by traditional type-casting on the networks, included Jane Wyman, Raymond Massey, Efrem Zimbalist Jr., Brian Keith, Vera Miles, Harvey Korman, Martin Sheen, Jack Albertson, Patty Duke, John Astin, Robert Lansing, William Shatner, John Forsythe, Carol Burnett, Flip Wilson, Ed Asner (who played God in an Adam-and-Eve story), and that bastion of the '60s counterculture, Peter Fonda. Major names continued to forego the big bucks to help Fr. Keiser deliver his message (and incidentally, to have a crack at the only continuing anthology still in existence) into the 1980's, a decade that saw *Insight* walk away with several Emmy Awards.

It's Light Time (1960). Often run Sunday mornings in tandem with *Davey and Goliath, It's Light Time* was a quarter-hour weekly filmed in Chicago on behalf of the Lutherans, hosted by Jim Stewart, a leading personality on Chicago's WBKB. Each episode was a comic or dramatic illustration of how to cope with the hazards of life through Faith. Though geared for children, *Light Time* was often quite challenging even on an adult level; its most compelling installment was mostly made up of Norman McLaren's award-winning nuclear-allegory short subject, *Neighbors.*

Rex Humbard (1966–). Though Rex Humbard had been preaching over his own UHF station in Akron, Ohio, since 1952, his national career got under way in the mid–60's. Humbard was the first television minister to make extensive use of color videotape (indeed, when he discovered that the channel in Chicago carrying his program had no color equipment, he moved his show to another Chicago outlet without so much as a by-your-leave); he was one of the first to expand his weekly program to 60 minutes; and it was Humbard's Cathedral of Tomorrow in the Akron suburb of Cuyahoga Falls that was the first church expressly designed to accommodate television cameras and equipment. By the early '70s, Rex Humbard had 350 "affiliates" nationwide, and was second only to Oral Roberts in pray-TV popularity.

Sports

"Fringe" sports considered too limited in appeal for extended network exposure prospered in syndication, especially once videotape helped to close the time-gap between a sports event and its television appearance. *Championship Bowling,* in its ninth season in 1960, was still going strong on color tape for its eighteenth year in 1969. Golf enjoyed live syndie coverage thanks to ad hoc operations like the Sports Network (purchased by Howard Hughes before the end of the decade); basketball, popular as a "regional," likewise had its own live hookups, generally underwritten by the teams themselves. Boxing, having worn out its network welcome amidst cries of brutality and corruption, was revitalized by the emergence of Muhammad Ali, whose closed-circuit TV bout with Sonny Liston in 1964 was heralded by extensive prefight syndicated specials, designed to help pack those theatres showing the televised fight itself. This pre-event coverage led the way to boxing's return to television by way of syndication. "Big-time" sports like baseball and football were given extra hype with weekly syndie highlight shows, which could now get onscreen with swifter speed thanks again to videotape. To annotate *all* the various syndicated sportsfests in the '60s would require a bigger volume than this, so let's touch upon some highlights.

Bullfights (1963). In 1963, the Spanish International Network got the bright idea of entering America's sports-syndie field with a series of taped, two-hour bullfights, direct from Mexico. Anticipating protests, the FCC at first blocked distribution of these bloody spectacles, then permitted their release on the condition that the gruesome "moment of truth" be clipped from each tape. The FCC forgot all about the violence leading up to that moment, including closeups of gorings and severed bull's ears. Bullfighting never quite caught on in American television.

Campy's Corner (1961). Former baseball star Roy Campanella, whose cheerful, upbeat public countenance virtually obliterated the tragedy of the auto accident which had crippled him for life, hosted a spirited half-hour interview show distributed by Heritage Films. Occasional non-sports guests included, at one point, voice-over actors Jackson Beck and Kenny Delmar, who visited Campy to promote the *King Leonardo* cartoon show!

Car and Track (1967). Self-explanatory weekly, from Spangler Productions.

Celebrity Billiards (1967). Earlier rack-'em-up series like *Championship Billiards* and *Ten-Twenty* spent most of their time figuring out clever camera angles to give visual dynamics to what was otherwise not an ideal television "sport." Medallion TV's *Celebrity Billiards* had the advantage of "star power." Its host was the amazing Minnesota Fats (Rudolph Wanderone Jr.), who spent most of his series' 39 weeks beating the tar out of such celebrities as Sid Caesar, Mickey Rooney, Milton Berle, Bill Cosby, Phyllis Diller, Donald O'Connor and Zsa Zsa Gabor.

Championship Billiards and ***Ten-Twenty*** see above

Championship Bridge (1961-62). More exciting than you'd think, *Championship Bridge* ran first on ABC in 1960-61, then was syndicated by ABC Films and usually shown on Sunday afternoons. The potential monotony of watching knitted-browed players palming pasteboards was broken up with "graphics," illustrating in weather-map style each player's progress. Hosting were bridge expert Charles Goren and newscaster Alex Dreier.

The Flying Fisherman (1963-67). In an overstocked stream of lookalike hunting-fishing shows, Roscoe Vernon "Gadabout" Gaddis stood above the rest with *The Flying Fisherman,* so titled because Gaddis was a licensed pilot who flew to select fishing spots throughout the western hemisphere. "Gadabout," a true television pioneer, started out in 1944 with a program over an experimental Schenectady, New York, channel, where he was sponsored by Hub Sporting Goods. (This made him the second-ever TV star with a regular sponsor, Lowell Thomas having been the first.) It was in Schenectady that Gaddis decided television would be his life, after a casual plug for Hub's line of wading boots caused the store to be sold out within a single day—this with only 500 television sets in the city! Gaddis entered sporadic filmed syndication in 1950, but it wasn't until 1963 that he became a national attraction. The head of Liberty Mutual decided that year that Gadabout's fans were the sort of rock-steady folks who'd make the best insurance risks; thus, *The Flying Fisherman* became the only 1963 syndie outside of *Death Valley Days* to debut with a single nationwide sponsor. It would be small of us to suggest that some of Gaddis' viewers tuned in to revel in the host's fractured English, such as Gadabout's pointing out which fish was "gooder" than another.

Football (1960-69). Most syndicated football shows of the decade followed the filmclip-and-interview format of the '50s, with videotaped highlights gradually easing out the "talking heads." After several years' syndication through Screen Gems, *The NFL Game of the Week,* a half-hour recap show, had its distribution handled by the National Football League itself in 1966. The sheer volume of gridiron activity in mid-decade forced this series to split in two: *NFL East* and *NFL West*. These programs were in turn consolidated in 1968 into the more generic *This Week in the NFL,* hosted by Pat Summeral. The strapping American Football League had to make do with a lesser recap weekly distributed by Tel-Ra, at least until the advent of the Super Bowl forced sportscasters and viewers to take the AFL a bit more seriously.

Gadabout Gaddis see **The Flying Fisherman**

Guest Shot (1962). Fifteen-minute Trans-Lux filler with a team of Hollywood columnists following celebrities in their private-life pursuits. If you really wanted to watch Fabian go lion-hunting, *Guest Shot* was right up your alley.

High and Wild (1966–67). Hunting, fishing and skiing, hosted by Don Hobart, once the emcee of an obscure '50s travelogue titled *The Vagabonds;* from Triangle Distribution.

International TV Bingo (1964). Distributed by Desilu to markets where on-the-air bingo was legal.

The Killy Challenge (1969–70). Olympic ski champ Jean-Claude Killy competing with celebrities on the slopes.

The Main Event (1960). One of the more engaging celebrity-conscious sports shows was Programs for Television's *Main Event.* The host, boxing great Rocky Marciano, spent goodly portions of each episode narrating clips from major fights of the past, but the show's highlights were its guest-star interviews. While some of the guests were from the boxing world, Marciano's interviewees included such non-ring favorites as Paul Newman, Nat King Cole, Joe DiMaggio, Eddie Bracken, Jack Carter, Gypsy Rose Lee, and Douglas Fairbanks Jr., who in one delightful half-hour was pitted against Marciano in an *epee* duel.

The Professionals (1967). A cinema-verite series of sports-star profiles, from 7 Arts.

Roller Derby and **Roller Game of the Week** (1962–   ). Those Lazarus-like wrestling shows, declared dead ever so often and revived with equal frequency, were joined in '60s syndication by another relic of television's caveman era. *Roller Derby* and *Roller Game of the Week* may have looked alike, but don't tell that to their fans or their executives; not only were the two shows produced by separate corporations, but competition between them was as deadly as the roller-skate races themselves. Both syndies were weekenders, with *Roller Game* getting a larger chunk of airtime by being offered in a two-hour format.

Sports International (1967). Filmed pocket version of *ABC's Wide World of Sports,* hosted by *Wide World's* Bud Palmer.

Surf's Up (1967). From Worldcorporation; a patchwork of water-sport footage, travelogue, and Beach Boys-style music, hosted by Stan Richards.

Talk/Interview

After a sluggish start, syndicated talk shows flourished during the decade. Like game shows, they were inexpensive to tape, had the allure of celebrity glamour, and many were flexible enough to schedule any hour of the day. A lot of talk shows, notably those sent out by the major station groups (Westinghouse, Metromedia, etc.), aped the *Tonight Show* desk-and-couch format, especially after that format veered from confrontation to pure entertainment when Jack Paar was replaced by Johnny Carson. A number of syndies were emceed by women, a bid for the more "intelligent" female that was supposed to have been created overnight in the early '60s. (The intelligent woman had, of course, always been there, but networks and sponsors were of the pregnant/barefoot/kitchen mentality and had trouble shaking this stereotype until women themselves forced the issue.) One development in the '60s talk field came about because syndies weren't bound to the same "broadcast-standards" dictates as the networks. This development was "shock-talk," a deliberately controversial and pugnacious chat-show style, which would eventually conquer the talk genre by the next decade.

The Al Capp Show (1968). The cartoonist creator of *Li'l Abner* graduated from favorite talkshow guest to short-lived talkshow host. Capp had lost old admirers and won new ones when he shifted from liberalism to conservatism in the mid-60's, but a lot of people from both political camps were turned off by his cackling bad manners.

The Alan Burke Show (1967). Former newsman and real estate executive Alan Burke was one of the '60s "gonzo" talk hosts who trotted out guests mainly to tear them apart and make fools out of them. Burke's nightly WNEW–New York series went into Metromedia syndication in early 1967, usually as a weekly. His stock-in-trade was the "fringe" guest, with causes or campaigns ranging from communicating with UFO's to dieting for Jesus. With his professorial air (and well-groomed beard), Burke undercut his guests with silent facial expressions of mounting incredulity when he wasn't assaulting them verbally. Most viewers got a therapeutic value from Burke's program; no matter how crazy one's personal beliefs may have been, in no way were they as nutzo as the opinions expressed by the characters on *The Alan Burke Show.*

Allen Ludden's Gallery (1969). After failing with several syndie attempts to make a go of the traditional interview, Metromedia gave the "magazine" concept a try. *Allen Ludden's Gallery,* available in either 60- or 90-minute versions, was evenly divided into six, or nine, ten-minute segments. These segments carried such headings as "First Portrait" (interviews of the famous *by* the famous, e.g. Steve McQueen queried by writer Harlan Ellison), and—inevitably in 1969—"The Kids." Only 21 markets carried *Gallery;* it was gone in 12 weeks. The magazine-style show would have to wait for the '70s popularity of CBS' *60 Minutes* and Group W's *PM Magazine* to gain strength.

Ask Julia Meade (1969). Actress and commercial spokeswoman Julia Meade hosted this antiseptic daily in which she answered, in Joyce Brothers fashion, letters from the viewers. One of a few efforts by Philadelphia-based Triangle Communications to crack the national talk market.

Bennett Cerf (1967). Authors and journalists were seen on this briefie hosted by famous publisher (and infamous punster) Bennett Cerf.

Blackbook (1969). The all-but-ignored black viewership was offered this daily interview by Triangle in 1969. The series' publicity people referred to host Matt Robinson as a "black Johnny Carson," ignoring the fact that blacks of the late '60s would have preferred to establish identities of their own.

Books and Brent (1961). In the manner of the above-mentioned Bennett Cerf (and years before Robert Cromie's *Book Beat* for PBS), Stuart Brent hosted this current literature interview show from the studios of WBKB–Chicago.

The David Frost Show (1969–72). The hottest non-network talk star of the '60s was neither an institution like Merv Griffin nor a nut-baiter like Alan Burke, but a brash young Britisher who'd been all but unknown in America until the middle of the decade. David Frost—comedy writer, satirist, scathing interviewer—managed to strike that happy (and often elusive) medium between friendly conversation and less-than-friendly confrontation. Frost's fullscale American stardom came after Merv Griffin left his Group W interview daily to host a CBS late-night effort in 1969. Several candidates were tested to fill Griffin's chair, among them Canadian television host Al Hamel; David Frost was selected on the strength of his similar "chat show" on London Weekend Television, as well as a series of monthly variety specials that Westinghouse had been importing from England for the past year. Unlike Merv Griffin, Frost did not leave one job to take another; he kept his London series even after his American debut, sticking to a timetable that would have killed a lesser man. Somehow, Frost found time for marathon American taping sessions, jet-shuttles to and from London, his always scrupulous research work, and even a highly publicized social life. *The David Frost Show* made a point of avoiding the three-on-a-couch approach of other programs. Frost revelled in probing one-on-one interviews; the looseness of some of his normally sedentary guests might be chalked up to the fact that Frost's "green room" (the guests' preshow waiting area) was next door to a well-known New York City watering hole.

After his July 1969 premiere, it looked as though David Frost would go the way of many another failed talkhost of past seasons. The opener was a textbook case of mediocrity, its nadir being a taped interview with England's

Prince Charles. Not only had British television censors chopped the interview into hash, but the post-production people had "sweetened" the segment with canned laughter! Also, sales of Frost's show outside the big cities were at first slim, since it was felt that the host's caustic wit wouldn't play in "the sticks." But Group W had faith in David Frost and gave him time to grow into an audience favorite. The daily 90 minutes gained in momentum, even snatching up an Emmy or two during its four-year run. David Frost's cancellation in the summer of 1972 was the result of hot-and-heavy competition from a new talkshow syndicated by Metromedia—starring none other than Merv Griffin.

The David Susskind Show (Open End) (1960–86). NTA's *Open End,* hosted by David Susskind, seemed in its first syndie days to be headed for the same oblivion as NTA's other talk efforts with such hosts as Henry Morgan and Alexander King. *Open End* had started over WNTA–New York in 1958 as a no-time-limit, uninhibited talkfest. It was syndicated in a two-hour form in 1960, but only thirteen stations (several of them "affiliates" left over from NTA's late lamented "fourth network") bothered to carry the weekly. Susskind's topics, which seemed centralized in radical politics and chi-chi showbiz palaver, didn't go over too well in Middle America. The series' turning point came in October of 1960. Soviet Premier Nikita Khrushchev, then making one of his frequent visits to New York, was eager to be interviewed by the media, especially in the wake of the recently intensified Cold War. Khrushchev loved his role as "troublemaker," and as a result was considered too much bother for most talk hosts, who figured that an evening with Nikita would end up an uninterrupted harangue on behalf of Communism. But David Susskind, a man not inclined to avoid controversy, invited Mr. K to appear on *Open End.* Susskind's main concession to the Russian's dignity was his promise not to interrupt the interview with commercials, which was the alleged reason that one of *Open End's* longtime New York sponsors pulled out, never to return. This wouldn't be the last Khrushchev-induced headache for Susskind.

On October 9, 1960, the Khrushchev interview aired live over WNTA and three other stations carrying *Open End,* and was tape-delayed for the remaining markets. The program started calmly enough, with Susskind hoping that his own heart-on-sleeve liberalism would encourage the Russian to respond openly to hard, probing questions. That wasn't quite what happened. Reviewers of the two hours were virtually unanimous in panning the show. Conservative columnist William F. Buckley pilloried Susskind for apologizing to Khrushchev whenever the Premier began rattling his saber over imagined insults; most other commentators merely found the interview to be deadly dull. When the smoke cleared, Susskind faced his critics. "I'm glad I done it," he said with an uncharacteristic lapse into vernacular. "I may be bruised but unbent. It's one thing for [Khrushchev] to stand on a rostrum in the U.N. and give out with his unplacable dogma of the Commie line; it's something else on a question-and-answer session. I just saw the transcript and you'd be surprised at the amount of information we elicited."

On a purely economic level, Susskind had every reason to be glad he "done it." Bad publicity can be good if it results in audience and sponsor interest. The

Khrushchev debacle placed *Open End* in the household-word category: within a year, Susskind's markets quadrupled, and he could be seen in virtually every major city in America by 1963. Not that the series' path was smooth by any means. In 1961, WNTA was sold and converted into an educational station, forcing Susskind to move his show to New York's more conservative WNEW-TV. In May of 1963, WNEW was announcing that Susskind had been fired, while the host was claiming that he'd quit; the brouhaha was over a pair of programs dealing with race relations and birth control respectively, two topics which could still stoke the fires of controversy in the '80s. In the fall of '63, *Open End* returned through the facilities of New York's WPIX; perhaps as a joshing reaction to WNEW's conservatism, Susskind's first WPIX show was a harmless outing featuring a panel of pre-teens.

WPIX might have remained Susskind's home had not the station cut the show from two hours to one, rather nullifying the "Open End" concept. So when good old WNEW dangled a two-hour slot before Susskind, the host returned to his old camp, amidst assurances that he'd temper his hot issues with occasional "fluff" shows. Since WPIX retained rights to the title *Open End,* the 1965 WNEW series was seen as *The David Susskind Show.* Syndication moved from NTA to WNEW's parent Metromedia company, an alliance which held firm until David Susskind taped his final program in 1986, one year before his death.

The Dennis Wholey Show (1969). Dennis Wholey specialized in not holding his own opinions, preferring to let his guests do the talking, then injecting a couple of devil's-advocate questions in the proceedings. Wholey was doing this on a Triangle syndie several years before toughening up his act as host of *PBS Latenight* in the '80s.

Dr. Albert Burke (1960–63). Conservative lecturer Albert Burke, whose intricate discussions on the dangers threatening American society won him written praise from the FCC itself, for several seasons hosted a Hartford, Connecticut, half-hour titled *Challenge.* This series was syndicated by Banner Films as *A Way of Thinking* in 1960, then by NTA as *Probe* in 1962.

The Donald O'Connor Show (1968). Metromedia's replacement for its flagging *Woody Woodbury Show* (which see) was hosted by musical-comedy star Donald O'Connor. While the company's admen heralded the daily series as "The Donald O'Conversation Show," the host was noticeably ill-at-ease in the interview department, so the program wisely concentrated on songs and skits. O'Connor's first guest was his *Singin' in the Rain* costar Debbie Reynolds; his director was Jim Jordan Jr., son of radio's "Fibber McGee." *The Donald O'Connor Show* lasted 26 weeks, replaced by *Allen Ludden's Gallery.*

The Ed Nelson Show (1969). Actor and erstwhile politician Ed Nelson helmed this 60- or 90-minute daily from ABC Films. It was seen in several markets as *The Morning Show,* the archetypical title given series designed as competition for NBC's *Today Show.*

Firing Line (1966–71). The deadly erudition of superconservative William F. Buckley Jr. was on display through the facilities of Worldcorporation beginning in 1966. Many *Firing Lines* were in the form of debates, with points awarded by moderators, most of whom were college students. The most fun occurred whenever Bill Buckley went nose-to-nose with old political foe (and longtime personal friend) John Kenneth Galbraith. *Firing Line's* most potent opposition, however, proved to be the American Federation of Television-Radio Artists, which for many years tried to bump Buckley off the air because he refused to join the union. *Firing Line* became part of the PBS lineup in May 1971, where, but for a few scattered commercial-syndie efforts, it has remained ever since.

The "Fringies" (1960–69). In contrast to responsible conservatives like William Buckley and Dr. Albert Burke, the airwaves of the '60s were festooned with the raving demagoguery of Clarence Mannion, Dan Smoot, H.L. Hunt, Billy James Hargis and "Reverend" Carl McIntyre. These self-styled patriots indulged in race-baiting, pro-bomb, anti-U.N. broadsides that were shunned by most responsible right-wingers. Things often got so inflammatory that the FCC had to step in and apply brakes, including suspending broadcast licenses. Still, these provacateurs had their audience, and when *TV Guide* ran an expose on their kind in 1967, quite a few readers cancelled their subscriptions instantly.

Girl Talk (1962–70). Virginia Graham, a secondary television hostess of the '50s, came into her own with ABC Films' daily *Girl Talk*. Although the series had its share of show-business froth and pointless bared-claw confrontation, Graham preferred to draw her female guests from the worlds of journalism and politics, erasing the demeaning tag of "Women's Show" from her series. *Girl Talk* prospered until Graham left for another program in 1969; she was replaced by Gloria DeHaven and Betsy Palmer.

Gypsy! (1964–65). Legendary "intellectual stripteaser" Gypsy Rose Lee (nee Louise Hovick) hosted a 7 Arts–released daily for a season and a half beginning in 1964. Rather than dwell on the expected candor and sex-talk, Gypsy surprised her fans by presiding over a "housewife" show, discussing the sort of topics it was supposed that housewives themselves discussed. On one early program, Gypsy, fellow "peeler" Ann Corio and Gypsy's actress-sister June Havoc engaged in a round-robin discourse over needlepoint!

Here's Barbara (1965). Not Barbara Walters but Barbara Coleman, whose interview show from WMAL–Washington, DC made it into a brief flurry of big-city syndication.

Hot Line (1964). This generic discussion-show title was bestowed upon a New York-based phone-in weekly hosted by waspish novelist and social critic Gore Vidal. *Hot Line* was never seen nationally, but did get sporadic East Coast syndication. When Vidal had to leave the show for a time, he was replaced by William F. Buckley — the man with whom Vidal would cross swords during a notorious televised name-calling session in 1968.

The Hy Gardner Show (1965). Moderately successful as a New York local, columnist Gardner's talk show barely got to first base as a syndie.

The Joe Namath Show (1969); **The Rosey Grier Show** (1969). As the dividing line between showbiz and sports grew thinner, a few sports figures got the notion that they were television stars. Two pro football players, Joe Namath and Rosey Grier, could be seen all over the tube in the late '60s, trying their best as actors, singers, dancers — and talk-show hosts. Rosey Grier's effort for ABC Films could at least rely upon the host's considerable piano-playing skill when conversation bogged down, while Joe Namath's weekly from Spangler Productions wasn't nearly as awful as expected. In fact, some TV critics got a kick from Broadway Joe's what-the-hey approach to the interview format — though many of the New York-based critics might have been watching Namath with visions of the '69 Super Bowl clouding their judgment.

The Joe Pyne Show (1966–69). Mr. Fist-in-your-Face himself, KTTV–Los Angeles talk host Joe Pyne made no pretense at politeness. An ex–Marine and amputee, Pyne seemed to have it in for the whole world as he snarled at his guests and studio audience, calling them "morons" and "meatheads," at one point offering to stuff a Jewish man's yarmulke down his throat. Like David Susskind, Joe Pyne's national ascendancy could be pinned down to a single telecast. On August 14, 1965, at the height of the riot activity in Los Angeles' Watts section, a black guest of Pyne's warned that a "race war" was at hand; whereupon Pyne pulled a gun from his vest and bellowed "Let 'em come! I'm ready for 'em!!" Whether or not this piquant moment was pre-planned is unimportant. It was enough for the FCC to seriously consider revoking KTTV's license — *and* for *The Joe Pyne Show* to enter national distribution through Hartwest. The series peaked at 85 markets, miles ahead of the coverage enjoyed by such other "controversials" as Alan Burke and William Buckley.

The June Havoc Show (1964). Actress June Havoc followed her sister Gypsy Rose Lee's lead with this briefly syndicated talk hour.

Kup's Show (1964–85). Chicago columnist Irv Kupcinet's television career began with a local chat show on that city's WBBM, *At Random*. He moved to rival station WBKB in 1962, and *Kup's Show*, as his talkfest was now known, went into national syndication three years later. It was a four-hour weekly devoted to "the lively art of conversation" — just conversation, minus theme, form, or any provocations or admonishments from "Kup" himself. Using his journalist's connections to line up incredibly varied panels (one 1972 session featured F. Lee Bailey, Eugene McCarthy, William Saroyan, Leroi Jones and "Happy Hooker" Xaviera Hollander!), Kupcinet sat back as his guests rambled on about anything and everything, politely interrupting whenever a new guest or a commercial break had arrived. If sparks ignited, as they did when Cleveland Amory engaged in a red-faced argument over vivisection with Morris Fishbein, or when Bob Hope and Robert Morley crossed words over Vietnam, well and good; if a guest like Imogene Coca was too timid to speak up and chose to listen, that was all right too. Some of the best *Kup's* moments occurred when guests *refused* to be drawn into fights; when a well-known anti-war activist who thrived on being challenged couldn't get anyone on the panel to respond to his taunts, he was reduced to giggling "Hey, let's all get stoned!" until his frustration became entertaining in itself. Through it all, Irv Kupcinet smiled and let his guests carry the ball. But the host's apparent laziness covered the fact that he was savvy (and powerful) enough to get all those important people on one set in the *first* place. The guest parade enabled *Kup's Show* to keep its viewers happy until 1985 — by which time the program had been streamlined to one hour and had for the past decade been seen over PBS — in a competitive market that eats talk-hosts for breakfast every morning.

Leave It to the Girls (1962). United Artists Television revived this onetime radio-television property of the '40s and '50s, with the same host (Maggie McNellis) and producers (Martha Rountree, Ted Bergman) as in its network days. The premise behind the taped, daily *Leave It to the Girls* was to have a lone male guest respond to questions and challenges from a female celebrity panel. Critics anticipating a mindless hen party were surprised when *Girls'* first guest was John Henry Faulk, who'd just won a lawsuit against CBS stemming from the days when he'd been blacklisted by the network, and who had plenty to say about it. *Leave It to the Girls* re-emerged in 1983 with the more applicable title *Leave It to the Women.*

Maurice Woodruff Predicts (1969). British psychic Maurice Woodruff, whose few correct predictions always received more press than his many miscalculations, hosted a celebrity-studded talk weekly from ever-hopeful Metromedia.

The Merv Griffin Show (1965–69; 1972–86). After several efforts at challenging the Johnny Carson juggernaut with latenight talk shows, Westinghouse remembered the critical praise given former band singer and later daytime host-producer Merv Griffin when Griffin had guest-hosted *Tonight* for a week in 1962. (This week had resulted in a short-lived NBC afternoon interview show for Griffin in the fall of that year.) Merv said "yes" to Westinghouse, and in April of 1965 the syndicated *Merv Griffin Show* began life from New York's "Little Theatre Just Off Times Square." On the surface, Merv's show was a *Tonight Show* clone, right down to a resident band, a couch, a desk, most of the same guests, and an "Ed McMahon" in the form of British character actor Arthur Treacher, who'd been a guest during Griffin's week on *Tonight* and whose curmudgeonly demeanor provided amusing contrast to Merv's boyish buoyancy. It appeared at first that Westinghouse was hoping that audiences would merely make a personality choice between Griffin and Carson, so alike were the two hosts' properties.

But there was more meat to Griffin's 90 minutes than met the eye. Merv's great talent was the ability to treat "hot issues" without the know-all pontification or hotheaded challenges common to other talk-hosts. When Griffin allowed philosopher Bertrand Russell to insist that Americans were committing atrocities in Vietnam, he did so after noting that he didn't agree with Russell, but that free speech transcended all personal beliefs. In later years, Merv was able to draw revealing comments from ex-vice president Spiro Agnew and Soviet ambassador Nikolai Federenko, merely by soft-pedalling tough questions with his own wide-eyed charm. Merv's aw-shucks style was able to accommodate more controversy and makers of controversy than most of the would-be Susskinds combined.

Merv Griffin's tenure with Westinghouse ended when he was lured to a CBS network latenight talk show with a contract calling for more money than even Carson was getting. It was on CBS that Griffin truly learned to appreciate the relative freedom accorded the syndie talk-host. The CBS "suits" immediately issued orders and edicts indicating that they felt they knew more about Griffin's show than Griffin did. One of the network's first acts was to fire Arthur Treacher, whom they felt appealed to the "wrong" (i.e. the older) audience. From minor irritations to major acts of censorial idiocy, CBS made Merv Griffin realize that if he was ever to be master of his own fate again, he'd have to escape the network decision-makers and return to syndication. His exit from CBS was a foregone conclusion anyway, since the network was never able to realistically compete on Carson's own ground.

When Griffin returned to syndication, he did so through Metromedia; within weeks after his March 1972 Metromedia debut, Merv won back his old audience, knocking his main competition, Group W's David Frost (who of course had replaced Griffin on Westinghouse), off the map. Metromedia made sure that most of Merv's markets ran him in the daytime hours, where he'd he performed best while at Westinghouse. (In the mid–1960's, many of Griffin's stations moved his show to late afternoons to compensate for the lack of "fresh" material in the 4-to-6 p.m. slots, which hitherto had belonged to network reruns and old movies. By 1966, only three of Merv's 26 stations were running his show at night; one year later, Merv's coverage was 100 percent daytime in 94 markets.) The new *Merv Griffin Show* proved an even bigger hit than his Group W series, earning a shelf-full of Emmy Awards for Griffin, his producers Bob Murphy and Peter Barsocchini, and his director Dick Carson (Johnny's brother). Merv's best programs during this period were his "theme" shows, wherein a group of guests with similar backgrounds would discourse on a single subject. Griffin had been a pioneer of the theme show back in the '60s, and in 1981 would pioneer another advance in the talkshow form: his show became the first daily series of its kind to be syndicated by satellite, beaming out its programs on the same day they'd been taped — "day and date," as this process is called in the industry. The shrinking talk/variety market in the early '80s led Griffin to experiment briefly with the "magazine" format, but by 1986 Merv was too busy packaging such syndie blockbusters as *Jeopardy* and *Wheel of Fortune* (both distributed by King World, which by then was syndicating *The Merv Griffin Show*) to bother coping with diminishing ratings. In November of 1986, Merv Griffin — looking youthful and chipper as ever — said goodbye to his fans after 21 years' steadfast service.

The Mike Douglas Show (1963–82). Mike Douglas' career bore an eerie resemblance to Merv Griffin's; Douglas had been a band singer, a game show host, and by the early '60s was conducting a Group W interview show. Westinghouse's KYW–Cleveland began its daily *Mike Douglas Show* in 1961. While at KYW, Douglas developed a neat utilization of guest stars; he'd feature a different celebrity co-host each week, who'd help Douglas introduce the other guests and move the program along for five whole days. This potentially expensive guest-star deployment was made cost-efficient when Westinghouse got a waiver from AFTRA, permitting Douglas to pay a lower guest rate than was required on the networks. That waiver nearly ended Mike's syndicated career before it began; when Westinghouse wanted to put Douglas' show in national distribution, AFTRA countered that they'd have to start paying network-level talent fees. Negotiations dragged on for months before a secret settlement enabled *The Mike Douglas Show* to "go national" in October of 1963.

In 1965, Westinghouse sold station KYW to Philadelphia, with Mike Douglas moving to Philly in the bargain. The host was ideal for daytime in *any* city. While he had his share of controversial guests, Douglas side-stepped the sort of off-color material that might offend his largely female following. (When Zsa Zsa Gabor made several censorable remarks about a popular comedian, Douglas' show went from "live" to videotape in the Philadelphia area.) Even so, both the FCC and the United States Senate once took Douglas to task for "contributing" to the glamourization of drug abuse! It seemed that young actor Paul Petersen revealed during a Douglas interview that he'd experimented with LSD. Few complained when Steve Allen admitted to the same thing soon afterward, but Allen wasn't the "role model" for teenagers that Petersen was. After a while, the only *Mike Douglas* guest who could remotely be accused of corrupting the Youth of America was The Three Stooges' Moe Howard.

The Mike Douglas Show was honored with the first Emmy ever awarded a syndicated daytime talk-variety show. It would turn out to be his only such award, but Douglas remained popular into the '70s, remaining fresh with such "Theme Shows" as his Our Gang reunion, and location jaunts to locales as remote as Moscow. In 1978, Group W decided that Philadelphia was not exactly Celebrity City, so *The Mike Douglas Show* was moved to Los Angeles. Douglas' ratings shot up, prompting Group W to offer Douglas a fat five-year contract; but by 1980, it became obvious that five years was only as long as Group W said it was. Ever searching for that elusive 18- to 34-year-old demographic group, Westinghouse declared that Douglas catered to a much-too-elderly crowd, and dropped him summarily in favor of youngish singer John Davidson. Douglas licked his wounds and started up a new daily talk show distributed by Syndicast. This new series never performed as well as the *Douglas Show* of old, so the format was rehauled in 1981 and the series was retitled *The Mike Douglas Entertainment Hour*. The only guests allowed on this latest venture were those who could sing, dance or tell jokes, which left such people as Carl Sagan and Betty Friedan out in the cold. Syndicast pulled the plug on *The Mike Douglas Entertainment Hour* after only 26 weeks. Mike Douglas' subsequent stab at a talk show through the auspices of Ted Turner's Atlanta "superstation" WTBS disintegrated amidst bitter accusations of betrayals and broken promises from both Turner and Douglas. After twenty years, *The Mike Douglas Show* was history.

The Morning Show see *The Ed Nelson Show*

The Oscar Levant Show (1960). NTA's replacement for its disastrous Alexander King talk show of 1959 was hosted by another frequent guest of *The Jack Paar Show,* pianist-raconteur Oscar Levant. A self-styled hypochondriac and "world's oldest living child prodigy," Levant parked his patented Neurotic routine long enough to demonstrate a real flair for interviewing, making it seem as though he really cared what his guests were saying. This didn't keep him on the air, however; apparently Levant's fans preferred the "sick sick sick" routine he habitually trotted out for Jack Paar.

Outrageous Opinions (1967). *Cosmopolitan* magazine editor Helen Gurley Brown presided over this daily from King Features Television. Brown made every effort to make her series live up to its title; *Outrageous Opinions* had a preoccupation with sex-talk, uninhibited for its time but nowhere near as raw as the body-function banter on Dr. Ruth Westheimer's program twenty years later. At its best, Brown's series offered some political and sociological views not normally given television airtime; at its worst, the show might as well have been titled *Obnoxious Opinions.*

The Pamela Mason Show (1965). Pamela Kellino Mason, onetime wife of actor James Mason, made her name in the talk show circuit with her habit of gleefully chattering away on virtually any subject, cheerfully admitting total ignorance on most subjects of importance. This habit led to a couple of talk shows of her own. The first was syndicated by Spangler Films in 1965; the second, in 1968, bore the unfortunate title *The Weaker(?)Sex.*

Pat Boone in Hollywood (1967). Co-produced by Boone's Cooga Mooga Productions and Filmways for Firestone Sales syndication, *Pat Boone in Hollywood* had a fairly good start with 26 presales. But the daily series' doom was sealed when *Pat Boone* was cancelled in the New York City market after a mere three months. The official reason given was that Boone was regarded as "too wholesome" for the Manhattan crowd.

Phil Donahue (1969–   ). It started in 1967. Youngish newscaster Phil Donahue was given a daily phone-in show on WLWD in Dayton, Ohio. Donahue was replacing an audience-participation show hosted by Johnny Gilbert, and reluctantly found himself with a studio audience when ticketholders for the Gilbert show had to be honored. Phil also found himself with such atypical (for Dayton) guests as militant atheist Madelyn Murray O'Hair; soon he was doing programs on such topics as anatomically accurate children's dolls. With this sort of material, it wasn't long before Phil Donahue would get national play, and that he did courtesy of WLWD's parent Avco company in 1969. The few television stations picking up the first Donahue shows tended to react to the controversial nature of his subject matter by running only 30 minutes of each daily hour, and running them in the fringiest of fringe periods — usually emulating WPIX–New York by showing Donahue very late at night. By 1970, Phil Donahue and the proverbial snowball in Hell were on the same chance-for-survival level.

Donahue persisted with a handful of markets until 1974, when Avco moved him out of Dayton and into Chicago, hoping to flesh out the guest-star roster. The move was a lifesaver. Donahue went from 40 markets in 1974 to 167 in 1979, the first year that *Phil Donahue* was the nation's Number One syndicated talk show. Hot issues and volatile guests may have been principal contributors to his fame and many Emmy Awards, but it was Donahue's talent for playing his studio audience, drawing them out with phrases like "Help me out here!" and "A show of hands, please!" that kept his viewers tuning in. Donahue always treated his audience as a participant, and this attitude extended to his call-in viewers. This technique led to a feeling of intimate involvement for Donahue fans across the nation (an involvement intensified when Donahue began shipping his programs out by satellite in 1981, allowing him to become a live or "day-and-date" commodity in many cities) — most of those fans being women, thanks to Phil's morning and afternoon time slots.

In 1984, Multimedia (a distributor who'd earlier absorbed Avco) moved Phil Donahue from Chicago to New York. Some fans protested that this removed the "middle America" ambience of his program, but Donahue was particularly happy with the move because he was able to remain close to his wife, actress Marlo Thomas. (Donahue met his future bride in romance-movie fashion when Marlo was a guest on his show in 1977.) Though Donahue's dominance of the talk show market has slipped in recent years due to a horde of competitors, he is still as of this writing a name to reckon with. He is also, after two decades of efforts by many female talk show stars, the one talk-host who's done most to bring respect and dignity to the "women's market." "When Phil Donahue started, people who were managers in television thought women were only interested in mascara tips and how to stuff a cabbage. Phil Donahue showed them women interested ... in leading the best possible lives." These grateful words were spoken in 1987 by Oprah Winfrey, the female talk-host who'd ultimately topple Phil Donahue from his Number One Syndie perch.

PM East — PM West (1961). Mike Wallace's NTA interview show slowed to a halt in early 1961. Wallace was then invited by Westinghouse to host the company's first try at taped syndication, a 90-minute nightly talk show which was first seen over Westinghouse's own stations, then distributed to the rest of the country. Wallace's co-host was Joyce Davidson, a Canadian TV personality who'd stirred up a tempest in 1959 when she declared that Canadians were rather apathetic concerning Queen Elizabeth's recent trip to the Western Hemisphere. (Davidson would later marry David Susskind; nothing strange about these bedfellows.) The new Westinghouse show was titled *PM East — PM*

West; Wallace and Davidson anchored from the East Coast in New York, while San Francisco television critic Terence O'Flaherty was the man from the West. Viewers hoping for flying sparks in the old Mike Wallace "interrogation" tradition were displeased as *PM* settled into a bloodless syndrome of cozy showbiz chat. The one time that the Wallace of old surfaced was when he enraged actor Burt Lancaster by suggesting that Lancaster had a reputation for being "difficult." Just when it looked as though *PM* would roar into life, however, Lancaster walked off the show. When *PM* died in July 1962, only 15 stations were carrying the program.

Probe see *Dr. Albert Burke*

The Rosey Grier Show see *The Joe Namath Show*

The Square World of Ed Butler (1969). The Marine-raiders type of talk show typified by Joe Pyne and Alan Burke had worn out its welcome by 1969. (It would enjoy, if that is the right word, a revival courtesy Wally George and Morton Downey Jr. in the '80s.) One of the last shock-talkers was Ed Butler, who called himself a "professional revolutionary." But *The Square World of Ed Butler* was so stale that it had to resort to the *Laugh In*-style fast-paced editing then in vogue to keep the audience from nodding off.

The Steve Allen Show (1962–64; 1968–71). The same month that *PM East — PM West* vanished in 1962, Westinghouse, still hopeful that a talk show would put the company on the syndie map, signed Steve Allen to preside over 90 nightly minutes for the Westinghouse-owned stations. When asked what sort of program he'd be doing, Allen replied that he'd just watched several kinescopes of the old *Tonight Show* he'd hosted for NBC from 1954 to 1957, decided they were pretty funny, and planned to do exactly the same type of show for Westinghouse. *The Steve Allen Show* went into national distribution in October 1962. Conditions couldn't have been better for a hit. Jack Paar had just abdicated from NBC's *Tonight Show* in March, but his successor, Johnny Carson, was tied to his ABC network contract until November; in the interim, *Tonight* was handled by a variety of guest hosts, and this lack of continuity had caused a slight dip in the ratings. Westinghouse counted on the "Paar dropouts" to latch on to Steve Allen, hoping that Allen's previous late-night-show track record would provide stiff competition against the (relatively) unfamiliar Carson. And at first, Steve Allen *did* manage to out-rate Carson in most of his 46 markets. In retrospect, it's easy to see why. Johnny Carson ran a relatively orderly ship; *The Steve Allen Show* was delightfully chaotic, with everything seemingly happening at once. Steve would indulge in a zany stunt like dressing as a tea bag and being dunked in a huge tank of hot water, then calm down to read a very serious report on drug abuse. Celebrities would make "funny phone calls" to unsuspecting people, then the stage would be given over to such then-chancy performers as Bob Dylan. "Kooky" guests like health-food faddist Gypsy Boots and "human woodchopper" Joe Interleggi would be followed by people like labor columnist Victor Reisel. And no sooner would a lengthy excerpt from something as brutally frank as the off–Broadway revue "In White America" be over than Steve Allen would be running around the stage yelling "Smock! Smock!" and "How's your bird?"

Eventually, this kitchen-sink approach wore itself down. Allen's "deep-think" pieces were lost on audiences of 1964 who had enough to be worried about from the real world. Inspiration began flagging on the comedy bits, especially when Allen began repeating his best sketches word for word, right down to the ad libs. Eyes began turning to the doggedly non-controversial and ever up-to-date Johnny Carson. While no less the Renaissance man he'd always been, Steve Allen ran out of gas, as it were, on Westinghouse. By mutual agreement, Allen and Westinghouse parted company in October of 1964.

After a few seasons with the networks, Steve Allen was back in 1968 with a new nightly syndie co-produced by Allen's Meadowlane Enterprises and Filmways. Firestone Sales used this 90-minute *Steve Allen Show* to replace its faltering *Pat Boone in Hollywood,* and managed to keep it in distribution for three years. Allen's new venture was a great deal more relaxed and conventional than his "madness-and-music" days at Westinghouse, but there were still a few prized Steve Allen moments. On one show, Steve was in a controlled drunk-driver test, and was so generous in his participation that he had to be carried out of the studio after taping.

That Regis Philbin Show (1964). Though the last few Westinghouse *Steve Allen Shows* of 1964 had been limp, there still remained some three dozen markets interested in a syndicated talk show. Westinghouse found a new host, Los Angeles daytime-television personality Regis Philbin. With assurances of more music and comedy and less talk, *That Regis Philbin Show* went on the week after Steve Allen's departure in October 1964. By early 1965, with only 16 markets hanging on, Regis Philbin's job security was shaky. It wasn't really his fault. Steve Allen was a tough act to follow, and Johnny Carson was all but unconquerable. What dealt the final blow to Philbin was the decision by several Westinghouse ex-"affiliates" to abandon talk-variety in favor of enticing new packages of first-run, full-color theatrical feature films. Thus when Regis Philbin accepted an offer to cohost an ABC late night show, Westinghouse said "Godspeed," and marked time until Merv Griffin came along.

That Show with Joan Rivers (1968–69). This Trans-Lux daily was the first television vehicle for comedienne Joan Rivers, who'd risen to prominence as a frequent Johnny Carson replacement on *The Tonight Show.* (Carson himself appeared in a somewhat sexist "bachelorette apartment" sketch on one of Rivers' early shows.) The level of humor on *That Show* was established on its opener, which featured Don Rickles "modelling" Vidal Sassoon's latest line of women's wigs. Even back in 1968, reviewers hacked away at Joan Rivers' "crass, aggressive style," but *That Show* managed to hang in there for 18 months.

A Way of Thinking see Dr. Albert Burke

The Weaker (?) Sex* see *The Pamela Mason Show

The Woody Woodbury Show (1967). Woody Woodbury, a Florida-based nightclub comic whose style was that of a risque Huck Finn, had been a suitable replacement for Johnny Carson on the ABC game show *Who Do You Trust?*, so in 1964 Westinghouse gave Woodbury a one-week tryout as a potential Steve Allen replacement. Woody didn't seem to have the organizational ability needed to pull together the loosely structured talk format, so Westinghouse went with Regis Philbin instead. In 1967, Metromedia made the first of three attempts to dent the chat-show market; the company's choice for host was our old friend Mr. Woodbury. In spite of the savvy of producer Ralph Edwards, a healthy number of sales and some encouraging reviews, *The Woody Woodbury Show* ended after 52 weeks (and at that, it was one of Metromedia's longest-running efforts). The ad campaign for this 90-minute nightly insisted that "Woody Woodbury is *not* a cartoon." Considering the thriving children's market of the 1960's, Woodbury might have done better if he *had* been a cartoon.

Travel/Documentary

The success story of travel shows in the '60s was the by-now old one: travelogues were cheap, flexible, and in glorious color. Documentaries did well because a market for such programs existed but wasn't being as well served by the networks as in the '50s, and hadn't yet been swallowed up by public television. Some of the more prestigious station groups began to package their documentaries as monthly or seasonal specials, a neat way to keep costs in check and draw more attention to programs that might have been taken for granted and ignored had they been presented on a weekly basis.

Across the Seven Seas (1962). Travel/documentary specialist Jack Douglas' color 1962 release was made in conjunction with Bing Crosby Enterprises and endorsed by Crosby himself, who usually remained aloof from his production company.

Adventure Calls (1965). Cardinal Films' *Adventure Calls* was a series of mountain/wilderness explorations narrated by Richard *(Sergeant Preston)* Simmons.

Almanac* see *Greatest Headlines of the Century

America (1964–65). No relation to the later PBS series hosted by Alistair Cooke, 1964's *America* was a two-season pictorial essay of cultural and natural wonders within the United States, produced and narrated by Jack Douglas. *America* was distributed by CBS Films, even though Douglas' brilliant color footage would have been lost on the CBS-owned stations, which like their parent network were color-blind in 1964.

The American Civil War (1960). A 13-part documentary first shown on the Westinghouse stations in 1959, then syndicated by Trans-Lux to coincide with the Civil War Centennial. Producers Roy Meredith and William J. Kelland relied upon the 4500 Civil War photographs made by Mathew Brady and his contemporaries. The word of the day was "montage"; Abraham Lincoln's mood-swings were indicated by swift cuts from one Lincoln photo to another, while tension was built on the Lincoln-assassination episode by inter-cutting pictures of the President and the assassination conspirators with a tight closeup of John Wilkes Booth's eyes. On one occasion, *The American Civil War* did have actual *moving* pictures, this for the half-hour on the Monitor-Merrimac sea battle, for which no contemporary photos existed. The producers themselves appeared on-camera to explain that they would recreate the famed battle in a Long Island pond, then did precisely that, with scale-model replicas of the two "ironclads."

The American West (1965); **Trails to Adventure** (1967). Perhaps because *The American West* and *Trails to Adventure* shared the same "line" producer, and perhaps because both series illustrated stories of the old West through location photography and recreations by professional actors, some television historians have assumed that the two programs were one and the same. But the fact is that *American West* was produced by the prolific Bill Burrud, while *Trails to Adventure* was assembled by Jack *(You Asked for It)* Smith—and when Burrud first laid eyes on *Trails to Adventure,* he sued Smith for infringement. The many documentaries clogging the airwaves in the '60s may have looked alike to the casual viewer, but their creators protected their individual projects with the jealousy of a mother lion.

Battle Line (1963). Following the success of David Wolper/Official's *Biography* (which see), Official Films adopted a policy of issuing one new documentary syndie per year. Its 1963 contribution, initially titled *Men in War,* was released to 120 markets as *Battle Line.* Produced by former Wolper associate Sherman Grinberg, *Battle Line's* novelty was having its World War II footage narrated not only by writer Jim Bishop, but by two veterans from both sides—e.g., an American and a Japanese reflecting upon the battle of Okinawa. The restraint of the narrative text and of Nelson Riddle's muted musical score gave the 39-week *Battle Line* a subtlety lacking in such earlier "Glories of War" series as *Victory at Sea.*

Biography (1962–63); **Biography II** (1980). Producer David Wolper had intended *Biography* to run on the CBS network, but the profitability and market share of his non-network special *The Race for Space* led Wolper to opt for syndication through Official Films. While many of the 20th century personalities covered on *Biography* (Roosevelt, Churchill, Hitler and so on) had been dwelt upon by other documentaries, Wolper strived to offer rarer film footage than had previously been seen on television. To that end, he pumped up his production staff (which included such later producers as Jack Haley Jr., Sherman Grinberg and Alan Landsburg, not to mention future *Exorcist* director William Friedkin) and began burrowing through film archives the world over: England's Imperial War Museum, Italy's Orbis Films and Vatican Archives, even Moscow's Sovexport and Artkim. Some of the precious filmclips on *Biography* included some rare *anti*–Hitler German propaganda from the '30s, John Barrymore's screen test for his never-filmed screen version of *Hamlet*, and, on the Helen Keller episode, a long excerpt from the 1919 silent *Deliverance*, a film dramatization of Keller's youth that played like *The Miracle Worker* without the soundtrack. Wolper also put together studies of such underused (by the networks) notables as Adm. Chester Nimitz and Eva Peron, as well as the first significant filmed study of astronaut John Glenn. Most admirably, Wolper was able by choosing his filmclips from several different sources to offer reasonably objective studies of his subjects, counterbalancing their positive and negative qualities — with the usual exceptions of such despots as Hitler, Stalin and Khrushchev.

Wolper's extra labors resulted in a weekly *Biography* budget of $35,000, at a time when most half-hour documentaries got by on $13,000 per week. But the added expenditures paid off. *Biography* parlayed its 75 presales into a 190-market peak by 1963; the series won a Peabody Award a year earlier, and its 65 episodes were still in active syndication into the '80s. Wolper's future as King of the Documentary was assured, and Official Films, having all but kissed off syndication after several failures a few years earlier, was in 1963 on top again. *Biography* was also a shot in the arm for the career of its narrator, Mike Wallace, who'd been in a slump after his NTA and Westinghouse syndies bit the dust.

In 1980, Television Representatives International put *Biography II* into circulation after the property had lain on the shelf for nearly two years. This new version, narrated by David Janssen, was made up of full-color studies of persons who'd risen to fame since 1963. But there were too many documentaries in the marketplace for *Biography II* to make a lasting impression, and sales were slim. The recent series on the Arts and Entertainment cable service hosted by Peter Graves and titled *Biography* was actually a package of unrelated documentaries from a variety of production sources.

Captured see *Wild Cargo*

Cesar's World (1968). Color travelogue hosted by Cesar Romero, from Akkad Productions/United Artists.

The Challenging Seas (1968). A coproduction of Bill Burrud and California's Marineland of the Pacific.

Communism RME (1962). A series of monthly specials from the Storer Stations group, narrated by Art Linkletter. The acronymic title was taken from Winston Churchill's description of Communism as "a Riddle, wrapped in a Mystery, wrapped in an Enigma."

Crime and Punishment (1961). Clete Roberts interviewed inmates of several American prisons in this Banner Films release produced by Collier *(One Step Beyond)* Young. The series met with some resistance from those who felt that the interviews tended to elicit sympathy for the convicts.

Danger Zone (1960). Narrated by war hero "Pappy" Boyington, this weekly look at danger-seekers was little more than a carbon copy of Jack Douglas' *Danger Is My Business. Danger Zone* was an issue of Bing Crosby's production company.

Decision: The Conflicts of Harry S Truman (1964). Screen Gems' *Decision* was a 26-week study of President Truman's six years in the White House. There'd been an earlier try at a Truman series by producer David Susskind and author Merle Miller, but the networks felt that Truman's stormy presidency was too controversial to dwell on without raising a passel of protests. More to the point was the observation of an ABC official: "Who wants to see *that* old man?" All that survives of Susskind's project is Merle Miller's entertaining volume of Truman interviews, *Plain Speaking.* In 1964, two years after the Susskind-Miller debacle, producer-director Ben Gradus secured the former president's services for *Decision,* this series designed for syndication and thus outside the trepidation and scrutiny of the networks. Truman's interviews were filmed in New York, Washington and Independence, Missouri; after many corporate-level ruminations at Screen Gems, it was decided to not edit out any of the ex-president's legendary profanities, since Truman wouldn't have been Truman without them. Sales were so strong on *Decision* that many network chieftains wished they'd weighed their opinions about "that old man" more carefully.

En France (1963). Ostensibly an educational foreign-language weekly, 7 Arts' *En France* was more an excuse to show off the scenic wonders of Gay Paree and series hostess Dawn Addams.

Field Communications Specials (late 1960's). Seasonally syndicated documentaries from the Field station group, a company headquartered at WFLD–Chicago. The organization's best-circulated effort (other than the kiddie spectacular *The Mean Mr. Firecracker*) was 1967's *The Price of a Record,* an in-depth look at the death of race-car driver Donald Campbell.

Fight for Life (1967). Stories of medical miracles narrated by Bing Crosby's wife Kathryn Grant, herself a registered nurse.

The Government Story (and other "sponsored" series) (1960–69). Group W's 1969 *Government Story,* placed on the air by the United States Treasury (and given "audience appeal" by hiring E.G. Marshall to narrate) was a prime example of the sort of syndie underwritten by special-interest organizations, in the manner of *Industry on Parade* in the '50s. These programs were sent out for free to local stations looking for programs to take up space in "fringe time." Earlier in the decade, the National Educational Association enjoyed wide distribution with *The School Story* (1960), a weekly documentary on the changing face of public education. Some of the *School Story* footage found its way into the Parent-Teacher Association's 1961 *Parents Ask About Schools.* In the early '60s, the United Nations expanded its 15-minute educational-station weekly *Dateline: UN* into the half-hour *International Zone,* hosted for several seasons by Alistair Cooke. *Social Security in Action* offered interviews with famous senior citizens benefited by old-age financial protection. And there was always *The Big Picture,* which in the '60s was hard-pressed to modify negative public reaction to Vietnam. All these efforts were reasonably watchable propaganda, but none of them broke any new stylistic ground.

The Great Adventure (1968). This all-purpose title was bestowed upon a Canadian contribution to the travelogue field, syndicated by Dudley Films. Yes, Dudley Films, not Snidely Films.

The Great War (1964). This British Broadcasting Corporation project was made up of priceless footage from the Imperial War Museum and narrated by Michael Redgrave, featuring top-rank actors like Emlyn Williams and Marius Goring assuming a variety of accents to read the actual words of World War One's participants. Though *Great War* was the BBC's biggest worldwide success of 1964, it didn't do very well in America, but neither did CBS' *World War One,* a network series of that same year. Even after half a century, most Americans apparently regarded the unpleasantness of 1914–18 as a "foreign" war.

Greatest Headlines of the Century (and other "fillers") (1960–63). After taking a bath on some expensive failed half-hour syndies, Official Films laid low for a couple of years to concentrate on "fillers" — three-to-five-minute vignettes used to fill dead air space on news or sports programs. Official's 1960 fillers included *Greatest Headlines of the Century* and *Sportfolio. Headlines,* the better of the two (even though its excellent filmclips were overladen with loud, near-hysterical voiceover narration), had an immediacy lacking in most other syndies. Its 366 episodes were each designed for release on a specific day; for example, the "Surrender of Germany" episode was meant to be shown on May 8. The Hearst Corporation followed the same pattern with its daily *Almanac,* first shown in 1960 and still in circulation as late as 1976. Pathé, one of the oldest newsreel firms in the business, came up with *Milestones of the Century* in 1961. Most of these vignettes were taken *not* from Pathé's film archives, but from a group of one-reel documentaries produced by Robert Youngson for Warner Bros./Pathé in the '40s and '50s. Much of the same footage crept into another Pathé filler, 1962's *Men of Destiny,* narrated by Drew Pearson. Anyone watching independent television stations in recent years will tell you that the "filler" is hardly a dead format, though most of the five-minute gapfillers seen in the '80s are less concerned with past news events than with such trivia as movie history and popular music.

Group W Specials (1960's onward). Westinghouse had been in the syndie-special business on a limited basis ever since its 1958 one-shot on the life and work of Benny Goodman. The company's schedule of specials increased as the '60s wore on, the best of these being 1968's *One Nation, Indivisible,* a very thorough three-hour investigation of American race relations which was distributed less than a month after the murder of Martin Luther King. This remarkable achievement wouldn't have been possible without the aid of the public-affairs departments from all five Westinghouse-owned stations. The same can be said of the *Spectrum* series, comprised of the top documentary offerings of the Group W channels; the best of the *Spectrums* were distributed to non–Westinghouse stations on a monthly basis. The year 1970 was particularly strong for *Spectrum,* including such efforts as *Assignment Vietnam, Runaway* (a tense study of teens on the streets), *Ho-Ka-He* (a tough look at living conditions on American Indian reservations), and two pieces on the plight of the urban blacks, *A Piece of the Action* and *The Man Nobody Saw.* Group W continued its tradition of special-event excellence into the '70s with such programs as the Bicentennially oriented 12-part *The Course of Human Events,* and into the '80s with its medical one-shots and its monthly *For Kids' Sake.* Mention also should be made of Group W's special "prime time editions" of its regular series, including *Merv Griffin* in the '60s, *Dinah!* in the '70s, and *PM Magazine* in the '80s.

International Zone see *The Government Story*

Island in the Sun (1965). A Bill Burrud-produced seafarer.

It's a Wonderful World (1963). Color travel/doc from Official Films, hosted by newsman John Cameron Swayze.

Keyhole (1962). A Jack Douglas/United Artists television "documatic," *Keyhole* offered up to three different self-made persons (or persons in offbeat occupations) per half-hour show, going through the recreated motions of whatever they did for a living.

Lawbreakers see below

Lee Marvin's Lawbreakers (1963). Produced by Marvin's own Latimer Productions for United Artists TV, *Lee Marvin's Lawbreakers* was the documatic to end them all. Marvin narrated on-location reenactments of major crimes, with the crime victims and police investigators involved playing themselves. The 26-week series' novelty value, color photography, and Lee Marvin's name power (bolstered by the syndie success of his old *M Squad* series) securely planted *Lawbreakers* into Syndication's Top Ten, even though most of the on-camera "real people" were prime contenders for the World's Worst Actor award. In one deathless show, two people who'd been kidnap victims couldn't quite stifle their smiles as they play-acted being scared of their "captors." The crooks were usually portrayed by police officers, since the actual lawbreakers would have likely been disinclined to recreate their mistakes, even if they'd been asked.

The Living Camera (1964). Person-on-the-street interviews and cinema-verite glimpses of America were featured in this Peter S. Robeck production.

Man in Space (1965). Six-part documentary from 7 Arts, suitable for reissue whenever NASA made its latest advance into the Great Beyond.

Men in Crisis (1964). His own distributor by 1964, David Wolper's release that year was an Alan Landsburg production, the 32-week *Men in Crisis.* Narrated by Edmond O'Brien, these half-hours concentrated on significant conflicts of history: "Hitler vs. Chamberlain," "Darrow vs. Bryan" and such. Sometimes the conflicts involved Man against Immovable Force, such as "Kefauver vs. Crime" and "Salk vs. Polio." The one crisis that was never filmed, "Wolper vs. Official Films," took place behind the scenes. Official sued Wolper in late 1964, claiming that their *Biography* contract prohibited Wolper from producing any independent documentaries involving famous persons of the 20th-century without first getting permission from Official. Wolper dismissed the suit as "hogwash."

Men of Destiny see *Greatest Headlines of the Century*

Milestones of the Century see *Greatest Headlines of the Century*

Nations at War (1963). Expert weekly prepared by the Canadian National Film Board and narrated by CBC radio personality Bud Knapp. *Nations at War* was syndicated in the U.S. by Desilu, and remained a staple of educational and commercial television outlets until the general switchover to color programming in the late '60s.

Of Lands and Seas (1965–70). Col. John D. Craig, he of *I Search for Adventure,* was back in 1965 with *Of Lands and Seas,* an outgrowth of the ABC-owned stations' *Passport Seven.* The Of Lands and Seas Corporation shipped out 260 hour-long color travelogue tapes, offering in-person appearances by the filmmakers responsible for the travel footage to local stations picking up the series. The sheer volume of episodes made *Of Lands and Seas* a Godsend for new UHF independents of the '60s and '70s who urgently needed first-class, first-run nightly color material.

Parents Ask About Schools see *The Government Story*

Passport Seven see *Of Lands and Seas*

Passport to Adventure (1963). Travel show produced at WBKB–Chicago, hosted by that station's all-purpose host Jim *(It's Light Time)* Stewart.

Perspectives on Greatness (1962–63). Hearst's 60-minute monthly *Perspectives on Greatness* was just what it promised; "perspective" accounts of famous persons and events, refusing to take sides even when it appeared that side-taking was called for.

Places and Faces (1965). Celebrated travelogue producers Don and Bettina Shaw helmed this Cardinal Films release.

Quest for Adventure (1965). Another Cardinal Films product; the "Quest" was a 60-foot sailing vessel. Michael O'Toole hosted.

The Race for Space (and other Wolper Specials) (1960–69). Capitalizing on America's space-program buildup after Russia's advances of the late '50s, David Wolper put together a 60-minute documentary titled *Race for Space,* a sublime assembly of NASA and Soviet news footage, rare clips of experiments in the 1920's, Nazi film of the V-2 in the '40s, and generous portions of Fritz Lang's prophetic 1928 feature film *Woman on the Moon.* The special's thesis was that America had a lot of catching up to do before she could hope to match the Russians in the new space race. For ultimate dramatic effect, Wolper engaged Elmer Bernstein to musically score the program, and Mike Wallace to narrate. Despite this talent lineup, Wolper was unable to peddle *Race for Space* to any of the networks. There was a new on-the-record policy amongst the networks of not accepting documentaries produced outside their own news staffs: *off* the record, the government was pressuring the networks not to play up the shortcomings of the space program, but to build confidence that America could beat the Reds to the moon any day (never mind that *Race for Space* was made with full cooperation from the Department of Defense). Also, Mike Wallace was "risky" because of the trouble he'd brewed up interviewing people like Mississippi's segregationist senator James Eastland and gangster Mickey Cohen on his last ABC network program in 1957–58. Added to this dilemma was the fact that Wallace's commercials for Parliament cigarettes would wipe out half the potential network sponsors for *Race for Space.*

Acquiring a national sponsor on his own, David Wolper set up an ad hoc network of 104 stations — 99 of them major-network affiliates. *Race for Space* was distributed the week of April 24–30, 1960, running circles around its competition, grabbing several awards, and eventually becoming part of the audiovisual curriculum at West Point. Wolper proved that a very powerful nonnetwork documentary-special market existed, and followed up *Race for Space* with a 1961 sequel, *Project Man in Space,* and a sports special, *The Rafer Johnson Story.* Wolper spent the rest of the decade supplying series and oneshots for both network and syndicated play. Starting in 1964, he began distributing six yearly specials on a non-network basis, dealing with such topics as the Berlin Crisis and Women in America; his 1966 release, *China: The Roots of Madness* (produced by Mel Stuart and written by Theodore H. White), won a pair of Emmy Awards. Wolper was still at it by the end of the decade, syndicating specials that were regarded as "hands-off" by the networks, including a 1965 rebuttal of the Warren Commission's findings, and Chicago's Mayor Daley's "answer" to critics of the Mayor's police excesses during the 1968 Democratic convention. (This last one was seen on 137 stations; the Democrats' response to Daley was seen on fewer than 13.)

The RKO Specials (mid–1960's). The RKO-General stations group provided occasional specials to non–RKO outlets; the company's watershed year was 1967, with *Marcel Marceau, Art in Peril* (covering the search for art treasures swiped by the Nazis during the war) and *Face of Genius* (a study of playwright Eugene O'Neill).

Safari (1969). An ABC Films release hosted by Murl Deusing, *Safari* was produced by WTMJ–Milwaukee, and was run by that station for many years in prime time in place of NBC's *The Virginian* — sweeping the ratings all the same.

The School Story see *The Government Story*

Sea War (1963). A BBC-produced 13-parter, *Sea War* bore the influence of NBC's *Victory at Sea* so deeply that it even appropriated *Victory's* opening-title design. But *Sea War* abandoned ship very quickly, not only because its filmclips weren't very well chosen or edited, but also because host Rear Admiral Ray Foster Brown had all the charisma of a kippered herring.

Silents Please (1962). A Paul Killiam-Saul Turrell production comprised of half-hour abridgments of silent-movie classics, *Silents Please* was the surprise hit of ABC's summer season in 1960. After another network summer go-round in 1961, the series entered syndication via Sterling Films, with 16 new episodes added to the package.

Social Security in Action see *The Government Story*

Spectrum see *Group W Specials*

Sportfolio see *Greatest Headlines of the Century*

The Story of... (1962). With *Biography* in full swing, David Wolper fulfilled a fall 1962 commitment to United Artists Television with *The Story of...*, a 39-week "docu-matic" narrated by John Willis. This series featured in-depth studies of people in various skilled professions: jockey, nightclub comic, dancer, and so on. ("The Story of a Writer" featured Ray Bradbury.) Since all the film used was brand-new and not library footage, *The Story of...* had a bulging budget of $48,000 per week — but more than paid its fare in 110 markets, including several highly competitive cities with but one or two television stations. An unforeseen added expenditure occurred thanks to the Cuban missile crisis of October 1962: five *Story of* segments, dealing with a marine, a jet pilot, an Allied soldier in Berlin, the California gubernatorial race, and a JFK press conference, had to be reshot or scrapped completely.

Survival (1964). Official Films' 1964 release was Sherman Grinberg's *Survival,* 38 explorations of notorious natural and man-made disasters, featuring survivors of those disasters and narrated by James Whitmore. Following the cycle of such 1970's "catastrophe" films as *The Poseidon Adventure* and *Earthquake, Survival* was re-released under the title *Disaster!*

Sweet Success (1960). Jack Douglas/Official Films docu-matic, featuring such self-made folks as the fellow who designed the "living billboards" in Times Square. *Sweet Success* was produced mainly so Jack Douglas could prove that the "alternative programming" allegedly craved by local stations could be provided at a reasonably low cost.

A Time to Remember (1963). British documentary, farmed out to the United States by Lakeside Films. *Time to Remember* anticipated Alan Landsburg's *Between the Wars* (1978) by offering weekly glimpses of the comings and goings of mankind between the two world conflicts. The mood was more lighthearted than Landsburg's show however, with Roger Livesy providing *Time to Remember's* tongue-in-cheek narration.

Trails to Adventure see The American West

True Adventure (1960–61). Full-color, 78-week nature study from the Bill Burrud Factory.

Untamed World (1968). In-the-wild documentary narrated by Phil Carey, syndicated before and after its 1968–69 NBC-network run by Metromedia.

Wild Cargo (1962). A Lakeside release, *Wild Cargo* tracked the exploits of hunters without bullets who rounded up rare species for the zoos of the world. Lakeside covered the same ground with new footage in 1965's *Capture.*

The Wolper Specials see Race for Space

World Adventure (1966). Long-running WWJ–Detroit local hosted by pleasantly plump George Pierrot, syndicated nationally by Field Communications.

The World of Lowell Thomas (1965). Peter S. Robeck Productions' pastiche of clips from Thomas' past television and movie work.

WPIX Specials (mid–1960's). WPIX-TV, a Manhattan independent owned by the New York *Daily News,* emulated Group W by shipping out its best specials to the rest of the country through the distribution of Bill Burrud's Teledynamics company.

The Xerox Specials (mid–1960's). Undaunted by a disastrous mid–60's series of United Nations dramatic specials for the networks, the Xerox

Corporation remained dedicated to bringing meaningful fare to the viewers. The company's best syndie showing from this period was *Storm in Summer,* an antidrug special widely distributed in 1966.

Westerns

"What westerns?" one asks. Like most television trends, the western burned itself out with too many series, too many lookalike stars and plots, too many gimmicks. *Death Valley Days* and its four rerun "spinoffs" (detailed in our 1950's notes) continued to prosper, but the 1960's produced only three new non-network horse operas — one of them a daily children's show.

Buckaroo 500 (1964). Fifteen-minute daily kiddie hodgepodge with a "cowboy" host (Buck Weaver), country-western songs, and audience-participation games — sort of a *Bozo* in buckskins.

Pony Express (1960). California National Productions' *Pony Express,* starring Grant Sullivan, Bill Cord and Don Dorrell (who could forget *them?*), was strategically released to coincide with both the Civil War centennial and the 100th anniversary of the founding of the real Pony Express. The original mail service lasted about 18 months; CNP's *Pony Express* rode for 39 weeks.

Two Faces West (1960). Screen Gems' cowboy syndie for the fall of 1960, originally titled *The Brothers January,* was renamed *Two Faces West* to avoid confusion with CBS Films' *Brothers Brannagan* (they paid people to worry about things like that). Television critics who'd had trouble telling the Brannagan brothers apart had even more difficulty differentiating between Ben January (a marshal) and his brother Rick (a doctor) — mainly because both parts were played by the same actor, *Manhunt* veteran Charles Bateman. Another "gimmick" western, perhaps? Not according to the series' producer Matthew Rapf, who insisted that having one actor play both roles was merely an economy move. Mr. Rapf of course was assuming that the average television viewer was not aware of the cost and production time involved in setting up split-screen sequences with tricky stand-in work. After a strong start, *Two Faces West* was abandoned by its audience, who recognized the series for what it was: a gimmick western, pure and simple, and not a very good one at that.

The 1970's

Guiding the destiny of most of the 1970's syndicated market were four little words: Prime Time Access Rule. The P.T.A.R. was a gathering of climaxes which began in the '50s. Back then, the television roost was ruled by the major advertisers, who not only determined what you'd see, but what you *wouldn't* see on what you saw—the *reductio ad absurdum* of this being such stunts as airbrushing the Chrysler Building off the New York skyline on a program sponsored by a rival auto firm. After certain sponsors' lust for high ratings resulted in the quiz show cheating scandals of 1958 (some contestants who'd proven popular with the viewers were given their quiz answers in advance), the Federal Communications Commission took a lot of the program control away from advertisers and handed it instead to the three major networks. Not that the networks' hands were much cleaner; the film studios producing many of the series began chafing because the networks had the last say over program content, but even more galling was what happened after those network film series went into syndication. Each network retained controlling interest in most of their shows, so it was they, *not* the film studios, who got the biggest share of residuals. Local stations also disliked the network monopoly; when time came for them to buy the best of those reruns for local play, the networks were likely to adopt a policy of "Buy *all* our reruns—even the dogs—or get nothing!" Shades of the movie industry's "block-booking" practices in the '40s.

Around 1965, the Westinghouse station group started a strong lobby against the networks' having all the best prime time slots; how, complained Westinghouse, could smaller firms hope to compete with ABC, CBS and NBC without having access to the best airtimes? At the same time, the FCC was stepping up its efforts to get the network to agree to a 50–50 profits split with local affiliates. When companies like Westinghouse agreed that they'd honor such a split if given the chance, the FCC paid attention—and by 1970 began taking decisive action. The first move was to insist that networks get out of the syndication business and give other distributors a break. CBS Films responded by changing its name to Viacom, getting FCC approval only after Viacom's executives sold all their CBS stock holdings. ABC

Films followed suit in 1973, transforming into Worldvision. NBC merely sold its network reruns to individual syndicators. At first this "get out of syndication" rule applied only to programs produced after 1971, but an antitrust suit resulted in the network's being forced to divest themselves of *all* their reruns from the beginning of filmed television.

Next, the FCC dictated that each network give back one nightly half-hour of airtime to their affiliates, a move designed to give other distributors a crack at prime time. The FCC also hoped that the extra local time would spark local stations and non-network station groups into a spurt of creative, bold, innovational new programming; this was called "diversification." And thus in September of 1971, the Prime Time Access Rule was born. P.T.A.R. didn't exactly inspire dancing in the streets. The networks weren't keen on losing three-and-a-half hours of weekly airtime, claiming that this loss stifled *their* creativity. Local stations for the most part hadn't a clue as to how to fill their new "access" time. Adding to the problem was that there was no official, unilateral decision as to just which half-hour per evening would be given back to the locals, so how in the world did anyone know what sort of new programming was called for if no one had any idea which demographic viewer group they'd be aiming at? An agreement was arrived at for the 1971-72 season: Access Time would in general be 7 to 8 p.m. (ET) on Monday, Wednesday, Thursday, Friday and Saturday. On Tuesday, the networks could keep 7:30 p.m., but NBC and CBS would give up 10:30–11:00. On Sunday, NBC stayed at 7:30–11 p.m., giving up 10:30 Fridays in exchange; CBS's Sunday schedule was 7:30–10:30, ABC's 8 to 11. And in order to keep 10:30 Tuesday night and to compensate for "network overtime" on their Monday night football games, ABC relinquished a half-hour (8:30–9 p.m.) in the *middle* of their Monday evening schedule. Why, a four-year-old child could understand this set-up. But most forty-year-old programming executives could not.

Taking advantage of access time, several syndicators "rushed to syndicate" in 1971, with wildly varying results. A few local outlets, most notably the Westinghouse-owned channels, made brave efforts at creating their own access fare. Other channels, emulating a couple of the big-city ABC-owned stations, expanded their nightly 7 p.m. newscasts to one hour. But most stations simply reran network repeats like *I Dream of Jeannie, Andy Griffith, Hogan's Heroes* and *Dragnet,* and did very well indeed. But the reruns lasted only until 1972, the year that the FCC, still craving "diversity," passed a binding rule that stations in the top 50 markets (representing 68 percent of the viewership) could *not* schedule reruns in access time. With very few exceptions, access programming had to be brand new and first-run. To make things easier in homogenizing access viewers into definite demographic targets, the FCC standardized access time as being 7 to 8 p.m. Monday through Saturday; Sunday remained the same as in 1971, but the networks were requested to run "educational" or family-oriented programs from 7:30 to 8:00.

In the earliest days of P.T.A.R., the problem of just what sort of programming would be most popular in syndication was partially solved with series that were merely new versions of old network favorites. *Hee Haw, Lawrence Welk, Lassie* and *Wild Kingdom,* dropped by their networks for a variety of reasons in 1971, went directly into syndication with new episodes and topped the syndie ratings charts for several seasons. This of course led other producers to create fewer untested first-runs like *Primus* and *Monty Nash,* and more warmed-over ex-network properties like *This Is Your Life* and *Let's Make a Deal.* By 1973, nearly 60 percent of the prime time access series were new syndicated editions of past network shows. Fresh, bold, innovative programming.

And where did the money come from to sustain these shows? A lot of the game programs were "cash sales" — sold for cash to local stations, who'd then have to line up their own sponsors — but these were low-cost enough to allow for this. The more expensive adventure, comedy and variety series couldn't make back their cost on a cash-sale basis. Most of these new syndies opted for the "Barter" system, which, as we've said several times before, was the practice of sponsors offering non-network programs free of charge (or at minimal cost) in exchange for gratis advertising time. Barter shows had long had a reputation of being Grade-Z efforts invented merely to showcase their sponsors. But as one NBC executive put it, "Barter is a dirty word, except when times are tough." Times were very tough after a national wave of inflation in 1971. Barter became respectable, and bartered series proliferated. This doesn't mean that the practice was 100 percent successful; after three years of syndication with a number of properties, Chevrolet left the barter field in 1974 for the more secure world of network advertising. Was Barter a failure, then? Not so far as Procter and Gamble was concerned; the company entered syndication the same year that Chevrolet left, and flourished for many years thereafter.

If the barter system was so hit-and-miss, why did so many sponsors subscribe to the policy during this period? The answer, like the P.T.A.R. itself, was rooted back in the 1950's. Many sponsors of 1971 yearned for the good old days of "program content control"; with bartered product, sponsors could once again call the shots. Several advertising agencies like J. Walter Thompson and Ogilvy and Mather became syndicators themselves during the '70s. So did a number of companies which bought television time for those agencies, companies like SFM and Syndicast.

As time went on, all syndicators realized that success in the access world was dependent upon big sales to the most influential station groups, like Group W and Metromedia, who'd guarantee them strong sales lineups in the biggest cities. And no more powerful station groups existed than the

15 outlets owned and operated by ABC, CBS and NBC. When the CBS o-and-o's purchased *Circus* in 1971, the NBC stations bought *Police Surgeon* in '72 and the ABC outlets went for *Ozzie's Girls,* hefty sales of these properties to smaller markets were in the bag, since those smaller markets tended to play follow-the-leader. It wasn't long before the network-owned stations began flexing their muscles, as when the NBC stations refused to allow a game show to make changes in its format, or when the CBS stations wouldn't permit another game show to raise its prize-ceiling above $25,000.

In September 1974, the FCC gave the networks back the 7–7:30 p.m. Sunday slot, maintaining the policy that the network offerings in this time period could only be news, public affairs, or family shows. Up until the '70s, the FCC had seldom dictated what sort of shows would be allowed on the air (else how could the more violent programs have survived?), but the days of non-interference were over. The next step in this power increase was the FCC's mandatory "Family Hour" ruling of 1975. Created under pressure from various private-interest concerns, this edict declared that neither networks nor local stations were permitted to run programs of an "objectionable" nature between the hours of 7 and 9 p.m. Ultimately, "Family Hour" was taken to court and declared a violation of the First Amendment, but the ruling wasn't dropped; it was merely altered to be on a "volunteer" basis—just like when you "volunteer" in the Marines. The Family Hour effect on syndication was instantaneous. No longer could action, heavy drama or "adult" comedy survive in access, nor could those series tainted with "mature" subject matter. To survive, syndicators would have to stick with programming that would please the whole family—and with costs mounting, those series would have to come cheap. Game shows, for example.

So by the end of the 1970's, the Prime Time Access Rule had succeeded not only in restoring control of program content to sponsors via barter and to networks via those networks' owned-and-operated outlets, but had restored to prominence the game show genre—the very genre that had inspired the cheating scandals which started this whole ball rolling in the first place.

Adventure/Mystery

This newly revitalized syndie genre offered the usual imitations of popular old network trends (spies, cops and cute animals), plus a refreshing—if not entirely successful—move toward Science Fiction/Fantasy, a form generally shunned by the networks on the bases of too-high cost and too-low appeal.

The Adventurer (1972). Bartered by Chevrolet, ITC's *The Adventurer* was filmed in Europe and starred Gene Barry, an international favorite thanks to his *Bat Masterson* and *Burke's Law*. Now get this: Barry played an American secret agent who posed as a millionaire businessman who posed as a famous movie star. Why a *secret* agent would choose two high-profile "covers," let alone how anyone could *pose* as a famous movie star, was as much a mystery as anything covered in *The Adventurer's* 26 half-hours. No matter. The scenery was lovely, Barry and the supporting cast (including Barry Morse and Catherine Schell) appealing, and the many stations who'd picked up the series (among them the NBC-owned) were happy with its returns during its single season. (See also *Double Action Theatre* and *The Protectors*.)

Adventures in Rainbow County (1972). A moderate success in its native Canada, *Rainbow County* was given a less-than-spectacular go in America by Group W in an effort to please the lobbyists for "more family entertainment." There was one familiar face in the cast: Lois Maxwell, "Miss Moneypenny" in the James Bond pictures.

Adventures of Black Beauty (1972). British half-hour version of Anna Sewell's girl-and-her-horse story, starring Judy Bowker (as the girl). Bartered for access by Johnson and Johnson (Fremantle handled the syndication), *Black Beauty* was acceptably nonviolent and family oriented. 52 episodes were filmed; 26 were run in syndication, while the remaining 26 didn't get much play until picked up by the Nickelodeon cable service in the 1980's.

***Black Beauty* see above**

Callan (1973). Throughout the '60s and '70s, innumerable foreign series were offered as ready-made syndie gapfillers (and also to satisfy the still-standing quota requirements). Many of the actioners of British or European origin, such as *Crane, The Rat Catchers* and *The Expert,* were in for a rough time Stateside; sales were minimal, usually going not to commercial outlets but to public television. One British cop series that might yet get wider exposure was a D.L. Taffner/Thames import, *Callan;* its star was Edward Woodward, recently "popularized" in America by the CBS series *The Equalizer*.

Department S (1973). A British favorite for four years before its American release (to 28 markets), ITC's *Department S* starred Peter Wyngarde as head of a special team of Paris-based Interpol agents. It was luxuriously produced by Monty S. Berman of *Saint* fame, but by the time the series made it to the states, spy shows were "out," especially nonbartered hour-long spy syndies with unfamiliar stars.

Dr. Simon Locke (1971); ***Police Surgeon*** (1972–73). *Dr. Simon Locke* was the series most frequently cited as proof of all that was "bad" about the barter system. Blame is frequently heaped upon Colgate-Palmolive for commissioning the series out of an allegedly callous lack of regard for quality;

since C-P already had doctor series in network daytime *(The Doctors)* and prime time *(Marcus Welby MD),* why not get out an access syndie as quickly and cheaply as possible? In all fairness, blame must also go to the Canadian Radio and Television Commission. In 1971, the CRTC decided that the overflow of American programs on Canadian TV was freezing out its homegrown product, so the old "quota system" of past years was reactivated. Canadian television people knew that most of their own country's series couldn't survive without American backing, so the old "co-production" gimmick was also brought back from the '50s and '60s. Canada's CTV and Valjohn productions, together with America's Four-Star and Colgate-Palmolive, developed *Simon Locke.* Its rural Canadian setting and Canadian production crew qualified the series as a "native" product, while its stars, Sam Groom (a regular on the NBC soaper *Another World*) as Locke and Oscar-winner Jack Albertson as Locke's crusty superior, were familiar favorites with American audiences. The participation of the CTV network seemed to assure a nationwide hookup for *Locke* in Canada with the attendant financial backing, but at the last moment, the CRTC rescinded its earlier quota ruling, permitting Canadian networks to run all the American programs that traffic would allow. Suddenly CTV wasn't interested in *Simon Locke,* which meant that the series would have to rely on its 100 American markets and several Canadian local stations to survive. All of these outlets picked up *Simon Locke* free, courtesy of Colgate-Palmolive's barter arrangement; with little production money available from its local markets and no funding from CTV, *Locke* had to make do on a budget of $50,000 an episode, less than half the average budget of a network half-hour—and every penny that wasn't spent showed up both on-screen and off.

Just how bad were things? Sam Groom, who'd left the lucrative world of soap operas because they had "no dignity," found himself sweating through all-night filming sessions in an old unventilated Toronto mansion (the series couldn't afford studio space) and changing costumes in the bushes on location because the budget hadn't allowed for dressing rooms. Jack Albertson, a veteran showman who in his time had endured the scuzziest of burlesque houses and vaudeville stages with nary a whimper, and who once hadn't batted an eyelash on a *Red Skelton Show* as he stood next to a cow that was overly relaxed, took one look at the first *Simon Locke* episode, let out a yell, and threatened to walk off the show. "After what I just saw," Albertson bellowed, "not a jury in the world would convict me!" As for the series itself, when the jerrybuilt sets weren't threatening collapse, the microphone was making guest appearances within camera range; one complex, extremely dangerous chase sequence had to be scrapped after a full day's shooting because the master camera covering the scene had failed to work. Ready when you are, C.B.

But it's very easy to tear something down (and it was a breeze for the television critics when *Dr. Simon Locke* first came out). We must note that the series did very well in the ratings, with most stations—including the NBC-owned channels—signing up for renewal. The fact that it was offered to these stations free of charge wouldn't really have mattered if it had done damage to the stations' overall nighttime ratings. *Dr. Simon Locke's* star Sam Groom registered strongly with the coveted 18- to 49-year-old female market; when Colgate-

Palmolive learned that these fans liked Groom but weren't overly fond of the series, the producers, promising more "network quality" (at a time when the phrase wasn't always a contradiction of terms), overhauled the property. Dr. Locke moved out of the sticks and set up shop with the Toronto Police — hence the new title, *Police Surgeon,* from the *Cowboy G-Men* school of catchall titles. Quality *was* improved, if only slightly, allowing for a generous helping of top guest-stars: Martin Sheen, Susan Strasberg, Keenan Wynn, Frank Gorshin, Nina Foch, William Windom, George Chakiris, Nehemiah Persoff, Leslie Nielsen, Michael Callan, Donald Pleasance. And definitely *not* Jack Albertson, whose "father figure" duties were taken over by Len Birman and Larry D. Mann. The superficial touch-ups enabled *Police Surgeon* to last until 1974, even though none of its staff was ever quite sure what a "police surgeon" was.

Doctor Who (1970–   ). This never-ending British sf favorite, the "mortgage lifter" of many an ailing American PBS station in the '80s, was given three chances at commercial syndication in 1970, 1972 and 1978 by Time-Life Television. Each time, most American station managers were underwhelmed. Those that bought the show ran it in serialized form, as intended, but its bizarre plot twists put those who caught a chapter halfway through a story at a complete loss as to what was going on. More damaging was the press reaction to the series; whenever the show was written up by a major American publication in the early '70s, the piece would dwell on *Dr. Who's* "silly" aspects. Dr. Who was a time-traveller who used a police call-box as his time machine: Ha ha ha. Whenever the actor playing Who would leave the series and be replaced, it was explained that the Doctor was allowed 13 "lives" in 13 different bodies: Ho ho ho. The costumes and special effects were strictly from Halloween, and the "faraway" lands visited by the Doc all seemingly had the same large stone quarry: Hee hee hee. *Doctor Who* was treated as though it were a bargain-counter *Batman,* and this bad press more than anything else ruined its chances at widespread American syndication in the '70s. But as hundreds of public television outlets of the '80s would happily discover, every Doc has his day.

Double Action Theatre see *The Protectors*

Elephant Boy (1973). Metromedia had hopes of appeasing the clean-up-TV brigades with the Sri Lanka–filmed *Elephant Boy,* but few markets were interested in the exploits of an elephant named Kala and his young master (played by "Esrom," of whom only Esrom's agent had ever heard).

Lassie (1971–74). *Lassie,* the ultimate clever-animal show, ran on CBS from 1954 to 1971, and though the human cast had undergone various changes of personnel, the series had three vital "constants." One was the doggie heroine herself (though that's not *entirely* true, since over the years Lassie was portrayed by six different collies, all of them certified — if camouflaged — males); the second was the series' 7 p.m. Sunday time slot; and the third was its sponsor, Campbell's Soups. In 1971, the FCC ordered CBS to give up *Lassie's* time slot to its affiliates, and it looked as though the old girl would be put to sleep after 17 years. But Ogilvy and Mather, the agency representing Campbell's Soups, struck a deal with the Wrather Organization, *Lassie's* production firm: Wrather would continue filming the show if Ogilvy and Mather could line up 100 markets for syndication. *Lassie* wound up with 202.

In terms of content and quality, the new *Lassie* wasn't much different than in its last CBS years. The dog had long since forsaken a single master and gone on the road from place to place, and this rootlessness was retained for the 1971–72 season, along with the series' superior photographic and production values. *Lassie* suffered no loss of its audience—in fact, since several stations ran the series in its old 7:00 Sunday berth, most fans never realized that CBS had cancelled it in the first place. By 1972, the budget was tightened a bit by having Lassie settle down to a single locale, a sprawling California Ranch maintained by Keith Holden (played by future *CHiPs* star Larry Wilcox). There Lassie remained until 1974, at which time Ogilvy and Mather decided the program had "run its course" as a first-run and put *Lassie* out to rerun pasture. The popularity of the syndicated *Lassie* seemed to indicate that adventure shows had a future in access time, even though later first-run series indicated mostly that *Lassie's* success might have been a law unto itself.

Monty Nash (1971). *Monty Nash* could at least boast of "network quality" in its production, understandably since the 26-week series had initially been packaged by producer Everett Chambers and writer Richard Jessup as an ABC network property, resorting to syndication after ABC decided that the market for half-hour adventure shows had dried up. On surface, *Monty Nash* seemed to have a lot going for it: Harry Guardino did a nice job as the government-agent hero (described in various publicity releases as a "James Bond type" or "Bogart type," fishing for an audience somewhere in there), and Four Star television made the costly but attractive decision to film each of the series' episodes in a different city. *Nash's* downfall was its scriptwork, uninspired at best, offensive at worst, even falling back in one installment on that most reprehensible of '70s TV cliches, "the crazed Vietnam veteran." With few decent story values, viewers had no reason to choose *Monty Nash* over rival telecasts of 1971's off-network rerun champ, *Dragnet.* Also, the different-city-per-week gimmick was eight years too late for the *Route 66* fans, two years too early to appeal to the new crop of stay-at-homes stranded thanks to the gasoline shortage. With a mere 31 markets, *Monty Nash* wouldn't have lasted even had the critics liked it, which they didn't; the San Francisco *Chronicle's* Terrence O'Flaherty crabbed that the series had "all the subtlety of *Highway Patrol.*" All the subtlety, perhaps, but little of the audience.

My Partner the Ghost (1974). This British ITC release favored conventional private-eye work with a decidedly unconventional twist. *My Partner the Ghost,* known in Britain as *Randall and Hopkirk (Deceased),* starred Mike Pratt as private dick Jeff Randall and Kenneth Cope as his partner Marty Hopkirk, the twist being that Hopkirk was stone dead, a ghost, who lent invisible aid to his surviving partner. *Ghost* tested extremely well during its January

1974 trial run on WNBC–New York. It didn't register as well in national syndication, but this was mostly due to an overload of access time product, and also because as a cop show, *My Partner the Ghost* was the sort of thing frowned upon by the professional killjoys who were lobbying for the "Family Hour." However, *Ghost* made enough of an impression in its brief life to warrant an American remake in 1980, the lead-footed *Landon Landon and Landon,* which died, died, died after its pilot.

Police Surgeon see *Dr. Simon Locke*

Primus (1971). *Sea Hunt* creator Ivan Tors decided that the new access viewers craved a high-tech variation on his old syndie property, and thus delivered *Primus* through Metromedia in 1971. Robert Brown, late of ABC's *Here Come the Brides,* played oceanographer Carter Primus, who often as not played second fiddle to his arsenal of equipment, which included a robot ocean-floor exploratory vehicle called "Big Kate." The series' color underwater filmwork maintained Tors' patented standard of excellence, but *Primus* was a hit only when wet. Whenever the series bobbed to surface, it was at the mercy of weakly developed characters and worn-thin storylines. Though the series managed a 94-station lineup even without barter assistance from a major sponsor, *Primus'* poor scripts, and Tors' efforts to do on $75,000 an episode what the networks were doing with $100,000 per half-hour, grounded the new show after 26 weeks.

The Protectors (1972–73). ITC's *The Protectors,* helped along by a strong sale to the CBS-owned stations, survived two full seasons, quite a feat in the cutthroat '70s syndie world. Filmed all over Europe, *Protectors* was created with both eyes on the American success of the British actioner *The Avengers.* The formula on both series was exactly the same: a man-woman team of international private eyes, the man a two-fisted fashion plate, the woman an aristocrat and expert in martial arts. Playing "protector" Harry Rule was American television star Robert Vaughn, who'd sworn up and down after *Man from U.N.C.L.E.* that he'd never do another series, but who had a lifestyle to maintain. (ITC's publicity hacks showed little shame when they sent out ad copy reading "Robert Vaughn makes the bad guys cry 'Uncle!' — as only he can.") Co-starring as "The Contessa" was Nyree Dawn Porter, likewise a familiar name to American viewers thanks to her work on the international smash *The Forsyte Saga.* Vaughn and Porter worked together well, considering that the half-hour series didn't waste much time on depth of character, and *The Protectors* might well have gone on to a third season. But Faberge cosmetics, the series' barter-sponsor, decided to abandon weekly television in 1974 to concentrate on "seasonal" ad-promotion campaigns. In the fall of '74, *The Protectors* and another ITC property, *The Adventurer,* were bundled together into a single 60-minute "cash-sale" syndie, *Double Action Theatre.* So alike were the two series that ITC might as well have called the new package *Double Vision Theatre.*

Salty (1974). 20th Century–Fox Television's Bahama-based *Salty* was 1974's variation on the *Flipper* format of father-figure (Julius Harris), freckle-faced boys and intelligent animal, in this case a sea lion. *Salty,* another balm to advocates of "family television," lasted but a year in the United States, but sold well enough overseas to inspire a feature-film version, directed as was most of the series by *Sea Hunt* and *Flipper* reliable Ricou Browning.

Space: 1999 (1975–76). The ongoing popularity of the *Star Trek* reruns led to a '70s renaissance of science-fiction series — though not on the networks, who couldn't forget that *Star Trek* was a major money-loser during its 1967–69 NBC network life. Syndication provided quite a few sci-fi affairs, but none of them were unleashed upon the world with as much pizzazz as ITC's *Space: 1999.* The Imperial Potentate of ITC (and much of British television), Sir Lew Grade, was approached by Gerry and Sylvia Anderson, producers of the "Supermarionation" kid's shows of the '60s, with the concept for a live-action outer-space opera. Grade went along with the plans only on the condition that *Space: 1999* be "the best space science-fiction program ever produced for televi-sion." To the mechanically minded Andersons, this meant that the new series would have to brim to overflowing with special effects, so they engaged the ser-vices of effects wizard Brian Johnson, who'd toiled on Stanley Kubrick's *2001: A Space Odyssey* and who'd later win Oscars for his work on *The Empire Strikes Back* (1980) and *Dragonslayer* (1983). The Andersons and ITC bankrolled *Space: 1999* at $250,000 per 60-minute episode, a price tag that would ultimately climb to $300,000 and require the financial cooperation of Italy's RAI TV network.

Lew Grade, of course, had his sights set on markets beyond England and Italy. To boost international sales, the stars of *Space: 1999* were Martin Lan-dau and Barbara Bain, known throughout the world for their work on America's *Mission: Impossible.* Eventually 104 different countries picked up *Space,* many of them, like Canada, planning to run the series on national net-works. Only the United States resisted a network commitment. So many "fresh, exciting" series concepts had failed in the years before 1975 that American network bosses weren't sure what the coming trend would be that year, and weren't about to risk valuable airtime on science fiction. So Grade aimed his "ultimate adventure series" at American syndication, using tactics that couldn't help but inspire admiration. In 1975, network-owned stations and the major station groups automatically got the best of the new syndies; also, UHF independent channels consistently lost out when these new non-networkers went directly to more profitable VHF network affiliates. In making sales, Sir Lew Grade deliberately bypassed the big station groups and VHF outlets, giving the "underdog" channels first dibs to *Space: 1999,* the sort of Grade-A product they'd always been denied in the past. The lag-behind UHF "indies" were especially responsive to this VIP treatment. Eventually, Grade was able to line up 156 American stations in time for *Space: 1999's* September 1975 debut — this without a single major station group in the line-up, *and* on a cash-sale basis.

This done, Grade's publicity team went to work. Hardly a day went by without a wire-service photo of Martin Landau, Barbara Bain or costar Barry Morse (who'd been on ITC's *The Adventurer*) shaking hands with this mayor or that club chairman. Press previews of the series' pilot were staged in such exotic but appropriate locales as planetariums and natural history museums. Sir Lew even wangled an endorsement for *Space: 1999* from rocket scientist Werner Von Braun, who since 1945 had had a genius for being on the right side at the right time. In the heat of enthusiasm, certain network affiliates began scanning their fall prime time network schedules to see which new shows could be bumped to make room for *Space: 1999*. (One frequently pre-empted sure fire loser was ABC's new *Welcome Back Kotter!*) When *Space* finally premiered, it disappointed no one. The special effects were all the fans had hoped for, the direction by Charles Crichton (previously a specialist in such light comedies as *The Lavender Hill Mob*) kept most of the first season's episodes moving at a fast clip. The music by John Barry was delightfully overblown, and even the unisex costumes by Rudi Gernreich seemed right at home in *Space: 1999's* streamlined, futuristic ambience. Critics were virtually unanimous in their praise, some overdosing on hyperbole and insisting that *Space* was superior to *Star Trek!* So carried away were people by the pyrotechnics of the first few episodes that the series' flaws were blissfully overlooked. Only nitpickers like Isaac Asimov were bothered that the series' whole premise — that several hundred space scientists colonized on "Moonbase Alpha" could be cast adrift in outer space when the moon was blown out of its Earth orbit by an atomic explosion, with no damage done to either the colonists, the moon or the Earth — was utterly lacking in any kind of scientific or natural logic. And because the special effects were so spectacular, it was easy to ignore that the characters on the show had about as much depth as a paper plate. By January 1976, the overwhelming success of *Space: 1999* made a second season of 24 episodes inevitable.

By mid–1976, attrition had set in. People began noticing that *Space's* scripts were so full of holes that last-minute bits of throwaway dialogue and "hidden" plot points were grafted on to make sense of the stories. Particularly damaging to fans suckled on *Star Trek* was *Space's* easy-out of making virtually all alien lifeforms on the series automatic villains, without a shred of *Trek's* respect and tolerance of lifeforms different from our own. The aliens on *Space: 1999* usually existed merely to be beaten by the heroes. (The producers got around "family hour" by observing that the baddies were seldom killed, merely stunned with lasers.) On top of this, Gerry and Sylvia Anderson split up. A new coproducer was hired: Fred Freiberger, the man perceived as the person who "destroyed" the third season of *Star Trek* with excessive gimmickry. Freiberger promised disenchanted fans that *Space's* scripts would get better and the characters be more "humanized," and that friendly aliens in the manner of *Trek's* Mister Spock would be introduced. Laudau's and Bain's characters developed a romance; Barry Morse was removed as the stiff-necked head officer, replaced with a younger, more "complex" character played by *Protectors* supporting player Tony Anholt. Catherine Schell (another veteran of *The Adventurer*) was brought in as a "resident alien" named Maya, denizen of the "Planet Psychon." Maya was typical of Fred Freiberger's obsession with gimmicks; she had the talent of being able to reorganize her molecular structure and take the shape of any other lifeform — human, animal or vegetable.

None of the "improvements" really helped, least of all Maya, whose transformations into monkeys and jaguars were mere special effects for their own sake, with barely any relevance to the plots. *Space: 1999* went out of production in 1976; the 1977 *Star Wars* film sparked a renewal of interest in science fiction and fantasy, enabling the 48 *Space* episodes to enjoy a brief rerun success, but the series was a dead issue by the end of the decade. It is important, however, that *Space: 1999* existed in the first place, for it proved beyond doubt that a very potent prime time market existed beyond the boundaries of the three major networks.

Starlost (1973). *Starlost,* filmed in Canada and syndicated by 20th Century–Fox Television, was created by the celebrated and very outspoken fantasy writer Harlan Ellison. Keir Dullea, the star of *2001: A Space Odyssey,* played a 28th-century youth who'd been condemned by his postapocalyptic society for speaking out against oppression; Dullea escaped his sentence by pilfering a space vehicle, *Earth Ship Ark,* taking along the girl he loved (Gay Rowan) and the girl's fiancé (Robin Ward). As suggested by the press releases, Harlan Ellison's original intention was to prove that mankind could survive and triumph despite the deprivations of war, prejudice and despotism faced by *Earth Ship Ark* each week. Alas, the series as filmed concentrated on the pessimistic aspects of a mismatched group lumbering in a derelict spaceship going from nowhere to nowhere — and the average 1973 viewer, beset by the antics of the Nixon administration and the headaches of the Energy Crisis, didn't need *Starlost* to remind them that life is a bitch. So appalled was Harlan Ellison by the series that he had his name removed from the credits, to be replaced by the alias, "Cordwainer Bird."

Star Maidens (1977). Hoping that *Star Wars* would keep the television sf market open past July 1977, Teleworld staged the American release of the bizarre 13-week German-British *Star Maidens*. Judy Geeson starred in this retread of the old one about a planet where women ruled and men were enslaved; in true B-spaceflick fashion, the ladies wore next to nothing and their "planet" looked more like a suburban shopping center. The saving grace of *Star Maidens* was the self-mocking direction of British horror-film specialist Freddie Francis.

Swiss Family Robinson (1976). The family hour situation compelled Fremantle to offer a Canadian network television hit in 1976, *The Swiss Family Robinson,* for U.S. syndication. Chris Wiggins as the Robinson *paterfamilias* was better suited to the role than Martin Milner had been in Irwin Allen's ill-fated ABC series version of the same property in 1975. But Canada's *Robinson* suffered in America because many station managers, regarding it as purely a "kiddie show" (which the Johan Wyss story had never really been, despite Disney's homogenized 1960 film version), relegated the series to the weekend

morning-afternoon ghetto, where *Swiss Family Robinson's* excellent production values lost out to competition from older — and far more violent —
animated cartoons.

U.F.O. (1972). Telecast in 91 American markets (five of the stations were
CBS-owned), *U.F.O.*, was a 1970 British series released to the United States by
ITC two years later to cash in on the *Star Trek* rerun boom. *U.F.O.* was the
first live-action project of puppet-show producers Gerry and Sylvia Anderson;
as previously mentioned, it was a retooling of the Andersons' 1967 kid's show
Captain Scarlet and the Mysterons, to the extent of hiring the actor who'd supplied the voice of Capt. Scarlet, Ed Bishop, as *U.F.O.'s* Commander Edward
Straker. Straker was head of a covert operation known as SHADO (Supreme
Headquarters, Allied Defense Organization), whose job was to repel any and
all invading Unidentified Flying Badguys, while maintaining utmost secrecy to
avoid worldwide panic. SHADO operated out of a base on the moon, and most
frequently out of a huge British motion picture studio, which looked
suspiciously like ITC's Pinewood headquarters. Fantasy television fans tend to
dismiss *U.F.O.* due to the woodenness of the actors, but the series' special
effects, utilizing an ultrasophisticated version of the "Supermarionation" process previously seen on the Andersons' children's shows of the '60s, were pretty
good for their time. And despite *U.F.O.'s* "save-the-world" mentality, the
series had a disarming lack of pretension when compared to the out-of-
proportion Anderson production *Space: 1999.* Still, it was hard to do well in
America with a 60-minute first-run syndie in 1972.

Children's

The formula espoused by PBS' *Sesame Street* — fast-cut music, comedy, information bites, positive social and personal reinforcement, and
plenty of puppets and marionettes — became the pattern to follow in the
early '70s. Even the lowliest local outlet could afford at least one weekly
kid's show that dispensed social values through the foam-rubber and felt
mouths of Muppet-like creatures. This trend of course continued in syndication.

Most crucial to the shape of '70s "kidvid" was the pressure exerted by
concerns like Action for Children's Television. Since 1968, the ACT had
tried to purge TV of what was perceived to be a glut of "useless" kid's entertainment. One of their main targets was the "Uncle" host who seemed more
interested in pushing commercial products than entertaining or enlighten-
ing his fans. By the mid-70's, this sort of host was all but extinct, thanks
to ACT. Also an "endangered species" was any children's program containing even a hint of violence (one old series frequently cited as harmful was
The Lone Ranger, for crying out loud!), and this put the onus on the thriving animated-cartoon trade of the previous decade. But what the ACT (and

smaller organizations like it) *really* wanted, so it seemed, was the total elimination of advertising on children's television. This made the organization the darling of people who didn't like TV, and the bane of TV producers who had a firmer grasp on the realities of show-biz survival. As can be seen in the *New Mickey Mouse Club* entry, the war against commercials managed to kill one of the few series that was given the unqualified endorsement of Action for Children's Television.

Battle of the Planets (1978). The syndie animation field of the late '70s had been blue-penciled into virtual oblivion by well-meaning pressure groups who screamed "excessive violence!" every time the Coyote fell into Grand Canyon after his latest acquisition from the Acme company had failed to capture the Road Runner. Knuckling under to pressure, the FCC made things tough with such actions as threatening to revoke the license of a Los Angeles television station if it did not, *at once,* cancel reruns of the cartoon series *Batman, Superman* and *Aquaman.* Hoping to make the status quo work in his favor, syndie producer Sandy Frank acquired a Japanese sci-fi cartoon series, *Gatchaman,* in 1977, then set about to "cleanse" it according to current policy. Frank edited out all scenes of intense jeopardy and violence, contracted Hanna-Barbera scrivener Jameson Brewer to write new scripts to fit the remaining footage, added new animation involving a cute talking robot (a bow to the *Star Wars* craze) to bridge the continuity gaps, and rerecorded the dialogue with such "harmless" voice-types as Alan Young, Ronnie Schell, Casey Kasem and Keye Luke. This whole package was released to the United States and Canada under the title *Battle of the Planets* in 1978. The series' initial wave of strong sales was, however, halted by the shifting sands of taste. As of late '77, the most popular syndie animation package was MGM's old *Tom and Jerry,* as mindless as violence could get! The swing *back* to fast action and mayhem made the expurgated *Battle of the Planets* look mighty toothless, and it's to Sandy Frank's credit that his expensive promotional campaign was able to keep the property alive and kicking for several seasons.

Big Blue Marble (1974–83). Taking the cue from its title, which referred to how the whole Earth looked when seen from outer space, *Big Blue Marble* was a magazine-style weekly presenting positive, nonstereotypical glimpses of children of various cultural, national and racial groups. Also spliced in were "pro-social" comic and dramatic vignettes, usually illustrating the virtues of Global understanding. One such playlet, "Hello in There," starred Jack Gilford, and won one of *Big Blue Marble's* several Emmies; the series also copped a Peabody Award. The series was financed by International Telephone and Telegraph, whose advertising approach endeared the company to those bemoaning the surplus of commercials on kid's programming. *Big Blue Marble* was shown without commercial interruption, the ITT logo appearing only at the beginning and end of each half-hour. Four minutes per show were left open to local advertisers — provided they agreed to leave the show uninterrupted and cluster their ads at the very end, just before the closing credits.

Call It Macaroni (1975). Another '70s series designed to broaden its young viewers' sociological scope, Group W's *Call It Macaroni* (bartered by Warner-Lambert and General Foods) leaned towards transplanting city kids into the great outdoors, and vice versa with rural children. A 1975 Peabody Award winner.

The Cliffwood Avenue Kids (1977). This Premore Productions release, starring a youngster named "Poindexter" (Randall Yothers Jr.) whose singular talent was the ability to cross his eyes, was an updated *Little Rascals,* featuring a group of young do-gooders who discoursed in a secret language and went after grown-up criminals. The bad guys were little more than non-threatening buffoons, and the series was low on real action-adventure; but the main thrust of *Cliffwood Avenue Kids* was to show how children of diverse racial and social backgrounds could live in harmony, and on this level the series scored.

Danny the Dragon (1970). Seldom-seen ITC British import; Danny the Dragon's young chum was played by Jack Wild, the "Artful Dodger" of the 1968 film *Oliver.*

Dipsy Doodle (1974). A bicentennially minded cartoon series, produced in Cleveland and distributed by SFM/General Foods, starring a bumpkinish descendant of the "original" Yankee Doodle.

Dusty's Treehouse (1971–76). A KNXT–Los Angeles production inspired by *Sesame Street* but good enough on its own to win a Peabody. Stu "Dusty" Rosen exchanged quips and educational tidbits with Tony Urbano's puppet troupe.

Earth Lab (1971). 60-minute Group W science weekly hosted by Rex Trailer and his computer "Philo."

Electric Impressions (and other Station-Group Syndies) (1971–79). Group W filled one of its 1971 access time slots with *Electric Impressions,* a music-and-interview preteen offering hosted by Ron Magers (age 27). *Impressions* was well produced, but never made it past the five Westinghouse channels. It was one of several kid's shows of the era created by various station groups to provide quality children's fare of their own, with the production costs evenly spread among their member stations. The RKO channels put together *The Froozles,* yet another *Sesame Street* lookalike. Taft Communications came up with *Max B. Nimble,* fun-and-info hosted by a professional magician. The ABC stations developed a weekend prime time access effort, *Rainbow Sundae,* in 1973, which hit the "Top Ten" in its chosen markets. NBC's five channels presented *The Shari Show,* with ventriloquist-puppeteer Shari Lewis presenting pro-social storylines within a takeoff of *The Mary Tyler Moore Show* (Lewis worked for "Bearly Broadcasting"); that same year, 1975, the NBC channels attempted to revive *Kukla Fran and Ollie,* which performed better on PBS. And in 1978, NBC offered a talking-machine weekender à la Group W's *Earth Lab, Whitney and the Robot.* All these series had aspirations of national syndication, but few got beyond the boundaries of their own station groups, a state of affairs that had less to do with quality than with an overstocked national market. (See also *Marlo and the Magic Movie Machine.*)

The Froozles see *Electric Impressions*

Gigglesnort Hotel (1979). A "local" that made it nationally, Bill Jackson's *Gigglesnort Hotel* emanated from Chicago, starring a puppet named Dirty Dragon. Vipro, Inc. distributed.

Hollywood Teen (1978). Since adults had their own "magazine" show *(60 Minutes)* and pre-teens were offered magazine weeklies *(Big Blue Marble, Kidsworld),* the 13- to 19-year-olds were served by *Hollywood Teen,* hosted by teenage heartthrob Jimmy McNichol.

Hot Fudge (1976–80). Originating at WXYZ–Detroit, *Hot Fudge* featured educational bites dispensed entertainingly by puppeteers Patti and Bob Elnicky. (Bob was co-producer of the show.) Bartered by General Mills and distributed by Lexington Broadcast Service, *Hot Fudge* was also available in a weekend "the best of..." package, *Hot Fudge Sunday.*

Howdy Doody see *The New Howdy Doody Show*

The Infinity Factory (and other Emergency School Aid Act Projects) (1975–79). One of the nicer by-products of the pressure brought to bear by Action for Children's Television was a bit of legislation known as the Emergency School Aid Act, which financed a number of series taped in ethnically mixed big cities that featured multi-racial and multi-lingual performers. *The Infinity Factory, Villa Alegre* and *Vegetable Soup,* stressing understanding and acceptance among children (and adults) of various colors and native languages, volleyed between commercial stations and PBS affiliates throughout the '70s. These series were distributed by TVaC (Television for All Children), as was the family-oriented *¿Qué Pasa USA?,* a marvelous bilingual situation comedy taped in Miami.

Jabberwocky (1975). From the adventurous WCVB–Boston and distributed by Boston Broadcasters Inc.; *Jabberwocky's* puppets interracted with children as well as the usual adult hosts.

Juvenile Jury (1970–72). One of the earliest projects of game show guru Jack Barry, *Juvenile Jury* had been a radio show as early as 1946, and a network television fixture (on both NBC and CBS) from 1949 through 1955. Barry and his partner Dan Enright brought the property back for syndication through Four Star in 1970, providing a ready-made "access" show when the new FCC rules went into effect one year later. Spotlighted each week were a panel of bright children who dispensed advice to the studio audience and the home viewers over issues both vital and trivial. *Juvenile Jury* was ideal for the "youth kick" of the early '70s, and as such was a shoo-in for weekend evenings, most notably on the ABC owned-and-operated outlets.

Kidsworld (1976–82). *Kidsworld* was developed by the Behrens Company with the hope of access-time sales; while the series ended up on weekend mornings and afternoons, the NBC owned-and-operated stations who'd intended to "prime-time" the show stayed with it. A weekly magazine series, *Kidsworld* bore some of the earmarks of *Big Blue Marble,* but was actually more a pocket edition of CBS' *60 Minutes,* with a team of hosts, three main features per show, and even its ticking-clock logo. In its own words, *Kidsworld* was "produced by kids, for kids"; this meant that the features were written or conceived by children, either the regular on-camera talent or the young home viewers. Concepts and filmclips were submitted to the *Kidsworld* staff from all over the country, in much the same way that Group W would later put together its *PM Magazine.* Features on *Kidsworld* ranged from profiles of youthful athletes and business entrepreneurs to pieces on the making of animated cartoons. Interview subjects included the then-current teen and postteen TV idols, along with adult role-models like *Happy Days'* Tom Bosley and the 86-year-old Groucho Marx! When asked how he got in the movies, Groucho replied feebly but firmly that he bought a ticket and sat down. The preteen interviewer giggled; who's to say that Mike Wallace wouldn't have done the same?

Kukla, Fran and Ollie see *Electric Impressions*

The Magic Garden (1975). Hostess Carol Demas held court over a gang of pro-social puppets in this daily half-hour taped at WPIX–New York and seen briefly on a national basis.

Marlo and the Magic Movie Machine (1977–79). One of the rare station-group kid's shows that flourished outside its five-station membership, *Marlo and the Magic Movie Machine* debuted April 3, 1977, over the CBS outlets, and before long could be seen in 70 markets outside the CBS orbit. Production and syndication were handled by a complex cartel including CBS, Hartford (Connecticut) TV station WFSB (where the series was taped), Fish Communications, Post–Newsweek, and the Corporation for Entertainment and Learning. Laurie Faso played happy-go-lucky Marlo, inventor of a machine known as "Machine" (its voice provided by Mert Koplin); this know-it-all creation dispensed filmclips focusing on past individual years and major historical events, as well as glimpses of current celebrities' baby pictures. The information-spewing computer concept was hardly new with *Marlo* (it wasn't new when utilized by *The Funny Company* in 1963), but was pulled off with a disarming freshness and smoothness. In the series' third and last season, the Magic Movie Machine offered quickie travelogues to distant lands. The series, and host Laurie Faso, were just the sort of ingredients calculated to placate even the most militant member of Action for Children's Television.

Max B. Nimble see Electric Impressions

Max the 2000-Year-Old Mouse (and other "inserts") (1970–79).
Although this educational cartoon-short series was produced by Steve Krantz in the late '60s, *Max the 2000-Year-Old Mouse* enjoyed its widest distribution when local stations were under fire to provide meaningful kiddie fare in the 1970's. *Max* was one of several animated fillers (their distributors preferred to call them "inserts") sandwiched into traditional afternoon cartoonfests to satisfy demands for instructional programming. The formula of these cartoons was usually to feature the animated "host" at the beginning and end, with filmclips or still pictures of an educational intent filling the three minutes in the middle. Other such inserts included Shamus Culhane's *The Wonderful Stories of Professor Kitzel,* syndicated by Worldvision and bartered by Bristol Myers, and *The Spirit of Freedom,* timed for release during the Bicentennial. Kaiser/Fields' series of *one*-minute information bites, *Snipets,* won a 1975 Peabody Award. (Trivia note: the theme music used for *Max the 2000-Year-Old Mouse* was later heard on Siskel and Ebert's PBS movie-review series *Sneak Previews.*)

The Mickey Mouse Club see The New Mickey Mouse Club

The New Howdy Doody Show (1976).
Throughout the decade, every effort was made to come up with perfect, inoffensive kid's series that would satisfy both the viewers and the media "watchdogs." This resulted in sifting through past television properties that had pleased the most and offended the fewest in earlier days; one such property was *Howdy Doody,* which ran on NBC from 1947 to 1960. In 1976, there were few Americans over the age of 25 that hadn't watched the fabled final *Howdy* telecast of September 23, 1960, when Clarabell the Clown (Lew Anderson) tearfully broke his on-camera silence with a whispered "Goodbye, kids." A decade after this finale, the members of Howdy Doody's home-audience "peanut gallery" were grown up enough to attend college, and when *Howdy* stars "Buffalo Bob" Smith, Lew Anderson and the little red-headed marionette himself began touring campuses in the early '70s, they played to S.R.O. crowds. This whiff of nostalgia was a welcome alternative to the sociopolitical dissension then sweeping colleges, and indicated that an audience for a *Howdy Doody* revival existed. A 1972 one-shot *Howdy* special on NBC was supposed to develop into a series, but went nowhere. Finally in 1976, *The New Howdy Doody Show,* taped in Buffalo Bob's home base of Miami, was ready for daily syndication through Metromedia and Victory Television. While its trade ads promised healthy doses of the series' old-style entertainment, there was special emphasis on up-to-date music and comedy for the youngsters. Some of the old *Howdy Doody* standbys retained included the basic puppet characters, the comedy skits, and the audience-participation segments. In respect to new racial sensitivities, the

character of dim-witted Indian "Chief Thunderthud" (of "Kowabunga!" fame) was eliminated; the actor who'd played Thunderthud in the old days, Bill LeCornec, was hired to play a new character, a Paul Lynde-like director named Nicholson Muir (after series producers Nick Nicholson and Roger Muir). The "girl sidekick" character, a descendant of such '50s *Howdy Doody* regulars as Princess Summerfall Winterspring and Peppy Mint, was brought into the '70s via "Happy Harmony" (Marilyn Patch), who was fetchingly attired in hot pants for the benefit of any "daddies" who happened to tune in. Also given a coat of 1970's paint were the tiny *Howdy* musician's band and the 50-seat Peanut Gallery, which gave way to a shrill brass combo and a studio audience of 400, typical of the decade's "bigger is better" theories.

While it was better than expected, *The New Howdy Doody Show* was a failure. The postmortem found that the series lacked the intimacy and spontaneity of the original, that its early-morning and late-afternoon time slots were inconvenient to the baby-boomers who might have been the new *Howdy's* most ardent fans, that the format was too antiquated to please the kids but too modernized to please adults, that no series can be sustained on nostalgia alone, and so on. But let's not dwell on negatives: Even though *Howdy* lost out as a syndicated strip, Howdy Doody, Buffalo Bob and Lew "Clarabell" Anderson remained very much in demand in the '70s and '80s for tours, personal appearances, municipal parades and much, much more. Audiences that had been unwilling to sustain nostalgia on a daily basis in 1976 have since proven more than happy to embrace it as a sometime thing.

The New Mickey Mouse Club (1977–78). *The New Mickey Mouse Club* was not Walt Disney Productions' first foray into non-network syndication. When the original *Mickey Mouse Club* (ABC 1955–59) went into off-net reruns in 1962, a few new sequences were filmed at Marineland of the Pacific, featuring USC physics professor Julius Sumner Miller as "Professor Wonderful." Ten years later, Disney came up with a first-run access syndie, a family-variety weekly called *The Mouse Factory,* which was reasonably successful but a financial drain on the faltering Disney empire. Part of the problem was that it was distributed by Disney's own Buena Vista; if the company was to enter syndication again, it would be with a less expensive property, and with some other company handling the headaches of distribution. Enter Stanley F. Moger, whose SFM company had recently switched from buying airtime for sponsors to becoming a syndicator itself. In January 1975, SFM acquired rights to the 390 *Mickey Mouse Club* reruns of the '50s, a property that carried no production costs because it had paid for itself years earlier.

Reissuing this property was the first step of a plan by SFM and Disney to develop the clean, positive first-run syndies that would pacify Action for Children's Television. The plan was to revive *Mickey Mouse Club* with new episodes and a new cast of Mouseketeers, but first the waters had to be tested with the old *MM Club* repeats to see if an audience existed for the new version. Results were phenomenal; despite the fact that they were shot in kiss-of-death black and white and the fact that they reflected an entertainment style of twenty years past, the *Mickey Mouse Club* reruns performed the old magic and soon were safely ensconced in the Top Ten syndicated kidvid properties (top five, in some cities!). Once certain of success, Disney began taping the flashy, full-color *New Mickey Mouse Club*. Aside from the expected clips from old Disney cartoons and features, the new series' choice of topics in the live-action scenes reflected the '70s; gone were such daily categories as "Talent Roundup Day" and "Guest Star Day," replaced by such typical abstractions of the decade as "Who, What, Where and Why Day." As for Mickey Mouse himself, the veteran star demonstrated his facility for changing with changing times by decking himself out in headband and jogging suit. And of course, the old "M-I-C, K-E-Y" theme music was rearranged into a disco beat. The most "1970's" aspect of the daily series was its choice of Mouseketeers. It was decided to avoid the all-white ambience of the '50s show (Annette Funicello was about as "ethnic" as the old series got); the twelve new Mouseketeers were comprised more equitably of blacks, Hispanics, and Asians, with the white kids less WASP than before. Strangely, these new performers were harder to tell apart than the Mousketeers of the '50s; despite the ethnic mix, they tended to act and sound alike. The only "star" to emerge from this new contingent was Lisa Whelchel, who later was cast in the NBC sitcom *The Facts of Life* as Blair, a character as white-bread and WASPish as they come.

The New Mickey Mouse Club premiered on 54 stations in January 1977, a debut geared to coincide with a year-long celebration of the Mouse's fiftieth birthday. The new series gained momentum, viewers, advertisers, and the dearly coveted endorsement from Action for Children's Television, which awarded the series with a special certificate. After 190 episodes, Disney decided that *New Mickey Mouse Club's* weekly $300,000 budget was too high to warrant any more new episodes; but no one was worried, since the series seemed assured of a long, fruitful rerun life. But then came 1979, and with it a fresh new Action for Children's Television attack, this time centered on the overabundance of children's advertising from breakfast cereals with heavy sugar content. It looked as though the FCC would once more buckle under to the ACT and impose a ban on such advertising. Cereal companies like Kellogg's and General Foods weren't about to bankroll future kid's syndies with this latest ACT sword dangling over their heads, nor were they willing to renew contracts on existing properties—such as *The New Mickey Mouse Club*. And so it came to pass that in December 1979, SFM withdrew *The New Mickey Mouse Club* from syndication. By managing to sabotage one of the few series which met with its complete approval, Action for Children's Television proved that it *is* possible to stab yourself in the back.

The New Zoo Revue (1972–75). The most blatant of the *Sesame Street* imitators was Fun-Co's *The New Zoo Revue,* bartered on a daily or weekly basis by Mattel Toys. The animal characters—Charlie the Owl, Henrietta Hippo, Freddie the Frog—were professional actor-dancers in costume, much like *Sesame Street's* Big Bird; in fact, the "Charlie Owl" suit was worn by former Mousketeer Sharon Baird—a onetime wearer of mouse ears ending up in the belly of an owl.... Producer Barbara Atlas co-created the series with Doug Momary, who appeared on camera with Emily Peden. Both Momary and

Peden were 23, a vital "selling point" for *New Zoo Revue's* youth-conscious publicity people. The series was cut from the same cloth as the other "singing animal" shows of the era, medicine-coating the sugar with songs and skits about self-improvement and tolerance. That it did so with gusto may be the reason that Lexington Broadcasting kept *New Zoo Revue* in active syndication well into the 1980's, despite the painfully dated quality of Doug Momary's flowered shirts and Emily Peden's miniskirts and go-go boots.

Pixanne (1973). *Pixanne* was a product of WNEW–New York, and sent out for syndication by Alcare Communications. Its hostess was made to appear teeny-tiny by use of an electronic process known as chroma-key.

Professor Kitzel see Max the 2000 Year Old Mouse

¿Que Pasa USA? see Infinity Factory

Rainbow Sundae see Electric Impressions

Rebop see Infinity Factory

The Shari Show see Electric Impressions

Snipets and Spirit of Freedom see Max the 2000 Year Old Mouse

Star Blazers (1979). Anticipating that the Japanese import *Battle of the Planets* would be a hit, the Claster company picked up Japan's *Space Cruiser Yamamoto* and ran it daily as *Star Blazers*. This cartoon sci-fier ran 65 episodes.

Summer Camp (1978). Instructional outdoors show, packaged by the YMCA; similar to the '80s *Camp Wilderness*.

Tony the Pony (1979). If anyone ever tells you that *Mister Ed* was the only series about a talking horse, refer them to Premore Productions' *Tony the Pony,* which enjoyed a brief multi-city exposure, first in access time and then on weekend afternoons. The horse, and other talking animals, were puppets with a predilection for dispensing information and advice; the "human" star was Poindexter, late of Premore's *Cliffwood Avenue Kids.*

Unicorn Tales (1977). A neat forerunner to Shelly Duvall's cable-television *Faerie Tale Theatre* of the '80s, Program Syndication Source's *Unicorn Tales* was a series of contemporized fairy tales, and an Emmy Award winner for Best Editing.

Vegetable Soup and Villa Alegre see Infinity Factory

Vision On (1972). One minority group studiously ignored by most television producers of the '70s was the handicapped, or disabled, presumably on the callous theory that physically and mentally impaired human beings weren't enough of a "consumer group" to worry about. Time-Life cared enough to import the BBC's *Vision On,* a 78-week series geared toward deaf and hearing-impaired children, with enough going on each week to appeal to non-afflicted viewers. The host was British cartoonist-comedian Tony Hart, who designed the animated "visual aids" used on the show. *Vision On* was an overdue but much welcome addition to many a market's access time slots.

Whitney and the Robot see *Electric Impressions*

The Wonderful Stories of Professor Kitzel see *Max the 2000 Year Old Mouse*

Comedy

If it's hard to remember most of the syndicated comedy series designed for access time in the '70s, it's understandable; this was the era of more memorable network comedies like *The Mary Tyler Moore Show, All in the Family, M*A*S*H* and *Happy Days.* A precious few syndie sitcoms were originals, but most dug back (sometimes way, *way* back) into previously successful formulae. The "comedy review" show did well on both sides of the debut of NBC's *Saturday Night Live.* Also on hand were a few syndie satires of other popular genres (soap operas, talk shows), though the satirical level was less Jonathan Swift and more *Cracked* magazine.

After Benny ... Thames Presents see *The Benny Hill Show*

All That Glitters (1977). The popularity of Norman Lear's soap-opera lampoon *Mary Hartman, Mary Hartman* (which see) had many industry pundits predicting that first-run syndie serials soon would dominate the airwaves. The first such syndie follow-up was Norman Lear's own *All That Glitters,* released by T.A.T. Communications on April 18, 1977, and run by many stations as part of a late-night "comedy block" with *Mary Hartman.* The premise of *All That Glitters,* established by Alan Jay and Marilyn Bergman's theme song at the beginning of each nightly episode, was that since the dawn of time, women had been the dominant sex, and men the subservient. The setting for this alternate-world fantasy was Globatron, a corporation run by flint-hearted women; the men on the series were simpering house-husbands or put-upon secretaries grousing about sexual harassment and not being appreciated as human beings. Role-reversal was *All That Glitters'* joke. Its only joke.

Viewer complaints came not from male chauvinists (few of whom bothered watching) but from feminists. The charge was that, by showing a world controlled by ruthless women in the same manner as ruthless men, the implication was that women would have botched up civilization just as much as men had if given the chance. Lest this make feminists sound like humorless killjoys, we must observe that most viewers *without* axes to grind were similarly ill-disposed toward the series. Though Norman Lear adroitly sidestepped admitting that *All That Glitters* was supposed to be a satirical reflection of A.D. 1977, the notion that the series was meant to mirror the sexual status quo of modern times was inescapable — and this was where the series really fell apart. The "joke" that women held executive positions ignored the fact that there were many real-life female execs, several of them in the entertainment business. The "helpless" attitude of the stay-at-home men on the series could not help but be offensive to men of 1977 who stayed home while wives worked and didn't feel helpless in the least. Also damaging was the fact that many of the jokes (one character went around planning to write a "rock opera") were generally three to five years out of date. Worst of all, despite the histrionic efforts of such pros as Lois Nettleton, Barbara Baxley, Jessica Walter, Chuck McCann, Eileen Brennan, and newcomers Gary Sandy and Linda Gray, there was not a single likeable *All That Glitters* character in the bunch. With brilliant material, a show with a cast full of unloveable jerks might have come off. But *All That Glitters* was just a step away from dreck.

We've gone on at length about *All That Glitters* because it managed to almost single-handedly destroy the syndicated-serial trend before it began. Anticipating another *Mary Hartman* bonanza, local stations running the series demanded and received top-dollar advertising rates. Once *Glitters* began to collapse, these same stations had to scrounge around for lower-cost sponsors, none of whom were able to cover the exorbitant prices the local channels had had to pay for Norman Lear's series. It was one thing to alienate viewers; when Lear started making enemies of television station managers, it was Goodbye Norman. *All That Glitters* was executed without ceremony four months after its debut.

America 2-Night see *Fernwood 2-Night*

The Baxters (1979–81). *The Baxters* started out as a five-minute sequence on *New Heaven, New Earth,* producer Hubert Jessup's weekly public-affairs series for the always-progressive WCVB–Boston. In each vignette, the Baxter family would come to loggerheads over a major crisis, at which point the sketch would end; then there'd be a cut to a studio audience, who'd debate the possible solutions to the problem posed in the sketch. So innovative did this concept seem that everyone quite forgot *Talk Back,* a religious anthology that had done the same thing nearly two decades earlier. Boston Broadcasters Inc. tried to syndicate *New Heaven, New Earth* to universal disinterest; but producer Norman Lear was intrigued by the potential of the "Baxters" sequence. He extended the sketch to 11 minutes, dressed it up with a Hollywood cast headed by Anita Gillette (late of Lear's *All That Glitters*), and issued his version of *Baxters* through Boston Broadcasters and his own T.A.T. firm in January, 1979. Given Lear's sitcom background, there was more emphasis on one-liners and set-ups than in the original Boston *Baxters;* otherwise, the format, with the sketch taking up half of each week's show, a studio audience threshing out its posed problems taking up the other half, was the same as before. Most local stations provided their own live audience and host; those outlets who couldn't afford studio work of their own were provided with live-audience sequences taped by Lear in Hollywood. *Baxters* did so well in its first 60 markets that it bade fair to be the syndie "sleeper" of its year. But it gradually developed that Norman Lear's production costs were outpacing his profits, so he dropped *Baxters* in 1980, at which time Boston Broadcasters shifted production to a cheaper Canadian studio and recast the series with less costly local professionals. *The Baxters'* novelty had worn off by 1981, but the series still managed to weather three syndicated seasons at a time when the average life expectancy of a syndie sitcom was roughly equivalent to that of a junebug.

The Benny Hill Show (1979–   ). Following the amazing success of the British satirical weekly *Monty Python's Flying Circus* over PBS in 1975, several attempts were made at bringing other British comedy shows to American shores. Gottlieb-Taffner, the American representative of England's Thames Television, used as its sales tactic the stringing of sample episodes from various imported series into "Thames Weeks" on WOR–New York and KHJ–Los Angeles; viewers then decided which of the sample series they'd like to see on a full-time basis. During 1979's Thames Week, Los Angeles viewers were treated to the antics of revue comic Benny Hill, whose preoccupation with things sexual wouldn't have gotten to first base (so to speak) in American television a decade or so earlier; by 1979, though, audiences inundated by "jiggle shows" like *Three's Company* and *Charlie's Angels* and the raunchy game show output of Chuck Barris were more than responsive to Benny Hill. Gottlieb-Taffner was encouraged to put together 65 half-hours culled from Benny's British comedy specials of the past ten years. For all its randy looseness, *Benny Hill* was really nothing new; the anatomy and body-function jokes were old when Grandpa heard them at his bachelor party, and the quickie editing and sped-up-action style had been done to death by *Laugh-In* in the early '70s. Benny Hill's real charm was a wide-eyed, ingenuous innocence in the face of the most outrageous sex-jokes, a whoops-my-dear comic style in the tradition of earlier British "naughty boys" like George Formby and Max Miller. Moreover, unlike other British comedy series which did hard-to-follow (for U.S. audiences) jokes about Parliament and General Assistance, Benny Hill did immediately understandable takeoffs on such American series as *Charlie's Angels* and *Ironside*. Never a ratings giant, *Benny Hill* nonetheless built up a large cult following which sustained the series into the '80s. To pad out its *Hill* package, Gottlieb-Taffner added a group of episodes with the title *After Benny, Thames Presents,* featuring such celebrated British funsters as Tommy Cooper and Frankie Howerd. Response to these comics wasn't remarkable, but it kept the fires burning until Benny Hill provided enough monthly specials to be sliced into more half-hour nightly doses.

Candid Camera see *The New Candid Camera*

Comedy Shop see *Norm Crosby's Comedy Shop*

Dave Allen at Large (1976). This British half-hour starred an iconoclastic monologist whose favorite target seemed to be organized religion. In the wake of *Monty Python,* Time-Life put *Dave Allen at Large* into American distribution, but got only a handful of PBS station sales for its trouble. *Dave Allen* didn't really take off in commercial syndication until the '80s, after *The Benny Hill Show* had opened the market for British "personality" comedy shows.

The David Frost Revue (1971–72). Chevrolet/Group W's *The David Frost Revue* starred the puckish talk show host and a corps of premiere comic talents, Jack Gilford and Marcia Rodd among them. The emphasis was on social satire, just as it had been on the precursor to the *Revue,* the 1967 British series *The Frost Report.* Few of the sketches bothered with subtlety, and most of them—notably a labored routine depicting the 1972 Presidential race as a "Miss America" contest—covered ground already staked out by *Laugh-In* and even *Mad* Magazine. As one dim viewer grumbled to *TV Guide,* "Hearing a new joke on [Frost's] show is as likely as hearing a revolving door slam."

Doctor in the House (1971–73). Based on a series of best-selling novels by Dr. Richard Gordon and an attendant string of popular British films, London Weekend Television's *Doctor in the House* was a racy, irreverent look at the lives and loves of a group of medical students at St. Swithins' Teaching Hospital. An international hit since its British debut in 1969, *Doctor* was bypassed by U.S. networks because it was deemed too risque for prevailing censorship standards, and mainly because it would probably result in legal headaches from the very sensitive American Medical Association. But Group W needed access material in a hurry, so *Doctor in the House* was packaged for syndication in the fall of 1971. By that time, irreverence and off-color humor were "in" thanks to CBS' *All in the Family;* in fact, the five stations owned by CBS made the first significant purchase of *Doctor in the House.* The following year, *Doctor's* American life was prolonged thanks to CBS' new *M*A*S*H,* which made "doctor" comedies palatable to even the most thin-skinned medico. Unlike *M*A*S*H, Doctor in the House* hadn't one iota of social consciousness. The series didn't try to change the world, it touched upon topics like disease and death strictly to induce belly-laughs, none of the stars (headed by Barry Evans as Dr. Michael Upton) indulged in Alan Alda-type pontificating, and the nurses looked more like the latest crop of *Sports Illustrated* bathing beauties. If the series' cheekiness was somewhat reminiscent of the *Monty Python* school of humor, it may be because its pilot show was written by *Python* members John Cleese and Graham Chapman, who named most of the characters after their own school buddies. The bulk of the series was written by another pair of satirical-revue scriveners, Bill Oddie and Graeme Garden, though John Cleese kept his hand in with some half-dozen episodes, one of which evolved into his later starring series *Fawlty Towers.* While only 72 *Doctor in the House* episodes made it to America, the series continued for years in England under such new titles as *Doctor at Large* and *Doctor in Charge.*

Dusty's Trail (1973). CBS' old *Gilligan's Island* comedy series never made much of a dent when it was network-run from 1964 through '67, but was a fantastic hit when it went into off-net reruns — much to the consternation of critics who'd consigned the sitcom to their "ten worst" lists. On the coattails of the *Gilligan's* success story, the producer, Sherwood Schwartz (who'd since had an even bigger hit, *The Brady Bunch*), sold Metromedia on a new access syndie sitcom for 1973, *Dusty's Trail*. Both *Gilligan's* and *Dusty* starred Bob Denver as the eponymous hero; both told of a group of people cut off from civilization and forced to fend for themselves. Both series even had the same seven character "types": Group Leader, Bumbling Assistant, Intellectual, Schoolmarm, Flashy Showgirl, Wealthy Married Couple. (On *Dusty's Trail,* these roles were filled by Forrest Tucker, Bob Denver, Bill Cort, Lori Saunders, Linda Kaye Henning, Ivor Francis and Lynne Wood. You *know* who played them on *Gilligan's Island*.) The difference was that *Gilligan's Island* took place on a desert isle, while *Dusty's Trail* was played out in a Conestoga wagon, separated from its wagon train in the 19th-century western wilderness. Since lost wagons tend to invoke memories of the Donner Party, the characters in *Dusty's Trail* came in regular contact with such outsiders as cavalrymen, Indians, outlaws and sharpsters. Thanks to *Gilligan's Island's* established appeal, *Dusty's Trail* sold like crazy (100 stations, including the CBS-owned) and opened big — then was shot down in flames after a single season. Beyond the fact that it wasn't even remotely good, *Dusty's* big mistake was Sherwood Schwartz' assumption that *Gilligan's* jokes and situations would work in any context. Desert islands can be funny, and lost wagons can be funny — *but not in the same way!* Schwartz' apparent belief that audiences who'd swallow *Gilligan* would swallow anything didn't work with *Dusty's Trail*. Audiences don't like to be reminded that they often act like sheep.

Everything Goes (1973). Canadian *Laugh-In*-style comedy series. This Winters-Rosen production was hosted by malaprop-happy monologist Norm Crosby and Tom O'Malley (the comedian who'd posed as a service-station attendant in a series of '60s gasoline commercials).

Fernwood 2-Night (1977); **America 2-Night** (1978). Norman Lear's talk-show lampoon *Fernwood 2-Night* was designed as a summer '77 interim series to bridge the gap between the last episode of *Mary Hartman, Mary Hartman* and the premiere of Lear's "new" satiric serial *Forever Fernwood*. A continuum was maintained by populating *Fernwood 2-Night* with the residents of Fernwood, Ohio, who'd come to prominence on *Mary Hartman*. It was hosted by two *Hartman* featured players, Martin Mull (as Barth Gimble) and Fred Willard (as Jerry Hubbard), and was allegedly telecast from their mythical hometown. Added to this undymanic duo was orchestra leader "Happy Kyne," played by real-life musician and sometimes comic actor Frank DeVol. Premiering on the 4th of July, *Fernwood* was self-consciously touted as the show "with something to offend everybody," although producer Alan Thicke drew the line at jokes about death — curious, since it had been a "running gag" on *Mary Hartman*. The main requirement for *Fernwood* material was that it be outrageous and unpredictable; outrageous it was, but its unpredictability was taken away first by critics who were quoting the series' best jokes before its premiere, and then by Norman Lear's tendency to hammer a joke to death. During its first few weeks, the nightly half-hour showcased a pianist encased in an iron lung, a segment titled "Talk to the Jew," a scientist who used laboratory rats to prove that leisure suits caused cancer, the grieving parents of a Roman Catholic priest who wanted their son "de-programmed," a bribe-taking consumer advocate, and a school principal who demonstrated corporal punishment on a well-endowed young lady. Later segments, many written just before taping time to keep up spontaneity, included hearing-ear dogs for the deaf, "The Church of the Divine Lemonade," and a specious telethon to keep the show on the air. More frantic than funny, *Fernwood 2-Night's* many weak spots were glossed over by the talent of its supporting cast, most prominently Dabney Coleman reviving his *Mary Hartman* role as Fernwood mayor Merle Jeeter, and Jim Varney, dry-running his "Ernest" character long before his string of popular "Hey, Vern!" commercials.

Fernwood 2-Night ended, as planned, on September 30, 1977. Had it clicked, the T.A.T. release would have returned in January 1978; evidence that it didn't click was the fact that *Fernwood* cut *Mary Hartman's* ratings by 50 percent. Even so, after *Hartman* sequel *Forever Fernwood* ran its last episode in March 1978, Lear and his creative supervisor Al Burton were back on April 19 with another talk show travesty, *America 2-Night*. The played-out Fernwood locale was replaced by a new location, Alta Coma, California (its top amusement spot was the Coma Cabana). By now, Norman Lear's audience not only expected the unpredictable, but could second-guess it. When *America 2-Night* regular Tony Rolletti (Bill Kirchenbauer), a self-enamored lounge singer, married his waitress girlfriend in a televised ceremony, viewers were way ahead of the game and knew that Rolletti's subsequent divorce would also be televised; and when a terrorist "took over" the show one night, it was easy to guess the moment, down to the second, that the terrorist would become starstruck and camera-conscious. When inspiration ran dry, the writers fell back on tested routines such as the "telethon" bit, this time a 24-minute fundraiser hosted by Jack Albertson, and the old gag of Martin Mull as Barth Gimble interviewing Martin Mull as Martin Mull (rendered twice as unfunny by having Fred Willard repeat the gag). The only people who seemed to have a genuinely good time with *America 2-Night* were its big-name guest stars who enjoyed spoofing themselves: Charlton Heston, Steve Allen, Jill St. John, Peter Frampton, Billy Crystal, Rita Moreno and, as the "prize" in a win-a-date-with-a-star contest, *Saturday Night Fever* costar Karen Gorney. Norman Lear insisted that *America 2-Night* was still commanding a major ratings share at the time of its August 18, 1978, cancellation, but that its high budget drove the show off the air.

Forever Fernwood see *Mary Hartman, Mary Hartman*

Half the George Kirby Comedy Hour (1972). Winters-Rosen's *Half the George Kirby Comedy Hour,* spun off from an earlier Canadian-taped syndicated special, starred impressionist George Kirby, whose talents were well mounted into some clever sketchwork. One of Kirby's writers and supporting players was a shaggy-haired young Steve Martin, who was then billed as a "comic magician." *Comedy Hour* reflected television's relative maturity in 1972 by not making a big deal over the fact that George Kirby was black (after all, in 1972 both Bill Cosby and Flip Wilson were starring in their own network variety shows). This didn't stop one eager publicist from going for a quick laugh in one of the series' trade ads, which ticked off the markets that had bought Kirby's series, then concluded with, "We were even sold in Jackson, Mississippi!"

Hilarious House of Frightenstein (1975). This Martin Grieve presentation ostensibly starred Vincent Price (who appeared only fleetingly), but was actually a vehicle for former *Sonny and Cher Show* regular Billy Van. *House of Frightenstein* was a five-a-week monster spoof (the main monster was named "Bruce") taped at CHCH in Hamilton Ontario by producer-writer-creator Rife Markowitz; it was touted as a kid's show but usually was telecast very late at night.

King of Kensington (1976). Canada's *King of Kensington* was released to the United States by Gottlieb-Taffner; because only 65 episodes made it to the states, and because most stations ran only half that many, it's not uncommon to see the sitcom written off as a "failure." In truth, *King of Kensington* was extremely popular in its own country, running a full four seasons and making a major star out of Al Waxman, an actor-director best known in America for his meaty supporting role in the '80s series *Cagney and Lacey*. *Kensington* stopped running only because Waxman was tired of the series, not because of diminishing Canadian ratings. Another charge levelled against the show was that it was merely a clone of *All in the Family,* with its middle-class hero's difficulty in coping with a changing world. Actually, Waxman's Larry King was nothing at all like Archie Bunker; King talked like a knee-jerk conservative, but was at base a soft-hearted liberal. He got into trouble not because he battled the other characters but because of his misguided efforts to do favors for them. Thanks to Al Waxman's *Cagney and Lacey*-inspired "stardom," Taffner gave *King of Kensington* a second American chance as a daily rerun strip in the mid–1980's.

The Lohman and Barkley (1976). Los Angeles radio comics Al Lohman and Roger Barkley, in concert with Four-Star Television, assembled what they described as "a comedy set in a talk-show." The series' wit quotient was established by its title, *The Lohman and Barkley* (no "Show" in the title; that was a joke, you see); by the assurance of its publicity that "Everyone's as zany as the hosts"; and by such highlights as "Celebrity Wrestling," pitting unathletic guest stars against the 300-pound "Masked Moron," who was actually the series' press agent. Maybe it wasn't any funnier than Norman Lear's *Fernwood 2-Night,* but at least Lohman and Barkley didn't get muscle-bound patting themselves on the back.

The Lorenzo and Henrietta Music Show (1976). Riding high with such networkers as *The Mary Tyler Moore Show* and *Bob Newhart Show,* MTM Productions decided to enter first-run syndication with a daily network comedy-variety series starring MTM producer Lorenzo Music (best known to viewers as the voice of Carlton the Doorman on *Rhoda*) and his wife Henrietta. This series had originally been packaged for potential network sale, but when the "big three" didn't want to risk the expense of a daily song-and-sketch affair, MTM took *The Lorenzo and Henrietta Music Show* to Metromedia, who lined up 40 interested markets. Geared for the comic temperament of 1976 with its neurosis-ridden hosts and you-can't-win comedy sketches, *L&H Music* looked like it had possibilities; in anticipation of its "stiff" competition, ABC began laying the groundwork for a rival network variety daytimer starring Hawaiian singer Don Ho. But with a wealth of excellent reviews notwithstanding, the 60-minute *Lorenzo and Henrietta Music Show* failed to lure viewers away from soap operas, game shows and Phil Donahue; when casual viewers did tune in, they were put to sleep by the Music's low-key approach to entertainment. As MTM president Grant Tinker put it bluntly, "the money wasn't there" for the company to continue first-run syndication. *Lorenzo and Henrietta Music* expired exactly one month after its September 13, 1976, debut; two weeks after the cancellation, ABC's *Don Ho Show* went on the air, only to die itself within four months. Neither ABC nor MTM would attempt daily comedy-variety again; as for Lorenzo Music, he went back "behind the scenes" as a producer, and most recently as the voice of the cartoon cat Garfield.

The Madhouse Brigade (1978). From Martin Grieve Productions; this Canadian-based political satire review was noteworthy only in that it gave early exposure to comic actor Joe Piscopo.

Mary Hartman, Mary Hartman (1976–77). Despite the fact that several talented people had tried and failed over the years to get a satirical soap opera off the ground, Norman Lear would not be dissuaded; after all, they'd told him that *All in the Family* wouldn't get anywhere either. Lear's first intention was to make a serial out of the old radio comedy sketch *The Bickersons,* but decided that its endlessly bickering-couple format was too limited; Lear then planned to use the continuing-story form as a takeoff of middle–America mores and values. He commissioned Gail Parent (who'd written the soap opera lampoon "As the Stomach Turns" for CBS' *Carol Burnett Show*), Ann Marcus (the head writer for the genuine serial *Search for Tomorrow*), Jerry Adelman and Daniel Gregory Browne to fashion a pilot script for a proposed comedy serial, *Mary Hartman, Mary Hartman.* With his solid success record as of 1975, Norman Lear had little trouble getting ABC to help develop *Hartman* (which the industry quickly dubbed *"MH2"*) and CBS to put up the money for the pilot. Neither network ended up buying the series, however. Lear, who revelled in publicly tilting at network windmills (there's no denying that the producer opened doors on television for previously "taboo" subject material, nor can one deny that he spent just as much time congratulating himself for doing so), would later insist that ABC thought a serial spoof "impossible," that

CBS declared the pilot too "weird," and that NBC, when offered *Mary Hart-man,* felt it was too "sexist." While it's true enough that all three networks turned the series down, Lear has tended to gloss over particulars. ABC would have bought the series had Lear included a laughtrack or studio audience to let the viewers know *MH2* was all in fun. CBS was on the verge of buying the series, but on a weekly prime time basis; Lear wanted the show to run daily in the afternoons, just after the "real" soaps. The producer's rejection of these network ideas indicated that he was weary of compromise, and turned to syndication as a way of getting a project across without corporate interference. (It was *not,* as has sometimes been suggested, merely to make more money; in fact, *Mary Hartman* lost $1.3 million in its first year, which prompted Lear to move distribution from Rhodes Communications, whose piece of the profits was perceived to be part of the reason for the loss, to Lear's own T.A.T.)

Even though there *had* been network interest, Lear representative Al Burton toured the nation to promote *MH2* for syndication armed with a sales approach that went something like this: *Mary Hartman* was the show no network wanted because of its risque subject matter, so why don't you "local" stations show how progressive you are by picking it up? Burton also used the "under-dog" approach adopted by Lew Grade when selling *Space: 1999; MH2* would always be pitched first to the lowest-rated station in each market to make them feel like they were at last on the ground floor of a "winner." Aided by laudatory prerelease articles by *Time* and *The Wall Street Journal, MH2* sold well enough outside the networks for Norman Lear to seriously consider creating a "fourth network" of his own.

Debuting over 101 stations on January 5, 1976, *Mary Hartman, Mary Hartman* grabbed instant attention with its overstocked (and Emmy-winning) pilot episode. Mary Hartman, a 34-year-old pigtailed housewife played in a near-catatonic state by Louise Lasser, was confronted by a down-the-block mass murder, the revelation that her grandfather was the "Fernwood Flasher" (the series took place in mythical Fernwood, Ohio) and by her dead-end sex life. All the while, Mary bemoaned the "waxy yellow buildup" on her floor. While it became less funny the more it was repeated by critics, the "waxy yellow buildup" line was a clue to *MH2's* premise: Life is *not* a television commercial, with instant solutions and happy endings. It was a good, solid premise that viewers could laugh at and relate to. Despite condemnation from a few (*Time* reversed its earlier opinion and labelled the series "Silly Stupid, Silly Stupid") and several soap-opera purists who felt that Norman Lear was demeaning their favorite "art form," *MH2* became a critics' darling and a viewer favorite. A few local stations objected to *MH2's* provocateur attitude towards risky material; WDCA–Washington, D.C., began censoring portions of each episode, while WTVR in Richmond, Virginia, dropped the show entirely. Boston's WCVB, on the other hand, ran the series untouched in a 3:30 p.m. slot because they *welcomed* the controversy it aroused. Except for WCVB, however, stations that followed Norman Lear's original intention of telecasting the series in late afternoons didn't do half as well as channels like WFLD–Chicago, who became top-rank ratings grabbers by running *MH2* late at night, opposite the other sta-tions' news broadcasts or Johnny Carson. This injection of adult humor in late-night slots led to a tradition of carrying "mature" sitcoms in this time period, leading in turn to the overwhelming rerun popularity of *M*A*S*H*.

Looking at *MH2* today, it's often hard to understand what made it work. The jokes seem obvious and repetitive, and the tendency to make death an ongoing "gag" (one character was drowned in a bowl of chicken soup, another was impaled on a Christmas tree, and so on) seems unduly self-conscious. What made the series click was the basic likeability of its cast. It was part of Norman Lear's genius (already demonstrated by *All in the Family*) to get the audience to "pull" for people they wouldn't want to know in real life; on *MH2*, this talent got viewers to follow the show faithfully, night after night, for two years. It also made stars out of character players like Louise Lasser, Mary Kay Place, Martin Mull, Ed Begley Jr., and Dabney Coleman (who insists to this day that his *MH2* role as Mayor Merle Jeeter is one of his favorites), just as *All in the Family* made a celebrity out of a former movie villain named Carroll O'Connor.

After a series of profound personal and professional difficulties, Louise Lasser left *MH2* in July 1977. After a summer season of a talkshow spoof titled *Fernwood 2-Night* (which see), Norman Lear returned in the fall with *Forever Fernwood*, utilizing *MH2's* supporting players. The star of this new series was Mary Kay Place, who'd won an Emmy as Mary Hartman's next-door neighbor, the enthusiastic but tasteless would-be country singer Loretta Haggers. Although the show was well put together, the loss of Louise Lasser as the "glue" that held the storylines together was fatal to *Forever Fernwood;* this and the general falling-off of interest in syndicated soap operas (only the largest-market cities were carrying *Fernwood,* the smaller markets having gone back to the security of network reruns) led to the new serial's cancellation in the spring of 1978. And as the dismal results that occurred when *Mary Hartman, Mary Hartman* reruns were syndicated in 1983 demonstrated, the Norman Lear "serial cycle" was definitely a product of its own time and none other.

The New Candid Camera (1974–78). The "old" *Candid Camera,* represented in various network versions in the '50s and '60s, had been available in rerun syndication for years; producer-host Allen Funt's venerable act of hiding a camera and catching people "in the act of being themselves" was a long-established favorite by the time it entered first-run syndication via Firestone Sales in 1974. *The New Candid Camera* offered the same silly stunts and humorous vignettes of "real life" as the older versions, only now in color instead of black-and-white. Assisting Funt at various junctures in *The New Candid Camera* were co-hosts Jo Ann Pflug and Phyllis George, and resident "stunt stager" Fannie Flagg. Longtime Funt associate Bob Banner produced the show.

Norm Crosby's Comedy Shop (1978–79). More giggles-and-yocks from Canada courtesy comedian-host Norm Crosby (see also *Everything Goes*). J. Walter Thompson Associates distributed this weekly offering of established and promising stand-up comics.

Ozzie's Girls (1973). This Viacom release was of course a continuation of ABC's old *Ozzie and Harriet,* which in 1973 held the record of being the longest-running network sitcom ever (it afflicted the airwaves from 1952 through '66). *Ozzie's Girls* starred, as ever, Ozzie Nelson (as stammering and "unemployed" as before), and his wife Harriet; son David Nelson functioned as the series' producer, while Ricky was off pursuing his sporadic singing career. The premise of the new series was that David and Ricky had left the Nelson house (at long last!), so Ozzie and Harriet, feeling lonely, decided to rent the boys' room. The new tenants turned out to be a pair of nubile co-eds (Brenda Sykes, Susan Sennett) who wandered in and out in various states of undress. The faintly risqué dialogue and situations arising from the presence of the girls was the series' only concession to the 1970's; otherwise, *Ozzie's Girls* was pure and simply a full-color *Ozzie and Harriet,* right down to the Nelson home's famous "living room," the same in practically every detail as the set in the old series. All that was missing was the enormous brass eagle that once had adorned the fireplace mantel; according to Ozzie, Harriet was sick of the sight of "that goddamned eagle." The pilot for *Ozzie's Girls* had been taped on the basis of what the Nelsons believed to be a firm commitment from NBC, but the network could find no room for the series on its 1972–73 schedule (at least that's what NBC told Ozzie). Filmways, the series' production company, took *Ozzie's Girls* to Viacom, which in turn sold the series to 100 stations (including the ABC-owned) with assurances of "ideal family entertainment." The buying markets were also banking on the general "nostalgia kick" of the early '70s, *Ozzie and Harriet's* previous track record, and the expected financial windfall that would accompany the issue of the *Ozzie and Harriet* reruns in 1973, to make *Ozzie's Girls* a winner. Indeed, when the new series premiered in October '73, ratings were strong and encouraging. But 24 weeks later, *Ozzie's Girls* was history. The people most affected by the "nostalgia kick," those aged 18 to 25, weren't in 1973 a significant enough consumer force needed to prompt *Ozzie's Girls'* sponsors to stay with the series; older viewers who'd tuned in the first episode to bask in the rosy glow of nostalgia found other things to do with their time once satisfied with briefly reliving their youth. Also, *Ozzie and Harriet's* longevity was established in another time for another audience. People unfamiliar with the old show couldn't "relate" to the '50s-suburbia ambience of the *Ozzie and Harriet* reruns, so *Ozzie's Girls* was merely a newer version of something those viewers didn't really want in the first place. And besides, *Ozzie's Girls,* while not exactly awful, wasn't awfully good, either. The series might have done better a decade later, when the "Baby Boomers" were determining the shape of television and were supporting the revivals of such older properties as *Perry Mason* and *Leave It to Beaver;* but this fact would have done little good for Ozzie Nelson, who died in 1975.

Please Stand By (1978). *Please Stand By,* the first syndicated sitcom since the double debacle of *Ozzie's Girls* and *Dusty's Trail,* came about because of economics. Network comedies like *Happy Days* and *Laverne and Shirley* were in 1978 being sold for syndication at costs determined by their network value, which was something in the neighborhood of a then-astronomical

$35,000 an episode. (Norman Lear was charging even more for a package of his network properties.) Local station managers found that the only way to avoid pawning the family jewels to afford these off-net repeats was to settle for lesser network castoffs at lower prices, many such series containing far fewer than the 100 episodes needed for a successful daily "strip." Viacom came up with what seemed an excellent solution: low-cost, first-run syndie sitcoms. If the idea took off, the syndicated comedies would build up their own fan followings and run long enough to provide local stations with economical strips; these stations could then tell producers of expensive network hits where they could go and what they could do with their high-priced reruns. *Please Stand By* was the vanguard of this proposed first-run movement. It was blessed with the attractive premise of having a well-to-do married couple encounter slapsticky situations after buying, then trying to maintain, a Tinker-Toy television station in New Mexico. Stars Richard Schaal and Elinor Donahue were already well established, thanks to their network contributions (especially Donahue, who's been on more comedy series than virtually any actor her age). Series creators Michael Warren and William Bickley had proven themselves as scriptwriters on such series as *Happy Days* and *Partridge Family* (and would continue to thrive into the '80s with such hits as *Mork and Mindy* and *Perfect Strangers*). And the producer was the superlatively successful Bob Banner. After the NBC-owned stations snapped up *Please Stand By* for their access lineups, expectations for the series ran so high that Viacom was drawing up plans for a spin-off series, *Pastor Prine*. The only way *Please Stand By* could fail was by doing too many episodes that had nothing to do with running a shoestring television station, or by not being funny. *Please Stand By* failed. It would be another five years before the spectre of first-run syndie sitcoms would again materialize.

Second City TV (SCTV) (1977–79). Though the words "Second City" tend to conjure up blissful memories of the Chicago-based comedy group which nurtured so many major comic talents, the locale of Rhodes Communication's *Second City TV* was Edmonton, Alberta. Series producer Andrew Alexander had set up a Toronto-based "Second City" troupe in that city's Old Firehall Theatre in 1973. Its first members included Dan Aykroyd, John Candy, Joe Flaherty, Eugene Levy and Gilda Radner. After Aykroyd and Radner were hired for NBC's *Saturday Night Live* in 1975, Andrea Martin, Catherine O'Hara, Harold Ramis and Dave Thomas joined the Canadian team. Following the lead of *Saturday Night,* producer Alexander moved his Second City into television, which turned out to be no cakewalk; Alexander was allotted only $35,000 to tape *five* half-hour shows. The resultant cheapness, at first a joke shared by the cast members, evolved into the premise of staging a weekly Second City series set in a super-low-budget television network — this leading to the concept of satirizing *all* network television. Opening fire on such targets as self-important TV personalities, pretentious "cultural" programs and copy-cat series formats, *Second City TV* maintained a satirical focus that *Saturday Night Live,* with its fire-at-random comedy approach, often lacked. It was easy to compare *SCTV* with *SNL,* since many markets ran the Canadian syndie just after the NBC weekly. *Second City* fans pointed out that the series' performers worked with each other rather than *at* each other, avoiding the ego clashes that marred some of the ensemble work on *Saturday Night Live; SNL's* devotees complained that *SCTV* was too timid, apparently scared of the "shock" material that was *Live's* stock-in-trade. Eventually, the two shows became network sisters when NBC, despite its president Fred Silverman's contention that *SCTV* was "too intellectual" for the weekend audience, picked up the show and expanded it to 90 minutes, complete with guest stars and musical numbers. This 1981 move was welcome relief to the Canadian cast's pocketbooks, but suddenly *SCTV* was at the mercy of the very network corporate minds it had been lampooning. Despite some very funny moments, the new *Second City* series suffered so much NBC interference that it frequently resembled one of its own "bad television" sketches.

Seymour Presents (1973). "Seymour" (Larry Vincent) was one of those television horror-film hosts who made wisecracks about the dreadful movies he was hosting; the Los Angeles-based emcee surrounded himself with such accoutrements as a "$10,000 hearse," and abetted his acid commentary with comedy skits of the pig-bladder variety. Syndicated by Rhodes, *Seymour Presents* was a series of 15-minute "wrap-arounds," to be used by local stations to pep up their own packages of horror movies.

Steve Allen's Laughback (1976). Other than his hosting stint on 1972's *I've Got a Secret,* Steve Allen's only syndicated contribution of the decade was a weekly, 90-minute retrospective of the best moments from his earlier series, distributed by Hughes Television.

Story Theatre (1971). Winters-Rosen's Vancouver-based *Story Theatre* was inspired by a well-received off–Broadway improvisational revue, created by Paul Sills. Sills' troupe ad-libbed its way through uproarious adaptations of famous fables and children's stories. Some of the best improv talent of the time appeared in the ensemble, including Peter Bonerz, Bob Dishy, Hamilton Camp, Melinda Dillon, Severn Darden, Richard Schaal, Richard Libertini and Eugene Troobnick. *Story Theatre* deserved far more than the handful of stations which picked it up for access time; most station managers dourly considered the series "too esoteric."

Take Five with Stiller and Meara (1977). J. Walter Thompson's *Take Five* was an enjoyable harkening back to the days of comic "fillers" like *Funny Manns,* though the five-minute vignettes were generally beneath the talents of stars Jerry Stiller and Anne Meara.

The Tom Smothers Organic Prime Time Space Ride (1971). Controversy-seekers were thrilled to learn that Group W planned to release *The Smothers Talent Company,* the title seeming to promise that Tom and Dick Smothers, who'd been booted off CBS for their censor-baiting political barbs in 1969, would be together again on the television screen. By September 1971, Group W fessed up that only Tom Smothers would appear on a permanent basis, while Dick would make occasional guest appearances. The series was released as *The Tom Smothers Organic Prime Time Space Ride;* with a pure-1960's title like that, you'd expect the sort of counterculture capers that Tom and Dick had been doing back in 1969, and you'd be right. Only now it was 1971. Tom Smothers' new half-hour had the look of a refurbished antique, and only 15 stations picked up his 13-week *Space Ride.*

The Trouble with Tracy (1971). This Canadian network sitcom starred Diana Nyland as a "zany" housewife who indulged in "wacky" stunts to advance her husband's career. While *Trouble with Tracy* was still doing rerun business in Canada as late as 1987, Rhodes Communications was less fortunate when it tried to syndicate the series below the border in 1971. American television already had one zany housewife too many.

The Wacky World of Jonathan Winters (1972–73). Chevrolet/Time-Life's *Wacky World of Jonathan Winters* — a rather limp title that at least was better than its original, even limper *Wonderful World of Jonathan Winters* — was heavily plugged as the only comedy-variety weekly that was totally ad-libbed (*Story Theatre* was long gone). Producer Greg Garrison knew from past experience that Jonathan Winters chafed under the yoke of formula television and written material, and that his greatest talent was improvising to his heart's desire. What Garrison didn't count on was that a half-hour was not the ideal length for Winters' expansive talents, especially when the comedian was saddled with mundane hosting chores and extraneous musical numbers; too often, Winters' bits were either too short to develop or too long to maintain comic balance. Perhaps Winters needed a co-host with the organizational ability to keep the show flowing, which might have happened had Garrison gone through with his original plan of making Steve Allen Winters' permanent "guest star." Instead, Jonathan was at the mercy of guest stars whose ad-lib talents were extremely variable. When a guest had the quick-wit skills of Debbie Reynolds (who appeared in the pilot), Burt Reynolds or Louis Nye, or when the guest was an agreeable straight man like Andy Griffith, *Wacky World* was home free. But all too often, Winters was up against the improvisational brilliance of people like singer/composer Paul Williams, who interrupted one of Jonathan's flights of verbal fancy by barking "Shuddup! I don't want to hear any of that!" Despite all creative roadblocks, *Wacky World of Jonathan Winters* delivered the goods often enough to keep spinning in access syndication until 1974 (its markets included the five NBC stations), at which time Chevrolet left syndication altogether in favor of the networks.

Wait Till Your Father Gets Home (1972–73). This Chevrolet/Rhodes release revived a format that had flourished briefly in the early '60s: the adult-oriented, half-hour animated cartoon. As the first such effort in years, *Wait Till Your Father Gets Home* was embraced by viewers as being off the beaten path; but a closer examination revealed that the series was nothing more than a Hanna-Barbera version of *All in the Family,* complete with conservative dad, ditsy mom, and rebellious offspring. Hanna-Barbera's animation was fixed at its usual level, about as visually stimulating as staring at a potato. The series' saving grace was its writing which, if not exactly Noel Coward, maintained a level of wit a step or two above the Hanna-Barbera norm. It also allowed Tom Bosley, who supplied the voice for leading character Harry Boyle, to test the "sitcom father" skills that would later serve him well on *Happy Days.* In its two-season existence, *Wait Till Your Father Gets Home* had the honor of being served legal papers. One of the series' gimmicks was a weekly "guest star," meaning that people like Don Adams, Jonathan Winters, Phyllis Diller and Monty Hall provided voice talent to their cartooned likenesses. This fantasy/reality crossover was extended to include lampoons of well-known people who didn't supply their own voices, but who were offered in caricatured form. No one complained when T.M. guru Maharishi Mahesh Yogi was parodied in one episode, since that bearded gent had been satire material since his Beatles days. But when a crooked used-car salesman on another *Father* episode was perceived to be a take-off of Los Angeles auto dealer Cal Worthington, Worthington sued not only Hanna-Barbera, Rhodes and Chevrolet, but also the five NBC-owned stations which carried the series. One wonders if Hanna-Barbera called forth Yogi Bear and Fred Flintstone as character witnesses.

Drama

Most syndicated straight-drama offerings of the '70s emulated that most popular form of the '50s, the anthology. What few continuing-character series there were mostly appeared in the limited-series format made acceptable to Americans by the PBS British import *Masterpiece Theatre.* (The most successful of these limited-series syndies, *Edward the King,* will be discussed later in the "Specials, Mini-Series and Mini-Networks" section.) A brace of serials appeared, one of them in the wake of the *Mary Hartman* mania. And quite a few mystery-and-macabre syndies came about when producers took stock of the fact that the old CBS series *The Twilight Zone* was still drawing crowds a decade after it left the network.

Against the Wind (1979). Thirteen-part gothic romance about a young woman (Mary Larkin) rising from squalor to success in 19th-century Australia. Taped on location, *Against the Wind* was brought to the United States by Worldvision/Taft (and in part by Hanna-Barbera!) as an answer to MCA's *Operation Prime Time* specials and *The Mobil Showcase Network.*

Crimes of Passion (1976). A series of 60-minute dramatizations of famed French *crimes passionel* and their resultant courtroom trials, produced in England and syndicated by ITC. This series managed a nightly prime time run on a New York independent station but was scarcely seen elsewhere.

The Evil Touch (1973). Allied Artists TV's *Evil Touch,* filmed in Australia, Canada and Hollywood, was in the *Whistler* tradition of giving unpleasant characters their just-desserts denouements, the reprobates forever making that one fatal slip which tripped up their perfect perfidy. A concession was made to *Twilight Zone* fans by having the wrong-doers on *Evil Touch* come to grief by sticking their noses into the supernatural and the occult. Hosting this anthology was Anthony Quayle, then best known to Americans via his lead role in NBC's short-lived *Strange Report*. *Evil Touch's* guest roster was of the usual mix, including Darren McGavin, Carol Lynley, Julie Harris, Kim Hunter and Susan Strasberg. Stories were on the whole well written, but most of them were compromised by *Evil Touch's* extra-low budget, which extended to the unconvincing wisps of "studio smoke" encircling Anthony Quayle's appearances.

Great Mysteries see *Orson Welles' Great Mysteries*

High Hopes (1978). As the syndicated-serial cycle of the '70s was in its death throes, Young & Rubicam and the Canadian Broadcasting Corporation were joining forces on a daily soap opera for simultaneous American and Canadian release. *High Hopes,* the series' rather supplicative title, premiered over the CBC and some 20 American channels (including the Metromedia group) on or about April 3, 1978. The barter sponsorship of Young & Rubicam's clientele made *High Hopes* a less costly purchase than Norman Lear's serial lineup (and at $10,000 an episode, less expensive to tape). But instead of offering an alternative to the general run of American network soaps, *High Hopes* looked and sounded exactly like its competition. Its college-town setting and lead performance by Bruce Gray (previously a regular on Canada's *Strange Paradise,* the star of which, Colin Fox, was in *High Hopes'* supporting cast) were inadequate ammunition against the long-established daytime favorites. The desperation-time inclusion of *Peyton Place* regular Dorothy Malone into *High Hopes'* waning days helped not a bit.

The Next Step Beyond (1978). ABC's Alcoa-sponsored *One Step Beyond* (1959–61) had been created by Merwin Gerard, produced by Collier Young, and hosted and directed by John Newland; it was a psychic-phenomena anthology, all its stories reputedly based on "documented fact." Procter and Gamble/Worldvision's 1978 access time revival, *The Next Step Beyond,* covered the same subject ground, many of its original lineup of television stations (including the ABC-owned channels), and returned Merwin Gerard, Collier Young and John Newland to their original production posts. Devotees of the original *One Step Beyond* tend to be unkindly disposed toward the 1978 revival, carping about the later version's cheapness and lack of atmosphere. The fans' hazy memories have blocked out the fact that the 1959 *One Step Beyond* was itself a quickie, studio-bound product with minimal production values. The sophistication of late–70's camera equipment allowed *Next Step Beyond* to forego the studio in favor of a rich variety of choice locations, including genuine crumbling mansions and dingy dark alleys. This verisimilitude permitted the newer series' stories to take on an immediacy and reality lacking in the earlier series. *One Step Beyond* faithfuls also maintain that its black-and-white photography was more conducive to sustaining a supernatural "mood" than the color tape used on the later series. These gripers didn't seem to notice that *Next Step Beyond's* use of muted color schemes was both eye-catching and creative; in fact, the company that supplied the series with its videotape equipment used the results seen on *Next Step Beyond* in its trade ads to "prove" that photographic excellence was possible even at low, low prices.

What ultimately worked against *Next Step Beyond* was not its look but its content. Beyond the fact that John Newland's lady-or-the-tiger story wrapups ("Did this happen, or didn't it? Can you explain it? Can anyone?") were less effective in 1978 than they were in the '50s and '60s, *Next Step Beyond* had a positively ruinous habit of avoiding brand-new stories in favor of remakes from the earlier series. In some cases, such as in the episode about the reporter who envisioned actual news events in his sleep, these remakes were virtually word-for-word. What was the point of shooting a new series if you were going to merely rehash old stories and bring nothing new to them, despite the advances in parapsychological research since the 1950's? In this respect, *The Next Step Beyond* was more like the First Step Backward.

Norman Corwin Presents (1971). In his glory years, Norman Corwin had, together with Arch Oboler and Archibald MacLeish, been one of the "star writers" of radio. Corwin's florid style, chock-full of imagery and alliteration, was heaven on the ears, especially when the writer indulged in whimsy and fantasy. Alas, his Canadian-taped *Norman Corwin Presents* was meant to be seen as well as heard, and what was seen frequently fell short of the words. Also, your average 1971 television station manager had only the dimmest notion of who Norman Corwin was. So despite a more satisfying longer run in Canada, Norman Corwin's brave, brilliant collection of half-hour playlets was sold by Group W to a paltry ten American markets — five of them belonging to Group W.

The Onedin Line (1976). Latching onto the *Masterpiece Theatre* fans, Time-Life did reasonably good American business with BBC's 26-week *Onedin Line,* a lavish costume drama (starring Peter Gilmore) about the British cargo-transport business of the 1860's. Any BBC series that could make a sale to a commercial outlet in Green Bay, Wisconsin, had it made.

Orson Welles' Great Mysteries (1973). His face framed by cigar smoke, Orson Welles did host duty for *Great Mysteries,* taped in Britain by Anglia Ltd. and distributed by 20th Century–Fox. The stories on this anthology weren't as much mysteries as they were tales of irony and revenge from the pens of Ambrose Bierce, Guy de Maupassant and O. Henry, with occasional Grand Guignol gracenotes as W.W. Jacobs' "The Monkey's Paw" (which had first been adapted for television as far back as 1939!) and room left over for a few contemporary tales. Familiar American faces popping through the sea of British actors included Victor Buono, David Birney and Clarence Williams III. Despite the series' title, Orson Welles appeared only in the introductions, and did not write, produce or direct the plays. He didn't even *claim* to have done so, which must qualify as a Hollywood First.

Paul Bernard, Psychiatrist (1972). A Fremantle American release, Canada's *Paul Bernard, Psychiatrist* wasn't a soap opera in the purest continuing-story sense, but it did have its own daily continuity. Bearded, pipe-smoked Dr. Bernard (played by Chris Wiggins, a Canadian who'd appeared in soaps on both sides of the border) listened to the travails of 19 women patients from different walks of life; as each woman made her return visits, her previous treatment would be mentioned, her future therapy hinted at. With the approval of the Canadian Mental Health Association, *Paul Bernard* hoped to enter the American consultation-syndie market opened up by Dr. Joyce Brothers and her colleagues. But beyond the Storer and CBS station groups, *Paul Bernard's* sales were meager indeed. Nor were those who tuned in the series satisfied with such smug, simplistic musings from "Dr. Bernard" as, "Have you ever tried to just relax and enjoy life?"

Roald Dahl's Tales of the Unexpected (1979–81). This wittily trenchant anthology from Anglia Ltd. was based on the works of Roald Dahl, whose stories had previously been put to work by such anthologies as *Alfred Hitchcock Presents* and Dahl's own brief 1961 CBS effort, *'Way Out*. Inevitably, some of the *Tales of the Unexpected* half-hours were retellings of Dahl stories previously seen on television, but unlike the *Next Step Beyond* situation, *Unexpected's* stories weren't so much remakes as they were alternative versions which could stand or fall on their own merit. Admittedly, nothing could have topped Alfred Hitchcock's 1958 version of Dahl's "Lamb to the Slaughter" (the one about the woman who clubs her hubby to death with a frozen leg of lamb, then cooks the evidence and serves it to the unwitting police), and the *Unexpected* version, with Judy Geeson miscast in the role so brilliantly played for Hitchcock by Barbara Bel Geddes, barely tried. But the 1979 reworking of "Man from the South," with Jose Ferrer betting a young man that his cigarette lighter won't light ten times in a row (the stakes being the young man's fingers) was every bit as good as the 1959 Hitchcock version starring Peter Lorre. And "A Dip in the Pool," previously filmed for the Hitchcock series with Keenan Wynn in the lead, was done far better in the *Unexpected* incarnation starring Jack Weston. (We must note that Norman Lloyd, who produced both *Alfred Hitchcock Presents* and the first season of *Tales of the Unexpected,* felt that the Dahl series was never as good as Hitchcock's — a peril, perhaps, of being too close to the situation for objectivity.) But *Tales of the Unexpected* was not exclusively devoted to remakes, offering a great many dramatizations of Roald Dahl stories never seen before on television, from the classic chiller "Royal Jelly" to the frightening true story "Genesis and Catastrophe," wherein Dahl demonically gets the audience to root for the survival of the 20th century's most infamous dictator. Roald Dahl himself hosted the series, proving a more relaxed emcee than he'd been on *'Way Out* back in 1961. Dahl helmed the British-taped *Unexpected* until succeeded by John Houseman in 1981, at which time the anthology became less the work of a single writer and more a grab-bag of famous "surprise" tales à la *Orson Welles' Great Mysteries.*

Tales of the Unexpected **see above**

Young Dr. Kildare (1972). One of the few dramatic syndies with continuing characters was Bristol-Myers/MGM's *Young Dr. Kildare.* This access offering followed the pattern established by NBC's *Kildare* series of 1961–66 by casting an unknown in the lead and pairing him with a "name" actor in the role of crusty old Doctor Gillespie. The magic had worked for Richard Chamberlain, who played 1961's Kildare opposite Raymond Massey's Gillespie; but the magic was gone for Mark Jenkins as young Dr. Kildare in 1972. In fairness to Jenkins, the poor guy never stood a chance opposite Gary Merrill, who as Gillespie could steal a scene by clearing his throat. The only "new star" to emerge from *Young Dr. Kildare,* albeit indirectly, was Marsha Mason, in the small occasional role of a nurse. Cursed with the sort of slapdash production values that represented the worst of the access "barter" shows, *Young Dr. Kildare* expired after 24 weeks. Its failure caused Columbia TV to abandon plans for the syndie revival of another old networker, *Father Knows Best.* Columbia had planned to go the *Kildare* route of casting its new *Father* without its familiar star of an earlier age, Robert Young; Young was then starring on ABC's top-rated *Marcus Welby MD*—the medical hit that had inspired the creation of *Young Dr. Kildare* in the first place.

Game/Quiz

The reasons for the rise of the syndie game show in the '70s have already been outlined in the introductory notes of this chapter. But if you're still laboring under the delusion that the Prime Time Access Rule encouraged diversity and originality in American television programming, read no further. The game shows will only depress you.

All About Faces (1972). Hosted by Richard Hayes, Screen Gems' *All About Faces* was a daily revision of an ABC networker of 1961, *About Faces,* and would later be reshaped for CBS' 1972 *Amateur's Guide to Love*—which in turn was reshaped into the 1978 syndie *Love Experts.* So many incarnations for so thin a premise: the celebrity contestant teams on *All About Faces* would view prefilmed sequences, then try to predict how the little "dramas" depicted in those sequences would turn out.

All-Star Anything Goes (1977). Once upon a time there was a British game show called *It's a Knockout!,* in which "normal" people partook in grueling, humiliating and ultimately silly indoor/outdoor stunts, for no other recompense than being seen on television. MGM Television optioned *It's a Knockout!* for an American version in 1975, but it was Bob Banner and Beryl Virtue who fashioned the stateside edition, retitled *Almost Anything Goes,* for the ABC network. For syndication, Viacom added the usual window-dressing of celebrity contestants (among them President Carter's brother Billy), and the result was *All-Star Anything Goes,* hosted by talk show emcee Bill Boggs. Like many game syndies of the '70s, *All-Star Anything Goes* was a weekly rather than a daily. The FCC was still going through its "diversification" charade, and preferred to "checkerboard" in the 7:30–8 p.m. access slot — running a different program each evening, rather than a nightly strip of the same show.

Anything You Can Do (1972). ABC Films' daily *Anything You Can Do* was originally produced for Canadian television by Bushnell/Don Reid Productions. As indicated by its Irving Berlin-inspired title, this series (hosted by both Gene Wood and Don Harron) boldly broke new ground by pitting the men contestants against the women. Another brand-new concept.

Bedtime Stories (1979). Hoping to tap the tickle-and-tease brand of "naughty" game shows that were the domain of Chuck Barris (whom we'll discuss in good time), Heatter-Quigley Productions developed *Bedtime Stories,* a spouse-tells-on-spouse affair of brief duration hosted by radio clowns Lohman and Barkley.

Break the Bank (1976; 1985). Hosted by coproducer Jack Barry, *Break the Bank* was the first of many fruitful collaborations between Barry-Enright and its off-network distributor, Colbert Sales. *Break the Bank* had begun on radio in 1945, had been seen on all three networks at various times between 1948 and 1956, and surfaced briefly on ABC Daytime in 1976. The object of the game was for the contestant to correctly answer a series of questions before being allowed a chance at the "bank-breaking" Final Question. In the first syndicated version, contestants had to guess which of the — yes — celebrities was providing the correct answer. The 1985 *Break the Bank* was produced by the late Jack Barry's partner Dan Enright for Blair Communications. The celebrities had vanished, unless you count the host, Gene Rayburn, who was eventually replaced by the gloriously named Joe Farago.

Can You Top This? (1970). So few game show syndies of this era survived past their first season that there sprouted up instant-replacement shows, much like the "second season" offerings waiting in the wings for the January cancellations on network television. Ready and able to fill in for any failed game show of 1969 was 1970's *Can You Top This?,* a Four-Star release based on an old joke-prone radio series. Wink Martindale and Dennis James hosted, while "human joke machine" Morey Amsterdam was permanent panelist.

Celebrity Charades (1979). Columbia Television's *Celebrity Charades* was hosted, appropriately, by a dummy — Squeaky the dummy, aided by his partner, comic ventriloquist Jay Johnson. The titular contestants played for charity, and the game of course was charades, the same parlor game deployed on the earliest of all syndicated game shows, *Pantomime Quiz.*

Celebrity Sweepstakes (1974–76). A 20th Century–Fox television weekly access version of a concurrently running NBC daily, *Celebrity Sweep-*

stakes was a which-famous-star-has-the-right-answer affair from producer Ralph Andrews. Jim McKrell hosted, with toothsome Carol Wayne the series' most often seen panelist.

The Cheap Show (1978). Another Chuck Barris-style "raunch" show, this one created by former Barris employee (and codeveloper of *The Gong Show*) Chris Bearde. Released by 20th Century–Fox/Firestone, *The Cheap Show* lived down to its name by having contestants indulge in ridiculous stunts for picayune prizes. Dick Martin hosted, valiantly.

Concentration (1973–78). This highly regarded "rebus" game, with the panelists trying to identify a famous phrase using a puzzle which was revealed piece by piece, ended its NBC daily run after 15 years on March 23, 1973. Six months later, Victory Television had a syndicated *Concentration* in a multitude of markets, which ran five seasons with Jack Narz at the emcee's post.

The Cross-Wits (1975–81; 1986). Ralph Edwards/Metromedia's *Cross-Wits* was a very simple, uncomplicated crossword-puzzle game; its one concession to Hollywood glitz was its use of the usual celebrities. In its review of the show, *Variety* opined that *Cross-Wits* "had legs." It sure did. Despite the stigma of not having a network history (usually the kiss of death for first-run syndie game shows), *Cross-Wits* lasted six seasons; it was never a big hit, but was a profitable timefiller, plugging up awkward gaps in many a local station's broadcast day. Jack Clark hosted the series' first go-round. In 1986, *Cross-Wits* was back, this time from ABR Productions (the initials stood for A. Burt Rosen, formerly of Winters-Rosen), "Crossed-Wit" Productions and Outlet Communications. ABR and company hoped to compete with bigger syndie guns like *Wheel of Fortune* by offering to subsidize local "cross wits" contests as a promotional tool. The new version, hosted by David Sparks, was generally seen in very early or very late "fringe time," though some emboldened stations, figuring they had nothing to lose, ran *Cross-Wits* smack-dab opposite the indestructable *Wheel of Fortune*.

The Dating Game see The New Dating Game

Dealer's Choice (1974); **Diamond Head** (1975). Producers Ed Fishman and Randall Freer tried to freshen up the game show market in 1974 by moving out of the big production centers of Hollywood, New York and Canada. There wasn't anything noticeably innovative in Fishman-Freer/Columbia's *Dealer's Choice,* with hosts Bob Hastings and Jack Clark presiding as contestants played games based upon such casino devices as dice, cards, and spinning wheels. What *was* new was *Dealer's Choice's* locale: it was widely plugged as the first-ever game show to emanate from Las Vegas. Sensing a future in game shows with out-of-mainstream locations, Fishman-Freer came up with a second Columbia release, *Diamond Head,* a mix of question-answer and the old ABC series *Supermarket Sweep.* (The winners had 15 seconds to scoop up as many dollar bills and gift certificates as possible.) As per its title,

Diamond Head was taped at Oahu's Kuilima Hotel. Bob Eubanks emceed (has Eubanks ever done anything *but* emcee?), and acting as "girl Friday" was former *Dealer's Choice* costar Jane Nelson, here keeping the audience alert by cavorting about in a bikini.

Diamond Head see above

Don Adams' Screen Test (1975). MCA Television had one of its fastest-selling first-run syndies in years with *Don Adams' Screen Test*. The series combined host/executive producer Don Adams' love of directing and his fascination with classic motion pictures. A few alumni of Adams' old sitcom *Get Smart* were along for the ride, including creative consultant Arne Sultan and writers Gerald Gardner and Dee Caruso; the producer-director was Marty Pasetta, whose yearly staging of the Academy Awards telecast made him as much a movie expert as Don Adams. On each weekly half-hour, Adams would select two members of the studio audience to help recreate famous movie scenes, costarring such showbiz pals of the host as James Caan, Don Rickles, Bob Newhart, Phyllis Diller and Shirley Jones. The resulting performances were judged by a panel of movie producers and directors, who'd then invite the lucky winner to play a role in their next production. Since many of these judges were well past retirement age, the winners were usually satisfied merely with a film of their *Screen Test* appearance and a new projector to run it on. Though its weekly $65,000 budget made it an expensive acquisition, *Don Adams' Screen Test* was considered enough of a sure thing to be picked up by the five NBC owned-and-operated stations and over 100 other outlets. As things turned out, those five NBC stations were instrumental in *Screen Test's* early cancellation. Most of the laughs on the show were engendered by the "bloopers" resulting from the recreated film scenes — missed lines, malfunctioning props, giggling actors. This meant that *Don Adams' Screen Test* was funny only if one found bloopers funny, and since most of these booboos were essentially manufactured ones, brought about by Adams' deliberate hectoring of the contestants, the humor got mighty thin after 13 weeks. Sensing that the series was about to wear out its welcome, MCA wanted to make changes in *Screen Test's* format. But the NBC-owned stations, all of whom were running the series in access time, liked the series as it stood and refused to let the changes go through (wasn't the Prime Time Access Rule created to *limit* network control?). By the summer of 1976, *Don Adams' Screen Test* was gone — but not forgotten. In 1984, an MCA-packaged series for ABC, *Foul-Ups, Bleeps and Blunders,* used generous portions of *Don Adams' Screen Test,* passing off its contrived foul-ups, bleeps and blunders as "genuine" Hollywood out-takes!

The Family Feud (1977–84). Goodson-Todman/Viacom churned out the 1970's Number One game-syndie hit, *Family Feud.* Typical of most access time quizzes, *Feud* had a network precedent, debuting as an ABC daytimer in 1976. Hosting both the network and non-network versions was Richard Dawson, he of the quickie Groucho-Laurel-Fields impressions and the "kiss the girls and make them squeal" school of game show emceedom. All manner of reasons were attributed to the unbelievable syndicated success of *Family Feud,* including its *sub rosa* contingent of intellectual fans, but what the attraction seemed to boil down to was the viewers' vicarious thrill of seeing common folks — all members of a family — winning big prizes by second-guessing not celebrities, nor one another, but the sample opinions given by a group of 100 *other* common folks. "If people like *that* can make wild guesses and win," mused the average viewer, "there's hope for me yet!" By 1979, *Family Feud* was running twice a week in access time, and by 1980, the NBC stations gave up all pretenses of "checkerboarding" their 7:30–8 p.m. schedule and started running *Family Feud* five nights a week, with nearly 200 stations nationwide following suit. Thus was the final nail on the coffin of the FCC's dreams of "diversification" driven home. So much revenue came the way of the stations carrying *Feud* that few were interested when Merv Griffin and King World offered their *Wheel of Fortune* as an access strip in 1983. The rise of *Wheel* and the fall of *Feud* were all but simultaneous, and by 1985 all that was left of the former syndie giant was a rerun package bearing the faintly oxymoronic title *The Best of Family Feud.* Perhaps the bell was tolling a year or so earlier, when *Feud's* format was showing signs of fatigue and rumors were circulating that Richard Dawson was an autocratic behemoth, rather than the loveable scamp he played before the cameras. (When a *Family Feud* revival was announced in 1988, Dawson's name wasn't mentioned.) But the NBC-owned outlets chose not to heed the warning signs, and permitted *Wheel of Fortune* to pass into other hands — an oversight from which the NBC stations haven't recovered to this day.

   The Gong Show (1976–80). Despite the moans and wails of critics who cite such Chuck Barris productions as *The Gong Show* as "typical" game shows, Barris was *not* your typical game show producer. He was a satirist, a self-avowed one, and designated as such by the earliest contemporary accounts of his output. He didn't start that way, but as audiences began to accept and expect more double and single entendres in Barris offerings like *The Newlywed Game,* the producer began treating the whole game genre as his own private joke, determined to see how far he could go in trampling on good taste before the public cried "Enough!" One hallmark of the Barris output was the willingness of contestants to make asses of themselves before millions of viewers. This spectacle culminated in Barris' summer 1976 NBC daily, *The Gong Show,* a zany "revival" of radio's old *Amateur Hour,* whose host Major Bowes had inaugurated the "gonging" of losers. Initially, the silliness of the talent competition was offset with the dignity of emcee Gary Owens. But when *Gong Show* went into weekly access syndication through Firestone Sales in the fall of '76 (it was quickly scooped up by the ABC stations group), Chuck Barris himself took over the hosting chores — perhaps precisely *because* of his utter lack of talent in this area. The syndie *Gong Show* offered wretched act after wretched act parading before the wise-lipped celebrity judges and the hooting and hollering audience. The audition procedure and resultant on-camera "talent" of *Gong Show* have been described by many television historians; suffice it to say that whenever bombarded by criticism, Chuck Barris would give his usual defense that the contestants had *wanted* to appear on *The Gong Show,* and that a world of alternative viewing awaited the critics on other channels. He also reiterated that the whole thing was a lampoon; the presence of a live band headed by Milton DeLugg (an anachronism in an era of canned music) and the presence of beautiful Sivi Aberg as Barris' assistant, a woman as classy and poised as Barris and his series were not, merely underlined the fact that no one should take *Gong Show* seriously. Eventually, Barris' "it's all a joke" approach resulted in the appearances of "regular" contestants like Gene-Gene the Dancing Machine, an enormous black stagehand with the agility of a Mack truck, and "The Unknown Comic" (Murray Langston), who understandably performed his routines with a paper bag over his head. The more popular *Gong Show* became, the less inclined critics were to accept Chuck Barris as a satirist, and soon these critics were taking the producer at face value as "The Sultan of Sleaze" and "King Leer." We imagine that Mr. Barris cried into his pillow every night.

The Guinness Game (1979). Paradine/Hill-Eubanks/20th Century–Fox Television's *Guinness Game* was inspired by the network "actuality" series *Real People.* Host Don Galloway grinned like a man possessed as contestants tried to beat the statistics written down in *The Guinness Book of World Records;* the most critical attention given this show was paid to the character who tried to beat the time-record for changing a tire. *Guinness Game* was getting somewhere in the ratings by early in 1980, but the NBC-owned stations dropped it and the station group's other access syndies in favor of *Family Feud,* leading *Guinness'* barter representatives Ogilvy and Mather to lose faith in the series.

High Rollers (1975; 1987). Heatter-Quigley's *High Rollers,* a daily dice-game thriller on NBC, was fashioned into a weekly Accesser by Rhodes as a companion piece for *Celebrity Sweepstakes;* Alex Trebek, less subdued than he'd be on *Jeopardy* a decade later, emceed. The 1987 daily syndicated *High Rollers* from Orion Pictures was hosted by the eternal Wink Martindale.

The Hollywood Connection (1977). A Barry-Enright/Colbert confection, with Jim Lange hosting as contestants once again predicted how questions would be answered by—do I have to say it?—celebrities.

The Hollywood Squares (1971–80; 1981; 1986–). This Peter Marshall-hosted celebrity tic-tac-toe game had premiered on NBC in 1966 thanks to the daytime success the network had enjoyed with *Let's Make a Deal* (which see); when NBC underwent a housecleaning of its daytime schedule in 1968, *Deal* was cancelled but *Squares* was retained. Ever since that time, there'd been a certain amount of rivalry between *Deal's* Hatos-Hall productions and *Square's* producing team of Merrill Heatter and Bob Quigley, so it stood to reason that when *Let's Make a Deal* became a winner in access syndication, *Hollywood Squares* would covet a piece of the action. Rhodes Communications premiered its weekly version of *Squares* so late in 1971 that it can legitimately be regarded as a 1972 release; *Let's Make a Deal,* with three months' worth of syndie popularity behind it, began to follow the progress of its rival series, just as *Squares* would enviously chart *Deal's* ratings. When the NBC stations insisted that *Hollywood Squares* be expanded to two nights per week, *Deal* followed suit. The two properties went nose-to-nose until Monty Hall briefly left *Let's Make a Deal* in pursuit of a desultory night club career in 1977, planting *Squares* firmly in the number one access game show slot it had always coveted; there it remained until the NBC-owned outlets went with *Family Feud* in 1979. 1981's daily version, taped in Las Vegas, did poorly enough to convince the industry that *Hollywood Squares* would have burnt itself out without the competition of *Family Feud* to kill it.

Taking sight of the fact that playing *Hollywood Squares* the way it had always been played was "old hat," Hearst Communications and Orion Productions' 1986 revival of *Squares* was a camped-up lampoon of the original series. Stunts included having each celebrity's "square" equipped with a grill so they could cook dinner while answering questions, and allowing the comics on the panel to indulge in quickie comedy routines before and after answering questions. And a more ludicrous sight is hard to imagine than seeing the series' famous giant tic-tac-toe board planted in front of a hotel or on a beach whenever the new series went on one of its location tours. Securing the new *Squares* firmly into the '80s was JM J Bullock, who frequented the center square inhabited for so many years by the late Paul Lynde. Bullock's manic one-liners about how brain-damaged his fellow celebrities seemed to be were far more attuned to their time and place than Lynde's effete sneering. John Davidson, all crinkly smiles and deliberately phony sincerity, was host for this latest *Hollywood Squares;* the announcer was Los Angeles deejay Shadoe Stevens, who frequently performed double duty as one of the star panelists.

The Honeymoon Game (1971). Because this weekly game show was supposed to have run a full 90 minutes per program, this writer was tempted to doubt that it ever made it into syndication, even though it was being pre-sold under the title *The Love Game* as early as 1970. However, the Jack Barry-produced *Honeymoon Game* has been listed in at least three reliable sources, so it's included here until we're all proven wrong. Jim McKrell hosted this marathon effort in which several newly married couples went through a labyrinthine series of elimination contests before winning a "dream honeymoon." The announcer was Harry Blackstone Jr., better known as a professional magician.

I've Got a Secret (1972). Goodson-Todman's long-running (1952–67) CBS series *I've Got a Secret* required its celebrity panel to guess the secrets that were whispered in the host's ear by the contestants. The syndicated version of *Secret* was initially slated to be emceed by Art Linkletter, but the reins of this Firestone release were turned over to Steve Allen, who'd been one of the series' network hosts.

It Pays to Be Ignorant (1973). Flushed with the success of *Let's Make a Deal* (which see), producers Stefan Hatos and Monty Hall put together this

Worldvision-released revival of the comedy quiz favorite *It Pays to Be Ig-norant,* which hadn't been seen on television (nor heard on radio) since 1951. Jokes and more jokes abounded, with comic actor Joe Flynn hosting and with laughmakers Jo Ann Worley, Charles Nelson Reilly and Billy Baxter on the panel (Billy Baxter?). But funny quiz shows didn't really catch on until after the Chuck Barris invasion a few years later.

It's Your Bet (1970–72). A Ralph Edwards production, created as a replacement for the NBC-owned stations' long-running *PDQ.* Hosted during its three-season run by a quiz-show Who's Who (Hal March, Tom Kennedy, Dick Gautier, Lyle Waggoner), *It's Your Bet* trod the well-worn path having celebrities spouses' guess the answers given by their famous husbands and wives.

Jeopardy (1974; 1984–   ). Merv Griffin's own story of how he came to develop *Jeopardy* for the NBC network in 1965 went as follows. Griffin was looking for a game format wherein he could not possibly be accused of cheating by giving the contestants the quiz answers in advance. At this point, either Griffin or his wife at the time suggested a program where the answers were given on-camera for everyone to see; it was then up to the contestants to provide the correct *questions.* NBC's *Jeopardy* ran daily for 11 seasons; its syn-dicated version from Metromedia was put on the market in late 1974 in an-ticipation of the series' imminent network cancellation in January of 1975. This first weekly syndie was an exact double of the network version, hosted as before by Art Fleming with off-stage announcing assistance from Don Pardo. But *Jeopardy's* vogue had passed (it was a game show that required the contestants to be intelligent, a trend halted by Chuck Barris in the mid–1970's) and its syn-die version died a quiet death after a year. A 1978 network *Jeopardy* tried to jazz things up with graphics and pretty colored lights, to no avail. Flash-forward to 1984: *Jeopardy's* first legion of fans, the baby-boomers, had grown up and were controlling the marketplace. Also, the enormous popularity of the Trivial Pursuit board game made the knowledge of useless information re-quired to play *Jeopardy* fashionable for the upwardly mobile set. Merv Griffin/King World's 1984 version of *Jeopardy* ended up taking off like a house afire. The original format and the series' wonderful tick-tock "think music" were happily retained, but Art Fleming was replaced by Alex Trebek, very likely the coolest, most unflappable host in game show history (although possessed with a delightful nasty streak that surfaced whenever a contestant failed to grasp the obvious). The new *Jeopardy* contestants probably spent their youth reading and memorizing trivia and minutiae while "real kids" were out getting fresh air and playing baseball. Twenty years later, these bookish types got their sweet revenge on their taunting childhood peers by raking in hundreds of thousands of dollars in *Jeopardy* prize money and becoming media celebrities in their own right — all because they retained in their heads the obscure, insignificant answers to obscure, insignificant questions. Rather like film and television historians.

The Joker's Wild (1976–86). Barry-Enright's *Joker's Wild,* a game predicated on the intricacies of the slot machine and the ability of the contestants to concentrate on the game rather than scream and/or wear a funny costume, ran on CBS daytime from 1972–75. It was revived locally by KHJ–Los Angeles starting July 1, 1976, knocked its L.A. competition out of the box, and went into a ten-year syndication career through Colbert Sales in the fall of '76. Jack Barry hosted the series, and was succeeded after his death in 1984 by Bill Cullen. (See also *The New Tic Tac Dough.*)

Let's Make a Deal (1971–76; 1980; 1984). Stephan Hatos and Monty Hall's *Let's Make a Deal* might never have gone into access syndication at all had Hatos-Hall gotten what it really wanted from the ABC network. Since acquiring *Deal* from NBC in 1968, ABC had done beautifully building its entire daytime schedule around the game show's "Door number three, Monty!" antics, extending this success into a sporadic nighttime version, which was stuck into ABC's schedule whenever the network had a weak spot, and which invariably won the ratings in that spot. Producer-host Monty Hall was promised by ABC that *Let's Make a Deal* was a "firm go" for the network's 1971–72 prime time season. But at the last minute, ABC reneged in favor of a couple of new sitcoms; the reason given was that game shows had "no prestige." To put it mildly, Monty Hall was mad as hell. He declared that unless ABC made some move towards getting *Let's Make a Deal* into prime time, he'd yank the daytime *Deal* off the network. Unconcerned about "prestige" when it came to dollars and cents, ABC compromised with a weekly syndicated *Let's Make a Deal* distributed by ABC Films (later known as Worldvision), clearing the series on the network's five stations and 130 other markets. Monty Hall's fit of pique paid off: *Deal* started big, and remained a smash until Hall left the show (temporarily) in 1976. Offensive though some may have found *Deal's* premise of allowing people with room-temperature I.Q.'s dressed in rooster and gorilla suits to make $100,000 deals with Monty Hall, on an historical level the series cannot be ignored; *Let's Make a Deal* opened the doors for the nightly syndicated versions of daytime network game shows that would come to dominate access time by the end of the '70s.

Let's Make a Deal made a pair of return visits to non-network television in the '80s, both of them taped in Vancouver (Monty Hall was himself a native of Canada), both of them dailies. The 1980 version was issued by Victory Television, while the 1984 edition came by way of Telepictures. By the mid-1980's, few viewers wanted to bother experiencing the second-hand thrill of seeing Monty Hall allow people in a TV studio to make fabulous deals and trades, when all these viewers had to do was pick up a phone and enjoy a real-life "deal" via one of the new, satellite-beamed home-shopping programs.

The Love Experts (1978). Viacom's *Love Experts* had been in development as early as 1970, and was (as mentioned earlier) fashioned somewhat along the lines of the 1971 syndie *All About Faces.* Host Bill Cullen would ask four celeb ... four you-know-whats to predict the outcome of a "civilian" contestant's romantic life, then to offer advice—and as we all know, no one is more qualified to handle affairs of the heart than television and movie stars.

Lucky Pair (1971). After running locally on KNXT–Los Angeles since 1969, *Lucky Pair,* produced by a consortium including Bob Barker, Al Hamel and Dick Clark, was given a chance at syndication in 1971. The object of the game was less important than the fact that *Lucky Pair* gave Richard Dawson a chance to cut his quiz-emcee teeth.

Make Me Laugh (1979–80). Based on a 1958 ABC summer-replacement series of the same name and format, *Make Me Laugh's* premise was that its contestant abstain from laughter for a given length of time, this task made difficult by having a battalion of professional comics bombard the contestants with jokes, puns and assorted schtick. ABC had had trouble lining up comics for 1958's *Make Me Laugh,* since few professional laughmakers wanted to risk their reputations should the contestants fail to chuckle. In 1979, however, with fewer nightclubs and variety shows around, there were plenty of hungry up-and-coming comics to supply the syndicated version for its two seasons. Among the mirth-makers were Gallegher, Murray Langston, and Howie Mandel; the host was Bobby Van. *Make Me Laugh* was one of many attempts to launch an ad-hoc syndicated "fourth network" in the '70s. The Program Development Group, comprised of leading independent stations including WPIX–New York, KTLA–Los Angeles and Field Communication's UHF outlets, was formed to provide strong first-run syndies for non-network-channel exposure. PDG got Paramount Television in on the plan, and as a result *Make Me Laugh* was Paramount's first-ever first-run syndicated series. Ultimately, PDG was absorbed by the leading light of the adhoc network movement, Operation Prime Time.

Masquerade Party (1974). Another Hatos-Hall revival of a long-dormant network favorite (see *It Pays to Be Ignorant*), *Masquerade Party* had built its reputation over both CBS and NBC from 1952 to 1960. This 20th Century–Fox syndie weekly was presided over by Richard Dawson, trying out all the bits and gags he'd have honed to perfection for *Family Feud.* Nipsey Russell, Jo Ann Worley and Bill Bixby were the permanent panelists whose task it was to guess the identity of famous people buried under mounds of latex makeup. During its first four weeks, *Masquerade Party* was New York City's top-rated game show syndie. Didn't hurt its national sales one bit.

Match Game PM (1975–81). Gene Rayburn hosted that "second-guess the celebrity" imbroglio known as *Match Game PM,* a Victory Television weekly based on the network daytime series of almost the same name. Score another one for Goodson-Todman, who'd gone from seeing all its prime time network shows cut down in one fell swoop in the late '60s, only to emerge as one of syndication's top bananas of the 1970's. *Match Game PM* graduated to Monday-through-Friday status after CBS cancelled its network version in 1979; the syndie's best customers were the CBS-owned channels.

Name That Tune (1970; 1974–80; 1984). This venerable musical guessing game ("I can name that tune in three notes!") was first seen on NBC and CBS from 1953 to 1959. Century Communications' 1970 weekly version was hosted by Richard Hayes. The series was squeezed out by its competition, only to reemerge in NBC-daytime in 1974, then in access syndication with Tom Kennedy as its host, Sandy Frank Productions as its distributor, and the NBC-owned stations in its manifest. In 1976, the prize ante was upped and the series rechristened *The $100,000 Name That Tune,* with typical late–'70s emphasis on songs with a disco beat. Ralph Edwards was executive producer for both these syndies. The warhorse property was back again in 1984 (once more reflecting the musical tastes of its time) as a daily; Sandy Frank developed this Jim Lange-hosted version, then sold the package to Television Program Entertainment.

The New Dating Game (1973; 1977–79); *The All-New Dating Game* (1986–   ). One of the first of the major network contributions of Chuck Barris, the original *Dating Game* graced ABC's airwaves from 1966 to 1970. This is the one where a "bachelorette" had to choose a date from three unseen bachelors on the basis of their answers to her questions. As television's standards of taste became looser, the questions and answers on *Dating Game* became more up-close and personal, as it were, and by the time the series was syndicated through Firestone Sales, conditions were as "raw" as the prevailing standards of the mid–'70s would allow. For many viewers, the series' high point occurred during its second syndicated run, when comedian Andy Kaufman appeared in the guise of a bemused bachelor from a foreign country. So real did Kaufman make his anguish over his failure of making himself "understood" that viewers wrote angry letters berating Chuck Barris for mistreating that poor little "European." Kaufman got off scot-free when the ruse was revealed, but Barris was still pilloried, this time for wantonly misleading the viewers! Both '70s syndie versions of *Dating Game* were emceed by the inescapable Jim Lange. After several years in reruns, the property was brought back to first-run by Barris' Bel-Air Productions as *The All-New Dating Game.* (This 1986 incarnation was very nearly titled *We Love the Dating Game.*) The choice of host on this version was amusing, in context. On an early *Gong Show,* actress Elaine Joyce had gonged a contestant who played music with his armpits, explaining that the act was the most tasteless thing she'd ever seen. By 1986, Miss Joyce had come to peace with her palate, and assumed the emcee's chair on *The All-New Dating Game.* (Jeff MacGregor took over that chair in 1987.)

The New Newlywed Game (1977–80; 1985–   ). Developed by Nicholson-Muir productions and brought to the tube by Chuck Barris, the first *Newlywed Game* joined Barris' *Dating Game* on ABC in 1966, where it remained until 1974 (it was back on the network for a while in 1984). This time, spouses had to guess how their husbands and wives would answer personal questions about their life together, and since married couples were on a deeper level of intimacy than people on their first date, *Newlywed Game* was raunchier than *Dating Game* could ever be. The syndicated version from Worldvision was one of Barris' biggest moneymakers, but also caused him a few headaches. The producer was forever threatening legal action against others who put their own imitation *Newlywed Games* on the air; and in the late '70s Barris filed suit against a Southern television station after it refused to pay for running both *Newlywed* and *Dating* because Barris had "lied" that the series met the station's "community standards." Such a statement may have been just one more joke for Chuck Barris, but the judge didn't share the laugh, and Barris lost. In 1985, Barris' Bel-Air productions managed to line up 150 stations for the most recent resurrection of *New Newlywed Game.* All television versions of this series, both off network and on, have been hosted by Bob Eubanks, whose job security has compensated for the attendant lack of dignity.

The New Price Is Right (1972–74; 1985). Goodson-Todman's entree into the nighttime edition of network-daytimer access sweepstakes (all their existing syndies were versions of programs long since cancelled by the networks) was Viacom's *New Price Is Right,* which had recently been revived on CBS' daily schedule after a network absence of seven years (its run on NBC and ABC had stretched from 1956 to 1965). Dennis James took over Bob Barker's daily "Come on down!" chores for the syndicated *Price,* which was picked up by the NBC owned stations rather than the CBS stations. (Could this be what the FCC meant by diversification?) Oddly, while CBS' *Price Is Right* became the top-rated network game show, even unto being the first such program to expand to a full hour, the syndicated versions never caught on. Television Program Source's 1985 daily syndie of the evergreen property, hosted by Tom Kennedy, was every bit as fun and frenetic as the bidding for fabulous prizes on the long-running network version, but its ratings ran well behind those for the league-leading *Wheel of Fortune.*

The New Tic Tac Dough (1978–86). Barry-Enright's NBC version of *Tic Tac Dough* was seen from 1957 to 1959, one of the few quiz shows to weather the cheating scandals of the era, probably because the contestants won "X"es and "O"s on the basis of questions from nine categories, rather than the single-category setup that allowed for preshow coaching. A "new" *Tic Tac Dough* had just wound up three months on CBS when Barry-Enright brought the property to syndication through Colbert Sales in 1978, where it frequently ran in tandem with the company's other game syndie, *Joker's Wild.* Both *The New Tic Tac Dough* and *Joker's Wild* ran to excellent business until 1986; both shows appealed to that faction of game show aficionados which demanded that contestants possess a semblance of human intelligence. One such contestant was *Tic Tac Dough's* Navy Lieutenant Thom McKee, who won more money and prizes than any other person in previous game show history — though the edge of this accomplishment was rather dulled when a few insensitive newspapers, taking advantage of the four-week delay between the series' taping and its telecast, revealed McKee's victory long before its airtime. This tape-to-telecast delay was responsible for a classic blunder in 1979, when *Tic Tac Dough* host Wink Martindale announced that the Grand Prize would be an all-expense-paid trip to exotic Iran—this episode being telecast well after the takeover by the Ayatollah.

The New Treasure Hunt (1974–77). Chuck Barris was responsible for this Sandy Frank Productions release, an exhumation of a giveaway show seen on ABC and NBC from 1954 to 1959. *New Treasure Hunt* specialized in heaping agonies and indignities on its contestants as they waited to learn the contents of their "treasure boxes," and it was this angle that brought the series to the attention of CBS' news-magazine show *60 Minutes*. The program devoted a lot of time to clips from a *Hunt* episode in which host Geoff Edwards grinned and guffawed while a woman contestant had humiliation after humiliation piled upon her, and then was so sadistically kept in suspense as to whether or not she'd won a fabulous prize that when it was revealed that she *had* won, she fainted dead away. How, queried *60 Minutes*, could Chuck Barris do such horrible things? Barris cheerfully replied that the woman had not been forced to appear on *Treasure Hunt* and that, if asked, the woman would say that her appearance was the greatest moment of her life. The woman was asked, and said exactly that.

The Newlywed Game see **The New Newlywed Game**

On the Money (1973). Avco Communications managed a dozen midwestern sales for this forgotten quiz show hosted by Bob Braun, taped in beautiful, bewitching Cincinnati, Ohio.

The $1.98 Beauty Contest (1978–79). After trashing game shows, giveaways and talent competitions, Chuck Barris took on beauty contests with his Sandy Frank Productions release, *$1.98 Beauty Contest*. Hosting was Rip Taylor, the sort of comic who makes packed houses laugh even while they feel guilty about it. Contestants were chosen mostly for their heft and or homeliness, and despite the apparent cruelty of allowing these resistable creatures to perform their artless songs and dances and parade in moth-eaten bathing suits, none of the ladies was forced to appear at gunpoint, and all of them had the time of their lives. Audiences who whined that they hated this sort of programming could blame only themselves when *$1.98 Beauty Contest* ended up as one of the few access releases of 1978 to be renewed for a second season. As for its tastelessness, was *Beauty Contest* really any worse than that yearly girlie show run each September which claims to emphasize talent and intellect but which still features baton twirlers and a swimsuit competition?

The $100,000 Name That Tune see **Name That Tune**

The $128,000 Question (1976–78). CBS' *$64,000 Question* was one of several network game shows purged during the cheating scandals of 1958. Viacom's plans to revive the series for 1975 access syndication included several "cheat-proof" emendations: Contestants would no longer be permitted to answer questions in only one field of expertise (thus avoiding preshow "cribbing"), and the answers would be kept secret with high-tech electronic gadgetry. Executive producer Steve Carlin, producer of the original *Question,* thought he had a time slot on the five CBS-owned stations sewn up, but CBS pulled the rug out, noting that the $64,000 ante was in violation of the network's prize-show ceiling of $25,000. There was actually more to the pulluot than that: CBS had been severely burned by the scandals during *Question's* first go-round, and thus wanted to divorce themselves from the series' newest version despite Carlin's protests of honesty. Viacom ended up pitching the new show to stations outside the CBS orbit, gaining toeholds in several other major station groups. Carlin then decided that, since he didn't have CBS to worry about, he'd up the prize ceiling to $128,000 as a bow to mid–1970's inflation. Hosting the weekly *$128,000 Question* were two Canadian boys, Mike Darrow and Alex Trebek.

The Parent Game (1972). A Chuck Barris/Sandy Frank weekly hosted by Clark Race. Race quizzed three married couples on how best to raise their children, then invited a professional child psychologist to award points to the "best" answers. *Parent Game* was rather sedate by Chuck Barris standards; it also lasted only one year, despite a large number of markets.

The Price Is Right see **The New Price Is Right**

Sale of the Century (1973; 1985). No sooner had *Sale of the Century* been cancelled after a four-year NBC daytime run than it popped up in weekly syndication through Rhodes Communications, hosted by Joe Garagiola. The object of the game was to attain big prizes at low cost by answering fairly easy questions. The format was purchased by Reg Grundy for an Australian version, which became that country's number one TV hit — with questions far tougher than anything heard on *Sale's* American runs. *Sale of the Century* returned to NBC daytime in 1983, and to syndication through Genesis/Colbert Sales in 1985. This last version, hosted by Jim Perry, emulated *Jeopardy* by adding a "trivial pursuit" twist to the questions.

The Seventh Sense (1978). A Rhodes release, emceed by Jim Peck. *Seventh Sense* had a real hypnotist, Elroy Schwartz, delve into the subconscious of the contestants; also tested was the contestants' prowess at extrasensory perception (ESP).

Sports Challenge (1971). Transmedia's *Sports Challenge,* bartered by Colgate-Palmolive and emceed by Dick Enberg, was a sports-trivia contest pitting a pair of three-person teams of pro athletes against each other. Like many sports-oriented syndies, *Sports Challenge* was often as not run on weekends.

Tattletales (1977; 1983–85). Goodson-Todman's winning streak of the '70s continued with *Tattletales,* which ran on CBS daytime from 1974–78 and as a Firestone syndie in '77. Bert Convy, seemingly put on this earth to host game shows, presided as celebrities and their spouses or current companions tried to second-guess one another. *Tattletales* was back, along with Bert Convy, for a short CBS daily run in 1982, and a two-season syndie hitch through Viacom in 1983.

Three's a Crowd (1979). Chuck Barris finally overreached himself with his Firestone-released *Three's a Crowd*. In this one, host Jim Peck asked the question that has been plaguing civilization since the time of the Pharaohs: "Who knows a man better—his wife or his secretary?" Having a secretary automatically put the contestants in the "upscale" bracket, a category hitherto untapped by Barris, most of whose previous contestants had trouble writing their *own* letters, let alone dictating them. Well-to-do people don't make the best Barris game-players; their innate dignity keeps them from relaxing and playing for laughs. Most of the husbands on *Three's a Crowd* merely looked uncomfortable as their wives and secretaries compared notes, and as a result, the home audience became equally edgy. At any rate, *Three's a Crowd* was voluntarily pulled out of syndication by Barris, along with all his other game shows, in 1980; the producer felt that the access-time market was becoming too congested, and he wanted to wait until things calmed down a bit before re-entering that market. He made a press-conference appearance in late 1980 to announce plans for a new property, *The Million-Dollar Talent Show,* which he promised would be a complete about-face of Barris' previous entertainment standards; the proposed new series would, he said, be "straightforward, dignified." We'll never know whether Chuck Barris was just kidding again or not, because no one picked up *The Million-Dollar Talent Show.* So Barris kept his original vow of staying out of television for awhile and concentrated on bold new fields of endeavor—like *The Gong Show Movie.*

Tic Tac Dough see *The New Tic Tac Dough*

Treasure Hunt see *The New Treasure Hunt*

TV Twin Double (1977). This franchised horse-race-based game show bore the inspiration of the long-running *Let's Go to the Races* (see "Game Show" notes in the 1950's section). George DeWitt, who'd once hosted the network version of *Name That Tune,* presided as home viewers guessed the outcome of prefilmed races.

The $25,000 Pyramid (1974–79); **The $50,000 Pyramid** (1981); **The $100,000 Pyramid** (1985–   ). CBS's daily *$10,000 Pyramid,* which debuted in 1973, inspired the Viacom weekly syndie retitled *$25,000 Pyramid* to make things more enticing to the prime time fans; Bill Cullen hosted the latter version. ABC picked up the network version in 1974, upping its ante (and altering its title) to $20,000 in 1976; the syndicated *Pyramid,* which fell under the jurisdiction of the CBS stations, remained constant at $25,000. Colgate-Palmolive's 1981 revival, no longer controlled by the CBS stations, was able to call itself *The $50,000 Pyramid* (the network version was cancelled in 1980).

This syndicated edition lasted 26 weeks, but a revival of interest in the series, inspired when CBS began running *$25,000 Pyramid* in daytime again in 1982, led to the 1985 20th Century–Fox nightly non-networker, which reflected the changing economy of the decade by establishing a grand prize of $100,000. All the network versions, and both syndies of the '80s, were emceed by Dick Clark, and the object of all *Pyramids* was for a celebrity-civilian team to work itself up a cash-prize pyramid using a word-association game, with clues like "Halloween" meant to lead to correct answers like "Pumpkin." Since their inception, all versions of *Pyramid* have been Bob Stewart Productions.

You Don't Say! (1978). Ralph Andrews Productions' guess-the-famous-name game, complete with the standard celebrity guests, was first televised on NBC from 1963 through 1969. An ABC revival had a less lengthy life in the summer of 1975; the Viacom syndie edition, hosted (like all its other incarnations) by Tom Kennedy, surfaced with equal brevity in 1978.

Informational

In addition to the programs listed below, "fillers" featuring well-known commentators like Paul Harvey, Earl Nightingale, Chet Huntley and Rona Barrett continued as did their prototypes of the 1950's, patching three- to five-minute holes in local schedules. Full-scale nightly news syndies still had to wait for the wider availability of satellites in the 1980's to make their mark.

Across the Fence (and other agriculture shows) (1970–79). Programs like *Across the Fence* used to be called "farm shows," and as such were seen mostly in the more agrarian portions of the country. But as "farming" gradually attained the monicker of "agribusiness," and urbanites became aware (as they'd been when the country was younger) that the nation's economy was as dependent on livestock as the stock exchange, agricultural programs began seeping into more and more cosmopolitan markets. The long-running "regional" *Agriculture USA* was streamlined into *AG-USA,* with John Stearns hosting, in 1974, eventually going Monday-through-Friday as *AG-Day.* Orion Samuelson's Chicago-based *National Farm Digest* would expand before the decade was over to include reports on international farming news. And there was also the ambitious *Country Day* from KSTP–Minneapolis, hosted by Gary Scheindel; for several years after its 1977 debut the only daily of its kind, *Country Day* built up a mininetwork of several midwestern stations before folding in 1982. It was one of the first rural programs to adopt the "magazine" format used on most agribusiness programs to this day.

AG-USA see above

The Butcher see *Celebrity Cooks*

Celebrity Cooks (1978). After Graham Kerr abandoned his *Galloping Gourmet* to devote his energies to spreading the word of God (see the "Informational" section in the 1960's), half-hour cooking shows folded in syndication, returning to the open arms (and well-stocked kitchens) of public television. There were a few 30-minute programs like the Canadian *Celebrity Cooks,* but most food-and-nutrition programs surfaced in the form of five-minute fillers like Merle Ellis' *The Butcher,* or were absorbed into segments of compartmentalized information shows like *PM Magazine* (which see).

Consultation (1974). Chicago-based health care program, produced by the University of Illinois Medical Center and hosted by Jack Righeimer.

Consumer Buyline (1978). With consumer advocates such as Ralph Nader applying the screws, the FCC decided to permit "comparative advertising"; now, a company like Anacin could compare its product to, say, Bufferin, without resorting to the euphemistic "Brand X" or "Another Leading Brand." This was done to encourage honest advertising, since the advertisers would be required by consumer watchdogs to *prove* their specific claims. *Consumer Reports on TV,* a series of five-minute vignettes released by the titular magazine in 1974, was the first consumer-advocacy offering. Four years later, Group W released the weekly *Consumer Buyline,* hosted by that ingratiating ham, David Horowitz. Horowitz enlivened what might otherwise have been a plodding tally of this product's plusses and that product's minuses with a weekly feature wherein he'd test, on-camera, an advertiser's claim — which generally involved tasting the "tastiest" and trying to break the "unbreakable." It was great theatre, and was expanded into Horowitz's even more enjoyable *Fight Back!* of the 1980's.

Consumer Reports on TV see above

Country Day see *Across the Fence*

Evening Magazine see *PM Magazine*

Family Counselor (1974). Legal and sociological advice was dispensed on this offering from WBZ–Boston.

For You, Black Woman (1977–79). *Two* increasingly influential groups were given airtime on this interview-information weekly, distributed by Gerber-Carter and the ABC Station Group, and hosted by Alice Travis, who'd previously helmed the morning program on the ABC flagship station in New York City.

Health Field (1978–83). A sprightly, informative medical daily, hosted by NBC science editor Frank Field, and cohosted at various junctures by Field's daughter Pamela and actress Lynn Redgrave. From Gray-Schwartz/Lexington Broadcasting.

House Call (1977). One of many projects featuring Harvard's Dr. Timothy Johnson. Johnson's output included *House Call* in the '70s, *Healthbeat* and *Update on Health* in the '80s, his monthly *Body Works* specials in both decades, and sporadic appearances as ABC's medical expert. The Boston-based Johnson, like David Horowitz, was as devoted to entertaining his viewers as informing them. Virtually all of Timothy Johnson's projects were taped in Boston and bartered by J. Walter Thompson.

It's Your Business (1979–   ). Weekly debate, produced by the U.S. Chamber of Commerce.

Life Around Us (1972). A Time-Life project designed to clarify biology for us ordinary mortals.

Loving Free (1977). This was the title of a best-selling book on the joys of marital sex, written under a pair of pseudonyms by a couple of Milwaukee-based advertising people, Dick and Paula McDonald. Their philosophies were extended to a series of three-minute fillers distributed by Taft/Hanna-Barbera.

Medix (1971–78). Like Chicago's *Consultation,* Los Angeles' *Medix* was a local health-care show that became a nationwide favorite on many weekend schedules. Dave Bell and Associates and Syndicast distributed this weekly, co-produced by the Los Angeles County Medical Association; one of *Medix's* hosts was Stephanie Edwards, in between her many talk-show stints.

Mr. Chips (1976). Hosted by Bill Brown and Don McGowan, Advertising Agency Associates' *Mr. Chips* was a woodworking show, the title of which virtually dared critics to come up with articles beginning with the word "Goodbye."

National Farm Digest* see *Across the Fence

The Pet Set (1971). This 39-weeker from Carnation Foods and Media Syndication starred celebrated animal lover Betty White and guest-starred plenty of pet-owning celebrities. Beyond the expected animal misbehavior (frequently on the laps of the Rich and Famous), *Pet Set* provided the valuable service of warning viewers that some animals could not and *should* not be domesticated; to that end, many of the "pets" seen on the series were actually full-grown jungle beasts!

PM Magazine (1978–   ). While it wasn't the first series to adopt a multisubject "magazine" format, CBS' *60 Minutes* was the one that "took," especially after the series' move into Sunday prime time in 1976 made the CBS weekly into a ratings champ—incentive enough to spur imitations on network and off. Group W's KPIX–San Francisco made the most dramatic move towards putting the magazine concept into access-time syndication with its

1976 daily, *Evening: The MTWTF Show.* Every night at 7:30, *Evening* presented three to four news/human interest vignettes, bound together by the series' ever-grinning young hosts. So impressed was Group W that it ordered its other stations to create *Evening Magazines* of their own in the fall of 1977; the five Westinghouse outlets supplied one another with the best of their videotaped featurettes. A nationwide saturation of this series was the next logical step; while the title remained *Evening Magazine* on the Group W's, the program was offered to syndication as *PM Magazine.* Group W would supply only 40 percent of each evening's half-hour, leaving the remaining 60 percent in the hands of the local buying markets. A costly proposal this, but one made enticing by Group W's invitation to the locals to ship their best material to *Evening Magazine's* San Francisco headquarters; from these, selected features would then be distributed to the other *PM Magazines* throughout the nation. Imagine how thrilled local news producers were at the prospect of showing off their best efforts all over America; now imagine further those local news anchors and announcers who now had a most expedient method of spreading their voices and faces from coast to coast — instant auditions for bigger things!

PM Magazine officially went national over WAGA–Atlanta on September 4, 1978. Within a year it was seen during access in all major markets except New York and Los Angeles, who by 1980 would be running *PM's* in the coveted prime time hours. Even tiny markets which really couldn't afford to tape their own local features were seduced by promises of national exposure. *PM* had the additional good fortune of meeting most of the FCC's "unofficial" criteria for quality access fare: it was information, public affairs, family entertainment, and local, all in one — and it even managed to succeed on those terms in the marketplace.

The series moved into the '80s with its largest-ever circulation and the added attraction of Group W's monthly *PM Magazine* specials, hosted by Bill Rafferty. But the popularity of *Family Feud* (and later *Wheel of Fortune*) gradually eroded *PM's* access-time ratings, and increasing costs forced many local stations to give up trying to produce local human-interest features for the series. During this time, *PM* underwent some reorganization. Group W began offering a complete half-hour program, taped in San Francisco, to smaller stations who had trouble producing their own vignettes. Rather than wait for good features to come their way, Group W began assigning the stations in *PM's* biggest markets to tape stories of Group W's choosing. To attract viewers who liked the "familiarity" inherent in rigidly formatted game shows, *PM* no longer had a "grab-bag" of subject matter, but settled into regularly scheduled feature subjects. And to keep apace of "info-tainment" programs like *Entertainment Tonight, PM* tried to retain freshness by cutting down its four-week tape-to-telecast delay, offering features on a day-and-date basis to channels equipped with satellite dishes. Ultimately in 1984, *PM Magazine* went the route of every program desperate for viewers, with "celebrity contributors": Sally Struthers spoke on children, Ben Vereen on show business, Robby Benson on "adventure," Loretta Swit on animals. But by now, the pioneering *PM Magazine* was merely one of a myriad of syndicated magazine shows — and not a particularly good or unusual one at that. *PM Magazine* survived, and its national version can still be seen in some markets, but only as a pale shadow of that eager, energetic and promising *Evening Magazine* which started it all back in the summer of '76.

Ruff House (1977–82). Financial advisor Howard Ruff, ever the "voice of doom" no matter what state the economy is in, hosted a feisty weekly from O'Connor Services.

Special Edition (1977). Weekly magazine show from Columbia Television. Wittily hosted by Barbara Feldon, *Special Edition* took its magazine concept literally, drawing its material from articles recently published in such periodicals as *Time, TV Guide* and *Reader's Digest.* When asked, the president of Columbia Television insisted that his new series was *not* trying to steal the thunder of Group W's *Evening Magazine,* but was produced in response to locals who really and truly were begging for "quality" access material to compete with the glut of game shows. After *Special Edition* wound up with only nine markets, Columbia's president had only four words to say about those quality-hungry locals: "They lie, they lie."

Tony Brown's Journal (1976–81). Host Tony Brown used filmclips and interviews to outline the past, present and future of blacks in America. His *Journal* began on PBS, was barter-syndicated by Pepsi-Cola, then returned to PBS, still with Pepsi's financial support.

Towards the Year 2000 (1971). Speculative access effort, from Group W. The emphasis was on the ecological future of the world, a subject that was usually confined to sporadic television specials — at least until the middle of this shortage-plagued decade.

Visual Girl (1971). The care and feeding of the teenaged female's face and figure, hosted by Ron Russell and bartered by a cabinet full of cosmetic products.

Wally's Workshop (1971–77). Wally and Natalie Bruner hosted this home-fixit weekly, distributed with the sponsorship of Young & Rubicam's household-improvement clientele.

Music/Variety

With rare exceptions like the programs starring Carol Burnett and Sonny and Cher, the weekly music/variety program became a vanishing breed on the three networks. It was considered a relic of past decades, and worse, it was deemed a money and ratings loser in large, urban communities whose economy (and TV sets) were controlled by the young and affluent. Two weeklies whose ratings were still strong in 1971, *The Lawrence Welk Show* and *Hee Haw,* were cancelled in an effort to "deruralize" the network scene. When those two properties set up shop in syndication, their subsequent spectacular success led the music/variety genre in general to follow suit. So the form didn't really disappear; it simply moved out of the "coast-to-coast" bracket and opted for "city-by-city."

One byproduct of the aforementioned *Hee Haw's* syndication perfor-mance was the shot in the arm it gave the country-western genre. Because the market for this form expanded, the programs were no longer essentially "regionals" that tended to look alike, but became more individualized, and as such will not be lumped together in this section as they have been previously. We'll reserve the "lumping" honor for the overabundance of "disco" shows in the 1970's.

The Amazing World of Kreskin (1972; 1975). Celebrated mindreader Kreskin (whose real last name was Kresge, but who'd watch a show called *The Amazing World of Kresge?*) had a star-studded, Canadian-produced variety vehicle distributed by Viacom. The company's ad copy devoted much space to Kreskin's "youthfulness" (he was 35; people over 40 didn't exist to these ad peo-ple) and to the star's long-standing offer of $20,000 to anyone who could prove that he performed his mental gymnastics with the aid of confederates. Kreskin didn't have to pay off in 1972, nor when he returned with a second batch of shows from Mizlou Productions (titled *The New Kreskin*) in 1975.

Andy (1976). One of the major victims of the networks' purging of music programs was Andy Williams, who'd starred an NBC weekly variety series from 1962 through '67, and then again from 1969 to '71 (this after a summer-replacement apprenticeship in the late '50s and early '60s). As in his network heyday, Williams featured as much comedy as music in his 1976 access series from Syndicast, most of it provided by puppeteer Wayland Flowers and his potty-mouthed puppet creation "Madame." And as before, Williams was loyal to the tuxedoed, "Let's hear it for one of our great, great stars" motif. Produc-ing the syndicated *Andy* was Pierre Cossette, whom we'll discuss further when we get to *Sammy and Company.*

Black Omnibus (1973). Distributed by Colgate-Palmolive/Syndicast starting in January of 1973, *Black Omnibus* was a new-talent variety series ex-uberantly hosted by James Earl Jones. Like *Soul Train* (which see), *Omnibus* broke through several long-standing barriers and enjoyed healthy distribution in the deepest of the Deep South.

The Bobby Goldsboro Show (1972–73). Country-western accesser, syndicated by Nashville's prolific Show Biz Inc. and bartered by General Mills. Goldsboro's weekly was graced with a dash of "high tech" in the person of a frog character, "Calvin Calaveras," who popped up on a computer-enhanced TV monitor.

The Bobby Vinton Show (1975–76). Syndicast's *Bobby Vinton Show* had a rather rocky start, thanks to the executive committee of the National Association of Television Program Executives. At the N.A.T.P.E.'s 1975 convention in Las Vegas (the organization's annual conclave is where virtually all syndicated series are bought and sold), Bobby Vinton was booked to perform, but was cancelled at the last minute. The reason was that the packager of Bobby's Canadian-taped series was rough-and-tumble Sandy Frank, whose self-described "go for the jugular" approach was resented by many of his competitors. It would seem that Frank's prime "offense" was that he told the blunt truth and refused to don silk gloves in a cutthroat business where most other distributors pretended to be ladies and gentlemen. Whatever the reason, Sandy Frank was regarded as a gadfly, and the N.A.T.P.E. tried to make Bobby Vinton suffer for it. But Frank was dearly loved by local station managers who'd been piling up the profits accrued by the producer-distributor's various syndies, so ill feelings or no, *The Bobby Vinton Show* was one of the big sellers of the 1975–76 season, and the season after that. Vinton's first batch of half-hours suffered from too much misfire comedy revolving around the star's Polish heritage (though these ethnic roots had the nice side effect of providing Bobby with such Polish-American guest stars as Loretta Swit and Ted Knight), but Vinton's 1976–77 offerings were right on the money, displaying the star as the versatile entertainer that his detractors are surprised to discover that he is. Originally aimed exclusively for access, *The Bobby Vinton Show* frequently played in the 8-to-11 p.m. hours, and did well no matter when or where it was scheduled.

Bonkers (1978). *Bonkers* was issued by ITC as a "humanized" companion piece to its musical-comedy marionette extravaganza *The Muppet Show* (which see). It shared the same British production facilities and the same producer (Jack Burns) as *Muppet Show,* and was picked up by most of the earlier syndies markets (the five CBS-owned stations included). The stars were the Hudson Brothers, who'd been touted in one failed network series after another as the "new Marx Brothers," though their style was more reminiscent of the old Ritz Brothers. Despite a surplus of comic energy, the Hudsons were unable to maintain viewer loyalty, perhaps because there was so little substance beneath their frantic antics. Attractively mounted, and with expert assistance from comedian-cartoonist Bob Monkhouse, *Bonkers* was at least superficially as good as *Muppet Show,* but a series doesn't always become an audience favorite by osmosis.

Celebrity Concerts (1977). Hour-long, self-explanatory weekly from Rhodes Communications.

Celebrity Revue (1976). Likewise summed up by its title was this music-and-interview program, taped, like *Celebrity Concerts,* in Canada.

Circus! (1971–72). 20th Century–Fox Television's *Circus!* was a 48-week variation of NBC's old *International Showtime* (put together by former

Showtime producers Patrick Pleven and Joe Cates), featuring location-taped circus acts from throughout the world. The series was a Friday-night access fixture on the five CBS stations, and a weekend attraction in most other markets. It pleased the crowd despite the critics' expected bashing of host Bert Parks, whom nobody ever liked but the public.

Country Club (1971). Billed in many cities as *The Hugh X. Lewis Show,* in honor of its singing host.

Dance Fever (1979–   ). Though spawned during the height of the "disco" craze, Merv Griffin/20th Century–Fox's *Dance Fever* weathered the loss of interest in disco-dancing by offering a weekly, big-prize dance competition, judged by a panel of (here we go again) celebrities. Produced by former *American Bandstand* dancer Paul Gilbert, *Dance Fever* was hosted for its first seven seasons by Deney Terrio, the man who'd taught John Travolta how to strut his stuff in the movie *Saturday Night Fever.* Terrio's profile was so low in 1979 that he once was blocked from attending a *Dance Fever* taping by a studio security guard who didn't recognize him. By 1980, *Fever* was so tightly tucked into Syndication's Top Ten that Terrio had no trouble gaining entrance anywhere. (He left the show in 1985, and was replaced by actor Adrian Zmed.) In recent years, the disco format has been abandoned, and a variety of terpsichorean techniques have been used by contestants.

Disco Break (and others in this vein) (1977–80). If quantity can be regarded as a yardstick, the most persuasive trend in rock-music syndies occurred after the runaway success of the 1976 feature film *Saturday Night Fever,* which almost single-handedly restored the discotheque industry to its prominence of the 1960's. It didn't take long for producers to drink the *Fever* well dry. Florida-based Steve Marcus came out with *Disco 77* (Witt Productions) in guess which year, followed in 1978 by *Disco Magic* (Disco Magic Productions); the latter was hosted by one Evelyn "Champagne" King, a disco queen so named, one supposes, to distinguish her from Evelyn "Seven Up" King. New Jersey was home base for Brookville Marketing's *Soap Factory* (1978), while Kip Walton/Viacom's *Hot City* (1978 again), hosted by Shadoe Stevens, beamed from Los Angeles. Rhodes' *Disco Break* (1978 once more) was a series of five-minute fillers aimed at locally produced record shows. And J. Walter Thompson's *Juke Box* (1978 — what a year!) was hosted its first season by actress-model Twiggy, then by movie star Britt Ekland. All the disco series featured strobe lights, illuminated floors, unbuttoned-to-navel shirts on the men, sprayed-on pants on the women, and a stubborn determination to ignore originality. Only *Juke Box* lasted into the 1980's.

Disco Magic and *Disco 77* see above

Dolly (1976). A Show Biz Inc. 39-week showcase for Dolly Parton, taped at Opryland, a Tennessee-based theme park and TV production center. The series concentrated on the talents of Miss Parton and her guests rather than the production trappings surrounding them, thereby avoiding the glitz-and-glamour overkill that ruined Parton's ABC series eleven years later.

Don Kirshner's Rock Concert (1973–82). The most widely distributed of the '70s rock syndies was Viacom's *Don Kirshner's Rock Concert*. Kirshner, a former studio music director and record executive (he nurtured such pre-fabricated groups as the Archies and the Monkees, as well as such "real" enter-tainers as Bobby Darin), had bolted ABC's *In Concert* in 1973, claiming that the network was forever thwarting his attempts to bring new, controversial rock artists to television, something he planned to do on a weekly basis in syn-dication. *Rock Concert* premiered in October of 1973; its first-week lineup of 105 stations was achieved thanks to Kirshner's premiere guest stars, the Rolling Stones, appearing on American television for the first time in seven years. As the weeks rolled by, Kirshner spent less airtime exposing underexposed talent and more time dipping into the standard guest-talent pool used by all the other rock shows. It was pretty embarrassing for the CBS-owned stations when they scheduled a *Rock Concert* featuring Sly and the Family Stone on the exact same evening that ABC's *In Concert* was *hosted* by Sly Stone and his aggregation. Still, the expensive veneer of Kirshner's 90-minute weekly, and his inclusion of brief biographies of his guest stars starting in *Rock Concert's* second season, kept the series blaring away until 1982 (by which time distribution had been taken over by Syndicast). The only gripe that any serious rock fan could make about the series was that the long-winded introductions of the guest stars were delivered by Don Kirshner himself, an on-camera job for which he was uniquely unqualified.

The Donna Fargo Show (1978). One of a handful of country-western shows not produced in Nashville, Metromedia's *Donna Fargo Show* was taped at the Osmond Family studios in Utah.

Flipside (1973). Concert clip-interview show spotlighting rock stars, from Mizlou Productions.

The Golddiggers (1971–72). Produced by Greg Garrison, Chevrolet/Time-Life's *The Golddiggers* was a continuation of a network series starring the female knee-and-navel musical group that had come to prominence on Gar-rison's old *Dean Martin Show*. While at first glance *The Golddiggers* would seem to offer greatest appeal to those droolers who'd later watch *Charlie's Angels* with the sound turned down, the girls were sweet and unthreatening enough, and Garrison's choice of guest stars conservative enough, to score with middle-agers who were terrified by hard rock. Charles Nelson Reilly, Jackie Vernon, Barbara Heller and Alice Ghostley were the resident comics on the syndicated *Golddiggers;* at the risk of sounding sexist, we must say that the Golddiggers themselves were interchangeable, all young, pretty, and devoid of individuality.

The Hank Thompson Show (1972). Country-westerner from Jimmy Dean Productions.

Hee Haw (1971–   ). Hastily pasted together to fill a Sunday night slot on the CBS network in 1969, *Hee Haw* was a countrified clone of NBC's *Laugh-In,* with fast-paced editing, comedy blackouts, groanable one-liners, pretty girls, and music. While the series was a ratings-grabber throughout its network life, CBS cancelled *Hee Haw* in 1971 as part of the network's de-ruralization policy which also killed such old favorites as *Mayberry RFD* and *The Beverly Hillbillies.* Hoping to take advantage of the wide-open syndication field created by the access time ruling, *Hee Haw* went into local distribution with seven barter-sponsors and a 181-station lineup in the fall of '71. To compensate for its loss of network revenue, the series cut its budget to a flat $175,000 per one-hour episode (an installment of CBS' half-hour *All in the Family* cost about $250,000 at that time), with the series' regulars willingly accepting union "scale" wages to keep the show alive. *Hee Haw* was almost instantly a smash in syndication, with most of its markets creating a "network" of their own by running the series at 7 p.m. (EST) on Saturdays. (Only in recent years has the series moved from the evening hours; many markets now run *Hee Haw* on Saturday mornings as an "adult alternative" to the network cartoon shows.) *Hee Haw's* success turned the country-western market from a regional consideration into a prime time, coast-to-coast selling ticket; the series' magic rubbed off on the plentitude of other C-and-W shows in syndication, the attendant audience encouraging the creation of the Nashville Network cable service in the 1980's, which has supplanted virtually every country-western syndie *except* the still-thriving *Hee Haw.*

Though created by a team of Canadians, Frank Peppiatt and John Aylesworth, and distributed by Canada's Youngstreet Productions, *Hee Haw* has always been taped in Nashville, first at the studios of WLAC–TV, and most recently at Opryland. Buck Owens and Roy Clark hosted the series during its network run and for most of its syndie career; in recent years, the series has adopted a guest-host format, though Owens and Clark still occasionally pop up, especially on *Hee Haw's* anniversary editions. As in its CBS days, *Hee Haw's* yearly consignment of 13 episodes has been taped in marathon sessions, with individual music and comedy vignettes shot in blocks and edited into several different installments. There is a discernable "family" feeling among the series' very large cast of regulars (including such veterans as Grandpa Jones and Minnie Pearl, as well as "newer" stars like The Hager Brothers), and this unforced warmth and camaraderie, as well as the American public's basic love of an old joke, have been cited as the secret of *Hee Haw's* continued success. Since the late 1970's, the emphasis on the series has shifted from cornpone comedy to music, and by 1979 *Hee Haw* was established as the Number One conduit for blue-ribbon country-western. Still, series producer Sam Lovullo never completely abandoned comedy, and to that end attempted a pair of *Hee Haw* spinoffs. The first, a 1977 pilot starring Don Knotts titled *Front Page Feeney,* went nowhere; but 1978's *Hee Haw Honeys,* a semi-sitcom set in a roadside diner and starring *Hee Haw* regulars Kenny Price, Lulu Roman, Misty Rowe, Kathie Lee Johnson and Gailard Sartain, got by for two seasons through Lexington Broadcasting Service, mostly on the strength of its musical guest stars. (Note: *Hee Haw* is now syndicated by Gaylord Communications).

The Hee Haw Honeys see *Hee Haw*

Hot City see *Disco Break*

The Hugh X. Lewis Show see *Country Club*

The Ian Tyson Show see *Nashville Now*

The Irish Rovers (1973). A 39-week Canadian network series featuring the titular folk-singing group, which never quite caught on in the States despite the earnest efforts of its distributor, Worldvision.

The Jimmy Dean Show (1974). In a syndicated market where the syndicator and sponsor get as much of the financial take as the star, C-and-W singer Jimmy Dean seemed to be living in the best of all possible worlds. His *Jimmy Dean Show* was distributed by Jimmy Dean Productions, and barter-sponsored by Jimmy Dean Pork Sausages.

Johnny Mann's Stand Up and Cheer (1971–72). One of Chevrolet's several access syndies, *Stand Up and Cheer* was a spinoff of a 1971 network special. Choral director Johnny Mann's "What's *right* with America!" musical tastes had been subject to stirring patriotic endorsements in some circles, stinging barbs in others, ever since a jaw-dropping production number seen on the 1970 Emmy Awards telecast, wherein Mann's singers bombarded a nation polarized by Vietnam and campus dissent with one flag-waving tune after another. Despite its critics, *Johnny Mann's Stand Up and Cheer* stayed in circulation for two years, supported by a viewership majority larger by far than the fabled "Silent" one. Contrary to the observations of many television historians, Mann's series did not dine on an exclusive diet of Sousa, Cohan, and Francis Scott Key. As early as its first season, *Stand Up and Cheer* featured tributes to such non-establishment groups as Chicago, the Mamas and the Papas, and Blood Sweat and Tears. Whether or not the honorees survived these tributes is something else again.

Juke Box see *Disco Break*

The Larry Kane Show (1972). Telecom-released dance show, taped in Houston.

The Lawrence Welk Show (1971–82); *Memories with Lawrence Welk* (1982). The Lawrence Welk story is virtually the same, blow by blow, as the story of *Hee Haw*. Bandleader Welk and his "champagne music" had been firmly established audience pleasers for years on the ABC network (since 1955), but in 1971 ABC decided to cater more to the "young, urban" crowd and abandon the middle–America middle-agers who were Welk's biggest fans. So producer Don Fedderson moved the 60-minute variety series into syndication, bringing along several of the demographically chosen sponsors (including

Geritol and Polident) who'd sustained Welk on ABC. As with *Hee Haw, The Lawrence Welk Show's* regulars — Welk included — graciously accepted large salary cuts to keep the syndie's weekly budget low. It is hardly a revelation at this late date to note that Welk enjoyed a larger station lineup in syndication (217 his first season) than he'd ever had during his network days. Welk's "outdated" style managed to weather eleven top-rated syndie seasons, and even after he decided to take it easy at age 80, Welk's face and musical style were still available via a retrospective weekly from MCA, *Memories with Lawrence Welk.*

The Magic Circus (1972); **The Magic of Mark Wilson** (1978). Illusionist Mark Wilson and his troupe (made up mostly of the Wilson family) appeared — and disappeared — in two '70s syndies, the first bartered by Pillsbury, the second available as a weekly 30 minutes or a daily 5 minutes from J. Walter Thompson.

The Mancini Generation (1972). Chevrolet's *Mancini Generation,* a youth-conscious weekly that tried to offer music pleasing to older ears as well, had two attractive gimmicks. One was a weekly location jaunt by Henry Mancini's musicians to famous tourist attractions; the other was the spotlighting of student-produced avant-garde film shorts set to popular music, anticipating the style and substance of MTV by nearly a decade.

Marty Robbins' Spotlight (1978–79). A Show Biz Inc. C-and-W version of *This Is Your Life,* with host Robbins offering tributes (usually in the form of pristine-quality movie and TV-show clips) of country-western greats, past and present.

The Mouse Factory (1972). Walt Disney Productions decided to enter first-run syndication by preparing a half-hour replacement series for any of the first wave of access syndies that hadn't scored a hit by the end of 1971. That pinch-hitting January '72 release was *The Mouse Factory,* a family-oriented comedy-variety confection hosted by celebrities and giving special attention to Disney's theme parks and filmclips from the company's best theatrical releases. Incredibly, the well-produced but antiseptic *Mouse Factory* found itself in the eye of a storm of controversy in mid-1972. One of the series' guest hosts was Pat Paulsen, then conducting a jocular campaign for the Presidency. Some of the other aspirants for that office didn't regard Paulsen's political bid as a joke, however, and insisted upon invoking the FCC-enforced "equal time" rule; they demanded a half-hour's free air time as a "response" to Paulsen's *Mouse Factory* appearance. Rather than give over a lot of expensive half-hours to these humorless politicos, most stations — including the NBC-owned — dropped Pat Paulsen's *Mouse Factory* episode entirely. Now think a minute: would *you* vote for a man who demanded equal time from a show titled *The Mouse Factory?*

The Muppet Show (1976–81). Jim Henson's Muppets (combination marionettes and puppets) had been poking gentle fun at things social and political since the '50s on such networkers as *The Today Show* and the Paar and Carson nightlies. But what had once been regarded as an adult-oriented act had by 1975 earned a "Kids Only" stigma by virtue of the Muppets' appearances on PBS' *Sesame Street*. Henson and his partner Frank Oz dearly coveted a prime time network slot, but none was forthcoming. It's often assumed that the Muppets' rebirth as a "grownup" act was due to the troupe's sequences on the first season of NBC's *Saturday Night Live;* the fact is that long before *SNL* premiered, Britain's Sir Lew Grade saw enough potential in the Muppets to commission a pilot for an ITC series, taped in the summer of 1975. In the autumn of that year (after ABC considered, then rejected, the notion of picking up the Muppets for its 1976–77 season), Grade capitalized on the "family hour" demands for more wholesome access-time entertainment by dishing up *The Muppet Show* for American syndication (though it was sold to various networks throughout the world, including Canada's CTV). A big sale to the CBS-owned outlets led to pickups in some 150 other American markets; *The Muppet Show* rapidly outstripped ITC's own *Space: 1999* as the fastest-selling first-run in syndication history, and by 1978 it was the number one non-network attraction.

The *Muppet Show* adopted a format made saleable by such past masters as Jack Benny and Milton Berle: doing a weekly show about the putting on of a weekly show. The Muppets' satiric focus was the foibles of Show Biz, specifically showbiz egos. Each of the Muppets was more concerned with upstaging his or her fellow performers than in pleasing the audiences, and none of the characters was more Me-oriented than the vainglorious Miss Piggy, who was second only in *Muppet Show* prominence to the series' host, Kermit the Frog. Sensing a good merchandising gimmick, Jim Henson and Frank Oz used Miss Piggy as a spoof of the "overnight superstar" syndrome then afflicting such luminaries as Suzanne Somers and Farrah Fawcett—and the results included Miss Piggy cheesecake posters, her own television variety specials, and a write-in candidacy for the "best actress" Oscar on the strength of Piggy's performance in 1979's *The Muppet Movie*. All this for a talking sock.

Viewers with a basic dislike of Muppetry were disarmed by *Muppet Show's* deft handling of guest stars. The Big Names were not only allowed to display their talents to the utmost, but to slyly parody their public images, and to do both tasks with equal dexterity and lack of self-consciousness. Henson and staff got top results by coddling and pampering their guest stars in the manner of Roman courtesans; in turn, the stars were expected to give their all, and to treat their Muppet costars with the same respect that they'd received. It was difficult to throw a celebrity tantrum in this mutual-admiration society—and impossible not to look pretty stupid if one started yelling and screaming at a chorus made of foam rubber. *The Muppet Show's* guest roster was one of the most impressive of any variety series, much less a syndicated one: included were Peter Sellers, Julie Andrews, Roger Moore, Helen Reddy, Danny Kaye, Beverly Sills, Elton John, Carol Burnett, Victor Borge, Jonathan Winters, Charles Aznavour, Dizzy Gillespie, and, in one of his last appearances, Jim Henson's idol Edgar Bergen. Rita Moreno even earned an Emmy for her 1977 appearance (one of *Muppet Show's* many such statuettes). But no guest was treated with more deference than one Chris Langham — who happened to be one of the series' head writers.

Though it stayed at the top of the ratings heap for five seasons, *The Muppet Show* was operating at a loss when it left first-run in 1981. The series cost $250,000 an episode (even though it was taped in the cost-conscious environs of England's Pinewood Studios), and couldn't hope to make back its cost until it went into reruns. Unfortunately, *The Muppet Show's* rerun career hasn't been as prestigious as its first-run life, mainly because many local stations, having learned nothing from Sir Lew Grade, still treat the Muppets as kiddie entertainers and schedule the series in the morning/afternoon kidvid fringe.

Music Hall America (1976). 60-minute series in the *Stand Up and Cheer* vein, minus a regular weekly host; taped in Nashville and distributed by Viacom.

Nashville Now (1970–71). Known in most markets as *The Ian Tyson Show,* this Young & Rubicam/Transmedia release's official title was *Nashville Now* — even though it was taped in Canada.

Nashville on the Road (1976–83). Another Show Biz Inc. release, this one featuring C-and-W acts from all over the country, taped on location. By 1981, the series was bridging its music with comedy supplied by regulars Jim Stafford and "Golly Dang, the Wonder Chimp."

Nashville Swing (1977). From Arcadia Productions; a combination of music styles in the manner of *Pop Goes the Country* (which see).

The Now Explosion (1970). Taped in Philadelphia and distributed by Spangler Films, *Now Explosion* cashed in on the (then fading) "psychedelic" craze by offering five-hour blocks of hallucinogenic filmclips and surrealistic light patterns overladen with Top-40 tunes; this was designed to be hosted by local-market radio disc jockeys. *Now Explosion* didn't last, but it was a step in the direction towards the "music videos" a decade up the road.

The Peter Marshall Variety Show (1976). Weekly 90-minute effort to turn the venerable *Hollywood Squares* host into a Sammy Davis Jr.-type comedy/variety host. While a fine singer and comedian in his own right, Peter Marshall couldn't keep this Group W release (produced by David Salzman) alive past 17 weeks.

Pop! Goes the Country (1974–83). One of the longest-lasting Show Biz Inc. releases, *Pop! Goes the Country* was also one of the slickest and most popular; it was one of the few C-and-W series other than *Hee Haw* to regularly crack Syndication's Top Ten. Ralph Emery handled the hosting chores for this weekly half-hour, which featured countrified versions of non-country hit tunes, as well as the latest hits from the Nashville contingent. In its last years, the series capitalized on the national popularity of nightclubs catering exclusively to C-and-W fans — hence its new title in the early '80s, *Pop! Goes the Country Club*. Tom T. Hall hosted this new version.

R.J. and Company (1976). More from that bottomless reserve of rock-and-roll, Philadelphia. The "R.J." of this Taft Communications release was Ron Joseph, who produced as well as hosted this *American Bandstand*-ish dance party.

Rockworld (1978–82). An NTN release, with the requisite music and interviews.

Rollin' on the River (1971); **Rollin' with Kenny Rogers and the First Edition** (1972). Canada's Winters-Rosen Productions issued several musical specials starring the likes of Sonny and Cher and Bobby Darin to American markets in the early '70s; one of these, featuring a soft-rock group called the First Edition, was expanded into a weekly access half-hour. It was titled *Rollin' on the River* (from a song made famous by Creedence Clearwater Revival) in honor of its setting, an old-time riverboat. Sponsoring this pleasant mix of rock, rhythm-and-blues, country-western and dentist-office music were Noxema and Coca-Cola. In deference to the prominence of First Edition member Kenny Rogers, the series was retitled *Rollin' with Kenny Rogers and the First Edition* for its second season; after this, the group broke up, and Rogers suffered several very lean years before hitting it big again.

Sammy and Company (1975–76). Syndicast's *Sammy and Company* has special significance as the only series starring Sammy Davis Jr. to make it to a second season. The always-exuberant Davis worked twice as hard as usual (that's four or five times harder than any normal human being) to make this 90-minute weekly series work; so desirous was Davis of "quality control" that he bought *Sammy and Company's* Las Vegas production facilities, Trans-American Video, for his very own. The series was produced by Pierre Cossette, a producer/personal manager best known for his annual Grammy Awards telecast. Cossette, who'd entered syndication as packager for Chevrolet's first access syndies (including *Stand Up and Cheer*) had definite notions about what made a series click; the producer was devoted to Las Vegas Baroque at its glitziest and gaudiest. In time-honored lounge-act tradition, Sammy Davis said "cat" and "dig" every few seconds, exerted stand-up energy during his sit-down celebrity interviews, thanked everyone "from the bottom of my heart," and risked a weekly hernia by breaking up with laughter at the slightest provocation. *Second City TV's* "Sammy Maudlin Show," with Joe Flaherty as Sammy and John Candy lampooning Davis' unctuous announcer William B. Williams, was but a slight exaggeration of the doings regularly dished up on *Sammy and Company*. Still, the Pierre Cossette approach worked then and works now, evidence that Glitz can be as much an Art Form as any other kind of entertainment.

Sha Na Na (1977–81). Bristol Myers/Lexington Broadcasting's *Sha Na Na* was first seen as a live special over the NBC-owned stations on January

11, 1977; it joined the access-syndie pool in the fall of that year, taking the NBC stations and 100-plus other markets into its fold. Sha Na Na was a rock group specializing in the doowah hits of the 1950's, and as such was treated as a "court jester" when appearing in hard-rock concerts (including Woodstock) from 1968 on. The growing fascination in all things having to do with the '50s and early '60s, amplified by movies like *American Graffiti,* Broadway shows like *Grease* and TV series like *Happy Days,* led Pierre Cossette to see series potential in Sha Na Na. Wisely, Cossette and producers Bernard Rothman and Jack Wohl placed the singers in a satirical setting, a "typical" tenement backyard of the '50s. Despite its musical content and its parade of "golden oldie" guest stars, *Sha Na Na's* strong suit was comedy, complete with a supporting cast including a teenaged groupie (Pamela Myers), spot-gag comics (Soupy Sales, Avery Schreiber, Kenneth Mars) and a long-suffering "neighbor lady" (Jane Dulo, who was given all the best comedy lines). Sha Na Na itself was molded into the back-talk, double-take style of the Bowery Boys, right down to a "Leo Gorcey" in the person of the group's unofficial head guy, Jon "Bowzer" Bauman. Bauman's well-publicized background as a serious, Juilliard-trained musician took some of the whammy off making TV "heroes" out of leather-jacketed punks. The fact that Sha Na Na's "greaser" image was pretty much a charade was underlined by having the group break character and offer Broadway ballads and Gilbert-and-Sullivan ditties. (Ironically, Jon Bauman reportedly incurred the wrath of *Happy Days* star Henry Winkler by intimating that Winkler's "Fonzie" character was a phony!) Audiences lapped up *Sha Na Na* for four full seasons, while serious rock critics were less enchanted, declaring that the group's treatment of '50s-style rock was tantamount to sacrilege. After the series folded, Lexington Broadcasting tried to spin Jon Bauman off into his own "Bowzer" series, but it turned out that Bauman's television future rested on his appearances as a conservative, well-groomed game-show host.

Soap Factory see Disco Break

Something Else (1970). Trendy, formless "youth" series from Metromedia, hosted first by comedian John Byner, then by singer-composer John Hartford.

Soul Train (1971–). This black-oriented dance show started on WCIU–Chicago in 1970 as a shoestring imitation of *American Bandstand.* The market for what once had been called "ethnic music" had broadened since the '60s, so even the touchiest of Southern markets were interested when Bozell and Jacobs (an ad firm representing several manufacturers catering to black consumers) put *Soul Train* into syndication in 1971. The series was still chugging away nearly 20 years later, distributed by Tribune Entertainment. *Soul Train's* producer-host has always been Don Cornelius, who is seemingly blessed with the same agelessness as his *American Bandstand* counterpart Dick Clark.

Speakeasy (1973). A man who insisted on calling himself Chip Monck interviewed rock stars in this J. Walter Thompson-distributed weekly.

Stand Up and Cheer see ***Johnny Mann's Stand Up and Cheer***

Supersonic (1976). Assemblage of rock concerts, taped in England and syndicated by Fremantle.

Superstars of Rock (1973). A Kip Walton production, replete with concert clips and interviews.

That Good Ole Nashville Music (1972–83). The first new C-and-W release to directly benefit from the 1971 *Hee Haw* syndie success was Show Biz Inc.'s *That Good Ole Nashville Music,* hosted its first few seasons by Dave Dudley. As the series' emphasis was shifted from old musical favorites to the newest hits, the title was altered to *That Nashville Music.*

Twiggy's Juke Box see ***Juke Box***

Vaudeville (1975). A Metromedia bid to revive the sort of old-fashioned variety hour that Ed Sullivan had pulled off for years. Mort Green was writer-producer, Burt Rosen executive producer for this weekly series in which veteran celebrities shared the stage with comparative newcomers.

The Wolfman Jack Show (1976). Wolfman Jack (real name: Bob Smith), the fabled "renegade" deejay who'd hosted NBC's *Midnight Special,* emceed this Canadian-taped music/comedy/interview outing from Jerry Dexter Programs, which during its formative stages bore the somewhat derivative monicker *Pop Goes the Wolfman.*

Religious

Someday someone ought to write an encyclopedic book on the history of religious television. This isn't that book, but we'll try to touch upon the highlights of this field in the 1970's.

Except for *This Is the Life* and *Insight,* the once-thriving religious anthology market had been economically squeezed off the map in the '70s. Coming fully into their own during the decade were the televangelists; these men (and women) functioned in syndication because they'd been phased out of the networks back in the early days of radio. The radio networks of the '30s and the various regulatory agencies that preceded the FCC determined early on that only the representatives of "established" or "mainline" religious groups — Protestant, Catholic, Jewish — would be given free network time, relegating the smaller, personality-oriented sects to local stations. This was done to avoid protests against the networks whenever a non-mainline minister indulged in a particular brand of outrageousness, such as Aimee Semple McPherson's cute trick of changing the frequency of her radio station whenever she felt like it, or when Father Charles Coughlin began blaming the woes of the world on Roosevelt and the Jews. Syndicated spiritual leaders, denied the free air space given to mainliners by the networks in the interest of public service, had to pay their own way on radio and later television—hence the now-familiar but always controversial over-the-air solicitations of funds.

By the 1970's, hundreds of new UHF stations were operating, and these outlets needed product for their low-rated weekend schedules. If the evangelists were willing to foot the bills, and they were, they found new homes on these new stations—and subsquently, many preachers like Bob Harrington (the Chaplain of Bourbon Street) and the Seventh Day Adventists' George Vandeman, heretofore strictly regional attractions, were beamed out on a wider, more national basis. Also wider was the range of religious programming available to viewers. Those who preferred music to preaching were rewarded with Show Biz Inc.'s *Gospel Singing Jubilee,* one of the top-rated religious offerings, and one of the few in the field that was syndicated on a barter-sponsor basis. Those who desired simple Bible studies without the haranguing could tune in to *Day of Discovery* (mentioned in our '60s section) and George Vandeman's *It Is Written* (a "regional" which went "national" in 1975). People who liked a little infighting and rivalry spicing their religious viewing could indulge in the father-son bickering between Herbert W. and Garner Ted Armstrong on Herbert's *World Tomorrow* and Garner Ted's *Plain Truth.* And those who longed for the days when Oral Roberts made the blind see and the lame walk could tune in on the laying-of-hands and fainting spells of Ernest Angley and Leroy Jenkins.

The most significant trend in religious syndication was its move away from the Sunday-morning ghetto and into the Monday-through-Friday class. There'd been some daily activity before this "big move," most notably from Garner Ted Armstrong's weekday messages, but the true leaders of the movement on a full national basis were Jim Bakker, Pat Robertson and Jimmy Swaggart—and it is this fact, rather than the individual fates that would befall these worthies in the '80s, that gives them their prominence in the world of syndication.

Billy James Hargis and His All-American Kids (1972). Right-wing Bible thumper Billy James Hargis forsook his behind-the-pulpit cannonades against the enemies of the American Way of Life in favor of a lavish, revue-style weekly featuring a clean-cut young chorus called the All-American Kids. Hargis still railed against moral and political turpitude in a manner that made all but the most intransigent conservatives blush, but whenever confronted by his critics, Hargis would laugh and say that no one had ever been able to bump him off the air. Ultimately, Billy James was done in by Billy James himself, when it was revealed that two of his recently married young followers discovered on their wedding night that *both* of them had known Hargis, in the Biblical sense. The downfall of Billy James Hargis should have served as a cautionary lesson for others who didn't quite practice all that they preached.

Captain Noah and His Magical Ark (1972). Children's religious programs never quite reached the heights of *Davey and Goliath* or *Off to Adventure* in the '70s. Most emcees of kiddie inspirational programs were well-meaning semi-professionals hampered by tacky production values, hand-me-down puppets and marionettes, and severely limited talents (some of these hosts did pretty well in spite of their problems, but not well enough for nation-wide success). One of the best of a negligible lot was *Captain Noah and His Magical Ark,* taped at WPVI–Philadelphia and distributed widely in the South and Midwest. The host was clergyman W. Carter Merbreier, who as the bewhiskered Captain Noah entertained children who'd otherwise have ignored his spiritual messages by carousing around a nicely detailed ship's-deck set and indulging in slapstick and pratfalls.

Hi, Doug see *700 Club*

Hour of Power see *Robert Schuller's Hour of Power*

James Robison (1970's onward). Rev. Robison was one of those evangelists whose program was seen in a great many markets, but whose name was unknown to the general public until that One Step Out of Line. The Texas-based Robison had had many individual installments of his Sunday series pre-empted because of his outspokenness against abortion and homosexuality; but when WSOC in Charlotte, North Carolina, cancelled Robison altogether because of his attacks on the liberal attitudes allegedly taken on "aberrant behavior" by certain highly regarded religious leaders, WSOC's action made national headlines. Actually, WSOC was already in the news for axing, on similar grounds, a fundamentalist weekly hosted by Rev. Charles Sustar, but since Robison's series was seen in more cities than Sustar's, it was Robison whom the public remembered. In fact, Robison's national coverage *increased* after the March 1980 WSOC incident, which said something about the hold televangelism was beginning to take in the syndie marketplace.

Jerry Falwell see *The Old-Time Gospel Hour*

Jim and Tammy and **Jim Bakker** see *The PTL Club*

Jimmy Swaggart see *A Study in the Word with Jimmy Swaggart*

Life in the Spirit see *The 700 Club*

The Old-Time Gospel Hour (1971–   ). This was for many years the official title of Rev. Jerry Falwell's weekly television church service. Falwell is better known to the public at large as the head of the Moral Majority; while it might be that this group is only one of the things it claims to be, its influence on everyday life on and off the TV tube cannot be taken lightly. To his credit, Falwell seldom mixed politics with religion on his show, especially after taking his lumps in 1976 for criticizing President Jimmy Carter's *Playboy* interview. Not only did the critique lose Falwell several markets, but it was levelled against the man whose own Born-Again Christianity helped sustain the televangelist movement of the mid-70's. Since that time, Falwell has for the most part separated his Moral Majority activities from his weekly electronic sermon.

Practical Christian Living see The 700 Club

The PTL Club (1975–87). If one is a believer, the initials stand for "Praise the Lord" or "People That Love"; if one is a cynic, they could very well stand for "Pass the Loot." Whatever the case, the *PTL Club* was the creation of Jim Bakker, who began his television career conducting a children's puppet show with his wife Tammy on Pat Robertson's *700 Club* (which see) in 1963. Guided by what seemed to be a sincere desire to spread God's word with the added ingredient of entertainment, Bakker suggested that Robertson's Virginia-based series adopt a couch-and-desk interview format similar to the *Tonight Show*. After inaugurating several other cosmetic changes in the Robertson operation, Bakker and his wife left to join Paul Crouch's Trinity Broadcasting Service. After a few harsh words with Crouch, Jim and Tammy went to Charlotte, North Carolina, there to launch the daily *PTL Club*. Using the entertainment trappings he'd employed on *700 Club*, and taking advantage of marketing techniques he'd learned from both Robertson and Crouch, Jim Bakker built up his own network of Southern television stations. When *PTL Club* went national in 1975, it had a slick assuredness far beyond its weekly $5,000 budget. Through the help of call-in and mail-in contributors, the Bakkers' operation was able to spend a million dollars per week by 1980. It was in fact Jim and Tammy's utilization of funds that attracted the attention of the *Charlotte Observer*, which conducted a long-term investigation into just how honest the Bakkers' evangelistic empire (which included worldwide missions, a home for the handicapped, and a glittery "theme park" called Heritage USA) really was. As with Billy James Hargis, Jim Bakker's Waterloo was apparently a sin of the flesh. In 1987, a former Bakker employee stepped forward with revelations of both sexual and financial hanky-panky on the part of the baby-faced Jim; within a month, people who'd never heard of the Bakkers were cracking jokes about Jim's alleged bedroom shenanigans and Tammy's eccentrically applied facial makeup. Jerry Falwell was called in to bail out the by-then financially ailing *PTL Club;* one of Falwell's first moves was to toss the Bakkers out of the operation they'd created. As of this writing, Jim and Tammy Bakker, with the support of many faithful followers willing to forgive and forget, are conducting a determined and frequently bizarre campaign to regain their former status in the PTL Ministry.

Reverend Ike and the Joy of Living Program (1973). Unique among televangelists, Dr. Frederick J. Eikenrotter II, better known as "Reverend Ike," was an unabashed advocate of "Green Power." He revelled in money and materialism, implored his followers to send in cash in exchange for "valuable gifts" of slightly less usefulness than those old box-top premiums, and was given to statements like "I wear $400 suits because God *wants* me to wear $400 suits!" It's hard to label someone as blatant as the Rev. Ike as a charlatan.

Robert Schuller's Hour of Power (1970–   ). Taped in Garden Grove, California, *Hour of Power* began in 1970 with a rotating team of four ministers hosting the program. Gradually the series became the sole responsibility of Robert Schuller, who, as a member of the Reformed Church of America, was one of the few "mainstream" ministers operating in syndication. This meant that Schuller could have made a bid for a major network slot if he'd wanted — but had he done so, he would never have enjoyed his 150-plus station lineup in syndication. Schuller's uplifting approach to his work and his message of "possibility thinking" looked and sounded a lot like the "positive thinking" sermons of Dr. Norman Vincent Peale — and no wonder, since Schuller has freely admitted that Dr. Peale was his role model and has invited the aging but still active Peale to be a frequent guest speaker on *Hour of Power*. Schuller has also proven to be as savvy as Peale in the ways of show business; philosophizing that something pretty spectacular was needed to keep the average viewer's eyes glued to the TV screen on Sunday morning, Schuller commissioned architect Philip Johnson to create the $15 million all-glass structure known as the Crystal Cathedral. It was a far cry from the days when Robert Schuller was preaching out of an old drive-in movie theatre.

The Rock and **The Ross Bagley Show** see entry immediately following

The 700 Club (1975–   ). The Yale-educated son of a United States Senator from Virginia, Marion G. "Pat" Robertson abandoned his silver-spoon existence for the hand-to-mouth life of a minister. In 1961, Robertson bought a dying UHF outlet in Portsmouth, Virginia, there to set up an all-religious TV service. The centerpiece of Robertson's tinker-toy operation was a phone-in prayer and guidance service created in 1963, *The 700 Club,* allegedly named for the 700 viewers whose cash contributions had kept Robertson's station on the air in its early days. By and by, and with the bright suggestions of Robertson employee Jim Bakker (see *The PTL Club*), *The 700 Club* developed into a sort of divinical *Johnny Carson Show,* complete with desk, couch, studio audiences, "Ed McMahon" sidekick (Jim Kinchloe) and celebrity guests, most of these in the "born again" category. Robertson's contribution as host was every bit as gladhanding and garrulous as Carson, Griffin and Douglas, though he displayed something less than Christian charity when discussing such problems as homosexuality and "secular humanism." When *700 Club* went into national syndication in 1975, Robertson already owned five southern TV stations which he dubbed "the Christian Broadcasting Network," had created several half-hour "satellite" programs to be run in tandem with the daily *700 Club* (including *Hi, Doug, Life in the Spirit, Practical Christian*

Living, The Rock, and *The Ross Bagley Show,* the latter hosted by a "gospel deejay"), and was laying the groundwork for the CBN Cable TV Network, which became one of the largest cable services of the '80s (and produced a whole slew of new series, which we'll discuss when we get to that decade). Robertson remained with *700 Club* until 1986, when he left both his host's chair and his ministry to conduct a campaign for the presidency — an office he'd been coveting since at least 1979. One wonders why a man with a powerful and influential commercial-TV talk show and cable-TV operation should want to step down into a mere public service job.

A Study in the Word with Jimmy Swaggart (1977–   ). After Jim Bakker and Pat Robertson made daily religious programming a viable commodity, Assemblies of God minister Jimmy Swaggart stepped in with his Monday-through-Friday *A Study in the Word,* taped in Swaggart's home base of New Orleans. Far more of a militant than many of his fellow televangelists, Swaggart could work himself up into a tear-stained frenzy when lambasting the enemies of Christianity. Some of his views were radical indeed for a man who wished to curry favor with a national audience. His comments on Jews were ill-chosen at best (and atypical, since many electronic evangelists were strong supporters of the State of Israel), and his declaration that Catholics weren't qualified to enter the Kingdom of Heaven must have come as quite a shock to people like Mother Theresa. And it was Jimmy Swaggart who blew the whistle on the improprieties of *PTL Club's* Jim and Tammy Bakker — which made Swaggart's ultimate disgrace following public revelations of his own sexual misconduct most ironic, and not a little gratifying to some.

Westbrook Hospital (1977). The one "new" dramatic religious program wasn't new at all, but a spinoff featuring characters and settings introduced on the Seventh Day Adventists' long-running anthology *Faith for Today.*

Specials, Miniseries, and Mini-Networks

This new category came about thanks to the wildly fluctuating American economy of the 1970's. Fewer syndie producers wanted to risk the financial pinch of a 26- or 32-episode series, so more producers opted instead for the monthly, bimonthly and quarterly special. Videotape enabled the music and news one-shots to have a "currency" not found on film, and also helped keep the costs further in check. And as a result of the demands of Action for Children's Television, a fresh new market opened up for one-shot or limited-series kid's programs, eminently suitable for the "non-violence," "culture" and "family hour" lobbyists. The limited-series format also embraced adult-oriented syndies, especially after the amazing network success of such "miniseries" as *Rich Man Poor Man* in 1976 and *Roots* in 1977. With television industry forecasters predicting that the miniseries movement would be the dominant force of the years to come, several companies, including MCA and Mobil Oil, used the limited dramatic series form to build up ad hoc syndicated "networks" to combat ABC, CBS and NBC, and to bolster the prime time lineups of independent stations, traditionally the weakest ratings hours of these unaffiliated outlets' broadcast days.

A note before beginning this section: Many of the so-called "specials" aimed at the family trade were actually made up of theatrical feature films. MGM's *Family Network* of 1973 and the still-visible *SFM Holiday Network* both offered old movies like *Ivanhoe, Knights of the Round Table, The Jungle Book, Jesse James* and *Friendly Persuasion* — many of these having already made the rounds in the syndicated film packages of the 1960's. And there were also things like Worldvision's *Specially for Kids* (1973), which at closer scrutiny was a bundle of children's films produced in Europe and Asia, including such imperishable classics as *Dogs to the Rescue!*

Bicentennial Specials (1974–80). Part of the general celebration of the 200th anniversary of the Declaration of Independence included a parade of television specials and fillers. The best-known of these were CBS' nightly, star-conscious *Bicentennial Minutes,* but syndication also serviced this onslaught of history lessons. Modest little one-minuters like Spot Bits' *21 Days of America* shared airtime with limited series like Gould/Post-Newsweek's *The Presidents: 76 Years on Camera,* narrated by James Garner, and its followup, *The American Documents,* hosted by William Shatner; and there were the more ambitious projects like Group W's 12-part *The Course of Human Events* (mentioned in our 1960's "Travel/Documentary" notes). These efforts provided viewers with more American history than they'd gotten in eight years of public school — and better still, without homework.

Capital Cities Specials (Mid 1970's–85). Before hitting the Big Leagues by purchasing the ABC TV network, the Capital Cities station group was most visible as a provider of specials to an average non-network lineup of 175 markets. Most Capital Cities one-shots were "crisis" oriented, including *The Trial of Eichmann, Why Can't I Learn?, Inflation: The Fire That Won't Go Out,* and the April 1977 grim prognostication of the long-term results of energy waste, *We Will Freeze in the Dark.* Capital Cities kept its hand in throughout the early '80s, most notably with 1985's antidrug piece, *High on the Job,* hosted by Stacy Keach, who at the time was in a British lock-up as a result of a cocaine bust.

The company also maintained a monthly schedule of children's specials. In keeping with the "crisis" policy of their adult programs, Capital Cities' kid's programs dealt with such dilemmas as drugs, delinquency and teen pregnancy. Specials like *This One's for Dad, It Can't Happen to Me, Loser Take All* and *When, Jenny, When?* in the '70s, and *Chicken!, Who Loves Amy Tonight* and *A Step Too Slow* (these last two spotlighting early performances by Laura Dern and Judge Reinhold, respectively), and Emmy-winning *Mandy's Grandmother* in the '80s, ran the gamut from peer pressure to understanding of adult senility and alcoholism. Circumventing accusations of sensationalism, Capital Cities included on-screen warnings of their specials' subject matter, and also shipped out pamphlets and study guides to schools and parent groups. These specials were originally aimed for late-afternoon and prime time access exposure; although dress-codes and teen slang have changed somewhat since their first telecasts, the Capital Cities one-shots hold up well enough to remain on the schedules of many 1980's cable services, usually on weekends.

Century Theatre (1973–74). A group of BBC adaptations of the classics, released in the United States by 20th Century–Fox, including limited-series versions of James Fenimore Cooper's *The Pathfinder,* Sir Walter Scott's *Fortunes of Nigel* and Frances Hodgson Burnett's *Little Princess.*

The Commanders (1974). From BBC/Time-Life; seven hour-length studies of wartime military decision-makers, including Eisenhower, MacArthur, Rommel, Yamamoto, Russia's Georgi Zhukov and Britain's Sir William Slim and Sir Arthur "Bomber" Harris.

The Dora Hall Specials (circa 1974). One of the oddest byproducts of the barter system came from Premore Productions, which issued several musical specials adorned with guest-stars like Ray Bolger and Sammy Davis Jr. — and starring a spunky middle-aged lady named Dora Hall. If you've never heard of Dora Hall, join the club. Rumors spread that Dora had put up the money for the specials herself, that her husband was a powerful advertising man, or that she was a onetime stage star making a comeback. Whatever the case, the local stations who telecast the specials cared not a whit that nobody had the vaguest idea who Dora Hall was, so long as her programs were offered free of charge by their barter sponsors.

Edward the King **see** *Mobil Showcase Network*

Family Classics (1972–74). An Ogilvy & Mather access-time package, comprised of multipart British adaptations of literary favorites like *Ivanhoe, The Black Tulip* and *Little Women.*

General Mills Fun Group (1974). Series of Canadian-made holiday specials, among them the animated *Tales of Washington Irving.*

I Am Joe's. . . (late 1970's). From J. Walter Thompson; monthly specials concentrating on various body parts (*I Am Joe's Liver,* etc.), based on a series of *Readers' Digest* articles.

Jack the Ripper (1976). Six-part speculative fiction about the most notorious serial murderer of all time. A British production (are you surprised?), syndicated by 20th Century–Fox.

Little Vic (1977). Joey Green played a ghetto youth whose life was turned around by his care and training of a horse named Little Vic. The six-parter was seen first in access (with the ABC-owned stations in its lineup) through Viacom, then as a regular visitor to local weekend schedules.

Metromedia Specials (1970–86). Many of the specials from this station group were of an ecological bent. The most startling of these was seen in two-hour form over the Metromedia outlets on June 1, 1970, then syndicated as an hour special to other markets. Titled simply *1985,* the special warned that, unless social and economic reforms were immediately effected, the world of 1985 could expect such catastrophes as power blackouts resulting in "civil war" between police and looters, martial law in Chicago, food and water rationing, DDT poisoning, killer smog, "black plagues" caused by poor public sanitation, and thousands of deaths in Mexico from rampaging dysentery. Metromedia's concern for the well-being of mankind continued into the '80s (until the station group was bought up by the Fox TV network in 1986) with specials about the escalating divorce rate, runaway teens, and one-shots like *The National Crime and Violence Test* (1982) and *The National Drug Abuse Test* (1983).

The Mobil Showcase Network (1977–   ). Although Operation Prime Time (which see) got all the glory, the first to seriously pursue the course of an ad hoc network in the mid–70's was Mobil Oil. One of the biggest contributors to the survival of public television, Mobil's entree in the commercial non-network game was *Ten Who Dared,* a ten-week series dramatizing the exploits of famed explorers. *Ten Who Dared* debuted on January 13, 1977, running in most cities on Thursdays at 8 p.m. (EST). The series established Mobil's policy of releasing British programs to American markets, as opposed to Operation Prime Time's insistence on producing its own, home-grown syndies: *Ten Who Dared* had previously been seen over the BBC as *The Explorers.* The 60-minute series was not a success, so Mobil retreated to bartering such access half-hours as *Between the Wars* for the next two seasons. The Mobil Showcase Network flowered again with another British import, Thames Television's *Edward the King,* a 13-parter starring Timothy West as the aging Edward VII (taking over from Charles Sturridge as the teenaged Edward). As mentioned in the introduction to this book, the networks refused to play *Edward* because of Mobil's editorial-like advertisements; so Mobil set up its own alignment of stations, running the series for 13 consecutive Wednesday evenings starting January 17, 1979. To attract the fans of the more popular, sensational fictional fare offered by Operation Prime Time, Mobil's ad copy for *Edward the King* was full of hubba-hubba come-ons like "Remembered as the Peacemaker King — but not forgotten as the Playboy Prince!" Tell-all tales of British royalty have always seemed to fascinate the American public, and *Edward* was no exception: the miniseries was the fourth-rated program in New York, number three in Chicago, number two in Los Angeles, and the top-rated show in Washington, D.C. CBS, one of the networks who'd originally rejected *Edward,* could only gnash its teeth as the 12 CBS affiliates who ran the Mobil series piled up their best Wednesday-night ratings of the year.

The Mobil Showcase Network's 1980 followup to *Edward the King* was another Thames Television product, *Edward and Mrs. Simpson,* a nonsensational dramatization of the events leading up to the 1936 abdication of Edward VIII (Edward Fox); Cynthia Harris played Edward's controversial American bride, Wallis Warfield Simpson. As with the first *Edward,* Mobil ran the six-parter on Wednesday evenings, uninterrupted by commercials (save for a three-minute message just before the drama started), and with introductory comments made by Robert MacNeil. Mobil pursued the Anglicizing of American television with its subsequent Showcase Network presentations, all of them run at the same time, same day on the buying stations. There were more historical dramas (1981's *Churchill and the Generals,* with *Edward the King* star Timothy West as Sir Winston Churchill); some Agatha Christie (*The 7 Dials Mystery* and *Why Didn't They Ask Evans,* both 1981); a 1984 duet of Frederick Forsyth stories, *A Careful Man* and *Privilege,* shown back-to-back on March 28; ample doses of Sir Laurence Olivier in two 1984 presentations, *King Lear* and John Morrison's *Voyage Round My Father;* and a summer 1980 try-out of various British music and comedy series, the best of which was *The Kenny Everett Video Show.* By far the most prestigious — and costliest — Mobil Showcase effort ran from January 10 through 13, 1983. It was *Nicholas Nickelby,* a televised version of the mammoth stage adaptation of the Dickens classic, starring Roger Rees as Nicholas and 39 other actors playing a total of 150 roles — changing costumes and characterizations before the audience's eyes, and wandering in and out of the audience in the true spirit of "living theatre." The Mobil television version lost a lot of the immediacy of the stage work, but viewers were happy, especially at not having to pay the flat $100 ticket fee charged when this Royal Shakespeare production moved to Broadway. One of the finest presentations from Mobil was also the simplest: a half-hour 1982 filmization of James Clavell's antidictator piece, *The Children's Story,* directed by the author.

The Nelvana Specials (1978). Most family specials were holiday tie-ins, such as J. Walter Thompson's *Miss Peach* Valentine and Easter offerings and *A Gorey Halloween.* The Canadian-based Nelvana animation studios came up with one of the best-circulated packages of holiday specials, distributed by Viacom and given a major build-up by the NBC-owned stations. These half-hour cartoons included *Romeo-0 and Julie-8* (for Valentine's Day), *The Devil and Daniel Mouse* (Halloween), *Intergalactic Thanksgiving* and *A Cosmic Christmas.* They weren't anything to crow about in terms of technique but were winners so far as clever character design, bright scripts and singable songs were concerned. The Nelvana specials won over the "better–TV" brigades with their soft-pedalled moral messages, lack of violence, and wide age appeal; they did well enough to be issued on a single videocassette in 1980, titled *Nelvanamation* (which did not include Nelvana's 1980 cartoon release, *Take Me Up to the Ballgame.*)

The Nixon Interviews (1977). Richard Nixon, three years into his retirement but as much in the public's consciousness as ever, was attempting (through his literary agent Irving Lazar) to set up a series of interviews over one of the major American networks — none of whom were interested in meeting Nixon's financial terms. David Frost, long out of the daily series rat race, had in 1977 just completed a series of British television interviews with such world leaders as Moshe Dayan and Harold Wilson. Frost and his producer John Birt became fascinated at the prospect of interviewing Nixon for television, and even better, they were willing to pay his price. Nixon, who recalled that the liberal-leaning Frost had been one of his fairest interviewers during the 1968 presidential campaign, went along with the plan — and thus it was David Frost who scored THE interview coup of the late '70s, and for syndicated television to boot.

Frost's questioning of the ex-president was taped in two 12-hour sessions. No guidelines regarding subject matter were imposed on either Frost or Nixon, and it was understood that Nixon would have no editorial control over the results; in return, Frost promised that the questions would be nonpartisan, based on the queries most likely to be asked by America's leading journalists on all sides of the political spectrum. The resulting miles of videotape were pared down to four 90-minute specials, to be broadcast on four consecutive Wednesdays at 9 p.m. starting May 4, 1977 (a fifth program of leftover material would be shown in October). Syndicast, the distributor, cleared 125 stations for the specials, allowing six minutes of barter ads per show; the programs were simulcast by the Mutual radio network, and subsequently seen in 70 foreign countries. Ever the showmen, Frost and Nixon kept the content of each special a secret until air time. As the first major televised appearance by the former president since 1974, *The Nixon Interviews* were ratings blockbusters — even though little was revealed that people didn't already know (or suspect) about Nixon, and despite the fact that many viewers were sorely disappointed that the unindicted co-conspirator didn't fall to his knees and beg forgiveness.

Operation Prime Time (1977–   ). In late 1976, MCA, in answer to pleas from independent stations for first-run, truly competitive prime time programming, formed a new station-by-station program service with the faintly militaristic name of Operation Prime Time. O.P.T. obtained financial support from major independents like WPIX–New York, WGN–Chicago and KCOP–Los Angeles, and used as its base of operations the vast expanses of MCA's Universal Studios. The first O.P.T. miniseries, a pulpish adaptation of Taylor Caldwell's *Testimony of Two Men,* showed the seams of a modest budget, but the property had a built-in readers' following, and the cast (headed by David Birney) was certainly "all-star" by TV standards. By the time of *Testimony's* premiere in May of 1977, Operation Prime Time's ad hoc network had grown from its first 17 stations to 91 markets, including several network affiliates disenchanted with what their networks had to offer. The six-hour *Testimony of Two Men* cinched a whopping 20 percent share of the audience, doing exceptionally well in the biggest cities.

Taking Operation Prime Time into consideration along with the Mobil Showcase Network and such first-runs as *Space: 1999,* industry prognosticators were saying that, with the added expedience of satellite transmission, network domination would diminish and ultimately disappear within the next decade, giving way to strong syndicated line-ups. Banking on these predictions, O.P.T.

began cranking out programming on a regular release schedule. In May of 1978, the mininetwork was back with a lavish picturization of *The Bastard* (a problematic title in certain markets), the first installment of John Jakes' early–America "Kent Family Chronicles." This $3.6 million enterprise in spot-the-star and sensationalism topped *Testimony's* ratings, earning an audience share ranging from 28 to 34 percent. O.P.T.'s 1978 docket also included Irwin Shaw's *Evening in Byzantium,* starring Glenn Ford in an improbable tale of terrorists at a foreign film festival, and Howard Fast's *The Immigrants,* released strategically at Thanksgiving time. *Immigrants* lost some of the ratings gleaned by Operation Prime Time's earlier efforts, so the consortium played safe with two more John Jakes "Kent Family" yarns in 1979, *The Rebels* and *The Seekers.* By the end of 1979, Operation Prime Time had 118 markets in its clutches with its dramatically shaky but ratings-grabbing specials.

As O.P.T. moved away from Universal to accept offerings from other major studios like Columbia, Fox and Paramount, it moved distribution out of the hands of MCA to its own distributor, Television Program Entertainment. In 1980 came O.P.T.'s biggest "push" (and best ratings) to date, with presentations like Harold Robbins' *The Dream Merchants,* John D. MacDonald's *The Girl, The Gold Watch and Everything,* soap opera–style stuff like *Tourist, The Gossip Columnist* and *Condominium,* a two-hour cartoon special from Hanna-Barbera titled *Yogi's First Christmas,* and a top-tune countdown with series potential, *Solid Gold '79.* The year 1981 gave the world a sequel *(The Girl, the Gold Watch and Dynamite!),* a "disaster-fantasy" about a society living in a capsized ocean liner *(Goliath Awaits),* and another musical special, a tribute to the celebrity alumnae of Northwestern University titled *The Way They Were.* With 1982 came a new trend, the biographical mini-series. The first of these, *A Woman Called Golda,* was by far the best, with Ingrid Bergman a tower of strength in her Emmy-winning (and tragically, her final) performance as Israeli prime minister Golda Meir. *Sadat,* in 1983, wasn't as good (nor was Mexico a completely satisfying location-filming replacement for the middle East), but the performances of Louis Gossett Jr. as Anwar Sadat and Barry Morse as Menachem Begin were first-rate. Other biographies ran from okay (1984's *The Jessie Owens Story* and *Helen Keller: The Miracle Continues*) to overbaked (1987's *Ford: Man and the Machine,* starring Cliff Robertson as Henry Ford). Then there were the dizzy absurdities of *Blood Feud,* with Robert Blake's Jimmy Hoffa vs. Cotter Smith's Robert Kennedy, which in one scene suggested that teamsters helped choreograph not only JFK's assassination but Lee Harvey Oswald's as well. This 1983 masterpiece was surpassed only by 1987's *Hoover vs. the Kennedys,* which had as a highlight a scene wherein "Marilyn Monroe," giving a rubdown to "John F. Kennedy" while the two of them share a hot tub (in 1962!), coos "Oooh! Your poor back!" With less historical trappings but with more dramatic integrity were O.P.T.'s various spy-novel adaptations of the '80s (LeCarre's *Smiley's People,* Ken Follett's *Key to Rebecca* etc.) and the lavish, British-produced versions of Barbara Taylor Bradford's society romances, *A Woman of Substance* (1985) and *Hold the Dream* (1986).

While not the first of the ad hoc network services, Operation Prime Time has proven the most durable, still giving its competition a run for the money even in the wide-open network/cable/pay market of the late '80s. Its yearly specials output has decreased in recent years, but its purpose of providing saleable first-run alternatives to the networks has been maintained by several series which have spun off from O.P.T. specials, including *Solid Gold, Star Search* and *Lifestyles of the Rich and Famous.* And its legacy has been handed down to any number of eager ad hoc hookups which have emulated O.P.T.'s steady stream of two-, four- and six-hour dramatic specials (see our notes in the 1980's section).

Scared Straight! (1978). The honor of "hottest" non-network special of the 1970's would have to go to KTLA–Los Angeles' *Scared Straight!* Produced and directed by Arnold Shapiro, this 60-minute documentary was a filmed record of the Rahway, New Jersey, State Prison's Juvenile Awareness Program—a mild cognomen for a program in which teenagers with police records were taken in groups through Rahway's maximum security facilities. Here the teens experienced the straight talk and verbal abuses of a team of convicts serving anywhere from 25 years to life, mostly for rape and murder. The 17 troublemaking teenagers seen in *Scared Straight!* were shown at the beginning of the program kidding around about their criminal activities and bragging that no visit to Rahway could possibly frighten *them.* The epilogue revealed a group of visibly shaken kids who for the most part had been frightened out of a life of crime by the convicts' bleak, brutal word-pictures of prison life, which included lovingly detailed descriptions of homosexual rapes and likely early deaths awaiting the teens should they end up "in stir." The uncompromising tone of the documentary was summed up by one convict's close-up scream of "Get that motherfuckin' camera OFF me!" Tacked on to dissuade more sensitive souls from watching the special was an introduction and narration by Peter Falk, who repeatedly warned the viewers that they were not about to see *The Partridge Family.* (Incidentally, Falk would not accept one penny more than Union minimum for his contribution.)

KTLA ran *Scared Straight!* on November 2, 1978. The resulting onslaught of phone calls to the station indicated that most viewers found the special (obscenities and all) an excellent deterrent for incipient hoodlumry. Since the networks would obviously reject a special which served up profanities at a rate of one per sentence, KTLA's parent company Golden West decided to offer the special to syndication through Dave Bell and Associates. Sixty stations ran the program in March of 1979; deciding that commercial interruptions would be inappropriate, Signal Oil underwrote the program and ran it without breaks. *Scared Straight!* earned a 26.1 Neilsen rating in New York City alone, and repeated its excellent performance throughout the nation; and as in Los Angeles, audience reaction was overwhelmingly positive. The special led to follow-up discussions on local stations, a fictionalized TV-movie, and the continuation of the "Scared Straight" program in Rahway, which was then under fire from the authorities as being only a temporary, and ultimately ineffective crime deterrent.

Did *Scared Straight!* succeed in its goal? A 1987 special titled *Scared*

Straight: Ten Years Later tracked down the 17 youths and nine convicts who appeared in the original special. Fifteen of the "kids" were shown to be settled down in honest, productive lives; of the other two, one had continued lawbreaking but was in the process of cleaning up his act, while the other, ruefully admitting that he should have paid attention back in 1978, was himself behind bars. The most poignant moment of the 1987 syndicated special was a scene in which this last-mentioned man was confronted by one of the former Rahway inmates, who'd conversely left prison and become a legitimate businessman. This time, it was the prisoner who was contrite, and the *visitor* who was roughly remonstrative. As the special's narrator Whoopi Goldberg observed, the far-reaching effects of any television program—or of television in general, for that matter—were strictly up to the individual.

Ten Who Dared see Mobil Showcase Network

Time-Life Classics (1972). More family fare, this time made up of foreign-filmed serializations of such standards as *Tom Brown's School Days* and *The Last of the Mohicans*.

Sports

There were few sports of any kind that one couldn't see on television in the 1970's; a larger TV market equalled a bigger hunger for major and minor televised sports events. In syndication, the basic field-and-stream, hunting and fishing half-hours persevered. The generic sports digest programs continued, as did the highlight-and-interview efforts. Wrestling was still around, still a "regional" attraction, as was its fellow early–TV denizen, the roller game. And for one brief, shining moment, it looked as though syndication would be on the ground floor of the latest advance in professional football. And then everyone woke up.

American Horse and Horseman (1973). A Les Walwork and Associates/Lasater release for the "upscale" sports enthusiast, appropriately hosted by western star Dale Robertson.

Ara's Sports World (1976). Onetime Notre Dame football coach Ara Parseghian hosted this chat-and-clips weekly from Viacom, which was almost released as *Ara's World of Sports* until ABC's legal department caught on.

Bowling for Dollars (1970–). This franchised series from the Claster Company (who started the business of franchising series formats to local stations with 1952's *Romper Room*) began in the '60s as a "regional," spotlighting top-drawer local contestants who competed for big cash prizes. A demand for first-run access material led *Bowling for Dollars* into more markets than ever it had enjoyed before 1971, but eventually the ranks thinned and the series prospered only in cities where TV bowling had an avid enough following.

Celebrity Bowling (1971–78); *Celebrity Tennis* (1974–78). The usual '70s tendency to combine gamesmanship with star-gazing led to the two above-mentioned weeklies, both put together by 7-10 Productions (the company stopped short of *Celebrity Cribbage*) and distributed by Syndicast. Jed Allen and Sherry Kominsky hosted the bowling show, while the tennis series was emceed by Tony Traubert and Bobby Riggs. After Riggs' "battle of the sexes" tennis match with Billie Jean King in 1973, King tried to emulate her rival with her own tennis weekly, which made little headway.

The Champions (1976). Half-hour snippets from legendary boxing bouts, from Marvin H. Sugarman productions.

Grambling Football (1972–late '70s). Louisiana's all-black Grambling College, long established as one of the foremost proving grounds for future pro football players, was represented with this taped series of 11 yearly football-game abridgments distributed by Black Associated Sports Enterprises.

Greatest Sports Legends (1974–   ). Hosted by a different sports celebrity or sports announcer each year, *Greatest Sports Legends* was first-run exclusively from April to September, bartered in its early career by Bristol-Myers and Continental Insurance and shipped out by Syndicast. Each half-hour episode spotlighted a celebrated athlete's past, present and likely future career.

Lee Trevino's Golf for Swingers (1972). Still more celebrities were on hand for this half-hour produced and directed by William *(New Zoo Revue)* Carruthers, taped at the way-beyond-your-lifestyle Talabasses Country Club Park in California.

Lloyd Bridges' Water World see *Water World*

Most Valuable Player (M.V.P.) (1971–72). This Roth Media release referred to two sports personalities of the M.V.P. category: Johnny Bench hosted the interview show during baseball season, while Willis Reed took over in the basketball months.

M.V.P. see above

NFL Game of the Week (1971–   ). A long-running weekender, *Game of the Week* was given a crack at prime time access by Hughes Television; there it stayed until games of another kind took over that time period, whereupon the NFL show returned to its weekend-afternoon homeland.

Outdoors with Julius Boros (1975). After parting company with Gadabout Gaddis, Liberty Mutual remained in the outdoor-sportsman syndie business with Julius Boros as host.

Outdoors with Ken Callaway (1975). A Transmedia release; not to be confused with *Outdoors with Julius Boros*.

The Racers (1976–77). Checkered-flag filmclips hosted by Curt Gowdy; from American-International/Syndicast.

Spartacade (1979). Ambitious, satellite-fed series from Moscow of pre–Olympic competition, intended as a lead-in to the 1980 Olympics from the same locale, which of course was going to be that year's premiere television sports event. Sure.

Water World (1972–74). A Heathertel field-and-stream show with more stream than field, bartered by such specialized sponsors as Mercury Marine and Champion Sparkplugs. Lloyd Bridges was the obvious choice to host the series, which bore Bridges' name in its title until James Franciscus succeeded Bridges for the final 13 half-hours.

The World Football League (1974). With occasional exceptions like the Grambling games, football was exclusively the domain of the networks, with the syndie efforts barely in the running. (Various attempts to make a non-network attraction out of Canadian football eventually shrivelled due to lack of interest.) Then came the valiant formation of the World Football League in 1974, designed to provide several cities with the only major-league sports franchises they'd ever had. Under the guidance of media-smart Eddie Einhorn, the WFL acquired a large line-up of television markets for its first summer season through the syndication facilities of TVS. (The only other serious bidder for the TV rights was the Hughes Network; the major networks' own football schedules were already filled to the brim.) Sadly, WFL's premiere happened at the worst possible time as far as building viewer loyalty was concerned. For one thing, the rather anemic pro-football lineups in the AFL and NFL in '74 had caused a severe dropoff in viewership. For another, few sports fans in the summer of 1974 could get worked up over football, what with baseball's Henry Aaron just having broken Babe Ruth's home-run record. Come 1975, the World Football League could not get one single solitary network or distributor interested in picking up its television option. The marketplace being what it was, there was soon no World Football League at all.

The World of Sports Illustrated (1971–72). The first sports digest specifically created with the access-time slots in mind, Chevrolet/Time-Life's *World of Sports Illustrated* was a special favorite of the CBS-owned stations, making the series' matriculation into a CBS-network weekly (retitled *CBS Sports Illustrated*) a logical chain of events.

Talk/Interview

Syndicated talk/interview abounded in the '70s for the same reasons as in the '60s: a bigger market, a demand for first-run entertainment, a comparative inexpensiveness. Donahue, Douglas and Griffin flourished by keeping apace of changing entertainment styles and public opinions.

Women continued making inroads in what was once the men's club of talkhosts, and at least one woman, Dinah Shore, matched and surpassed her male counterparts for a time. And there were the usual casualties, including program concepts that didn't take, "favorite" personalities who couldn't transfer their popularity to the daily chat routine, and a few good shows that had the misfortune of being squeezed out of an increasingly overpopulated field.

America's Black Forum (1976–   ). From Telecommunications; discussion, debate and interviews of and by blacks.

Bob Braun see Paul Dixon

Comeback (1979). As always, producers were on the prowl for "sure-fire" series concepts, sure-fire because they'd worked once before. American-International's *Comeback* was a reheating of a 1950's series starring George Jessel, which focussed on great names from yesteryear who'd fallen upon hard times and who were coaxed before the camera to tell how they'd overcome the doldrums. *Comeback* host James Whitmore exerted every ounce of his acting talent to keep his guests from wallowing in self-pity. Strangely, this videotaped series was sent into rerun syndication on blurry, second-generation kinescope films; apparently also making a "comeback" on this series was the most obsolete of 1950's-style technology.

Dinah! (1974–80). After NBC's daily *Dinah's Place* fell victim to that network's preoccupation with game shows, host Dinah Shore moved to 20th Century–Fox Television; thanks to a firm early commitment from the CBS-owned channels, her new syndicated *Dinah!* toted up 100 markets less than six months after its 1974 debut. (It was, surprisingly, *not* seen that first year in Nashville, Dinah's hometown.) A master blend of talk, music, and home-improvement and cooking tips, *Dinah!* added several Emmies to Miss Shore's already cluttered trophy room, as well as a 1976 honor for the star as "Broadcaster of the Year." Jokesters liked to point out that Dinah had a habit of running off at the mouth when she was supposed to be listening to her guests, but that was technique, not carelessness: being in the presence of a gabby hostess encouraged her interviewees to open up and contribute to the conversation. The cleverest aspect of the series was Dinah's habitual undercutting of her peaches-and-cream public image with a tendency to gently go for blood in her interviews, often by digging up skeletons from her guests' past. Ann-Margret turned several shades of crimson at the sight of her baby pictures, Johnny Carson averted his eyes as a kinescope of his first television series from 1950 flickered on screen in all its ticky-tacky glory, and Dick Cavett wailed "Oh, spare me!" as Dinah unspooled an old Signal Corps film featuring Cavett overacting horrendously as a foppish West Point cadet.

We're not about to insult anyone's intelligence by suggesting that many of these extemporaneous moments weren't planned in advance. This, in fact, led to the ultimate atrophying of *Dinah!* (not, as has been assumed, Miss Shore's diminishing singing voice; even with a range considerably smaller than in her network days, Dinah could out-belt most younger song stylists). The rigors of taping a daily 90 minutes began to erode Shore's patented spontaneity, and by the late '70s, her gaiety and her "astonishment" at the direction her conversations were taking seemed forced and, worst of all, rehearsed. With the show faltering (it had long before lost the CBS stations), the producers retooled *Dinah!,* toning down talk in favor of music and comedy. The rechristened *Dinah and Friends* was lively at first, but ultimately fell into the old pattern of "celebrity surprises"—you know, when McLean Stevenson or somebody rides in on an elephant or shows up dressed as a waiter, and oh, what a *surprise* it is! *Dinah and Friends* lingered until 1980.

Evans and Novak (1976). Washington columnists Rowland Evans and Robert Novak presided over this news-behind-the-news discussion weekly from RKO, nearly a decade before their similar series for the Cable News Network.

Everyday (1978). With the ink barely dry on their *PM Magazine* contracts, Group W added a spanner to the works to saturate the daytime market with magazine-style entertainment. Expensively taped at Hollywood's Television City, Group W's *Everyday* made its national bow on October 2, 1978. A true potpourri, *Everyday* threw in generous amounts of interview, music, comedy, news, health hints and cooking advice. It was decided that this melange needed a team of hosts, rather than a single emcee. Filling the bill were Stephanie Edwards, late of ABC's *AM America,* actor John Bennett Perry, and a troupe of regulars including comic Murray Langston and singer Tom Chapin. Too much of anything can bury rather than buoy a series, and this was what happened to *Everyday*. Group W suggested that the daily's demise was because *Everyday* wasn't *Phil Donahue:* there was little give-and-take with the studio audience, nor were timely issues or controversies touched upon. Indeed, anything timely would have been old stuff by airtime, since the show was taped several weeks in advance—its last hour, taped the first week of February, wasn't aired until March 30, 1979. So *Everyday* was gone, but not Group W. The company retained most of *Everyday's* production staff and planned a magazine-show comeback for 1980, tentatively titled *This Afternoon* and tentatively hosted by Gary Collins.

For Adults Only (1971). Two very sharp "personality" journalists, Joyce Davidson and Barbara Howar, teamed for the weekly *For Adults Only,* produced by Talent Associates (whose boss, David Susskind, was Joyce Davidson's husband). Unworthy of its lurid title, *For Adults Only* (in some markets known as *The Joyce and Barbara Show,* a cognomen more suited to a singer-sister act) was an excellent showcase for issues of importance.

Good Day (1976–78). A daily interview hosted by John Willis, from the busy studios of WCVB–Boston.

Imus, Plus (1978). New York "shock radio" pioneer Don Imus wasn't able to build a national following for his commando style, but his 90-minute weekly had its moments.

Jerry Visits (1971–75). KNXT–Los Angeles' *Jerry Visits,* featuring Jerry Dunphy and an array of high-profile guest stars interviewed at their homes or recreation spots, was well circulated thanks in part to KNXT's sister CBS-owned stations.

The Jim Nabors Show (1978). Syndicast tried to make a Merv Griffin out of comic actor Jim Nabors, playing safe with Nabors' fans by including his *Gomer Pyle* co-star Ronnie Schell as a regular. *The Jim Nabors Show* was a catch-as-catch-can hour of interviews, music, audience participation, and contests. Nabors allowed at the time that his daily wouldn't show a profit until its second season. He never had the chance to find out. Sur-prise, sur-prise!

Joanne Carson's VIPs (1972). If tabloids are to be believed, Joanne Carson split with her husband Johnny partly because she wished to be recognized for her own talent, rather than merely as an appendage to Johnny's fame. *Joanne Carson's VIPs* proved on a daily basis that the ex–Mrs. Carson could hold her own as an interviewer (she'd been a journalist before her marriage), and even more valuable was her talent for drawing out many of her famous friends who otherwise steered clear of television. Sadly, most station managers in 1972 figured that the only bankable Carson was Johnny. In fact, the name of *VIP's* production firm — Wing-It/Jay M. Kholos Advertising/Universal Entertainment — ran longer than the series. Well, almost.

Joyce and Barbara see *For Adults Only*

The Joyce Jillson Show (1978). The onetime starlet and fulltime astrologer had her own vehicle from a company appropriately named Jupiter Entertainment.

Living Easy with Dr. Joyce Brothers (1972). The presence on this Capricorn Productions release of announcer Mike Darrow, a band, and a guest-roster with names as diverse as Douglas Fairbanks, Jr., Larry Storch, Dr. Margaret Mead, Marlo Thomas, Rex Reed, Helen Gurley Brown, Irene Ryan, Stiller and Meara, Soupy Sales and Mickey and Sherri Spillane, would seem to indicate that the days of Dr. Joyce Brothers sitting behind a desk and merely dispensing psychological sagacity were numbered. Indeed, around the time that this daily half-hour series premiered, Dr. Brothers was just becoming a member of the Screen Actors Guild. Still, she had time for another series of five-minute television talks in 1973.

Mantrap (1971). This Dick Clark Production somewhat miscalculated the purpose of the Women's Movement. At a time when many women were pressing for sexual equality, *Mantrap* often resorted to an adversarial approach in its pitting a panel of female celebrities against one lone man (series host Alan Hamel). Even the series' opening credits, which were overladen with the sound of a lot of women's voices chattering formlessly all at once, was more suited to the days of "woman driver" and "mother-in-law" jokes than the supposedly enlightened '70s.

Not for Women Only (1971–79). Inaugurated locally on WNBC–New York as *For Women Only,* this Colgate-Palmolive daily series wisely changed to a non-polarizing title when entering syndication in 1971. Barbara Walters, then busy on *The Today Show,* was the first host. *Not for Women Only* adopted a theme-per-week policy: five consecutive half-hours devoted in depth to a single issue. Sustaining one subject for a whole week works only when the host is up to the challenge, a fact brought home when Barbara Walters was briefly replaced by her old *Today* colleague Hugh Downs. A self-confessed "jack of all trades, master of none," Downs was unable to confine himself to one single topic for two-and-a-half hours weekly, and has since opted for the magazine approach of PBS' *Over Easy* and ABC's *20–20.* Seasoning the heavier material on *Not for Women Only* were occasional doses of "standard talkshow procedure." On one program, young magician Doug Henning accomplished what many a harried interviewee might have wished to do when he sawed Barbara Walters in half. *Not for Women Only* was one of the most durable women-oriented programs; it lasted nine seasons, by which time Barbara Walters had been succeeded by Polly Bergen and Dr. Frank Field and Colgate-Palmolive's barter sponsorship had been taken over by Alpo Dog Food (which, like Hugh Downs, had followed Barbara Walters from *The Today Show*).

The Paul Dixon Show (1974). After Avco's *Phil Donahue* hit it big, the company cast about for more local talk hosts who might succeed in the national market. Avco-owned WLWT in Cincinnati provided what seemed to be a likely candidate in the station's "morning man" Paul Dixon, who already had something of a national reputation; Dixon had hosted a widely seen daily variety show on the old DuMont network in the '50s. Unfortunately, Dixon seemed to have never really left that decade behind, and his varsity-show approach to entertainment did not translate well to national syndication in 1974. Avco tried again later on with another long-established WLWT personality, Bob Braun, whose noontime daily got some decent coverage in a number of midwestern markets, but Braun was still small potatoes compared to Phil Donahue.

The Real Tom Kennedy Show (1970). Game-show host Tom Kennedy went the daily-variety route with this Century Communications release. The curious title was slightly inaccurate. Even Tom Kennedy was not the "real" Tom Kennedy; his real name was Narz, and he was the brother of another game-show veteran, Jack Narz.

The Sheila MacRae Show (1971). This 20th Century–Fox daily should have won the 1971 award for Nepotism in Action: Sheila MacRae's cohosts were her actress-daughters Heather and Meredith, and the series' producer was Sheila's husband Ron Wayne.

Tom Kennedy see *The Real Tom Kennedy Show*

The Virginia Graham Show (1970–72). Virginia Graham bolted *Girl Talk* in 1969 to launch a more issue-oriented daily, which carried her name in the title and which was distributed by Rhodes. Telecast in prime time in many cities, the 90-minute *Virginia Graham Show* helped to spearhead a thriving '70s market of talk shows hosted by women.

What Every Woman Wants to Know (1972). To fill the gap left when *Not for Women Only* changed sponsors, Colgate-Palmolive cooked up a January 1972 release hosted by Bess Myerson and titled *What Every Woman Wants to Know.* The new daily concentrated as much on self-improvement and self-protection (it displayed its New York origins by featuring police officers who'd tell women how to guard against muggers and home intruders) as it did with the woman's role in '70s society.

Woman (1971). This one was helmed by WOR–New York's candid radio talk-host Sherrye Henry.

Travel/Documentary

The story here was the same as in the 1960's, only more so. Travel and documentary shows appealed to all age groups, and were cheap to make in the bargain. Thus they were just what the doctor ordered when the FCC exerted pressure for more "family" programming, and when production costs on many other '70s syndies went through the roof.

American Adventure (1972). Travel-and-adventure show bartered by American Motors with instructions that the series be shown on weekend afternoons, just prior to the network sportscasts.

American Lifestyle (1972). E.G. Marshall hosted this Showcorporation release, which centralized the growth of the United States by concentrating on movers and shakers like Edison and Ford.

American Wilderness (1973). A David Wolper production, sponsored by International Harvester.

Animal World (1973–80). One of Bill Burrud's best and longest-lasting projects, *Animal World* began on NBC in 1968 and ran for three years on all three networks (sometimes titled *Animal Kingdom*) before settling into syndication. Its barter-sponsors included Kal-Kan, Procter and Gamble and

Westclox; reruns of *Animal World* were issued on a cash-sale basis under the title *Wildlife Adventure.*

Audubon Wildlife Theatre (1971–72). ABC Films and 20th Century–Fox teamed up for *Audubon's* 78 half-hours, which like many wildlife syndies of the era placed a concern for ecology above the mere showing of "pretty pictures."

Between the Wars (1978). Alan Landsburg had initially planned that his 16-week *Between the Wars* be shown on PBS with support from Mobil Oil, but Mobil, busy with its off-and-on "Showcase Network," opted for commercial stations. Officially, *Between the Wars* and two other Mobil-sponsored half-hours, *When Havoc Struck* and *World War II: GI Diary,* were Mobil Showcase Network presentations, and buying stations were requested to run the programs on the same evening during the same access time-period; but many markets couldn't clear the time, and ran the Mobil shows wherever they could. *Between the Wars* was narrated by Eric Sevareid, with contributions from an impressive array of historians and eyewitnesses; it concentrated on the period of 1918–1941, during which the sociopolitical lessons not learned from the First World War led to World War II.

The Big Battles (1973). British actors Paul Rogers and Peter Bond narrated this compilation of war footage, coproduced by French Pathé and the BBC. Home International handled U.S. syndication.

Charles Blair's Better World (1973). Blair's documentary series insisted that it would cover only "upbeat" topics, but frequently the good aspects of the world were counterbalanced with the bad, as in one episode which dwelt on famous political assassins.

The Coral Jungle (1976). Exquisitely photographed Group W underwater series, narrated by Leonard Nimoy.

David Niven's World (1974). From J. Walter Thompson; David Niven's jaunty narration was provided to films depicting everything from mountain-climbing to dope smuggling!

The Explorers (1972). David Wolper Productions again, this time in concert with Hughes Television. Leslie Nielsen hosted.

Friends of Man (1974). A Mediavision wildlifer, hosted by Glenn Ford.

Great Roads of America (1973). A journey down America's asphalt avenues, narrated by Andy Griffith and released in a year that O.P.E.C. kept many *off* the Great Roads.

In Search of... (1976–82). In 1973, Alan Landsburg purchased the American rights for what he'd later describe as an "overlong, pretentiously narrated and absolutely fascinating" German documentary film. *Chariots of the Gods?* was based on a book by Eric Von Däniken which used "archeological evidence" of the rag, bone and hank of hair variety to prove that the ancient civilizations had been influenced by visitors from outer space. Landsburg decided to show this film as a one-shot television special; at the insistence of his sponsor, he whittled the film to a playable, less ponderous length and dubbed in new-and-improved narration by Rod Serling. Under the title *In Search of the Ancient Astronauts,* Landsburg's "new" speculative documentary made off with a juicy ratings slice. Although he himself was no real fan of "what if..." movies, Landsburg was partial to good ratings, so he put together a second, similar network special, *In Search of the Ancient Mysteries.* The subsequent success of this program (and of a best-selling book written by Landsburg's staff as a tie-in) led to Landsburg's creation of a weekly series of speculations, titled, as if you hadn't guessed, *In Search of....*

Bristol-Myers began pitching *Search* as an access syndie in early 1976; the NBC-owned stations were so bowled over by the concept that they picked up the show immediately, and other markets wasted no time in following suit. For six seasons, Landsburg kept *In Search of...* in production, with his crack team of researchers and a diligent globe-trotting camera crew supplying stories of possible supernatural events, probable instances of psychic phenomena, and "maybe" stories about people like Jack the Ripper and events like the Hindenburg disaster. Few long-standing mysteries were solved, and Landsburg never let the facts get in the way of a good story, but *Search* was ultraenjoyable "pop" documentary entertainment.

While the saturnine and stentorian Leonard Nimoy would seem the obvious choice to narrate *Search,* he wasn't Landsburg's *first* choice. Robert Vaughn, replacing the late Rod Serling, had narrated the pilot, but was either not asked or not available to host the series itself. At the same time, David Wolper was trying to sell his own "speculation" series, *The Unexplained.* Wolper's program was optioned by the NBC-owned stations, but they dropped it in favor of *Search.* After this, Landsburg hired the narrator of *The Unexplained's* pilot as permanent *In Search of...* host. That narrator happened to be Leonard Nimoy, and the rest, as they say, is history. Incidentally, after being knocked out of the running by his former employee Alan Landsburg, David Wolper left syndication in favor of the networks. After the premiere of his ABC miniseries *Roots* in 1977, Wolper felt no pressing urge to return to the non-network field again.

Inner Space (1974). From Four-Star/Fremantle; William Shatner narrated the breathtaking underwater camerawork of Ron and Valerie Taylor, shortly before their celebrated contributions to the Universal feature film *Jaws.*

Last of the Wild see below

Lorne Greene's Last of the Wild (1974). Not narrated by Pernell Roberts, this popular half-hour was produced by Ivan Tors of *Sea Hunt* fame and bartered by General Electric.

Other People — Other Places (1974). This J. Walter Thompson release, narrated by Peter Graves, first ran in England over BBC as *Strange Places*. After the *In Search of. . .* success, *Other People — Other Places* was redistributed as *Strange People — Strange Places.*

Passport to Travel (1974). More world views from Entertainment Corporation of America, produced by prolific Los Angeles travelogue host Hal Sawyers.

Safari to Adventure (1971–73). Bill Burrud again, this time with the added advantage of the ABC-owned outlets in his access-time lineup.

Secrets of the Deep (1974). Four-Star's companion show to its *Thrillseekers* (which see), with astronaut Scott Carpenter joining his space-travel "colleagues" Leonard Nimoy and William Shatner as a narrator of underwater films.

Seven Seas (1971). Hour-long specials series, from Four-Star.

Strange People — Strange Places see *Other People — Other Places*

That's Hollywood (1977–81). Onetime David Wolper employee Jack Haley Jr. had produced a hit MGM feature in 1973, a pastiche of the studio's past musical highlights titled *That's Entertainment.* This feature, and its sequel, had roots in a never-produced television series of Haley's called *Hooray for Hollywood.* Once Haley assumed presidency of 20th Century–Fox television, any future sifting of the MGM archives was out of the question, but this didn't stop Haley from pursuing his dream of creating a weekly nostalgic TV journey through a major studio's film vaults. Ultimately, Fox issued Haley's *That's Hollywood;* hosted by Tom Bosley, this series spotlighted not only choice clips from past Fox film classics, but also managed to show vignettes from several RKO, United Artists, and public-domain features. Adding to the spice of the series were out-takes, bloopers, deleted scenes (including Shirley Temple imitating Jimmy Durante in a scene cut from *Little Miss Broadway*), and, naturally, self-congratulatory previews of upcoming 20th Century–Fox attractions.

This Is Your Life (1970–72; 1983). The "documentary" section is as good a place as any for *This Is Your Life,* Ralph Edwards' marathon radio and television weekly which documented the lives and times of celebrated persons. From 1948 through 1961, Edwards had been tricking the famous into appearing before his microphones or cameras, then relating their life stories to them and trotting out their friends and family for warm (at least they *seemed* to be warm) reunions. Lever Bros.' bartered syndie *This Is Your Life* was taped, as opposed to its live days on the networks, so some of the old "surprise" quality was lost to viewers since the honorees were listed in *TV Guide* well in advance. (Radio historian Jim Harmon had it on the good authority of a former radio star that in fact many of the honorees were themselves tipped off that they'd be honored by Edwards, to avoid on-camera heart attacks or confrontations with old "friends" whom the honored guests actually despised.) Still, the '70s version of *This Is Your Life* had a few classic moments: when *Hee Haw* comedian Junior Samples was the special guest, he couldn't stop crying, and by and by his nonstop blubbering turned into unintentional high comedy. A 1981 *This Is Your Life* retrospective special on NBC was supposed to have led to a network revival of the series; instead, the property turned up briefly as a weekly syndie from Lexington Broadcasting/Telepictures in 1983. Producer Edwards himself hosted the first syndicated *Life*, as he'd done back in the '40s, '50s and '60s; Joseph Campanella emceed the 1983 version, which like the NBC special featured clips from past episodes.

Three Passports to Adventure (1970). Hal, Halla, and David Linker, stars of the long-running '50s travelogue *Wonders of the World,* were back with more high-class home movies in 1970.

Thrillseekers (1972–73). Four-Star's enthusiastic update of *Danger Is My Business,* with Chuck Connors narrating filmclips of daring people in deadly occupations (or recreational pursuits), had enough sheer nonstop action for *Variety* to gush that "No one will turn off once they switch on the set."

The Unknown War (1979). Thanks to the quicksilver quality of world events, Air Time International's *The Unknown War* was for the most part The Unseen Series. *Unknown War* was produced in cooperation with Russia's Sovietfilm and was a sympathetic (and apolitical, or at least as apolitical as it could be under the circumstance) account of the Soviet Union's struggle to survive World War II. Isaac Kleinerman, whose documentary experience included the Pathé newsreels and CBS' *20th Century,* produced; Burt Lancaster narrated; Harrison E. Salisbury wrote the narration, John Lord assembled the scripts, and poet Rod McKuen adapted both script and narration into a more lyric style, in addition to handling the musical direction. As a compassionate look at human courage under pressure rather than a political endorsement, *Unknown War* was created in the spirit of U.S.-U.S.S.R. "detente." But the series was doomed to obscurity, not by anti–Russian sponsors or television stations, but indirectly by President Jimmy Carter. In 1980, Carter withdrew the American athletes from the Moscow Olympics in protest against Russia's invasion of Afghanistan. Local stations then considered it politic, in every sense of the word, to drop *The Unknown War* — a gesture that did about as much good as Jimmy Carter's.

When Havoc Struck (1977). A Mobil "Showcase Network" 12-parter, featuring half-hour filmed records of famous natural disasters, narrated by Glenn Ford. The series' working title was *Catastrophe* — and what an opening for a jaundiced television critic *that* would have been.

Wild Kingdom (1971–   ). An NBC Sunday afternoon fixture since 1963, *Wild Kingdom* was cancelled for the same reason that CBS got rid of

Lassie in 1971; NBC had to give its time slot back to local stations to stay in line with the new Prime Time Access Rule. Also as in the *Lassie* situation, *Wild Kingdom's* sponsor, Mutual of Omaha, was willing to barter the series in syndication if enough local markets were interested. 215 markets were interested indeed, and *Wild Kingdom* was in syndication ever afterward, even surviving the death of its creator-host, Marlin Perkins, in 1986. (Its most recent host has been Jim Fowler, who'd been pretty much in charge of the series for several seasons anyway.)

In addition to ultimately benefitting, in terms of national coverage, from the Prime Time Access Rule, *Wild Kingdom* represented the first "test case" for that piece of legislation. *Kingdom's* producers dared to ask permission to waive the new access rules in 1972 and be allowed to include reruns from the series' network days in its manifest. The explanation was that, with its around-the-world filming itinerary, *Wild Kingdom* was able to come up with only 13 new episodes per year. The FCC decided that the series had enough "educational" value to warrant a waiver of the no-network-reruns-in-access policy, but only if *Wild Kingdom* maintained a future yearly schedule of 13 new episodes, 13 reruns from the syndicated programs, and *then* 13 network reruns. Thus *Wild Kingdom* was able to maintain a full 39-week schedule in its first few years and was able to stay alive, pleasing everyone except producers of other network shows-cum-syndies like *Lawrence Welk, Hee Haw* and *You Asked for It,* who wished that *they* could have made *Wild Kingdom's* money-saving compromise with the FCC.

So far as content was concerned, *Wild Kingdom* was virtually the same rare-animal show it had been on network (and, once again like *Lassie,* it was frequently shown in its old network time slot). Also the same were Marlin Perkins' delightfully kitschy lead-ins to his insurance commercials: "We took a real gamble filming that charging white rhino, but if *you* don't want to gamble with your family's future, protect yourself with Mutual of Omaha."

Wild, Wild World of Animals (1973–79). If the title reminded the viewer of both *Wild Kingdom* and *Animal World,* then the title-thinker-uppers did their job well. William Conrad narrated this one, a co-production of Windrose, Dumont (not the old network), the BBC and Time-Life.

Wildlife Adventure see Animal World

Wildlife in Crisis (1976). A Viacom release, more cautionary than most of its kind.

The World at War (1974). Laurence Olivier provided the terse commentary for Thames Television's *World at War,* which won an Emmy after Gottlieb-Taffner brought the series to America. This may well be the best, most thorough World War II chronicle ever made for television. In the course of its 26 one-hour installments, *World at War* offered seldom-seen clips of British radio and music-hall comics keeping up morale, of the kangaroo-court trials of the Hitler assassination attempt conspirators, of vicious anti–Semitic German newsreels and "documentaries," and some absolutely stomach-churning color footage of the carnage at Okinawa. These and other sequences brought home the sadness and obscenity of war with far greater clarity than any previous documentary series.

The World of Survival (1971–77). Produced on behalf of the World Wildlife Fund, *World of Survival* was hosted — frequently on location — by John Forsythe. So lucrative was this property that its distributor, Anglia Ltd., changed its name to Survival Anglia.

World War 2: G.I. Diary (1978). Just what its title promised, a first-hand look at the war narrated with foot-soldier simplicity by Lloyd Bridges. This last of the Mobil Showcase Network's half-hour access shows (before Mobil's move into syndicated prime time) had its sales path smooth by a strong alliance with the CBS-owned stations; and like the other Mobil Accessers *(Between the Wars* and *When Havoc Struck),* it was released concurrently with the publication of a paperback book of the same title.

You Asked for It (1972); **The New You Asked for It** (1981–82). More access material culled from an earlier TV era, American-International's *You Asked for It* followed the format of its more famous network predecessor (it ran on both DuMont and ABC from 1950 to 1959), by presenting scenes of unusual occupations, out-of-ordinary or celebrated people, and strange stunts, which purportedly had been requested by write-in viewers. Jack Smith, who'd succeeded Art Baker on the network *You Asked for It,* hosted the 1972 weekly. Sandy Frank Productions cooked up the 1981 revival, which ran five nights a week and was hosted by Rich Little, who felt the urge to throw in his celebrity impressions whether he was asked to or not. Jack Smith was on hand with vignettes from the series' black-and-white past. When the budget was cut for *The New You Asked for It's* 1982 season, Jack Smith had taken over as host again, and the series was almost completely comprised of clips from older episodes.

The 1980's

The new trends and new technologies — especially that marvel of the age, the satellite — affecting syndication in this incredibly busy decade are best treated on a genre-by-genre basis. But first, a general overlook at the 1980's.

In 1971, there were many local stations who hoped that the Prime Time Access Rule would go away because of the difficulty at the time in coming up with saleable programming in the 7:30–8 p.m. slot. This was no problem at all by 1980; the glut of moneymaking syndies that came to dominate access time made P.T.A.R. more popular with each passing season. In fact, when the three networks made noises about expanding their half-hour evening newscasts to full hours, these plans were scuttled by the locals, who didn't want to lose their lucrative runs of *Wheel of Fortune, Entertainment Tonight* and other access favorites. Formerly an awkward interim between daytime and nighttime schedules, the access time period was now frequently the most valuable half-hour in a station's broadcast day — and thus, in the early '80s, syndicators concentrated their energies on access.

But as the decade moved forward, syndication began to establish itself as a formidable prime time (8–11 p.m.) force as well. Henry Siegel, chairman and president of Lexington Broadcasting (one of the most powerful syndie operations of the '80s), claimed that first-run syndies flourished because, at long last, non-network producers were coming up with "network quality" programs. This quality had, however, always existed in some form or other in syndication. The fact is that it wouldn't have mattered how quality-conscious the new syndies were if the '80s hadn't offered a large enough market to sustain them. From 1980 to 1985, over 300 new independent UHF channels went on the air, a result of the FCC's loosening of rules as to how many stations a single company could own. While it's true that many of these fledgling UHFers were filing bankruptcy within a year or so after their debuts, the important thing is that a whole new, very hungry market was opened up to syndicators — a market that demanded the sort of high-class product that would allow independent television to compete realistically with its long-established VHF competition. Producers responded with programs that *had* to look better than mere time-fillers or cheap "barter" product slapped together merely to advance the cause of their sponsors. (Of course, "barter" was still very much alive—but producers could no longer get by with minimal production and entertainment values simply to fill their advertisers' airtime.)

Syndies looked classier also because the independents weren't competing merely with the networks anymore. The cable industry had grown from a tightly restricted (by the once more diligent FCC) service bringing faraway television shows to poor-reception areas, into a multi-channel monster offering a wealth of "superstations," specialized services, call-in shopping outlets, ethnic and religious forums, and pay-TV channels which ran the sort of unfettered, uncensored fare that commercial stations could only dream about. Thrown in to this new embarrassment of riches was the videocassette industry, which sent network, non-network and cable TV into tizzies. No longer was the viewer enslaved by rigid scheduling thought up in New York or Hollywood. With a flick of a VCR button, average viewers became their *own* schedulers, watching favorite programs whenever they felt like watching them.

With so much competition from so many sources, local stations demanded—and got—superior-quality syndies that enabled the locals to go head-to-head with the best the networks, cable, and home video had to offer. This intensified competition aided syndication further when the networks, scrambling to retain the control they'd once had over the airwaves, began switching programs around on their schedules with all of the fast-shuffle rapidity (but none of the finesse) of a riverboat cardsharp; they also started cancelling new shows after only one or two episodes if the ratings weren't overnight blockbusters, and in desperation, the networks stepped up their "stunting" with one-shot musical, comedy and "reality" specials. Viewers who craved at least a modicum of consistency in their vieweing began turning with more frequency to independent outlets, where one could be fairly certain that syndie favorites like *Solid Gold* and *Star Search* would remain at the same time, same channel, at least long enough for the viewer to develop something resembling a regular viewing pattern. And producers, unable to get a firm 13- or 26-week commitment from the networks, found syndication welcoming them with open arms. Syndication's new prominence, which never could have happened so long as the networks monopolized the industry, thrived from the "thrill of the chase" that only extra competition made possible.

Despite the weakening of the networks' hold over the airwaves, there were still some operations that wished to organize their non-network offerings into new "fourth networks" of their own. It looked in 1986 that the Fox Network, created when newspaper mogul Rupert Murdoch purchased the 20th Century–Fox studios and the Metromedia station group, was about to make the long-elusive fourth-network dream a reality. With a lineup of some 110 independent channels (many of them those spanking-new UHF outlets), Fox went on the air with a nightly talk show, followed in early 1987 by a weekend prime time service of comedy, adventure and variety shows. Though the service has undergone a lot of tough sledding, as of this writing the Fox Network is in its second year of operation.

Which raises the inevitable question: should the Fox Network series be discussed in these pages, or does the "network" tag disqualify them from a book devoted to syndicated television? Fox's status in the industry is an uncertain one. In its first months, Fox's ratings were discussed as part of the "Top 20" syndicated programs; by the fall of 1987, Fox's weekly programs were being listed in the regular network ratings (usually as "proof" that few viewers were interested in a fourth network. It's problematic that when Fox picked up the annual Emmy awards telecast, the program resulted in the best ratings the service had had to date—yet it was overall the *lowest*-rated Emmy show of all time!). As 1988 rolled around, industryites described Fox variously as a network, an ad hoc network, a dressed-up syndication service, a serious threat to the Big Three, and a flash in the pan that soon would give up the notion of a nationwide hookup and devote itself to city-by-city syndication.

And how does Fox see itself? In its *TV Guide* listings, its advertising and its over-the-air announcements, Fox describes itself as a network, and expects its affiliates to run the Fox programs on the same day at the same time, just like any other network. And yet, Fox's senior vice president of programming, Garth Ancier Sr., insists that Fox is *not* a network, but a "satellite-delivered national program service." On its first anniversary, Fox was still being officially described by its executives as anything *but* a network. This seeming duplicity has a purpose. So long as Fox does not qualify as a "real" network, it is permitted to syndicate its series to non–Fox affiliates—because one of the very few old FCC rulings still in effect is the one that prohibits the networks from syndicating their own series.

This being the status quo, we'll treat the Fox series as syndicated offerings, and list them according to genre along with all the other syndies of the 1980's.

Adventure/Mystery

A onetime front-runner of the syndication business, Adventure/Mystery was a rather barren field in the '80s, seemingly conceding to the dominance of the genre enjoyed by the networks. But it was a field that began to show signs of fertility in 1987 with the latest docking of the Starship *Enterprise*.

The Beachcombers (1985). No relation to Cameron Mitchell's syndie vehicle of 1961, *The Beachcombers* was a Canadian family-oriented outdoor-adventure series, and a prime time favorite in its own country since 1973. Blair Communications made 130 of the best episodes available to the states as a daily strip, but *The Beachcombers'* no-star cast proved something of a detriment.

Captain Power and the Soldiers of the Future (1987). Although regarded by many as a children's series, *Captain Power* proved broad enough in its appeal to qualify as "all ages" entertainment. This Landmark Corporation release, shot in Ontario, starred Tim Dunigan as Captain Jonathan Power, leader of a ragtag but dedicated group of freedom fighters battling their repressive rulers in a futuristic society where the "Volcanians" (robots) ruled and human beings were trodden upon. Captain Power's principal enemy, Lord Dread, was played with lip-sneering relish by David Hemblin. The computer-enhanced special effects were something like those seen in the 1982 Disney movie *Tron,* though better executed and without the earlier film's self-consciousness. And the storylines were more than a little reminiscent of *Star Wars* and its sequels, not only in terms of the Luke Skywalker–Darth Vader atmosphere inherent in the Captain Power–Lord Dread relationship but in the series' emphasis (on the heroes' side anyway) on loyalty, fidelity, relative fair play, and a sense of genuine loss and bereavement whenever one of the good guys was killed.

Captain Power might well have been judged solely on its own terms as a rousing, meticulously produced adventure show where the audiences actually cared what happened to the people on screen, had it not become a *cause célèbre* to kiddie-TV critics of 1987. Produced at the behest of Mattel toys, *Power* was the first of the 1980's "inter-active" programs. At certain points in each week's half-hour, the young viewers at home were called upon to help Capt. Power out by zapping the villains with their Official Captain Power Power Jets — a toy found at your local stores at prices ranging from 30 to 40 dollars. Each time a player scored a "hit" through an electronic signal which worked something like the activator of a garage-door opener, the player's score would be toted up on the TV screen. This wasn't what educators and media critics had in mind when they begged young viewers to stop being passive TV watchers. The toys, it was charged, would turn youngsters into trigger-happy nihilists; the Power Jets would supposedly gum up all the grown-up electronic devices around the house; and worst of all, according to Action for Children's Television's Peggy Charren, the price-tag on the toy weapons would unfairly divide the home audience into "haves and have-nots." Perhaps some of the critics should have taken a look at the show itself — beyond its strident, obnoxious ad campaign, that is. Not only was *Captain Power* above-average entertainment, but its storylines did not, as expected, rely upon the viewers' ownership of the Power Jets for full enjoyment. While the toy *enhanced* the fun, the fun was not wholly dependent upon that toy, and *Captain Power* had just as many fans that sat back and watched as it did devotees who zapped the screen. It's typical of the forest-and-trees attitude of the pressure groups that, with so many other children's series which lowered the kids' standards with poor animation and offered them false sets of values by showing characters dressing and behaving in a trendy, me-first manner, the target of television's nay-sayers should be *Captain Power,* simply because Mattel wanted to take advantage of the free enterprise system.

Dempsey and Makepeace (1985). *Dempsey and Makepeace* was a slick, stylish detective series, extremely popular in its native Britain (and a winner of a 1985 gold medal from the International Film Festival) before making its American syndie debut through Tribune Entertainment. The original intention was to revive the old *Avengers* format, pairing a Cambridge-educated policewoman with an erudite, elegant millionaire American detective. By the time it went before the cameras, *Dempsey and Makepeace* was about a scruffy Serpico type named James Dempsey (Michael Brandon), who after embarrassing his police-department superiors by blowing the whistle on high-level political corruption was "disciplined" by being sent out of America to study British police techniques (a punishment devoutly to be wished by many American cops!). At Scotland Yard, Dempsey became part of a dog-and-cat team with a martial-arts-savvy electronics wizard, ace policewoman Harriet "Harry" Makepeace (Glynis Barber). As expected, the resulting tensions were sexual as well as professional, with "macho vs. lib" and "let's discuss this at my place over a few drinks" well in the forefront. Refereeing the pair was their supervisor, Inspector Spikings (Ray Smith). As in past TV years, the British production crew did wonders on a budget far tinier than that on any 60-minute American adventure weekly, though the stories played safe with the usual cop-show emphasis on crazed killers, shifty stoolies and car chases. But at least the female cop rescued the male cop once in a while, more than can be said for the damsel-in-distress attitude on most American detective series. Though the 48 *Dempsey and Makepeace* episodes available to the United States were not a major hit, they paid their way.

Friday the 13th (1987). Like *Captain Power,* Paramount Television's *Friday the 13th* was condemned by professional TV-bashers before they'd even seen it, because it borrowed its title from a gruesome (but profitable) series of theatrical feature films devoted to mask-wearing ax-wielders and chopped-up teenagers. Actually, beyond its title, the 60-minute *Friday the 13th* had nothing to do with the movies, but was instead a supernatural thriller, a curious amalgam between *Twilight Zone* and *The Fugitive.* Two cousins, a boy named Ryan (John D. LeMay) and a girl named Mickey (Robey), discovered that several items sold from their late uncle's store were "cursed" antiques, and thereafter the cousins devoted themselves to hunting down the new owners of the demonic artifacts before it was — shudder — too late. Dolls with diabolical powers, trick mirrors and all the old horror-story gimcrackery abounded in this inexpensive (shot in Canada, a fact made obvious by the recurring role played by Canadian television stalwart Christopher Wiggins) but smartly assembled and atmospheric chiller. *Friday the 13th* was initially slated to be aired late at night, but proved too popular to be shunted away to the after-midnight slots and ended up in prime time in many markets; in some cities, it was shown back-to-back with Paramount's other first-run syndie hit, *Star Trek: The Next Generation.*

Sea Hunt see "Adventure/Mystery" notes in the chapter on the 1950's.

Star Trek: The Next Generation (1987). The most eagerly anticipated syndicated series of all, *Star Trek: The Next Generation* had been on the drawing board in one form or another since 1972. Throughout the '70s, Paramount Television issued statements that it planned to use the "new" *Star Trek* as the nucleus of a prime time fourth network, and these plans included the participation of old *Trek* regulars like William Shatner, Leonard Nimoy and DeForest Kelley. But the former *Trek* personnel were sidetracked into a series of high-grossing *Star Trek* feature films, so Paramount shelved the revival and concentrated its fourth-network notions into the studio's participation in Operation Prime Time. By the mid–80's, fascination in the old *Star Trek* series was at fever pitch, and Paramount got back into the action by pitching a weekly revival to the three major networks. All of the Big Three showed interest, but none were willing to purchase a full 26-week season of 60-minute episodes, and Paramount had to have such a commitment to justify the new series' $30,000,000 yearly budget. For a time, the new Fox Network looked as though it would pick up the series, but Fox could only deliver some 100 markets, while station-by-station syndication could offer twice as many. So *Star Trek: The Next Generation* became a syndie, with first-dibs sales going to the 150 or so stations already beaming the old *Trek* reruns (many of them buying the new *Trek* so it wouldn't be thrown into competition with the repeats).

That "Next Generation" qualifier in the title grew from necessity. Since none of the old *Star Trek's* stars were available, executive producer Gene Roddenberry justified a totally new cast by thrusting the new *Trek* seven decades after the time-period of the first series. While diehards moaned that *Star Trek* would never be the same without its original actors, the new people were every bit as personable and charismatic as the old favorites. Taking command of the Starship *Enterprise* was Shakespearean actor Patrick Stewart as Capt. Jean-Luc Picard, who was grayer and less emotional than William Shatner, while Jonathan Frakes was cast as Picard's right-hand man, Cmdr. William "Number One" Ryker. Roddenberry's new supporting-cast choices were made in some cases to improve upon what many considered shortcomings in the first series. Denise Crosby (Bing's granddaughter) played security chief Tasha Yar, while the ship's medical officer, Dr. Beverly Crusher, was essayed by Gates McFadden; putting women into authoritative positions was a bid to make the new series more equitable and less "sexist" than the 1960's edition. (The opening narration was altered in this spirit: the *Enterprise's* mission was now "to boldly go where no *one* has gone before.") The inclusion of Wil Wheaton as Dr. Crusher's son, and the visibility of the other crew members' children on board the *Enterprise,* helped to make the characters more family-oriented and less all-business than in the earlier series. And to avoid an imbalance in the ensemble playing by creating a new "Mr. Spock" cult, there were now *several* characters who were either aliens or possessed of strange character traits. Michael Dorn played Klingon officer Lt. Worf, evidence that the warmongering Klingons had at last reached "detente" with the United Federation of Planets. Marina Sirtis was cast as Deanna Troi, a half-human, half-"Betazoid" starfleet counselor who was a psychic in the bargain. Brent Spiner was Lt. Cdr. Data, an android who delighted in behaving like a human being. And LeVar Burton, who as the onetime star of 1977's *Roots* was the biggest name in the cast, played the blind Lt. Geordi LaForge, who "saw" thanks to the aid of his Visual Input Sensory Optical Reflector (or "VISOR," which is what the device looked like).

To deter the grousing of Trekkies that the production values on *The Next Generation* weren't up to snuff, Roddenberry and company saw to it that the new *Star Trek* was far more elaborately produced than the old one. The new *Enterprise* was now supposed to be eight times larger than the first, and there were a lot more extras milling about; we now truly believed that the Captain was responsible for the lives of several hundred crew members, a belief made difficult by the sparsely populated corridors of the old *Enterprise.* And the special effects were in the hands of the miracle workers at Industrial Light and Magic; the outerspace scenes were both spectacular and convincing (even though there were still noises in the Great Beyond) and there was a whole new arsenal of futuristic hardware, including a device that could change the atmosphere and surroundings of a room to suit the fancy of its occupants. As in the original *Star Trek,* the sophisticated machinery and off-beat characters were treated naturally and casually, as though the characters were truly living in an era where the remarkable was commonplace and where they'd conquered old race prejudices and come to terms with new technology. The humanity and optimism of the series were never allowed to take a back seat to the science-fiction trappings.

Star Trek: The Next Generation debuted officially in October 1987, a month after a two-hour TV *Trek* movie which set up the characters and even offered a surprise cameo by DeForest Kelley, the earlier series' Dr. McCoy (who hobbled around in old age makeup and didn't get to say "He's dead, Jim"). Everyone expected the new *Star Trek* to perform well — but it's likely that no one expected it to do as well as it did! By December, it was the fourth highest-rated syndie on the market, and was receiving the ultimate accolade of being shown in prime time by several network stations in lieu of their networks' comparatively feeble offerings. Opinions were divided as to whether the new *Star Trek* would achieve the immortality of its ancestor; for every viewer who raved that *The Next Generation* was the best television series ever, there was a curmudgeon who complained that the series was too cluttered with gimmickry and that its storylines tended to echo those of the "Classic 79" episodes of 1966–69. We'll have to leave *Star Trek: The Next Generation's* place in history to the next generation of TV historians.

21 Jump Street (1987). Premiering April 12, 1987, Stephen Cannell Productions' *21 Jump Street* (originally *Jump Street Chapel,* a title done away with lest viewers think it a religious show), was the first action-adventure offering from the Fox Network. The hour-long series bore traces of ABC's old *Mod*

Squad: a group of youthful-looking cops, whose callow demeanor made them difficult to take seriously as on-the-street lawkeepers, were told to pose as teenagers in order to bust criminals who preyed on high-schoolers. Tom Hanson, the unofficial "lead kid," was played by Johnny Depp (taking over from Jeff Yagher, who starred in the two-hour pilot). The others were an ethnically balanced mix, including black actress Holly Robinson as Judy Hoff, Dustin Nguyen as Ioki, and Peter DeLuise as Penhall. (DeLuise, son of comedian Dom, was hired because his chunky frame made him something of a "comedy relief," but he eventually lost so much weight that he was given many of the action scenes that previously had all gone to Dustin Nguyen.) Though it was plunked into the Sunday evening "suicide slot" opposite CBS' *60 Minutes, 21 Jump Street's* masterful combination of adventure and compassion towards the problems facing modern youth quickly made it the highest-rated of the Fox series. It was also embraced by special-interest concerns for its realistic, thoughtful and noncondescending approach to such touchy teen issues as drugs, parental abuse, peer pressure and pregnancy. Fox established a "hot line" that allowed *Jump Street's* young viewers to call in and share their opinions or personal experiences concerning the dilemmas faced on each week's episode. The Fox executives listened when the "kids" spoke up, even on points of program content. When the young viewers complained that they couldn't "relate" to the character played by Frederick Forrest, that of an ex-flower child of the '60s who was now the young police officers' principal supervisor on the force, Forrest was replaced by a more traditional head cop (Steven Williams), whose adversarial relationship with the younger cops was on the adult vs. kid level that made the stories more compelling to the teenaged fans. Like so many other cost-conscious syndies of the 1980's, *21 Jump Street* was filmed in Canada, where labor was cheap but the results were just as professional as anything out of Hollywood. Executive producer: Patrick Hasburgh.

Werewolf (1987). A kinky horror-adventure series produced by Tri-Star Pictures, *Werewolf* debuted as a two-hour movie on the Fox Network on July 11, 1987, and thereafter settled down into a half-hour weekly. Eric Cord (John York), a young man bitten by a werewolf and thus himself a victim of lycanthropy, was forced to track down the "source" werewolf who originally infected the person who'd bitten Eric. All the while, Eric was himself being tracked down for the murder of the fellow who of course was the werewolf who'd sunk his dentures into him; pursuing Eric was flamboyant bounty hunter Alamo Joe, played by Lance LeGault. LeGault might have been the most excessive performer on *Werewolf* had it not been for Chuck Connors, who portrayed a one-eyed sea captain (complete with outrageous mittel–European dialect) who turned out to be the "source werewolf" that Eric had to kill in order to rid himself of his curse. *Werewolf's* storylines were gloriously awful, and its acting and directing on the level of *The Perils of Pauline,* but the series was beautifully photographed, and its man-to-werewolf transition scenes, designed by makeup wizard Rick Baker, were brilliantly repellent. Best of all, the Canadian-filmed series was a compendium of inside jokes. Two of the better examples: Chuck Connors' character's name, Janos Skorzeny, was also the name of the vampire in the 1972 television-movie classic *The Night Stalker;* and the rifle wielded by Alamo Joe was the very same weapon used by Connors in his '60s network series, *The Rifleman.* Unfortunately, Chuck Connors, easily the best thing about *Werewolf,* fell victim to the Fox Network's never-ending pursuit of the under-30 crowd. His character was killed off, and the villainy was inherited by a younger, handsomer, and purportedly sexier actor.

Children's

This subheading should perhaps be "cartoon shows," because that's virtually all the kiddie-syndie field had to offer in the '80s. The upsurge in assembly-line animation was brought about by certain changes affecting the FCC. It once had been forbidden for a children's (or even an adult) show to be a half-hour commercial disguised as entertainment. But under the aegis of new FCC chairman Mark Fowler, this ruling was relaxed. Cartoon producers were complaining that the only way they could survive in syndication was by merchandising their cartoon characters, and by advertising those characters within their series so they could offer their shows on a barter basis. Typical of the Reagan years, Fowler was on the side of Big Business. Noting that free enterprise worked only in a spirit of competition, and noting too that pay and cable services, unbound by FCC rulings, were starting to run away with the ratings, Fowler adopted a "let the marketplace decide" policy—that is, let the cartoon producers do their over-commercialized series to stay alive in an increasingly tougher market. Then let the kiddie viewers decide whether or not they liked the new, merchandising-happy cartoon shows. The kiddies liked them—and watched, and watched, and watched. In 1983, there was only a handful of first-run children's syndies. By 1987, there were over 40.

To counteract the sabre-rattling of Action for Children's Television and like-minded groups, cartoon producers began insisting that their offerings were "pro-social." This meant that the heroes loved and cared about one another, that they were concerned about matters like tolerance and ecology, and that villains were clearly shown to be in the wrong and were duly punished for their wicked deeds—and sometimes were even redeemed and reformed. When these moral lessons weren't overly obvious in the storylines themselves, the half-hour cartoons began inserting (with a shoehorn, it seemed) half-minute bits of sage advice at the end of each program, such as "Don't get into a stranger's car," "Respect the rights of others," and so forth. Overseeing these 30-second lessons were children's specialists like Dr. Gordon Berry and Stanford's professor of communications Donald F. Roberts, who were engaged as technical advisors for many of the new cartoon shows. It wasn't the cartoon producers' fault if the kids preferred to ignore the messages and revel in the action and violence, or if the kids happened to be out of the room when those pro-social pearls were offered at episode's end. The producers had done their duty, were absolved, and washed their hands of sin.

It's pointless to criticize, on an individual basis, the quality of animation in most of the new shows (the level was slightly lower than that of penny-arcade flip pictures); better to concentrate on the concepts and the scripts. At their best, the new series were okay; at their worst, one could turn off the TV and make one's child go outside or read a book.

The Adventures of Teddy Ruxpin (1987). Teddy Ruxpin was a toy bear who told stories to its owner courtesy of a long-playing audio tape deep within its bowels. Like so many other cuddly playthings of the period, Teddy became the star of his own daily animation series, and like many of his brethren, Mr. Ruxpin was test-marketed with an ad campaign for the toy and a five-part "limited series" on television to see if the character would "fly." *Adventures of Teddy Ruxpin* was put together by DIC Productions, who with Hanna-Barbera and Filmation was one of the "big three" of '80s TV animation.

Adventures of the Galaxy Rangers (1986). This daily cartoon half-hour was a 21st-century outer-space "western," complete with extraterrestrial sheriffs and rustlers (see also *Bravestarr* and *Saber Rider and the Star Sheriffs*). From Gaylord Communications/Transcom/ITF.

Animal Express (1986). Joan Embry of the San Diego zoo hosted this live-animal study, produced by the Corporation for Entertainment and Learning and first telecast over the USA Cable Network. The 130 half-hours were then syndicated by 20th Century–Fox.

Barbapapa (1981). Dutch cartoon series reminiscent of *The Smurfs,* initially targeted for a late '70s release by LBS (Lexington Broadcasting System) but not generally shown until another LBS Dutch import, *Dr. Snuggles* (which see), made headway in 1981.

Beverly Hills Teens (1987). Just what the world was begging for; a cartoon series about rich teenagers who drove around in hot rods equipped with swimming pools, attended a palatial high school the size of San Simeon, and had their butlers carry their schoolbooks for them. This DIC Production from Access Syndication contained somewhat worse animation than usual, in itself an accomplishment.

Big Foot and the Muscle Machine see *Super Sunday*

The Bionic Six (1987). MCA Television joined forces with LJN Toys for this weekly (and later daily) cartoon series about the escapades of two bionic (part-human, part-machine) parents and their four multiracial adoptees — all of whom burst into rock music in between crime-fighting engagements. It made one yearn for the days of *Crusader Rabbit*.

Bravestarr (1987). Marshal Bravestarr was the law and order on a planet called "New Texas" in this animated daily from World Events Syndication.

Camp Wilderness (1980). Not unlike 1977's *Summer Camp,* this was an outdoors and arts-and-crafts weekender; from Montani Entertainment and Gold Key Television.

Captain Harlock (1985). British cartoon adventure, issued by Ziv International and Harmony Gold in two separate packages: *Captain Harlock and the Space Pirates* and *Captain Harlock and the Queen of 1000 Years.* Somewhere there must be someone who can tell them apart.

The Centurions (1986). On this Monday-through-Friday cartoon from Worldvision, computer scientist Crystal Kane and her "Centurions" (computer-generated battlers) battled Doctor Terror's "Doom Drones."

Challenge of the GoBots (1985). From Hanna-Barbera/TeleRep: the good-guy GoBots from the planet Gobotron emigrated to planet Earth, still locked in combat with their arch enemies, the Cykills.

Children's Theatre (1983). Saturday-morning fare from LBS: Chuck McCann and a group of toothy child actors hosted cartoons based on comic strips like Bill Keane's "The Family Circus." After leaving the weekly grind, *Children's Theatre* devoted itself to seasonal specials.

Chuck Norris' Karate Kommandos (1986). This was one of the less shining examples of what happened when the FCC decided to "let the marketplace decide." This short-lived Worldvision cartoon daily was inspired by the movie exploits of karate-champ film star Chuck Norris (who supplied his own voice); the villains included "Super Ninja" and an "evil empire" known as VULTURE. As in many of these artistically and morally suspect animated bloodlettings, a psychiatrist-technical advisor was engaged to oversee a daily "pro-social" coda to the program. Would that one of the pro-social messages have been "Stop watching crummy cartoon shows!"

Comic Strip (1987). A Filmation marathon of made-for-television cartoons, which could be run either as a 2½ hour weekly or a 30-minute daily. In the manner of *Funtastic World of Hanna-Barbera* and *Super Sunday* (which see), *Comic Strip* featured several "stars" in their own self-contained adventures: "The Mini-Monsters," "The Street Frogs," "The Tigersharks" and "Karate Kat."

Dangermouse (1986). Extremely funny British cartoon series, first shown in the United States on the Nickelodeon cable service, then syndicated by D.L. Taffner. Created by Brian Trueman, Dangermouse was an eyepatched, musclebound secret agent battling various animal villains, most of whom spoke in hilarious provincial British accents and were either cursed by inept henchmen or monumentally stupid themselves. In the spirit of *Rocky and Bullwinkle* and *Monty Python,* there was a stentorian narrator who changed the subject whenever he felt like it, straight-to-the-camera comments on the silliness of the situations, and an underlying satire of society as a whole.

Defenders of the Earth (1986). Produced in 1985 but not released until the following year (there was no room), *Defenders of the Earth* spotlighted several King Features comic-strip characters who fought against evil — and also introduced the natural and adopted offspring of these funny-paper favorites. Mandrake the Magician was paired with his adopted son, a martial-arts wizard named Kshin. Mandrake's assistant Lothar was teamed with his natural son L.J., the Phantom was aided by *his* son Kit Parker, and Flash Gordon was helped by his daughter Jedda. The parent-child device had previously been used on the network cartoon series *Superfriends.* While *Defenders of the Earth* made just as little advance in the art of animation as its predecessor, it at least deserved — and received — plaudits for taking its "pro-social" ad promises seriously. *Defenders* pleased adult observers with its clear-eyed approach to genuine problems facing the children of the '80s — notably in an episode wherein Flash Gordon had to wean his son Mark away from a dangerous flirtation with drugs.

Dennis the Menace (1986). Distributed by DFS and bartered by General Mills, *Dennis the Menace* was a cartoon show based on the bratty-kid comic strip created by Hank Ketchum (previously adapted as a live-action CBS sitcom in the early '60s). Dennis' usual pranks were amplified with occasional "super-powers" and international intrigue, and tempered with short moral platitudes. Brennan Thicke, son of actor/talkshow host Alan Thicke, supplied the voice of Dennis.

Dinosaucers (1987). A DIC/LBS daily pitting dinosaur-like aliens from the planet Reptillion against one another on Earth. The good "guys" were the Dinosaucers, and the villains were the Tyrannos. Four Earth kids calling themselves the "Secret Scouts" were on the Dinosaucers' side. At least this one was occasionally funny on purpose.

Dr. Snuggles (1981). A droll Dutch animated weekly starring veterinarian Dr. Snuggles, who travelled from one animal friend to another via pogo stick. This LBS release took the "talking beast" concept a step further by giving the power of speech to *everything,* including suitcases and stepladders. Peter Ustinov provided most of the voices.

DuckTales (1987). Buena Vista's *DuckTales* was the Disney Studios' first foray into daily, made-for-television syndicated animation. Many of the characters, including Scrooge McDuck, the Beagle Boys and Gyro Gearloose had their roots not in the studio's theatrical cartoons but in the wonderful Disney comic books of the '40s and '50s, most of them written or illustrated by the matchless Carl Barks. *DuckTales* was fast and furious fun for adults as well as children, especially adept at kidding the cliches of animated cartoons; when a character found himself standing in mid-air on *this* show, he didn't plummet to Earth in the traditional fashion, but was likely to be joined in mid-air by all the *other* characters! The animation was farmed out to Japanese studios and mostly computer-generated, but the Disney staff had full creative control, so that *DuckTales,* while well below the usual Disney standard, was head and shoulders above most of the other cartoon series infesting the airwaves.

Fat Albert and the Cosby Kids (1984). Created and produced by Bill Cosby, Filmation's *Fat Albert* had had a 12-year run on CBS before entering syndication, with several brand-new episodes, via Group W in 1984. As in their CBS days, the animated Fat Albert and his gang of kids faced the perils of daily life with good humor and song. And as always, Bill Cosby treated his audience not like know-nothing kiddies but like the adults they would some day become. As a result, many of the syndicated *Fat Alberts* were amazingly mature, especially an episode in which the kids participated in a "Scared Straight"-like visit to a maximum-security prison.

Funtastic World of Hanna-Barbera (1985–). Weekend 90-minute animation block, featuring several separate series, including "The Paw Paws" (cute Indian animals) and "Galtar and the Golden Lance" (sword-and-sorcery). In 1986, the series was expanded to two hours to accommodate new episodes of an old Hanna-Barbera network favorite, *Johnny Quest.* The centerpiece of *Funtastic World* was "Yogi's Treasure Hunt," which attempted to feature *every one* of Hanna-Barbera's "funny animal" characters from the '50s, '60s and '70s — sort of a couch-potato purgatory.

Galaxy Rangers see *Adventures of the Galaxy Rangers*

Galtar and the Golden Lance see *Funtastic World of Hanna-Barbera*

The Get-Along Gang see *Kiddeo TV*

Ghostbusters: The Original Ghostbusters (1986); **The Real Ghostbusters** (1987). Someday, the people involved will look back at the Great *Ghostbusters* Controversy and laugh — which may be the biggest laughs ever generated by the two cartoon series in question. Here's the whole story. Back in 1975, the CBS Saturday morning schedule boasted a live-action comedy titled *The Ghost Busters,* in which "Spencer, Tracy and Kong" did battle with the spirits of historical characters. Larry Storch was Spencer, Forrest Tucker was Kong, and Bob Burns cavorted in a gorilla suit as Tracy. The series was produced by Filmation's Lou Scheimer and Norm Prescott; it ran for a year, then was deservedly forgotten. In 1984, Columbia released a multimillion-dollar feature film title *Ghostbusters,* which featured Dan Aykroyd, Bill Murray and Harold Ramis as a tacky team of "paranormal investigators" who ended up rescuing New York from an invasion of spooks, hobgoblins and demons. *Ghostbusters* was an all-time box-office champ, so it took a while before it was released on videocassette. In the meantime, Filmation gathered its wits and issued Beta and VHS cassette versions of its old 1975 TV series, which was rechristened *The Original Ghostbusters.* Now we move to 1986: Columbia TV was readying a cartoon series version of *Ghostbusters* (the movie) for Saturday morning network exposure. Wasting no time, Filmation prepared its own animated *Ghostbusters* (inspired by its TV series) as weekday syndicated fare. Columbia's lawyers and Filmation's lawyers began firing volleys at one another, the result being that the Filmation series was retitled *Filmation's Ghostbusters* (what wit!), and then, again, *The Original Ghostbusters.* Columbia's version went out to the ABC network in 1986, and subsequently to syndication (with different episodes), as *The Real Ghostbusters.* Many station managers, displaying the imagination and originality common to station managers, ran the rival *Ghostbusters* opposite one another the first few weeks of September 1987, until they realized that they were cancelling each other out. No matter: despite the fact that the two shows had different leading characters and went after different varieties of ghosts (the *Original* spooks were from fairy tales and mythology, while the *Real* spectres were more urban and up-to-date), the two *Ghostbusters* were so alike in animation style and humor quotient that they might as well have been the same program.

GI Joe: A Great American Hero (1985). A Sunbow Production for the Claster Company and DIC, *GI Joe* was among the first animated syndies devoted to five-a-week illustrated commercials for its "action figure" counterpart. The cartoon was based not on the original Hasbro GI Joe doll of the '60s, but on the 1983 revival of that product as a "fighting force" of five *different* dolls — the "team of heroes" concept popularized by the *Star Wars* films. "GI Joe" was no longer one man, but a quintet of specialized soldiers battling the minions of the evil organization known as "Cobra." After a two-hour cartoon special and several one-week miniseries, *GI Joe* became a daily in 1985 — and turned DIC Productions into a name to reckon with (and sometimes make fun of).

GoBots see *Challenge of the GoBots*

The Great Space Coaster (1981–86). Emmy-winning daily children's show, from the people who brought you *Romper Room. Great Space Coaster's* format, embracing live action, cartoons, puppets (with character names like "M.T. Promises") and educational overtones, owed more than a little to *Sesame Street;* but the series' good-natured enthusiasm, energy and positive results on its young audience kept *Space Coaster* in orbit for five seasons. A

Sunbow/Claster production (before those folks plunged into commercialized cartoon series), with barter participation from Kellogg's Cereals.

He-Man and the Masters of the Universe (1983–   ). Prepare your brickbats or bouquets: here's the first of the animated thirty-minute commercials. He-Man, a superstud superhero, resided on the planet Eternia, where he clashed with the forces of evil. But mainly, this creation of the Filmation thinktanks was put on the air to promote a line of He-Man dolls, toys and games from the factories of Mattel. When Group W first offered *He-Man* in 1983, a lot of stations shunned the series, fearful of fallout from concerned-citizen groups who felt that kid's television was already commercialized to death. But after FCC regulations were relaxed (some dropped altogether) in 1984, a great many local markets jumped on *He-Man's* bandwagon, and the daily series ended up the second highest-rated kid's show of the year — and the He-Man action figure accordingly was the nation's second biggest-selling toy (dear old Barbie was the first). Also seen amidst the muscle-flexing, sword-and-sorcery and 30-second "moral messages" on each *He-Man* episode were He-Man's twin sister She-Ra and the villainous Skeletor; both these characters subsequently appeared in fast-selling toy form, and She-Ra was later spun off into a carefully timed and planned TV series of her own in 1985 *(She-Ra: Princess of Power)*. Two years later, a live-action feature film, *Masters of the Universe,* appeared, a middling effort saved by the enthusiastic perfidy of Frank Langella as Skeletor.

Heathcliffe (1984). Claster/DIC Japanese-animated daily, starring the snide, sneaky feline created for the funnies by George Gately. Featured as the voice of Heathcliffe in this LBS release was Mel Blanc, in his 50th year in the voice-over business.

Hugga Bunch (1984). Limited-run SFM puppet series which managed an Emmy award for "model shop supervision."

Inhumanoids (1986). At first glance just another animated advertisement from Claster/DIC/LBS, *Inhumanoids* turned out to be a real hoot for adults who chanced to tune in. Forget the "Middle Earth goodies vs. baddies" concept of the series; *Inhumanoids* had some hilarious plot complications worthy of *Rocky and Bullwinkle.* One week's installment had the giant-sized, wicked "Mutors", infected by a love potion, proceed to kidnap every large *statue* of a female figure in sight. One smitten Mutor abducted the Statue of Liberty, bringing it to life in his underground home; he learned to regret his rashness when Miss Liberty turned out to be a henpecking harridan, lounging before the TV and eating bonbons while forcing her evil "boy friend" to exercise away his excess blubber!

Inspector Gadget (1983). DIC Productions' first major release, *Inspector Gadget* starred what might best be termed a Bionic Moron, a bumbling semirobot doing battle against Dr. Claw and M.A.D. ("Mean and Dirty"). Don

Adams used his Maxwell Smart voice as Gadget, but he bailed out before the series' 65 half-hour cartoons were completed, to be replaced by a distressingly obvious imitator. Like many another syndie, *Inspector Gadget* tried to compensate for its mindlessness by wedging in an "important lesson" at the climax of each installment — though Gadget was hardly the ideal spokesman for common sense.

Jayce and the Wheeled Warriors (1985). An SFM release, not surprisingly tied in with a line of toys. Jayce (short for Jason) was a young man searching throughout the universe for his father; opposing him at every far-flung point in space were the evil Monster Minds.

Jem see *Super Sunday*

The Jetsons (1985). In an era when revivals of old television favorites like *Leave It to Beaver* and *Perry Mason* were commonplace, Hanna-Barbera got into the act with 41 new half-hour episodes of *The Jetsons,* a futuristic cartoon sitcom that had originally run on ABC way back in 1962–63. Hanna-Barbera had an advantage in the revival business; unlike the rediscovered human television stars of yore, cartoon characters never grew old and fat. (Even their voices didn't betray their ages, surprising since *The Jetsons* used the same voice-talent as in its first run, including George O'Hanlon, who was well past 70, and Penny Singleton and Mel Blanc, who were approaching 80.) This Worldvision package also included the original 24 *Jetsons* episodes, having the good taste to remove their intrusive laugh-tracks. The new installments deployed the same characters and settings as the older show, with the addition of a "pet alien" named Orbity.

Johnny Quest see *Funtastic World of Hanna-Barbera*

Karate Kat see *Comic Strip*

Kid-a-Littles (1984). Puppetry from a company called T.E.N. (The Entertainment Network).

Kiddeo TV (1986). A DIC/LBS omnibus of cartoon series, designed to be shown in weekend 90-minute chunks, including such commercial tie-ins as *The Get-Along Gang, The Popples* and *Rainbow Brite.* In its earliest months, the package featured a Japanese-made adventure cartoon, *Ulysses 31.*

Kids Are People Too (1986). After a long Sunday-morning ABC run (1978–82), this "you're special!" fun-and-instruction series entered syndication by way of JM Entertainment and EJ III Productions. Barry Glazer produced, and one of the series' network hosts, Michael Young, kept things moving on-camera.

Kids, Incorporated (1985). Sincerely pro-social live-action/puppet series from Orbis Productions, MGM TV, and Hal Roach Studios (the offshoot of the company which started kiddie entertainment with *Our Gang* back in 1922). *Kids, Incorporated* copped an Emmy for "Outstanding Lighting."

Lady Lovelylocks and the Pixietails (1987). Still another "loveable" kid's toy transformed by LBS into a weekly series. If you like the title. . . .

Macron 1 (1985). Hoping to combine the best of two syndie worlds, Sudan/Orbis' *Macron 1* had its cartoon outer-space escapades backed up with the latest Top-40 rock tunes.

Maple Town (1987). More from Sudan/Orbis. *Maple Town* animated the exploits of a group of cute animal characters otherwise available as overpriced dolls in your local store. Janet Adams appeared as the live-action narrator, "Mrs. Maple."

M.A.S.K. (1985). The letters stood for "Mobil Armored Strike Kommand," adding illiteracy to the other shortcomings of this quickie DIC/LBS animated toy ad. The bad guys' group was called V.E.N.O.M.; we don't even care what *that* stood for.

Mini Monsters see Comic Strip

Mister Moon's Magic Circus (1982). John Saranto played Moon in this Century/Telepictures weekend show, from the *Sesame Street* school of live action intermingled with puppets.

My Little Pony and Friends (1986). Daily promotion for a whole bunch of Hasbro toys, from our good friends Sunbow/Claster/DIC. This cartoon series has the distinction of offering for the first time in animated form the "Mr. Potato Head" characters. Perhaps the producers felt an affinity.

The Original Ghostbusters see Ghostbusters

The Paw Paws see Funtastic World of Hanna-Barbera

Photon (1986). Half-hour combo of live action and laser/computer animation, from SFM. The hero, Christopher, was supposedly an average teenager, but was in reality "Bhodi Li," alien defender of the Universe against the baddies from the planet Arr (one of whom was named Buggarr). This "Ultimate Game on Planet Earth" was remindful of other video-game-inspired entertainments like the movies *The Last Starfighter* and *Tron*, though *Photon's* special effects were cheap to the point of absurdity.

The Popples and Rainbow Brite see Kiddeo TV

Rainbow Patch (1982). Puppets and lessons on life, designed for weekend play on the NBC-owned outlets.

Rambo (1986). From Worldvision: an expurgated animated version of the guerrilla fighter with an attitude problem, played by Sylvester Stallone in a series of high-grossing (and highly gross) feature films. Rambo (his voice was not supplied by Stallone, but by someone we could understand) blammed and slammed against the diabolical superorganization "Savage." What's next....

The Real Ghostbusters see *Ghostbusters*

Robotech (1985). Harmony Gold animated daily, described in its ads as a "Multi-generational epic space soap opera." *Robotech's* setting was an outer-space training school for humans and androids. Character names included "Risa," "Lisa" and "Minmei," but the series' oddest duck was a nightclub chanteuse who turned out to be a transvestite!

Robotix see *Super Sunday*

Saber Riders and the Star Sheriff (1987). Another outer-space western in the less-than-honored tradition of *Bravestarr* and *Galaxy Rangers,* DIC's *Saber Rider* featured a number of Clint Eastwood and Charles Bronson types.

She-Ra: Princess of Power see *He-Man and the Masters of the Universe*

Silverhawks (1986). After scoring with the cartoon daily *ThunderCats* (which see), Rankin-Bass and Lorimar-Telepictures issued this Monday-through-Friday walking and talking commercial featuring Commander Stargazer and his confrères. The Silverhawks were the space-age equivalent of the "Untouchables," fighting a variety of extraterrestrial gangsters and robber barons, foremost among these the scurrilous Mon Star and his Mob.

The Spiral Zone (1987). An Orbis daily release. On this one, the Earth was held captive beneath the "Spiral Zone" by the evil scientific genius Overlord. Could Dirk Courage and his Zone Riders come to the rescue? And could the animation style keep anyone over 12 years old awake?

Sport Billy (1982). Well-intentioned cartoon weekly from Filmation. Sport Billy was a young super-athlete who promoted integrity and fair play. (Billy's voice was provided by Lane Scheimer, who in the spirit of fair play was the son of a Filmation executive.) Like many other made-in-Japan cartoons, the eyes of the Occidental characters were so inordinately round and wide that they seemed to be hysterical hypothalamics.

Starcom (1987). Weekly DIC cartoon. Starcom battled the unspeakable Emperor Dark. What price George Lucas?

Street Frogs see *Comic Strip*

Super Sunday (1985). Another multicharacter weekend animation cluster, this time from DIC/Claster. Included were "Robotix," "Big Foot and the Muscle Machine" (featuring truck driver Yank Justice), and "Jem," the sage of a female rock-group called The Holograms whose lead singer, Jem, had inclinations toward the Supernatural. Armed with a best-selling record titled "Truly Outrageous," *Jem* branched out into a separate daily series in 1987.

The Sylvanian Families (1987). By now, you've guessed that the two major toys promoted in 1980's kiddie cartoon shows were action figures and cute li'l furries. *The Sylvanian Families* (whose adventures were concocted by DIC/Claster) weren't action figures—either on or off the screen.

Teddy Ruxpin see *The Adventures of Teddy Ruxpin*

Terrahawks (1985). Gerry Anderson, onetime kappelmeister of the "Supermarionation" process that graced many syndies of the '60s, was back in the '80s with this puppetized sci-fi weekly from Primetime Television/ITC. *Terrahawks* was reminiscent of Anderson's 1967 *Captain Scarlet and the Mysterons:* 21st-century heroes vs. invading space villains.

ThunderCats (1985). First put on the market by Rankin-Bass/Telepictures in 1983, *ThunderCats* didn't get released until after the cartoon-commercial form was well established via *He-Man* and *GI Joe.* Armed with his Secret Sword, the noble Lion-O led the ThunderCats (who were lionlike humans, or humanlike lions, or whatever) against the sinister Mutants. If you didn't catch the characters daily on television, you couldn't miss them elsewhere: the ThunderCats showed up as action-figure toys, on the backs of cereal boxes, and immortalized in rubber on the sides of tennis shoes.

Tiger Shark see *Comic Strip*

Transformers (1985). "More than meets the eye," promised the theme-song for this Sunbow/Claster/DIC effort. That's because the Transformers could change themselves from robots into cars, tanks, or weapons (and so could the toys that the series huckstered). These heroes battled the nasty Decepticons, bringing their battle to Earth after a million-year conflict on their home planet. After a few five-day pilots and two-hour TV-movies, *Transformers* began beaming its message on behalf of Hasbro Toys on a daily basis in 1985, sweeping the kid-syndie ratings that year and inspiring an unending parade of imitators.

Tranzor Z (1985). Superheroes battled super-sorcerers in this 3B/T.E.N. cartoon daily.

Ulysses 31 see *Kiddeo TV*

Visionaries (1987). The Visionaries, also known as The Spectral Knights of the Planet Prysmo (whose kiddie-toy counterpart was a hologram device) clashed with the Darkling Lords, a cartel of wicked sorcerers. The virtue of this Marvel/Claster release was that it appeared only once a week.

Voltron, Defender of the Universe (1985). "Ultimate Super-Robot" cartoon series, produced in Japan for World Events Television.

Way to Go! (1980). Combination children's activity series, hosted by Peter Kastner, and kid's game show, the latter part emceed by Bill Armstrong of *Liar's Club* fame.

We're Movin' (1981). Teen-oriented Group W magazine weekly hosted first by Scott Baio, then by Willie Aames. Baio and Aames later appeared onscreen at the same time in the syndie sitcom *Charles in Charge.*

Yogi's Treasure Hunt see ***Funtastic World of Hanna-Barbera***

Young Universe (1986). Weekend newsmagazine for the 10-to-14-year age group, produced by the Behrens Company.

Zoobilee Zoo (1986). SFM's daily *Zoobilee Zoo* dispensed lessons about life with song, dance and clever sayings, featuring a group of musical-comedy performers dressed as animals. Hosting was Ben Vereen, who between this series and the music/variety weekly *You Write the Songs* was a busy man indeed in 1986. *Zoobilee Zoo* was produced and directed by Steve Binder, a veteran variety-show man who'd been responsible for Elvis Presley's "comeback" special in 1968.

Comedy

Sketch comedy, a network moneymaker since the introduction of *Saturday Night Live,* was tried out in many ways in '80s syndication, few lasting into a second season. But the big news in this decade was the remarkable growth of the syndicated sitcom industry. Around about 1984, it looked as though network sitcoms were fading. Long-runners like *M*A*S*H* and *Happy Days* were fewer and farther between; many programs with syndie-rerun potential, such as *WKRP in Cincinnati,* fell short of the 100 or so episodes needed for a healthy Monday-through-Friday "strip." Syndicators had no way of knowing that Bill Cosby's as-yet-unpremiered series would pump new life into the sitcom form, so other means of keeping the genre alive on a non-network basis were attempted. One method was to take a reasonably popular network series that hadn't run more than 65 or 70 episodes and film new half-hours, with same cast and format, to pad out the syndie package. Another was the *Leave It to Beaver* syndrome of reviving past series and formats for first-run, occasionally with new cast members but seldom with new jokes. A third method, one followed in particular by a consortium called the New Program Group, was to create brand-new sitcoms without any network history, to create long-running (it was hoped) series that would first make their grade in access time and then make their profits in stripped reruns. Perhaps these new shows could even stand up and hold their own against the network competition; perhaps more of them would have, had they provided a choice rather than an echo of time-worn network-sitcom formats. At any rate, the long-dormant syndie-sitcom industry was a booming, healthy one before 1987 was cold—inspiring a daring scheme to counter-program against the indestructable *Wheel of Fortune* with a different access-time first-run comedy each evening.

'Allo, 'Allo (1982; 1987). A British World War II sitcom that put such American projects as *Hogan's Heroes* to shame. Gordon Kaye starred as Rene, a larcenous, philandering French innkeeper caught between the proverbial rock and hard place in the early 1940's. Rene had to curry favor with the Nazi bigwigs of the occupying troops, but also was forced to aid a group of Resistance fighters who'd set up camp in his pantry. German officer Von Strohm (Richard Marner) got wind of the underground activity, but had to keep mum lest his own crooked activities, particularly the confiscation of valuable art treasures, become known to the Gestapo. What we had here was an old-fashioned door-slamming farce, given substance by its historical trappings. This often excruciatingly funny series was initially distributed to PBS stations by Lionheart (who'd taken over from Time-Life as the BBC's American representative) in 1982. When demand increased for first-run sit-comery in syndication in early 1987, the ready-made *'Allo 'Allo* made its long-overdue commercial television bow.

Bizarre (1984). First seen on the Showtime Cable service in 1981, this comedy-sketch series hosted by John Byner seemed to be an endurance test for people who thought that words beginning with the letter "F" were the ultimate in humor. Viacom cleaned up much of the language when it syndicated a package of the best *Bizarre* episodes to non-cable television.

Bustin' Loose (1987). This one began as a successful Richard Pryor movie about a charming lawbreaker who was paroled in the care of a female social worker and forced to act as handyman and surrogate parent to a group of unruly "problem" kids. Taking Richard Pryor's place in MCA-TV's series version of *Bustin' Loose* was Jimmy Walker, who'd skyrocketed to TV fame in the '70s by shouting "Dy-no-mite!" once a week on CBS' *Good Times.* Alas, the Jimmy Walker we saw on *Bustin' Loose* was merely another actor (not a terribly good one) who fielded wisecracks from a pack of standard sitcom kids—children so bereft of talent that they defied critical comment. The only performer who was able to bring humor and humanity to her role was Vonetta McGee, a veteran of low-budget "blaxploitation" pictures who was superb in the role of the no-nonsense social worker. *Bustin' Loose* was an example of the syndie sitcom at its feeblest, despite the technical-advisor presence of Dr. Gordon Berry, whose job it was to inject "pro-social" values in the series. (Dr.

Berry performed the same function on several cartoon syndies.) The best advice Dr. Berry could have given the producers of *Bustin' Loose* was to hire some kids who could act.

Canned Film Festival (1986). LBS' *Canned Film Festival,* bartered in syndication by Dr. Pepper, was a byproduct of a popular (if somewhat risible) book of the '70s, *The Fifty Worst Films of All Time.* Laraine Newman, formerly of *Saturday Night Live,* portrayed the chief usherette in a rundown movie house (presiding over a cluster of "comics" who lent unfunny support), acting as host for half-hour abridgments of classic movie turkeys. Included was the usual revival-house "bad-movie" repertoire of films like *The Terror of Tiny Town,* an all-midget western, and the legendary *Robot Monster,* which starred a bubble-blowing gorilla in a diving helmet. Since *Canned Film Festival* could only clear rights for public-domain films, it never got around to spotlighting two of the biggest bombs of the '80s, *Yellowbeard* and *Perfect* — both of which costarred Laraine Newman.

Charles in Charge (1987). Typical of the '80s tendency to cook up "new" first-run syndies from defunct network series, MCA's *Charles in Charge* featured Scott Baio in the title role and Baio's offscreen best friend Willie Aames as Charles' on-screen best friend Buddy. During its 1984–85 network run, the series had young Charles "in charge" of the children of a working couple. In syndication, Charles and his pal Buddy had moved to Seattle, where Our Hero was hired to care for the three kids of a working mother (Sandra Kerns). The children, who like most TV urchins seemed to be majoring in Wisecracking 101 in school, were played by Nicole Eggert, Josie Davis and Alexander Polinsky. (These may well be the stars of the future; after all, Scott Baio started as a child actor.) MCA and Tribune Entertainment made the syndicated *Charles in Charge* episodes primarily to flesh out its network-rerun package, but thus far only the new episodes have gotten anywhere in the non-network market. The quality of the new half-hours was on a par with the old ones.

Charlie Horse (1982). There were several syndicated packages of old television series episodes like *TV Classics* and *The Golden Age of Television* making the rounds in the '80s. *Charlie Horse,* a Hearst production out of Minneapolis, was hosted by Charles McCarty. It "dressed up" repeats of old '50s favorites like *My Little Margie* and *Public Defender* with sound effects and occasional comic commentary — undoubtedly entertaining viewers who thought that all old TV programs were pretty ridiculous anyway, but irritating those who would have liked to watch a flash from the past without latter-day adornment.

Check It Out (1986). Ever since *Three's Company,* it had been the specialty of D.L. Taffner Productions (formerly Gottlieb-Taffner) to create American-market versions of British sitcoms originally created by Brian Cooke. Cooke's *Tripper's Day,* a Thames Television effort about the manager of a small grocery store, was reborn on Canadian TV as *Check It Out* in 1985; it ran first on Canada's CTV, then America's USA Cable, and ultimately in syndication (through Taffner) in April of 1986. Don Adams, curiously lacking much of the comic timing he'd exhibited in the old *Get Smart* days, starred on *Check It Out* as Howard Bannister, the beleagured manager of Cobb's Groceries. The remaining cast was comprised of stock TV types: officious assistant manager (Dinah Christie), pushy young man on the way up (Jeff Pustel, sexpot (Kathleen Lasky), timorous "nellie" (Aaron Schwartz), and so on. One of this series' developers was Arne Sultan, who'd worked with Don Adams previously on *Get Smart* and *Don Adams' Screen Test*. Somehow, *Check It Out* lasted three seasons, despite such shortcomings as lukewarm direction, misfire pacing, tepid comedy content, and a production-value cheesiness that was manifested in its second-hand costumes and paste-and-paper sets.

Comedy Break (1985). One of a brace of 1985 syndicated comedy-revue shows designed for late-night syndication over independent channels (see also *Comedy Tonight*), *Comedy Break* was known in many markets as *Mack and Jamie,* in honor of its hosts, Mack Dryden and Jamie Alcroft. The stars and the "new talent" featured on this nightly half-hour usually ran a poor comedy second to the filmclips of W.C. Fields and Abbott and Costello used as buffers between routines. A Tribune/Gaylord release.

Comedy Tonight (1985). The other 1985 half-hour nightly comedy syndie, Orbis Productions' *Comedy Tonight* was test-marketed in March of that year and released for Monday-through-Friday play in September. Taped at New York's Metromedia studios and emceed by its producer, Manhattan talk show host Bill Boggs, *Comedy Tonight* offered a steady flow of young comics on the way up (and down). Neither this series nor *Comedy Break* sold as well as another package of syndicated sketches, *Carson's Comedy Classics,* a compilation of Johnny Carson's best *Tonight Show* moments of the past 15 years which also debuted in 1985.

DC Follies (1987). A wickedly hilarious British series, *Spitting Image,* made its mark on the American public via filmclips on news programs and two U.S. network television specials in mid–1987. *Spitting Image* used grotesquely caricatured puppets of real-life political leaders and celebrities in a series of tasteless but devastatingly funny satirical skits. It scored a hit in America, but when time came to syndicate the concept, the concept did not appear in its original form. Syndicast teamed with puppeteers Sid and Marty Krofft to develop a *Spitting Image* clone, which went out to 130 markets in the fall of 1987 as *DC Follies* (also the title given a pre-series special). Fred Willard played the bartender in a Washington watering hole known as DC Follies, where the elite — in this case, the puppet-marionette likenesses of politicos and media and movie stars — met to eat, drink and crack jokes. The results were softer, less vicious, and far less funny than in the British original. Most of the political jokes were so old they were toothless, even though the series prided itself on its topicality. (Carter, Nixon and Ford were frequent targets, never mind that their humor potential had been wrung dry a decade earlier.) And for every amusing bit involving current luminaries like Oprah Winfrey, Michael Jackson or Jim and Tammy Bakker, there were pointless routines that tried to get laughs merely by name-dropping. (One early sketch had Jack Nicholson putting the make on British prime minister Margaret Thatcher. Why?) The worst was saved for the end of each episode; to avoid potential lawsuits, Syndicast included a disclaimer in the closing credits saying that the show was all in fun and that no offense was intended. *DC Follies* therefore didn't even have the courage of its very few convictions, and its shrill laughtrack only emphasized its hollowness: artificial laughs for artificial characters.

Dr. Science (1987). Limited-series takeoff on the old "Mr. Wizard" type of junior-science programs; based on a lampoonish radio show syndicated to FM stations.

The Dom DeLuise Show (1987). Producer Greg Garrison apparently found it irresistible to star Dom DeLuise in a semisitcom with funny supporting characters and glamourous guests like Burt Reynolds and George Peppard, cashing in on the "in-joke" quality of such series as ABC's *Moonlighting* and Cable's *It's Gary Shandling's Show* by having the characters break up, forget their lines, drop character and talk directly to the audience. Though no fictional persona was really possible under the conditions set up by Multimedia's *Dom DeLuise Show,* the star played Dominick DeLuca, a Hollywood barber whose shop was conveniently close to all the major studios (justifying the drop-in guest stars). The supporting cast included George Wallace as Dom's partner, Charlie Callas as an overzealous private eye, various blue-collar types enacted by Lois Foraker, Angela Aames and Michael Chambers, and Wil Scudder doing the Charlie Chaplin imitation he'd made famous on a series of IBM commercials. As with earlier syndies like *Don Adams' Screen Test* and Greg Garrison's *Wacky World of Jonathan Winters,* DeLuise's series appealed the most to those who found incessant ad-libbing to be the funniest thing on earth. To some viewers, the most appealing aspect of *The Dom DeLuise Show* was a little monkey with whom Dom shared the finale of each episode; the monk was also an ad-libber, but far less self-conscious about it than his co-stars.

Down and Out in Beverly Hills (1987). Inspired by the 1985 hit comedy film (itself based on the 1932 French film *Boudu Saved from Drowning*), this Buena Vista release was test-run over the Fox Network on April 26, 1987, joining Fox's lineup on a weekly basis in late July. Hector Elizondo and Anita Morris played the *nouveau-riche* Whitemans, whose trendy California lifestyle was interrupted — and challenged — by live-in hobo Jerry Baskin (Tim Thomerson). Since the stars of the film version were Richard Dreyfuss, Bette Midler and Nick Nolte, the cast of TV's *Down and Out in Beverly Hills* couldn't help but suffer in comparison. This and the fact that what might have been funny in a 100-minute movie could be very trying on a weekly half-hour basis, doomed TV's *Down and Out* to the "honor" of being the very first program cancelled by the Fox Network. The one character who emerged unscathed was also the only "actor" who carried his role over from the movie into the sitcom: Mike the Dog, who for a brief time challenged Spuds McKenzie as America's favorite Canine Celebrity of the '80s.

Duet (1987). While many of the early Fox Network series were met with derision or indifference by the media critics, such was not the case with *Duet*, a Paramount television weekly which was a "critics' darling" from the moment of its April 19, 1987, debut. Ben Coleman played mystery writer Matthew Laurence, whose daydreamed adventures involving his detective hero Murdoch — a name also coincidentally borne by the owner of the Fox Network — were staged in a Raymond Chandlerish *film noir* fashion. Laurence's 80s-bachelor lifestyle was altered by the arrival of chic caterer Laura Kelly (Mary Page Keller). Matthew's best friends were the upwardly mobile Richard (Chris Lemmon), whose idea of a crisis was to have the refrigerator in his limousine conk out, and Richard's wife Linda (Alison LaPlaca), whose answer to any disagreement with her spouse was a threat to withhold sex. Jody Thelan rounded out the cast as Laura's ditsy sister Jane. Highly praised as the first "yuppie sitcom," *Duet* had a satisfyingly consistent level of cleverness, though its format — nice but fallible leading characters, eccentric friends, and klutzy siblings all coping with modern life — wasn't too far removed from the sitcoms of earlier days. The one aspect of *Duet* that had the critics doing hand-springs was that the episodes were shown in sequential, continuing-saga form, with Matthew and Laura's relationship growing warmer from show to show. Many of the critics were evidently as young as the characters in the series, for they forgot that there were many earlier comedies *(Burns and Allen, The Beverly Hillbillies)* that had been doing continuing stories, without fanfare, long before *Duet*. But young and trendy were the bywords of the day, and critics played along with those bywords rather than put *Duet* in historical perspective. Produced by Gary David Goldberg's Ubu Productions with Ruth Bennett as executive producer (Goldberg and Bennett had been responsible for NBC's *Family Ties*), *Duet* was perhaps overpraised by the press, but was certainly one of the wittier and more enjoyable sitcoms of its era.

Elvira's Movie Macabre (1983). Actress Cassandra Peterson, a conservative-looking redhead, created a whole new career for herself when she donned a long black wig, heavy "vampire" makeup and revealing black gowns, then adopted a California "valley-girl" speech pattern. In this guise, Peterson was KHJ–Los Angeles' "Elvira," host of a horror-movie weekly. Reminiscent of LA's Vampira in the 1950's, Elvira spent most of her screen time lounging on a sofa and making atrocious jokes about the even more atrocious movies which unspooled on her *Movie Macabre*. As with earlier horror-show hosts like Philadelphia's Zacherly, Elvira was soon the subject of mammoth fan clubs, look-alike contests, and sold-out personal appearances. KHJ put *Elvira's Movie Macabre* into syndication in 1983, complete with the bow-wow movies Elvira had been running in the L.A. market, and with campy guest appearances from people like Ed McMahon and Barbara Billingsley. Once established nationally, Elvira began popping up as a special guest on various comic and dramatic television programs—and all the while her "alter ego" Cassandra Peterson continued to accept featured roles in such movies as *Pee-Wee's Big Adventure* (which ironically starred another actor who parlayed a 1950's persona into a 1980's supercareer, Paul "Pee-wee Herman" Rubens).

Evening at the Improv (1981–82). Two-season 60-minuter produced by Bud Friedman, the operator of the famed Los Angeles comedy cabaret known as The Improvisation. Hosts on *Evening at the Improv* were an eclectic bunch, ranging from old masters like Phil Silvers to newer comics like Andy Kaufman and even straight actors like Sally Kellerman. Though a troupe of supporting actors appeared regularly as the waiters, waitresses and bartenders serving the Improv's live audience, the emphasis was on monologues (most of them heavily laundered for television) from America's leading and soon-to-be-leading stand-up comics. American TV Syndication distributed on behalf of New Form Television and The Improvisation, Inc. In 1987, a new batch of *Evening at the Improvs,* with noticeably less stringent censorship, began appearing on the Arts and Entertainment cable service.

FTV (1986). Just as MTV stood for "Music Television," FTV stood for "Fun Television" on this MTV spoof produced by Chris Bearde and distributed by Metromedia. In the tradition of music satirists like Alan Sherman and "Weird Al" Yankovic, *FTV's* regulars (Khandi Alexander, Stephen Bishop, Vin Dunlop, Don Felder, Pat Matterson, Mark McCollum and John Paragon) played fast-and-loose in their own versions of currently popular rock videos.

George and Mildred see *Thames Originals*

George Schlatter's Comedy Club (1987). This King World weekly hour (initially titled *Laugh Machine*) was done in the spirit of George Schlatter's television hit of the late 1960's, *Rowan and Martin's Laugh-In.* Vignettes edited from the stand-up routines of various comedians would be rearranged into "themes," such as Sex, Dining Out, and TV Commercials. Not all comics were shown to their best advantage in this fragmentary fashion, nor did *Comedy Club* jell whenever clips of the better comedians were interspersed with those of lesser talents.

Hangin' In (1986). *Hangin' In* was a popular Canadian prime time comedy with serious sociological undertones about the tribulations of social worker Kate Brown (Lally Cadeau) and her streetwise teenage charges. When Orbis Communications picked up *Hangin' In* for the American market, it adopted the brave policy of syndicating the series as a Monday-through-Friday strip. But daily doses of social comment left audiences accustomed to the frivolities of *Three's Company* cold, and *Hangin' In,* though still a favorite in Canada, died in the U.S.

Honeymoon Hotel (1987). This Access Syndication Corporation release starred Isabel Sanford as the titular hotel's owner, and was the launching pad of a plan by producer Fred Silverman to create a market for *daily* first-run syndie sitcoms. Silverman's dream lasted for five days; so did *Honeymoon Hotel.*

It's a Living (1985–). *It's a Living* lived first from 1981 through '82 on ABC, during which time it was briefly retitled *Making a Living.* The series followed a group of waitresses who worked at a top-of-the-skyscraper L.A. restaurant. Retained from the ABC series for syndication's *It's a Living* were Ann Jillian as Cassie, Barrie Youngfellow as Jan, Gail Edwards as Dot, Marian Mercer as field-marshal headwaitress Nancy, and Paul Kreppel as Sonny, a slimy cocktail pianist. While the ABC original had a number of critic-defenders, no one but the viewers liked the syndie version, which featured as its two jokes the hardships of waitressing and the sexual yearnings of the characters. Ann Jillian, whose very appearance in a 22-episode series was a testament to the grit and courage of an actress who'd just undergone a dangerous double mastectomy, stayed with the non-network *It's a Living* until her contract terminated, then left for more satisfying projects; she was replaced by Shirley Lee Ralph as Ginger. Ralph exerted as much energy into this sitcom as she did on her "nighttime job" on the NBC series *LA Law.* Also added to the cast in 1986 was another waitress, Amy, played by Crystal Bernard. *It's a Living* was a Witt-Thomas production, made in conjunction with Golden West TV, Lorimar Telepictures and LBS; Procter and Gamble handled the barter-advertising end.

Karen's Song (1987). The new Fox Network just couldn't seem to do at all well on Saturday evenings, and *Karen's Song,* which debuted on July 19, 1987, didn't help matters any. Patty Duke played Karen Mathews, a 40-year-old literary agent and divorcee with a teenage daughter (Teri Hatcher). Karen managed to shock everyone — including herself — when she fell in love with a 28-year-old caterer named Steven Forman, played by Lewis Smith. (Does anyone remember when the fans of 18-year-old Patty Duke were equally shocked when she married a man twice her age?) Costarring as a brash friend of Karen's was Lainie Kazan, whose antic performance was one of the series' few sources of genuine laughs. *Karen's Song's* premise soon flew out the window in favor of dumb one-liners and infantile storylines; the series earned the distinction of being the shortest-lived of the first Fox Network efforts.

Keep It in the Family see *The Thames Originals*

The Kenny Everett Video Show (1980). High-tech comedy sketch series from Britain, distributed by D.L. Taffner as part of a summer 1980 attempt by Mobil Oil to syndicate an entertainment "block" to independent stations. Everett's best bits would later be seen on the *Night Flight* series over the USA Cable service.

L.A.T.E.R. see *The Life and Times of Eddie Roberts*

Laugh Trax (1982). *Rock Comedy* was the working title for this LBS/Company III/Sunn Classics production, as good a title as any for this conglomeration of wacky humor and rock music. Jim Stahl hosted, while Gail Mathias, Lucy Webb and Frank Welker contributed to the sketches. The producer was old *Laugh-In* hand Carol Raskin; Bristol-Myers bartered the 60-minute weekly.

The Laurel and Hardy Show (1986). Normally a package of theatrical films that had been TV staples since the late 1940's wouldn't rate a mention as a "first-run syndie." But Hal Roach Studios did with the old comedies of Stan Laurel and Oliver Hardy what every film distributor should do with every old movie on TV. The company went to the trouble of preparing pristine, 35-millimeter prints of L&H's films, and also restored "lost" footage that hadn't been seen since the early '30s. Even when this 90-minute series edited the old movies to accommodate commercials (all the team's features were pared to a uniform 60–65 minutes), the re-editing was done with a keen sense of rhythm and continuity — something that the distributors of other feature films ignore when they hack their films to bits to fit into two-hour slots. The Roach people even included newsreel and home-movie clips of the comedians, well-researched tributes to Laurel and Hardy's "stock company" of supporting comics, and brief scenes from the foreign versions of the Laurel and Hardy comedies, with the stars speaking their words phonetically in Spanish and French. Whether or not Hal Roach's "colorization" process (wherein old black-and-white films were turned into color via computer) added anything to such L&H films as *The Music Box* and *Way Out West* will probably always be a matter of hot debate, but otherwise, *The Laurel and Hardy Show* was a tip of the hat to film preservation societies everywhere, as well as a treat to fans of the team in particular and lovers of vintage films in general. Rob Word of Hal Roach, Inc. was executive producer; production consultant was renowned film historian (and lifelong Laurel and Hardy buff) Leonard Maltin.

The Life and Times of Eddie Roberts (1980). Popularly known as *L.A.T.E.R.*, the Columbia TV nightly series was a satirical soap opera in the *Mary Hartman* tradition, and was in fact developed by former *Hartman* writer Ann Marcus and her husband Ellis. Renny Temple played Eddie Roberts, professor at Cranepool University, who was stuck in a mire of soapish situations, including the insatiable sexual cravings of his wife Dolores (Udana Power). Others in the cast were Allison Balson (as the Roberts' daughter Chrissie), Allen Case, Joan Hotchkis, Jon Lormer and Darryl Roach. The syndicated-serial fad had run its course by the time *L.A.T.E.R.* first appeared on January 7, 1980; the series' final episode ran less than four months later. The series' failure led 20th Century–Fox to shelve plans for releasing another serial spoof, *T.H.E. Hospital* (what was this fascination with initials?), even after taping several episodes.

Mack and Jamie see *Comedy Break*

Mad Movies with the LA Connection (1985). The LA Connection was a comedy troupe which ran old movies before live audiences, turned off the soundtrack, and interpolated their own comic dialogue. The group first gained prominence on the 1983's talk show syndie *Thicke of the Night,* and later were rewarded with their own half-hour series by Four-Star Television. Public domain movies were used to keep costs low: thus, Shirley Temple's 1939 *The Little Princess* was transformed into the tale of a girl possessed by her demonic doll, while the 1950 melodrama *D.O.A.* became an *I Love Lucy* episode thanks to the vague resemblance between *D.O.A.* star Edmond O'Brien and Desi Arnaz. Political humor was made possible by the public-domain status of two Ronald Reagan pictures, *Santa Fe Trail* (in which Raymond Massey, decked out in a beard for his role as John Brown, was suddenly converted into the Ayatollah Khomeini) and *This Is the Army.* There was even time to hoke up family home movies sent in by the viewers. As one can see, subtlety was left in the lobby on *Mad Movies,* which was as funny as this rather parasitic style of humor ever gets. Kent Scov, one of the voice-actors and writers, was executive producer: other LA Connection members were Bob Buchholtz, Connie Sue Cook, Steve Pinto and Stephen Rollman.

Madame's Place (1982). Wayland Flowers' "dirty-old-lady" puppet Madame had been tooling around the game show/talk show circuit for years when Paramount TV took a chance and gave the old dear her own nightly series. *Madame's Place* cast the star as the host of her own talk show; supporting cast regulars included Johnny Haymer as Madame's butler Walter, Judy Landers as Madame's niece, a busty would-be starlet, and Hector Elias as Robin Espinoza, leader of. "Madame's All-Divorced Band." When the talk show parody faltered, the emphasis shifted to the prickly puppet's home life; when that concept also faltered, the 110 stations who'd bought 26 weeks' worth of *Madame's Place* went back to their *Odd Couple* reruns and old movies. Maybe Paramount would have had better luck syndicating the fictional series that was supposed to have been Madame's talk show competition: *Naked All-Star Bowling.*

Mama's Family (1986–). A spinoff of the funny-bitter "Family" sketches on the old *Carol Burnett Show, Mama's Family* appeared as an NBC sitcom in 1983. Carol Burnett made only token appearances as Eunice, the vindictive daughter of domineering Mama. In the title role, Vicki Lawrence (all of 25 when she created the role in 1974) was brilliant as the blunt, bullying matriarch of a very sorry household. NBC's *Mama's Family* was critically acclaimed but short-lived. When Lorimar-Telepictures dug up the series to make new first-run syndie episodes in 1986, Miss Lawrence was back as Mama, as were two more of the NBC cast, Ken Berry as Mama's doltish son Vint and Dorothy Lyman as neighbor Naomi Oates. New regulars included Allan Kayser as Bubba and Beverly Archer as Iola. All the characterizations were top-rank, even when the scripts were merely rank; too many of the syndie episodes relied on cheap bathroom and sex jokes at the expense of believable storylines. But series producer Joe Hamilton (Carol Burnett's ex-husband) evidently understood his audience; as of 1987, *Mama's Family* was the top-rated syndicated sitcom, playing to excellent business in 147 markets.

Man About the House see *The Thames Originals*

Marblehead Manor (1987). Paramount's *Marblehead Manor* was a run-of-the-mill servant-master farce, with emphasis on bosoms, bottoms and funny costumes. Paxton Whitehead was top-billed as Albert, head butler in the home of vegetable-oil millionaire Randolph Stonehill (played by series coproducer and co-creator Bob Fraser). Linda Thorson, who two decades earlier made very little impression as Diana Rigg's replacement on *The Avengers,* had developed into a droll, polished farceur for her middle-aged role as Mrs. Stonehill. The supporting-cast servants were the standard mix of fools, sexpots and cute foreign accents, all adept at double-takes, pratfalls and embarrassed smiles. The comedy on the series was of the "Who's been sleeping in my bed?" school of the average suburban dinner theatre, but *Marblehead Manor* was well produced and extremely well directed, and entertained without changing your life.

Normally, the previous paragraph would be the end of the story—but *Marblehead Manor* was more than just a standard syndie sitcom. Premiering September 14, 1987, it was the Monday-night entry in a plan by the NBC-owned TV stations to combat the unconquerable access time hit, *Wheel of Fortune.* After several years of unsuccessful Monday-through-Friday strip gameshows in the 7:30–8 p.m. slot, NBC Television Stations' president Al Jerome decided to revive the "checkerboard" concept—running a different program each night of the week, a practice NBC had given up seven years earlier. The first step was to get all five NBC-owned stations to go along with the plan and run all the new shows on the same evenings, else the plan would be abandoned as cost-inefficient. The five stations complied, and Al Jerome commented that this was quite a coup since "It's never been our practice for the stations to program together." (Apparently Jerome didn't know, or chose to forget, that the NBC stations had ceased checkerboarding back in '80 when they unilaterally agreed to run *Family Feud.*) The next move was to choose five programs that would thrive in access. Out of 75 possibilities, the five were narrowed down to *Marblehead Manor, She's the Sheriff, You Can't Take It With You, Out of This World* and *We Got It Made.* This new syndie-sitcom crop was described, without much team spirit, by NBC Entertainment chief Brandon Tartikoff as "the United States Football League of comedy."

Married ... with Children (1987). Premiering Sunday, April 5, 1987, *Married ... with Children* was the first regular half-hour sitcom to appear on the new Fox Network; it was run three times that evening to reach the widest possible audience (some of whom might have liked to reach back). Executive producer Ron Leavitt claimed that he based the series on his own marriage, to which we can only say "poor fellow." Opening each week to the strains of

Frank Sinatra singing "Love and Marriage," *Married . . . with Children* told of the Bundy family, an upper-middle-class bunch who spent most of their time tearing each other down. Ed O'Neill was foul-tempered Al Bundy, Katie Sagal was his lazy, viper-tongued wife Peggy, and the kids (as repulsive a pair as one was likely to find outside a real high school) were Christina Applegate as Kelly and David Faustino as Bud. Rich Shynder costarred as Al's neurotic coworker, while Amanda Bearse and David Garrison were around for contrast (and as a target for many of the nastier jokes) as the Bundys' kissie-huggie newlywed neighbors. The critics and viewers who liked the show applauded it for providing, with its nonstop barrage of insults, defamations and refusals to play nice, an antidote to the happy-family sweetness of Bill Cosby's top-rated network sitcom (indeed, Fox insisted that *Married . . . with Children's* working title was *Not the Cosby Show,* a good story if nothing else). Detractors observed that the series' constant putdowns were wearisome, and that *The Honeymooners* had done a better job of depicting a lasting marriage based on open conflict some thirty years earlier. Either way, stars Ed O'Neill and Katie Sagal managed to pull off the near-impossible task of conveying the notion that the Bundys really loved each other despite the guerrilla warfare. *Married . . . with Children* was never a mega-hit in the Cosby tradition, but remained one of Fox's few consistently popular comedy shows.

Mister President (1987). After resisting series television for nearly 25 years, George C. Scott joined this Fox Network show about the private life of an American president. Scott, at $100,000 per episode Fox's highest-paid star (the previous holder of that honor, talk show host Joan Rivers, was on her way out when *Mr. President* debuted on May 3, 1987), played former Wisconsin governor Sam Trench, an honest and down-to-earth fellow who used common sense and a lot of soul-searching to cope with the pressures of the presidency. Johnny Carson, whose production company put this series together, claimed that this was the story of how an "average American family" coped with being thrust into the political limelight. Thus the stories were not about politics per se, but about their ramifications on the individual: Sam Trench found that he had to curry favor with people he despised, wife Meg (Carlyn Glynn) found her love life taking second priority to the world situation, and kids Cynthia (Maddie Corman) and Nick (Andre Gower) had to suffer the constant supervision of their social life by the CIA. Conrad Bain and Allen Williams were around as two of the president's advisers, but mainly as straight men for George C. Scott's laugh lines. *Mr. President* suffered from the sort of indecision that would be fatal to any chief executive. The series was first filmed, then videotaped, then filmed again; it had a laughtrack and then it didn't; it played for subtle humor but then backslid into vaudeville one-liners. Throughout all this, George C. Scott masked any dissatisfaction he might have had with the series by playing his part with the air of a man who had his mind on more important acting assignments, and couldn't be bothered with expending any extra energy on his Sam Trench role. When the ratings dropped, the format was tinkered with. It was contrived to have Trench's wife walk out on her husband (happens all the time in the White House), with her position as "first lady" sort of filled by Sam's sister-in-law, played to maximum effect by comedienne Madeline Kahn. Ultimately the show was axed because it was costing Carson Productions too much money — certainly the first time an American president has been voted out of office after only one year of overspending.

Morecambe and Wise (1980). The popularity of *Benny Hill* inspired other efforts at syndicating half-hour nightly abridgments of foreign comedy specials. One of these was from BBC/Time-Life and featured the British comedy duo of Eric Morecambe and Ernie Wise, whose humor fell somewhere between the Bob and Ray school and the Rowan and Martin league.

National Lampoon's Hot Flashes (1984). Test-marketed several times, this comedy/music review never seemed to have enough staying power to survive as a weekly. Franklin Ajaye was the biggest name on this sometimes satire of current events, underwritten by the humor magazine of the title.

The New Adventures of Beans Baxter (1987). Beans Baxter (Jonathan Ward) was a typical '80s high-school kid with a typical '50s sitcom home (complete with white picket fence) and mother (Elinor Donahue). Most of his problems before his "new adventures" began were of the usual teenage run, including his hot-and-cold relationship with his girlfriend Cake (Karen Mistal). That was until Beans' father (Rick Lenz), allegedly a postman, disappeared, whereupon Beans learned that Dad was actually a top-secret courier for American Intelligence and had been kidnapped by the dastardly international spy organization known as U.G.L.I. So Beans pursued the villains, was in turn pursued by them, tried to maintain a "normal life" in between assignments, and no one took anything seriously — least of all the bad guys, who were given to saying "Have a nice day" after killing their victims. And there you had Fox's *New Adventures of Beans Baxter,* a lunatic mixture of *Leave It to Beaver* and *The Man from U.N.C.L.E.* that was alternately praised and damned by viewers and critics after its July 18, 1987, premiere. Occasionally joining the asylum-like atmosphere was Shawn Weatherly as a gorgeous Russian double-agent defector, who paraded around in very little clothing and used the hapless Beans' bedroom as a hideout. ("If you have an explanation for a naked tuba-playing blonde, I'd like to hear it!" wailed Beans' girlfriend Cake in one of the saner moments of this series.) John Vernon and Jerry Wasserman played Beans' secret-agent superiors, and "played" is the correct word. Stealing everything but the cameras each week was the aforementioned Elinor Donahue, who remained oblivious to the espionage stuff despite the most conclusive evidence that her son was not merely working a part-time job after school hours, and who was inclined to send Beans to his room for beating up a hired assassin on their front lawn. No potential laugh-getting situation was overlooked on *Beans Baxter,* and usually the strain showed (by way of "impossible" jokes and kinky villains like punk-rocker Wendy O. Williams); but credit the Fox Network for at least *trying* (albeit briefly, since the ratings were lousy) to offer something that wasn't a clone of every other sitcom on television.

The New Gidget (1986–87). The "old" *Gidget* was the 1965 ABC series, based on a novel and series of movies about a Malibu teenager and her surfing pals, which made a star out of Sally Field. The new Francie "Gidget" Lawrence of 1986 was played by soap-opera actress Caryn Richman, a more sedate, less hyper type than the Gidgets of the past. In her new syndicated series from Ackerman-Riskin Productions and Colex (an amalgam of Columbia TV and Lexington Broadcasting), Gidget had miraculously aged only ten years since her last television appearance two decades earlier; she was now the owner of a Malibu travel agency, in partnership with her best friend LaRue (Jill Jacobsen, then concurrently appearing on CBS' nighttimer *Falcon Crest*). The Gidge had married her old boyfriend Moondoggie, who'd become a city councilman and who was played by former *Little House on the Prairie* regular Dean Butler. William Schallert, a past master at playing understanding fathers, played Gidget's understanding father. Not forgetting that the appeal of the original *Gidget* was in watching the adventures of a bunch of fun-loving teens, the producers created the character of Gidget's high-schooler niece Danni; she was portrayed by Sydney Penny, who in 1983 had become a "name" thanks to her appearance on the ABC miniseries *The Thorn Birds* (she played Rachel Ward as a young girl). Contrary to the worst expectations, *The New Gidget* managed to capture the carefree, sun-baked ambience of the 1965 series thanks to Ackerman-Riskin's decision to film rather than videotape the new show: film added a deep-tanned density to the outdoors scenes that tape would have been hard-pressed to convey. And though it was burdened with the usual heavy-handed sitcom trappings (including supporting appearances by Richard Paul, who played exactly the sort of prissy, self-important mayor that he'd essayed on the old ABC series *Carter Country*), *The New Gidget* was a pleasant, amiable, and at times quite heart-warming little series, especially noteworthy for its espousal of ecological and family values. The warmth generated by the three-dimensional performances of the leading actors at times transcended the first *Gidget* series; whether or not Caryn Richman would scale the same career heights enjoyed by Sally Field was debatable, but there was no truth to the rumor that her next series would be *The Flying Mother Superior*.

The New Monkees (1987). *The New Gidget* notwithstanding, not every sitcom of the '60s lent itself well to revival in the '80s: *The New Monkees* bore this out. On the credit side, Columbia TV didn't rush headlong into a quickie update of the NBC *Monkees* series of 1966–68; the creation and release of the new series was painstakingly planned and calculated. First there was the return of the original Monkees on the concert trail starting in 1985. This imitation–Beatles singing group included Mickey Dolenz, Davey Jones, Mike Nesmith and Peter Tork; only Nesmith, who by the mid-80's was a fabulously successful film and rock-video producer, declined to participate in the comeback tour. The "old Monkees" concerts, somewhat amazingly, played to packed houses and caused traffic jams in virtually every city they graced. (Much of the enthusiasm had been passed to the teens of the '80s by the singers' first fans of the '60s, now grown up.) This euphoria was followed by a "rerun blitz" of the original *Monkees* series, first in a two-day marathon on the MTV Cable service, then in summer 1986 local-market syndication. The vintage episodes were captivating in their fast-cut, slapstick exhilaration (this style had been inspired by the Beatles films of the '60s directed by Richard Lester), and generated a willing audience for Columbia's final step, the creation of "The New Monkees" for a new first-run syndie. "New" they were. Just as had happened with the formation of the first quartet in 1966, a nationwide talent search was conducted to come up with four fresh faces to portray the utterly up-to-date Monkees of 1987. The four new boys hired were Marty Ross, Dino Kovas, Larry Saltis and Jared Chandler, who like the original "pre-fab four" were engaged more for their comic ability than for their musical merits. For music fans, *The New Monkees* offered two elaborate "rock videos" per episode; for comedy fans, all the old schtick and stock characters (crooked managers, mad scientists, et al.) were dragged out of the woodwork. The results were so strident that *The New Monkees* looked exactly like what it was: a misguided mess concocted out of past brilliant ideas by businessmen who had no idea of what teenagers *really* wanted to see. The same charge *might* have been levelled at the original *Monkees,* but the difference was that Dolenz, Jones, Nesmith and Tork all had genuine personality and charm, qualities lacking for the most part in the four faceless men who called themselves the New Monkees.

Nine to Five (1986–87). One of the box-office biggies of 1980 was a feminist comedy film titled *Nine to Five,* which told the world what secretaries have always known: Male bosses were sexist and unreasonable, and if female secretaries ran things, society would be better off. This was a workable premise, but if you're going to do a television series based upon that premise, stick to it, and don't show the same fluctuation and lack of backbone displayed by the boss in the original movie. The first network version of *Nine to Five* in 1982 tried to stay faithful to the original, but was sabotaged by lukewarm ratings and an eventual descent into standard sitcomery. 20th Century–Fox TV's syndicated *Nine to Five* had almost no relation to the movie's attack on sexism. The new series' emphasis was on maintaining a home life while retaining a 40-hour job, with hints that the secretaries on the series were secretly in love with their boss, and hoped that he'd provide one of them the security of marriage. Happy New Year, 1936. Sally Struthers joined the legion of former network sitcom stars who emigrated to syndication in the mid-80's as *Nine to Five's* Marsha, a character not found in the original film. Back from the earlier network weekly *Nine to Five* were Valerie Curtin as Judy Bernley (the Jane Fonda role in the movie) and Rachel Dennison as Doralee, the part taken in the 1980 film by Dennison's sister Dolly Parton. Ed Winter, who'd had better material as the zealous CIA agent on *M*A*S*H,* was cast as boss William "Bud" Coleman (an inside joke, we suppose, since the larcenous boss in the original film was played by Dabney Coleman). One question: if the producers were going to throw out the chauvinism angle in favor of a secretary-loves-boss routine, why bother taping a new *Nine to Five* at all? Why not just bring back reruns of Ann Sothern's *Susie?*

Off the Wall (1986). Yet another comedy-sketch syndie of a single year's duration. Gaylord/Fries distributed *Off the Wall:* its comedy troupe consisted of Joe Baker, Louise Duart, Susan Elliot, Pat Fraley, Shelley Herman and Terry Kiser. The jokes were about Ronald Reagan's hair, Ronald Reagan's memory, Ronald Reagan's attitudes, and, for variety, Ronald Reagan's wife.

One Big Family (1986). Tony Thomas, part of the production team of Witt-Thomas-Harris (with Paul Junger Witt and Susan Harris), brought his father Danny Thomas back to the weekly-sitcom grind with Lorimar/LBS' *One Big Family*. Just because this series was one of the few 1986 comedy syndies that was not based on an earlier network show didn't mean that *One Big Family* was any different from the usual sitcom syndrome, outside of the welcome return of the elder Thomas. Danny played Uncle Jake, an ex-vaudevillian living in Seattle, whose happy solitude was interrupted when his suddenly orphaned nieces and nephews moved in with him. The eldest of these relatives was Don (Anthony Starke), who with wife Jan (Kim Gillingham) acted as surrogate parents for the younger brothers and sisters, one of whom was played by Dom DeLuise's son Michael. The final episode of this single-season wonder was a "retrospective" of the series' highlights—a barren half-hour indeed.

Out of This World (1987). This MCA issue was the Thursday-night entry in the NBC stations' access "checkerboarding" attempt (see notes on *Marblehead Manor*). Maureen Flannagan played Evie Garland, who on her 13th birthday discovered that her presumed-dead father was actually alive and an alien from the planet Antares—and that she was half-alien herself, with the ability to stop all movement around her with a gesture of her fingers. This of course resulted in no end of complications for Evie and her literally down-to-Earth mother Donna (played by Donna Pescow, herself a series ingenue on her own 1978 networker, *Angie*). Evie's dad made occasional appearances in the form of a voice emanating from a crystal cube. Surprisingly, the single basic joke on *Out of This World* was not overplayed, and the series was easily the best of the five sitcom syndies chosen for the checkerboard project; it was certainly worthy of being selected by the NBC stations as the lead-in for NBC's Thursday winner *The Cosby Show,* and was one of the two new checkerboarders renewed for a second season (see also *She's the Sheriff*). All this in spite of the fact that *Out of This World* was at base merely a variation of the previous season's ABC series *Starman,* and the fact that the rest of *World's* supporting cast was from the Acme TV-Cliche Factory. The most precious of the secondary characters was played by Doug McClure, who labored under the apprehension that he was a master comedian in the role of a macho movie star who became the mayor of a small California town (where did they get *that* idea?).

Paul Hogan (1982). Imported on the heels of *The Benny Hill Show* was this raunchy series of comic vignettes from Australia. A major television and film star "down under," Paul Hogan had the ability to go from one finely detailed comic character to another without batting an eyelash, though his talents were usually compromised in pedestrian skits involving his series' two favorite subjects, soccer and beer. Primetime/Gould/Post-Newsweek didn't do too well with this series in 1982, but only because they were four years too early. Paul Hogan didn't graduate to international superstardom until the release of the feature film *Crocodile Dundee* in 1986.

Punky Brewster see Silver Spoons

Robin's Nest see The Thames Originals

Second Chance (1987). Another attempt by the Fox Network at offering out-of-the-norm entertainment, *Second Chance,* which premiered September 26, 1987, had a premise that all but defies description, but here goes anyway. Charles Russell (Kiel Martin) was dead, his soul in Limbo. St. Peter (Joseph Maher) gave Charles a second chance by returning him to Earth, there to guide the destinies of Charles' own 15-year-old self, nicknamed "Chazz" (Mathew Perry). The dead Charles had to keep the living Chazz from following the life of crime that had condemned the dead Charles to a bleak afterlife. Randee Heller played Chazz' mother, which meant that she was also *Charles'* mother. The audience was just as confused as you probably are at this point, so in 1988, Fox dropped the whole alter-ego concept and transformed *Second Chance* into a traditional teen sitcom, *Boys Will Be Boys.*

She's the Sheriff (1987). Suzanne Somers, a modestly talented actress elevated to television superstardom in the late–70's ABC sitcom *Three's Company,* left that show because she wanted five times the money she was making. In the years that followed, Somers managed a good income as a nightclub performer, but the public was cool to her attempts at moviemaking and her occasional TV specials — and the critics and industry heads, unimpressed that she'd once been a number-one pinup poster personality, froze her out as effectively as did her former fans. In 1987, Lorimar-Telepictures announced that a new syndicated comedy was in the works, a project that had been kicking around at CBS for several years under the title *Suddenly Sheriff.* In an ironic twist that any fiction writer would reject as ridiculous, Suzanne Somers was hired to replace the original star of *Suddenly Sheriff,* Priscilla Barnes — who'd been Somers' replacement on *Three's Company!* Somers played the widow of the sheriff of a small Nevada county, who found herself taking over her late husband's job. Her character, Hildy Granger, was given two sitcom-style kids and an overenergetic mother (Pat Carroll). Most prominent of Hildy's deputies was Rubin (George Wyner), who openly coveted the sheriff's job and did everything within his underhanded means to discredit his new boss. The series, retitled *She's the Sheriff,* was picked up by the NBC-owned stations as the Tuesday entry in their access checkerboard project (see *Marblehead Manor*) and by 159 other markets. Produced by Somers' husband Alan Hamel, *She's the Sheriff* was the standard mulligan's stew of wisecracking criminals, "funny disguise" scenes and ultraloud laughtracks, but it was nowhere near as bad as a lot of people expected it to be; if you didn't expect the series to be any more than it was, you could tolerate the half-hour taken out of your life each week. *She's* *the Sheriff* and *Out of This World* were the only two "checkerboard" sitcoms to earn a second season renewal (though a projected spinoff of *She's the Sheriff,* a series starring Don Knotts as a hairdresser [!], never materialized). As for Suzanne Somers, she played her role as well as it could be played; all that was missing was that extra spark that makes the difference between a star and a superstar.

Silver Spoons (1986); **Punky Brewster** and **Webster** (1987). The syndicated extension of NBC's *Silver Spoons* appeared to be one of several efforts in the manner of *Too Close for Comfort* (which see) to pad out a skimpy network-rerun package with first-run episodes. There was a little more to the story than that. When this saga of a rich kid (Ricky Schroder) and his equally wealthy but childish dad (Joel Higgins) started its NBC run in 1982, its production company, Embassy Communications, was so certain it has a long-running hit that it guaranteed that 116 episodes of *Silver Spoons* would be available for syndication in 1986. Local stations made their scheduling plans in accordance with those guarantees. But *Silver Spoons* took an unexpected ratings dip, so NBC reached for the ax after only 94 installments. Still, Embassy had an iron-clad guarantee that they had to honor, so 22 more episodes of *Silver Spoons* were ground out for syndication and the package ended up as a Monday-through-Friday late-afternoon kid's strip. Much the same happened to Columbia TV's *Punky Brewster* (another clever-kid opus, the kid in question being an orphan's-shelter runaway played by a young lady with the awe-inspiring monicker of Soleil Moon Frye). NBC was so certain of the lasting success of *Punky* that it even commissioned a Saturday-morning cartoon version of the property. But as with *Silver Spoons,* the nighttime viewers grew weary of *Punky Brewster* long before they were supposed to, so Columbia, having made *Silver Spoons*-like promises of a fat syndication package, was obliged to churn out extra *Punky Brewsters* for the afternoon trade. And in early 1987, Paramount announced that it would produce first-run episodes of *another* wisecracking-kid networker, *Webster* (starring Emmanuel Lewis), that had failed to live up to expectations of a long ABC run; as before, the new *Websters* would be sent directly into strip syndication. Most viewers couldn't tell the difference between the three series' network reruns and their made-for-syndication episodes. Some viewers couldn't tell the difference between the three series.

Small Wonder (1985–   ). Sitcom distributors were painfully aware that the big money would always go to those former network series with 100 or more episodes to their names — and that profits would have to be split with and scads of money paid out to those network series' producers. A solution was previously adopted by 1978's *Please Stand By* (see notes on "Comedies" in the 1970's section) of creating first-run syndie sitcoms to allow syndicators to tote home more of the revenue, as well as control the number of episodes produced for future rerun sales. *Please Stand By* was a bomb, but by 1985 the market for fresh first-run product was bigger than ever before, so an organization devoted to the production of new-for-syndication comedy half-hours was created, comprised of such powerful station-group concerns as Hearst, Metromedia, Gannett, Taft and Storer. This was the New Program Group—a group of such formidability that 20th Century–Fox TV listened up when the group commissioned a new non-network sitcom titled *Small Wonder*. The premise: 11-year-old Tiffany Brissette played Vicki, whose name was an anagram for "Voice Input Child Identificant." Vicki was an android assembled by computer engineer Ted Lawson (Dick Christie). For the usual reasons, Vicki's true nature had to be kept secret, so she was passed off as an adoptee of Lawson and his wife Joan (Marla Pennington). Jerry Suprian rounded out the family unit as the Lawson's natural son Jamie. The stories were predicated on the notion that little Vicki was ten times stronger and smarter than any human being, and could do anything and everything—plus, she had a conscience to make sure that "the right thing" was accomplished before each week's half-hour faded out. The scripts weren't what one could call brilliant or innovative (there were even snoops, suspiciously in the manner of *Bewitched's* Gladys Kravits and *I Dream of Jeannie's* Dr. Bellows, who forever threatened to tumble to Vicki's secret); additionally, Tiffany Brissette tried to convey the idea that she was a robot by speaking in a lifeless monotone, which for a while seemed to be the limit of the girl's acting abilities. All the same, the novelty of watching a sitcom that hadn't already been factory-tested on the networks drew many curious viewers, many of whom enjoyed the show and supported it through several seasons, during which time *Small Wonder* was frequently the Number One-rated syndie comedy. The financial and ratings rewards for the weekly *Small Wonder* revived a market for first-run syndicated comedies that had been hibernating since the early '60s, and led to the syndie-sitcom explosion that was just around the corner.

The Ted Knight Show see Too Close for Comfort

The Thames Originals: George and Mildred, Keep It in the Family, Man About the House, Robin's Nest (1983–85).

Having made a network industry out of converting the British series created by Brian Cooke into popular American sitcoms, D.L. Taffner Productions went one step further by offering for American syndication the original British series; all were produced by Thames Television, hence the package name of *Thames Originals*. *Man About the House,* the inspiration for ABC's *Three's Company,* had already been seen on a test-market basis seven years before its "official" American syndie-strip debut in 1983 (in fact, it was the strong showing of a week's worth of *Man About the House* in the New York and Los Angeles markets in 1976 that led ABC to give the go-ahead for *Three's Company*). And just as *Three's Company* inspired two spinoff series, so too had *Man About the House,* and both originals were part of the Thames package: *George and Mildred* was the English version of ABC's *The Ropers,* while *Robin's Nest* was the precursor of ABC's *Three's a Crowd.* Moving past *Three's Company* (and about time), the *Thames Originals* also included *Keep It in the Family,* the British series that provided the blueprint for *Too Close for Comfort*—also originally on ABC. The American Taffner productions wouldn't have been possible without their

British forebears; conversely, few American markets would have been interested in the *Thames Originals* without the track records of the Taffner remakes.

Throb (1986–   ). A sitcom lampoon of the recording business, *Throb* was produced and bartered by Procter and Gamble and distributed by Worldvision-Taft; it was shown on the NBC-owned stations in Saturday access and run prime-time in most other markets. Diana Canova starred as Sandy Beatty, a Buffalo divorcee who kicked over the traces and moved to New York City with son Jeremy; Sandy then took an administrative assistant job at Throb Records, a ramshackle firm run on little more than chutzpa by boss Zack (Jonathan Prince). Other Throb employees included Jane Leeves as Blue, a cockney rock singer whose deep dark secret was her advanced age (she was 27), and Robert Picardo as Rob. Appealing production values and lively cameo performances by major musical stars kept viewers from noticing that *Throb* didn't throb very much in the script department. The series emulated ABC's *Moonlighting* by having the characters comment that they knew they were on a television series and that they were saying words written by someone else. It was a device that worked only when it seemed to be off-the-cuff, and *Throb* was about as off-the-cuff as D-Day. Sy Rosen and Freddy Towbin were executive and line producer, respectively.

Too Close for Comfort (1983–86); *The Ted Knight Show* (1986). Fat and sassy thanks to *Three's Company,* ABC contracted D.L. Taffner Productions to Americanize another of Brian Cooke's British sitcoms (see *Thames Originals*). Taffner chose Cooke's *Keep It in the Family,* the story of a father who became obsessively overprotective when his sexy young daughters moved out, then moved in to the flat one floor down from the father's. ABC was looking for a vehicle for comic actor Ted Knight, so Knight became the star of Taffner's version of *Keep It in the Family,* which debuted in the fall of 1980 as *Too Close for Comfort.* Knight played newspaper cartoonist Henry Rush (a job that kept him home and in the midst of the action), Nancy Dussault was wife Muriel, and the nubile daughters were Lydia Cornell (as blonde Sarah) and Deborah Van Valkenburgh (brunette Jackie). The series took place in San Francisco, an ideal locale since it provided a steady stream of supporting characters who were either sexually overstimulated or sexually ambiguous. Amidst the series' smirks, sneers and smarms were occasional highlights like the appearances of Audrey Meadows as Ted Knight's mother-in-law and the "mid-life" pregnancy that the writers concocted for Nancy Dussault, which resulted in baby son Andrew. When sexy sitcoms wore out their welcome in 1983, *Too Close for Comfort* was cancelled. With only 63 episodes in the can, Taffner would have trouble assembling the reruns into a daily strip, so *Too Close for Comfort* became the first ex-network sitcom of the 1980's to tape additional episodes for first-run syndication — and to fatten the package. The opening episode of *Too Close's* 42 syndie installments premiered over the Metromedia stations on April 2, 1984. This was during a time that Metromedia was having fourth-network ambitions, so the company (through LBS distribution) shipped out the new episodes on a weekly basis to the rest of the country. The resulting excellent ratings opened new doors for the long-moribund syndicated sitcom market; in terms of quality (and merit), no new doors were opened on *Too Close for Comfort,* but audiences were responsive.

In April of 1986, some changes were made. The series didn't get any funnier, but it underwent some shifting of format when the two actresses playing the daughters left the show, leaving *Too Close for Comfort* without a justification for its title. So Henry and Muriel Rush were moved out of Frisco (along with another regular, the girls' addled friend Monroe Ficus, played by JM J. Bullock) and settled in Marin County, where Henry became co-owner of a small newspaper. The series was retitled *The Ted Knight Show;* new regulars included Pat Carroll as Mrs. Stinson, Henry's antagonistic partner; Lisa Antelle as an Hispanic maid; and Warren Berlinger and Beverly Sanders as Henry's co-worker Herb and wife Marsha. These pros knew how to make the most of their stock characters and wheezy old laughlines, so *The Ted Knight Show* seemed assured of a long run. But after only 22 episodes, the series came to a sudden, tragic halt when Ted Knight lost a long battle with cancer late in 1986.

The Tracey Ullman Show (1987). British singer-comedienne Tracey Ullman had had an English television variety series *(Three of a Kind)* and the 1985 song hit "They Don't Know" to her credit by the time that producer James L. *(Terms of Endearment)* Brooks and the Fox Network fashioned a half-hour weekly for her. Considering that Fox felt *The Tracey Ullman Show* enough of a winner to feature the series as one of its two "Prime Time Premiere" programs on April 5, 1987 (see also *Married . . . with Children*), and considering that hers was the only comedy-variety series on any network at the time, viewers would have been remiss if they hadn't given the girl at least one look. *The Tracey Ullman Show* tended to scare off viewers used to more conventional variety shows, wherein the star would do a monologue, bring on the guest stars, and set up the sketch situations. On *Ullman,* a sketch would frequently begin halfway through its plotline; well-known supporting actors like Julie Kavner (formerly of *Rhoda*) would be brought into the proceedings without fanfare; and so adept was Tracey Ullman at assuming a multitude of comic characters with an astonishing range of accents and ages, that the more casual viewers were often uncertain whether they were watching Ullman or some other actress! Those that stayed with the series were treated to that rare species, the show that had the decency not to imitate what everyone else was doing on the air. The only detraction was the dreadfully unfunny animated sequences used as buffers between the sketches. Hardly a household word in 1986, Tracey Ullman walked away with an Emmy and a whole new legion of fans in 1987.

Wayne and Shuster (1980). In the spirit of *Benny Hill,* the 80 half-hours of Taffner's *Wayne and Shuster* were culled from several 60- to 90-minute Canadian television specials. Johnny Wayne and Frank Shuster, who'd been entertaining Canada since the '40s and had been familiarized to the

United States through *The Ed Sullivan Show* in the '50s and '60s, suffered more than most comedians from the fragmentation of their work, since their routines were carefully paced for the more relaxed rhythm of longer running times, and often played from 20 to 45 minutes before building to a punchline. Also, the intellectual and literary references used by the team (one of their best bits was a restaging of Shakespeare in a baseball setting) were often lost on the meat-and-potatoes *Benny Hill* fans to whom Taffner usually aimed its imports.

We Got It Made (1987). Described accurately by one critic as "the ultimate bimbo show," *We Got It Made* first oiled its way through a brief NBC run in 1983. Matt McCoy and Tom Villard played two NYC roommates who advertised for a housekeeper, hired one named Mickey McKenzie, and horrified their girlfriends when Mickey turned out to be a well-endowed young lady (played by Teri Copley). Viewers who couldn't anticipate the sort of complications that sprang from this concept had probably never seen a situation comedy in their lives. The only surprise was that the series was seen on NBC and not 1983's repository of dreck, ABC. Though its first-week ratings were quite good, *We Got It Made* rapidly supplanted 1965's *My Mother the Car* as prime candidate for the worst-ever sitcom, and wore out its welcome with equal rapidity. In 1987, the NBC-owned channels sent out a call for first-run comedy material to checkerboard in access time (see *Marblehead Manor*). Executive producer Fred Silverman revitalized his old *We Got It Made,* fashioned a pilot, and won out over 70 other pilots. (God only knows how wretched those programs must have been.) Back again for MGM-UA's syndicated *We Got It Made* was Teri Copley, older but just as pulchritudinous as ever in the role of Mickey, and Tom Villard as spacey, useless-merchandise dealer Jay Bostwick. John Hilner replaced Matt McCoy as lawyer David Tucker. The new series was usually taped before a live audience, and most of the dirty chuckles emanating from the crowd seemed to suggest that the audience was corralled from the local house of corrections. *We Got It Made* was selected as the Friday night entry in the NBC stations' checkerboard lineup, a decision ultimately proving fatal to NBC's 8 p.m. Friday entry, *Rags to Riches.*

Webster **see** *Silver Spoons*

What a Country! (1986). Russian-born Yakov Smirnoff (a stage name for a largely unpronounceable real name), a top comedian in his native land, fled to the United States when his jokes failed to amuse the Soviet higher-ups. Mastering English in no time at all, Smirnoff scored a hit in America with his self-deprecating monologues about life in Russia and about the adventures of an alien in the states. Smirnoff was sworn in as an American citizen along with thousands of other applicants during the televised celebration of the Statue of Liberty's centennial in July of 1986, an event that proved advantageous for the sales of a syndicated sitcom starring Yakov Smirnoff, *What a Country!* This Viacom/Primetime/Tribune offering, inspired by the British sitcom *Mind Your Language,* debuted in the fall of '86. Smirnoff played Nikolai, a Russian emigre attending an American citizenship class. Supporting Smirnoff were Garrett M. Brown and Gail Stickland as teachers, and a melting-pot crew of classmates including George Murdock as Lazlo, pro tennis star Vijay Amritraj as Ali, Donna Dixon as the traditional sexy Swede Inga, Leila Hee Olson as Yung Hi, and Daniel Reyes (also a semiregular on *Miami Vice*) as Victor, an Hispanic. A strong cast indeed — *too* strong. *What a Country* was supposed to be a vehicle for Yakov Smirnoff, but the poor fellow barely got a word in edgewise — especially when center stage was taken by the funniest of the supporting players, Harry Waters Jr., who played Robert, a self-absorbed young man who'd been a royal prince in his own African country but who had to fend for himself in the United States. Mid-season, Don Knotts was brought in as "cast insurance" in the role of Bud McPherson, an ex-marine who tried to use boot-camp tactics on the night-school class as the school's principal. Not only was Knotts' character irritating, but it tended to drive Yakov Smirnoff further into the background. Perhaps Smirnoff was better off keeping a low profile, for *What a Country!* was a labored effort, predicated on the premise that foreigners had funny accents and seemed to be bumblers but were okay when the chips were down. Yakov Smirnoff continued to pack 'em in on the comedy-concert circuit, but *What a Country!* proved an insufficient passport for Smirnoff's TV-series stardom.

What's Happening Now!! (1985–86). Colex (Columbia TV and LBS) started its syndie-sitcom career with a 1985 exhumation of an ABC series, *What's Happening!,* which first was seen from 1976 through '79. Though it claimed to be inspired by the gritty, street-smart 1975 film *Cooley High,* the original *What's Happening!* looked more like *The Bowery Boys in Blackface.* The stars, all of them supposed to be students in a predominantly black Los Angeles high school but all of whom looked well past the age of consent, were Ernest Thomas as Raj, Haywood Nelson Jr. as Dwayne, and tubby Fred Berry as comedy-relief Rerun. (A situation comedy with comedy relief. It was that kind of show.) Mabel King as Raj's Mom and Shirley Hemphill as a wisecracking waitress at the boys' local hangout were excellent, but Danielle Spencer quickly won the honor of the Most Obnoxious Brat of 1977 in her role as Raj's kid sister Dee. Like many black sitcoms of the era, *What's Happening!* had an overabundance of put-downs and one-liners, with plotlines neatly tied up with moralizing, coping, hugging and a lot of "Awwwwwws" on the laughtrack. Subtle it wasn't, but the series did well in reruns, especially in big markets like New York and Chicago. When Colex looked around in 1985, it discovered that virtually all of *What's Happening's* leading actors were "between projects" and at liberty: the result was *What's Happening Now!!* Raj was now married to Nadine (Anne-Marie Johnson); Dwayne was a computer programmer; Shirley Hemphill was now the owner of the diner where she previously had been employed; Danielle Spencer was still pitching jokes at any and all targets as the grown-up (but no more appealing) Dee; and Fred "Rerun" Berry had grown up(?) as a used-car salesman. *What's Happening Now!!* breezed through its first season, and all might have been smooth at renewal time had not Fred Berry decided to pull a "Suzanne Somers." Indicating that he'd have been better off speaking through a press agent, Berry publicly balked at the measly $5000 per episode he was getting (in all fairness, this *was* measly by network-television standards), but just when a mutual agreement between the actor and the producers was about to be reached, Berry declared to the press that he wouldn't work for less than $20,000 per show. And then he iced the cake by saying "I'm the most popular person on the show, and I know it!" The producers didn't see things as clearly as Berry saw them; they fired Berry on the spot, and *What's Happening Now!!* did just fine without "Rerun" for its second season.

The Wilton-North Report see notes on *The Late Show with Joan Rivers* in the 1980's "Talk-Interview" Section.

Women in Prison (1987). The absolute nadir of the Fox Network sitcoms, Embassy's *Women in Prison* was thrust upon an unwilling public on October 11, 1987. Julia Campbell played a pretty, pampered young wife whose slimy lawyer husband (Thomas Callaway) got her thrown into the slammer on a phony shoplifting charge. The tough cons and merciless guards were played by Peggy Cass, C.C.H. Pounder, Holly Colburn, Denny Dillon and Wendy Jo Sperber, talented actresses all who didn't deserve the dreck served to them by this poor excuse for a comedy. Viewers could have gotten more laughs by watching an old Ida Lupino prison picture on *The Late Show*.

You Can't Take It With You (1987). This was Procter and Gamble/LBS' Wednesday night offering for the NBC stations' access checkerboard lineup (see *Marblehead Manor*). *You Can't Take It with You* had originally been a 1936 Pulitzer Prize-winning play by Moss Hart and George S. Kaufman; it told of a zany family who, in the middle of a depression, ignored money and did just what they pleased, disdaining the crumbling, tradition-bound world around them. The play dates rather painfully when seen today, and is so reliant on its Depression-era framework that attempts to update the work have always come a-cropper. This didn't stop the television-series version of *You Can't Take It with You* from planting the eccentric characters into the 1980's. In an era where everyone did what they felt like doing anyway, the leading characters, a family named Sycamore, seemed more aloof and preoccupied then genuinely zany. The otherwise reliable Harry Morgan appeared over-rehearsed and underenthused as Grandpa Vanderhoff, head of the Sycamore clan (evidently confusing Kaufman and Hart with Thornton Wilder, the producers saddled Morgan with *Our Town*-like direct-to-audience monologues). The equally accomplished Lois Nettleton was merely vacant in the potentially whimsical role of dilettante authoress Penny Sycamore, while Richard Sanders suffered by having his character of Penny's husband Paul transformed from the hobby-happy tinkerer of the play to the boobish inventor of such useless items as a "talking dartboard." Heather Blodgett as Essie Sycamore and Teddy Wilson as Mr. Pinner (a combination of the play's Mr. DePinna and Donald the Handyman) were other talented cast members whose characters were rendered tiresome by reducing them to a cliched sitcom level. Executive

producer Hal Kanter (recently the head writer for Bob Hope) and director Norman Abbott (of *Sanford and Son* fame) kept the doings on *You Can't Take It
with You* moving at a swift pace, but somehow with no real sense of enjoyment. In fact, the only "sense" one derived from the series was of a lot of potent
talent being wasted.

Whether or not this series, or any of the other NBC stations' checker-
boarded sitcoms, had any real merit was a moot point. In late December of
1987, the NBC Station Group executives took a long hard look at their access
time ratings and realized that none of the five new shows were even within
shouting distance of the ratings of *Wheel of Fortune*. It was decided that the
checkerboard concept would be abandoned in the fall of 1988 (and three of the
five syndie sitcoms cancelled), and that the NBC channels would try to beat out
Wheel of Fortune with a new version of *Family Feud*. And to think that there
once was a time that some people actually believed that the Prime Time Access
Rule would result in radically innovative programming.

Drama

Dominating this genre in the '80s was the return of the courtroom
drama, a phenomenon brought about by *The People's Court*. Though this
series was technically a "reality" show, it will be regarded in these pages as
a drama, since its producers' policy of whittling down each court case to
fit *People's Court's* half-hour time slot accommodated Alfred Hitchcock's
definition of drama as "real life with the dull parts cut out."

Fame (1983–87). To paraphrase its theme song, *Fame* began "living
forever" as a 1980 MGM movie, ostensibly about the lives and loves of the
students and faculty of New York's High School of the Performing Arts, but
mostly about a lot of talented kids who broke into production numbers at a
moment's notice. NBC's weekly 60-minute version of *Fame* began its run in
1982, where it built up a wide-eyed youthful following. Young, would-be
"stars" loved to vicariously live their lives through the showbiz hopefuls on the
series, even though *Fame* took some liberties with reality. (The actual performing arts high school upon which the locale of the series was based did not give
weekly public performances, but such events, usually staged beyond the means
of *any* high school, were the order of the day on *Fame*.) Carried over from the
movie version were Debbie Allen as the tough disciplinarian dance instructor
Lydia Grant (Allen also choreographed the series' dance numbers); famed
composer-conductor Albert Hague as iconoclastic music teacher Benjamin
Shorofsky; and Lee Curreri and Gene Anthony Ray as two of the gifted
students. Though *Fame* withered in the ratings, its teenaged fan-following was
sufficient for MGM-UA and LBS Communications to keep the series alive after
its network demise in the form of a weekly syndie. Metromedia got in on the
act, hoping that *Fame* would serve as the cornerstone for its planned "fourth
network." A budget cut on the series went by virtually unnoticed, and *Fame*

went on to even greater glory as a non-network attraction, though by this time the series had lost most of its contact with real life and was indulging in an episode based on "A Christmas Carol" (has there ever been a weekly show that hasn't done one of those?) and an installment in which one of the kids discovered that he was the spitting image of a young foreign prince, leading to a Manhattan version of *The Prisoner of Zenda!* The main attraction on *Fame* remained the production numbers, which suggested that at the very least, Bob Fosse and Busby Berkeley were on the high school's tenured staff.

Most of the cast of NBC's *Fame* made the transition to the syndie version, among them the aforementioned Debbie Allen, Albert Hague, Lee Curreri and Gene Anthony Ray, as well as "faculty members" like Carol Mayo Jenkins (as English teacher Elizabeth Sherwood) and the students portrayed by Valerie Landsburg and Carol Imperato. New students over the years have included Cynthia Gibb, Billy Hufsey, Jesse Borego, Nia Peeples, Elisa Heinsohn, Tanya Fenmore, Michael Cerveris, Michael Jackson's sister Janet and Carol Burnett's daughter Carrie Hamilton (who was joined by her mother in a rousing rendition of "We're a Couple of Swells" on one of *Fame's* final episodes in 1987). In an effort to inject some dramatic conflict on the series, Ken Swofford was added to the cast in 1983 as vice-principal Morloch, who saw his appointment to the high school as an insult and did everything he could to thwart the students' desires to artistically express themselves (that was like the principal of a manual arts school denying his students the right to build furniture, but as we've already said, reality was not *Fame's* strong suit). Off-screen, Swofford was one of the series' biggest boosters, even after he was written out of the show and replaced by Graham Jarvis as vice-principal Dyrenforth. In its last season, *Fame* added Eric Pierpont as a new faculty member, a disillusioned actor who'd recently turned to cabdriving. *Fame* left the air in 1987, a victim not of drooping ratings but of budgets in excess of profits. During its four-run syndie run, the series was deservedly honored with several Emmies; despite its plotline shortcomings, *Fame* was a shining beacon of youth, talent and imagination, and a welcome relief to the game-and-talk syndrome afflicting the non-network world of 1983.

Guilty or Innocent (1984). This absurd combination of courtroom drama and game show from Genesis/Colbert was comprised of a 15-minute reenactment (in grade-school pageant style) of a real-life court case, followed by a session wherein contestants had to figure out the trial's outcome. Whoever guessed correctly was showered with the sort of big cash prizes that game shows dispense like jellybeans. Hosting the daily *Guilty or Innocent* was attorney Melvin F. Belli, with John Shearin moderating the quiz portion. At the time, Belli was quoted as saying that *Guilty or Innocent* was "a hell of a lot better" than fellow attorney F. Lee Bailey's recent syndie flop, *Lie Detector* (which see). Bailey said nothing, allowing *Guilty or Innocent* to hang itself.

The Judge (1986–). As *Guilty or Innocent* has just demonstrated, the popularity of *The People's Court* (which see) reinstated the market for courtroom syndies. Unlike *People's Court,* most of the new dailies were in some way or other fictionalized: *Divorce Court* (see "Drama" notes in the chapter on the 1950's) had a real judge and real attorneys, but the litigants were actors; *Superior Court* (which see) had a real judge, but the litigants *and* attorneys were actors. Sandy Frank and Gary Ganaway's *The Judge* (from Genesis/Colbert) had not one solitary "real" participant. Actor Robert Franklin starred as Judge Robert Shields, and the reenacted cases brought before him were usually of the child-custody variety; the series had, in fact, started production as *Custody Court,* and there were rumors that the original intention was to display *genuine* custody hearings, tears, anguish and all (wouldn't *that* have been American Television at its best?). The actors on *Judge* playing the lawyers and contestants played in a manner not seen since the last road-show production of *East Lynne,* and the series, though supposedly based on fact, was topheavy with soap-opera contrivances and Dickensian coincidences. *The Judge* was the outgrowth of an access time weekly locally produced by WBNS-TV in Columbus, Ohio.

Lie Detector (1983). "What *60 Minutes* is to network TV," *Lie Detector* would be to daily syndication, promised the trade ads. Attorney F. Lee Bailey, ever willing to parade before the cameras, hosted, costarring with polygraph expert (and series creator) Ed Gelb. Gelb's polygraph was supposed to determine whether or not the claims of guest contestants were true or false. But we didn't know any more about the veracity of Melvin Dummar's claim that he'd been willed a fortune by Howard Hughes after his *Lie Detector* appearance than before, nor did the convicted criminals who volunteered to be strapped to the polygraph accomplish any more than a brief vacation from the slammer. Sandy Frank Productions handled this one; they can't lie their way out of it.

People's Court (1981–   ). Here's the Edwards-Billett/Telepictures series that started it all. One wonders if *People's Court* would have enjoyed its popularity and longevity (which after seven seasons in 1987 showed no signs of abatement) had the series been picked up by the network which wanted to make a few "minor" alterations in its format. Instead of a real judge listening to real small-claim cases, this network wanted to have comically re-enacted hearings, with Nipsey Russell playing the prosecutor and Charles Nelson Reilly as the defense attorney! Happily, producers Ralph Edwards and Stu Billett opted for syndication and went with the original concept of series creator John Masterton, who'd done all right with the "reality" concept on the old CBS game show *Bride and Groom* (which frequently culminated in an on-camera wedding). Besides, "reality shows" were all the rage in 1981 thanks to *Real People* and its progeny. Selected to preside over the daily *People's Court* was a retired 61-year-old California jurist named Joseph Wapner. Judge Wapner rapidly became a celebrity in his own right, as did host-narrator Doug Llewelyn (an entertainment journalist and producer, later responsible for such slices of life as Geraldo Rivera's "Al Capone's Vault" special) and court clerk Rusty Burrell. Cases on the series were chosen from some twenty small-claim courts within a 60-minutes'-drive-radius from *Court's* studio; from these, those cases with the most audience appeal (such as the oft-quoted case of a stripper who was sued for an allegedly inadequate performance at a stag party) were selected for television exposure. The contestants chosen agreed to waive their rights to a court trial in exchange for cash compensation for appearing on television. Wapner's decisions were binding, but since both plaintiff and defendant were paid for their "performances," no one really went home broke, though some losers were out of joint after losing in front of a nationwide audience.

People's Court was an instant hit, but not without its detractors. Critics griped that Judge Wapner was unduly harsh on the litigants, bullying them into proper court behavior, and that many of the series' participants who seemed most deserving of courtroom victory went down to defeat. Actually, Wapner's gruff act was reserved only for those who came into court ill prepared, or who refused to behave like adults. (On one show, Wapner remonstrated with a loudmouthed plaintiff for his obnoxious behavior *after* the plaintiff had won his case.) And the fact that some of the more likeable litigants lost their cases merely proved what the series allegedly set out to prove, that you'd better have your court arguments well thought out or you'll lose, deserving or no. Not by any means a "hanging judge," Wapner held fast to strict rules of evidence, and if your evidence was shaky or nonexistent, that was too bad (though in cases where *both* litigants' evidence was shaky or nonexistent, Wapner relied on his own gut feelings as to whose story held the most credibility). Another complaint was that Wapner rushed through his cases to adhere to *People's Court's* half-hour format. This complaint was not only fatuous but ill-informed, since there was a careful disclaimer at the end of each installment that the cases were often edited for time before telecast. Wapner always gave the litigants ample time to prove their cases — as well as make fools of themselves.

Prisoner: Cell Block H (1980). Nightly serial, produced by Reg Grundy, which premiered in its native Australia as *Prisoner* in February of 1979. (Australia is a country devoted to prime-time serials; among its most popular television attractions of the '70s were reruns of America's *Peyton Place*.) Set in a violence-prone women's prison, the series told of the sexual and emotional travails of the wardens and guards (played with varying degrees of compassion and sadism by Patsy King, Gerald McGuire and Fiona Spence) and the prisoners (foremost among them convicted murderer "Queen Bea" Smith, played to the hilt by Val Lehmann). The series' frankness in matters of sex and violence went over better in Australia than they would have on American network TV, but Firestone Sales, anxious to find something that would match the popularity of *Mary Hartman, Mary Hartman,* picked up *Prisoner* for stateside syndication anyway, tacking *Cell Block H* to the title so as not to confuse the series with the cult-favorite vehicle for Patrick McGoohan, *The Prisoner*. Firestone test-marketed the serial on a Monday-through-Friday basis over KTLA–Los Angeles in August 1979, where its excellent ratings justified a nationwide syndication starting in January 1980. *Prisoner: Cell Block H* did just fine whenever it played in prime time or access, but the media watchdogs were up in arms over the essential sleaziness of the project (including *TV Guide,* which editorialized against the series while some of its regional editions accepted advertising for the show). Under fire from the professional cleaner-uppers, most markets ran *Prisoner* very late at night, where it languished and died after about a year. We would say that the serial got what it deserved, but that might suggest that there weren't equally offensive American-made series pumping through the airwaves at the same time.

Rituals (1984–85). Another attempt to restore life to the syndie-serial form which hadn't really flourished since the 1977 demise of *Mary Hartman, Mary Hartman.* Set in a Virginia college town (though exteriors were taped in North Carolina), Metromedia/Telepictures' *Rituals* was one of those "the world is full of sexy predators" yarns, its chief predator played by Christina Jones. The strong cast included Tina Louise, Julie Sommars, Peter Haskell, and Sharon Farrell; Jo Ann Pflug played a major part until her born-again Christianity compelled her to exit the tawdry plot proceedings. *Rituals* also featured the sort of "stunt casting" that would guarantee some viewers would tune in on occasion out of sheer curiosity. George Lazenby, famous as a one-time-only movie James Bond, played a leading role, as did ex–*Mary Hartman* lead Greg Mullavey and Olivia Newton-John's then-boyfriend Matt Littanzi. Patti Davis, Ronald Reagan's daughter, was supposed to have had a recurring role, but her alleged lack of artistic discipline put the kibosh on that. To curry journalistic favor, executive producer Frank Koenigsberg invited a number of TV critics to appear as well-fed extras in one of the party scenes; but the press wasn't to be bought that easily, especially with the below-average refreshments they received. Desperate for the big ratings that never came, the producers ran a mid-season contest, allowing viewers to vote on which of *Rituals'* characters should live and which should be killed off. Few viewers were interested in playing God, even with cash prizes involved. So almost a year to the day that the daily series debuted (on September 10, 1984), *Rituals* closed up camp on the Columbia-Burbank lot.

Romance Theatre (1982). The NBC-owned stations were very keen on this daily drama from Commworld International, but before long they (like most other buying stations) were running off this loser in "fringe" time-periods. *Romance Theatre* can be termed a semi-soap or a mini-serial; each of its stories, based on the works of the Romance Writers of America Guild, was wrapped up after five half-hour installments. Louis Jourdan hosted, and there were such ratings-boosting gimmicks as casting Ronald Reagan's daughter Patti Davis (who later proved as talented a writer as she was an actress), in several roles, and a brief contest permitting viewers to nominate "The Most Romantic Couple in America." Problem: the producers of the series made an inviolate promise to the viewers that each of the five-part stories would end happily, and what true soap-opera fan really wanted to see *that?*

The Sullivans (1980). Anticipating that Australia's *Prisoner: Cell Block H* (which see) would score a hit, T.A.T./Embassy, the same concern that had distributed *Mary Hartman, Mary Hartman,* acquired American television rights for another Aussie soaper, Crawford Productions' *The Sullivans.* The serial was set during World War II, and the titular family was played by Paul Cronin, Lorraine Bayly, Andrew McFarlane, Steven Tandy, Richard Morgan and Susan Hannaford. Though well produced, *The Sullivans* lasted about as long in the states as did *Prisoner: Cell Block H:* the market for syndie serials was nonexistent by mid–1980.

Superior Court (1986–   ). With its *People's Court* going great guns, Edwards-Billett/Lorimar-Telepictures offered another courtroomer into the daily-syndie pool, *Superior Court*. Genuine jurist William E. Burns presided (his role taken over by a rotating cast of guest judges for Season Two); the cases were allegedly "drawn from the headlines," and the lawyers, litigants and spectators were actors, usually actors of the waving-arm furrowed-brow category. The soap-opera style dialogue heard on the series was supplied by its producer-writers, William and Joyce Covington, whose previous credits included such serials as *Capitol, General Hospital, One Life to Live, Search for Tomorrow,* and the unlamented syndie *Rituals.* While *Superior Court* went through the motions of presenting several potent legal issues of the late '80s, its honorable intentions were often laid low by the histrionics.

Tales from the Darkside (1984–   ). One of the few successful efforts at reviving the horror/science fiction anthology motif for the '80s (*Amazing Stories* and the revivals of *Twilight Zone* and *Alfred Hitchcock Presents,* network programs all, failed to attract crowds), *Tales from the Darkside* benefitted from the creative input of executive producer George Romero. The producer-director-writer who finessed a cheap little 1968 chiller called *Night of the Living Dead* into a thriving film career, Romero imbued *Tales from the Darkside* with all of his by-now familiar trademarks: the anthology was scary, unpretentious, made the most of its low budget, and it possessed a jet-black sense of humor. The series premiered as a one-shot special titled "Trick or Treat" (the original name of *Darkside* when it was being prepared for a potential sale to CBS), which ran during the obvious October weekend in 1983 and starred Barnard Hughes as a despotic moneylender whose sadistic Halloween pranks eventually backfired. Stars of the series proper (which began its run in the fall of 1984) included such time-saving pros as E.G. Marshall, Jerry Stiller, Tammy Grimes, David Huddleston and, in a 1985 episode tied in with the return of Halley's comet, Fritz Weaver as the ghost of Halley himself, riding in on the tail of the cosmic phenomenon bearing his name. Jerry Gorod and Rick Rubinstein were the line producers for the 92 *Tales from the Darkside* installments, which ran first as weekly, then were run as a daily rerun strip starting in 1987. The series was a Tribune/Laurel/JayGee Production for LBS release.

Tales of the Haunted (1981). For every success like *Tales from the Darkside,* there were a multitude of neverweres. Barry-Enright/Colbert offered a five-day trial run of *Tales of the Haunted,* hosted by Jack Palance. The first and last terror on this busted pilot was "Evil in the House," in which Palance also starred.

True Confessions (1986). Bill Bixby, who'd run the television gamut as the Favorite Martian's nephew, Eddie's Father, and the Magician, hosted this expensive (but not very expensive-looking) Alan Landsburg production, seen Monday through Friday. Each day, a different heart-tugging tale from the pages of *True Confessions* Magazine was dramatized, covering a wide range of topics from sex to sensationalism to sex. Ironic for a series with the word "True" in its title was its team of producers, Terry Keegan and Arthur Fellowes, best known for their mini-series *Washington: Behind Closed Doors,* a comic-book version of H.R. Haldeman's novel of a Nixonish presidential administration. Stars of the half-hour Entertainment McNuggets seen on *True Confessions* ranged from reliables like Burgess Meredith, Mickey Rooney, June Lockhart, Shelley Winters and Robert Culp, to "incredibles" like Marjoe Gortner and Engelbert Humperdinck. King World distributed; after six months, King World was grateful indeed that it still had *Wheel of Fortune* and *The Oprah Winfrey Show* to pay the bills.

Young Lives (1981). Extremely brief soap opera, test-run on some 16 stations by Post-Newsweek and attempting to dramatize the genuine difficulties of teenage life. Older viewers were of the opinion that the problems of teens were "off-color" and had no business infesting the airwaves. These viewers preferred the clean, wholesome entertainment offered by *General Hospital* and *One Life to Live.*

Game/Quiz

The entries in this section will be confined to those game shows which debuted in syndication during or after 1980. Readers wishing to bone up on the '80s careers of such favorites as *Truth or Consequences, Family Feud* and *The Newlywed Game* are referred to the Game/Quiz notes in the chapters on the '60s and '70s.

Anything for Money! (1984). Hosted by comedian Fred Travalena, Paramount's *Anything for Money!* combined the worst aspects of *Real People* and *Candid Camera.* The daily series took to the streets to prove that people would undergo any display of aberrant behavior or humiliation for financial rewards. After indulging in such stunts as pretending to enjoy eating a pudding that tasted like last year's tennis shoes, the "real people" were handed large sums of paper money and congratulated for being such good sports. (Once the cameras were turned off, the money was taken back and cashier's checks were substituted, the proffering of cold cash being for the titillation of the home viewers.) Evidently the one thing the producers couldn't get a lot of people to do for love *or* money was watch *Anything for Money!;* it survived past 1985 only on cable-TV reruns.

Bullseye (1980). A Colbert release, emceed by Jim Lange. The object was to answer questions chosen from three spinning wheels—one of which spun out of control on one episode, providing the high point of this indifferent effort.

Camouflage (1980). Futile attempt by Worldvision and host Tom Campbell to generate interest in the old ABC network "hidden picture" game show of the 1960's.

Card Sharks (1982; 1986). Jonathan M. Goodson, scion of a famous game-producing family, created this game show for CBS daytime in 1978, wherein contestants tried to guess if a card was of higher or lower value than the card preceding it. The 1982 syndie version, a Mark Goodson/Firestone release, was hosted by Jim Perry and retained the network format. The 1986 non-network revival, hosted by Bill Rafferty and distributed by Lorimar-Telepictures, added the "Family Feud" angle of allowing contestants to play the card game only after correctly determining how a group of 100 people would answer specific questions.

Catch Phrase (1985); *Perfect Match* (1986). Telepictures' highly touted game show release of 1985, produced by Marty Pasetta, top-billed Art James, who presided over a video-screen tic-tac-toe game. *Catch Phrase's* last-word technology enabled its producers to promote the series as the most up-to-date game show on the market; they even went so far as to offer an "insurance policy" to local buying stations. Should *Catch Phrase* not be a major success, Telepictures would provide a free-of-charge replacement. *Catch Phrase* wasn't even a minor success, so Telepictures had to make good its promise in January 1986 with *Perfect Match,* a "choose-the-ideal-date" panel show. *Perfect Match* did fairly well in the ratings, and might have been extended into a second season had not Chuck Barris brought about legal action by claiming that *Perfect Match* was a rip-off of Barris' *Dating Game* and *Newlywed Game.*

Chance of a Lifetime see *The $1,000,000 Chance of a Lifetime*

Every Second Counts (1984). A Group W-produced quizzer hosted by Bill Rafferty, in which couples "won time" in order to compete for a $20,000 prize.

Face the Music (1980). This was the first "in-house" production from Sandy Frank; that is, Frank not only distributed *Face the Music,* but put the show before the cameras in the first place. Ron *(Tarzan)* Ely presided as famous song titles, matched with celebrity photographs, resulted in off-color comments from the contestants. That's all.

Headline Chasers (1985). From the purveyors of *Wheel of Fortune,* Griffin Productions and King World, came this daily hosted by co-producer Wink Martindale. The contestants had to complete a "newspaper headline" ("_____ Crosses the Atlantic"), or guess what the headline was about ("_____ Crosses the _____").

Joker! Joker!! Joker!!! (1980). Weekend children's version of Barry-Enright/Colbert's *Joker's Wild* (see "Game/Quiz" in the 1970's section), hosted, like its parent program, by Jack Barry.

Lingo (1987). The main attraction of this minor-league build-the-word game from A. Burt Rosen Productions was its host, President Reagan's son Michael.

Love Connection (1983–   ). Developed by creator Eric Lieber under the titillating cognomen *For Singles Only,* Telepictures' *Love Connection* was a smirk-filled but successful daily based upon video dating; couples matched up via their videotaped "resumes" would come back on the show after their dates to give the audience the low-down. Chuck Woolery hosted.

Matchmaker (1987). First offered by Four Star TV in 1985, this *Dating Game*-style quizzer was hosted by Dave Hull, who as the "matchmaker" of the title paired up six singles who could neither see each other nor be seen themselves. The pairing was accomplished on the basis of answered questions. In many markets, those who cared had to stay up quite late to experience *Matchmaker.*

The $100,000 Pyramid see *$25,000 Pyramid* in the 1970's "Game/Quiz" section.

The $1,000,000 Chance of a Lifetime (1986–   ). The first "in-house" production of the distribution firm of Telepictures (just before that company's lucrative merger with Lorimar), *The $1,000,000 Chance of a Lifetime* was the newest version of a venerable giveaway show first seen from 1950 through '56. Its million-buck ante was the largest cash prize of any game show to date, and *Lifetime's* producer Bob Synes was quoted as saying that he hoped there wouldn't be any winning streaks that would bankrupt the program. Jim Lange was the daily's host.

Perfect Match see *Catch Phrase*

Play the Percentages (1980). *Family Feud* stuff again, this time produced by Barry-Enright, released by Colbert, and emceed by Geoff Edwards. A $25,000 jackpot awaited winners who successfully matched answers to questions in accordance with answers given by a certain percentage of a previously surveyed group.

The Pop 'n' Rocker Game (1983). Jon Bauman, formerly the duck-tailed "Bowzer" of the rock group *Sha Na Na,* hosted this MCA weekly, an R-and-R variation of *Name That Tune.*

So You Think You Got Troubles?! (1982). From Edwards-Billett/Telepictures. Ventriloquist Jay Johnson, who had with his dummy Squeaky hosted 1979's *Celebrity Charades,* pulled another of his wooden pals, "Bob," out of the suitcase to emcee *So You Think...etc.* "Real people" with problems ranging from hilarious to heartrending asked a panel of experts how to grapple with those problems. Then, to compete for big prizes, the people with the problems had to guess which of the experts' solutions went along with the majority opinion of the studio audience. Sort of an "I'm okay if everyone says I'm okay" endeavor. The sole redeeming factor of *So You Think You got Troubles?!* was that it got enough markets to keep an even stupider game-show daily, *That... Quiz Show,* off the air.

Starcade (1983); **Video Game** (1984). Ted Turner, busy with his own Atlanta "superstation" and various cable services, found time to syndicate *Starcade,* a video arcade game contest hosted by Geoff Edwards. Neither this nor Edwards-Billett/Viacom's *Video Game* (emceed by Greg Winfield and Karen Lea) survived the eventual cooling off of the video-arcade mania.

Strike It Rich (1986). Not to be confused with a 1950's series of the same title which wallowed in human misery (with fabulous prizes for the unfortunates), Blair Communications' syndicated *Strike It Rich* was a simple man vs. woman quiz session. Gimmicks included a million-dollar grand prize (matched only by the earlier release *Chance of a Lifetime,* which see), a "bandit" figure who popped up electronically on-screen to whisk away winnings from those who guessed wrong, and an arch made up of nine video screens. Joe Garagiola presided.

Take My Word for It (1982). San Francisco-based gamefest given small-scale syndication by Worldvision. Celebrity panelists tried to bluff contestants with ludicrous definitions of obscure words.

Video Game see *Starcade*

Wheel of Fortune (1983–   ). As of this writing the highest-rated daily syndicated series of all time, *Wheel of Fortune* had a modest beginning. Based by producer-creator Merv Griffin on an old children's word game called "Hangman," this spin-the-wheel, choose-the-letter, guess-the-phrase-and-get-rich affair premiered on the NBC daytime schedule in 1975 doing adequate but far from spectacular business. Chuck Woolery (replacing the star of the pilot, Edd "Kookie" Byrnes) hosted, with Susan Stafford as the game's letter-turner. In 1982, Pat Sajak took over (though according to Merv Griffin, Sajak made no impression at all with the NBC executives) as host; Susan Stafford retired from show business and was replaced by a comely blonde model, Vanna White, whose previous connection with game shows had been as a contestant on *The Price Is Right.* Merv Griffin decided at this time to syndicate a nightly *Wheel of Fortune* to improve its revenue, but found that few distributors were interested; besides, the top-dog game syndie of the time was *Family Feud,* and no non-network gamefest had yet been able to compete with *Family Feud* and live. Griffin found a distributor literally at the bottom of the barrel: King

World, a hotel-room operation with little more than the *Little Rascals* theatrical shorts to its name, felt it had nothing to lose by taking on *Wheel of Fortune*. Determining that trying to saturate all 200-plus syndie markets at once would result in unmanageable expense, not to mention inadequate time slots in large markets already glutted with game show product, King World decided to pitch *Wheel* only to those stations who evinced a genuine interest — which meant only nine stations in 1983. Within a few months, the series had 50 markets in its manifest, though three of the biggest markets, New York, Chicago, and Los Angeles, still saw no promise in the program. And then the miracle happened: *Wheel of Fortune* began beating *Family Feud* in those cities which ran the programs opposite one another in access time. Since the NBC-owned stations shortsightedly held firm to the ailing *Family Feud* in the larger markets, the newly desirable *Wheel of Fortune* was gobbled up by the NBC stations' eager competitors — particularly the ABC-owned. By 1985, *Family Feud* was heading toward the Exit, and *Wheel of Fortune* was Number One, where it remained for several seasons to come.

Determined not to mess up a good thing, King World did some research to find out just why *Wheel* was so popular. (Merv Griffin was usually averse to "market research," but only when the experts would tell him ahead of time what *wouldn't* work rather than tell him how to take advantage of what *did* work.) The multitude of reasons for success seemed to boil down to "Please One, Please All." *Wheel* appealed to fans of shows where no particular talent was needed to be a contestant, since the players' progress was determined mainly by the luck of spinning wheel. But it also appealed to fans of game shows where knowledge and intelligence were necessary, since the contestants had to figure out what the hidden words or phrases were after winning the vowels and consonants via the wheel-spinning. The contestant who guessed the answer on the puzzle-board got first dibs on the best prizes at the same time, the player won something simply by guessing which letters were hidden. Finally, the series held great appeal to folks at home who dreamed that someday, they too would be given a chance to choose from a variety of fantastic prizes after winning the game portion of the show. (In recent seasons, the choosing of prizes has been replaced by simply giving the contestants cash awards; still, it's the stuff that dreams are made on.)

King World's research also revealed that the stars of *Wheel of Fortune* were perfect and virtually irreplaceable. Pat Sajak proved the ideal emcee for a show wherein winners were given to jumping and squealing, simply because he was cool, courteous and pleasant, and never indulged in the jumping and squealing himself. Then there was lovely letter-turner Vanna White. In the first few seasons of *Wheel,* King World's publicity made little if any mention of Vanna. Then after doing its homework, the syndicator learned that it was the wholesome beauty and winning personality of Miss White that kept most of the male viewers, many of whom usually ignored game shows, tuning in. King World could have gone the obvious route of making Vanna a more vocal and active participant of the show, maybe with a little singing and dancing thrown in. Wisely, they retained her appeal by *not* overemphasizing it on-screen. It was up to the off-screen publicity boys to do their job with magazine articles and personal appearances for Miss White. Before 1987 was over, Vanna White had a thriving family of fan clubs, a line of women's clothing, and an autobiography to her name.

Also by 1987, the onetime last-placed King World was in the megabucks category, distributing not only *Wheel of Fortune* but other smashes like *Jeopardy* and *The Oprah Winfrey Show.* But it was *Wheel* upon which the King Empire was built, and the company has sagaciously left the program's format alone, avoiding the tinkering, tampering and gimmickry that have ruined many other television property. The day will come eventually that *Wheel of Fortune* will revolve no longer. (It was losing some of its audience by 1988, even though its 35 percent share of the audience was still the envy of the industry.) One hopes that the series' death will be one with quiet dignity, and not self-destruction by excess, the sad fate that befell *Family Feud* with its last desperate efforts to knock off the upstart *Wheel of Fortune* before *Feud's* own demise in 1985.

Win, Lose or Draw (1987). When movie star Burt Reynolds dreamed up this Buena Vista–released daily, he claimed it evolved from a parlor game he'd played with friends in his living room; indeed, the set of *Win, Lose or Draw* was a carbon copy of that selfsame room. The presence in the first week's episodes of Reynolds himself, along with his future bride Loni Anderson, made the whole thing seem like an elaborate home video. The game was to have celebrity and "civilian" contestants guess a word, phrase, or popular song or what-have-you on the basis of the other contestants' hastily drawn sketches on an easel. If you've recognized this as a variation of 1969's *Fast Draw,* then you've read the 1960's section thoroughly. The "artists" on *Win, Lose or Draw* were at their most entertaining when they could draw very well, or when they drew as if their fingers had been broken at birth. Co-producer Bert Convy hosted, working with Spartan-like diligence to convince the viewers that he and the contestants were having the best possible time in the world. An NBC network daily version of *Win, Lose or Draw,* which ran concurrently, was hosted by Vicki Lawrence.

You Bet Your Life (1980). Hill-Eubanks/SFM had the unmitigated gall to revive Groucho Marx's old quiz show without the one reason that this modest giveaway series had flourished in the '50s and '60s — namely, Groucho himself (who was admittedly dead at the time and thus unable to participate in the revival). Reasoning the Marx appeal was his way with an insult, the creators of 1980's daily *You Bet Your Life* selected as host comedian Buddy Hackett, who likewise didn't suffer fools well and said as much. But Hackett's sneering, naughty-boy comic persona wasn't anything like Groucho's raffish yet appealing curmudgeon act, nor was the syndie's announcer Ron Hussman as memorable as the original's George Fenneman. *You Bet Your Life* had been a game show where the host, not the format, prevailed, but this didn't work for the 1980 version. It's not for nothing that Groucho Marx was billed as "The One, the Only."

Informational

The overabundance of news and "magazine" shows in the 1980's was a direct result of technology. No longer did informational or instructional shows have to wait for a month, or several months, after their inception before being telecast. Thanks to the growing usage of satellite transmission, syndication could operate on the same "Day and Date" footing as had the networks for the past four decades. And as mentioned in the introduction to this decade, a larger market of new stations existed, as willing to be fed by satellite as their forebears in earlier years had been willing to be serviced by film and tape—anything to avoid the costs of producing local programs of their own.

One sort of "information" show that *doesn't* appear in the upcoming section is the magazine or documentary-style program, often hosted by a celebrity but usually emceed by a team of "investigative reporters" you've never seen before, which turns out to be a half-hour commercial for anything from a hair restorer to tinted sunglasses. These are out-and-out advertisements, without even the thin veneer of entertainment which accompanies such toy tie-in cartoon series as *He-Man* and *GI Joe,* and like those cartoon series are the results of the FCC's laissez-faire policies of the '80s.

Afternoon (1982). An attempt by the Corinthian Stations Group to cash in on the audience for programs like *Hour Magazine.*

Agronsky and Company (1980). Weekly news analysis hosted by Martin Agronsky, a television regular since the early '50s. Outside the Post-Newsweek stations, this series generally showed up unsponsored on PBS outlets.

Alive and Well (1984). After a healthy run on the USA Cable service, this daily magazine was given a syndie go by Orbis Communications. Marion Ross, Linda Arkin and Mike Jerrick were regular hosts, with frequent contributions from former Olympic athlete Cathy Rigby and one-time chatshow host Joanne Carson.

All About Us see *Inday*

America (1985). Paramount/Post-Newsweek had every expectation of a long and fruitful run when the 60-minute daily *America* premiered on September 16, 1985. Industry soothsayers predicted that the show would be the hit of the syndie season, and a big sale to the CBS-owned stations for late afternoon telecast seemed to cinch the predictions. The hosting trio included soap-actor regular Stuart Damon, former *Real People* costar Sarah Purcell, and actor McLean Stevenson. Woody Fraser, *America's* creator-producer, had been in the syndication game ever since the first *Mike Douglas Show* in 1963. (Another bankable name, sex therapist Ruth Westheimer, had been slated as an *America* regular, but bowed out a week before the series' debut.) With a strong behind-the-scenes team and a formidable on-screen lineup, it looked like *America* was on its way. It was, but not in the right direction. Less than a month after the debut, *America* was dropped by those all-important CBS stations (as was the series' weekend wrapup edition, *America This Week*); it took little time for other markets to follow suit, and by December 20, *America* had had it. Paramount's official reason was that the series' low ratings didn't justify its $22 million budget, while insiders have suggested that severe budget cutbacks at the CBS Network led its owned-and-operated stations to drop the information-oriented *America* in favor of more "entertaining" shows. In any case, the series' demise had little to do with the presence of McLean Stevenson, despite the observations of wise-guy critics that the poor man seems to carry around his own cloud of failure ever since leaving the cast of *M*A*S*H*.

America This Week see above

America's Value Network see *The Home Shopping Network*

Ask Dr. Ruth (1987). Pixielike sex psychologist Dr. Ruth Westheimer, victim of a thousand-and-one impressionists, emceed this frank give-and-take daily devoted to everyone's favorite topic. Essentially the same series as her Lifetime Cable service's *Good Sex,* Dr. Ruth's syndie effort was toned down considerably for commercial television by King Features Television but was still pretty ripe nonetheless. Nell Carter was the first of many celebrity guests on the doctor's January 1987 debut show; Larry Angelo cohosted. But watered-down Ruth Westheimer didn't play as well as the no-holds-barred version seen on cable and read in her newspaper column, so after 13 weeks Dr. Ruth's daily appearances were confined to the Lifetime service, as before.

At the Movies (1982–   ). Originally titled *Movie Views, At the Movies* was a film-review weekly cut from the same cloth as PBS' *Sneak Previews,* even starring that series' Chicago-based movie critics Gene Siskel and Roger Ebert. *Sneak Previews* retained the rights to Siskel and Ebert's policy of voting for films with a "Yes" or "No," so the co-hosts adopted a "Thumbs Up – Thumbs Down" system for *At the Movies.* Syndicated by Tribune Entertainment (Siskel's home newspaper was the *Chicago Tribune*), *At the Movies* lost its stars when they emigrated to yet another *Sneak Previews* lookalike, cleverly titled *Siskel & Ebert* (which see). Their chairs on *At the Movies* were kept warm by critic and celebrity interviewer Rex Reed, and tweedy Showtime Pay-Cable showbiz commentator Bill Harris, who worked together well despite their obvious differences in personal taste and personality. This time, Siskel and Ebert took their "thumb" reviewing system with them, leaving Reed and Harris to utilize a "star system": Four stars for a great film, one star for a woof-woof.

A Better Way (1984). This weekly's official title was *Good Housekeeping: A Better Way,* and was a consumer-report offering underwritten by that influential magazine. Co-hosting were talk show stalwarts Pat Mitchell and John Mack Carter.

Beyond 2000 (1986). An LBS limited-series weekender, with host David Birney guiding viewers (mainly of the five NBC-owned outlets) through the world of modern science.

Biznet News (1983). A satellite-piped daily business report, with one foot in commercial television and the other in a cable service also bearing the name Biznet. Meryl Comer and Carl Grant hosted (see also *The Financial News Network*).

Body Buddies (1980). A husband-and-wife exercise show.

Breakaway (1983). Satellite-cast by Orion/Colbert live from New York but shown on a tape-delay basis in most cities, *Breakaway* — originally titled *Project 83* — was another in an ongoing series of efforts to lure away some of Phil Donahue's and *Hour Magazine's* devotees. Adopting the by-then time-honored "magazine" format, this daily hour enlisted a battalion of hosts: Monte Markham, Martha Lambert, Garry Owens and Peggy Cass. After a few weeks of negative reviews, *Breakaway's* producers retained the most popular of the hosts, Martha Lambert, but confined Garry Owens to offscreen announcing and dropped Markham and Cass entirely. Peggy Cass had once been a "draw" on television in the '50s, but made no impression on audiences 25 years later; the official reason that Monte Markham was replaced by Chicago radio personality Norman Mark was that Markham was "too stiff," but it might have been because the actor had played the surprise killer on so many TV mystery shows that the *Breakaway* viewers expected him to end each program by shouting, "I did it! I did it! Hahahahahah!!" Either way, neither Markham nor Cass was as annoying as the *Breakaway* correspondent who gratingly referred to herself as "Your fearless girl reporter." This lady's superciliousness carried over into the rest of the series, which though budgeted at $280,000 per week looked tacked together hurriedly and cheaply nonetheless.

But before fading away a year after its September 1983 premiere, *Breakaway* managed to contribute a priceless moment of notoriety. This occured when series correspondent Steve Wilson cornered CBS newsman Dan Rather leaving a courtroom where a sticky lawsuit involving Rather was under way. Pressed for a comment, Rather smiled, cheerfully asked that Wilson bring his microphone closer, then suggested that Wilson commit upon himself an impossible sexual act. Later, Rather called *Breakaway's* producers, apologized, offered to give a full interview, and asked that the embarrassing tape not be shown. Steve Wilson imagined what Rather himself would do in such a situation — and ran the tape, with the profanity (but not the lip movements) bleeped out, thereby earning *Breakaway* a place in the hearts of those who delighted in watching a respected television newsman's chickens come home to roost.

Business This Morning see *The Financial News Network*

Car Care Central (1981). The more expensive automobiles became, the more valuable was advice on keeping one's present car alive. Thus there was an instant market for SFM's *Car Care Central,* hosted each week by Peter Brown.

Christian Science Monitor Report see *Independent Network News*

Cinematractions (1987). Brief, undistinguished imitation of the Siskel and Ebert school. While it must look awfully easy to take film clips and critique them, the end results often just look awful.

CNN2 Headline News (1982–   ). Ted Turner's Cable News Network was the first 24-hour television service devoted to reporting, digesting and editorializing on the day's events. In 1982, Turner set up a headline service, offering news recaps on the quarter-hour, and calling it CNN2. This headline service was offered not only to cable companies, but also gratis to local stations who either couldn't afford full news staffs of their own or who needed something to keep them on the air overnight.

Couples (1982). Psychiatrist Walter Brackelmanns asked real-life folks to discuss their most intimate difficulties, then offered advice, in this ancestor to 1987's *Getting in Touch. Couples* was released by Golden West Television.

Cover Story (1986). Actress Lisa Hartman, who proved an apt interviewer in spite of her "bad girl" television image, hosted this average weekly magazine-style show from Fries Communications.

Crook and Chase (1986–   ). They were Lorriane Crook and Charlie Chase, and they were hosts of this nightly magazine show which emphasized country-western stars. *Crook and Chase* was seen over the Nashville Network cable service, and syndicated by Jim Owens Television; it originated from Nashville, and was taped before a studio audience.

A Current Affair (1987). A nightly magazine produced at WNYW–New York, this half-hour was the first series to be syndicated by the Fox Network outside its 100-plus independent-station lineup. The tone of the features presented tended to be less *PM Magazine* and more in line with the checkout-counter tabloids ("Tough Judge Throws Teens in Jail for Poor Grades!") *Current Affair* was anchored by Maury Povich.

Dayton Hudson Direct see *The Home Shopping Network*

Ebony/Jet Celebrity Showcase (1983; 1985–   ). First offered by Syndicast in 1983, then put on production hiatus for two years, this weekly black-oriented newsmagazine was put together by Johnson Publishing, the firm responsible for *Ebony* and *Jet,* America's leading black periodicals. Among the hosts were Deborah Grables, Tom Joyner, and sportscaster Greg Gumbel.

Entertainment Tonight (1981–); **Entertainment This Week** (1981–). First titled *Entertainment Today,* but renamed when most prospective markets picked it up for late-afternoon and evening time slots, *Entertainment Tonight* premiered September 14, 1981, a coproduction of several concerns, including Paramount, TeleRep and Cox Communications (it was a Paramount/TeleRep project for Operation Prime Time). *E.T.* was the first magazine show to take full advantage of the "[same] day and date" service offered by satellite relay, and to that end, Paramount sold the series to several smaller markets by offering to throw in a satellite dish free of charge! The purpose of the half-hour strip was to encapsulate the major events of the day in the entertainment industry, mostly through interviews and previews of coming attractions. Tom Hallick, Marjorie Wallace and Ron Hendren were the first team of hosts; later, Hallick and Wallace left, and Hendren was teamed with Dixie Whately. Robb Weller, Leeza Gibbons and Steve Edwards were other helmspersons for *E.T.* (along with its weekly roundup program, *Entertainment This Week*); occasional contributors ranged from "ambush journalist" Geraldo Rivera to movie critic/historian Leonard Maltin. Columnist Rona Barrett appeared for a while, but left when she decided that *Entertainment Tonight* favored frivolous fluff over serious journalism. Conversely, roving interviewer Robin Leach bolted to host his own *Lifestyles of the Rich and Famous* when he determined that *E.T.* had too much journalism and not *enough* fluff and frivolity. Though it has fluctuated between the "news" and "fun" schools since its inception, and has as a result risen and fallen in the ratings time and again, *Entertainment Tonight* was well on its way to an eighth season by 1987; its hosts that year were the intelligent and attractive Mary Hart and Jon Tesh. *E.T.,* and its subsequent imitators, have proven showman Mike Todd's adage that everyone has two businesses — their own and show business.

Essence (1984–). Raymond Horn Productions' *Essence* drew its name and format from a magazine aimed at an upscale black audience. The weekly bowed on May 5, 1983, over WPIX–New York and went national the following year. Susan L. Taylor and Felipe Luciano hosted.

Eye on Hollywood (1986); **Hollywood Closeup** (1985). A pair of *Entertainment Tonight* clones. *Eye on Hollywood* was initially seen over the ABC network, then distributed station-by-station through Harmony Gold. *Hollywood Closeup,* first produced at KABC–Los Angeles for the ABC-owned channels, was sent out to the nation by both Syndicast and Access. One of its hosts was former *Entertainment Tonight* star Steve Edwards.

Fan Club (1987). Teen-oriented interview magazine show from Blair Entertainment, done up in the flashy, quick-cut style of MTV's rock videos.

Olympic star Mitch Gaylord hosted amidst a welter of laser beams and digital-slow-motion effects.

Fight Back! With David Horowitz (1980–). An offshoot of Horowitz's earlier *Consumer Buyline, Fight Back!* was decked out with a hooting-and-hollering studio audience and with comedy sequences wherein various products were tested to see if their advertisers' claims were true; counterpointing the fun were more serious studies of the consequences of misleading advertising. While *Fight Back!* did brisk business in the first 19 markets carrying the weekly, it didn't really take off nationally until distribution moved from Group W to Paramount in 1984, implanting itself as a weekend favorite in nearly 100 cities.

The Financial News Network (1982–); ***Business This Morning*** (1987). FNN, a 24-hour cable service offering interviews, stock reports and "caveat emptor" consumer advice, was relayed via satellite to commercial stations seeking worthwhile "plugs" for holes in their daily schedules. Eventually, FNN's non-cable service was manifested in an early-morning daily distributed by Fox-Lorber, *Business This Morning*. This series was taped, with live inserts of overseas-trading reports.

From the Editor's Desk see ***Independent Network News***

Getting in Touch (1987). Following in the footsteps of fellow "radio therapists" Sally Jessy Raphäel and Ruth Westheimer, NBC-radio personality Dr. David Viscott launched his own nightly television half-hour in the fall of 1987, through Access Communications and Baruch Productions. Unlike Dr. Ruth, Viscott's emphasis was not on carnal knowledge but on family crises; his modus operandi was to bring before the cameras several members of the same family to hash out their problems and hopefully to come to terms. Voyeuristic, true—but a positive step towards mending the "fragmented family" dilemma of the late 1980's.

Good Housekeeping: A Better Way see ***A Better Way***

Headlines on Trial (1987). Despite its lurid title, this Orbis release was an intelligent round-robin debate pitting legal experts of various inclinations against one another apropos the "hot" topics of the day. Harvard Law professor Arthur Miller (see also *Miller's Court*) presided.

Healthbeat (1982). Harvard's Dr. Timothy Johnson, back again with his own version of a magazine show. Produced by WCVB–Boston, *Healthbeat* gained much of its reputation thanks to a well-received prime time run on a New York City independent outlet.

Hollywood Closeup see ***Eye on Hollywood***

The Home Shopping Network (and other over-the-air "markets")
(1985–   ). Granddaddy of all the televised bargain basements, *The Home
Shopping Network* first saw the light of day in 1977. Two Florida-based
retailers, Lowell "Bud" Paxson and Roy Speer, took the industry fortune tellers
seriously vis-a-vis the prediction that, in the future, most shopping would be
conducted over two-way TV, with the consumer having only to pick up a phone
to shop. Paxson and Speer's first home-shopping service took place over a
Florida radio station, then spread to cable television. Within a decade, the
Home Shopping Network would expand to *two* satellite-beamed services (one
operating around the clock) and a passel of owned-and-operated TV stations.
As Paxson explained, home shopping combined "America's love of television,
their love of shopping and the love of a bargain." The home viewer called in
an order for the lovely piece of simulated-china dinnerware or "cubic zirconia"
he or she had just seen on the tube at that low, low price, and felt as though
a genuine bargain had been struck at the expense of those rich folks running
television. Once the FCC dropped its rulings against over-the-air solicitations,
The Home Shopping Network and its brethren added commercial television to
its marketplace. In the two-year period between 1985 to 1987, viewers were
treated to San Diego's *Telephone Auction;* to the all-night *America's Value
Network;* to USTV's *Dayton Hudson Direct* (hosted by Jim Peck and occasionally by Charlene Tilton); to Lorimar/Fox's daily strip *Value Television*
(produced by former *Good Morning America* exec Susan Winston, and emceed
first by *Jeopardy's* Alex Trebek, then by Richard Simmons; this one was
financed by the New York restaurant firm of Horn and Hardart); and even to
a quiz show, *The Home Shopping Game,* picked up in 1987 by the CBS-owned
stations and distributed by *Home Shopping Network's* syndicator, MCA. The
saturation point was reached early on, but home shopping continued past 1987
to weave its spell over shut-ins and couch potatoes of all ages, sexes, and financial situations.

Hour Magazine (1980–89). Rising phoenix-like from the ashes of Group
W's disastrous 1978 syndie *Everyday, Hour Magazine* entered the daily-strip
market in the fall of 1980, utilizing the compartmentalized-subject format that
was doing so well for Group W's nightly *PM Magazine.* Tying things together
before the *Hour Magazine* studio audience was Gary Collins, a television actor
who like *Good Morning America's* David Hartman proved that his real metier
was as "info-tainment" host. In the first months, Collins tended to giggle over
any subject of even a slightly sexual nature, but he rapidly matured, eventually
winning an Emmy for his contributions to *Hour Magazine.* He even managed
not to look ridiculous and uncomfortable (as some male hosts did) when don-
ning an apron for the cooking segment, a popular *Hour Magazine* feature that
spawned several best-selling cookbooks. Pat Collins co-hosted *Hour's* first few
seasons; she was replaced by Bonnie Strauss. Eventually, Group W abandoned
the notion of a permanent co-host, going the *Mike Douglas Show* route with
weekly celebrity guest hosts. While the series had its moments of puffery, particularly in the appearances of "hairdresser to the stars" Jose Eber, *Hour
Magazine* was at its best with brief but in-depth information bites, such as the

frequent visits from health and science expert Dr. Isadore Rosenfeld. Never a major hit in big markets like New York and Chicago, *Hour Magazine* sustained a faithful following in the "hinterlands," and bade fair by the end of the '80s to remain a middle–America favorite.

Inday (1985). Grandiose (to the tune of $24 million) attempt to create a two-hour info-tainment block for the benefit of independent stations, *Inday* was broadcast by Tribune Entertainment starting October 7, 1985, using as its hub the half-hour *Inday News*. *Inday* was actually a patchwork, comprised of daily series from various producers which had been offered, but rejected, as individual syndies. *What's Hot — What's Not,* a fads-and-foibles half-hour hosted by Fred Willard and Melanie Chartoff, was produced by Lorimar. *All About Us,* 30 minutes of news-behind-the-news starring Ron Hendren, came from Barry-Enright. And rounding out the two hours was *It's a Great Life,* wherein Robert and Rosemary Stack told us what fun it was to be senior citizens. (Columbia Television, *Great Life's* packager, had, incredibly, at first wanted the 30ish Ed Begley Jr. to host the program!) LBS Communications distributed *Inday* via satellite on behalf of the Tribune company, hoping to provide tantalizing competition for the soap operas and game shows on the other channels. But like another 1985 issue, *America, Inday* was way too costly to survive with only its hundred or so markets supporting it. The package had the added handicap of failing to appeal to the various audience factions to whom it was targeted; *It's a Great Life* in particular merely alienated elderly viewers who tended to be envious or resentful of Mr. and Mrs. Stack's sumptuous lifestyle. As the months wore on, many local stations began running only 60 or 90 minutes of the daily *Inday* feed, preferring the profitable security of sitcom reruns and old movies to the insecurity of the "untested." By the spring of 1986, all that was left of the lofty project was *Inday News,* and even this was gone by fall. *Inday's* losing gamble proved once more that it took more than a lush budget and splashy ad campaign to win the viewers' hearts and minds.

Inday News see above

Independent Network News (1980–   ). The first successful effort at creating a national TV news broadcast outside the network mainstream, *Independent Network News* (or *I.N.N. News,* as it came to be called) was telecast from a cramped corner of the *New York Daily News* building by Manhattan's WPIX over a modest hookup of some thirty independent outlets beginning in the spring of 1980. As the "indie" market grew, and more ambitious station managers wished to compete with rival news shows at minimal price (and also to satisfy the FCC's then-existing policy that all commercial stations *had* to provide some form of informational programming), *I.N.N. News* found its way via the Westar Satellite into 57 markets by 1981, 73 by 1982, and over a hundred from 1983 onward. Since *I.N.N.'s* parent Tribune Company lacked the lavish television budgets of the Big Boys, the nightly report kept apace by focussing on the human element behind the news. When major events occurred, *I.N.N.* concentrated on their after-effects because there wasn't enough money to cover the stories "on the spot." For several years after 1981, *I.N.N.* offered two daily broadcasts, one for afternoons. Anchorpeople for both editions have included Pat Harper, Bill Jorgenson, Steve Bausch, Carl Rowan, Marvin Scott, Brad Holbrook, Clare Carter and Morton Dean, none of whom showed the slightest discomfort over broadcasting from a set roughly the same size as Walter Cronkite's dressing room. Over the years, *I.N.N. News* has spawned several spin-off half-hour weeklies, including *From the Editor's Desk, The Wall St. Journal Report* and *The Christian Science Monitor Report*. Recently, the nightly news program has been retitled *USA Tonight*.

I.N.N. News see above

It's a Great Life see *Inday*

Jack Anderson Confidential (1982). The shoot-from-the-hip investigative reporter combined expose and consumer advocacy in his brief weekly from Barry-Enright.

Joy of Gardening (1982). A bartered weekly hoe-and-grow show, taped in Troy, New York, hosted by Dick Raymond, and shipped out by Garden Way Marketing Association.

Learn to Read (1987). Anti-illiteracy daily distributed first to the ABC-owned stations, then nationally, and finally offered to public television.

Look at US (1981). Advertising itself as "the giant killer," the young distribution firm of Telepictures slew no Goliaths with its magazine daily *Look at US* (the "US" stood for "United States"), produced by George *(Real People)* Schlatter and hosted by Richard Crenna.

Louis Rukeyser's Business Journal (1981). A Viacom/Gateway release; financial news and advice from the know-it-all star of PBS's *Wall Street Week*.

Miller's Court (1982). Harvard's Arthur Miller, the sort of law professor who liked to dress up as historical characters to liven up his classroom, worked with a studio audience to thrash out complex legal problems on this WCVB–Boston weekly syndicated by Metromedia.

Morning Stretch with Joanie (1981–). The aggressively healthy Joanie Greggains was asked by KPIX–San Francisco to conduct a daily exercise show, to fill an early morning time slot until a projected talk show could be put together for that slot. The talk show came and went, but Joanie's daily pushup-and-jumping-jack outing continued to thrive nationally, complemented by a series of best-selling books and videotapes.

NCTV (1987). The initials stood for "National College Television," and one would think that the students putting this series together would want to bowl the audience over with originality. Instead, this hour weekly offered *Richard Brown's Screening Room,* a movie-review/interview show, and *New Grooves,* more interviews interspersed with rock-video previews. Evidently the kids learned a valuable lesson in college: you can't go wrong with someone else's ideas.

New Grooves see above

Newscope (1983). An attempt by Gannett/Telepictures/LBS to go the *I.N.N. News–PM Magazine* formula one better, *Newscope* was a daily "localized" magazine show. Local hosts would read the news as prepared by the *Newscope* staff, then would introduce the series' pre-recorded special features. Done in by time slots with poverty-stricken ratings, *Newscope* was soon offering nothing but five-minute fillers.

The Prime of Your Life (1983). Magazine program aimed at senior citizens, with Arlene Francis one of its hosts, *Prime of Your Life* was off before most people knew it had ever been on. After all, this was early '83; old people with useful lives plain didn't exist on television.

Richard Brown's Screening Room see *NCTV*

The Richard Simmons Show (1981–84). "Hips, Hips, Go Away! Give Them All to Doris Day!" sang out weight-loss guru Richard Simmons as he led a sweat-suited legion of ladies through a series of calorie-burning exercises on his popular daily from Golden West Television. Simmons, in his youth so grotesquely fat that he'd appeared as a "freak" in foreign films, saw the light one day when an anonymous friend sent a note begging Simmons not to eat himself to death. With his "Y-R-U FAT" license plates as his talisman, Simmons worked his way into the Hollywood circle of celebrity weight-losers, ending up with a supporting part (as himself) on the ABC soap opera *General Hospital.* This in turn led to his own daily program, where he spiced up the usual exercise sessions with cooking tips and comedy sketches. (Simmons was able to play so many roles in these skits that it's said he was under the scrutiny of the various performing unions, who didn't understand why they weren't getting talent vouchers from Simmons' unbilled "supporting cast"!) So successful was *The Richard Simmons Show* that some stations took to running it in prime time, or twice each day. Director Jerry Kupcinet (son of Irv Kupcinet of *Kup's Show* fame) certainly deserved his Emmy award for bringing coherence to Simmons' crazy combination of exercises, laughs, kitchen hints, audience participation and celeb interviews. The star's overexposure on his own and other people's shows led to the inevitable ennui on the part of his fans, and his ultimate cancellation. After the demise of Simmons' daily, Richard made a stab at hosting a home-shopping syndie, *Value Television,* where his infectious enthusiasm now seemed forced; he also helmed a daily program on the Lifetime Cable service. In 1987, Syndicast put Simmons back on the syndie trail (albeit in fewer markets) with *Richard Simmons' Slim Cooking.*

***Richard Simmons' Slim Cooking* see immediately previous**

Rock and Roll Evening News (1986). Producer Andy Friendly left *Entertainment Tonight* when he felt that the series was eschewing journalism for glitz; he went on to produce King World's *Rock and Roll Evening News,* a weekly magazine-style roundup of the comings and goings in the music world. Hosting were Steve Kmetko and Eleanor Mondale (daughter of former vice president Walter Mondale).

Siskel & Ebert (1986). Buena Vista release; a film-review weekly featuring the former stars of *At the Movies* (which see). The series, known briefly as *Siskel & Ebert & the Movies,* was at its best whenever it looked like the two critics would come to blows over their frequent disagreements.

Soap Opera Digest; Soap Spots; Soapworld (all 1982). The ever-increasing popularity of soap operas from fans of all sexes and walks of life led to a brief spate of serial recaps and reviews, and interviews with soap stars. Sandy Frank's *Soap Opera Digest,* hosted by *Days of Our Lives'* Bill and Susan Hayes, lost out in the open market to *Soapworld,* an interview show from Edwards-Billett Colbert. It was supposed to have starred John Gabriel (a veteran serial actor himself); but Gabriel went with a five-minute-filler series called *Soap Spots,* so *Soapworld* made do with Michael Young.

Taking Advantage (1983–84). A Paramount release, from the production team that brought you *Entertainment Tonight.* Jerry Graham, Sybil Robson, Pat Crowley and Terry Savage dispensed financial advice and interviewed self-made rich folks.

Telephone Auction* see *The Home Shopping Network

Today's Black Woman (1981). Successor to *For You, Black Woman,* this Syndicast effort was hosted by Freda Payne.

Today's Business (1986). Another of the Reaganomics Era's daily financial reports, this one distributed by Buena Vista. Consuelo Mack of the ESPN Cable service's *Business Times* (and later the emcee of *The Wall St. Journal Report*) co-hosted with Tom Peters, the author of *In Search of Excellence.* Also appearing were Bill Wolfman (an editor of *Business Week*) and Andrew Tobias (of *The Daily Business Guide*). The only thing these worthies couldn't seem to foresee was that the television market would itself feel a financial pinch in early 1987, forcing *Today's Business* off the air.

:20 Minute Workout (1982). Exercise daily from Tantra Productions, and similar to the same company's five-minute "Aerobicize" vignettes that had appeared on cable television and as a semiregular feature on NBC's *Tomorrow Show.* The warning at the beginning of each program that the aerobics presented therein might be dangerous seemed best applied to male viewers, who risked coronaries from the excitement of watching a team of leotard-clad young ladies thrusting their pelvises toward the camera.

Update on Health (1980 onward). The tireless Dr. Timothy Johnson (see *Healthbeat*) in a batch of five-minute health tips; from J. Walter Thompson.

USA Tonight **see** *Independent Network News*

USam (1981). The Christian Broadcasting Network's version of the *Good Morning America* brand of sunrise fare, with no overt religious overtones but with emphasis on "good news." Former Miss America Terry Ann Meeuwsen co-hosted this live hour-long daily with gospel music deejay Ross Bagley; Bagley would later be replaced by Brian Christie. Terry Casey handled news, Tom Mahoney weather, Scott Hatch sports. *USam* suffered from its enormous cost and its inaccessible 6 a.m. time slot; viewers hadn't yet been conditioned by NBC's *News at Sunrise* to get up that early for world events.

Value Television **see** *The Home Shopping Network*

Wall St. Journal Report **see** *Independent Network News*

World of People (1980). Time-Life Television's bid at the TV-magazine market; this was a half-hour video version of the company's *People* Magazine. The daily series succeeded in offering none of *People's* virtues and all of its faults, including its superficiality. Bill Hillier, who'd worked on *PM Magazine,* was *World of People's* creator; Steve Edelman, Jane D'Atri and Sarah Edwards were correspondents.

Yan Can Cook (1981). Kitchen series starring Martin Yan; followed by Cable TV's *Wok with Yan.* Mediacast handled distribution.

Your New Day (1980). Daily SFM news and information show spiced with beauty tips; hosted by Vidal Sassoon, who despite his success in the women's wear and cosmetic fields has never developed into a satisfying television personality.

Music/Variety

Two observations here. For one, the tendency for music/variety programs to gather together in syndication after being given the boot by sitcom- and cop-happy networks continued from the '70s. For another, the overriding musical trends were dictated by the advent of a cable service known as Music Television, or MTV, which offered rock videos and star interviews (presided over by "veejays") on a 24-hour basis. Most musical syndies emulated — if not carbon-copied — MTV, to the extent that several UHF independent stations (mostly in areas not serviced by Cable) became fulltime rock-video conduits themselves. It was an easy thing to do; for many years, music videos were offered to local stations free of charge.

America Rocks (and many other such) (1982–). The various and sundry music-video/interview outings looked so much the same that to the untrained eye, they may seem to all be part of a cacophonous continuum of never-ending twanging and wailing. They are listed alphabetically in the next paragraph. Those programs evincing a hint of originality will be treated separately in the "Music/Variety" section.

First on the list, the undistinguished *America Rocks*. Next, *The Dance Show,* produced concurrently by Metromedia in New York and Cox Communications in Atlanta, hosted by New York's Carl Dupree and Atlanta's Townsend Coleman. Then, 1985's *The Great Record Album Collection*. Next, the unmemorable *Hit City.* Next there was *H.O.T.,* or *Hits of Today,* a Bob Banner production from Group W, hosted by Lloyd Mann. *Melba Moore's Collection of Love Songs* was next, followed by Music Television's own *MTV Top 20 Video Countdown,* then *Music Magazine. New York Hot Tracks,* first seen on the Big Apple's WABC in July 1983, was hosted by Carlos De Jesus; it was picked up for the rest of the nation by Golden West, and lasted until 1987, occasionally offering live as well as prerecorded music. *The Rock 'n' Roll Show,* from Blair Communications, was an attraction on the CBS-owned stations. Mathis and Gold Associates' *Rock 'n' Roll Tonight* was initially titled *In the Midnight Hour* in deference to its inspiration, NBC's concert-oriented *Midnight Special. Rock Palace,* from LBS, was snatched up by the NBC-owned outlets. *Rockworld* continued its run from the '70s, supplanting interviews with music videos in its last months in the early '80s. *This Week's Music* is next on the list, then Columbia TV's *Top 40 Videos.* And finally, the daily *We're Dancin',* hosted by Townsend *(Dance Show)* Coleman, who later graduated to *New York Hot Tracks*).

America's Top Ten (1980–). Casey Kasem transferred his long running radio series, based on the top ten songs as determined by *Billboard* magazine, to television through the auspices of All American Television/Gold Key/LBS. Its ads promised that the series would have wide-ranging appeal to the "Teen-Ult" audience, and that it did. Despite stiff competition from MTV and its imitators, the half-hour weekly *America's Top Ten* was one of the longest-lasting "countdown" shows, entering 1988 with a new host, Shadoe Stevens.

American Bandstand (1987). No one seriously entertained the notion that Dick Clark would let his 35-year-old *American Bandstand* die after its cancellation by ABC in 1987. Less than a week after the last, tearful network show, Clark was back at his old stand in syndication through LBS, bringing with him many of his teen-oriented sponsors (including Clearasil). Clark's clout in the industry was enough to allow him the luxury to retain his dance party's 60-minute format, despite the general rule that half-hour syndies were the most cost efficient.

The Blue Jean Network (1981–82). Summertime concert series, produced by Jackie Barnett and distributed by the Osmond Family's syndication service.

The Dance Show see *America Rocks*

Dancin' to the Hits (1986). A weekly half-hour with echoes of *Solid Gold* (which see), Gaylord/ITF's *Dancin' to the Hits* featured beautiful bodies "synch-dancing" to popular records. Hosting was *Falcon Crest's* Lorenzo Lamas, who hoped that this show would prove that he, too, could dance and sing. Lamas' back-up group, originally called "The Street Talkers," were later re-christened "The Sweet Dreams."

Dick Clark's Nitetime (1985). Weekend variety hour which underwent several title changes *(Good Times 85, Nitetime Bandstand)* and distributors (Syndicast, King World) before its release. This one took longer to get on the air than it did staying there.

Dream Girl USA (1986). Music and dance were part and parcel of this weekly beauty contest, a 20th Century–Fox release (complete with weekly disclaimer insisting that it *not* be confused with the Miss USA Pageant). The emcee was noted actor Ken Howard, who admittedly took the job because it was easy work and paid a bundle.

FM-TV (1984). Rock-video effort of various lengths (anywhere from one to two hours) from On the Air Productions, spotlighting clips from classic rock concerts of the late 1960's.

Glen Campbell Music Show (1982). Another attempt by producer Pierre Cossette to "Las Vegas-ize" a popular middle-of-the-road entertainer (as witness Cossette's 1976 venture with Andy Williams). LBS distributed.

The Great Record Album Collection; Hit City; Hits of Today (H.O.T.) see *America Rocks*

Hollywood Heartbeat (1980). Bob Welch, onetime member of Fleetwood Mac, introduced rock-concert snippets for this Gold Key Television weekend interview/music half-hour.

It's Showtime at the Apollo (1987). Reportedly, there was a similar syndie produced at Harlem's legendary Apollo Theatre in the '50s, but the 1987 version is the only one we can find any conclusive information about. Produced by Bob Banner for Apollo Enterprises, *It's Showtime* featured (and was hosted by) the top black singers, dancers and comedians of the day, and took time out to offer film-clip tributes of past greats in the field of black entertainment. This hourly weekly was telecast by the NBC-owned stations and its other markets on late weekend evenings.

Let's Rock (1980). 1950's-style rock 'n' roll; from ITC.

Love Songs (1985). A musical "newspaper of the air," interspersing its rock videos with "personals" sent in by viewers in quest of romance. An On the Air television release.

The Magic Music Machine (1984). We *tried* to dispose of all the clone-ish video shows in one paragraph, but they breed like rabbits. This one was from 20th Century–Fox TV.

Melba Moore's Collection of Love Songs* see *America Rocks

The Monte Carlo Show (1980). A 20th Century–Fox release, produced by Marty Pasetta and hosted by Patrick Wayne. This variety "spectacular" from Monte Carlo's Sporting Club lasted only one year in America, but was 20th Century–Fox's biggest international moneymaker of that year.

MTV Top 20 Video Countdown* see *America Rocks

Music City USA (1984–   ). Also known as *New Music City USA,* this Top-20 country-and-western countdown (one of the few C-and-W's not absorbed by the Nashville Network Cable service) was released by Multimedia.

Music Machine (1987). Weekly singing-dancing contest, not far in design from the well-established *Dance Fever.* Taped at Detroit's Club Taboo and presided over by singer-songwriter Curtis Gadson. From LBS.

Music Magazine* see *America Rocks

New Music City USA* see *Music City USA

New York Hot Tracks* see *America Rocks

Odyssey (1985). This might have been just another music-video opus, except that it was produced by the National Christian Network; there was still a lot of rock, but none of the violence, profanity or nudity that characterized several contemporary rock videos.

On Stage America (1984). Dreaming once more of a fourth network, Metromedia hoped that the elaborate *On Stage America* would spark just such a network. Los Angeles Raider Tod Christiansen was host, and among the producers were battle-scarred variety veterans Dwight Hemion and Nick Vanoff. The best program was a sentimental tribute to comic George Kirby, then making a comeback after a disastrous bout with narcotics; but *On Stage America* succumbed to its overpowering budget and to its lack of local-station support.

Puttin' on the Hits (1984–   ); ***Puttin' on the Kids*** (1986). Broadway and soap opera star Allen Fawcett hosted both of these Dick Clark Productions. *Puttin' on the Hits* featured regular people competing for cash awards by lip-synching to records by their favorite rock stars. (There were a lot of incipient Michael Jacksons in the series' first season.) The lip-synchers on *Puttin' on the Kids* were drawn from the 5-through-13 age group. Judging on the adult show were a panel of celebrities, and the judges on the kid's show were *child* celebs from various sitcoms. (You know you've outgrown TV when you don't recognize *any* of these "celebrities.") The two *Puttin' Ons* were created by Chris Bearde, who once worked for Chuck Barris and can thus be forgiven for a cynical "they'll watch anything" viewpoint.

Rock-n-America (1984). Comedy was the drawing card for this rock-video weekly from Counterpoint Television. The host was Rick Ducommun, playing a "gizmo-savvy genius."

The Rock 'n' Roll Show; Rock 'n' Roll Tonight; Rock Palace* see *America Rocks

Salute! (1983). This MCA musical hour was to have been hosted by Burt Bacharach and his wife Carol Bayer Sager, but it was old reliable Dick Clark who emceed for this weekly tribute to major music personalities.

Solid Gold (1980–   ). Arguably the best of the syndicated "countdown" shows, *Solid Gold* first appeared as an *Operation Prime Time* special on February 29, 1980, hosted by Glen Campbell and Dionne Warwick. Warwick remained as host when Paramount Television turned the special into a weekly; other emcees over the years have included Andy Gibb, Marilyn McCoo, Rex Smith and Rick Dees. The format consisted of having the week's top ten tunes either performed by their original artists, or interpreted in movement form by the Solid Gold Dancers, a co-ed troupe dominated by statuesque young ladies wearing as little as possible. Allowing occasional breathers for the dancers and singers have been several stand-up and sit-down comics, all of whom seemed to deserve far fewer laughs than the studio audience awarded them. Those not interested in the human element on *Solid Gold* were kept happy by the series' vast inventory of lighting effects and flashy editing tricks; it's no surprise that several Emmies have gone to the *Solid Gold* technical crew. The series has offered annual review specials, and a brief daily strip of highlights, *Solid Gold Hits,* a 1984 release hosted by Grant Goodeve.

Solid Gold Hits see above

Star Search (1983–   ). Television Program Entertainment (a branch of Operation Prime Time) featured a Bob Banner-produced "new talent" special,

Star Search, in April of 1983. At the end of this special, local stations were besieged with thousands of calls from aspirant entertainers asking how they, too, could be allowed to strut and fret before the cameras. In September of 1983, *Star Search* not unexpectedly went weekly, hosted by Ed McMahon. The new faces who, after several elimination rounds, won the big prizes, went on to movie, television and record contracts: as of this writing, the biggest "name" to emerge from *Star Search* has been a superb song stylist named Sam Harris, whose *Search* appearances spawned a diligent fan club virtually overnight. Several other winners have gotten positions on other Bob Banner productions.

Star Tracks (1980). Pre–MTV interview/concert-clip series, from Fremantle.

This Week in Country Music (1983–87). Magazine-style countdown.

This Week's Music and *Top 40 Videos* see *America Rocks*

TV 2000 (1986). Comedy and music from Bob Banner Productions, principally a vehicle for *Star Search* contest winner John Kassir.

We're Dancin' see *America Rocks*

You Write the Songs (1986). Conceived originally as a daily show, this weekly music contest, produced by Bob Banner and Al Masini for Television Program Entertainment, was hosted by Ben Vereen and populated by nearly naked chorus persons. The object was to do a *Star Search*-style program for would-be songwriters.

Religious

The sexual and financial scandals which rocked the televangelism industry in the late '80s will have been documented to death by the time this book is published, so we refer you to the notes on Jim and Tammy Bakker and Jimmy Swaggart in the 1970's chapter, and have done with it. Dwelling on those scandals would throw this book off balance just as surely as would listing *all* the religious programs available in syndication (not to mention over cable) in the 1980's. A random sampling of ten regional editions of *TV Guide* in the spring of 1987 revealed that over *80* such first-run programs were being distributed nationwide, and even this may have only been a fraction. Included were the big-timers from past decades like Robert Schuller and Oral Roberts; second-echelon personalities who'd risen since 1980 like Kenneth Copeland, Jack Van Impe, Arthur DeKruyter and Lowell Lundstrom (and family); people with the marketing know-how to build up mininetworks of independent stations, such as Lester Sumrall; persons with large followings in smaller markets, from Arthlene Rippy to Zola Levitt; more laying-on-of-hands entrepreneurs like W.V. Grant; children-oriented efforts with titles like *The Black Buffalo* and *That's Inkidable;* musical programs such as *Lightmusic* and *Jamboree;* and even the taped-at-home efforts of such celebrated "lay persons" as Art Linkletter and Dale Evans. Most of these programs fell into two categories: straight preaching (either to a single camera or a packed studio audience), or documentary-style studies of the crises facing people of Faith.

As with our religious-programming notes of past chapters, we offer a sampling of the more remarkable efforts in this field in the '80s. As to the reasons *why* this field was so full in this decade (beyond the wider accessibility of satellites and video equipment), we can only note the never-ending habit, throughout history, of humankind trying to find spiritual solace from increasingly difficult times.

Another Life (1981–84). This often incomprehensible melange of soap opera and religiosity was an effort by the Christian Broadcasting Network to broaden its appeal to daytime-drama aficionados. *Another Life,* co-created by former NBC daytime chief Bob Aaron and with the semiretired Roy Winslow (late of *Search for Tomorrow* and *Secret Storm*) as its first story consultant, was initially titled *The Inner Light* and originally intended to display a group of typical soap opera characters who faced their problems by applying "Judeo-Christian principles." The serial was set in the town of Kingsley (an alias for CBN's headquarters, Portsmouth, Virginia); playing the Davidson family were John Corseau, Mary Jean Feton and Darrel Campbell. The Davidsons were swept into the traditional serial runaround of infidelities, deep dark secrets and criminal activities, but the difference was that all the characters tried to wipe their slates clean (and wrap up the plotlines) by becoming born-again Christians. Though well-meaning, *Another Life* was as subtle and tasteful as those little pamphlets one finds stuffed under one's windshield which tell in comic-book style that you'll go to Hell if you don't stop looking at the opposite sex and driving too fast. "Highlights" of *Another Life* included a vain, selfish woman "finding Jesus" after being kidnapped, and an astounding hospital sequence wherein a gangster *literally* sees the light. Despite the professionalism of such serial vets as Dorothy *(Edge of Night)* Stinette and Nick *(Another World)* Benedict, *Another Life* confounded fans of both daytime drama and religious programming by playing both ends down the middle. Despite the respectable ratings for its June 1, 1981, debut, the serial never picked up steam; except for reruns on the CBN Cable service, *Another Life* wasn't seen or heard from after its last new program on October 5, 1984. Thereafter, CBN Cable confined its efforts to grab the less religiously inclined viewers to repeats of old network sitcoms, cop shows and westerns.

Dr. Eugene Scott (early 1980's onward). Few electronic evangelists were more fun to watch than Dr. Eugene Scott, he of the eternal chomped-down cigar and wide-brimmed hat. The leader of Faith Center Inc., Dr. Scott used his daily program principally (it seemed) to raise funds for himself and his cause; indeed, it was virtually a telethon, with all interview sequences and musical numbers directed at the purpose of getting viewers to phone in donations. Because Dr. Scott piped his program over satellite on a 24-hour-a-day basis (usually taping three to four hours per day, then rerunning them over and over), local stations looking to fill scheduling gaps could run Scott's program any time of the day or night. Dr. Scott's biggest moment in the sun occurred when, for various reasons, the FCC decided to pull the plug—literally—on Faith Center's KHOV-TV in Los Angeles on May 24, 1983. Before disappearing in mid-sentence into a field of static, Dr. Scott used his last KHOV telecast as a lectern to rail against TV bigwigs in general and the FCC in particular; the last-mentioned agency was depicted on-camera as a group of wind-up toy monkeys.

The Flying House and **Superbook** (both 1983). Children's religious programming ranged from puppet playhouses *(Secret Place)* to Biblical quiz shows *(Bible Bowl)*, with room left over for a brace of made-in-Japan cartoon series, syndicated by the Christian Broadcasting Network. Both *Flying House* and *Superbook* told of a group of modern-day kids who were magically whisked off to witness the great events recorded in the Bible.

Peter Popoff (early '80s onward). Here was another televangelist who might never have been heard of outside his own following had not a scandal elevated him to national notoriety. Peter Popoff was a faith healer who amazed his flock with his uncanny talent of picking members of his audience at random, then guessing these persons' life stories and reasons for attending his program; he'd then cure their various ailments through the laying on of hands, a gift which, like his "mind-reading," Popoff attributed to the Almighty. James Randi, a professional illusionist and self-styled "hoax-buster," saw several holes in Popoff's routine, just as a few years earlier Randi had seen through some of the so-called miracles accomplished by mentalist spoon-bender Uri Geller. Using the same dogged attention to detail that he'd used on Geller, Randi discovered that Peter Popoff's messages were not precisely coming from God; he was able to guess his audience's past histories through the help of Mrs. Popoff and a radio device implanted in Popoff's ear. This electronic enhancement also allegedly enabled Popoff to determine which of his congregation's afflictions and illnesses were "curable." As a result of Randi's investigation, Popoff's multi-million dollar operation took a severe dip in the donation department.

The downfall of Peter Popoff, and those of Jimmy Swaggart and the Bakkers, overshadowed the sincerity and accomplishments of the many other television evangelists who operated with openness and honesty. Televised religion had endured so much bad press by the end of 1987 that some religious leaders were demanding that the TV personalities start adhering to a book of ethics. A curious demand, since there already was such a Book; it came in two volumes and had been available for a couple of thousand years.

Specials, Miniseries, and Mini-Networks

Many offerings in this category followed the lead of Operation Prime Time, which long before 1980 had moved from the new-kid-on-the-block category to old and trusted friend. By mid-decade, a new trend was in the making: The live, one-shot "stunt" special, designed for shock, amazement and network-busting ratings. A few things are left out of the upcoming section for space reasons, including those ever-proliferating specials that pose as science-fiction documentaries or film histories, but are really promotional flackery for major motion pictures. Also excluded are the offerings of the strapling Fox Network, which are covered elsewhere in our '80s chapter; it's hard to call a hookup with over 100 stations, and with a fixed prime time schedule, a "mininetwork."

Air Time International Specials (1981–   ). Miniseries documentaries, concentrating on the sociopolitical history of mankind, distributed by Air Time International. Included were such undertakings as *History of the World* (minus Mel Brooks), *The Race for the White House,* and perhaps the best of the batch, a star-studded six-parter titled *The Roots of Rock 'n' Roll.*

American Caesar (1984). Miniseries biographical documentary of General Douglas MacArthur, based on the book by William Manchester. Seen first on Ted Turner's Atlanta superstation, then syndicated by Alan Enterprises.

"Awareness" and "Benefit" Specials (mid–1980's onward). To call some of the offerings in this category "one-shots" would be minimizing them. Many of these specials, designed either to present the facts of a crisis, debilitating illness or the like before the public, or to offer entertainment on behalf of worthy causes, were more like telethons in terms of TV air time. USTV's *The AIDS Connection,* a live overnight program relaying the known facts, many fallacies and possible medicinal balms concerning the single most dangerous communicable disease of our times, ran a full eight hours in most markets after its sign-on July 24, 1987. *LiveAid* and *FarmAid,* two celebrity concerts devoted to raising funds for the ill and destitute in America, were picked up fitfully by the networks, but run from beginning to end (over two days, in the case of *FarmAid*) on cable and in syndication.

Blood and Honor (1982). Six-hour dramatization of the rise of the Hitler Youth, distributed by D.L. Taffner and Field Communications. The drama was filmed in Germany with a native cast, and was introduced for American audiences by actress Taina Elg.

Buchanan H.S. (1985). Group of drama specials revolving around the staff of a high-school newspaper; this was one of the last Metromedia presentations before that company's seven owned-and-operated outlets became the nucleus of the new Fox Network.

CBN Specials (early '80s onward). One-shots shipped out by the Christian Broadcasting Network ranged from semi-whimsical pieces like *Ask God* (in which people were queried as to the one question they'd like to pose to the Almighty), to the unrelenting frankness of *X-Pose,* a study of the pornography industry hosted by Efrem Zimbalist Jr.

Citizen's Summit (1986). Christmas-season "international special," organized in part by entrepreneur Ted Turner, in which talk-host Phil Donahue exchanged views, via satellite, with Soviet Union spokesman Vladimir Posner. Conceived in the spirit of "glasnost," *Citizen's Summit* succeeded mostly in making Donahue look incredibly naive as the crafty Mr. Posner wrapped him, and the special, around his little finger.

Commworld Prime Time Showcase (1983). A bid by Commworld to emulate Operation Prime Time with a series of made-for-syndication, videotaped two-hour dramas. The "series" yielded only two productions: *Emergency Room,* a hospital meller starring Sarah Purcell and LeVar Burton, and *Desperate Intruder,* a weary retread of the one about a blind woman (Meg Foster) vs. escaped criminals (Claude Akins, Nick Manusco). Procter and Gamble bartered this short-lived project.

Dave Bell & Associates Specials (1980–   ). After tasting glory as distributor for the controversial 1977 special *Scared Straight,* Dave Bell & Associates remained in the syndie-special business, with emphasis on exposing society's darker side. The distributor started the decade with *Angel Death,* a searing Metromedia-produced special on the horrors of the deadly drug P.C.P. ("Angel Dust"). *Hard Time* was a 1980 prison documentary narrated by George Kennedy, and was followed later that year by a teen-runaway study, *Whatever Happened to Lori Jean Lloyd. Shoot—Don't Shoot* (1982) delineated the most unnerving decisions made by cops on the beat when confronted with armed felons, while two more 1982 ventures, *Going Straight* and *Goodbye Again* dealt respectively with rehabilitation of criminals and divorce. Concentrating on the cinema verite method utilized in *Scared Straight,* Dave Bell & Associates' offerings managed to temper potential sensationalism with equal doses of dispassionate journalism and compassionate humanity.

Fight Against Slavery (1982). Meticulously produced (by the BBC) six-hour dramatization of the ultimate abolishment of mankind's "peculiar institution"; Lionheart Television distributed.

Golden Circle Specials (1980). Metromedia's answer to Operation Prime Time came in the form of a projected group of miniseries, featuring colorful characters who were either self-made or empire builders. The first of these, *Wild Times,* was a sprawling document of the career of Wild West show impresario Hugh Cardiff (played by Sam Elliot), and was released in January of 1980. In July of that same year, Golden Circle offered *Roughnecks,* a serial-like saga of the oil industry, starring Cathy Lee Crosby, Sam Melville and Steve Forrest. *Roughnecks* was also the last Golden Circle special; Metromedia halted the series before filming could begin on such tantalizing titles as *Sitka, Blue Grass* and *Columbia Gold.* (See also *Metroprime Specials.*)

Liberty Mutual Specials (1980–82). Taking a brief leave from its weekend hunting-and-fishing excursions, Liberty Mutual Insurance underwrote a quintet of one-hour dramas. The first, *Wilson's Reward* (June 1980) was based on Somerset Maugham's "Vessel of Wrath" (already twice-filmed under the title *The Beachcomber*), starred Gerald S. O'Loughlin and Sandy Dennis, and was directed by actor Patrick O'Neal. O'Neal wielded the megaphone for the next Liberty Mutual special, December 1980's *Mr. Griffin and Me,* a Hollywood-based mystery with Burgess Meredith, Gloria Grahame and Rosemary Murphy. *The Best of Friends,* a shooting-the-rapids adventure based on Hemingway's "Three Day Blow" and featuring Peter Graves, Carol Lynley and Alex Cord, was seen in August of 1981. January of 1982 brought *Bush Doctor,* filmed in Australia, with Hugh O'Brian in the title role. Liberty Mutual's final endeavor was a "Love Comes to Red China" piece titled *Peking Encounter,* filmed on location with Diana Canova, June Lockhart and Mason Adams in the leads, and released the last week of August, 1982.

Metroprime Specials (1984–86). In its last two years before its sale to the Fox Network, Metromedia distributed several BBC-produced two- to four-hour dramas, filmed in England and Australia. The most notable of the *Metroprime Specials* was 1985's *Jamaica Inn,* an over-glamourized adaptation of Daphne Du Maurier's yarn about 19th-century smugglers; Jane Seymour and Patrick McGoohan starred in the roles created by Maureen O'Hara and Charles Laughton in Hitchcock's 1939 filmization of the same novel.

The Mormons' Specials (1980–83). Seasonal playlets, produced by the Mormons, with major names coping with ultrasentimental plotlines. The first, *Mr. Krueger's Christmas,* was a half-hour's worth of loveable curmudgeonliness by James Stewart, and has been shown annually since 1980. Equally well circulated was *The Last Leaf,* a leisurely adaptation of an O. Henry story, featuring Art Carney as a misanthropic artist who sacrificed himself so that a young girl might live.

The Mystery of Al Capone's Vault (and other "Events") (1984–   ). The above-mentioned one-shot may have been one of the biggest of the syndie "stunt specials" of the '80s, but it wasn't the first. On August 16, 1984, *Andrea Doria: The Final Chapter* was telecast live to those outlets with satellite or microwave relay facilities, and tape-delayed elsewhere. Most of the two-hour special was comprised of a 1975 filmed documentary on the famed sunken luxury liner; the live portions consisted of host George Plimpton overseeing the opening of a safe salvaged from the ship's wreckage. The results, both in terms of recovered riches and ratings, weren't what the producers had hoped, so it would be two years before another "buried treasure" event would be foisted on the American public. This occurred on the evening of April 8, 1986. Through the auspices of Westlake Entertainment and the Tribune Company, virtually all markets were treated to a live two-hour excavation of the "hidden vaults" beneath the headquarters of 1920's gangland czar Al Capone in Chicago's Lex-ington Hotel. Otherwise reasonable people who would normally shun such an exercise in empty voyeurism (would the explorers *actually* find untold millions of dollars, and maybe a few cement-encased skeletons?) tuned in by the droves, some out of casual interest, some because they really cared, and many because they wanted to watch the host of the special, "gonzo" TV journalist Geraldo Rivera, fall flat on his face. As the whole world knows by now, all Rivera and his team of drillers and blasters discovered were a few mouldy liquor bottles. Viewers got their laugh at Rivera's expense, but it was Rivera and the special's producers, John Joslyn and Doug Llewelyn, who laughed last and loudest. *The Mystery of Al Capone's Vault* proved to be the single highest-rated syndicated program *in history*. Geraldo Rivera and his accomplices could now write their own ticket and be assured of an enormous viewership in all future "stunt" endeavors. Rivera's follow-ups included *American Vice: The Doping of a Nation* in December of '86 (which resulted in an embarrassing lawsuit for Rivera by a person who was caught up in a live, on-camera "drug raid"); *Innocence Lost: The Erosion of American Childhood* in April of 1987; *Sons of Scarface: The New Mafia* in August of the same year; and a 1988 special on murder, which had as its centerpiece an interview with mass killer Charles Manson. These specials were in the usual Geraldo Rivera vein of unquestioned sincerity mixed with appalling tastelessness, while the non–Rivera "event" specials from the *Capone* production team were sincere only in their desire for monster ratings. As 1987 drew to a close, viewers were honored with a Halloween special hosted by William Shatner, *The Search for Houdini,* which featured a live seance that proved as much as all the other efforts to contact Houdini's spirit had in the past; and, full-circle from the *Andrea Doria* affair, October 28's *Return to the Titanic—Live,* featuring host Telly Savalas, endless pretty shots of Paris in the fall, and a few baubles, bangles and beads drawn from another waterlogged ship's vault.

Omni: The New Frontier (1981). Monthly specials drawn from the pages of the scientific-speculation periodical *Omni* magazine, narrated by Peter Ustinov and syndicated by Mag-Net.

On the Air Specials (1982–   ). Historical specials distributed by On the Air Television and produced by such concerns as Golden West Television and TCA/Drew Associates. The 1982 offerings were concentrated on the tenth anniversary of the Watergate Hotel break-in, and included *784 Days that Changed America,* hosted by Nancy Dickerson and Robert Drew. In recognition of the twentieth anniversary of the Kennedy assassination, the On the Air product for 1983 included *Being with JFK* and *America Remembers John F. Kennedy.* Other On the Air titles: *Television: Our Life and Times,* a 1985 retrospective of the Great Tube; and another 1985 presentation, *Years of Hope—Years of Danger: The PostWar World,* a scrupulously fair-handed history lesson featuring such varied commentators as Carroll O'Connor, Carl Sagan, Jerry Falwell, John Kenneth Galbraith and Tom Hayden (though not all at once!).

Return to Eden (1984). Australian miniseries, delivered to American audiences by Worldvision. Rebecca Gilling starred as a woman seeking revenge on the husband who tried to murder her. It took Ms. Gilling six television hours to do what Barbara Stanwyck used to accomplish in 90 minutes flat.

Shaka Zulu (1986). Filmed on location in Africa, this Harmony Gold/Gaylord release was widely touted as the most expensive non-network miniseries ever made. Certainly it raised one of the biggest ruckuses with its depiction of Zulu warriors as human beings with such human frailties as lust for power and desire for revenge. Many viewers found offense with the series' display of bare female breasts (in scenes that were about as erotic as a 1947 issue of *National Geographic*). As a result of the brouhaha, most markets didn't get to see *Shaka Zulu* until a year or two after its initial release.

Stars with David Steinberg (1984). Not every Operation Prime Time special could be a *Solid Gold* or *Star Search* and stand on its own as a series. This celebrity-interview affair hosted by comedian Steinberg was given several tryouts, but failed to catch on as a weekly.

The Tribune Specials (1984–). In addition to releasing the "stunt specials" mentioned in our notes on *The Mystery of Al Capone's Vault,* Tribune Entertainment offered a number of dramatic and variety one-shots. Prominent among the Tribune releases were a 1984 domestic melodrama, *A Married Man,* starring Anthony Hopkins; *Nadia,* a 1984 biopic about Olympic star Nadia Comaneci, with Talia Balsam in the title role; *Anzacs,* a story of Australia's participation in World War I, made several years before its 1987 American premiere and released at that time to take advantage of the *Crocodile Dundee*-generated celebrity of *Anzacs* star Paul Hogan; and 1986's *Salute to Jimmy Doolittle,* an all-star tribute to the World War II general hosted by Bob Hope.

Young People's Specials (1984–). Half-hour "message" dramas, done up entertainingly by Multimedia, sponsored by Campbell's Soups, and released on a monthly basis to several big-city markets including those served by the NBC-owned channels. Some of the self-descriptive titles included *That Funny Fat Kid, The Day Dad Got Fired,* and *Danny and the Killer Rain* (the rain, of course, being of the acid variety). *My Mother the Witch* was an anti-prejudice story set in 17th-century Massachusetts; *Rosie* was a touching tale involving the terminal illness of a loved one; *Little Arliss* was a sequel to Fred Gipson's love-my-dog novel *Old Yeller;* and *Umbrella Jack* was a tale of the homeless, featuring an Emmy-winning performance by John Carradine.

Sports

With all three networks going full-blast with sports events, with PBS offering everything from badminton to soccer, with one cable service (ESPN) devoted exclusively to round-the-clock athletic activity, one would think that there wouldn't be anything left over for syndication. Yet still, the sports syndies bloomed, and still they made nationwide sales.

Al McGuire On Sports (1982). Never at a loss for words, basketball coach Al McGuire could be seen in his first nationally syndicated sports show over 17 stations, including the NBC-owned operations, thanks to the distribution channels of D.L. Taffner.

Babe Winkelman's Good Fishing (1984). What can one say? Not much different from all the other fishermen on television, Babe Winkelman was representative of the sort of entrepreneur who went in for this sort of programming in the '80s; he supplemented his TV weekly with personal appearances, personalized fishing gear, and a series of fast-selling video cassettes. The popularity of Winkelman, Rowland Martin, Bill Dance and all other television outdoorsmen is amazing; by rights, watching a picture of a man catching a fish should be as exciting as smoking a picture of a cigar.

The Baseball Bunch (1980–). Seasonal, youth-oriented sports weekly from Major League Baseball Promotion Corporation (also responsible for the weekly Mel Allen-narrated recap *This Week in Baseball*). The "regulars" were a crew of pre-teen ballplayers and their "friend," the San Diego Chicken. The emphasis was on good sportsmanship, and the guests were those few sports celebrities who actually practiced good sportsmanship. Though quite elementary material, *Baseball Bunch* was well-crafted enough to earn two Emmies for film editing.

Bob Uecker's Wacky World of Sports (1986–). If you looked for the dictionary definition of "workaholic," you'd probably find a picture of Bob Uecker. The former major league ballplayer was in 1986 acting in the ABC sitcom *Mr. Belvedere,* busy with a series of beer commercials, and doing play-by-play broadcasts for the Milwaukee Brewers when he took on this comedy sports syndie for Orbis Communications. Several miles removed from the wit of Ring Lardner, *Wacky World of Sports* offered such highlights as surfing reports and "the shooting chef," as well as the usual film-clips of sports bloopers and fat people playing beachball.

Fight of the Month (1981). LBS monthly hosted by Marvelous Marvin Hagler.

Fights of the '70s (1980). Retrospective from 20th Century–Fox TV.

G.L.O.W. and *P.O.W.W.* see *Wrestling*

Golden Gloves see *Sugar Ray Leonard's Golden Gloves*

Goodwill Games (1986). Another of millionaire Ted Turner's attempts to warm up relationships between the Americans and the Soviets was this semi-Olympic series of sports contests, pitting the U.S. and U.S.S.R. against one another in good, clean, friendly athletic rivalry. *The Goodwill Games* were carried on Turner's cable services, and on those independent stations evincing interest, from July 5 through 19, 1986. Alternately fascinating and boring, these muscle matches between America and the Iron Curtain countries suffered from the fact that, unlike the Olympics, there were no recognizable personalities amongst the athletes. When there was talk that there'd be another session of Goodwill Games in a few years, Ted Turner did not commit himself; he'd lost several million dollars in two full weeks of events that most people didn't bother to watch, and that many others were unaware had even taken place.

Greats of the Game (1984). Another retrospective, this one from DFS.

The Road to Moscow (1980); **The Road to Los Angeles** (1984); **The Road to Calgary** (1987). No, these aren't rejected titles for Bob Hope–Bing Crosby pictures. The *Roads* listed above, distributed variously by Syndicast and MCA, were lead-in weeklies to the Olympic contests of the '80s. *Road to Moscow* proved a worthless title when Jimmy Carter, angered at the Soviets' ongoing violations of "human rights," pulled America out of the Olympics; the series was "disguised," not very successfully, with the new title *American Athletes*. The Russians themselves pulled out of the 1984 Games, but this had no effect on sales of *The Road to Los Angeles*. While *Road to Seoul* would have been the logical title for the 1987 lead-in show, the distributor was wary of the tinderbox political situation in Korea; the *Seoul* show was held out of release until late 1988, replaced in the autumn of '87 by a weekly preview of the winter Olympics, *Road to Calgary*.

Smash! see *Wrestling*

Sports: Pros and Cons (1987). Weekly debate from SFM, with Bob Trumpy moderating as athletes, managers and columnists were pitted against one another over current sports controversies.

Star Games (1984). Pamela Sue Martin and Bruce Jenner hosted this weekly celebrity sports contest from Viacom, inspired by those ubiquitous (and matter-of-taste) "Battle of the Stars" network specials.

Sugar Ray Leonard's Golden Gloves (1982). From MCA; youthful boxers on their way up (and sometimes down and out).

Super Chargers (1983). Auto-racing weekly.

This Is the NFL; This Week in Baseball; This Week in the NFL; This Week in the USFL; Weekend Sports Wrapup (early 1980's onward). It's difficult to critique these recap shows, since they were only as good as the previous week in sports. Guess, however, which of these shows was no longer on the air by 1987?

Weekend Heroes (1981). Another wrap-up show, seasoned with interviews, from Gold Key/Syndicast; Paul Hornung was its first host, followed by Jayne Kennedy. *Weekend Heroes* was one of the earliest series of its kind to benefit from satellite technology, enabling it to cover sports events that had occurred only days before telecast time.

World Wrestling Federation (WWF) Wrestling see *Wrestling*

Wrestling (1983 onward). Though it had always been a lucrative syndicated property, wrestling remained a "regional" throughout the '70s, with the individual wrestling weeklies playing to selected markets where the sport was popular or which had weekly arena matches of their own to promote. Entrepreneur Vincent K. MacMahon changed all that when he consolidated several regional weeklies into a single attraction, *World Wrestling Federation Wrestling* (known less redundantly as *WWF Wrestling*), and managed to sell the series to virtually every major market in every state in the nation. MacMahon's early-1980's marketing strategy was followed by other wrestling leagues and associations (each with their own sets of World champions, deadly rivalries, and "good" and "bad" guys); this syndie saturation was enhanced by weekly grappling matches over the country's various cable services. The increased exposure made national heroes (and villains) of wrestlers who previously had been famous only regionally. And the bigger wrestling got, the gaudier it became: the already outrageously attired athletes' clothes got even more flamboyant; packed-house bouts were staged, like prizefights, at major Vegas and Atlantic City gambling houses arenas; and the audiences began to include high-profile movie, television, recording and sports personalities. Despite isolated incidents where showmanship crossed over into senseless brutality (who could forget David "Doctor D" Schultz punching out ABC interviewer John Stossel on-camera?), many viewers watched wrestling matches as a harmless way to enjoy the euphoria of brute force, or to laugh at the more obvious moments of pre-rehearsal, or both. What these viewers got out of *Smash!,* a nightly talk show wherein wrestlers engaged in conversations that usually degenerated into dire threats, or such women's-wrestling extravaganzas as *Gorgeous Ladies of Wrestling (G.L.O.W.)* and *Powerful Women of Wrestling (P.O.W.W.)* is a question best left to the sociologists and sex therapists. With *WWF Wrestling* established as the third top-rated syndicated weekly of 1987, and with the annual *Wrestlemania* videocassettes breaking sales records all over, it's a safe bet that TV wrestling isn't about to fade away day after tomorrow.

Talk/Interview

For the first time since the late '60s, this field was dominated not by the established Old Masters (many of whom, including Griffin and Douglas, had been elbowed off the air by the early '80s) but by a whole flock of fairly new faces. That the subject matter heard on talk shows tended to remain the same from personality to personality was one of the risks run when trying to give the public what it thinks it wants.

The Barry Farber Show (1982). Undaunted by a poorly received stab at national television in 1978, New York radio personality Barry Farber, who described himself as belonging to the "Big Bang School" of controversy ("A conservative is a liberal who's been mugged!" was all too typical of Farber's style) went before the cameras for a 1982 weekly from 20th Century–Fox TV. Viewers soon grew tired of such fabricated Farber confrontations as a Ku Klux Klanner and a black militant shouting "You're another!" for 60 minutes.

Born Famous (1987). A limited-series revision of Cable's *Are You Anybody?,* which delineated the accomplishments of celebrities' spouses, Fries Communications' *Born Famous* interviewed the sons and daughters of the famous. Kathy Cronkite, Walter's daughter, hosted.

Charlie Rose (1981). Half-hour daily taped at WRC in Washington, D.C., and distributed by Post-Newsweek. Host Charlie Rose held court over the standard conglomeration of celebrities and special-interest proponents; his most poignant program was an interview with a befuddled, emaciated David Niven, shortly before the actor's death. Charlie Rose later built up a following of red-eyed fans when he became a co-host on the all-night *CBS News Nightwatch.*

David Brenner see *Nightlife with David Brenner*

The Don Lane Show (1980). American-born Don Lane, a very popular television personality in Australia, had been hosting an essay-to-take talk-variety program taped in Sydney since 1974 when Worldvision decided to introduce Lane to U.S. viewers in the fall of 1980. The results were pleasant, but slim competition to Merv, Phil and the rest of the talk show establishment.

Geraldo (1987). Investigative journalist Geraldo Rivera was the sort of personality one either revered or despised. Fans would point to the positive results of his jump-out-of-the-bushes technique, which included sweeping social reforms and the routing of rascals operating within the law. Non-fans considered Rivera a self-promoting pest, spending most of his time over-sensationalizing news stories that had already been covered, and researched, by less colorful journalists. Rivera's public reason for walking off his contributor's job on ABC's *20-20* was completely in character; he claimed that the network had suppressed his report about the "truth" of the 1962 death of Marilyn Monroe, another old news story that Rivera planned to milk to the utmost. (The Monroe material in question was later syndicated as a one-shot special by Silverbach-Lazarus, without Rivera's participation; it was a sow's ear of stories that everyone had been hearing for nearly 25 years, but there was no doubt that Geraldo would have used his magic touch to transform the special into a silk purse.) Operating on a free-lance basis, Rivera made his syndie mark with the notorious *Mystery of Al Capone's Vault* (see notes in "Specials, Miniseries, and Mininetworks" section). His next top-rated non-network specials had Rivera fielding questions from live studio audiences, where he showed considerable talent. What more logical step afterwards than a *daily* audience-participation series? The logical move was made with Paramount/Tribune's *Geraldo* in the fall of 1987. Derided by some as the "male Oprah Winfrey" for his tendency to ooze emotionalism from every pore, Rivera was actually quite adept at handling his new job, tempering his melodramatics by taking a seemingly sincere interest in the opinions of his guests and his audience members, no matter how obtuse or obscene those opinions may have been. There was never anything "quiet" about Rivera's shows: he'd bring the same intensity to a program about child molesters as he would a "fun episode" featuring male strippers. Like it or not, *Geraldo* was lively entertainment, one of the few new talk shows of the late '80s to match *The Oprah Winfrey Show* (which see) as an equal on Winfrey's home turf.

Good Company (1984). A brave but foredoomed effort by KSTP–Minneapolis to crack the morning chat-show market with hosts Steve Adelman and Sharon Anderson.

Hot Seat with Wally George (1985). Everything old is new again, and that goes for the "fist-in-your-face" talk shows of the '60s. In the early '80s, Wally George, an ultra-ultra conservative talk-host who made his mark on KDOC in Anaheim, California (a station owned by another right-wing entertainer, Pat Boone), got his name and face plastered over every major magazine and weekly tabloid after his go-for-blood interview style began building a solid California audience. Videotape clips of Wally George programs wherein a peace activist was so steamed by Wally's badgering that the guest kicked the host's desk over before storming off, or when a stripteaser was goaded into demonstrating her talent on-camera, were circulated far and wide by novelty-hungry TV newsmagazines, so it was a "given" that *Hot Seat with Wally George* would be given a chance at national syndication. The man who gave George that chance was former network executive Fred Silverman, who was then trying to promote Metromedia into a major competitor of the established networks. Wally George was "hot," so Wally George was Silverman's newest acquisition. Alas, Silverman forgot what so many others have forgotten in the past, that Southern California is not The Whole World. While Wally George was able to pack his studio audience with oddly garbed beerbellies who'd scream "Wal-LEE! Wal-LEE!" in praise or "JERK! JERK! JERK!" in condemnation, the rest of the country was less enthusiastic. Whereas even in the old days of such earlier "guerrilla" talk-hosts as Joe Pyne there was *some* give-and-take with the guests, with Wally George it was all "take." George would viciously and deliberately hector his guest into flashes of bad temper, then just when the guest would try to counter with his or her views, George would prompt his audience to scream so loud that no exchange of views was possible, or have the guest thrown out with the aid of the two armed guards he kept in attendance. Sometimes, Wally would get so mad himself that he'd walk off his own show, though usually about five minutes before sign-off time (this wasn't the only element of *Hot Seat* that smelled of contrivance). While admittedly most of Wally George's guests were the sort of fringies who wouldn't be given the time of day by Carson or Donahue, Wally's take-no-prisoners approach was the very antithesis of "discussion." For most viewers, one or two exposures to *Hot Seat* were more than enough, and Wally George, the man who once earned himself a cover on *People* magazine, was back in his local market — and nowhere else — by 1986, less than a year after his national "break." But those who sighed in relief and assumed that George was the last of the fist-in-face types were blissfully unaware that Morton Downey Jr. was hovering in the wings.

Jerry Lewis see *Thicke of the Night*

Joan Rivers see *The Late Show with Joan Rivers*

The John Davidson Show (1980–82). Demonstrating the sort of loyalty one finds all the time in Showbiz, Group W signed a five-year contract with talk show star Mike Douglas in 1978, then less than two years later decided Douglas was too old a host performing to too old an audience, and dropped him after 18 years. Group W's idea of a "young, trendy" type was John Davidson, who replaced Douglas in 1980. (Douglas and Davidson remained friends, though it's reported that Mike was put out because John knew about the upcoming switch in hosts but said nothing.) Davidson did his twinkly best, but *The John Davidson Show* was itself axed in 1982, a victim, claimed Group W, of the fact that the talk-interview format was played out, over-populated, and too costly to survive much longer. Oprah Winfrey hadn't happened yet.

The Larry King Show (1983). Talkmeister Larry King was in the sixth season of his fantastically successful Mutual Radio Network all-night chatfest when he signed with MCA/Post-Newsweek for a Sunday night television series, telecast live in most markets from March 13 through July 10, 1983. No effort was made to dress up the series for the camera — in fact, it was little more than "illustrated radio." Not bad, but not really for the Sunday night crowd. King did rather better when he took over Sandy Freeman's nightly call-in show on the CNN Cable Network in 1985. As with his syndie, King's cable effort emanated from Washington, D.C.

The Late Show with Joan Rivers (1986–87); ***The Late Show*** (1987–   ). This nightly hour-long talk program, intended as the cornerstone of the brand-new Fox Television Network, wound up more a stone of the "mill" variety. Joan Rivers, a long-established comedienne whose routines involved ridiculing her own appearance as well as the personal and physical defects of the Rich and Famous, had a lucrative contract as Permanent Guest Host on Johnny Carson's NBC *Tonight Show,* but was offered several millions more to helm the Fox show. Rivers broke not only her *Tonight* contract but any future relations with Johnny Carson by publicly trashing him and his staff at the slightest opportunity. *The Late Show* premiered on October 9, 1986, over all but one of the Fox affiliates (its Milwaukee affiliate stuck fast, and as it turned out wisely, to its *Bob Newhart Show* reruns); the ratings were respectable, if short of the 6 percent share of the audience that Fox had promised its stations. But respectable ratings have a way of evaporating: *The Late Show* turned out to be a bomb of Hiroshima-like dimensions, very nearly sinking Fox before it was launched, virtually destroying Joan Rivers' quarter-century reputation as a reliable laugh-getter, and making it harder than ever to promote potential Johnny Carson competition for late-night consumption.

Since the press as a whole was against Rivers from the beginning, it's hard to make an objective assessment of what happened. It was true that Joan Rivers would alternate between insulting her guests so arbitrarily that she alienated half her audience, and fawning over other guests like a moonstruck autograph hound—which the audience members that remained disliked even more than the insults. Those close to the program claimed that too much power was wielded in a negative manner by Rivers' husband, series co-producer Edgar Rosenberg (now deceased and unable to defend himself). It was also charged that Rivers wanted nothing to do with "new talent," preferring to chat only with the Upper Crust of celebrities (although *The Late Show* made a major star of a comparatively obscure comedian named Arsenio Hall). One thing that was certain was that Rivers and staff closed their ranks and refused to listen to criticism, offering the same mistakes over and over in the apparent hope that eventually they'd be proven right and the rest of the world proven wrong. Even changing producers didn't help: Bruce McKay was replaced by JoAnn Goldberg, who'd softened Barbara Walters' hard-shell image for a series of ABC interviews and who, it was hoped, would do the same for Rivers. It didn't work. But what hurt *The Late Show* most was that, after all of Fox's assurances that the series would be a bold new alternative to *The Tonight Show,* and after all of Joan Rivers' cutting remarks about Johnny Carson, the best Fox and Rivers could come up with was a virtual *Tonight Show* clone: same couch, same desk, same opening monologue, practically the same set and in-house band.

Continually trounced in the ratings, Fox finally agreed with public consensus that *The Late Show with Joan Rivers* was a lost cause, and that while Rivers may have been an excellent guest host, she was either not enough or too much on a night-after-night basis. Guests on Rivers' last program, which aired May 15, 1987, included two of her opening-night guests, David Lee Roth and Pee-wee Herman. Fox tested several potential new *Late Show* hosts, including Carol Bayer Sager (and there were rumors that the show would be taken over by the recently ousted emcees of *The PTL Club,* Jim and Tammy Bakker!)

before briefly replacing the series with a nightly *David Letterman Show*–like satirical news-and-interview show (produced by onetime *Letterman* staffer Barry Sand) titled *The Wilton-North Report*. When this project threatened to be a disaster rivalling anything dished up by Joan Rivers, Fox revived *The Late Show* with a team of alternating comic-hosts, Jeff Joseph and John Mulrooney. By the end of 1987, *The Late Show* was showing signs of returning to life, but its future was still very iffy.

The ultimate blame for the failure of *The Late Show* must rest not with Joan Rivers, but with the Fox Network itself. Fox could have jumped in early on, reshuffled the format, tried to reason with Rivers and her staff, and made something workable out of the whole mess. Instead, Fox sat on its hands, presumably hoping that the notoriety of Joan Rivers' rift with Johnny Carson would be incentive enough for viewers to tune in. When will TV executives realize that notoriety results in fame and audience favor only until something even more notorious comes along — or until the supposedly dull-witted public wakes up?

Leave It to the Women (1981). Woody Fraser, in 1981 busy producing *The Richard Simmons Show,* teamed with wife Norma to oversee a daily revival of the old '50s and '60s series *Leave It to the Girls* (see the "Talk/Interview" section of the 1960's chapter), with title altered to suit the mood of the times. Stephanie Edwards, formerly of ABC's *AM America* and Group W's *Everyday,* moderated. Executive producer, of all people, was Chuck Barris, who exhibited the good taste lacking in his many game shows during his tenure on *Leave It to the Women.* Mag-Net Productions distributed.

The Next President (1987). Series of 60-minute interviews conducted with the 1988 presidential-race hopefuls by a non-partisan David Frost. Sponsored by *US News and World Report* and distributed by Orbis Communications.

Nightlife with David Brenner (1986). Next to Joan Rivers, comedian David Brenner was most often seen occupying Johnny Carson's *Tonight Show* desk when Carson was away. When Brenner took a job as host of Motown/King World's new Monday-through-Friday *Nightlife* (which debuted September 8, 1986), he had the good grace not to speak ill of Mr. Carson, as Joan Rivers had done before launching her nightly talk show. And a good thing, too, since Brenner remained a welcome visitor to the Carson set after *Nightlife* died in mid–May of 1987. Admittedly, many markets ran the program at impossible hours (a Dallas station telecast *Nightlife* at five in the morning!), but the head of King World had a more blunt explanation for Brenner's failure: "He should have been funnier."

The Oprah Winfrey Show (1986–   ). The remarkable Oprah Winfrey, who worked her way up from high-school misfit and troublemaker (the result of an unhappy, unstable home life) to local television talk host, had everything working against her in terms of attaining nationwide popularity — at least according to those "researchers" who made such life-or-death decisions. Oprah was a woman; she was slightly overweight; she wasn't a raving beauty; she wasn't deferential to men; she was black. Her first syndicated exposure was with a daily chat show produced at WJZ–Baltimore and distributed by Program Syndication Service, *People Are Talking,* which Winfrey co-hosted with Richard Sher. This series managed to beat Phil Donahue in the local ratings (a portent of the future), but dead-ended on a national basis. Of course, cried the "experts," it was all Oprah's fault. She was all wrong. She had no future in the business.

A few seasons later, Oprah was hired to host WLS–Chicago's low-rated *AM* program, and the magic began. Viewers who at first found Winfrey brash and irreverent were ultimately enchanted by her no-nonsense, practical approach to weighty and controversial topics; one observer pointed out that, while rival talk-host Phil Donahue was forever prefacing his questions with "Help me out," Oprah gave the impression that she needed no help whatsoever. Balancing her unpretentious outspokenness was Winfrey's unabashed fan-worship whenever interviewing a major celebrity. *AM's* ratings went through the roof, and was retitled *The Oprah Winfrey Show.* The star quickly gained a national reputation thanks to adulatory magazine and newspaper articles about the fresh young kid on the talk show block. And, as had happened in Baltimore, Oprah Winfrey knocked Phil Donahue out of his Number One ratings slot in Chicago. (Ironically, Donahue had been one of Winfrey's role models in her formative years.) In addition, there seemed to be no end to Winfrey's talents: when chosen by Steven Spielberg for a plum supporting role in his feature film *The Color Purple,* she made good to the extent of an Oscar nomination!

The King World distribution firm would have had to be peopled by idiots not to take advantage of Oprah's fame, so on September 8, 1986, King World put *The Oprah Winfrey Show* into national distribution. Within a few months, Winfrey toppled Donahue and all her other rivals off the top-of-the-ratings plateau; within six months, an Emmy award rested on Winfrey's shelf. The Oprah Winfrey style included the ability to exude an Earth-mother aura whenever guiding interviewees through her daily hour; to put troublemakers in their place, no question about it; to sympathize with the tragedies of others to the point of weeping more copiously than any talk-host since Jack Paar; to work into her interviews discussions of her *own* travails, including her well-publicized suicide attempt; and to cheerfully and immodestly plug her outside television and movie projects. What might otherwise seem cloying and obnoxious from any other talk show host was transformed by Oprah Winfrey into an appealing on-camera persona — and a winning ratings ticket. The one negative aspect of *The Oprah Winfrey Show* was King World's tacky ad campaign when it first promoted the series: "Had your Phil?"

The Paul Ryan Show (1983; 1985). Another local-market big fish who made no splash when diving into national syndie waters, KTLA–Los Angeles' Paul Ryan struck out twice; his second series was also known as *Trendsetters.*

People Are Talking see The Oprah Winfrey Show

Sally Jessy Raphäel (1984–). Initially *In Touch with Sally Jessy Raphäel,* this 30-minute (later 60-minute) daily featured the St. Louis-based sex therapist whose fame rested on her nightly network radio call-in advice show. Raphäel, whose red-tinted glasses and casual approach to the weightiest topics won her new fans when she moved to television, did not, like her fellow radio therapists Dr. Ruth Westheimer and David Viscott, merely move her radio format before the cameras. Sally Jessy's daily was a *Phil Donahue*-style parade of social and political issues, with a studio audience to provide feedback and plenty of sex-talk and "fluff" pieces to satisfy the home viewership. In fact, Raphäel's program and Donahue's shared the same distributor: Multimedia.

Stanley Siegel (1981). Siegel, the host of WABC–New York's morning show, became a national figure after baring his soul on a David Susskind program which featured several other noted talk-hosts. As his Manhattan fans well knew, soul-baring was nothing out of the ordinary for Stanley Siegel, who frequently brought his psychiatrist on his talk show (couch and all) for live, televised therapy sessions. On the Air Syndication felt in 1981 that the rest of America might see what New York saw in Stanley Siegel. The tepid results undoubtedly sent Siegel galloping back to his couch.

Star's Table (1986). Restaurant-based table-hopping interview show distributed by the Christian Broadcasting Network and emceed by onetime *Entertainment Tonight* star Dixie Whately.

Thicke of the Night (1983–84). Perhaps *this* time Metromedia would launch its ever-unrealized fourth network. The program would be another late-evening challenge to Johnny Carson (haven't we been here before?). Former NBC head Fred Silverman felt that the man to take on Carson was Canadian comedian/talk host/producer/songwriter Alan Thicke, who'd done fine with the *Tonight*-style format on Canadian TV. Perhaps if *Thicke of the Night* had had a format — *any* format — it might have survived. But from the moment of its September 5, 1983, debut, *Thicke of the Night* was plagued with profound schizophrenia. One night, it was an interview hour-and-a-half; the next night, it was a series of carefully rehearsed comedy sketches; the next, it was totally ad-libbed by its supporting comedy cast; the next.... The next, it was as big a turkey as it had been the night before. *Thicke of the Night* never had more than the tiny viewership it had started with. When the comedy material was good, its sketches ran too short, and when the material was bad, the sketches ran and ran and ran. There were potential star faces in the troupe of comedy regulars: Richard Belzer would go on to host his own talk show for the Lifetime Cable service, Gilbert Gottfried would parlay his "kvetching" act into a series of well-received candy bar commercials, and Charles Fleischer would rise to fame as the voice of the title character in the 1988 movie hit *Who Framed Roger Rabbit?* But none of these comics were particularly brilliant on *Thicke of the Night.* Not that it would have mattered; Metromedia and MGM/UA Television doomed the series from the start with an ad campaign that promised to dethrone the Mighty Carson—a campaign that has never, but *never* worked for anyone. Moreover, Alan Thicke himself looked ill-at-ease and often downright ill-prepared. (On one classic evening, Thicke asked Keith Carradine about Keith's "late" father John, who wasn't quite late yet.) The series' added burden was that it was taped four weeks before it was telecast, which meant that all its topical jokes were a month behind those of the ever up-to-date Carson. Metromedia eventually moved Thicke out of Carson's way by having its owned-and-operated stations run the program a half-hour after *The Tonight Show* signed off. When *Thicke of the Night* folded in late 1984, the show had ceased production and was into reruns, Alan Thicke's career and personal life were in tatters (but would happily revive with the ABC sitcom *Growing Pains*), and Metromedia was desperately trying to maintain a late-night continuum by giving Jerry Lewis a week's tryout as host of his own series. Lewis was better than usual, and lots more sure of himself than Thicke, but Metromedia's dream of late night dominance had been utterly shattered months before. Fred Silverman would later complain that doing *Thicke of the Night* was "like trying to do *Saturday Night Live* five nights a week," while Alan Thicke adopted a *mea culpa* attitude about the whole affair. Thicke and Silverman would work together again in 1986 for a *Perry Mason* TV movie—in which Thicke played a nasty, manipulative talk show host who was murdered before the first commercial!

Tom Cottle: Up Close (1982). Boston-based psychologist Tom Cottle, a familiar face to PBS fans, hosted this Metromedia daily from Boston's WCVB. Cottle conducted probing interviews (often probing so deep that the program seemed like a counseling session) with celebrity guests. What might have been *Up Close's* liveliest half-hour never got aired; mega-millionaire Ted Turner was so burned up when Cottle asked a rather innocuous personal question that Turner stormed off the set, threatening to sue Mr. Cottle's hindquarters should any portion of the interview be televised.

The Toni Tennille Show (1980). Talk-variety from MCA, starring the prettier half of the "Captain and Tennille" singing team. After running through several producers and production companies since first conceived in early 1979, *The Toni Tennille Show* settled for the producing duo of Bob Eubanks and Michael Hill. Beyond the fact that the talk show market was overstocked to the point of suffocation, *The Toni Tennille Show* was made inaccessible to most of Toni's fans by the NBC-owned stations, which scheduled the program just after *The Tomorrow Show* at 2 a.m. Adding insult to injury was the fact that those viewers up at that hour complained that Toni Tennille had replaced their beloved reruns of *The Mary Tyler Moore Show*.

Wally George see *Hot Seat with Wally George*

The Wil Shriner Show (1987). "Conceptual comedian" Wil Shriner (son of legendary humorist Herb Shriner), launched this Group W daily talker in 1987 as part of industrywide effort to take advantage of the "new" chat-show market opened up by Oprah Winfrey. But there was trouble afoot before the cameras even started turning; Shriner planned to do a laugh-filled mockery of the talk genre à la David Letterman, but Group W demanded an "infotainment" format as exemplified by its *Hour Magazine*. The resultant marriage of styles was a shaky and not terribly happy one, and *The Wil Shriner Show,* though given a vote of confidence by being picked up by the NBC-owned outlets, was hanging by its fingernails, mostly in fringe time slots, before it was six months old.

Woman to Woman (1983). From Golden West Television; daily, hour-long panel show hosted by Pat Mitchell, late of *Hour Magazine. Woman to Woman* won an Emmy as best new talk show of 1983–84, but once more, the market was too swamped with talk-talk-talk for the series to have a decent chance at survival.

Travel/Documentary

There has always been, and probably always will be, a market for this type of programming. Not only was it welcome on the syndicated scene, but cable services like Arts and Entertainment and the Discovery Channel devoted practically their entire broadcast days to Travel/Documentary.

America Works (1983). Sporadically released half-hours, produced at the behest of the AFL-CIO Labor Institute, narrated by Marie Torres, and syndicated by Fox/Lorber/All-American Television. Essentially a streamlined, elongated update of old working-man documentaries like *Industry on Parade.*

American Diary (1982). E.G. Marshall hosted this limited biographical-historical series, aimed at weekend broadcasts by American National Productions.

Crime, Inc. (1985). A D.L. Taffner British import, concentrating on the gangster kings of the '20s and '30s. The package got nowhere until after Geraldo Rivera's top-rated assault on Capone's vault; *Crime, Inc.* was then picked up by the Arts and Entertainment cable service and run as *Crime in America.*

Exciting World of Speed and Beauty (1983). Globetrotting celebration of fast and/or luxurious automobiles, designed by Access Syndication Service as a companion piece for reruns of *Lorne Greene's New Wilderness* (which see).

Heroes: Made in the USA (1986). Some of the heroes in this Post-Newsweek/Access weekender were self-made captains of industry. Host: Craig T. Nelson.

Lifestyles of the Rich and Famous (1984–   ). This voyeuristic paean to conspicuous consumption began as a feature on *Entertainment Tonight;* when the feature's creator-host, Robin Leach, left that nightly magazine, he took *Lifestyles of the Rich and Famous* with him, transforming the property into a group of two-hour specials, the first of these syndicated by Television Program Entertainment in April of 1984. *Lifestyles* went weekly in the fall of that year; the series' fans apparently couldn't get enough of its lavishly photographed studies of how movie stars, famous authors and the like spent their hard-earned millions while cavorting in Malibu, South America or the Cote d'Azur. Any resentment at watching these privileged people do and buy things beyond the audience's means was undercut by the peppy narration of Robin Leach. The Harrow-born journalist spoke with such a thick British working-class dialect that his observations had the air of the poor little kid at his first fancy dress ball; audiences could identify with this attitude, which kept Leach's peeks at financial excess "down to Earth." After unduly emphasizing the newest TV and movie stars in its first few months, *Lifestyles* gave some air-time to "old money" celebrities of an earlier age, who sometimes displayed a sweet modesty about their wealth that was lacking in the arrogant so-and-sos who'd just recently attained their fame and fortune. What might have come as a surprise to the viewers was that several of Leach's on-camera subjects received compensation for their appearances, including free limousine and hotel service and $1400 expense money! Starting with its 1985–86 season, *Lifestyles of the Rich and Famous* began running a short feature called "Runaways," showing celebrities at their favorite private vacation spots. This feature was in turn spun off into yet another Robin Leach weekly, *Runaway with the Rich and Famous,* released by T.P.E. in 1986.

Lorne Greene's New Wilderness (1982). Lorne Greene, by 1982 a 40-year veteran of the broadcasting business, produced and narrated this American Television Syndication weekly followup to his earlier *Last of the Wild. New Wilderness* went on to win an Emmy for Best Editing, while Greene went on as a commercial spokesman. The actor died in 1987, just before he was to begin work on his final syndicated project, a two-hour movie revival of his old *Bonanza* series.

Runaway with the Rich and Famous see *Lifestyles of the Rich and Famous*

The Spectacular World of Guinness Records (1987). David Frost was on hand to ooh and aah over the fantastic achievements recorded (or about to be recorded) in *The Guinness Book of World Records,* just as he'd been for a short group of specials based on that same publication back in the '70s. *Spectacular World* was concocted by Peregrin and Together Again Productions, and shipped out by Orbis Communications.

The Start of Something Big (1985). Steve Allen (with the off-screen help of his crack research staff) hosted this Television Program Entertainment weekly devoted to behind-the-scenes glimpses of major events, success stories, and strange-but-true facts. *Start of Something Big* was hyped with a $500,000 giveaway contest just prior to and during its release. Steve Allen would tape several of his narrative contributions in 12-hour sessions, leaving time for his multitude of other projects.

Vietnam: The 10,000 Day War (1981). Alan Enterprises' 26-week essay on the bloodiest undeclared war in recent history was narrated with a decidedly anti-military slant by Richard Basehart. Few stations would touch the series in 1981, and when it was given an occasional chance by a commercial or public outlet, it faced contributor and sponsor boycotts and unrelenting attacks from such right-wing groups as Accuracy in Media. *Vietnam* would later run on the Arts and Entertainment cable service; after the late–80's success of several movies about the war, Vietnam was suddenly "saleable," so Arts and Entertainment had no want of sponsor for this superbly (and selectively) edited documentary.

Where Were You? (1981). Year-by-year retrospective documentary, mainly seen in weekend access time on the five ABC-owned channels.

Annotated Bibliography

Here is a list of books that went into my research. The Introduction to this book mentions the periodicals of critical importance to a researcher in this field, as well as five of the books listed here. Some of the works below were devoted to specific syndication or syndie-related information, some spoke of specific syndicated programs in a page or two, and some offered but a sentence or throwaway phrase. Those books that were of special help (and might benefit the reader who wishes to pursue the history of syndication further) are summarized in an annotation. Those that were of marginal help, or whose significance to my text is summed up by their titles, are listed without comment.

General Reference

Barnouw, Eric. *A Tower in Babel: The History of Broadcasting in the United States to 1933*. New York: Oxford University Press, 1966.
_____. *The Golden Web: The History of Broadcasting in the United States 1933–1953*. New York: Oxford, 1968.
_____. *The Image Empire: The History of Broadcasting in the United States from 1953*. New York: Oxford, 1970.
Barnouw's large, scholarly, opinionated and highly readable trilogy spends more time on the influence of the networks and advertisers on broadcasting, but does provide brief chronologies of various moments of importance in syndication — particularly the pioneering syndie effort *Amos 'n' Andy*.

Brooks, Tim, and Earle Marsh. *The Complete Directory to Prime Time Network TV Shows, 1946–Present*. New York: Ballantine, 1979. Rev. editions: 1981, 1985, 1988.
The most thorough of the "popular" source books, with complete cast lists, dates of series premieres and cancellations, and a section on major television awards. Brooks and Marsh began adding selected syndicated series, by popular demand, in their 1981 revision, noting that they'd chosen only those syndies deemed significant in their eyes. The most recent revision, which appeared in late 1988, has included the inaugural offerings of the new Fox network. The book does not include public television programs, nor does it list daytime or early-afternoon series.

Clift, Charles, and Archie Greer. *Broadcast Programming: The Current Perspective*. Washington, D.C.: University Press of America, 1978.
This summary of programming trends was printed annually for many years.

The 1978 edition contains valuable information on the state of syndication since the Prime Time Access Rule went into effect seven years earlier. It also provides a list of syndie-series ratings for the year.

Dunning, John. *Tune in Yesterday: The Ultimate Encyclopedia of Old-Time Radio 1925–1976.* Englewood Cliffs, N.J.: Prentice-Hall, 1976.

This book admittedly owes a great deal to *The Big Broadcast,* a radio-series encyclopedia compiled in the early '70s by Frank Buxton and Bill Owen. But Dunning, a Denver radio personality and old-time radio show collector, adds the touch of the fan and enthusiast, making the reader wish that he or she could hear those old programs instead of just reading about them. *Tune in Yesterday* was useful in tracing the roots of several 1950's syndicated adventures, dramas, comedies and westerns, as well as a number of '60s and '70s game shows.

Eisner, Joel, and David Krinsky, *Television Comedy Series: An Episode Guide to 153 TV Sitcoms in Syndication.* Jefferson, N.C.: McFarland, 1983.

Enormous — and enormously rewarding — volume covering much of what is available in syndication in the comedy field. Includes an episode-by-episode breakdown of the following made-for-syndication series: *Colonel Flack, The Goldbergs, The Great Gildersleeve, How to Marry a Millionaire, The Jim Backus Show, Mr. Ed, This Is Alice,* and that syndie champion of champions, *The Abbott and Costello Show.* Also included are the episodes of such cartoon series as *Huckleberry Hound, Yogi Bear* and *Wait Till Your Father Gets Home.*

Eliot, Marc. *American Television: The Official Art of the Artificial Style and Tactics in Network Prime Time.* New York: Anchor/Doubleday, 1981.

More opinionated than factual, not to mention more arch than funny, Eliot's book skewers several syndies that made it into prime time, especially *I Led Three Lives.*

Fireman, Judy, ed. *TV Book: The Ultimate Television Book.* New York: Workman Press, 1977.

Includes very brief but entertaining studies of Ziv Television by Tim Onosko, and of the business of game-show syndication by Joyce Jaffe.

Gertner, Richard, ed. *International Motion Picture Almanac.* Quigley Publications, New York.

_____, ed. *International Television and Video Almanac.* Quigley.

These two books were once printed under one title: *The International Motion Picture Almanac,* which first appeared in 1929. This *Almanac* began listing TV information in 1952; in 1956, the first edition of *International Television Almanac* was published, a title which was changed to incorporate the word "Video" (a nod to the cassette industry) in 1987. *The Television Almanac* is useful in offering information on international producers and distributors of syndicated TV shows, while the *International Motion Picture Almanac* maintains an up-to-date biographical section of "who's who" in the industry.

Grossman, Gary H. *Saturday Morning TV.* Dell, New York, 1981.

Intensely nostalgic look at what we've been watching Saturday mornings for the past three decades. Passing references to innumerable syndies, with emphasis on adventures and westerns. Includes a list of programs that have been seen on or off network on Saturday morning — though I'd question the inclusion of such night-time syndies as *Highway Patrol* and *Sea Hunt* which, though they may have been rerun in the kiddie hours, were not specifically designed for that market.

Horn, Maurice, ed. *World Encyclopedia of Comics.* New York: Chelsea House, 1976.

Though not all-inclusive, this astounding 700 plus-page work offers thumbnail sketches of major international comic strips and comic artists. Extremely useful in tracking the origins of many syndie cartoon series, and especially helpful in offering a history of newspaper syndication, a few elements of which I've incorporated in my own "Syndication in a Nutshell" section of this book.

McNeil, Alex. *Total Television: A Comprehensive Guide to Programming from 1948 to the Present.* New York: Penguin, 1980. 2d ed., 1984.

A handy companion to Brooks and Marsh's *Complete Directory to Prime Time Network TV Shows,* McNeil's book provides far more information on syndicated offerings; he also includes public television and daytime programs. McNeil writes as a fan, not a pedant; frequently his cast and production credits are skimpy, but his enthusiasm for his subject is contagious. But *Total Television* isn't precisely "total"; McNeil does not include series made up of reruns and pilot episodes from other series, nor does he list programs comprised of theatrical feature films and short subjects.

Norback, Craig T., and Peter G. Norback, and eds. of TV GUIDE. *TV Guide Almanac.* New York: Ballantine, 1979.

A compendium of television facts, including brief histories of the major networks, a list of existing television broadcasting stations in the Western Hemisphere, a tally of prominent advertising firms, and a rundown of virtually all syndication firms and their wares.

Shulman, Arthur, and Roger Youman. *How Sweet It Was!* New York: Bonanza, 1966.

A superficial history of American TV up to 1966, lavishly illustrated. Definitely reflects the attitudes of its time, especially in assuming that spy shows would continue in popularity for years to come and in titling its section on soap operas "While the Dishes Wait"! Still, it's as good a reference for a number of syndies as any that could have been compiled in that pre–VCR era — and surprisingly noncondescending towards TV at a time when Television History was considered to be as frivolous as collecting beer cans.

Terrace, Vincent. *Encyclopedia of Television: Series, Pilots and Specials (1937–1984).* New York: Zoetrope, 1986. 3 vols.

Terrace's mammoth three-volume set, an outgrowth of his pioneering effort *Complete Encyclopedia of Television Programs 1947–1979* (New York: Barnes, 1979), is quite simply the best and most comprehensive source book on the subject of American television.

Thomey, Ted. *The Glorious Decade.* New York: Ace, 1970.

Thomey, a veteran magazine writer and "ghost" for many a celebrity autobiography, provides a chatty observation of why the good shows of the "golden years" were as good as they were. Concentrates almost exclusively on the networks, with brief notes on such syndie–TV personalities as Georgie Jessel.

Wilk, Max. *The Golden Age of Television: Notes from the Survivors.* New York: Dell, 1976.

    Devoted virtually *in toto* to the recollections of the veterans of "live TV," Wilk's book concludes with a chronicle of how hard it was to sell the major movie studios on the notion of producing TV films.

Winship, Michael. *Television,* 1st U.S. ed. New York: Random House, 1988.

    Written as a tie-in for a PBS series on the world history of TV narrated by Edwin Newman, who provides an introduction to Winship's book, *Television* offers observations on the business end that the TV series glossed over. Amusing are the observations of many new honchos in the syndication game, who speak as if they were the first to discover the rewards inherent in non-network TV.

Specific Genres

Biskind, Peter. *Seeing Is Believing.* New York: Pantheon, 1983.

    Biskind's contention is that all films made in the 1950's were either subliminally or overtly sociopolitical. Some of his side comments, such as his notes on the authors of the book *New York Confidential,* bear some relation on the adventure/mystery and drama syndies of the era.

Edmondson, Madeline, and David Rounds. *From Mary Noble to Mary Hartman: The Complete Soap Opera Book.* Briarcliff Manor, N.Y.: Stein and Day, 1976.

    Originally published in 1973 as *The Soaps,* this book was expanded in 1976 to include a thorough study on the origin, the premiere and the aftermath of *Mary Hartman, Mary Hartman* — though it speaks not at all on such earlier syndie serials as *Strange Paradise.*

Everson, William K. *The Detective in Film.* Secaucus, N.J.: Citadel, 1972.

    Celebrated film historian Everson is no big fan of TV, but his study of detective-movie trends provides tidbits on such syndies as *Sherlock Holmes, Colonel March* and *The Falcon.*

Fabe, Maxine. *TV Game Shows.* Garden City, N.Y.: Doubleday, 1979.

    Offers a list of virtually all game programs seen in the years 1946–1979, with the usual emphasis on network shows and a mere nod of acknowledgment to syndication.

Gerani, Gary, and Paul H. Schulman. *Fantastic Television.* New York: Harmony Books, 1977.

    Well-researched history of science-fiction and fantasy programs, with complete episode logs of selected TV series. The only syndies treated in depth are *Superman* and *Space: 1999,* but there's a list of lesser series both network and syndicated in the last section of the book.

Glut, Donald, and Jim Harmon. *The Great Television Heroes.* Garden City, N.Y.: Doubleday, 1976.

    Good companion piece to Grossman's *Saturday Morning TV;* offers further insight into such syndies as *Cisco Kid* and *Time for Beany.*

Hadden, Jeffrey K., and Charles E. Swann. *Prime Time Preachers.* Reading, Mass.: Addison-Wesley, 1981.

Objective overview of "televangelism," with short studies of up-and-coming stars like Pat Robertson and the Bakkers. Offers the actual TV ratings of ministers whose own estimate of their viewership was somewhat exaggerated. Divides the major personalities into groups: "The Supersavers," "The Mainliners," "The 'Talkies'" (i.e., those whose programs emulate *The Johnny Carson Show*), "The Entertainers," "The Teachers" and "The Unconventional." Excellent pre–PTL scandal study of the genre.

Higham, Charles, and Joel Greenberg. *The Celluloid Muse.* Chicago: Regnery, 1969.

Contains interviews with a number of film directors both brilliant and pedestrian. Directors such as Robert Aldrich and John Frankenheimer offer much that is valuable on the TV-production experience.

Maltin, Leonard. *The Great Movie Comedians.* New York: Crown, 1978.

_____. *Of Mice and Magic.* New York: New American Library, 1980. Rev. ed., 1987.

Maltin's painstakingly researched work is always a treat. *Great Movie Comedians* touches on the TV work of such comic giants as Keaton and Abbott and Costello; *Of Mice and Magic* is a sweeping history of American animated cartoons, with additional notes on the television work of such sterling cartoon factories as UPA, Hanna-Barbera and Famous Studios.

Miller, Don. *Hollywood Corral.* New York: Big Apple/Popular Library, 1976.

Freewheeling history of the "B" Western, including a solid chapter on such low-budget TV jobs as *Wild Bill Hickok, Range Rider* and *26 Men.*

Mitz, Rick. *The Great TV Sitcom Book.* New York: Richard Malek, 1980 (several rev. editions).

Mitz' wise-guy attitude grates at times, but his is the best general look at the sitcom form and its influence on TV as a whole; the book is constantly being revised, usually with the melancholy realization that TV comedy isn't always something to be laughed at. Syndicated sitcoms are treated casually, but perhaps the recent upsurge in such syndies will oblige Mitz to spend as much time on non-network shows as he lavishes on *I Love Lucy, M*A*S*H,* or even *Rhoda.*

Morganstern, Steve, ed. *Inside the TV Business.* New York: Sterling Publishers, 1979.

Drawn from seminar and convention speeches given by many of TV's prime movers, *Inside the TV Business* gives generously of its space to syndication specialists such as Alan *(In Search of...)* Landsburg.

Morris, James. *The Preachers.* New York: St. Martin's Press, 1973.

Traces the lives and times of a number of electronic-religion purveyors, among them Oral Roberts, Billy James Hargis, Reverend Ike and the Armstrong family.

Parish, James Robert, ed. *The Great Movie Series.* Cranbury, N.J.: A.S. Barnes, 1971.

Provides the cinematic roots of such TV series as *Jungle Jim, The Falcon, Boston Blackie* and *Dr. Christian.*

Rose, Brian G. *Television and the Performing Arts*. Westport, Conn.: Greenwood
    Press, 1986.
    A history of cultural counterprogramming along the lines of syndication's *Play
of the Week*.

Schemering, Christopher. *Soap Opera Encyclopedia*. New York: Ballantine, 1985.
    Everything you want to know, including complete cast lists, about every TV
soap since the medium began. Indispensible for information on such syndies as
Mary Hartman, All That Glitters, Paul Bernard: Psychiatrist and *Rituals*.

Schneider, Cy. *Children's Television: The Art, the Business and How It Works*.
    Introduction by Fred Silverman. Lincolnwood, Ill.: NTC Business Books, 1987.
    Matter-of-fact, hard-nosed, but easy-to-read book by a longtime advertising
executive. Schneider sees nothing wrong in creating kid-oriented commercials,
pointing out effectively that children's programming could not exist without some
sort of financial support, and that every program can't and shouldn't be *Sesame
Street*. He's particularly rough on Action for Children's Television, which he
perceives as having created more problems than it has solved for TV.

Stewart, Sandy. *From Coast to Coast: A Personal History of Radio in Canada*.
    Toronto: CBC Enterprises, 1985.
    First published in 1975 as *A Pictorial History of Radio*, Stewart's work takes
on added value as more and more made-in-Canada product finds its way into U.S.
TV syndication. *From Coast to Coast* provides a historical foundation for one of
the most thriving entertainment industries in the Western Hemisphere.

Wilmut, Roger. *From Fringe to Flying Circus: Celebrating a Unique Generation of
    Comedy*. London: Methuen, 1983.
    Superb history of British television's satirical-comedy boom of the '60s and
'70s, of special interest vis-a-vis the syndie career of David Frost and the 1971 Access
Time import *Doctor in the House*.

Woolery, George. *Children's Television: The First Thirty-Five Years 1946–1981*.
    Metuchen, N.J.: Scarecrow, 1983. 2 vols.
    How I wish I could have found this excellent two-volume work while laboring
on my own book! Volume One covers animated cartoons; Volume Two covers live,
film and tape programs. Woolery includes broadcast dates, cast and production
credits (where available), and cross-references whenever the programs in his book
contain historical, literary or non-children's-TV elements. Had I discovered this
book, however, I would probably not have done a lot of my own primary research
and come up with the very few programs *not* covered in Woolery's pages.

Specific Series, Production Companies and Personalities

Arnold, Edwin T. *The Films and Career of Robert Aldrich*. Knoxville: University
    of Tennessee Press, 1986.

Balio, Tino. *United Artists: The Company That Changed the Film Industry*. Madi-
    son: University of Wisconsin Press, 1987.

Buckley, William F., Jr. *The Jeweler's Eye.* New York: Berkeley/Putnam, 1969.
_____. *Quotations from Chairman Bill.* Compiled by David Franke. New Rochelle, N.Y.: Arlington House, 1970.
Contains observations on confrontational talk shows in the years before Morton Downey, Jr., was invented.

Culhane, Shamus. *Talking Animals and Other People.* New York: St. Martin's Press, 1986.
Inside glimpses of the TV-animation racket.

Dixon, Wheeler, ed. *Producers Releasing Corporation: A Complete History and Filmography.* Introduction by William K. Everson. Jefferson, N.C.: McFarland, 1986.

Donahue, Phil, et al. *Donahue: My Own Story.* New York: Simon and Schuster, 1979.

Douglas, Mike. *Mike Douglas: My Story.* New York: Putnam, 1978.

Fairbanks, Douglas, Jr., and Richard Schickel. *The Fairbanks Album.* Boston: New York Graphic Society, 1975.

Fates, Gil. *What's My Line?* Englewood-Cliffs, N.J.: Prentice-Hall, 1978.

Gargan, William. *Why Me? An Autobiography.* Garden City, N.Y.: Doubleday, 1969.

Griffin, Merv, with Peter Barsocchini. *Merv: An Autobiography.* New York: Simon and Schuster, 1980.

Grossman, Gary H. *Superman: Serial to Cereal.* New York: Big Apple/Popular Library, 1976.

Hall, Monty, with Bill Libby. *Emcee Monty Hall.* New York: Grosset and Dunlap, 1973.

Higby, Mary Jane. *Tune in Tomorrow.* New York: Cowles, 1968.
An actress' personal account of old-time radio.

Hurst, Richard Maurice. *Republic Studios: Between Poverty Row and the Majors.* Metuchen, N.Y.: Scarecrow, 1979.

Irvine, Reed. *Media Mischief and Misdeeds.* Chicago: Regnery Gateway, 1984.
Alternative view of news and talk shows, from the chairman of Accuracy in Media.

Jewell, Richard B., with Vernon Harbin. *The RKO Story.* New York: Arlington House, 1982.

Kotsilibas-Davis, James. *The Barrymores: The Royal Family of Hollywood.* New York: Crown, 1981.

McGee, Mark Thomas. *Fast and Furious: The Story of American International Pictures*. Jefferson, N.C.: McFarland, 1984.

Maltin, Leonard, ed. *Hollywood Kids*. New York: Popular Library, 1978.
_____, ed. *The Laurel and Hardy Book*. New York: Curtis Books, 1973.
_____, and Richard W. Bann. *Our Gang: The Lives and Times of the Little Rascals*. New York: Crown, 1977.
   Contains information on the Hal Roach Studios, one of the earliest TV-film plants.

Metz, Robert. *CBS: Reflections in a Bloodshot Eye*. Chicago: Playboy Press, 1975.

Miller, Merle. *Plain Speaking: An Oral Biography of Harry Truman*. New York: Berkeley/Putnam, 1975.

Mulholland, Jim. *The Abbott and Costello Book*. New York: Big Apple/Popular Library, 1975.

Nelson, Ozzie. *Ozzie*. Englewood Cliffs, N.J.: Prentice-Hall, 1973.

Russell, Nicole (a.k.a. the Duchess of Bedford). *Nicole Nobody*. Garden City, N.Y.: Doubleday, 1974.
   First-hand information on the modus operandi of maverick TV series producer Sheldon *(Foreign Intrigue)* Reynolds.

Sanders, Connie Steven and Gary Weissman. *Champagne Music*. New York: St. Martin's Press, 1985.
   The story of *The Lawrence Welk Show*.

Simmons, Garner. *Peckinpah: A Portrait in Montage*. Austin: University of Texas Press, 1982.

Singer, Kurt. *The Laughton Story*. Philadelphia: John C. Winston publishers, 1954.

Swanson, Gloria. *Swanson on Swanson*. New York: Random House, 1980.

Thomas, Bob. *Bud and Lou*. Philadelphia, J.P. Lippincott, 1977.
   Rather vitriolic bio of Abbott and Costello.

Thomas, Tony, Rudy Behlmer, and Clifford McCarthy. *The Films of Errol Flynn*. Secaucus, N.J.: Citadel Press, 1969.

Wallace, Mike and Gary Paul Gates. *Close Encounters*. New York: Berkeley Press, 1985.

Yablonsky, Lewis. *George Raft*. New York: McGraw-Hill, 1974.

Index

383